Women
in
Western
European
History

Women in Western European History

RETIRED

A Select Chronological, Geographical,
and Topical Bibliography
FROM ANTIQUITY TO THE
FRENCH REVOLUTION

Compiled and edited by
Linda Frey, Marsha Frey,
and Joanne Schneider

GREENWOOD PRESS

Westport, Connecticut

Library of Congress Cataloging in Publication Data

Frey, Linda.
    Women in western european history.

    Includes indexes.
    Contents: [1] From antiquity to the French Revolu-
tion—[etc.]
    1. Women—Europe—History—Bibliography—Collected
works. I. Frey, Marsha. II. Schneider, Joanne.
Z7961.F74   016.3054   81-20300
ISBN 0-313-22858-2 (lib. bdg. : v. 1)   AACR2

Library of Congress Catalog Card Number: 81-20300
ISBN: 0-313-22858-2

First published in 1982

Greenwood Press
A division of Congressional Information Service, Inc.
88 Post Road West, Westport, Connecticut 06881

Printed in the United States of America

10 9 8 7 6 5 4 3 2 1

To Dolores and Art,
our West and East Coast research assistants

CONTENTS

PREFACE

"All that has been written about women by men should be
suspect, for the men are at once judge and party to the lawsuit."
Poulain de la Barre
(1647-1723)

The problem that this quote highlights, the accuracy of the historical
perception of women, haunts us today. The bias to which Poulain de la
Barre refers still exists. Often neglected or underestimated, women's roles
are now being uncovered or recovered. Fortunately, the recent efforts of
greater numbers of historians and social scientists, men and women alike,
have provided growing legitimacy to research about women. The spurt in
publications on women's history reflects in part the increased interest in
social history. The crucial place of women in that schema is undeniable.
Our historical perception of women's roles is constantly changing, in part as
a result of the fusion of interdisciplinary perspectives. New questions and
methodologies provide insight into how ordinary people lived and died.
These new perspectives do not discount traditional history, but stress
research in areas heretofore neglected. Social history skillfully integrated into the standard divisions of the discipline provides a more informative view
of the past and promotes a rethinking of some major issues.

Women's history is not without its problems. Traditionalists question its
validity, branding it a pseudoscholarly offspring of the feminist movement
of the 1960s and 1970s. Nevertheless, serious scholarship in the field
abounds. The very interdisciplinary nature of the inquiry makes this
scholarship difficult to locate. The plethora of historical and nonhistorical
journals and anthologies, which continue to appear in large numbers, make
the task of locating current research a formidable one.

With these problems in mind, this bibliography was planned to make
available to the scholar and the nonspecialist recent and past research on

women. It will enable instructors to implement the historical study of women in their classes and to provide supplementary reading lists for their students. The material can be used within a separate conceptual framework of women's studies or integrated into more traditionally oriented courses. The compiled citations highlight issues peculiar to women's history. Scholarship about women has been and is part of the historical canon, but the greatest concentration of work in topics related to women dates from the decades around the turn of the twentieth century and the years after 1965. It is no coincidence that both periods were associated with activism by women for greater rights. The bibliography also underlines the predominance of work focusing on the role of women in France and England. In highlighting the research made available through publication, it also points to the areas in which much work remains to be done.

In spite of the drawbacks of historical periodization, this work has been organized according to traditional time divisions. The present volume covers women's history in Western Europe from antiquity roughly to the French Revolution A second volume now in process will continue the survey through the contemporary period. We realize that social realities are rarely confined to the time limits of a given historical era because of the long term nature of social change. Nevertheless, the need to have some recognizable organization dictated that we adopt the traditional framework. Terms such as Renaissance are used as reference guides despite the fact that women's position may not have significantly changed as a result of humanist thought.

The work is further organized into geographical/political divisions and, within these, into broad and narrow topics, including individual figures of historic importance. Citations covering more than two broad periods are entered in the opening Historical Surveys section. Citations dealing with a particular period in general are entered within topical categories under a General division preceding the geographical ones. The detailed Historical Outline and Topical Guide to Citations, which serves as a specific table of contents for the work, demonstrates the order of citations, proceeding from the most general to the most specific. Cross-references are utilized where helpful. To further facilitate use of the bibliography, subject, name, and author indexes also are included, with reference to entry numbers of pertinent citations. Pithy, pointed quotations have been added as illustrative material introducing broad topical sections of the bibliography. Their authors are noted in the Guide to the Quotations.

The following is a list of criteria used and procedures followed in compiling this volume.

- The entry must focus *directly* on the *historical* condition of women.

- It must deal with Western European countries.
- It must cover a period within the time span from antiquity to approximately 1789.
- It must be published material.
- It must be accessible in the United States. In the case of a periodical, it must be available (full edition) in at least ten libraries nationwide. No rare editions or obscure periodicals are included.
- It may be a monograph or an article from a scholarly journal or anthology.
- The entry must be in English or one of the major Western European languages.
- The latest, and if possible, the English edition is listed.
- For well-known figures such as Elizabeth I, the number of entries is usually limited to fifteen.
- An entry on an individual must focus on the life or historical setting of the figure. A purely literary or artistic analysis usually would not be included.
- This bibliography does not include primary sources such as memoirs or letters; nor does it include literary sources such as novels or poems.
- To avoid confusion, no abbreviations have been used.
- The most common usage has dictated the spelling of names, for example, Vittoria Colonna.
- Women are listed under the country with which they are most commonly associated.

Some people may question the need for another printed bibliography in this age of computers with their instant recall capabilities. The expense involved in utilizing databanks and their inclusion of mainly recent research are but two drawbacks. While women's history is certainly a beneficiary of the newest scholarship, older research also must be consulted.

There is no published bibliography now available on women in Western European history. In extant bibliographies, women's history is treated only tangentially, if at all. The present work will serve to bring women's issues into the mainstream of historical research, to underscore the contribution of an evolving field which focuses on often inarticulate groups. From the numerous citations it is evident that a great deal of scholarship has been done. But more work needs to be undertaken. New research can only raise more questions and encourage the re-evaluation of traditionally accepted views of society. To encourage the pursuit of new scholarship, this bibliography is offered as a guide.

ACKNOWLEDGMENTS

We would like to acknowledge the unfailing support of our immediate families. They have encouraged and oftentimes assisted us in what otherwise would have seemed a Sisyphean task. We must extend a note of thanks to the librarians at the Farrell Library, Kansas State University; the John D. Rockefeller Library, Brown University; the Maureen and Mike Mansfield Library, University of Montana; and the William O. Thompson Memorial Library, Ohio State University. The very existence of this work would not have been possible without the dedicated labors of generations of historians and the encouragement of our colleagues, especially James Carey. The invaluable labors of Betty Bailey, Kansas State University, and of Elaine Gerard and Tania Ruzaeff of the University of Montana typing services deserve special mention.

HISTORICAL OUTLINE
AND TOPICAL GUIDE
TO CITATIONS

GUIDE TO QUOTATIONS

The definitive statement about the female sex has yet to be made. The quotations introducing sections in the bibliography come from famous and not-so-famous men and women throughout history, listed below with the pages on which the quotations are given. Many positive remarks appear, but also do the negative ones. The incredible variety of comments about women illuminates the constant fluctuations in the historical experience of women.

Women
in
Western
European
History

I. HISTORICAL SURVEYS

A. GENERAL

1. BIBLIOGRAPHIES

"And God created man to his own image: to the image of
God he created him: male and female he created them."
Bible

00001. Arora, Ved Parkash. _Women; a Selected Bibliography_. Regina,
Sask.: Provincial Library, Bibliographic Services Division,
1972.

00002. Astin, Helen S. _Women; a Bibliography on their Education and
Careers_. New York: Behavioral Publications, 1974.

00003. Backscheider, Paula R. and Nussbaum, Felicity A. _An Annotated
Bibliography of 20th Century Critical Studies of Women and
Literature, 1660-1800_. (Reference Library of the Humanities
Series.) New York: Garland Publishing, 1977.

00004. Ballou, Patricia K. "Bibliographies for Research on Women."
Signs 3 (Winter 1977): 436-450.

00005. Davis, Audrey B. _Bibliography on Women; with special Emphasis
on their Roles in Science and Society_. New York: Science
History Publications, 1974.

00006. Eastern Michigan University. Library. _The Role of Women in
Society_. Ypsilanti: Eastern Michigan University Library,
1971.

00007. Een, Jo Ann Delores and Rosenberg-Dishman, Marie B., eds.
Women and Society. Vol. 2. Beverly Hills: Sage Publications, 1978.

00008. Freeman, Leah. The Changing Role of Woman: a Selected Biblio-
        graphy. Rev. ed. Sacramento: Sacramento State College
        Library, 1972.

00009. Hinding, Andrea and Chambers, Clarke A. Women's History
        Sources. New York: Bowker, 1978.

00010. Jacobs, Sue-Ellen. Women in Perspective: A Guide for Cross-
        Cultural Studies. Chicago: University of Illinois Press,
        1974.

00011. O'Connor, Patricia et al. Women: A Selected Bibliography.
        Springfield, Ohio: Wittenberg University, 1973.

00012. Rader, Hannelore B. and Butterfield, Mary. The Role of Women
        in Society. Ypsilante: Eastern Michigan University Library,
        1972.

00013. Rosenberg, Marie Barovic and Bergstrom, Len V. Women and
        Society: A Critical Review of the Literature with a
        Selected Annotated Bibliography. Beverly Hills, Calif.:
        Sage Publications, 1975.

00014. Rowbotham, Sheila, ed. Women's Liberation and Revolution: A
        Bibliography. Bristol, England: Falling Wall Press, 1973.

00015. Salzer, Elizabeth M.A. Selected Bibliography of Books on
        Women in the Libraries of the State University of New York
        at Albany. Albany, New York: University Libraries Biblio-
        graphy Division, 1972.

00016. Tobias, Sheila. "The Study of Women." Choice 8 (December
        1971): 1295-1304.

2. ENCYCLOPEDIAS AND DICTIONARIES

"Wise men never say what they think of women."
Samuel Butler

00017. Browne, William Hardcastle. Famous Women of History. Phila-
        delphia: Arnold and Co., 1895.

00018. Chiappe, Jean-François. Le Monde au féminin. Encyclopédie
        des femmes célèbres. Paris: Editions Aimery Somogy, 1976.

00019. Enciclopedia Salvat de la mujer y la familia. Pamplona:
        Salvat, 19__ .

00020. Encyclopédie de la femme et de la famille. . . Paris:
        Hachette, 1968-70.

00021. Ireland, Norma Olin. Index to Women of the World from Ancient
        to Modern Times. Westwood, Mass.: F.W. Faxon Co., 1970.

00022. Jourcin, Albert. Dictionnaire des femmes célèbres. Paris:
        Larousse, 1969.

00023. Lexicon der Frau. Zurich: Enzyclios Verlag, 1953.

00024. Macksey, Joan and Macksey, Kenneth, eds. The Book of Women's
        Achievements. New York: Stein and Day, 1976.

00025. Magrini, Gigliola. Donna 70. Azzate: Varesina grafica, 1970.

00026. Rocamora, Maria Luisa. El Libro de la mujer. Barcelona:
        Ediciones Danae, 1973.

00027. Two Thousand Women of Achievement. Totowa, N.J.: Rowman and
        Littlefield, 1970.

00028. Uhlmann, Irene and Mallachow, Lore. Die Frau. Leipzig:
        Bibliographisches Institut, 1973.

00029. The World Who's Who of Women. Cambridge, England: Melrose
        Press, 1973.

3. SURVEYS

"These miserable creatures who have no other knowledge than
that they were made for the use of man."
                                        J. Richards

00030. Abel, Johann Joseph. Historisches Gemälde der Lage und des
        Zustandes des weiblichen Geschlechts unter allen Völkern der
        Erde bis auf die neuesten Zeiten. Leipzig: Schumann in
        Zwickau, 1803.

00031. Acworth, Evelyn. The New Matriarchy. London: V. Gollancz,
        1965.

00032. Adams, Elsie, and Briscoe, Mary Louise, eds. Up Against the
        Wall Mother. . .: On Women's Liberation. Beverly Hills,
        Calif.: Glencoe Press, 1971.

00033. Agonito, Rosemary. History of Ideas on Women: A Source Book.
        New York: G.P. Putnam's Sons, Paragon Books, 1979.

00034. Aikin, Lucy. Epistles on Women; Exemplifying their Character
        and Condition in Various Ages and Nations. London: J.
        Johnson & Co., 1810.

00035.   Alba, Victor. *Historia Social de la Mujer*. Barcelona: Plaza
         and Janes, 1974.

00036.   Alexander, William. *The History of Women*. 2 vols. 1796.
         Reprint. New York: AMS Press, 1976.

00037.   Alpern, Mildred. "Images of Women in European History."
         Social Education 42 (March 1978): 220-224.

00038.   Altbach, Edith Hoshino, comp. *From Feminism to Liberation*.
         Cambridge, Mass.: Schenkman Pub. Co., 1971.

00039.   Antoine, Thomas. *An Account of the Character, the Manners
         and the Understanding of Women, in Different Ages of the
         World*. Translated by Mrs. Kindersley. London: J. Dodsley,
         1800.

00040.   Ardiner, Shirley. *Perceiving Women*. London: Malaby Press,
         1975.

00041.   Bakan, David. *And They Took Themselves Wives: The Emergence
         of Patriarchy in Western Civilization*. New York: Harper
         and Row, 1979.

00042.   Barbey d'Aurevilly, Jules Amedée. *Femmes et moralistes*. 1906.
         Reprint. Geneva: Slatkine, 1968.

00043.   Bardèche, Maurice. *Histoire des femmes*. 2 vols. Paris:
         Stock, 1968.

00044.   Beard, Mary R. *On Understanding Woman*. 1931. Reprint. New
         York: Greenwood Press, 1970.

00045.   _____. *Woman as Force in History*. 1946. Reprint.
         New York: Collier Books, 1962.
         Also refer to #73.

00046.   Beauvoir, Simone de. *The Coming of Age*. New York: G.P.
         Putnam's Sons, 1972.

00047.   _____. *The Second Sex*. New York: Vintage
         Books, Random House, 1974.

00048.   Bebel, August. *Woman in the Past, Present and Future*. Inter-
         national Library of Social Sciences Series, vol. 1. 1885.
         Reprint. New York: AMS Press, Inc., 1976.

00049.   Beckmann, Emmy and Stoss, Irma, eds. *Quellenhefte zum
         Frauenleben in der Geschichte*. 4 vols. Berlin: F.A. Herbig
         1928.

00050.   Bell, Raley Husted. *Woman from Bondage to Freedom*. New York:
         The Critic and Guide Company, 1921.

00051. Bell, Susan G., ed. Women: From the Greeks to the French
       Revolution. Belmont, Calif.: Wadsworth Publishing Co., 1973.

00052. Borgese, Elisabeth Mann. Ascent of Woman. New York: George
       Braziller, 1963.

00053. Bosmajian, Hamida, and Bosmajian, Haig, eds. This Great
       Argument: The Rights of Women. Reading, Mass:
       Addison-Wesley Publishing Company, 1972.

00054. Boulding, Elise. The Underside of History: A View of Women
       through Time. Boulder, Co.: Westview Press, 1976.

00055. Brada, Fini. Die Stellung der Frau in der Gesellschaft. Eine
       soziologische Studie auf Grund eines historischen Ruckblickes.
       Prague: Karda, 1936.

00056. Bradbury, Harriet B. Civilization and Womanhood. Boston:
       Richard Badger, 1916.

00057. Branca, Patricia. Women in Europe Since 1750. Princeton,
       N.J.: Princeton University, 1978.

00058. Bridenthal, Renate, and Koonz, Claudia, eds. Becoming Visible:
       Women in European History. Boston: Houghton-Mifflin, 1977.

00059. Brockett, Linus Pierpont. Woman: her Rights, Wrongs,
       Privileges, and Responsibilities. Freeport, N.Y.: Books
       for Libraries Press, 1970.

00060. Bullough, Vern L., and Bullough, Bonnie. The Subordinate Sex:
       A History of Attitudes Toward Women. Urbana: University
       of Illinois Press, 1973.

00061. Calverton, V.F., and Schmalhausen, S.D. Woman's Coming of Age.
       New York: Horace Liveright, 1931.

00062. Carroll, Berenice A., ed. Liberating Women's History: Theo-
       retical and Critical Essays. Urbana: University of Illinois
       Press, 1975.

00063. Child, Lydia Maria (Francis). Brief History of the Condition
       of Women in Various Ages and Nations. 1854. Reprint. New
       York: Scholarly Press, 1977.

00064. Chombart de Lauwe, Marie Jose, et. al. La Femme dans la
       société. Paris: Centre national de la recherche scienti-
       fique, 1963.

00065. Christie, Jane Johnstone. The Advance of Woman: From the
       Earliest Times to the Present. Philadelphia: J.B. Lippin-
       cott Co., 1912.

00066. Cohart, Mary, ed. Unsung Champions of Women. Albuquerque:
       University of New Mexico Press, 1975.

00067. Comer, Lee. Wedlocked Women. Leeds, England: Feminist Books, 1974.

00068. Coolidge, Mary Elizabeth Burroughs Smith (Roberts). Why Women are So. 1912. Reprint. New York: Arno Press, 1972.

00069. Corro, Jose Cantu. La Mujer traves de los siglos. Botas: Mexico Ediciones, 1938.

00070. Davies, John Langdon. A Short History of Women. New York: Literary Guild of America, 1927.

00071. Davis, Elizabeth Gould. The First Sex. Baltimore: Penguin Books, Inc. 1972.

00072. Deckhard, Barbara. The Women's Movement Political, Socio-economic and Psychological Issues. New York: Harper and Row, 1975.
           [See especially Part 2 Historical Struggle for Liberation, Chs. 8 and 9.]

00073. Degler, Carl N. "Woman as Force in History by Mary Beard." Daedalus 103 (Winter 1973): 67-73.

00074. De Leeuw, Hendrik. Woman: The Dominant Sex. New York: T. Yoseloff, 1957.

00075. Delmar, Rosalind. "Looking Again at Engel's Origin of the Family: Private Property and the State." In The Rights and Wrongs of Women, edited by Juliet Mitchell and Ann Oakley, pp. 271-287. New York: Penguin Books, 1976.

00076. Deutsch, Helene. The Psychology of Women: A Psychoanalytic Interpretation. 2 vols. New York: Grune and Stratton, 1945.

00077. Diner, Helen. Mothers and Amazons: The First Feminine History of Culture. Edited and translated by John Philip Lundin. 1932. Reprint. New York: Doubleday, 1973.

00078. Dobash, R. Emerson and Dobash, Russell. Violence Against Wives A Case Against the Patriarchy. New York: Macmillan Publishing Co., The Free Press, 1979.

00079. Eaubonne, Françoise d'. Y a-t-il encore des hommes? Paris: Flammarion, 1964.

00080. English, Jane, ed. Sex Equality. Englewood Cliffs, N.J.: Prentice Hall, 1977.

00081. Figes, Eva. Patriarchal Attitudes: Women in Society. New York: Stein and Day, 1970.

00082. Fort, Gertrud von le. The Eternal Woman: The Woman in Time:
       Timeless Woman. Translated by Placid Jordan. Milwaukee:
       Bruce, 1962.

00083. Freeman, Jo, ed. Women: A Feminist Perspective. 2nd ed.
       Palo Alto, Calif.: Mayfield Publishing Co., 1979.

00084. Friedan, Betty. The Feminine Mystique. New York: Norton,
       1963.

00085. Gamble, Eliza Burt. The Sexes in Science and History, an
       Inquiry into the Dogma of Woman's Inferiority to Man. New
       York: G.P. Putnam's Sons, 1916.

00086. George, Walter Lionel. The Story of Woman. New York: Harper
       and Bros., 1925.

00087. Geschichte der Frauen und ihrer Stellung in der menschlichen
       Gesellschaft bei allen Volkern und zu allen Zeiten. Eine
       Weihegabe für die Frauenwelt. Leipzig: Dyk, 1853.

00088. Giele, Janet Zollinger. "Centuries of Womanhood: An Evolu-
       tionary Perspective on the Feminine Role." Women's Studies
       1 (1972): 97-110.

00089. Gilman, Charlotte (Perkins) Stetson. The Man-Made World: or,
       Our Androcentric Culture. 1911. Reprint. New York:
       Johnson Reprint Corp., 1971.

00090. Gleichen-Russwurm, Alexander v. Eva mit dem Apfel: Frauenraub,
       Frauenkauf, Frauenrecht. Berlin: Drei Masken Verlag, 1928.

00091. Goldberg, Steven. Sex in the Social Order: The Inevitability
       of Patriarchy. New York: Morrow, 1973.

00092. Griffiths, Naomi Elizabeth Saundaus. Penelope's Web: Some
       Perceptions of Women in European and Canadian Society.
       Toronto: Oxford University Press, 1976.

00093. Grimal, Pierre, ed. Histoire mondiale de la femme Paris:
       Nouvelle librairie de France, 1965.

00094. Groult, Benoite. Le féminisme au masculin. Paris: Editions
       Denoel, 1977.

00095. Hamilton, Roberta. The Liberation of Women: A Study of
       Patriarchy and Capitalism. Boston: George Allen and
       Unwin, 1978.

00096 Hammond, Dorothy and Jablow, Alta. Women in Cultures of the
       World. Reading, Mass.: Benjamin Cummings Publishing Co.,
       1976.

00097. Harding, Mary Esther. The Way of all Women, a Psychological
       Interpretation. New York: Longman's, Green and Co., 1936.

00098.   Harrison, Austin. Pandora's Hope: A Study of Woman. London:
          Heinemann, 1925.

00099.   Hartley, C.G. The Truth about Woman: Biological, Historical,
          Anthropological, Sociological. Brooklyn: Revisionist
          Press, 1974.

00100.   Hartman, Mary S., and Banner, Lois, eds. Clio's Consciousness
          Raised: New Perspectives on the History of Women. New York:
          Octagon Books, 1976.

00101.   Havil, Anthony. The Making of a Woman. London: Wales
          Publishing, 1969.

00102.   Hays, Hoffmann Reynolds. The Dangerous Sex: The Myth of
          Feminine Evil. New York: G.P. Putnam's Sons, 1964.

00103.   Hecht, Marie B.; Berbich, J.D.; Healy, S.A.; and Cooper, C.M.
          The Women, Yes. New York: Holt, Rinehart & Winston, 1973.

00104.   Heywood, Thomas. The General History of Women, containing the
          Lives of the most holy and prophane, the most famous and
          infamous in all Ages. London: W.H., 1657.

00105.   Higgins, Ardis O. Windows on Women. North Hollywood: Halls
          of Ivy Press, 1975.

00106.   Holtby, Winifred. Women in a Changing Civilization. 1936.
          Reprint. Chicago: Academy Ltd., 1978.

00107.   Iglitzin, Lynne B. "Women as Property: the Persistence of
          Patriarchal Thinking." The Center Magazine 7 (May-June
          1973): 44-47.

00108.   Jameson, Anna Brownell (Murphy). Characteristics of Women;
          Moral, Poetical, and Historical. New York: Houghton-
          Mifflin, 1898.

00109.   Jewitt, Paul K. Man as Male and Female. Grand Rapids, Mich.:
          Eerdman's, 1975.

00110.   Johnson, George William. The Evolution of Woman from Subjec-
          tion to Comradeship. London: R. Holden and Co., 1926.

00111.   Justin, Dena. "From Mother Goddess to Dishwasher." Natural
          History 82 (Fall 1973): 40-45.

00112.   Kaplan, Justin, ed. With Malice Toward Women: A Handbook for
          Women-Haters Drawn from the Best Minds of All Time. London:
          W.H. Allen, 1953.

00113.   Keller, Frances Richardson, ed. The Struggles of Eve. Santa
          Barbara, Calif.: ABC-Clio Press, 1980.

00114. King, William C., comp. Woman: Her Position, Influence, and
       Achievement throughout the Civilized World; her Biography,
       her History, from the Garden of Eden to the Twentieth Century.
       Springfield, Mass.: The King-Richardson Co., 1902.

00115. Klein, Viola. The Feminine Character: History of an Ideology.
       1949. Reprint. Urbana: University of Illinois Press, 1972.

00116. Koepcke, Cordula. Die Frau und die Gesellschaft. Munich:
       G. Olzog, 1973.

00117. Koven, Anna de. Women in the Cycles of Culture: A Study
       of Women's Power through the Centuries. New York: G.P.
       Putnam's Sons, 1941.

00118. Langdon-Davies, John. A Short History of Women. New York:
       The Viking Press, 1927.

00119. Latour, Anny. Kulturgeschichte der Dame. Hamburg: Marion
       Von Schroder Verlag, 1963.

00120. Lea, Eduard and Masters, R.E.L. The Anti-Sex: The Belief
       in the Natural Inferiority of Women. New York: Julian
       Press, 1964.

00121. Lederer, Wolfgang. The Fear of Women. New York: Harcourt,
       Brace, Jovanovich, 1970.

00122. LeFort, Gertrud, Freiin von. The Eternal Woman. The Woman in
       Time and Timeless Woman. Translated by Marie Cecilia Buehrie,
       with preface by Max Jordon. Milwaukee: Bruce Publishing
       Co. 1954.

00123. Lerner, Gerda. The Majority Finds its Past: Placing Women in
       History. New York: Oxford University Press, 1979.

00124. Letourneau, Charles. La Condition de le femme dans les diverses
       races et civilisations. Paris: V. Giard and E. Briere, 1903.

00125. Ludovici, Anthony Mario. Lysistrata; or Woman's Future and
       Future Woman. New York: E.P. Dutton and Co., 1925.

00126. _____. Woman: A Vindication. London:
       Constable and Co., 1929.

00127. Luria, Gina and Tiger, Virginia. Everywoman. New York:
       Random House, 1976.

00128. Malinowski, Bronislaw. Sex, Culture and Myth. New York:
       Harcourt, Brace, 1962.

00129. Mallet, Francine. La Victoire de la femme, histoire univer-
       selle de la condition feminine. Paris: Pont-Royal, 1964.

00130. Mandrou, Robert. "Les femmes dans l'histoire." Revue historique 242 (Oct.-Dec. 1969): 339-346.

00131. Marcuse, Herbert. Eros and Civilization. Boston: Beacon Press, 1955.

00132. Martin, Louis Auguste. Histoire de la femme, sa condition politique, civile, morale et religieuse. Paris: Didier, 1862-1863.

00133. Martin, M. Kay and Voorhies, Barbara. Female of the Species. New York: Columbia University Press, 1975.

00134. Mead, Margaret. Male and Female. New York: New American Library, 1955.

00135. Meiners, Christoph. Geschichte des weiblichen Geschlechts. 4 vols. Hannover: Helwing, 1788-1800.

00136. Merchant, Carolyn. The Death of Nature: Women, Ecology and the Scientific Revolution. San Francisco: Harper and Row, 1980.

00137. Miqueli, Violeta. Woman in Myth and History. New York: Vantage Press, 1962.

00138. Mitchell, Juliet. Woman's Estate. New York: Pantheon, 1972.

00139. _____. Women and Equality. Cape Town, So. Africa: University of Cape Town Press, 1975.

00140. Monestier, Marianne. Femmes d'hier et de demain, d'ici et d'ailleurs. Paris: Plon, 1967.

00141. Montagu, Ashley. The Natural Superiority of Women. Rev. ed. New York: Collier Books, 1970.

00142. Morgan, Elaine. The Descent of Woman. New York: Stein and Day, 1972.

00143. Muir, Charles S. Women, the Makers of History. New York: The Vantage Press, 1956.

00144. Muzzey, Artemas Bowers. The Young Maiden. 4th ed. Boston: William Crosby, 1843.

00145. Nachtigall, Horst. "Das Problem einer mutterrechtlichen Kultur." Archiv für Kulturgeschichte 40 (1958): 275-288.

00146. O'Faolain, Julia, and Martines, Laura, eds. Not in God's Image: A History of Women in Europe from the Greeks to the Nineteenth Century. New York: Harper and Row, 1973.

00147. Oriège, Guy d'. Histoire et géographie de la femme. Paris: Editions du Scorpion, 1958.

00148.   Osborne, Martha Lee, ed. Woman in Western Thought. New York:
         Random House, 1979.

00149.   Ploss, Hermann Heinrich; Bartels, Max; and Bartels, Paul.
         Woman: A Historical Gynaecological and Anthropological
         Compendium. Edited and translated by Eric John Dingwal.
         3 vols. London: Heinemann, 1935.

00150.   Plumb, J.H. "The Woman's Burden." In In the Light of His-
         tory, pp. 140-146. Boston: Houghton-Mifflin, 1973.

00151.   Putnam, Emily James. The Lady: Studies of Various Significant
         Phases of Her History. 1910. Reprint. Chicago: University
         of Chicago Press, 1970.

00152.   Reed, Evelyn. Woman's Evolution from Matriarchal Clan to
         Patriarchal Family. New York: Pathfinder Press, 1975.

00153.   Reeves, Nancy. Womankind Beyond the Stereotypes. Chicago:
         Aldine Publishing Company, 1971.

00154.   Reich, Emil. Woman through the Ages. 2 vols. London:
         Methuen and Company, 1908.

00155.   Reik, Theodore. The Creation of Woman. New York: George
         Braziller, 1960.

00156.   Reiter, Rayna R., ed. Toward an Anthropology of Women. New
         York: Monthly Review Press, 1975.

00157.   Rey, Pierre Louis. La Femme; de la belle Hélène au movement
         de liberation des femmes. Paris: Bordas, 1972.

00158.   Richard, Gaston. La femme dans l'histoire. Etude sur
         l'evolution de la condition sociale de la femme. Paris:
         Doin, 1909.

00159.   Riencort, Amaury de. Sex and Power in History: How the
         Differences Between the Sexes has Shaped our Destinies.
         New York: Dell, 1975.

00160.   Rosaldo, Michelle, and Lamphere, Louise, eds. Woman, Culture
         and Society. Stanford, Calif.: Stanford University Press,
         1974.

00161.   Rougemont, Denis de. Love in the Western World. New York:
         Pantheon Books, 1956.

00162.   Rowbotham, Sheila. Hidden from History: 300 Years of Women's
         Oppression and the Light against it. New York: Pantheon
         Books, 1975.

00163.   _____. Women, Resistance, and Revolution. New
         York: Vintage, 1974.

00164.   Ruether, Rosemary Radford. New Woman, New Earth, Sexist
          Ideologies and Human Liberation. New York: Seabury Press,
          1975.

00165.   _____ and Bianchi, Eugene. From Machismo
          to Mutuality: Essays on Sexism. New York: Paulist Press,
          1975.

00166.   Sa, Irene Tavares de. A Condicao da mulher. Rio de Janeiro:
          Agir, 1966.

00167.   Sabrames, Demosthenes S., comp. Das sogenannte schwache
          Geschlecht. Munich: List, 1972.

00168.   Sabrosky, Judith A. From Rationality to Liberation, the
          Evolution of Feminist Ideology. Westport, Conn.: Greenwood
          Press, 1979.

00169.   Safilios-Rothschild, Constantina. Toward a Sociology of Women.
          Lexington, Mass.: Xerox College Pub., 1972.

00170.   Sanday, Peggy R. "Toward a Theory of the Status of Women."
          American Anthropologist 75 (October 1973): 1682-1700.

00171.   Sayers, Dorothy L. Are Women Human? Grand Rapids: William B.
          Eerdman's Publishing Company, 1971.

00172.   Scharlieb, Mary. Womanhood and Race-Generation. New York:
          Moffat, Yard, and Co., 1912.

00173.   Scheinfeld, Amram. Women and Men. New York: Harcourt,
          Brace, 1943.

00174.   Schmalhausen, Samuel and Calverton V.F., eds. Woman's Coming
          of Age. New York: Horace Liveright Inc., 1931.

00175.   Schuster, Ernest Joseph. The wife in ancient and modern
          times. London: Williams and Norgate, 1911.

00176.   Ségur, Alexandre Joseph Pierre de. Les Femmes, leur condition
          dans l'ordre social chez les differents peuples anciens et
          modernes. Paris: Treuttel et Würtz, 1803.

00177.   Semaine de la Pensée Marxiste. Les femmes, la vie et l'amour.
          Paris: Les Editions du Pavillon, 1967.

00178.   Spencer, Anna Garlin. Woman's Share in Social Culture. 1912.
          Reprint. New York: Arno Press, 1972.

00179.   Stuart, Dorothy M. The Girl Through the Ages. 1933. Reprint.
          Detroit, Mich.: Singing Tree, 1970.

00180.   Sullerot, Evelyne. Woman, Society and Change. New York:
          McGraw-Hill, 1971.

00181. Sumner, William Graham. _War_ and _Other_ _Essays._ Freeport,
        N.Y.: AMS Press, 1970.

00182. Swiney, Frances. _The_ _cosmic_ _Procession;_ _or,_ _the_ _Feminine_
        Principle _in_ _Evolution._ London: E. Bell, 1906.

00183. _____. _Women_ _among_ _the_ _Nations;_ _a_ _Short_ _Treatise._
        London: "The Awakening", 1913.

00184. _____. _Woman_ _and_ _Natural_ _Law._ London: C.W.
        Daniel, Ltd., 1912.

00185. Tanner, Nancy, and Zihlman, Adrienne. "Women in Evolution.
        Part 1: Innovation and Selection in Human Origins." _Signs_
        1 (Spring 1976): 585-638.

00186. Tarbell, Ida M., ed. _The_ _Book_ _of_ _Woman's_ _Power._ New York:
        Macmillan Co., 1911.

00187. Theobald, Robert, ed. _Dialogue_ _on_ _Women._ Indianapolis: Bobbs-
        Merrill, 1967.

00188. Thième, Hugo Paul. _Woman:_ _in_ _all_ _Ages_ _and_ _all_ _Countries._
        Philadelphia: Barre and Sons, 1907-1908.

00189. Thomas, Antoine Leonard. _An_ _Account_ _of_ _the_ _Character,_ _the_
        Manners, _and_ _the_ _Understanding_ _of_ _Women_ _in_ _Different_ _Ages,_
        and _Different_ _Parts_ _of_ _the_ _World._ London: J. Dodsley, 1800.

00190. Thomas, Edith. _Eve_ _et_ _les_ _autres._ Paris: Gizard, 1952.

00191. Thomson, Katherine (Byerley). _Queens_ _of_ _Society._ London:
        J.W. Jarvis, 1890.

00192. Truc, Gonzague. _Histoire_ _illustre_ _de_ _la_ _femme._ Paris: Plon,
        1940-1941.

00193. Vaerting, Mathias and Vaerting, Mathilde. _The_ _Dominant_ _Sex._
        Translated by Eden and Cedar Paul. New York: George H.
        Doran Co., 1923.

00194. Van Baal, J. _Reciprocity_ _and_ _the_ _Position_ _of_ _Women:_ _Anthro-_
        pological _Papers._ Atlantic Highlands, N.J.: Humanities
        Press, Inc., 1976.

00195. Vigman, Fred K. _Beauty's_ _Triumph:_ _Or,_ _the_ _Superiority_ _of_ _the_
        Fair _Sex_ _Invincibly_ _Proved._ N. Quincy, Mass.: Christopher
        Publishing House, 1966.

00196. Walsh, Elizabeth. _Women_ _in_ _Western_ _Civilization._ Cambridge,
        Mass.: Schenkman, 1981.

00197. West, Uta. _Women_ _in_ _a_ _Changing_ _World._ Hightstown, N.J.:
        McGraw-Hill Book Company, 1975.

00198.   White, Eben Minerva. Woman and Civilization. London: J. Bale
          and Staples, 1940.

00199.   White, Sarah Parker. A Moral History of Woman. Garden City,
          N.Y.: Doubleday, Doran, 1937.

00200.   Whiting, Lilian. Women Who Have Ennobled Life. Philadelphia:
          University Press, 1915.

00201.   Whyte, Martin K. The Status of Women in Preindustrial Societies.
          Princeton, N.J.: Princeton University Press, 1978.

00202.   Wieth-Knudson, Knud Asbjern. Feminism: A Sociological Study
          of the Woman Question from Ancient Times to the Present Day.
          London: Constable & Company, Ltd., 1928.

00203.   _____. Understanding Women: A Popular
          Study of the Question from Ancient Times to the Present Day.
          Translated by Arthur G. Chater. New York: Elliot Holt, 1929.

00204.   Winter, Alice Ames. The Heritage of Women. New York: Minton,
          Balch and Co., 1927.

00205.   Women's History Research Center. The Synopsis of Women in
          World History. Berkeley, Calif.: 1972.

00206.   Woodward, Emma H. Men, Women and Progress. London: Dulav
          and Co., 1885.

00207.   Wormser-Migot, Olga. Les Femmes dans l'histoire. Paris:
          Correa, 1952.

00208.   Wright, Thomas. Womankind in Western Europe from the Earliest
          Times to the 17th Century. 1869. Reprint. Boston: Long-
          wood Press, 1977.

4. BIOGRAPHICAL SKETCHES

          "Man, who has never neglected an opportunity of exerting
          his power, in paying homage to [women's] beauty, has always
          availed himself of their weakness. He has been at once
          their tyrant and their slave."
                                        Antoine-Léonard Thomas, 1772

00209.   Abbot, Willis J. Notable Women in History: The Lives of Women
          Who in All Ages, All Lands, and in All Womanly Occupations
          Have Won Fame and Put their Imprint on the World's History.
          Philadelphia: John C. Winston Co., 1913.

00210. Adelman, Joseph. Famous Women, an Outline of Feminine Achieve-
        ment through the Ages with Life Stories of Five Hundred Noted
        Women. New York: Ellis M. Lonow Co., 1926.

00211. Armour, Richard. It all Started with Eve. New York: McGraw
        Hill Book Co., Inc., 1956.

00212. Bäumer, Gertrud. Bildnis der Liebenden; Gestalt und Wandel
        der Frau. Tübingen: Rainer Wunderlich Verlag, 1958.

00213. _____ . Gestalt und Wandel; Frauenbildnisse. Berlin:
        F.A. Herbig, 1939.

00214. Betham-Edwards, Matilda. Six Life Studies of Famous Women.
        Freeport, N.Y.: Books for Libraries Press, 1972.

00215. Biographium Faemineum. The Female Worthies: or Memoirs of
        the Most Illustrious Ladies of all Ages and Nations. 2 vols.
        London: S. Crowder, 1766.

00216. Blashfield, Evangeline Wilbour. Portraits and Background. 1917.
        Reprint. Freeport, N.Y.: Books for Libraries Press, 1971.

00217. Blei, Franz. Glanz und Elend berühmter Frauen. Berlin: Ernst
        Rewohlt, 1927.

00218. _____ . Himmlische und irdische Liebe in Frauenschick-
        salen. Berlin: Ernst Rowohlt, 1928.

00219. Boccaccio, Giovanni. Concerning Famous Women. Translated
        by Guido A. Guarino. New Brunswick, N.J.: Rutgers Univer-
        sity Press, 1963.

00220. Bolton, Sarah Knowles. Famous Leaders Among Women. 1895.
        Reprint. Freeport, N.Y.: Books for Libraries Press, 1972.

00221. _____ . Famous Types of Womanhood. 1892.
        Reprint. Freeport, N.Y.: Books for Libraries Press, 1971.

00222. _____ . Lives of Girls Who Became Famous. New
        York: Thomas Y. Crowell, 1947.

00223. Borer, Mary Irene Cathcart. Women Who Made History. London:
        Fredrick Warne, 1963.

00224. Bradford, Gamaliel. Daughters of Eve. 1930. Reprint. Port
        Washington, N.Y.: Kennikat Press, 1969.

00225. Brantôme, Pierre de Bourdeille. Vues des dames illustres
        francoises et étrangères. Paris: Gannier Freres, 1873.

00226. Brophy, Brigid. Don't Never Forget. New York: Holt, Rinehart
        and Winston, 1961.

00227. Brown, Ivor. Dark Ladies. London: Collins, 1957.

00228. Buckmaster, Henrietta. <u>Women who Shaped History</u>. New York: Crowell-Collier, 1966.

00229. Castelot, André. <u>Femmes tragiques de l'histoire</u>. Paris: Presses Pocket, 1969.

00230. Child, Lydia Maria (Francis). <u>Good Wives</u>. Boston: Carter, Hendee and Co., 1833.

00231. Christophe, Robert. <u>Les Grandes amoureuses de l'histoire</u>. Paris: Editions France-Empire, 1972.

00232. Clarke, Mary Cowden. <u>World-Noted Women: Or, Types of Womanly Attributes of all Lands and Ages</u>. New York: Appleton, 1868.

00233. Dantas, Julio. <u>Revoada de musas as mulheres na vida dos homens celebres</u>. Lisbon: Portugalia Editora, 1965.

00234. Dark, Sydney. <u>Twelve More Ladies: Good, Bad and Indifferent</u>. 1932. Reprint. Freeport, N.Y.: Books for Libraries, 1969.

00235. D'Auvergne, Edmund. <u>Adventuresses and Adventurous Ladies</u>. London: Hutchinson and Co., 1929.

00236. Delacoux, P.A. <u>Biographie des sages-femmes célèbres, anciennes, modernes, et contemporaines</u>. 1834. Reprint. New Haven, Conn.: Research Publications Inc., 1975.

00237. Demeuse, Pierre. <u>Les Amoureuses de l'amour; les immoralités légendaires</u>. Brussels: P. de Meyer, 1967.

00238. Diagram Group. <u>Mothers. One Hundred Mothers of the Famous and the Infamous</u>. London: Paddington Press, Ltd., 1976.

00239. Dufour, Antoine. <u>Les Vies des femmes célèbres</u>. Edited by G. Jeanneau. Geneva: Droz, 1970.

00240. <u>Eccentric Biography; or, Memoirs of Remarkable Female Characters, Ancient and Modern</u>. Worcester: Isaiah Thomas, 1804.

00241. Edwards, Mathilda Barbara Betham. <u>Six Life Studies of Famous Women</u>. Freeport, N.Y.: Books for Library Press, 1972.

00242. Effinger, John R. <u>Women in All Ages and in All Countries</u>. Philadelphia: G. Barrie and Sons, 1907-08.

00243. _____. <u>Women of the Romance Countries</u>. Philadelphia: Rittenhouse Press, 1908.

00244. Ewart, Andrew. <u>The World's Wickedest Women: Intriguing Studies of Eve and Evil through the Ages</u>. New York: Taplinger Publishing Co., 1965.

00245. Fassbinder, Klara Maria. Frauenleben durch die Jahrhunderte. 2 vols. Münster: Aschendorffsche Verlagshandlung, 1928.

00246. Fry, Peter George Robin Somerset. The Zebra Book of Famous Women. London: Evans Brothers, 1972.

00247. Goldsmith, Margaret. Seven Women Against the World. London: Methuen and Co., Ltd., 1976.

00248. Goodrich, Samuel Griswold. Lives of Celebrated Women. Boston: J.S. Locke and Co., 1876.

00249. Hale, Philip L. Great Portraits: Women. Boston: Bates and Guild, 1909.

00250. Hale, Sarah J. Women's Record or Sketches of All Distinguished Women from the Creation to A.D. 1854. 1855. (Source Library of the Women's Movement.) New York: Hacker Art Books, 1971.

00251. Hays, Mary. Female Biography: Or Memoirs of Illustrious and Celebrated Women of all Ages and Countries. 3 vols. Philadelphia: Fry and Kammerar, 1807.

00252. Henriot, Emile. D'Héloïse à Marie Boshkirtseff, portraits de femmes. Paris: Librarie Plon, 1935.

00253. _____. Portraits de femmes. Paris: A. Michel, 1951.

00254. Hewitt, Mary Elizabeth M. Lives of Illustrious Women of all Ages. 1860. Reprint. New Haven, Conn.: Research Publications Inc., 1975.

00255. Humy, Fernand Emile de. Women Who Influenced the World. New York: Library Publishers, 1955.

00256. James, Bartlett B. Women in All Ages and All Countries. 10 vols. Philadelphia: Rittenhouse Press, 1907-08.

00257. James, George Payne, ed. Memoirs of Celebrated Women. 1876. Reprint. Freeport, N.Y.: Books for Libraries, 1974.

00258. Jameson, Anne Brownell (Murphy). Lives of Celebrated Female Sovereigns and Illustrious Women. 1870. Reprint. New Haven, Conn.: Research Publications, Inc., 1976.

00259. Jenkins, Elizabeth. Ten Fascinating Women. London: Odhams Pr., 1955.

00260. Kaeser, Hildegard Johanna. Frauen erobern die Welt; Lebensbilder berühmter Frauen. Zurich: Orell Fussli, 1961.

00261. Klock, Frank. The Predators: Tales of Legendary Liberated Women. New York: Drake Publishers, 1974.

00262. Knapp, Samuel L. Female Biography; Containing Notices of
        Distinguished Women in Different Nations and Ages. New
        York: J. Carpenter, 1834.

00263. Mayne, Ethel Colburn. Enchanters of Men. Philadelphia:
        George W. Jacobs and Co., 1909.

00264. Parton, James. World's Famous Women: A Series of Sketches
        of Women Who Have Won Distinction by their Genius and Achieve-
        ments as Authors, Artists, Actors, Rulers, or within the
        Precincts of Rome. New York: John W. Lovell, 1890.

00265. Pomeroy, Sarah Gertrude. Little-Known Sisters of Well-Known
        Men. Boston: Dana Estes and Co., 1912.

00266. Robertson, Clyde. Fifty Famous Women. Atlanta: Banner
        Press, 1936.

00267. Rogers, Cameron. Gallant Ladies. New York: Harcourt, Brace
        and Co., 1928.

00268. Schmidt, Minna Moscherosch, ed. Four Hundred Outstanding
        Women of the World and Costumology of their Time. Chicago:
        Author, 1933.

00269. Schnittkind, Henry Thomas and Thomas, Dana Lee. Living
        Biographies of Famous Women. Garden City, N.Y.: Halcyon
        House, 1942.

00270. Seillière, Ernest Antoine Aime Leon, Baron. Nouveaux por-
        traits de femmes. Paris: Emile-Paul Freres, 1923.

00271. _____. Portraits de
        femmes. Paris: Emile-Paul Freres, 1923.

00272. Sergeant, Philip Walsingham. Dominant Women. 1929. Reprint.
        Freeport, N.Y.: Books for Libraries, 1969.

00273. Shepherd, Don. Women in History. Los Angeles: Mankind
        Pub., 1973.

00274. Starling, Elizabeth. Noble Deeds of Women. Boston: Crosby,
        Nichols, Lee & Co., 1860.

00275. Strong, Joanna and Leonard, Tom B. A Treasury of the World's
        Great Heroines. New York: Hart Pub., 1963.

00276. Taylor, Kathryn. Generations of Denial, Seventy-Five Short
        Biographies of Women in History. New York: Times Change
        Press, 1971.

00277. Vincens, Cécile. Portraits de femmes. Paris: Libraire
        Hachette et Cie, 1906.

00278. Vincent, Arthur. Lives of Twelve Bad Women: Illustrations
        and Reviews of Feminine Turpitude Set Forth by Impartial
        Hands. 1897. Reprint. Plainview, N.Y.: Books for
        Libraries, 1972.

00279. Wharton, Grace and Wharton, Philip. The Queens of Society.
        2 vols. New York: Worthington Co., 1890.

00280. Witt, Henriette Elizabeth (Guizot), dame de. Les Femmes dans
        l'histoire. Paris: Hachette, 1889.

00281. Woodward, Helen. Bold Women. Freeport, N.Y.: Books for
        Libraries Press, 1971.

00282. Wortham, Hugh Evelyn. Three Women: St. Teresa, Madame
        de Choiseul, Mrs. Eddy. Boston: Roberts Brothers, 1873.

00283. Wyzewa, Teodor. Some Women: Loving or Luckless. Translated
        by C.H. Jeaffreson. London: John Lane, 1909.

00284. Zahm, John Augustine. Great Inspirers. New York: Appleton,
        1917.

5. POLITICAL

"A woman of sense and breeding would scorn as much to
encroach upon the prerogatives of the man as a man of
sense will scorn to oppress the weakness of the woman."
Daniel Defoe

a) Generic

00285. Elshtain, Jean Bethke. "Moral Woman and Immoral Man: A
        Consideration of the Public-Private Split and its Political
        Ramifications." Politics and Society 4 (1974): 453-473.

00286. Hecker, Eugene Arthur. A Short History of Women's Rights
        from the Days of Augustus to the Present Time. 1914. Re-
        print. Westport, Conn.: Greenwood Press, 1971.

00287. Okin, Susan Moller. Women in Western Political Thought.
        Princeton, N.J.: Princeton University Press, 1979.

00288. Woolsey, Kate Trimble. Republics Versus Woman: Contrasting
        the Treatment accorded to Women in Aristocracies with that
        Meted out to her in Democracies. New York: Grafton Press,
        1903.

b) Legal

00289. Bridel, L. La Femme et le droit; étude historique sur la
        condition des femmes. Paris: F. Pichon, 1884.

00290. Bryce, James. "Marriage and Divorce under Roman and English
        Law." In Studies in History and Jurisprudence, 2: 782–859.
        New York: Oxford University Press, 1901.

00291. Cooper, J.P. "Patterns of Inheritance and Settlement by
        Great Landowners from the Fifteenth to the Eighteenth
        Centuries." In Family and Inheritance: Rural Society in
        Western Europe, 1200–1800, edited by Jack Goody, Joan Thirsk,
        and E.P. Thompson, pp. 192–327. New York: Cambridge Uni-
        versity Press, 1976.

00292. Gide, Paul. Étude sur la condition privée de la femme, dans
        le droit ancien et moderne et en particulier sur le senatus-
        consulte velleien, suivi du: caractère de la dot en droit
        romain, et de la condition de l'enfant naturel et de la con-
        cubine dans la legislation romaine. 2nd ed. Paris: L.
        Larose et Forcel, 1885.

00293. Goody, Jack. "Inheritance, Property and Women: some Compara-
        tive Considerations." In Family and Inheritance: Rural
        Society in Western Europe, 1200–1800, pp. 10–36. Cam-
        bridge: University Press, 1976.

00294. _____. "Marriage Prestations, Inheritance and Descent
        in Pre-Industrial Societies." Journal of Comparative Family
        Studies 1 (1970): 37–54.

00295. Mansfield, Edward D. The Legal Rights, Liabilities and Duties
        of Women with an Introductory History of their Legal Condi-
        tion in the Hebrew, Roman and Feudal Systems. Salem: John P.
        Jewett and Co., 1845.

00296. Marie, J. Essai sur la condition civile des femmes. 1865.
        Reprint. New Haven, Conn.: Research Publications, 1975.

00297. Ostrogorskii, Moisei Iakovlevich. The Rights of Women: A
        Comparative Study in History and Legislation. New York:
        C. Scribner's Sons, 1893.

00298. Weber, Marianne. Ehefrau und Mutter in der Rechtsentwicklung.
        Eine Einführung. Tübingen: J.C.B. Mohr, 1907.

c) Feminism

00299. Abensour, Léon. Histoire generale du féminisme des origines
a nos jours. Paris: Delagrave, 1921.

00300. _____. Le Probleme féministe; un case d'aspiration
collective vers l'egalité. Paris: Radot, 1927.

00301. Eaubonne, Françoise d' Histoire et actualité du féminisme.
Paris: Alaine Moreau, 1972.

00302. Fuente, Jaime de la. La Mujer, a Debate. Madrid: Editorial
Alamenda, 1970.

00303. Giffin, Frederick C., ed. Woman as Revolutionary. New York:
The New American Library, Inc., 1973.

00304. Rossi, Alice S., ed. The Feminist Papers: From Adams to
DeBeauvoir. New York: Columbia University Press, 1973.

00305. Roszak, B. and Roszak, T., eds. Maculine/Feminine: Readings
in Sexual Mythology and the Liberation of Women. New York:
Harper and Row, 1969.

00306. Schneir, Miriam ed. Feminism: The Essential Historical
Writings. New York: Random House, 1972.

00307. Walters, Margaret. "The Rights and Wrongs of Women: Mary
Wollstonecraft, Harriet Martineau, Simone de Beauvoir."
In The Rights and Wrongs of Women, edited by Juliet Mitchell
and Ann Oakley, pp. 304-378. New York: Penguin, 1976.

d) Political Roles

00308. Dark, Sydney. Twelve Royal Ladies. 1929. Reprint. Freeport,
N.Y.: Books for Libraries, 1970.

00309. Gooch, George Peabody. Courts and Cabinets. New York: Longmans, Green, 1944.

00310. Hutton, J. Bernard. Women in Espionage. New York: Macmillan,
1972.

00311. Jameson, Anna Brownell (Murphy). Celebrated Female Sovereigns.
New York: The Werner Co., 1910.

00312. Singer, Kurt D. The World's Thirty Greatest Women Spies. New York: Wilfred Funk, 1951.

e) Military

00313. Gribble, Francis G. Women in War. New York: Dutton, 1917.

00314. Hansbrough, Henry Clay. War and Women. New York: Duffield, 1915.

00315. Hargreaves, Reginald. Women-at-Arms: Their Famous Exploits throughout the Ages. London: Hutchinson and Co., 1930.

00316. Laffin, John. Women in Battle. New York: Abelard-Schuman, 1967.

00317. Romain, Col. Charles Armand. Les guerrières. Paris: Berger-Lavrault, 1937.

6. ECONOMIC

"If they all married [their families] would go poor through providing so many dowries."
                    Arcangela Taraboti

00318. Ankarloo, Bengt. "Agriculture and Women's Work: Direction's of Change in the West, 1700-1900." Journal of Family History 4 (Summer 1979): 111-120.

00319. Barker, Diana Leonard and Allen, Sheila, eds. Dependence and Exploitation in Work and Marriage. New York: Longman Inc., 1976.

00320. Bickner, Mei L. and Shaughnessey, Marlene. Women at Work: Annotated Bibliography. Los Angeles: University of California Press, 1977.

00321. Boulding, Elise. "Familial Constraints on Women's Work Roles." Signs 1 (Spring 1976): 95-117.

00322. Campbell, Mrs. Helen. Women Wage-Earners, Their Past, Their Present, and Their Future. Boston: Roberts Brothers, 1893. [See esp. ch. 7, "General Conditions for English Workers, pp. 142-160; and, ch. 8, "General Conditions for Continental Workers," pp. 161-187.]

00323. Engels, Friederich. The Origins of Family, Private Property,
        and the State. New York: Pathfinder Press, 1972.

00324. Gardiner, Jean. "Political Economy of Domestic Labor in
        Capitalist Society." In Dependence and Exploitation in
        Work and Marriage, edited by Diana Leonard Barker and
        Sheila Allen, pp. 109-120. New York: Longman Inc., 1976.

00325. Gilman, Charlotte. Women and Economics. A Study of the
        Economic Relation between Men and Women as a Factor in
        Social Evolution. New York: Harper and Row, 1966.

00326. Kahne, Hilda and Hybels, Judith. Work and Family Issues: A
        Bibliography of Economic and Related Social Science Re-
        search. Wellesley, Mass.: Wellesley College Center for
        Research on Women, 1979.

00327. Leser, C.E.V. "Trends in Women's Work Participation."
        Population Studies 12 (1958-59): 100-110.

00328. McFarland, Joan. "Economics and Women: A Critique of the
        Scope of Traditional Analysis and Research." Atlantis 1
        (Spring 1976): 26-41.

00329. Medick, Hans. "Zur strukturellen Funktion von Haushalt und
        Familie im Übergang von der traditionellen Agrargesellschaft
        zum industriellen Kapitalismus: die protoindustrielle
        Familienwirtschaft." In Sozialgeschichte der Familie in der
        Neuzeit Europas, edited by Werner Conze, pp. 254-282.
        Stuttgart: Ernst Klett Verlag, 1976.

00330. Pleck, Elizabeth H. "Two Worlds in One: Work and Family."
        Journal of Social History 10 (1976): 178-195.

00331. Slicher van Bath, B.H. Agrarian History of Western Europe,
        AD 500-1850. London: Edward Arnold Publishers, Ltd., 1963.
        [See especially ch. "Population," pp. 77-97.]

00332. Spencer, Anna Garlin. "Primitive Working Woman," Forum 46
        (1911): 546-558.

00333. Stearns, Peter W. Lives of Labor: Work in Maturing Industrial
        Societies. New York: Holmes and Meier Publishers Inc.,
        1975.

00334. Sullerot, Evelyne. Histoire et sociologie du travail féminin.
        Paris: Gonthier, 1968.

00335. Thompson, Dorothy Lampen. Adam Smith's Daughters: Six Dis-
        tinguished Women Economists from the 18th Century to the
        Present. Jericho, New York: Exposition Press, 1973.

        Also refer to #641, 642, 643, 653, 669, 674, 718.

7. RELIGION

"Beautiful, yet chaste, modest, steeped in the fear of the
Lord."   Guibert of Nogent about his Mother

a) Generic

00336. Alvarez, L.R. Feminismo y espiritualidad. Madrid: Taurus,
1964.

00337. Christ, Carol P. and Plaskow, Judith, eds. Womanspirit Rising:
A Feminist Reader in Religion. New York: Harper and Row,
1979.

00338. Clark, Elizabeth and Richardson, Henry W., eds. Women and
Religion: Readings in the Woman Tradition from Aeschylus
to Mary Daly. New York: Harper & Row, 1976.

00339. Crook, Margaret Brackenbury. Women and Religion. Boston:
Beacon, 1965.

00340. Culver, Elsie Thomas. Women in the World of Religion. New
York: Doubleday & Co., 1967.

00341. Govaart-Halkes, Tine. Frau, Welt, Kirche. Wandlungen und
Forderungen. Vienna: Styria, 1967.

00342. Gross, Rita M., ed. Beyond Androcentrism: New Essays on
Women and Religion. Missoula, Mt.: American Academy of
Religion and Scholars' Press, 1977.

00343. _____. "Methodological Remarks on the Study of Women
in Religion: Review, Criticism and Redefinition." In
Women and Religion, edited by Judith Plaskow and Joan
Arnold Romero, pp. 153-165. Missoula, Mt.: American Academy
of Religion and Scholars' Press, 1974.

00344. Harkness, Georgia Elma. Women in Church and Society: A
Historical and Theological Inquiry. Nashville: Abingdon
Press, 1972.

00345. Heiler, Friedrich. Die Frau in den Religionen der Menschheit.
Edited by Anne M. Heiler. Theologische Bibliothek Toepel-
mann, vol. 33. Hawthorne, N.Y.: Walter de Gruyter, Inc.,
1977.

00346. Matossian, Mary Kilbourne. "In the Beginning, God Was a Woman."
Journal of Social History 6 (Spring 1973): 325-343.

00347. Riquet, Michel. "Point de vue d'historien et de théologien
        catholique." In Prévention des naissances dans la famille,
        edited by Hélène Bergues, pp. 329-340. Paris: Presses
        universitaires de France, 1960.

00348. Ruether, Rosemary Radford, ed. Religion and Sexism: Images
        of Women in the Jewish and Christian Tradition. New York:
        Simon & Schuster, 1974.

00349. _____. "The Theological Roots of Misogynism
        and the Prospects of Liberation Today." In Women and Reli-
        gion. Ann Arbor, Mich.: Office of Religious Affairs,
        University of Michigan, 1972.

00350. _____. "Women's Liberation in Historical
        and Theological Perspective." In Women's Liberation and the
        Church, edited by Sarah Bently Doely, pp. 26-36. New York:
        Association Press, 1970.

00351. _____ and McLaughlin, Eleanor, ed. Women of
        Spirit, Female Leadership in the Jewish and Christian
        Traditions. New York: Simon and Schuster, 1980.

00352. Scherer, Alice. Frauen im Alltag. Dusseldorf: Haus der
        katholischen Frauen, Verlags-Abeilung, 1966.

00353. Van Vuuren, Nancy. The Subversion of Women as Practiced by
        Churches, Witch Hunters and other Sexists. Philadelphia:
        Westminster Press, 1973.

00354. White, Eben Minerva. Woman in World History: her Place in
        the Great Religions. London: Herbert Jenkins, 1924.

00355. Williams, Jay G. "Yahweh, Women and the Trinity." Theology
        Today 32 (October 1975): 234-242.

00356. Women and Religion: Bibliography and Directory. Berkeley,
        Calif.: Women's History Research Center, 1974.

00357. Women in Ritual and Symbolic Roles. Edited by Judith Hoch-
        Smith and Anita Spring. New York: Plenum Press, 1978.

                    b) Women and Judaism

00358. Belkin, Samuel. "Levirate and Agnate Marriage in the Rabbinic
        and Cognate Literature." Jewish Quarterly Review 60 (April
        1970): 275-329.

00359. Berman, Saul. "The Status of Women in Halakhic Judaism." In
        The Jewish Woman: New Perspectives, edited by Elizabeth
        Koltun, pp. 114-128. New York: Schocken, 1976.

00360.   Christ, Carol. "Women's Liberation and the Liberation of God:
          An Essay in Story Theology." In The Jewish Woman: New
          Perspectives, edited by Elizabeth Koltun, pp. 11-17. New
          York: Schocken, 1976.

00361.   Epstein, Louis M. The Jewish Marriage Contract: A Study in
          the Status of the Woman in Jewish Law. 1927. Reprint.
          New York: Arno Press, 1973.

00362.   _____. Marriage in the Bible and the Talmud. Cam-
          bridge, Mass.: Harvard, 1942.

00363.   _____. Sex, Law, and Custom in Judaism. New York:
          KTAV Publishing Co., 1968.

00364.   Feldman, David M. Birth Control in Jewish Law, Marital Rela-
          tionships, Contraception and Abortion. New York: New York
          University Press, 1968.

00365.   Fink, Greta. Great Jewish Women. New York: Bloch Publishing
          Company, 1978.

00366.   Friedman, Mordechai. "Annulling the Bride's Vows: A Pales-
          tinian Ketubba Clause." Jewish Quarterly Review 61 (Janua-
          ry 1971): 222-233.

00367.   Ginzberg, Louis. The Legends of the Jews. Translated by
          Henrietta Szold. 7 vols. Philadelphia: Jewish Publication
          Society, 1909-1938.

00368.   Greenberg, Blu. "Judaism and Feminism." In The Jewish Woman:
          New Perspectives, edited by Elizabeth Koltun, pp. 179-192.
          New York: Schocken, 1976.

00369.   Hands, L. Some Difficulties which beset the Jewess, with
          special reference to her Legal Position, London: Burt and
          Sons, Printers, 1917.

00370.   Hyman, Paula. "The Other Half: Women in the Jewish Tradition."
          In The Jewish Woman: New Perspectives, edited by Elizabeth
          Koltun, pp. 105-113. New York: Schocken, 1976.

00371.   Kahana, Rabbik. The Theory of Marriage in Jewish Law. London:
          E.J. Brill, 1966.

00372.   Katz, Jacob. Tradition and Crisis, Jewish Society at the End
          of the Middle Ages. New York: Schocken Books, 1971.
          [See especially Ch. 14 "The Family", pp. 135-148.]

00373.   Kayserling, M. Die judischen Frauen in der Geschichte,
          Literatur und Kunst. Leipzig: Brockhaus, 1879.

00374.   Lacks, Roslyn. Women in Judaism: Myths, History and Struggle.
          Garden City, N.Y.: Doubleday, 1980.

00375. Loewe, Raphael. The Position of Women in Judaism. London:
        S.P.C.K., 1966.

00376. Meiselman, M. Jewish Woman in Jewish Law. Library of Jewish
        Law and Ethics, vol. 6. New York: KTAV Publishing House,
        Inc.

00377. Montefiore, C.G. and Loewe, H., eds. A Rabbinic Anthology.
        London: Macmillan and Co., 1938.
            [See especially, pp. 507-515, Rabbinic pronouncement on
            wives.]

00378. Patai, Raphael. The Hebrew Goddess. New York: KTAV Publ.
        House, 1967.

00379. Plaskow, Judith: "The Jewish Feminist: Conflict in Identi-
        ties." In The Jewish Woman: New Perspectives, edited by
        Elizabeth Koltun, pp. 3-10. New York: Schocken, 1976.

00380. Schlesinger, Benjamin. The Jewish Family: A Survey and
        Annotated Bibliography. Toronto: University of Toronto
        Press, 1971.

00381. Smith, J.M. Powis. The Origin and History of Hebrew Law.
        Chicago: University of Chicago Press, 1931.

00382. Trachtenberg, Joshua. Jewish Magic and Superstition. New
        York: Behrman's Jewish Book House, 1939.

00383. Unna, Rabbi Isaac. "Marriage in Judaism." In The Jewish
        Library, First Series, edited by Leo Jung, pp. 311-335.
        New York: Macmillan Co., 1928.

                        c) Women and the Bible

00384. Allen, Christine. "Who was Rebekah? On me be the curse, my
        son." In Beyond Androcentrism, edited by Rita Gross, pp.
        183-216. Missoula, Mt.: Scholars Press for the American
        Academy of Religion, 1977.

00385. Baab, O.J. "Woman." In The Interpreter's Dictionary of the
        Bible 4: 864-867. New York: Abingdon Press, 1962.

00386. Batten, J. Women alive: Twenty-five Talks on Women of the
        Bible. Grand Rapids: Zondervan Pub. House, 1964.

00387. Bennett, Anne McGrew. "Overcoming the Biblical and Traditional
        Subordination of Women." Radical Religion 1 (Spring 1974):
        26-33.

00388. Besant, Annie. Women's Position According to the Bible.
        London: A. Besant and C. Bradlaugh, 1885.

00389   Bird, Phyllis. "Images of women in the Old Testament." In
          Religion and Sexism, edited by Rosemary Ruether Radford,
          pp. 41-88. New York: Simon and Schuster, 1974.

00390.   Boucher, Madeleine. "Some Unexplored Parallels: to 1 Cor. 11,
          11-12, and Gal. 3, 28: The New Testament on the Role of
          Women." Catholic Biblical Quarterly 31 (January 1969):
          50-58.

00391.   Brueggemann, Walter. "Of the Same Flesh and Bone (Genesis 2:
          23a)." Catholic Biblical Quarterly 32 (October 1970):
          532-542.

00392.   Carmichael, Calum. "A Ceremonial Crux: Removing a Man's Sandal
          as a Female Gesture of Contempt." Journal of Biblical
          Literature 96 (September 1977): 321-336.

00393.   Caspar, Adelheid. Die Frau in der Bibel. Quellenhefte zum
          Frauenleben in der Geschichte, edited by Emmy Beckmann and
          Irma Stoss, vol. 1. Berlin: F.A. Herbig, 1928.

00394.   Chappell, Clovis G. Feminine Faces. Grand Rapids, Mich.:
          Baker Books, 1978.

00395.   Cole, William Graham. Sex and Love in the Bible. New York:
          Association Press, 1959.

00396.   Deen, Edith. All the Women of the Bible. New York: Harper,
          1955.

00397.   Dumas, Francine. L'Autre semblable. Hommes et femmes.
          Neuchatel: Delachaux and Niestle, 1967.

00398.   Farnon, Alice Craig. Women and Jesus. Philadelphia: United
          Church Press, 1973.

00399.   Gendler, Mary. "The Restoration of Vashti." In The Jewish
          Woman: New Perspectives, edited by Elizabeth Koltun,
          pp. 241-247. New York: Schocken, 1976.

0400.   Gilliland, Dolores S. Selected Women of the Scriptures of
          Stamina and Courage. Spearfish, S.D.: Honor Books, 1978.

00401.   Herr, Ethel. Chosen Women of the Bible. Chicago: Moody
          Press, 1976.

00402.   Higgins, Jean M. "The Myth of Eve: the Temptress." Journal
          of the American Academy of Religion 44 (December 1976):
          639-648.

00403.   Hoftijzer, J. "David and the Tekoite Woman." Vetus Testamentum
          20 (1970): 419-444.

00404.   Holladay, William. "Jeremiah and Women's Liberation." Andover
          Newton Quarterly 12 (March 1972): 213-223.

00405. Kruijf, T. C. de. The Bible on Sexuality. Translated by
       F. Van der Jeijden. De Pere, Wisc.: St. Norbert Abby
       Press, 1966.

00406. Lee, G. Avery. Great Men of the Bible and the Women in Their
       Lives. Waco, Tex.: Word Books, 1968.

00407. Legrand, Lucien. The Biblical Doctrine of Virginity. New
       York: Sheed and Ward, 1963.

00408. Levenson, Jon. "1 Samuel 25 as Literature and History."
       Catholic Biblical Quarterly 40 (January 1978): 11-28.

00409. Lockyer, Herbert. The Woman of the Bible. 1st ed., Grand
       Rapids, Mich.: Zondervan Pub. House, 1967.

00410. Macartney, Clarence E. Great Women of the Bible. Grand
       Rapids, Mich.: Baker Books, 1974.

00411. Maertens, Thierry. The Advancing Dignity of Women in the
       Bible. De Pere, Wisc.: St. Norbert Abbey Press, 1969.

00412. Mulliken, Frances H. and Salts, Margaret. Women of Destiny
       in the Bible. Independence, Mo.: Herald House, 1978.

00413. Ockenga, Harold J. Women Who Made Bible History. Grand
       Rapids, Mich.: Zondervan Pub. House, 1971.

00414. Overby, Coleman. Bible Women. Austin, Tex.: Firm Foundation
       Publishing House, 1936.

00415. Patai, Raphael. Family, Love and the Bible. New York:
       Pershill House, Ltd., 1960.

00416. _____. Sex and Family in the Bible and the Middle
       East. Garden City, N.Y.: Doubleday and Company, 1959.

00417. Price, Eugenia. The Unique World of Women. Grand Rapids,
       Mich.: Zondervan Pub. House, 1973.

00418. San Sebastian, Carmen. El árbol de la vida; pecados y virtudes
       de las mujeres biblicas. Madrid: Ediciones Studium, 1962.

00419. Schepps, David D. Remarkable Women of the Scriptures. Phila-
       delphia: Dorrance and Company, 1976.

00420. Scherer, Alice. Biblische Frauen. Frankfurt: M. Knecht,
       1966.

00421. Southard, Madeline. Attitude of Jesus toward Women. New
       York: Doran, 1927.

00422. Souza, Geraldo Pires de. Elas na Biblia; espôsas e maes no
       antigo testamento. Sao Paulo: Ed. Paulinas, 1968

00423. Speiser, E. "The Wife-Sister Motif in the Patriarchal Narratives." In Biblical and Other Studies, edited by Alexander Altman, pp. 15-28. Cambridge, Mass.: Harvard University Press, 1963.

00424. Stagg, Evelyn and Stagg, Frank. Woman in the World of Jesus. Philadelphia: The Westminster Press, 1978.

00425. Starr, Lee Anna. Bible Status of Women. New York: Revell, 1926.

00426. Stendahl, Krister. The Bible and the Role of Women. Philadelphia: Fortress, 1966.

00427. Swidler, L.J. "Jesus was a Feminist." Southeast Asia Journal of Theology 13 (1971): 102-110.

00428. Terrien, Samuel. "Toward a Biblical Theology of Womanhood." Religion in Life 42 (Autumn 1973): 322-333.

00429. Trible, Phyllis. "Depatriarchalizing in Biblical Interpretation." In The Jewish Woman: New Perspectives, edited by Elizabeth Koltun, pp. 217-240. New York: Schocken, 1976.

00430. Vos, Clarence J. Women in Old Testament Worship. Delft: Judels and Brinkmann, 1968.

00431. Wilson, Martha. "Woman, Women and the Bible." In Women and Religion: 1972, edited by Judith P. Goldberg, pp. 141-148. Missoula, Mt.: American Academy of Religion, 1973.

d) Christianity

(1) Non-specific

00432 Arnaud D'Agnel, G. Le Mariage. Paris: E. Flammarion, 1933.

00433. Bailey, Derrick Sherwin. Homosexuality and the Western Christian Tradition. London: Longmans, Green, 1955.

00434. _____. The Man-Woman Relation in Christian Thought. London: Longmans, Green, 1959.

00435. _____. Sexual Relations in Christian Thought. New York: Harper & Row, 1959.

00436. Bainton, Roland H. "Christianity and Sex, an Historical Survey." In Sex and Religion Today, edited by Simon Doniger, pp. 17-96. New York: Association Press, 1953.

00437. Blenkinsopp, Joseph. Sexuality and the Christian Tradition.
        Dayton, Ohio: Pflaum Press, 1969.

00438. Cairncross, John. After Polygamy was made a Sin: The Social
        History of Christian Polygamy. London: Routledge & Kegan,
        1974.

00439. Cole, William Grahm. Sex in Christianity and Psychoanalysis.
        New York: Oxford University Press, 1955.

00440. Dawson, Christopher Henry. Christianity and Sex. London:
        Faber and Faber, 1930.

00441. Dermine, J. La Doctrine du mariage chrétien. Louvain: n.p.
        1938.

00442. Farley, Margaret A. "Sources of Sexual Inequality in the
        History of Christian Thought." Journal of Religion 56
        (April 1976): 162-176.

00443. Flandrin, Jean Louis. "Contraception, Marriage, and Sexual
        Relations in the Christian West." In Biology of Man in
        History, edited by Robert Forster and Orest Ranum, pp. 23-47.
        Baltimore: Johns Hopkins University Press, 1975.

00444. _____. L'église et le contrôle des naissances.
        Paris: Flammarion, 1970.

00445. Lea, Henry Charles. History of Sacerdotal Celibacy in the
        Christian Church. London: Watts, 1932.

00446. Rengstorf, Karl. Mann und Frau im Urchristentum. Cologne:
        Westdeutscher Verlag, 1954.

00447. Riquet, Michel. "Christianity and Population." In Popular
        Attitudes toward Birth Control in Pre-Industrial France and
        England, edited by Orest and Patricia Ranum, pp. 21-44. New
        York: Harper and Row, 1972. Also in Population 4 (1949):
        615-630.

00448. Troeltsch, E. The Social Teaching of the Christian Churches.
        New York: Macmillan Press, 1961.

00449. Underhill, Evelyn B. The Mystics of the Church. New York:
        Schocken Books, 1964.

00450. Volz, Carl A. "Christianity and the Family A.D. 100-1400."
        In Family Relationships and the Church, edited by Oscar E.
        Feucht, pp. 76-98. Saint Louis, Mo.: Concordia Publishing
        House, 1970.

00451. Weber, Max. The Sociology of Religion. Translated by E.
        Fischoff. Boston: Beacon Press, 1964.

00452.   Westermarck, Edward. Christianity & Morals. London: Paul,
          Trench, Trubner & Co., 1939.

                          (2) Women

00453.   Aubert, Jean Marie. L'Eglise et la femme. Paris: C.T.I.C.,
          1969.

00454.   _____. L'Eglise et la promotion de la femme.
          Paris: Editions Fleurus, 1969.

00455.   Azione cattolica italiana. Unione donne. Per una riflessione
          sulla donna. Rome: Tip. Città Nuova, 1969.

00456.   Bacon, L.D. Women in the Church. London: Butterworth, 1945.

00457.   Beccaria, Marie Josephe. Les Femmes ont-elles leur place dans
          l'église? Paris: Editions du Centurion, 1967.

00458.   Cebolla, Lopez, Fermin. La mujer como subiglesia. Madrid:
          Alameda, 1971.

00459.   Collins, Sheila D. "Toward a Feminist Theology." The Christian
          Century 89 (1972): 796-799.

00460.   Daly, Mary. Beyond God the Father: Toward a Philosophy of
          Women's Liberation. Boston: Beacon, 1973.

00461.   _____. The Church and the Second Sex. New York: Harper
          and Row, 1968.

00462.   _____. Gynecology, the Metaethics of Radical Feminism.
          Boston: Beacon Press, 1979.

00463.   Dantier, Alfonse. Les Femmes dans la société chrétienne.
          Paris: Firmin-Didot et Cie., 1879.

00464.   Daughters of St. Paul. Twenty Women who met a Challenge.
          Boston: St. Paul Edition, 1972.

00465.   Deen, Edith. Great Women of the Christian Faith. New York:
          Harper, 1959.

00466.   Evoy, John J. Real Women in Religious Life. New York: Sheed
          and Ward, 1967.

00467.   Gage, Mathilda J. Woman, Church and State: A Historical
          Account of the Status of Women through the Christian Ages,
          with Reminiscences of the Matriarchate. 2nd ed. New York:
          Arno Press, 1972.

00468. Garside, Christine. "Good and Evil for Women." In Women and
        Religion, compiled by Joan Arnold Romero, pp. 104-127.
        Tallahassee, Fla.: American Academy of Religion, 1973.

00469. Goltz, Eduard Alexander, Freiherr von der. Der Dienst der
        Frau in der Christlichen Kirche. Potsdam: Stiftungsverlag,
        1914.

00470. Kavanagh, Julie. Women of Christianity. New York: Appleton,
        1852.

00471. Lexau, Joan M., ed. Convent Life: Roman Catholic Religious
        Orders for Women. New York: Dial, 1964.

00472. McGrath, Sister Albert Magnus O.P. Women and the Church.
        Garden City, New York: Doubleday and Co., Inc., 1976.

00473. McKenna, Sister Mary Lawrence. Women of the Church. New
        York: Kennedy, 1967.

00474. Moll, Willi. The Christian Image of Women. Translated by
        Elizabeth Reinecke and Paul C. Bailey. Notre Dame: Fides
        Publishers, Inc., 1967.

00475. Morris, Joan. The Lady was a Bishop: The Hidden History of
        Women with Clerical Ordination and the Jurisdiction of
        Bishops. New York: Macmillan Company, 1973.

00476. Peters, Jan. "Is there Room for Women in the Functions of the
        Church?" Concilium 34 (1968): 126-138.

00477. Prohl, Russell. Women in the Church. Grand Rapids, Mich.:
        Eerdmans, 1957.

00478. Raming, Ida. The Exclusion of Women from the Priesthood:
        Divine Law or Sex Discrimination? Translated by Norman R.
        Adam. Metuchen, N.J.: Scarecrow Press, 1976.

00479. Raymond, Janice G. "Nuns and Women's Liberation." Andover
        Newton Quarterly 12 (March 1972): 201-212.

00480. Ryrie, Charles. The Place of Women in the Church. New York:
        Macmillan, 1958.

00481. Sertillanges, Antonin Gilbert. Féminisme et christianisme.
        Paris: V. Lecoffre, 1908.

00482. Tavard, George H. Woman in Christian Tradition. Notre Dame,
        Ind.: University of Notre Dame Press, 1973.

00483. Thrall, Margaret E. The Ordination of Women to the Priesthood:
        A Study of the Biblical Evidence. London: SCM Press, 1958.

00484. Ulanov, Ann Belford. The Feminine in Jungian Psychology and
        in Christian Theology. Evanston: Northwestern University
        Press, 1971.

00485. Van Eyden, Rene. "The Place of Women in Liturgical Functions."
        Concilium 72 (1972): 68-81.

00486. Vinatier, Jean. La femme: parole de Dieu at avenir de l'homme.
        Paris: Les Editions ouvrieres, 1972.

00487. Von Arx, Walter. "The Churching of Women after Childbirth:
        History and Significance." Concilium 112 (1979): 63-72.

00488. Walsh, James Joseph. These Splendid Sisters. 1927. Reprint.
        Freeport, N.Y.: Books for Library Press, 1970.

00489. Zarri, Adriana. "Woman's Prayer and Man's Liturgy." Concilium
        52 (1970): 73-80.

e) Saints/Religious Women

00490. Baring-Gould, Sabine. Lives of the Saints. Edinburgh: John
        Grant, 1914.

00491. _____. Virgin Saints and Martyrs. London:
        Hutchinson, 1906.

00492. Blunt, Hugh Frances. The Great Magdalens. 1928. Reprint.
        Freeport, N.Y.: Books for Libraries, 1969.

00493. Delehaye, Hippolyte. The Legends of the Saints: An Intro-
        duction to Hagiography. Translated by V.M. Crawford. New
        York: Longmans, Green and Co., 1907.

f) Mariology

00494. Ashe, Geoffrey. The Virgin. London: Routledge and Kegan
        Paul, 1976.

00495. Boslooper, Thomas David. The Virgin Birth. Philadelphia:
        Westminster, 1962.

00496. Brown, Raymond; Donfried, Karl P.; Fitzinyer, Joseph A.; and
        Reumann, John. Mary in the New Testament. Philadelphia:
        Fortress Press, 1978.

00497. Bruteau, Beatrice. "The Image of the Virgin-Mother." In Women and Religion, edited by Judith Plaskow and Joan Arnold Romero, pp. 93-104. Missoula, Mt.: American Academy of Religion and Scholars' Press, 1974.

00498. Jameson, Anna Brownell (Murphy). Legends of the Madonna as Represented in the Fine Arts. New York: Houghton, Mifflin, 1911.

00499. Kolb, Karl. Eleusa. A 2000 year Madonna Archetype. Regensburg: Institution Marianum, 1968.

00500. _____. Das Madonnenland; 500 Madonnen in Taubergrund. Wurzburg: Echter-Verlag, 1970.

00501. O'Meara, Thomas. Mary in Protestant and Catholic Theology. New York: Sheed and Ward, 1966.

00502. Rahner, Karl. Mary Mother of the Lord. Translated by W.J. O'Hara. New York: Herder and Herder, 1963.

00503. Ruether, Rosemary Radford. Mary, the Femine Face of the Church. Philadelphia: Westminster Press, 1977.

00504. Scheeben, M.J. Mariology. Translated by T.L.M.J. Genkers. St. Louis: B. Herder Book Company, 1946.

00505. Thurian, Max. Mary, Mother of the Lord, Figure of the Church. London: Faith Press, 1963.

00506. Warner, Marina. Alone of all Her Sex: The Myth and the Cult of the Virgin Mary. New York: Alfred A. Knopf, 1976.

g) Canon Law

00507. Esmain, Adhemar. Le mariage en droit canonique. 2 vols. 1891. Reprint. Philadelphia: Franklin, 1969.

00508. Genestal, R. Histoire de la légitimation des enfants naturels en droit canonique. Paris: E. Leroux, 1905.

00509. Huizing, Peter. "La dissolution de mariage depuis le concile de Trente." Revue de droit canonique 21 (1971): 127-145.

00510. Janssens, L. "Morale conjugale et progestogènes." Ephemerides theologicae lovanienses 39 (1963): 787-826.

00511. Melia, E. "Le lien matrimonial à la lumière de la théologie
        sacramentaire et de la theologie morale de l'Eglise ortho-
        doxe." Revue de droit canonique 21 (1971): 180-197.

00512. Noonan, John T., Jr. Contraception: A History of its Treat-
        ment by the Catholic Theologians and Canonists. Reprint.
        1965. New York: Mentor, 1967.

00513. _____, ed. The Morality of Abortion: Legal
        and Historical Perspectives. Cambridge, Mass.: Harvard
        University Press, 1970.

00514. _____. Power to Dissolve: Lawyers and Marriages in
        the Courts of the Roman Curia. Cambridge, Mass.: Harvard
        University Press, 1972.

00515. Voeltzel, R. "Le lien matrimonial en climat protestant."
        Revue de droit canonique 21 (1971): 149-179.

h) Witchcraft

00516. Anglo, Sydney, ed. The Damned Art Essays in the Literature
        of Witchcraft. Boston: Routledge and Kegan Paul, 1977.

00517. Barnett, Bernard. "Witchcraft, Psychopathology, and Hallu-
        cinations." British Journal of Psychiatry 111 (May 1965):
        439-445.

00518. Baschwitz, Kurt. Hexen und Hexenprozesse: Die Geschichte
        eines Massenwahns. 2nd ed. Munich: DTV, 1966.

00519. Cabanes, Augustin. Moeurs intimes du passé. (onzième série).
        Le sabbat a-t-il existé? Paris: A. Michel, 1935.

00520. Caro Baroja, Julio. The World of the Witches. Translated by
        O.N.V. Glendinning. Chicago: University of Chicago Press,
        1964.

00521. Cohn, Norman. Europe's Inner Demons: An Enquiry Inspired
        by the Great Witch-Hunt. London: Chatto and Heinemann,
        1975.

00522. Ehrenreich, Barbara and English, Deirdre. Witches, Midwives,
        and Nurses: A History of Women Healers. Old Westbury, N.Y.:
        Feminist Press, 1973.

00523. _____. "Witches, Midwives,
        and Nurses." Monthly Review 25 (October 1973): 25-40.

00524. Eliade, Mircea. _Occultism, Witchcraft, and Cultural Fashions: Essays in Comparative Religions_. Chicago: University of Chicago Press, 1976.

00525. Forbes, Thomas Rogers. _The Midwife and the Witch_. New Haven: Yale University Press, 1966.

00526. _____. "Midwifery and Witchcraft." _Journal of the History of Medicine_ 17 (1962): 264-283.

00527. _____. "Witch's Milk and Witches' Marks." _Yale Journal of Biology and Medicine_ 22 (January 1950): 219-225.

00528. Frazer, Sir James George. _The New Golden Bough_. Edited by Theodor H. Gaster. New York: Criterion Books, 1959.

00529. Fritscher, John. _Popular Witchcraft, Straight From the Witch's Mouth_. Bowling Green, Ohio: Bowling Green University Popular Press, 1972.

00530. Garcon, Maurice, and Vinchon, Jean. _The Devil_. London: Victor Gollancz, 1929.

00531. Grillot de Givry, Emil. _Witchcraft, Magic and Alchemy_. 1931. Reprint. New York: Dover, 1972.

00532. Haining, Peter. _Anatomy of Witchcraft_. New York: Taplinger Pub. Co., 1972.

00533. Harris, Marvin. _Cows, Pigs, Wars & Witches: The Riddles of Culture_. New York: Random House, 1974.

00534. Hole, Christina. _Mirror of Witchcraft_. London: Chatto and Windus, 1957.

00535. Horsley, Richard A. "Who Were the Witches? The Social Roles of the Accused in the European Witchcraft Trials." _Journal of Interdisciplinary History_ 9 (Spring 1979): 689-715.

00536. Hueffer, Oliver Madox. _The Book of Witches_. 1908. Reprint. Totowa, N.J.: Rowman and Littlefield, 1973.

00537. Hughes, Pennethorne. _Witchcraft_. 1952. Reprint. Harmondsworth: Penguin Books, Ltd., 1971.

00538. Jones, W.R. "Abracadabra--Sorcery and Witchcraft in European History." _History Teacher_ 5 (November 1971): 26-36.

00539. Langin, G. _Religion und Hexenprozess_. Leipzig: O. Wigand, 1888.

00540. Lea, Henry Charles. _Materials Toward a History of Witchcraft_. 1939. Reprint, New York: T. Yoseloff, 1957.

00541. Lehner, Ernst and Johanna. <u>Devils, Demons, Death, and</u>
        <u>Damnation</u>. New York: Dover, 1972.

00542. Lewis, I.M. <u>Ecstatic Religion: An Anthropological Study of</u>
        <u>Spirit Possession and Shamanism</u>. Baltimore: Penguin, 1971.

00543. Maple, Eric. <u>The Dark World of Witches</u>. New York: A.S.
        Barnes and Co., Inc., 1962.

00544. Monter, E. William, ed. <u>European Witchcraft</u>. New York:
        Wiley, 1969.

00545. Murray, Margaret Alice. "Child-sacrifice among European
        Witches." <u>Man</u> 18 (1918): 60-62.

00546. _____. <u>The God of the Witches</u>. London:
        Oxford University Press, 1970.

00547. _____. <u>The Witch-Cult in Western Europe</u>.
        Oxford: University Press, 1921.

00548. Nelson, Mary. "Why Witches were Women." In <u>Women: A Feminist</u>
        <u>Perspective</u>, edited by Jo Freeman, pp. 335-350. Palo Alto,
        Calif.: Mayfield Publishing Co., 1975.

00549. Newall, Venetia, ed. <u>The Witch Figure</u>. <u>Folklore Essays by a</u>
        <u>Group of Scholars in England Honouring the 75th birthday of</u>
        <u>Katharine M. Briggs</u>. Boston: Routledge and Kegan Paul,
        1973.

00550. Parrinder, Geoffrey. "The Witch as Victim." In <u>The Witch</u>
        <u>Figure</u>, edited by Venetia Newall, pp. 125-138. Boston:
        Routledge and Kegan Paul, 1973.

00551. _____. <u>Witchcraft European and African</u>. London:
        Faber & Faber, 1963.

00552. Robbins, Russell Hope. <u>The Encyclopedia of Witchcraft and</u>
        <u>Demonology</u>. New York: Crown Publishers, 1959.

00553. Rose, Elliot. <u>A Razor for a Goat: A Discussion of Certain</u>
        <u>Problems in the History of Witchcraft and Diabolism</u>.
        Toronto: University of Toronto Press, 1962.

00554. Ruether, Rosemary Radford. "The Prosecution of Witches: A
        Case of Sexism and Agism?" <u>Christianity and Crisis</u> 34
        (23 December 1974): 291-295.

00555. Russell, Jeffrey B. <u>A History of Witchcraft, Sorcerers,</u>
        <u>Heretics and Pagans</u>. New York: Thames and Hudson, 1980.

00556. Seligmann, Kurt. <u>Magic, Supernaturalism and Religion</u>.
        London: Allen Lane, 1971.

00557.   Seth, Ronald. Witches and their Craft. New York: Taplinger, 1968.

00558.   Simons, G.L. The Witchcraft World. New York: Barnes and Noble, 1974.

00559.   Soldan, Wilhelm Gottlieb. Geschichte der Hexenprozesse. Munich: G. Muller, 1912.

00560.   Starhawk. "Witchcraft and Women's Culture." In Womanspirit Rising, edited by Carol P. Christ and Judith Plaskow, pp. 259-268. New York: Harper and Row, 1979.

00561.   Summers, Montague. The Geography of Witchcraft. 1927. Reprint. Boston: Routledge and Kegan Paul, 1978.

00562.   _____. The History of Witchcraft and Demonology. 1926. Reprint. New York: University Books, 1956.

00563.   _____. A Popular History of Witchcraft. New York: Barnes & Noble, 1973.

00564.   Thorndike, Lynn. A History of Magic and Experimental Science. 8 vols. New York: 1922-1958.

00565.   Widdowson, John. "The Witch as a Frightening and Threatening Figure." In The Witch Figure, edited by Venetia Newall, pp. 200-220. Boston: Routledge and Kegan Paul, 1973.

00566.   Williams, Charles. Witchcraft. New York: Meridian, 1959.

00567.   Williams, Selma R. Riding the Nightmare. New York: Atheneum, 1978.

8. SOCIAL

"Men have many faults, women have but two: There's nothing good they say; there's nothing good they do."
                              The Great Advocate and Orator
                              for Women, 1682

a) Generic

00568.   Banner, Lois W. "Why Women Have Not Been Great Chefs." The South Atlantic Quarterly 72 (Spring 1973): 198-212.

00569.   Baudrillart, Henri Joseph Leon. Histoire du luxe privé et public depuis l'antiquité, jus qu'à nos jours. 4 vols. 2nd ed. Paris: Hachette et Cie, 1878-1880.

00570. Bauer, Bernard A. <u>Woman</u> <u>and</u> <u>Love</u>. Translated by Eden and
        Cedar Paul. New York: Liveright, 1949.

00571. Bendix, Reinhard and Lipset, Seymour Martin, eds. <u>Class,</u>
        <u>Status,</u> <u>and</u> <u>Power,</u> <u>Social</u> <u>Stratification</u> <u>in</u> <u>Comparative</u>
        <u>Perspective</u>. New York: Free Press, 1966.

00572. Brinton, Crane. <u>A</u> <u>History</u> <u>of</u> <u>Western</u> <u>Morals</u>. New York:
        Harcourt, Brace and Co., 1959.

00573. Finck, Henry T. <u>Primitive</u> <u>Love</u> <u>and</u> <u>Love</u> <u>Stories</u>. New York:
        Charles Scribner's Sons, 1899.

00574. _____. <u>Romantic</u> <u>Love</u> <u>and</u> <u>Personal</u> <u>Beauty:</u> <u>Their</u>
        <u>Development,</u> <u>Casual</u> <u>Relations,</u> <u>Historic</u> <u>and</u> <u>National</u> <u>Pecul-</u>
        <u>iarities</u>. New York: Macmillan, 1912.

00575. Fuchs, Edward. <u>Illustrierte</u> <u>Sittengeschichte</u> <u>vom</u> <u>Mittelalter</u>
        <u>bis</u> <u>zur</u> <u>Neuzeit</u>. 5 vols. Munich: Albert Longen Verlag,
        1909-1912.

00576. Harkness, Georgia Elma. <u>The</u> <u>Sources</u> <u>of</u> <u>Western</u> <u>Morality</u>. New
        York: Scribner's Sons, 1954.

00577. Lecky, William E. <u>History</u> <u>of</u> <u>European</u> <u>Morals</u>. 1869. Reprint.
        New York: George Braziller, 1955.

00578. Oakley, Ann. <u>Sex,</u> <u>Gender</u> <u>and</u> <u>Society</u>. London: Maurice Temple
        Smith, 1972.

00579. _____. <u>Woman's</u> <u>Work:</u> <u>The</u> <u>Housewife</u> <u>Past</u> <u>and</u> <u>Present</u>.
        New York: Pantheon Books, 1976.

00580. Rivers, W. H. R. <u>Social</u> <u>Organisation</u>. New York: A. A. Knopf,
        Inc., 1924.

00581. Salomon, Alice. <u>Heroische</u> <u>Frauen</u>. <u>Lebensbilder</u> <u>sozialer</u>
        <u>Führerinnen</u>. Zurich: Verlag für Recht und Geschichte, 1936.

00582. Schultz, Alwin. <u>Das</u> <u>häusliche</u> <u>Leben</u> <u>der</u> <u>europäischen</u>
        <u>Kulturvolker</u> <u>vom</u> <u>Mittelalter</u> <u>bis</u> <u>zur</u> <u>2.</u> <u>Halfte</u> <u>des</u> <u>18.</u>
        <u>Jahrhunderts</u>. Handbuch der mittelalterlichen und neueren
        Geschichte, vol. 4. Munich: R. Oldenbourg, 1903.

00583. Shorter, Edward. "Différence de classe et sentiment depuis
        1750." <u>Annales:</u> <u>économies,</u> <u>sociétés,</u> <u>civilisations</u> 29
        (July-August 1974): 1034-1057.

00584. Tiger, Lionel. "The possible biological Origins of Sexual
        Discrimination." <u>Impact</u> <u>of</u> <u>Science</u> <u>on</u> <u>Society</u> 20 (1970):
        29-44.

00585. Wachsmuth, Wilhelm. <u>Europäische</u> <u>Sittengeschichte</u>. Leipzig:
        F.C.W. Vogel, 1831-39.

b) Demography

00586. Bardet, Jean-Pierre. "La démographie des villes de la
        modernite, XVIe-XVIIIe siècles; mythes et realites."
        Annales de démographie historique (1974): 101-126.

00587. Biraben, Jean Noel. "Evolution de la fécondité dans l'Europe
        occidentale." In Official Documents of the European Popula-
        tion Conference, I, C2, pp. 1-29. Strasbourg: n.p., 1966.

00588. Chaney, Elsa. "Women and Population." In Population and
        Politics, edited by Rich L. Clinton, pp. 233-246. Lexington,
        Mass.: Lexington, 1973.

00589. Chaunu, Pierre. Histoire quantitative, histoire serielle.
        Paris: Librairie Armand Colin, 1978.

00590. Drake, Michael. "Age at Marriage in the Pre-Industrial West."
        In Population Growth and the Brain Drain, edited by Frank
        Bechhofer, pp. 196-208. Edinburgh: Edinburgh University
        Press, 1969.

00591. Dupâquier, Jacques and Demonet, Michel. "Ce qui fait les
        familles nombreuses." Annales: économies, sociétés,
        civilisations 27 (1972): 1025-1045.

00592. Flinn, Michael W. The European Demographic System, 1500-1820.
        Baltimore: Johns Hopkins University Press, 1981.

00593. Gasken, Katherine. "Age at First Marriage in Europe before
        1850: A Summary of Family Reconstitution Data." Journal
        of Family History 3 (Spring 1978): 23-36.

00594. Glass, David Victor, and Eversley, D.E.C., eds. Population in
        History, Essays in Historical Demography. Chicago: Aldine
        Pub. Co., 1965.

00595. _____ and Revelle, Roger, eds. Population and
        Social Change. London: Edward Arnold, 1972.

00596. Habbakkuk, H.J. Population Growth and Economic Development
        Since 1750. Leicester: Leicester University Press, 1972.

00597. Hollingsworth, Thomas. "On the Marriage Rate in Pre-Malthusian
        Europe; Comparison with the under-developed Countries of
        today; The Marriage Rate in Europe today; Comparison with
        the Marriage Rate in former Days." In Official Documents
        of the European Population Conference, I, C2, pp. 1-11.
        Strasbourg: n.p., 1966.

00598.   Laslett, Peter and Wall, Richard, eds. Household and Family
in past Time: Comparative Studies in the Size and Structures
of the Domestic Group over the last three Centuries in
England, France, Serbia, Japan and Colonial North America.
Cambridge: Cambridge University Press, 1972.

00599.   Lavergne, Bernard. "Le mystère des oscillations de la natalité
en France et dans les pays occidentaux." Année politique et
économique 44 (1971): 435-443.

00600.   Lee, Ronald Demos, ed. Population Patterns in the Past
Studies in Social Discontinuity, New York: Harcourt, Brace,
Jovanovich, Publishers, 1977.

00601.   Menken, Jane; Trussell, James; and Watkins, Susan. "The
Nutrition Fertility Link: An Evaluation of the Evidence."
Journal of Interdisciplinary History 11 (Winter 1981): 425-
441.

00602.   Mols, Roger. Introduction a la démographie des villes d'Europe
du XIVe au XVIIIe siècle. Louvain: Université de Louvain,
1954-1956.

00603.   Noonan, John T., Jr. "Intellectual and Demographic History."
Daedalus 97 (1968): 463-485.

00604.   Ohlin, G. "Mortality, Marriage and Growth in Pre-Industrial
Populations." Population Studies 14 (March 1961): 190-197.

00605.   Rotberg, Robert I. and Rabb, Theodore K., eds. Marriage and
Fertility. Studies in Interdiscriplinary History. Princeton, N.J.: Princeton University Press, 1980.

00606.   Russell, Josiah Cox. "Demographic Patterns in History." In
Demographic Analysis: Selected Readings, edited by Joseph J.
Spengler and Otis Dudley Duncan, pp. 52-68. Glencoe, Ill.:
Free Press, 1956.

00607.   Schofield, Roger S. "The Relationship between Demographic
Structure and Environment in pre-industrial Western Europe."
In Sozialgeschichte der Familie in der Neuzeit Europas,
edited by Werner Conze, pp. 147-160. Stuttgart: Ernst
Klett Verlag, 1976.

00608.   Taylor, K.W. "Some Aspects of Population History." In
Demographic Analysis: Selected Readings, edited by Joseph J.
Spengler and Otis Dudley Duncan, pp. 44-51. Glencoe, Ill.:
Free Press, 1956.

00609.   Tilly, Charles, ed. Historical Studies of Changing Fertility.
Princeton, N.J.: Princeton University Press, 1978.

00610.   _____. "The Historical Study of Vital Processes."
In Historical Studies of Changing Fertility, edited by
Charles Tilly, pp. 3-55. Princeton: University Press, 1978.

00611.   Van de Walle, Etienne and Van de Walle, Francine. "Allaite-
         ment, sterilité, et conception: les opinions jusqu'au XIX
         siècle." Population 27 (July–October 1972): 685–701.

00612   Vann, Richard T. "History and Demography." History and
         Theory 9 (1969): 64–78.

00613.   Wrigley, E. Anthony Population and History. New York:
         McGraw-Hill, 1969.

c) *Family*

(1) Bibliographies

00614.   Aldous, Joan and Dahl, Nancy S., ed. International Biblio-
         graphy of Research in Marriage and the Family. Vol. 2,
         1965-1972. Minneapolis: University of Minnesota Press,
         1974.

00615.   Aldous, Joan and Hill, Reuben, eds. International Bibliography
         of Research in Marriage and the Family. Vol. 1, 1900-1964.
         Minneapolis: University of Minnesota Press, 1967.

00616.   Bardis, Panos D. "Family Forms and Variations Historically
         Considered." In Handbook of Marriage and the Family, edited
         by Harold T. Christensen, pp. 403-461. Chicago: Rand
         McNally, 1964.

00617.   Berkner, Lutz K. "Recent Research on the History of the
         Family in Western Europe." Journal of Marriage and the
         Family 35 (August 1973): 395-405.

00618.   Harris, Barbara J. "Recent Work on the History of the Family:
         A Review Article." Feminist Studies 3 (Spring-Summer 1976):
         159-172.

00619.   Katz, Jacob. "Family, Kinship and Marriage among Ashkenzaim
         in the Sixteenth to Eighteenth Centuries." Jewish Journal
         of Sociology 1 (April 1959): 4-22.

00620.   Milden, James Wallace. The Family in Past Time. A Guide to
         the Literature. New York: Garland Publishing Inc., 1977.

00621.   Olson, David H.L. and Dahl, Nancy S., ed. Inventory of
         Marriage and Family Literature. Vol. 3, 1973-1974. St.
         Paul: University of Minnesota, 1975

00622.   Sinofsky, Faye, et. al. "A Bibliography of Psychohistory.
         Section II, The History of Childhood." History of Child-
         hood Quarterly 2 (Spring 1975): 531-541.

00623.   Soliday, Gerald L., ed. History of the Family and Kinship:
          A Select International Bibliography. Millwood, N.Y.: Kraus
          International, 1980.

(2) Non-specific

00624.   Anderson, Robert T. "Changing Kinship in Europe." Kroeber
          Anthropological Society Papers 28 (1963): 1-48.

00625.   Ariès, Philippe. "Les familles d'Ancien Régime." Revue des
          travaux de l'Académie des sciences morales et politiques
          4th ser. 109 (1956): 46-55.

00626.   _____. "The Family and the City in the Old World
          and the New." In Changing Images of the Family, edited by
          Virginia Tufte and Barbara Myerhoff, pp. 29-41. New Haven:
          Yale University Press, 1979. Also in Daedalus 106 (Spring
          1977): 227-235 and Esprit 1 (1978): 3-12.

00627.   Berkner, Lutz K. "Rural Family Organization in Europe: A
          Problem in Comparative History." Peasant Studies Newsletter
          1 (1972): 145-156.

00628.   _____. "The Use and Misuse of Census Data for the
          Historical Analysis of Family Structure. Journal of
          Interdisciplianry History 5 (1974-1975): 721-738.

00629.   Burgess, Ernest Watson, and Locke, Harvey J. The Family from
          Institution to Companionship. 3rd ed. New York: American
          Book Company, 1960.

00630.   Cohen, Joel. "Childhood Mortality, Family Size, and Birth
          Order in Pre-Industrial Europe." Demography 12 (February
          1975): 35-55.

00631.   Conze, Werner, ed. Sozialgeschichte der Familie in der
          Neuzeit Europas. Stuttgart: Ernst Klett Verlag, 1976.

00632.   _____. "Sozialgeschichte der Familie." Viertel-
          jahresschrift fur Sozial und Wirtschaftsgeschichte 65 (1978):
          357-369.

00633.   Cuisenier, Jean and Segalen, Martine, eds. The Family Life
          Cycle in European Societies. The Hague: Mouton, 1977.

00634.   Erikson, Erik. Life History and the Historical Moment. New
          York: Norton, 1975.

00635.   Farber, Bernard. Kinship and Family Organization. New York:
          Wiley, John and Sons, Inc., 1966.

00636. Forster, Robert and Ranum, Orest, eds. Family and Society:
        Selections from the Annales. Baltimore: Johns Hopkins
        University Press, 1976.

00637. Gilman, Charlotte (Perkins) Stetson. The Home: Its Work and
        Influence. 1903. Urbana: University of Illinois
        Press, 1972.

00638. Goodsell, Willystine. A History of Marriage and the Family.
        Rev. ed. New York: MacMillan, 1934.

00639. Goody, Jack, ed. The Character of Kinship. Cambridge:
        University Press, 1973.

00640. _____. "The Evolution of the Family." In Household and
        Family in Past Time, edited by Peter Laslett and Richard
        Wall, pp. 101-124. Cambridge: University Press, 1972.

00641. _____; Thirsk, J.; and Thompson, E.P. Family and In-
        heritance--Rural Society in Western Europe, 1200-1800. New
        York: Cambridge University Press, 1976.

00642. Greenfield, S.M. "Industrialization and the Family in
        Sociological Theory." American Journal of Sociology 67
        (1961): 312-322.

00643. Grosse, Ernst. Die Formen der Familie und die Formen der
        Wirtschaft. Freiburg: J.C.B. Mohr, 1896.

00644. Hammel, Eugene and Laslett, Peter. "Comparing Household
        Structure over Time and Between Cultures." Comparative
        Studies in Society and History 16 (1974): 73-109.

00645. Hareven, Tamara K. "Family Time and Historical Time."
        Daedalus 106 (Spring 1977): 57-70.

00646. _____. Transitions: The Family and the Life
        Course in Historical Perspective. New York: Academic Press,
        1978.

00647. Hartland, Edwin S. Primitive Paternity: The Myth of Super-
        natural Birth in Relation to the History of the Family.
        London: D. Nutt, 1910.

00648. Hausen, Karin. "Familie als Gegenstand historischer Sozial-
        wissenschaft: Bemerkungen zu einer Forschungsstrategie."
        Geschichte und Gesellschaft 1 (1975): 171-209.

00649. _____. "Die Polarisierung der 'Geschlechtscharaktere'--
        Eine Spiegelung die Dissoziation von Erwerbs-und Familien-
        leben." In Sozialgeschichte der Familie in der Neuzeit
        Europas, edited by Werner Conze, pp. 363-393. Stuttgart:
        Ernst Klett Verlag, 1976.

00650   Laslett, Peter. "Characteristics of the Western Family con-
         sidered over Time." In Family Life and Illicit Love in
         earlier Generations, pp. 12-49. New York: Cambridge Uni-
         versity Press, 1977. Also in Journal of Family History 2
         Summer 1977): 89-116.

00651.   _____. "The Comparative History of Household and the
         Family." Journal of Social History 4 (1970): 75-87.

00652.   _____. "Le cycle familial et le processus de social-
         isation: caractéristiques du schéma occidental considéré
         dans le temps." In The Family Cycle in European Societies,
         edited by Jean Cuisenier, pp. 317-338. Paris: Mouton, 1977.

00653.   _____. "Familie und Industrialisierung: eine
         'starke Theorie'." In Sozialgeschichte der Familie in der
         Neuzeit Europas, edited by Werner Conze, pp. 13-31. Stutt-
         gart: Ernst Klett Verlag, 1976.

00654.   _____. Family Life and Illicit Love in earlier
         Generations. New York: Cambridge University Press, 1977.

00655.   _____. "Introduction: The History of the Family."
         In Household and Family in Past Time, edited by Peter Laslett
         and Richard Wall, pp. 1-89. Cambridge: The University Press,
         1972.

00656.   Letourneau, Charles. The Evolution of Marriage and the
         Family. New York: C. Scribner's Sons, 1908.

00657.   Levi-Strauss, Claude. The Elementary Structures of Kinship.
         Boston: Beacon Press, 1969.

00658.   McArdle, Frank. "Another Look at 'Peasant Families East and
         West'." Peasant Studies Newsletter 3 (1974): 11-14.

00659.   Malkin, H.J. "Observations on Social Conditions, Fertility
         and Family Survival in the Past." Proceedings of the Royal
         Society of Medicine 53 (1960): 117-132.

00660.   Messer, Mary B. The Family in the Making, an Historic Sketch.
         New York: Putnam, 1928.

00661.   Michel, Andree, compiler. Sociologie de la famille et du
         mariage. Paris: Mouton, 1970.

00662.   Mogey, John. "Residence, Family, Kinship: Some Recent Re-
         search." Journal of Family History 1 (August 1976): 95-105.

00663.   Nash, Arnold S. "Ancient Past and Living Present." In
         Family, Marriage and Parenthood, edited by Howard Becker
         and Reuben Hill, pp. 84-103. Boston: Heath, 1955.

00664.   Ortigues, Edmond. "La psychanalyse et les institutions
         familiales." Annales: économies sociétés, civilisations 27
         (1972): 1091-1104.

00665.   Phillpotts, Bertha Surtees. Kindred and Clan in the Middle
         Ages and After: A Study in the Sociology of the Teutonic
         Races. Cambridge: University Press, 1913.

00666.   Plumb, J.H. "The Dying Family." In The Light of History,
         pp. 147-152. Boston: Houghton Mifflin, 1973.

00667.   Queen, Stuart A., and Habenstein, Robert. The Family in
         Various Cultures. Philadelphia: Lippincott, 1961.

00668.   Rabb, Theodore, and Rothberg, Robert, eds. The Family in
         History. New York: Harper & Row, 1973.

00669.   Rosenbaum, Heidi. Familie und Gesellschaftsstruktur: Material-
         ien zu den sozio-okonomischen Bedingungen von Familienfor-
         men. Frankfurt: Fischer Taschenbuch-Verlag, 1974.

00670.   _____. "Zur neueren Entwicklung der historischen
         Familienforschung." Geschichte und Gesellschaft 1 (1975):
         210-225.

00671.   Rosenberg, Charles E., ed. The Family in History. Phila-
         delphia: University of Pennsylvania Press, 1975.

00672.   _____. "Introduction: History and Exper-
         ience." In The Family in History, pp. 1-12. Philadelphia:
         University of Pennsylvania Press, 1975.

00673.   Sabean, David. "Aspects of Kinship Behaviour and Property
         in Rural Western Europe before 1800." In Family and Inheri-
         tance: Rural Society in Western Europe, 1200-1800, edited
         by Jack Goody, Joan Thirsk and E.P. Thompson, pp. 96-111.
         New York: Cambridge University Press, 1976.

00674.   Sawhill, Isabel V. "Economic Perspectives on the Family."
         Daedalus 106 (Spring 1977): 115-125.

00675.   Schmidt, Wilhelm. Gebräuche des Ehemannes bei Schwangerschaft
         und Geburt. Mit Richtigstellung des Begriffes der Couvade.
         Vienna: Verlag Herald, 1955.

00676.   Shorter, Edward. The Making of the Modern Family. New York:
         Basic Books, Inc., Publishers, 1975.

00677.   Skolnick, Arlene S. and Jerome H. Family in Tradition.
         Boston: Little, Brown, 1971.

00678.   Stern, Bernhard J., ed. The Family: Past and Present. New
         York: Appleton, 1938.

00679. Swerdlow, Amy; Bridenthal, Renate; Kelly, Joan; Vine, Phyllis.
        Household and Kin, Families in Flux. Old Westbury, New
        York: Feminist Press, 1981.

00680. Tufte, Virginia and Myerhoff, Barbara, ed. Changing Images
        of the Family. New Haven: Yale University Press, 1979.

00681. Verdon, Michael. "The Stem Family: Toward a General Theory."
        Journal of Interdisciplinary History 10 (Summer 1979):
        87-106.

00682. Wells, Robert V. "Family History and Demographic Transition."
        Journal of Social History 9 (Fall 1975): 1-19.

00683. Wheaton, Robert. "Family and Kinship in Western Europe: the
        problem of joint Family Household." Journal of Interdiscip-
        linary History 5 (Spring 1975): 601-628.

00684. Wrigley, E. Anthony. "Reflections on the History of the
        Family." Daedalus 106 (1977): 71-85.

00685. Zimmerman, Carl C. Family and Civilization. New York:
        Harper, 1947.

        Also refer to #323, 329, 330, 380, 415, 416, 450, 591, 598.

                          (3)   Motherhood

00686. Beil, Ada. Inhalt und Wandel der Idee der Mutterlichkeit.
        Individuum und Gemeinschaft, vol. 1. Munich: J.F.
        Bergmann, 1926.

00687. Crepaz, Adele. Mutterschaft und Mutter. Kulturgeschichtliche
        Studien. Leipzig: O. Wiegand, 1905.

00688. Hall, Nor. Mothers and Daughters: Reflections on the Arche-
        typal Feminine. Minneapolis: Rusoff Books, 1976.

00689. Minturn, Leigh, and Lambert, William Wilson. Mothers of Six
        Cultures. New York: John Wiley and Sons, Inc., 1964.

00690. Shorter, Edward. "Der Wandel der Mutter-Kind Beziehungen zu
        Beginn der Moderne." Geschichte und Gesellschaft 1 (1975):
        256-287.

                          (4)   Childhood

00691. Aries, Phillipe. Centuries of Childhood: A Social History of
        Family Life. Translated by Robert Baldick. New York:
        Random House, 1965.

00692. Brouardel, Paul Camille Hippolyte. L'Infanticide. Paris:
        J.B. Bailliere et Fils, 1897.

00693. De Mause, Lloyd. "The Evolution of Childhood." In The History
        of Childhood, edited by Lloyd de Mause, pp. 1-74. New York:
        Harper Torchbook, Harper and Row, 1975.

00694. _____., ed. The History of Childhood. New York:
        Psychohistory Press, 1974.

00695. Despert, J. Louise. The Emotionally Disturbed Child - Then
        and Now. New York: Vantage Press, 1965.

00696. Erikson, Erik. Childhood and Society. 2nd ed. New York:
        W.W. Norton, 1963.

00697. _____. Identity, Youth and Crisis. New York: W.W.
        Norton, 1968.

00698. Flandrin, Jean-Louis. "L'attitude a l'egard du petit enfant
        et les conduites sexuelles dans la civilization occidentale."
        Annales de demographie historique (1973): 143-210.

00699. Haffner, Carl. "The Changeling: History and Psychodynamics of
        Attitudes to Handicapped Children in European Folklore."
        Journal of the History of Behavioral Sciences 4 (January
        1968): 55-61.

00700. Langer, William L. "Further Notes on the History of Infanti-
        cide." History of Childhood Quarterly 2 (Summer 1974):
        129-134.

00701. _____. "Infanticide: A Historical Survey."
        History of Childhood Quarterly 1 (Winter 1974): 353-366.

00702. Laslett, Peter. "Introduction: Comparing Illegitimacy over
        Time and between Cultures." In Bastardy and its Comparative
        History, edited by Peter Laslett, Karla Oosterveen and
        Richard M. Smith, pp. 1-68. Cambridge, Mass.: Harvard
        University Press, 1980.

00703. _____, Oosterveen, Karla, and Smith, Richard M., eds.
        Bastardy and its Comparative History. Cambridge, Mass.:
        Harvard University Press, 1980.

00704. Lopez, Manuel D. "A Guide to the Interdisciplinary Literature
        of the History of Childhood." History of Childhood Quarterly
        1 (1973-74): 463-494.

00705. Mattessich, Paul W. "Childlessness and its Correlates in
        Historical Perspective: A Research Note." Journal of
        Family History 4 (Fall 1979): 299-307.

00706. Payne, George Henry. The Child in Human Progress. London:
        G.P. Putnam's Sons, 1916.

00707. Piers, M.W. "Kindermord: Ein historischer Ruckblick."
        Psyche 30 (1976): 418-435.

00708. Theopold, Wilhelm. Das Kind in der Votivmalerie. Munich:
        Thiemig Verlag, 1981.

00709. Weber-Kellermann, Ingeborg. Die Kindheit. Frankfurt am
        Main: Insel Verlag, 1979.

        Also refer to #508, 545, 622, 630.

                        d) Marriage

00710. Blum, Leon. Marriage. Translated by Warre Bradley Wells.
        Philadelphia: J.B. Lippincott Co., 1937.

00711. Briffault, Robert and Malinowski, Bronislaw. Marriage: Past
        and Present. Boston: Porter Sargent, 1956.

00712. Caird, Mona. Morality of Marriage and Other Essays on the
        Status and Destiny of Women. London: George Redway, 1897.

00713. Davidson, Terry. "Wifebeating: A Recurring Phenomenon
        Throughout History." In Battered Women: A Psychosociologi-
        cal Study of Domestic Violence, edited by Maria Roy, pp.
        2-23. New York: Van Nostrand Reinhold Company, 1977.

00714. Flandrin, Jean-Louis. "Mariage tardif et vie sexuelle: Dis-
        cussions et hypothèses de recherche." Annales: Economies,
        sociétés, civilisations 27 (November-December 1972):
        1351-1378.

00715. Foerster, Frederick Wilhelm. Marriage and the Sex Problem.
        Translated by Meyrick Booth. New York: F.A. Stokes Co., 1912.

00716. Hajnal, J. "European Marriage Patterns in Perspective." In
        Population in History, edited by D.V. Glass and D.E.C. Eversley,
        pp. 101-143. Chicago: Aldine Publishing Co., 1965.

00717. Hamilton, Cicely M. Marriage as a Trade. 1909. Reprint.
        Detroit: Singing Tree Press, 1971.

00718. Hughes, Diane Owen. "From Brideprice to Dowry in Mediterranean
        Europe." Journal of Family History 3 (Fall 1978): 262-296.

00719. James, E.O. Marriage Customs through the Ages. New York:
        Collier Books, 1965.

00720. Jeaffreson, John Cordy. Brides and Bridals. 2 vols. 1872.
        Reprint. New Haven, Conn.: Research Publications Inc., 1977.

00721.   Joyce, George Hayward, S.J. Christian Marriage: An Historical
         and Doctrinal Study. New York: Sheed & Ward, 1948.

00722.   Kitchin, Shepherd Braithwaite. A History of Divorce. London:
         Chapman and Hall, Ltd., 1912.

00723.   Kramer, S.N. The Sacred Marriage Rite. Bloomington, Ind.:
         Indiana University Press, 1969.

00724.   Kühn, Joachim. Ehen zur linken Hand in der europäischen
         Geschichte. Stuttgart: K.F. Koehler, 1968.

00725.   Mair, Lucy. Marriage. London: Scolar Press, 1977.

00726.   Marriage: Past and Present. Boston: Porter Sargent, 1956.

00727.   Michelet, Jules. L'Amour. Paris: Calmann-Levy, 1926.

00728.   Murstein, Bernard I. Love, Sex and Marriage through the Ages.
         New York: Springer Publishing Co., Inc., 1974.

00729.   Pitt-Rivers, Julian. The Fate of Shechen, or the Politics of
         Sex; Six Essays in the Anthropology of the Mediterranean.
         Cambridge: Cambridge University Press, 1977.

00730.   Pomerai, Ralph de. Marriage, Past, Present and Future: An
         Outline of the History and Development of Human Sexual
         Relationships. New York: R.R. Smith, 1930.

00731.   Swiney, Frances. The Bar of Isis, or, the Law of the Mother.
         London: C.W. Daniel, 1909.

00732.   Thiel, Josef Franz. "The Institution of Marriage: An Anthro-
         pological Perspective." Concilium 55 (1970): 13-24.

00733.   Turner, E.S. A History of Courting. New York: E.P. Dutton
         and Co., 1955.

00734.   Westermarck, Edward Alexander. The History of Human Marriage.
         1891. Reprint. New York: Johnson Reprint Corp., 1971.

00735.   _____. A Short History of Marriage. London:
         Macmillan, 1926.

         Also refer to #290, 294, 319, 358, 361, 362, 366, 371, 383,
         432, 438, 441, 443, 507, 509, 510, 511, 514, 515, 590, 593,
         593, 597, 604, 605, 614, 615, 619, 621, 638, 656, 661.

e) Sex Life and Morals

(1) Non-specific

00736. Aranguren, José Luis L. Erotismo y liberación de la mujer.
Ariel: Esplugues de Llobregat, 1972.

00737. Bloch, Ruth H. "Untangling the Roots of Modern Sex Roles: A
Survey of Four Centuries of Change." Signs 4 (Winter 1978):
237-252.

00738. Braxton, Bernard. Women, Sex and Races: A Realist View of
Sexism and Racism. Washington, D.C.: Verta Press, 1973.
[See especially "Handmaids of the Devil (witchcraft), pp.
31-59 and "Woman as Prostitute," pp. 147-158.]

00739. Briffault, Robert. Sin and Sex. New York: Macaulay Co., 1931.

00740. Bullough, Vern L. Sex, Society and History. New York:
Science History Publications, 1976.

00741. _____. Sexual Variance in Society and History.
New York: John Wiley and Sons, 1976.

00742. Bullough, Vern and Bonnie. Sin, Sickness, and Sanity: A
History of Sexual Attitudes. New York: Garland, 1977.

00743. Calverton, V.F., and Schmalhausen, S.D., eds. Sex in
Civilization. Garden City, N.Y.: Garden City, 1929.

00744. D'Arcy, M.C. The Heart and Mind of Love, Lion and Unicorn:
A Study in Eros and Agape. London: Faber and Faber Ltd.,
1954.

00745. Ellis, Albert and Abarbanel, Albert. The Encyclopedia of
Sexual Behavior. 2 vols. New York: Hawthorn Books, 1961.

00746. Fere, Charles Samson. Scientific and Esoteric Studies in
Sexual Degeneration in Mankind and in Animals. Translated
by Ulrich Van der Horst. New York: Anthropoligical Press,
1932.

00747. Fitch, Robert. The Decline and Fall of Sex. New York:
Harcourt, Brace, 1957.

00748. Foucault, Michel. The History of Sexuality. New York:
Pantheon Books, 1978.

00749. Frischauer, Paul. L'Archéologie de la sexualité. Paris:
Stock, 1969.

00750. Fromm, Erich. The Art of Loving. New York: Harper and Row, Co., 1956.

00751. Geddes, Patrick and Thompson, J. Arthur. The Evolution of Sex. London: W. Scott, 1897.

00752. Henriques, Fernando. Love in Action: The Sociology of Sex. New York: E.P. Dutton and Co., 1960.

00753. Hunt, Morton M. The Natural History of Love. New York: Funk and Wagnalls, 1967.

00754. Jeanniere, Abel. The Anthropology of Sex. Translated by Julie Kernan. New York: Harper & Row, 1967.

00755. Kern, Stephen. Anatomy and Destiny: A Cultural History of the Human Body. Indianapolis: The Bobbs-Merrill Co., Inc., 1975.

00756. Kinsey, Alfred C., et. al. Sexual Behavior in the Human Female. Philadelphia: W.B. Saunders, 1953.

00757. _____. Sexual Behavior in the Human Male. Philadelphia: W.B. Saunders, Co., 1948.

00758. Laslett, Peter. "Age at sexual maturity in Europe since the Middle Ages." In Family Life and Illicit Love in Earlier Generations, pp. 214-232. New York: Cambridge University Press, 1977.

00759. Lewinsohn, Richard. A History of Sexual Customs. New York: Harper and Row Publishers, 1958.

00760. Lucka, Emil. Eros: The Development of the Sex Relation through the Ages. New York: G.P. Putnam's Sons, 1915.

00761. Ludovoci, Laurence James. The final inequality; a critical assessment of women's sexual role in society. New York: Norton, 1965.

00762. Mantegazza, Paola. The Sexual Relations of Mankind. Translated by Samuel Putnam. 11th ed. Reprint. New York: Eugenics Publishing Company, 1957.

00763. Maranón, Gregorio. Ensayos sobre la vida sexual: Sexo, trabajo y deporte; Maternidad y feminismo: Educacion sexual y differenciación sexual; Amor conveniencia y eugenesia. Madrid: Espana Calpe, 1960.

00764. Nygren, Anders. Eros and Agape. Translated by Philips Watson. 1953. Reprint. New York: Harper, 1969.

00765. Parsons, Elsie Worthington (Clews). The Old-Fashioned Woman: Primitive Fancies About the Sex. 1913. Reprint. New York: Arno Press, 1972.

00766. Perella, N.J. The Kiss Sacred and Profane: An Interpretive
        History of Kiss Symbolism. Berkeley: University of Cali-
        fornia Press, 1969.

00767. Robinson, Victor, ed. Encyclopedia Sexualis. New York:
        Dingwall-Rock, 1936.

00768. Rubin, Gayle. "The Traffic in Women." In Toward an Anthro-
        pology of Women, edited by Rayna Reiter, pp. 157-210. New
        York: Monthly Review Press, 1975.

00769. Seward, Georgene Hoffman. "Sex roles, ancient to modern." In
        Sex Roles in Changing Society, edited by Georgene H. Seward
        and Robert C. Williamson, pp. 109-125. New York: Random
        House, 1970.

00770. _____. Sex Roles in Changing Society. New
        York: Random House, 1970.

00771. Shorter, Edward. "Capitalism, Culture and Sexuality: some
        competing Models." Social Science Quarterly 53 (1972):
        338-356.

00772. _____. "Sexual Change and Illegitimacy: The
        European Experience." In Modern European Social History,
        edited by Robert Bezucha, pp. 231-69. Lexington, Mass.:
        D.C. Heath and Co., 1972.

00773. Simons, G.L. Sex and Superstition. London: Abelard and
        Schuman, 1973.

00774. Solé, Jacques. L'amour en Occident à l'époque moderne.
        Paris: A. Michel, 1976.

00775. Tannahill, Reay. Sex in History. New York: Stein and Day,
        1980.

00776. Taylor, Gordon Rattray. Sex in History. New York: Vanguard
        Press, 1954.

00777. Thomas, William. Sex and Society. 1907. Reprint. New York:
        Arno Press, 1974.

00778. Ussel, Josvan. Histoire de la répression sexuelle. Paris:
        Robert Laffont, 1972.

00779. Walters, R.G. "Sexual Matters as Historical Problems: A
        Framework of Analysis." Societas 6 (Summer 1976): 157-175.

00780. Wright, Helena. Sex and Society. Seattle: University of
        Washington Press, 1969.

00781. Young, Wayland. Eros Denied: Sex in Western Society. New
        York: Grove Press, 1964.

        Also refer to #654, 698, 714, 715, 727-729.

(2) Prostitutes and Courtesans

00782. Bassermann, Lujo. The Oldest Profession: A History of Pros-
        titution. Translated by James Cleugh. New York: Stein
        and Day, 1968.

00783. Bauer, Willi. Geschichte und Wesen der Prostitution: Eine
        geschichtliche und sozial-ethische Darstellung der Prostitu-
        tion in Wort und Bild und ihrer Folgen im Zeitraum von uber
        4000 Jahren. Stuttgart: Weltspiegel-Verlag, 1965.

00784. Bloch, Iwan and Loewenstein, Georg. Die Prostitution.
        Berlin: Louis Marcus Verlagsbuchhandlung, 1925.

00785. Boiron, N.M. La Prostitution dans l'histoire--devant la
        droit--devant l'opinion. Nancy: Berger-Levrault, 1926.

00786. Bullough, Vern L. History of Prostitution. New Hyde Park,
        N.Y.: University Books, 1964.

00787. _____ and Deacon, Margaret, eds. A Bibliography
        of Prostitution. New York & London: Garland Publishing Co.,
        1977.

00788. Burgess, William. The World's Social Evil: A Historical
        Review and Study of the Problems Relating to the Subject.
        Chicago: Saul, 1914.

00789. Dieckmann, Heinz. Hetärenkatalog. Munich: Heyne, 1970.

00790. Das Dirnentum und der Dirnengeist in der Gesellschaft. Leipzig:
        Verlag von Max Spohr, 1918.

00791. Evans, Hilary. Harlots, Whores and Hookers: A History of
        Prostitution. New York: Tapplinger Publishing Co., 1979.

00792. Fischer, Wilhelm. Die Prostitution. Leipzig: Verlag
        Curt Ronninger, 1920.

00793. Flexner, Abraham. Prostitution in Europe. 1914. Reprint.
        New York: Patterson Smith Pub. Corp., 1969.

00794. Greer, Joseph H. Prostitution, its History, Cause and Cure.
        Seattle: Crucible Pub., 1920.

00795. Guyot, Yves. La Prostitution. Paris: G. Charpentier, 1882.

00796. Harriet, W. Geschichte der Prostitution aller Volker. Berlin:
        Schoneberg, Jawerstahl, 1912.

00797. Harris, G. La prostituzione, sue origine suo sviluppo e sua
        organizzazione. Milan: G. Gnocchi, 1885.

00798. Hayward, C. The Courtesan: The Part she has played in
        Classic and Modern Literature and in Life. London: The
        Casanova Society, 1926.

00799. _____. Dictionary of Courtesans--an Anthology, sometimes
        Gay, sometimes Tragic, of the Celebrated Courtesans of
        History from Antiquity to the Present Day--Arranged in
        Alphabetical Order. New York: University Books, 1962.

00800. Henriques, Fernando. Prostitution and Society: A Survey.
        New York: Citadel Press, 1963.

00801. _____. Prostitution in Europe and the Americas.
        2 vols. New York: Citadel Press, 1962.

00802. Hervas, Ramon. Historia de la Prostitution. Barcelona:
        Telestar, 1969.

00803. Kuhn, Franz. Femes derrière un voile. Paris: Calman-Levy,
        1972.

00804. Lacroix, Paul. History of Prostitution among all the Peoples
        of the World, from the most remote antiquity to the present
        Day. New York: Covici Friede, 1931.

00805. Leonhard, Stephan. Die Prostitution. Munich: E. Reinhardt,
        1912.

00806. McCabe, Joseph. The Story of the World's Oldest Profession.
        Girard, Kansas: Haldeman-Julius Publications, 1932.

00807. Rabutaux, A.P.E. De la prostitution en Europe depuis
        l'antiquite jusqu'a la fin du XVI siecle. Paris: Lebigre
        Duquesne Freres, 1851.

00808. Regnault, F. L'evolution de la prostitution. Paris: E.
        Flammarion, 1906.

00809. Sanger, William. History of Prostitution: Its Extent, Causes
        and Effects throughout the World. 1859. Reprint. New
        York: Arno Press, 1972.

00810. Schreiber, Hermann (Lujo Bassermann). The Oldest Profession.
        New York: Stein and Day, 1968.

00811. Scott, George Ryley. A History of Prostitution from Antiquity
        to the Present Day. 1936. Reprint. London: T. Werner
        Laurie, 1954.

00812. Servais, J.J. and Laurend, J.P. Histoire et dossier de la prostitution. Paris: Editions Planete, 1965.

00813. Seymour-Smith, Martin. Fallen Women. London: Thomas Nelson, 1969.

00814. Sorge, Wolfgang. Geschichte der Prostitution. Berlin: Potlhof and Co., 1919.

00815. Waldegg, Richard and Heinz, Werner. Geschichte und Wesen der Prostitution. Stuttgart: Weltspiegel Verlag, 1956.

Also refer to #738.

f) Fashion/Manners

00816. Aretz, Gertrude. The Elegant Woman: From the Rococo Period to Modern Times. New York: Harcourt, Brace, 1932.

00817. Bell, Quentin. On Human Finery. London: Hogarth Press, 1947.

00818. Bergler, E. Fashion and the Unconscious. New York: Brunner, 1953.

00819. Binder, P. Muffs and Morals. New York: Morrow, 1954.

00820. Boucher, François. A History of Costume in the West. London: Thames and Hudson, 1970.

00821. Brooke, Iris. Western European Costume. New York: Macmillan, 1940.

00822. Colas, Rene. Bibliographie genérale du costume et de la mode. 1933. Reprint. New York: Hacker Art Books, 1963.

00823. Cunnington, Cecil Willett. Perfect Lady. London: M. Parrish, 1948.

00824. Cunnington, Phillis and Lucas, Catherine. Charity Costumes of Children, Scholars, Alsmfold, Pensioners. New York: Barnes and Noble, 1978.

00825. _____. Costumes for Births, Marriages and Deaths. New York: Barnes and Noble, 1972.

00826. _____. Costume of Household Servants. New York: Barnes & Noble, 1975.

00827. Cunnington, Phillis, and Cunnington, Willett Cecil. The History of Underclothes. London: Michael Joseph, 1951.

00828. Davenport, Millia. Book of Costume. New York: Crown Publishers, 1948.

00829. Evans, Mary. Costume Throughout the Ages. Rev. ed. Philadelphia: Lippincott, 1950.

00830. Grand-Carteret, John. La femme en culotte. Paris: Flammarion,
1899.

00831. Hiler, H. and Hiler, M. Bibliography of Costume. New York:
H.W. Wilson, 1939.

00832. Kelly, Francis Michael and Schwabe, Randolph. Historic Costume,
a Chronicle of Fashion in Western Europe, 1490-1790. New
York: C. Scribner's Sons, 1929.

00833. Kybalová, Ludmilla; Herbenová, Olga; and Lamarová, Milena. The
Pictorial Encyclopedia of Fashion. Translated by Claudia
Rosoux. London: Hamlyn, 1968.

00834. Langner, Lawrence. The Importance of Wearing Clothes.
London: Constable, 1959.

00835. Laurent, Jacques. A History of Ladies Underwear. London:
Joseph, 1968.

00836. Laver, James. Clothes. New York: Horizon Press, 1953.

00837. _____. Dress: How and Why Fashions in Men's and
Women's Clothes have Changed during the Past Two Hundred
Years. London: J. Murray, 1950.

00838. Ostier, M. Jewels and the Woman: The Romance, Magic and
Art of Feminine Adornment. New York: Barnes & Noble, 1958.

00839. Planche, James Robinson. A cyclopedia of costume or dictionary
of dress. New York: J.W. Bouton, 1877.

00840. Robida, A. Mesdames nos aieules, dix siècles d'élégance.
Paris: Librarie illustree, 1891.

00841. Uzanne, Louis Octave. The Sunshade, the Glove and the Muff.
London: J.C. Nimmo and Barn, 1884.

00842. Veblen, Thorstein. "The Economic Theory of Women's Dress.
Popular Science Monthly 46 (December 1894): 198-205.

00843. Villermont, Comtesse Marie de. Histoire de la coiffure
feminine. Paris: Renouard, 1892.

00844. Waugh, Norah. Corsets and Crinolines. London: B.T. Batsford,
1954.

00845. Wykes-Joyce, M. Cosmetics and Adornment: Ancient and Con-
            temporary. New York: Philosophical Library, 1961.

        Also refer to #268.

g) Health/Medical

(1) Birth Control

00846. Bergues, Hélène, et. al. La prevention des naissances dans
            la famille, ses origines dans les temps modernes. Paris:
            Presses universitaires de France, 1960.

00847. Finch, Bernard and Green, Hugh. Contraception through the
            Ages. Springfield, Ill.: Thomas, 1964

00848. Green, Shirley. The Curious History of Contraception. New
            York: St. Martin's Press, 1971.

00849. Himes, Norman E. Medical History of Contraception. New York:
            Gamut Press, 1963.

00850. _____. "Medical History of Contraception." New
            England Journal of Medicine (1934): 567-581.

00851. Oakley, Ann. "Wise Woman and Medicine Man: Changes in the
            Management of Childbirth." In The Rights and Wrongs of
            Women, edited by Juliet Mitchell and Ann Oakley, pp. 17-58.
            New York: Penguin, 1976.

00852. Wood, Clive and Suitter, Beryl. The Fight for Acceptance: A
            History of Contraception. Aylesbury, England: Medical
            and Technical Publishing Co., Ltd., 1970.

        Also refer to #364, 443, 444, 447, 510, 512, 514.

(2) Women in Medicine

00853. Ackerman, Emma M. "Progress of Women in Medicine." Journal
            of Iowa State Medical Society 23 (July 1933): 361-362.

00854. Aitken, Janet. "Women in Medicine in the Ages." Journal of
            the Medical Women's Federation 46 (July 1964): 175-179.

00855. Angwin, Maria L. "Woman in Medicine." Woman's Medical
            Journal 6 (August 1897): 241-249.

00856.   Austin, Margaret. "History of Women in Medicine: A
         Symposium: Early Period." Bulletin of the Medical Library
         Association 44 (January 1956): 12-15.

00857.   Baudouin, Marcel. Femmes médecins d'autre fois. Paris:
         Jules Rousset, 1906.

00858.   Bolton, H. Carrington. "The Early Practice of Medicine by
         Women." Popular Science Monthly 18 (December 1880): 191-
         202.

00859.   Brunton, Lauder. "Some Women in Medicine." Canadian Medical
         Association Journal. 48 (January 1943): 60-65.

00860.   Bullough, Bonnie and Bullough, Vern L. Emergence of Modern
         Nursing. New York: Macmillan Co., 1969.

00861.   Bullough, Vern L. The Development of Medicine as a Profession.
         New York: Hafner Press, 1966.

00862.   Bullough, Vern L. and Bullough, Bonnie. The Care of the Sick:
         The Emergence of Modern Nursing. New York: Prodist, 1978.

00863.   Caldwell, Ruth. "Women in Medicine: Chapter III. Women in
         Medicine--'Modern History'." Medical Woman's Journal 37
         (April 1930): 96-98.

00864.   Chadwick, James Read. "The Study and Practice of Medicine by
         Women." International Review 7 (October 1879): 444-471.

00865.   Chaff, Sandra L., et. al. Women in Medicine: A Bibliography
         of the Literature on Women Physicians. Metuchen, N.J.:
         Scarecrow Press, Inc., 1977.

00866.   Cordell, Eugene F. "Woman as a Physician. Illustrious
         Examples Drawn from History. The Advantages of the Female
         Medical Students of Today Compared with those of her Pre-
         decessors, with Suggestions as to their Proper Utilization."
         Maryland Medical Journal 10 (6 October 1883): 353-356.

00867.   Cuthbert, Sister M. "Women in Medicine." Medical Missionary
         32 (January-February 1958): 7-9.

00868.   Cutter, Irving S. and Viets, Henry R. A Short History of
         Midwifery. Philadelphia: Saunders, 1964.

00869.   Dock, Lavinia L. and Stewart, Isabel Maitland. A Short History
         of Nursing. New York: G.P. Putnam's Sons, 1936.

00870.   Feldman, Jacqueline. "The Savant and the Midwife." Impact of
         Science on Society 25 (1975): 125-136.

00871. Fontanges, Haryett. Les femmes docteurs en medecine dans tous
        les pays: étude historique, statistique, documentaire et
        anecdotique sur l'art de la medecine exercé par la femme.
        4th ed. Paris: Alliance Cooperative du Livre, 1901.

00872. Ghrist, Jennie. "President's Address. Women in Medicine."
        Woman's Medical Journal 22 (July 1912): 147-149.

00873. Glasgow, Maude. "Women in the Medical Profession."
        Medical Record 88 (4 December 1915): 951-955.

00874. _____. "Women Physicians." Journal of the American
        Medical Women's Association 9 (January 1954): 24-25.

00875. Goodnow, Minnie. Goodnow's History of Nursing. Philadelphia:
        W.B. Saunders, Co., 1916.

00876. Gordon, J. Elise. "Some Women Practitioners of Past
        Centuries." Practitioner 208 (April 1972): 561-567.

00877. Hellstedt, L.M., ed. Women Physicians of the World: Auto-
        biographies of Pioneer Medical Women from 27 Nations.
        Vol. 1. Washington, D.C.: Hemisphere Publishing Corp.,
        1978.

00878. Hurd-Mead, Kate Campbell. "A Contribution to the Study of
        Women in Medicine. Were There Qualified Women Doctors
        Before the Nineteenth Century?" New England Journal of
        Medicine 199 (13 September 1928): 527-534.

00879. _____. "History of Medicine." Women in
        Medicine 72 (April 1941): 21-22.

00880. _____. A History of Women in Medicine:
        From the Earliest Times to the Beginning of the Nineteenth
        Century. 1938. Reprint. New York: AMS Press, 1976.

00881. _____. "The Seven Ages of Women in
        Medicine." Bulletin of the Medical Women's National
        Association 35 (January 1932): 11-15.

00882. _____. "A Study of the Medical Education
        of Women." Journal of the American Medical Association 116
        (25 January 1941): 339-347.

00883. Jamieson, Elizabeth M. and Sewall, Mary F. Trends in Nursing
        History. Philadelphia: W.B. Saunders Co., 1950.

00884. Jex-Blake, Sophia. Medical Women: A Thesis and a History.
        1886. Reprint. New York: Source Book Press, 1970.

00885. _____. Medical Women: Two Essays. London:
        Hamilton, Adams, & Co., 1872.

00886. Landau, Richard. Geschichte der jüdischen Ärtzte. Berlin:
        S. Karger, 1895.

00887. Lipinska, Melanie. Les femmes et le progrès des sciences
        medicales. Paris: Masson et Cie, 1930.

00888. _____. Histoire des femmes médecins depuis dans
        l'antiquité jusqu'à nos jours. Paris: Jacque et Cie, 1900.

00889. _____ and Mackenzie, Muir. "Women Doctors: An
        Historic Retrospect." Contemporary Review 108 (October
        1915): 504-510.

00890. Loyola, Sister M. "Women in Medicine." Catholic World 157
        (May 1943): 156-164.

00891. Marks, Geoffrey and Beatty, William K. Women in White. New
        York: Charles Scribner's, 1972.

00892. "A Medico-Literary Causerie: The Evolution of the Medical
        Woman (Part I)." Practitioner 52 (February 1896): 288-292;
        (April 1896): 407-412.

00893. Minor, T.C. "The Doctresses of Medicine." Interstate Medical
        Journal 8 (March 1901): 97-108.

00894. Radcliffe, Walter. Milestones in Midwifery. Bristol: Wright,
        1967.

00895. Robinson, Victor. White Caps: The Story of Nursing. Phila-
        delphia: J.B. Lippincott Co., 1946.

00896. Salzi, Francesco. Medical Women. Rome: Tipografia Romana,
        1877.

00897. Sandelin, Ellen. "On the Status of Female Doctors in Various
        Countries." Hygiea 63 (1901): 297-325.

00898. Schönfeld, W. Frauen in der abendländischen Heilkunde vom
        klassischen Altertum bis zum Ausgang des 19. Jahrhunderts.
        Stuttgart: Enke, 1947.

00899. Scoutetten, Henri. "The History of Women Physicians from
        Antiquity to the Present." La France médicale 14: 98-99
        (1867): 331-336.

00900. Seymer, Lucy Ridgely (Buckler). A General History of Nursing.
        New York: Macmillan and Company, 1936.

00901. Shryock, Richard. The History of Nursing. Philadelphia:
        Saunders, 1959.

00902. Siebold, E.C.J. von, M.D. Versuch einer Geschichte der
        Geburtshilfe. Berlin: Enslin, 1838-1849.

00903.   Steinberger, S.   "The History of Women Physicians."
          Gynaekologia (Budapest) (1902):   36-41.

00904.   Stenhouse, Evangeline E.   "Women: Patients and Physicians."
          Journal of the American Medical Women's Association 7
          (September 1952):   333-339.

00905.   Steudel, Johannes.   "Medical Women of the Occident." _Journal_
          of the American Medical Women's Association 17 (January
          1962):   52-55; (February 1962):   139-142.

00906.   Walker, Jane.   "The Return of Women to Medicine." _Contemporary_
          Review 137 (January 1930):   46-50.

00907.   Walsh, James J.   "Women in the Medical World." _New York_
          Medical Journal 96 (28 December 1912):   1324-1328.

00908.   Whitten, Kathryn M.   "Women and the Practice of Medicine."
          Medical Woman's Journal 50 (November 1943):   273-276.

00909.   Winner, Dame Albertine.   "Women in Medicine." _Nursing Mirror_
          and Midwives Journal 140 (6 March 1975):   41.

00910.   Wollstein, Martha.   "The History of Women in Medicine."
          Woman's Medical Journal 18 (April 1908):   65-69.

00911.   "Women Doctors: An Historic Retrospect." _Contemporary_
          Review 108 (October 1915):   504-510.

          Also refer to #522, 523, 525, 526.

                        (3)   Women and Health

00912.   Bloch, Iwan.   _Der Ursprung der Syphilis._   2 vols.   Jena:
          Gustav Fischer, 1911.

00913.   Delaney, Janice; Lupton, Mary Jane; and Toth, Emily. _The_
          Curse, A Cultural History of Menstruation.   New York:
          Dutton, 1976.

00914.   Graham, Harvey.   _Eternal Eve, the History of Gynaecology and_
          Obstetrics.   New York: Doubleday, 1951.

00915.   Jeanselme, E.   _Histoire de la syphilis._   Paris: G. Doun et
          Cie, 1931.

00916.   LeRoy Ladurie, Emmanuel.   "Famine Amenorrhoea (17-20th
          Centuries)."   In _Biology of Man in History,_ edited by Robert
          Forster and Orest Ranum, pp. 163-178.   Baltimore: Johns
          Hopkins University Press, 1975.

00917.   Veith, Ilza.   _Hysteria: The History of a Disease._   Chicago:
          University of Chicago Press, 1965.

00918. Whitwell, J.R. Syphilis in Earlier Days. London: H.K. Lewis
        and Co., 1940.

00919. Witkowski, Gustave Joseph. Histoire des accouchements chez
        tous les peuples. Paris: G. Steinheil, 1889.

9. CULTURAL

"Why then was I born a woman, to be scorned by men in words
and deeds?"   Isotta Nogarola

a) Generic

00920. Biedermann, Karl. Frauen-Brevier Kulturgeschichtliche
        Vorlesungen. Leipzig: Weber, 1856.

00921. Clarke, Isabel C. Six Portraits. 1935. Reprint. Freeport,
        N.Y.: Books for Librairies Press, 1967.

00922. Dorland, W.A. Newman. The Sum of Feminine Achievement: A
        Critical and Analytical Study of Woman's Contribution to the
        Intellectual Progress of the World. Boston: The Stratford
        Company, 1917.

00923. Endres, Franz Karl. Kulturgeschichte der Frau. Bern: Verlag
        Hallway, 1942-1944.

00924. Hamill, Frances. "Some Unconventional Women before 1800:
        Printers, Booksellers, and Collectors." Publications of
        the Bibliographical Society of America 49 (1955): 300-314.

00925. Henne am Rhyn, Otto. Die Frau in der Kulturgeschichte. Berlin:
        Allgemeiner Verein fur deutsche Literatur, 1892.

00926. Klemm, Gustav. Die Frauen kulturgeschichtliche Schilderungen
        des Zustands und Einflusses der Frauen in den verschiedenen
        Zonen und Zeitaltern. 6 vols. Dresden: Arnold, 1854-1856.

00927. Moore, Virginia. Distinguished Women Writers. 1934. Reprint.
        Port Washington, N.Y.: Kennikat Press, 1968.

00928. Pilz, Walter H. Kleine weibliche Kulturgeschichte. Vienna:
        Amandus-Verlag, 1954.

00929. Russell, Dora W. Hypatia: or, Woman and Knowledge. 1925.
        Reprint. Folcroft, Pa.: Folcroft, 1977.

00930. Schrader-Klebert, Karin. "Die kulturelle Revolution der
        Frau." Kursbuch 17 (June 1969): 1-45.

00931.   Stannard, Una. Mrs. Man. San Francisco, Calif.: Germain
         Books, 1977.

b) Education

00932.   Barrau, Caroline de. La femme et l'éducation. Paris:
         J. Cherbuliez, 1870.

00933.   Boslooper, Thomas and Hayes, Marcia. "How the game began."
         In The Feminity Game, pp. 115-135. New York: Stein and
         Day, 1973.

00934.   Brink, J.R. Learned Women: A Tradition of Female Scholars
         Before 1800. Montreal: Eden Press, 1980.

00935.   Friedrich, Theodor. Formenwandel von Frauenwesen und
         Frauenbildung. Leipzig: Armanen Verlag, 1934.

00936.   Halsall, Elizabeth. "The Sex Factor: A Comparative View."
         Aspects of Education 19 (June 1977): 1-31.

00937.   Kirchhoff, Arthur. Die akademische Frau. Berlin: H. Steinitz,
         1897.

00938.   Labalme, Patricia H., ed. Beyond their Sex, Learned Women of
         the European Past. New York: New York University Press,
         1980.

00939.   May, B. Die Mädchenerziehung in der Geschichte der Pädagogik
         von Plato bis zum 18. Jahrhundert. Strassburg: J. Singer,
         1908.

00940.   Stock, Phyllis. Better than Rubies: A History of Women's
         Education. New York: G.P. Putnam's Sons, Capricorn Books,
         1978.

00941.   Women's Education--A World View: Annotated Bibliography of
         Doctoral Dissertations. Westport, Conn.: Greenwood Press,
         Inc., 1979.

c) Literature

(1) Bibliographies

00942.   Schwartz, Narda Lacey. Articles on Women Writers 1960-1975:
         A Bibliography. Oxford: Clio Press, 1977.

00943   Stansbury, Sherry A. "A Bibliography of Feminist Criticism."
         Canadian Newsletter of Research on Women 6 (May 1977): 84–
         114.

00944.   Women and literature: an annotated Bibliography of Women
         Writers. Cambridge, Mass.: Cambridge–Goddard Women and
         Literature Group, 1976.

(2)   Non-specific

00945.   Anderson, Margaret. "Feminism and the Literary Circle."
         Atlantis 1 (Fall 1975): 3–13.

00946.   Arnold, R. and Chandler, O., eds. Feminine Singular Triumphs
         and Tribulations of the Single Woman. London: Femina
         Books, Ltd., 1974.

00947.   Bernikow, Louise. Among Women. New York: Harmony Books,
         1980.

00948.   Coffin, Tristam P. The Female Hero in Folklore and Legend.
         New York: Seabury Press, 1975.

00949.   Fletcher, Jefferson B. The Religion of Beauty in Women. New
         York: Macmillan Co., 1911.

00950.   Foster, Jeannette H. Sex Variant Women in Literature: A
         Historical and Quantitative Survey. London: Muller, 1958.

00951.   Goulianos, Joan, ed. By a Woman Writ: Literature from Six
         Centuries by and about Women. New York: Penguin Books,
         1974.

00952.   Hagstrum, Jean H. Sex and Sensibility: Ideal and Erotic
         Love from Milton to Mozart. Chicago: University Press, 1980.

00953.   Kostman, Samuel. Women of Valor. New York: Richard Rosen
         Press, Inc., 1978.

00954.   La Rochefoucauld, Edmée (de Fels) duchesse de. Le rôle
         politique international des femmes jugé par les grands
         écrivains. Rome: A. Staderini, 1964.

00955.   Moore, John C. "The origins of western ideas: Irving Singer's
         'The nature of love: Plato to Luther'." Journal of the
         History of Ideas 29 (1968): 144–151.

00956.   Morton, Frederick W. Woman in Epigram. Chicago: A.C.
         McClurg, 1895.

00957.   Murray, Michele. A House of Good Proportion: Images of
         Women in Literature. New York: Simon & Schuster, 1973.

00958. Patai, Daphne. "Utopia for Whom." _Aphra_ 5 (Summer 1974):
        2-16.

00959. Rogers, Katherine M. _The Troublesome Helpmate: A History of
        Misogyny in Literature_. Seattle, Wash.: University of
        Washington Press, 1966.

00960. Sullerot, Evelyne. _Histoire et mythologie de l'amour. Huit
        siècles d'écrits féminins_. Paris: Librairie Hachette, 1975.

00961. Thiselton-Dyer, Thomas F. _Folk-Lore of Women, as Illustrated
        by Legendary and Traditional Tales Folk-Rhymes, Proverbial
        Sayings, Superstitions, etc_. 1906. Reprint. Williamstown,
        Mass.: Corner House Press, 1968.

                         (3) Poetry

00962. Barnstone, Aliki and Barstone, Willis, eds. _A Book of Women
        Poets from Antiquity to Now_. New York: Schocken Books, Inc.
        1978.

00963. Bodkin, Maud. _Archetypal Patterns in Poetry: Psychological
        Studies of Imagination_. 1934. Reprint. London: Oxford
        University Press, 1963.

00964. Jameson, Anna Brownell (Murphy). _The Romance of Biography;
        or Memoirs of women loved and celebrated by poets from the
        days of the troubadours to the present day_. 1837. Reprint.
        New Haven, Conn.: Research Publications Inc., 1975.

                         (4) Satire

00965. Larcher, L.J. _Satire et diatribes sur les femmes l'amour et le
        mariage_. Paris: Adolphe Delahays, 1860.

                         (5) Prose

00966. Davis, Natalie Zemon. "Gender and Genre: Women as Historical
        Writers, 1400-1820." In _Beyond their Sex: Learned Women of
        the European Past_, edited by Patricia Labalme, pp. 153-182.
        New York: New York University Press, 1980.

00967. Marzolf, Marion. _Up from the Footnote: A History of Women
        Journalists_. New York: Hastings House Publishers, Inc.,
        1977.

00968. White, Cynthia L. _Women's Magazines 1693-1968_. London:
        Michael Joseph, 1970.

d)   Literary Salons

00969.   Tornius, Valerian.   Salons 1400-1900. A Pageant of Beauty
          and Wit. London: Thornton Butterworth, 1929.

e)   Art and Artifacts

(1)   Women in Art

00970.   Brown, Lyvia Morgan.   "Sexism in Western Art."   In Women:
          A Feminist Perspective, edited by Jo Freeman, pp. 309-322.
          Palo Alto, Calif.: Mayfield Publishing Co., 1975.

00971.   Feininger, Andreas.   Maids, Madonnas and Witches: Women in
          Sculpture from Prehistoric Times to Picasso. Translated by
          Joan Bradley. New York: Abrams, 1961.

00972.   Freixas, Emilio.   Dibujando la figura femenina. Barcelona:
          Sucesor de E. Meseguer, 1968.

00973.   Garland, Madge.   The Changing Face of Beauty: Four Thousand
          Years of Beautiful Women. New York: M. Barrows, 1957.

00974.   Gervaso, Roberto, ed.   Le donne di Borra. Verona: Edizioni
          Ghelfi, 1971.

00975.   Hess, Thomas B., and Nochlin, Linda, eds. Women as Sex
          Object: Studies in Erotic Art 1730-1970. New York: News-
          week, 1972.

00976.   Hirsch, Anton.   Die Frau in der bildenden Kunst, ein kunst-
          geschichtliches Hausbuch. Stuttgart: Verlag von Ferdinand
          Enke, 1905.

00977.   Malvern, Marjorie M.   Venus in Sackcloth: The Magdalen's
          Origins and Metamorphosis. Carbondale: Southern Illinois
          Press, 1975.

00978.   Relouge, I.E., ed.   The Nude in Art. Translated by Mervyn
          Savill. London: B.T. Batsford, 1959.

00979.   Roe, Frederic Gordon.   The Nude from Cranach to Etty and
          Beyond. Essex, England: F. Lewis, 1944.

00980. Ungherini, Aglauro. Manuel de bibliographie biographique et
        d'iconographie des femmes celebres. Naarden: A.W. van
        Bekhoven, 1968.

00981. Vandoyer, Jean-Louis. The Female Nude in European Painting
        from Pre-history to the Present Day. London: Longmans,
        Green, 1957.

00982. Wagner, Anni. Die Frau im Rampenlicht der Kunst. Munich:
        K. Theimig, 1963.

00983. Waters, Clara E.C. Women in the Fine Arts from the 7th
        Century B.C. to the 20th Century A.D. 1904. Reprint.
        Boston, Mass.: Longwood Press, 1977.

                        (2) Women Artists

                        (a) Actresses

00984. Gilder, Rosamond. Enter the Actress: The First Women in
        the Theatre. Boston: Houghton Mifflin Co., 1931.

                        (b) Dancers

00985. Migel, Parmenia. The Ballerinas: From the Court of Louis XIV
        to Pavlova. New York: Macmillan, 1972.

                        (c) Musicians/Singers

00986. Bohillier, Marie. La musique dans les couvents de femmes depuis
        le moyen âge jusqu'à nos jours. Paris: Scholar Cantorum, 1898.

00987. Drinker, Sophie. Music and Women: The Story of Women in
        their Relation to Music. New York: Coward-McCann, 1948.

00988. Elson, Arthur. Woman's Work in Music. 1931. Reprint.
        Washington, D.C.: Zenger Publishing Company, Inc., 1976.

00989. Neuls-Bates, Carol. "Five women composers 1587-1875."
        Feminist Art Journal 5 (Summer 1976): 32-35.

                        (d) Painters/Sculptors

00990. Bachmann, Donna G. and Piland, Sherry. Women Artists: An
        Historical, Contemporary and Feminist Bibliography.
        Metuchen, N.J.: Scarecrow Press, 1978.

00991. Clement, Clara Erskine. Women in the Fine Arts: From the Seventh Century B.C. to the Twentieth Century A.D. 1904. Reprint. New York: Hacker Art Books, 1975.

00992. Ellet, Elizabeth F. Women Artists in all Ages and Countries. New York: Harper Bros., 1859.

00993. Female artists past and present. Berkeley, Calif.: Women's History Research Center, 1974.

00994. Fine, Elsa H. Women & Art: A History of Women Painters & Sculptors from the Renaissance to the 20th Century. Montclair, N.J.: Abner Schram, 1978.

00995. Fournier, Charles Antoine. Le livre d'art des femmes. 1877. Reprint. New Haven: Research Publications, 1976.

00996. Fowler, Carol. Contributions of Women: Art. (Contributions of Women Series.) Minneapolis: Dillon Press, Inc., 1976.

00997. Greer, Germaine. The Obstacle Race: The Fortunes of Women Painters and their Work. New York: Farrar, Straus, and Giroux, 1979.

00998. Harris, Ann Sutherland and Nochlin, Linda. Women Artists, 1550-1950. New York: Alfred A. Knopf, Inc., 1976.

00999. Hess, Thomas B. and Baker, Elizabeth C. Art and Sexual Politics, Women's Liberation, Women Artists and Art History. New York: Macmillan, 1973.

01000. Hill, Vicki L. Female Artists, Past and Present. Berkeley, Calif.: Women's History Research Center, Inc., 1974.

01001. Moe, Louisa, ed. Female Artists Past and Present: International Women's Year 1975 Supplement. Berkeley, Calif.: Women's History Research Center, Inc., 1975.

01002. Munsterberg, Hugo. The History of Women Artists. New York: Clarkson N. Potter, Inc., 1975.

01003. Nochlin, Linda. "Why have there been no great women artists? Art News 69 (January 1971): 22-39, 67-71.

01004. Petersen, Karen and Wilson, J.J. Women Artists: Recognition and Reappraisal from the Early Middle Ages to the Twentieth Century. New York: Harper and Row Publishers, Inc., 1976.

01005. Sparrow, Walter Shaw, ed. Women Painters of the World: from the times of Caterina Vigri (1413-63) to Rose Bonheur and the Present Day. 1909. Reprint. New York: Hacker Art Books, 1976.

01006. Tufts, Eleanor. Our Hidden Heritage: Five Centuries of Women Artists. New York: Paddington Press, 1974.

01007.   "Women Artists--What Has History Done to Them?" Rama Pipien:
         The Peoplesmedia Digest 3 (May-June 1973): 19.

                            f) Science

01008.   Coolidge, Julian L. "Six Female Mathematicians." Scripta
         Mathematica 17 (March-June 1951): 21-31.

01009.   Emberlin, Diane D. Contributions of Women: Science. (Con-
         tributions of Women Series.) Minneapolis: Dillon Press,
         Inc., 1977.

01010.   Harless, Johann Christian Friedrich. Die Verdienste der
         Frauen um Naturwissenschaft Gesundheits-und Heilkunde.
         Göttingen: Van den Hoeck-Ruprecht, 1830.

01011.   Lonsdale, Kathleen. "Women in Science: Reminiscences and Re-
         flections." Impact of Science on Society 20 (1970): 49-59.

01012.   Maccoby, Eleanor E. "Feminine Intellect and the Demands of
         Science." Impact of Science on Society 20 (1970): 13-28.

01013.   Osen, Lynn M. Women in Mathematics. Cambridge, Mass.: MIT
         Press, 1974.

01014.   Tosi, Lucia. "Woman's Scientific Creativity." Impact of
         Science on Society 25 (1975): 105-114.

01015.   Zahm, John Augustine. Women in Science. 1913. Reprint.
         Cambridge, Mass.: MIT Press, 1974.

         Also refer to #937.

B. BRITISH ISLES

1. BIBLIOGRAPHIES

         "He for God only, she for God in him."
                                        Milton

01016.   "Bibliography for the Study of Women in English History."
         Canadian Newsletter of Research on Women 6 (October 1977):
         136-146.

01017. Kanner, Barbara. "Introduction: Old and New Women's History."
        In The Women of England from Anglo-Saxon Times to the
        Present, edited by Barbara Kanner, pp. 9-31. Hamden, Conn.:
        Archon Books, 1979.

01018. _____, ed. The Women of England from Anglo-Saxon
        Times to the Present: Interpretive bibliographical Essays.
        Hamden, Conn.: Archon Books, 1979.

2. SURVEYS

"I am sure you will love it though it be a Girle."
                              Lady Frances Hatton

01019. Hill, Georgiana. Women in English Life: From Mediaeval to
        Modern Times. 2 vols. London: Richard Bentley and Son,
        1896.

01020. James, Bartlett Burleigh. Women of England. Philadelphia:
        Rittenhouse Press, 1908.

01021. Kerst, Henri. La Femme dans la société anglaise, étude et
        témoignages littéraires. Paris: Mason et Cie, 1971.

01022. MacCurtain, Margaret and O'Corrain, Donncha, eds. Women in
        Irish Society: The Historical Dimension. Contributions in
        Women's Studies, no. 11. Westport, Ct.: Greenwood Press,
        Inc., 1979.

01023. Morrison, M. "The British Isles." In Women of all Nations,
        edited by T.A. Joyce, 4: 756-62. New York: Funk &
        Wagnalls, 1915.

01024. Murray, Eunice G. Scottish Women in Bygone Days. 1930.
        Reprint. Norwood, Pa.: Norwood Editions, 1976.

01025. O'Malley, Ida Beatrice. Women in Subjection: A Study of the
        Lives of Englishwomen before 1832. London: Duckworth, 1933.

01026. O'Tuathaigh, Gearoid. "The Role of Women in Ireland under the
        New English Order." In Women in Irish Society: The His-
        torical Dimension, edited by Margaret MacCurtain and Donncha
        O'Corrain, pp. 26-36. Westport, Conn.: Greenwood Press,
        1979.

01027. Ray, John Philip. The Place of Women, 1700 to the present
        Day. London: Nelson, 1971.

01028. Schneider, Joseph. "Class Origin and Fame: Eminent English
        Women." American Sociological Review 5 (October 1940):
        700-712.

01029. Staars, David. The English Woman: Studies in her Psychic
        Evolution. London: Smith, Elder, 1909.

01030. Stenton, Doris May. The English Woman in History. 1957.
        Reprint. New York: Schocken, 1977.

3. BIOGRAPHICAL SKETCHES

        "Most women have no character at all."   Pope

01031. Barton, Felix. The Most Beautiful Women in British History.
        Albuquerque, N.M.: Gloucester Art Press, 1978.

01032. Bradford, Gamaliel. Portraits of Women. 1916. Reprint.
        Freeport, N.Y.: Books for Libraries Press, 1969.

01033. Casey, Elizabeth. Illustrious Irishwomen. 2 vols. London:
        Tinsley Brothers, 1877.

01034. Cassidy, James F. The Women of the Gael. Boston: Strafford
        Co., 1922.

01035. Costello, Louisa Stuart. Memoirs of Eminent Englishwomen.
        4 vols. London: R. Bentley, 1844.

01036. Darton, J.M. Famous Girls who have Become Illustrious Women:
        Forming Models for the Young Women of England. 1864. Re-
        print. New York: Arno Press, 1979.

01037. Ffrench, Yvonne. Six Great Englishwomen: Queen Elizabeth I,
        Sarah Siddons, Charlotte Bronte, Florence Nightingale,
        Queen Victoria, Gertrude Bell. London: Hamilton, 1953.

01038. Northcroft, Dora. Famous Girls of the Past. Mystic, Conn.:
        Lawrence Verry, Inc., 1966.

01039. Pollitt, Ronald, and Curry, Herbert, eds. Portraits in
        British History. Homewood, Ill.: The Dorsey Press, 1975.

01040. Sitwell, Edith. English Women. London: William Collins, 1932.

01041. Six Brilliant English Women. 6 vols. Representative Women
        Series. London: G. Howe, 1930.

4. POLITICAL

"Ah, woman, woman! Come, we have no friend
But resolution and the briefest end."
                                        Shakespeare

a) Generic

01042.   Blease, Walter Lyon. The Emancipation of English Women.
         New York: B. Blom, 1971.

b) Legal

01043.   Chapman, Annie Beatrice Wallis and Chapman, Mary Wallis. The
         Status of Women Under the English Law. New York: E. P.
         Dutton and Co., 1909.

01044.   Cleveland, Arthur Rackman. Woman under the English Law from
         the Time of the Saxons to the Present Time. London: Hurst
         and Blackett, Ltd., 1896.

01045.   Crofts, Mrs. Maud Isabel, ed. Women under English Law.
         London: Butterworth and Co., Ltd., 1928.

01046.   Holdsworth, William Searle. A History of English Law. 12
         vols. Boston: Little, Brown and Co., 1938.

01047.   Howell, Cicely. "Peasant Inheritance Customs in the Midlands,
         1280-1700." In Family and Inheritance: Rural Society in
         Western Europe, 1200-1800, edited by Jack Goody, Joan
         Thirsk, and E. P. Thompson, pp. 112-155. New York: Cam-
         bridge University Press, 1976.

01048.   Kenny, Courtney Stanhope. The History of the Law of England
         as to the Effects of Marriage on Property and on the Wife's
         Legal Capacity. London: Reeves & Turner, 1879.

01049.   Kidd, Margaret. "Women under Scots Law." In Women under
         English Law, edited by Mrs. Maud Isabel Crofts, pp. 95-101.
         London: Butterworth and Co., Ltd., 1928.

01050. Mitchell, Juliet. "Women and Equality." In The Rights and
        Wrongs of Women, edited by Juliet Mitchell and Ann Oakley,
        pp. 379-399. New York: Penguin, 1976.

01051. Stopes, Charlotte (Carmichael). British Freewomen: Their
        Historical Privilege in Common Law and Equity. London:
        S. Sonnenschein and Co., Ltd., 1894.

01052. Strachey, Rachel Conn (Costello). Struggle. New York:
        Duffield, 1930.

01053. Thompson, E. P. "The Grid of Inheritance: a Comment." In
        Family and Inheritance: Rural Society in Western Europe,
        1200-1800, edited by Jack Goody, Joan Thirsk, and E. P.
        Thompson, pp. 328-360. New York: Cambridge University

        Also refer to #290, 1137, 1150, 1165.

c) Criminal

01054. Cockburn, J. S., ed. Crime in England, 1550-1800. Princeton,
        N.J.: Princeton University Press, 1977.

01055. Jenkins, Elizabeth. Six Criminal Women. 1949. Reprint.
        Freeport, N.Y.: Books for Libraries, 1971.

01056. Sharpe, J. A. "Domestic Homicide in Early Modern England."
        Historical Journal 24 (March 1981): 29-48.

d) Political Roles

01057. Cook, E. Thornton. Royal Marys. London: Murray, 1929.

01058. Fattorusso, Joseph. Kings and Queens of England and of
        France: a genealogical, chronological History. London:
        David Nutt, 1953.

01059. Fraser, Antonia, ed. The Lives of Kings and Queens of
        England. New York: Knopf, Borzoi Books, 1975.

01060. Green, Mary Anne Everett (Wood). Lives of the Princesses of
        England from the Norman Conquest. 6 vols. 1849-1855.
        Reprint. New Haven, Conn.: Research Publications Inc.,
        1975.

01061.   Jenner, Heather. Royal Wives. London: Gerald Duckworth, 1967.

01062.   Richardson, Mrs. Aubrey. Famous Ladies of the English Court. London: Hutchinson and Co., 1899.

01063.   Strickland, Agnes. Lives of the Queen of England, from the Norman Conquest. Philadelphia: G. Barrie and Son, 1902–1903.

01064.   _____. Lives of the Queens of Scotland and English princesses concerned in the regal Succession of Great Britain. New York: Harper, 1857–1864.

01065.   _____. The Queens of England; a series of portraits of distinguished female sovereigns. Rev. ed. New York: D. Appleton, 1866.

01066.   Thornton–Cook, Elsie. Her Majesty: The Romance of the Queens of England, 1066–1910. 1926. Reprint. New York: Arno Press, 1979.

01067.   _____. Royal Daughters. London: Heath Chanten Ltd., 1935.

01068.   _____. Royal Elizabeths: The Romance of Five Princesses, 1464–1840. New York: E. P. Dutton, 1929.

01069.   _____. Royal Marys, Princess Mary and her Predecessors. New York: E. P. Dutton and Co., 1929.

01070.   Trease, Geoffrey. The Seven Queens of England. London: William Heinemann Ltd., 1953.

01071.   Villiers, Elizabeth. Our Queen Mothers. London: Melrose, 1936.

01072.   Wakeford, Geoffrey. The Princesses Royal. London: Robert Hale, 1973.

5. ECONOMIC

"[Chastity] is out of the question when starvation is the case."
                                        Defoe

01073.   Franz, Nellie Alden. English Women Enter the Professions. Cincinnati, Ohio: Privately Printed, 1965.

01074. Richards, Eric. "Women in the British Economy since about
        1700: An Interpretation." History 59 (October 1974):
        337-357.

01075. Tickner, F. W. Women in English Economic History. London:
        J. M. Dent, 1923.

01076. Tilly, Louise and Scott, Joan. Women, Work, and Family.
        New York: Holt, Rinehart and Winston, Inc., 1978.

        Also refer to #1100, 1106, 1150.

6. RELIGION

The time is coming when "not only men but women will
prophesy."   Mary Cappe, 1645

a) Religious Orders

01077. Concannon, Helena (Walsh). The Poor Clares in Ireland (A.D.
        1629-1929). Dublin: Gill and Son, 1929.

b) Witchcraft

01078. Anderson, Alan, and Gordon, Raymond. "The Uniqueness of
        English Witchcraft: A Matter of Numbers?" [reply to J.K.
        Swales and Hugh V. McLachlan]. British Journal of Socio-
        logy 30 (September 1979): 359-361.

01079. Byrne, Patrick F. Witchcraft in Ireland. Cork: Mercier
        Press, 1967.

01080. Campbell, J. G. Witchcraft and Second Sight in the Highlands
        and Islands of Scotland. Glasgow, Scotland: n.p., 1902.

01081. Davies, R. Trevor. Four Centuries of Witch-Beliefs. 1947.
        Reprint. New York: B. Blom, 1972.

01082. Ewen, Cecil Henry L'Estrange. Witchcraft and Demonianism; A
        concise Account derived from sworn Depositions and Con-
        fessions obtained in the Courts of England and Wales (1538-
        1717). 1933. Reprint. London: Heath Cranston, 1970.

01083. _____, ed. Witch Hunting and Witch Trials; The Indict-
        ment for Witchcraft from Records of 1373 Assizes Held for
        the Home Circuit, 1559-1736. London: K. Paul, Trench,
        Trubner and Co., Ltd., 1929.

01084. Hole, Christina. *Witchcraft in England*. Totowa, N.J.:
        Rowman and Littlefield, 1977.

01085. Holmes, Ronald. *Witchcraft in British History*. London:
        Frederick Muller Ltd., 1974.

01086. Kittredge, George Lyman. *Witchcraft in Old and New England*.
        Cambridge, Mass.: Harvard University Press, 1929.

01087. Monter, E. William. "The Historiography of European Witch-
        craft: Progress and Prospects." *Journal of Interdiscipli-
        nary History* 2 (Spring 1972): 435-451.

01088. Notestein, Wallace. *A History of Witchcraft in England from
        1558 to 1718*. 1911. Reprint. New York: Thomas Y. Crowell
        Co., 1968.

01089. Sergeant, Philip Walsingham. *Witches and Warlocks*. 1936.
        Reprint. Detroit: Gale Research Co., 1974.

01090. Swales, J. K., and McLachlan, Hugh V. "Witchcraft and the
        Status of Women: A Comment." *British Journal of Socio-
        logy* 30 (September 1979): 349-358.

01091. Thomas, Keith. "Witchcraft and its Social Environment." In
        Religion and the Decline of Magic, pp. 535-569. New York:
        Charles Scribner and Sons, 1971.

01092. _____. "Witchcraft in England: The Crime and its
        History." In *Religion and the Decline of Magic*, pp. 435-
        468. New York: Charles Scribner and Sons, 1971.

7. SOCIAL

"Tho' she thinks and speaks as a man would do, still it is
as woman ought to do. . . "
                                    Gentleman's Magazine, 1737

a) Generic

01093. Barley, M. W. *The English Farmhouse and Cottage*. England:
        University of Nottingham Press, 1967.

01094. Chambers, Jonathan David. *Population, Economy, and Society
        in Pre-Industrial England*. Edited by W. A. Armstrong.
        New York: Oxford University Press, 1972.

01095. Escott, Thomas Hay Sweet. *Society in the Country House*.
        Philadelphia: G. W. Jacobs and Co., 1907.

01096. Fussell, George E. The English Country Woman: A Farm House
       Social History, AD 1500-1900. London: A. Melrose, 1953.

01097. Girouard, Mark. Life in the English Country House: A Social
       and Architectural History. New Haven: Yale University
       Press, 1978.

01098 Hamilton, Henry. "The Place of Women in Society." In
       England History of the Homeland, pp. 315-341. New York:
       Norton, 1948.

01099. Laslett, Peter. The World We Have Lost. 2nd ed. New York:
       Charles Scribner's Sons, 1971.

01100. Marshall, Dorothy. The English Domestic Servant in History.
       Historical Association, General series G 13. London:
       George Philip and Son, Ltd., 1949.

01101. Owen, David. English Philanthropy, 1660-1960. Cambridge,
       Mass.: Harvard University Press, 1962.

01102. Phillips, Margaret and Tomkinson, W. S. English Women in
       Life and Letters. London: H. Milford, 1926.

01103. Quennell, Marjorie and Quennel, C.B. A History of Everyday
       Things in England. 4 vols. 1918. 4th ed. London:
       B. T. Batsford Ltd., 1957.

01104. Synge, Margaret Bertha. A Short History of Social Life in
       England. London: Hodder and Stoughton, 1908.

01105. Timbs, John. Nooks and Corners of English Life, Past and
       Present. London: Griffith and Farran, 1867.

01106. Turner, E. S. What the Butler Saw: Two Hundred Years of the
       Servant Problem. New York: St. Martins, 1963.

01107. Watt, Margaret. The History of the Parson's Wife, London:
       Religious Book Club, 1945.

                    b) Demography

01108. Beaver, M. A. "Population, Infant Mortality and Milk."
       Population Studies 27 (1973): 243-254.

01109. Cowgill, Ursula. "The People of York, 1538-1812." Scientific
       American 222 (January 1970): 104-113.

01110. Eversley, D.E.C.; Laslett, Peter; and Wrigley, E.A. An Intro-
        duction to English Historical Demography: From the Sixteenth
        Century to the Nineteenth Century. New York: Basic Books,
        1966.

01111. Flinn, Michael. Scottish Population History from the Seven-
        teenth Century to the 1930's. New York: Cambridge Univer-
        sity Press, 1977.

01112. Hollingsworth, Thomas. "A Demographical Study of the British
        Ducal Families." Population Studies 11 (1957): 4-26.

01113. Hoskins, William George. "The Population of an English
        Village, 1086-1801: A Study of Wigston Magna." In Provin-
        cial England: Essays in Social and Economic History, pp.
        181-208. London: Macmillan, 1964.

01114. Kennedy, Robert, Jr. "The Social Status of the Sexes and
        Their Relative Mortality Rates in Ireland." In Readings in
        Population, edited by William Petersen, pp. 121-135. New
        York: Macmillan, 1972.

01115. Laslett, Peter. "Mean household size in England since the
        sixteenth century." In Household and Family in Past Time,
        edited by Peter Laslett and Richard Wall, pp. 125-158.
        Cambridge: The University Press, 1972.

01116. _____. "Size and Structure of the Household in
        England over Three Centuries." Population Studies 23 (July
        1969): 199-223.

01117. Levine, David. Family Formation in an Age of Nascent
        Capitalism. New York: Academic Press, 1977.

01118. _____. "Proletarianization and Population Growth."
        In Sozialgeschichte der Familie in der Neuzeit Europas,
        edited by Werner Conze, pp. 247-253. Stuttgart: Ernst
        Klett Verlag, 1976.

01119. Schofield, Roger S. "Perinatal Mortality in Hawkshead, Lanca-
        shire, 1581-1710." Local Population Studies 4 (1970): 11-16.

01120. Trantner, N. L. Population since the Industrial Revolution:
        The Case of England and Wales. New York: Barnes and Noble,
        1973.

01121. Wall, Richard. "Mean household size in England from printed
        sources." In Household and Family in Past Time, edited by
        Peter Laslett and Richard Wall, pp. 159-203. Cambridge:
        The University Press, 1972.

01122.   Wrigley, Edward Anthony   "Family Limitation in Pre-Industrial
         England."   Economic History Review 2nd ser. 19 (1966):
         82-109.
         Also in Population in Industrialization, edited by Michael
         Drake, pp. 157-194. London: Methuen, 1969.
         Also in Popular Attitudes Toward Birth Control in Pre-
         Industrial France and England, edited by Orest and
         Patricia Ranum, pp. 53-99. New York: Harper & Row, 1972.

01123.   _____. Introduction to English Historical
         Demography. London: Weidenfeld and Nicholson, 1966.

01124.   _____. "Mortality in pre-industrial England:
         the example of Colyton, Devon over three centuries."   In
         Population and Social Change, edited by D.V. Glass and Roger
         Reville, pp. 243-273. New York: Crane, Russak, 1972. Also
         in Daedalus 97 (Spring 1968): 546-580.

         Also refer to #1157.

                          c) Family

                      (1) Non-specific

01125.   Bosanquet, Helen Dandy. The Family. New York: Macmillan
         Co., 1926.

01126.   Hill, Christopher. "Sex, Marriage and Family in England."
         Economic History Review 31 (August 1978): 450-463.

01127.   McGregor, O. R. "Some Research Possibilities and Historical
         Materials for Family and Kinship Study in Britain." British
         Journal of Sociology 12 (1961): 310-317.

01128.   Marx, R. "La vie familiale des pauvres dans l'Angleterre pré-
         industrielle." Recherches anglaises et américaines 8 (1975):
         13-29.

01129.   Mousnier, Roland. La famille, l'enfant, et l'éducation en
         France et en Grande-Bretagne du XVIe au XVIIIe siècle. 3
         volumes. Paris: Centre de documentation universitaire,
         1975.

01130.   Parsons, Elsie Worthingon (Clews). The Family: An Ethnogra-
         phical and Historical Outline with Descriptive Notes,
         Planned as a Text Book. New York: G. P. Putnam, 1926.

01131.   Pillorget, Rene. La tige et le rameau: familles anglaise et
         francaise XVIe - XVIIIe siècle. Paris: Calmann-Levy, 1979.

01132.   Pillorget, René. "La tige et le rameau: familles anglaise
         et francaise XVIe - XVIIIe siècle." Journal of Modern
         History 52 (June 1980): 372.

01133.   Queen, Stuart A.; Habenstein, Robert W.; and Adams, John B.
         "The Later English Family--Romantic Love and a Power
         Struggle." In The Family in Various Cultures, pp. 247-270.
         New York: J.B. Lippincott, 1961.

01134.   Seabrook, Jeremy. The Unprivileged. London: Longmans, Green
         and Co., 1967.

01135.   Stone, Lawrence. The Family, Sex and Marriage in England,
         1500-1800. New York: Harper and Row, 1977.

01136.   _____. "The Rise of the Nuclear Family in Early
         Modern England." In The Family in History, edited by
         Charles E. Rosenberg, pp. 13-57. Philadelphia: University
         of Pennsylvania Press, 1975.

01137.   Vann, Richart T. "Wills and the Family in an English Town:
         Banbury, 1550-1800." Journal of Family History 4 (Winter
         1979): 346-367.

         Also refer to #1076.

                        (2) Childhood

01138.   Ashdown, Dulcie M. Royal Children. London: Robert Hale,
         1979.

01139.   Bedford, Jessie [Elizabeth Godfrey]. English Children in
         the Olden Times. New York: E. P. Dutton and Co., 1907.

01140.   Gathorne-Hardy, Jonathon. The Unnatural History of the Nanny.
         New York: Dial Press, 1973.

01141.   Godfrey, Elizabeth. English Children in the Olden Time. 1907.
         Reprint. Williamstown, Mass.: Corner House Publishers,
         1980.

01142.   Laslett, Peter. "The Bastardy prone Sub-culture." In
         Bastardy and its Comparative History, edited by Peter Las-
         lett, Karla Oosterveen and Richard M. Smith, pp. 217-246.
         Cambridge, Mass.: Harvard University Press, 1980.

01143.   _____ and Oosterveen, Karla. "Long-term trends in
         bastardy in England." In Family Life and Illicit Love in
         earlier generations, pp. 105-159. New York: Cambridge
         University Press, 1977.

01144.   Newman, Anthea. "An evaluation of bastardy recordings in and
          east Kent parish." In Bastardy and its Comparative History,
          edited by Peter Laslett, Karla Oosterveen, and Richard M.
          Smith, pp. 141-157. Cambridge, Mass.: Harvard University
          Press, 1980.

01145.   Oosterveen, Karla; Smith, Richard M.; and Stewart, Susan.
          "Family reconstitution and the study of bastardy: evidence
          from certain English parishes." In Bastardy and its Com-
          parative History, edited by Peter Laslett, Karla Oosterveen,
          and Richard M. Smith, pp. 86-140. Cambridge, Mass.: Har-
          vard University Press, 1980.

01146.   Owen, G. R. "Illegitimacy at Ilsington, 1558-1830." Devon
          and Cornwell Notes and Queries 31 (1968-70): 220-221.

01147.   Pinchbeck, Ivy and Hewitt, Margaret. Children in English
          Society. 2 vols. Toronto: University Press, 1969-1973.

01148.   Stuart, Dorothy Margaret. The English Abigail. London:
          Macmillan and Co., Ltd., 1946.

          Also refer to #1108, 1129.

                         d) Marriage

01149.   Carter, Ian. "Marriage Patterns and Social Sectors in Scot-
          land before the Eighteenth Century." Scottish Studies 17
          (1973): 51-60.

01150.   Clay, C. "Marriage, Inheritance and the Rise of Large Estates
          in England, 1660-1815." Economic History Review 2nd ser.
          21 (1968): 503-518.

01151.   Cole, Margaret. Marriage: Past and Present. 1939. New
          York: AMS Press, 1975.

01152.   Guthrie, Charles John. "The History of Divorce in Scotland."
          Scottish History Review 8 (1911): 39-52.

01153.   Hair, P.E.H. "Bridal Pregnancy in Rural England in Earlier
          Centuries." Population Studies 20 (November 1966): 233-243.

01154.   _____. "Bridal Pregnancy in Earlier Rural England,
          Further Examined." Population Studies 24 (March 1970):
          59-70.

01155. Howard, George Elliott. A History of Matrimonial Institutions, Chiefly in England and the United States, with an Introductory Analysis of the Literature and the Theories of Primitive Marriage and the Family. 1904. Reprint. New York: Humanities Press, 1964.

01156. Mueller, Gerhard J.W. "Inquiry into the State of a Divorceless Society: Domestic Relations, Law and Morals in England from 1660-1857." University of Pittsburgh Law Review 18 (1957): 545-578.

01157. Outhwaite, R. B. "Age at Marriage in England from the Late Seventeenth to the Nineteenth Century." Transactions of the Royal Historical Society 5th ser. 23 (1973): 55-70.

        Also refer to #290, 1048, 1126, 1135.

e) Sex Life and Morals

01158. Bloch, Iwan. Ethnological and cultural studies of the sex life in England illustrated as revealed in its erotic literature and art. Translated and edited by Richard Deniston. New York: Falstaff Press, 1934.

01159. _____. A History of English Sexual Morals. London: F. Aldor, 1936.

01160. _____. Sexual Life in England, Past and Present. London: F. Aldor, 1938.

01161. Bristow, Edward J. Vice and Vigilance: Purity Movements in Britain since 1700. Totowa, N.J.: Rowman and Littlefield, 1978.

01162. Epton, Nina Consuelo. Love and the English. London: Cassell, 1969.

01163. Fryer, Peter. Mrs. Grundy: Studies in English Prudery. London: D. Dobson, 1963.

        Also refer to #1126, 1135.

f) Fashion/Manners

01164. Ashdown, Emily Jessie. British Costume during XIX Centuries. (Civil and Ecclesiastical). London: T. C. and E. C. Jack, 1910.

01165. Baldwin, F.E. Sumptuary Legislation and Personal Regulations
       in England. Baltimore: The Johns Hopkins Press, 1926.

01166. Bradfield, N. Historical Costumes of England from the
       Eleventh to the Twentieth Century. London: G.G. Harrap and
       Co. Ltd., 1938.

01167. Brooke, Iris. A History of English Costume. London: Methuen,
       1937.

01168. Calthrop, Dion Clayton. English Costume from William I to
       George IV, 1066 - 1830. London: A. & C. Black Ltd., 1937.

01169. _____. English Costume, Painted and Des-
       cribed. 4 vols. London: A. and C. Black Ltd., 1923.

01170. Clinch, George. English Costume: From Prehistoric Times to
       the Eighteenth Century. Totowa, N.J.: Rowman and Little-
       field, 1975.

01171. Cunnington, Cecil Willett. A Dictionary of English Costume.
       New York: Barnes and Noble, 1968.

01172. _____. A Picture History of English
       Costume. New York: Macmillan, 1960.

01173. Cunnington, Phillis and Lucas, Catherine. Occupational
       Costume in England; From the Eleventh Century to 1914.
       New York: Barnes and Noble, 1967.

01174. DeCourtais, Georgine. Women's Headdress and Hairstyles in
       England from A.D. 600 to the Present Day. London: B.T.
       Batsford, 1973.

01175. Fairholt, Frederick William. Costume in England; a History of
       Dress Till the Close of the Eighteenth Century. 1885.
       Reprint. Detroit: Singing Press, 1968.

01176. Hill, Georgiana. A History of English Dress from the Saxon
       Period to the Present Day. 2 vols. New York: Putnam, 1893.

01177. Kelly, Francis Michael and Schwabe, Randolph. Short History
       of Costume and Armour, Chiefly in England, 1066-1800.
       New York: C. Scribner's Sons, 1931.

01178. Laver, James. English costume from the Fourteenth through
       the Nineteenth Century. New York: The Macmillan Company,
       1937.

01179. Mansfield, Alan. Ceremonial Costume: Court, Civil, and
       Civic Costume from 1660 to the present. Totowa, N.J.:
       Barnes and Noble, 1980

01180. Planché, James Robinson. History of British Costume. London:
       G. Bell, 1913.

01181. Walker, George. The Costume of Yorkshire. Sussex: Caliban
        Books, 1978.

01182. Wildeblood, J. and Brinson, P. The Polite World - A Guide to
        English Manners and Deportment from the Thirteenth to the
        Nineteenth Century. Oxford: University Press, 1965.

01183. Williams, Neville. Powder and Paint: A History of the
        English Woman's Toilet, Elizabeth I to Elizabeth II.
        London: Longmans, Green and Co., 1957.

01184. Wright, Thomas. The Homes of Other Days: A History of Domestic
        Manners and Sentiments in England from the Earliest Known
        Period to Modern Times. London: Trubner and Co., 1871.

g)   Health/Medical

(1)   Abortion/Birth Control

01185. Brown, P. S. "Female Pills and the Reputation of Iron as an
        Abortifacient." Medical History 21 (July 1977): 291-304.

01186. Ranum, Orest and Patricia, eds. Popular Attitudes toward
        Birth Control in Pre-Industrial France and England. New
        York: Harper Torchbooks, 1972.

        Also refer to 1122.

(2)   Women in Medicine

01187. Abel-Smith, B. A History of the Nursing Profession in Great
        Britain. New York: Springer, 1960.

01188. Aveling, James H. English Midwives: Their History and Pros-
        pects. London: J. and J. Churchill, 1872.

01189. Donnison, Jean. "Medical Women and Lady Midwives." Women's
        Studies 3 (1976): 229-50.

01190. _____ . Midwives and Medical Men, a History of Inter-
        professional Revalues and Women's Rights. New York:
        Schocken, 1977.

01191. Ringland, John. Annals of Midwifery in Ireland. Dublin: John
        Falconer, 1870.

01192. Webb-Johnson, Alfred. "Mainly About Women." British Medical
        Journal 2 (8 August 1942): 165-166.

8. CULTURAL

"The revolution of the years has now produced a generation of
Amazons of the pen, who with the spirit of their predecessors
have set masculine tyranny at defiance, asserted their claim
to the regions of science and seem resolved to contest the
usurpation of virility."   Samuel Johnson

a) Education

01193. Barnard, Howard Clive. A History of English Education from
1760. 2nd ed. London: University of London Press, 1961.
[See esp. Ch. 18 "The education of girls and women" pp.
156-166.]

01194. Borer, Mary Cathcart. Willingly to School, History of Women's
Education. London: Lutterworth, 1976.

01195. Cressy, David. "Literacy in Pre-Industrial England."
Societas 4 (Summer 1974): 229-240.

01196. Gardiner, Dorothy Kempe. English Girlhood at School, A Study
of Women's Education through Twelve Centuries. London:
Humphrey Milford, 1929.

01197. Kamm, Josephine. Hope Deferred: Girls' Education in English
History. London: Methuen and Co., 1965.

01198. Turner, Barry. Equality for Some: The Story of Girls' Education. London: Ward Lock Educational, 1974.

Also refer to #1129.

b) Literature

(1) Non-specific

01199. Ballard, George. Memoirs of British Ladies who have been
celebrated for their Writings or Skill in the Learned Languages, Arts and Sciences. London: T. Evans, 1775.

01200. Boos, Florence, ed. "1976 Bibliography of Literature in
        English by and about Women: 600-1960." Women and Litera-
        ture 5 Supplement (Fall 1977): 1-168.

01201. Kavanaugh, Julia. English Women of Letters: Biographical
        Sketches. 2 vols. London: Hurst and Blackett, 1863.

01202. Mahl, Mary R. and Koon, Helen, eds. The Female Spectator
        English Women Writers before 1800. Old Westbury, N.Y.:
        Feminist Press, 1977.

01203. Manley, Seon and Belcher, Susan. O, Those Extraordinary
        Women! Or the Joys of Literary Lib. Philadelphia: Chil-
        ton Book Company, 1972.

01204. Springer, Marlene, ed. What Manner of Woman: Essays on
        English and American Life and Literature. New York:
        New York University Press, 1977.

01205. Utley, Francis Lee. The Crooked Rib: An Analytical Index to
        the Argument about Women in English and Scots Literature to
        the End of the Year 1568. Columbus, Ohio: Ohio State Uni-
        versity Press, 1944.

01206. Utter, Robert Palfrey and Needham, Gwendolyn Bridges. Pamela's
        Daughters. New York: Macmillan Company, 1937.

01207. Wilson, Mona. These Were Muses. 1942. Reprint. Port Wash-
        ington, N.Y.: Kennikat Press, 1970.

        Also refer to #1102.

(2) Poetry

01208. Salomon, Louis B. The Devil Take Her; A Study of the Rebel-
        lious Lover in English Poetry. Philadelphia: University of
        Pennsylvania Press, 1931.

01209. Wardroper, John. Love and Drollery. London: Routledge and
        Kegan Paul, 1969.

(3) Prose

01210. Johnson, Reginald Brimley. The Women Novelists. 1919.
        Reprint. Freeport, N.Y.: Books For Libraries Press, 1967.

01211. Mews, Hazel. Frail Vessels: Woman's Role in Women's Novels
        from Fanny Burney to George Eliot. London: Athlone Press,
        1969.

01212. Whitmore, Clare H. Woman's Work in English Fiction from the
        Restoration to the Mid-Victorian Period. New York: G. P.
        Putnam's Sons, 1910.

c) Art and Artifacts

01213. Bouchot, Henri. La femme anglaise et ses peintres. Paris:
        Libraire de l'art ancien et moderne, 1903.

01214. Clayton, Ellen C. English Female Artists. 2 vols. St. Clair
        Shores, Mich.: Scholarly Press, Inc., 1977.

        Also refer to #1199, 1206.

C. FRANCE

1. SURVEYS

"A woman of wit is the scourge of her husband, her children,
her friends, her servants, of everybody."   Rousseau

01215. Carroll, Paulette. "The French woman: Privileges and Prob-
        lems." The Colorado Quarterly 21 (1973): 479-490.

01216. Decaux, Alain. Histoire des Francaises. 2 vols. Paris:
        Libraire academique Perrin, 1972.

01217. Destable, M. De l'evolution feminine comparee en France et
        en Amerique. Rouen: Lecerf, 1898.

2. BIOGRAPHICAL SKETCHES

"During [Madame de Pompadour's] last moments she let it be
seen that her soul was a mixture of strength and weakness,
never suprising in a woman. Nor does it surprise me to see
that she is now as much mourned as she used to be despised
or hated."   Madame de la Tour Franqueville

01218. Beaunier, Andre. <u>Visages</u> <u>des</u> <u>femmes</u>. Paris: Plon Nourrit
        et Cie, 1913.

01219. Bordeaux, Henry. <u>Portraits</u> <u>de</u> <u>femmes</u> <u>et</u> <u>d'enfants</u>. Paris:
        Plon-Nourrit, 1919.

01220. Collins, Marie and Sayre, Syvie Weil, eds. <u>Les</u> <u>femmes</u> <u>en</u>
        <u>France</u>. New York: Scribner's Sons, 1974.

01221. Gearey, Caroline. <u>French</u> <u>Heroines;</u> <u>eminent</u> <u>for</u> <u>Piety</u> <u>and</u>
        <u>Virtue</u>. London: J. Blackwood and Co., 1884.

01222. Haggard, Andrew Charles Parker. <u>Remarkable</u> <u>Women</u> <u>of</u> <u>France</u>
        <u>(from</u> <u>1431</u> <u>to</u> <u>1749)</u>. London: S. Paul and Co., 1914.

01223. Haussonville, Gabriel Paul Othenin de Cléron, comte d'.
        <u>Femmes</u> <u>d'autrefois;</u> <u>hommes</u> <u>d'aujourdhui</u>. Paris: Perrin
        et Cie, 1912.

01224. Lefevre, Maurice. <u>La</u> <u>femme</u> <u>à</u> <u>travers</u> <u>l'histoire</u>. Paris: A.
        Fontemoine, 1902.

01225. Legouvé, Ernest. <u>Histoire</u> <u>morale</u> <u>des</u> <u>femmes</u>. Paris: J.
        Hetzel et cie, 1896.

01226. Mennechet, Edouard, ed. <u>Le</u> <u>Plutarque</u> <u>français,</u> <u>vies</u> <u>des</u>
        <u>hommes</u> <u>et</u> <u>femmes</u> <u>illustres</u> <u>de</u> <u>la</u> <u>France,</u> <u>avec</u> <u>leurs</u> <u>por-</u>
        <u>traits</u> <u>en</u> <u>pied</u>. 4 vols. Paris: Longlois et Leclercq,
        1844-1847.

01227. Mongredien, Georges. <u>Libertins</u> <u>et</u> <u>amoureuses</u>. Paris: Perrin,
        1929.

01228. Sainte-Beuve, Charles Augustin. <u>Portraits</u> <u>des</u> <u>femmes</u>. Paris:
        Garnier frères, 1869.

01229. Watson, Paul Barron. <u>Some</u> <u>Women</u> <u>of</u> <u>France</u>. 1936. Reprint.
        Freeport, N.Y.: Books for Libraries, 1969.

        Also refer to #1032.

3. POLITICAL

"Women are not in the wrong when they decline to accept the
rules laid down for them, since the men make these rules
without consulting them."   Montaigne

a) Legal

01230. Aubenas, Roger. Cours d'histoire du droit privé 3 vols.
        Aix-en-Provence: Libraire de l'université, 1954.

01231. Brissaud, Jean. A History of French Private Law. Translated
        by R. Howell. Boston: Little, Brown and Company, 1912.

01232. Chénon, Emile. Histoire générale du droit français public et
        privé des origines à 1815. 2 vols. Paris: Recueil Sirey,
        1926-1929.

01233. Chevailler, Laurent. "Remarques sur la condition juridique du
        batard en droit valdotain et en droit coutumier français."
        31° Congresso storico subalpino, Aosta 1956 1 (1959): 187-
        197.

01234. Droit privé et institutions regionales: études historiques
        offertes à Jean Yver. Paris: Presses universitaires de
        France, 1976.

01235. Gilissen, John. "Le privilege de masculinité dans le droit
        coutumier de la Belgique et du Nord de la France." Revue
        du Nord 43 (1961): 201-216.

01236. _____. "Puissance paternelle et majorité emancipa-
        trice dans l'ancien droit de la Belgique et du nord de la
        France." Revue historique de droit français et étranger
        4th ser. 38 (1960): 5-57.

01237. Lefebvre, Charles. Lecons d'introduction générale à
        l'histoire du droit matrimonial français. Paris: L.
        Larose, 1900.

01238. Martin, Oliver. Histoire de la coutume de la prevote et
        vicomté de Paris. Paris: Ernest Leroux, 1930.

01239. Morange, G. La femme dans la fonction publique. Paris:
        Recueils Dalloz et Sirey, 1955.

01240. Ourliac, Paul and Malafosse, J. de la. Histoire du droit
        privé: Le droit familial. Paris: Presses universitaires
        de France, 1968.

01241. Paillot, Pierre. Etude sur la représentation successorale et
        sa place dans le droit familial du Nord de la France.
        Paris: Domat-Montchrestien, 1935.

01242.   Petot, Pierre and Vandenbossche, André. "Le Statut de la
          femme dans les pays coutumiers français du XIIIe au XVIIIe
          siècle." Recueils de la Société Jean Bodin 12 (1962):
          243-254.

01243.   Thabaut, Jules. L'Evolution de la législation sur la famille.
          Paris: A. Rousseau, 1913.

01244.   Yver, Jean. Egalité entre héritiers et exclusion des enfants
          dotés: essai de géographie coutumière. Paris: Sirey, 1966.

          Also refer to #1296, 1310, 1316, 1332, 1472.

                          b)   Feminism

01245.   Albistur, Maite and Armogathe, Daniel, eds. Le grief des
          femmes. Anthologie des textes féministes du moyen âge à
          la séconde république. Vol. I. Paris: Editions Hier et
          Demain, 1978.

01246.   _____. Histoire du féminisme
          français. Paris: Editions des femmes, 1977.

01247.   Ascoli, Georges. "Essai sur l'histoire des idées féministes
          en France du XVIe siècle à la Revolution." Revue de
          synthese historique 13 (August 1906): 25-57, 161-184.

01248.   Faguet, E. Le féminisme. Paris: Societe francaise
          d'imprimerie et de librairie, 1910.

01249.   Joran, Theodore. Les féministes avant le féminisme. Paris:
          G. Beauchesne et ses fils, 1935.

                    c)   Political Roles/Military

01250.   Aulneau, Joseph. Les Grandes Dames du Palais - Royal (1635-
          1870). Paris: Denoel, 1943.

01251.   Bearne, Catherine Mary Charlton. Heroines of French Society
          in the Court, the Revolution, the Empire, and the Restor-
          ation. London: E.P. Dutton, 1907.

01252.   Bingham, Denis Arthur. The Marriages of the Bourbons. New
          York: Scribner and Welford, 1890.

01253.   Brooks, Geraldine. Dames and Daughters of the French Court.
          1904. Reprint. Freeport, N.Y.: Books for Libraries, 1968.

01254. Castries, René de la Croix, duc de. The Lives of the Kings
        and Queens of France. Translated by Anne Dobell. New York:
        Alfred A. Knopf, 1979.

01255. Cocteau, Jean. Reines de la France. Paris: Bernard Grasset,
        1952.

01256. Gearey, Caroline. Two French Queens and other Sketches.
        London: Digby, Long and Co., 1896.

01257. Hamel, Frank. The Dauphines of France. New York: J. Potts
        and Co., 1910.

01258. _____. Fair Women at Fountainebleau. London: E. Nash,
        1909.

01259. La Varende, Jean de. Les belles esclaves. Paris: Flammarion,
        1949.

01260. Lescure, Mathurin François Adolphe de. Les grandes epouses.
        Paris: Firmin-Didot et cie, 1884.

01261. Madinier, Renée. Amours et destins des reines de France.
        Paris: Librairie académique Perrin, 1969.

01262. _____. Amours royales et imperiales. Paris:
        Perrin, 1966.

01263. Thornton-Cook, Elsie. The Royal Line of France-the Story of
        the Kings and Queens of France. London: J. Murray, 1933.

01264. Vigne, René Rouault de la. "Women who have Fought for
        France." American Society Legion of Honor Magazine 21
        (Summer 1950): 139-156.

4. ECONOMIC

            "girls of common extraction. . .
            all they need [to know] is to keep
            all their accounts and memoranda. . ."
                            Fénelon

01265. Bouvier, Jeanne. Histoire des dames employées dans les postes,
        télégraphes et telephones de 1714 à 1929. Paris: Les
        Presses universitaires de France, 1930.

01266. Bruhat, J.; Cerati, M.; Charle-Roux, E.; Gilles, Ch.; Guil-
        bert, M.; and Ziegler, G. Les femmes et le travail du moyen-
        âge à nos jours. Paris: Ed. de la Courtille, 1975.

01267. Chatelain, Abel. "Migrations et domesticité féminine urbaine
        en France, XVIIIe siècle-XXe siècle." Revue d 'histoire
        économique et sociale 47 (1969): 506-528.

01268. Guilbert, Madeleine. Travail et condition féminine. Biblio-
        graphie commentee. A partir de 1,084 livres et articles
        de 1890 a 1976. Paris: Ed. de la Courtille Odeon, 1978.

01269. Paulin, V. "Le travail à domicile en France. Ses Origines,
        son evolution, son avenir." Revue Internationale du Travail
        37 (February 1938): 205-240.

        Also refer to #1076, 1320, 1326.

5. RELIGION

"Thou shalt not suffer a witch to live."
                                        Exodus, xxii:18

01270. Biver, Paul and Biver, Marie-Louse. Abbayes, monastères,
        couvents de femmes a Paris des origines a la fin du XVIIIe
        siècle. Paris: Presses universitaires de France, 1975.

01271. Burguière, Andre. "The Charivari and Religious Repression in
        France during the Ancien Regime." In Family and Sexuality
        in French History, edited by Robert Wheaton and Tamara K.
        Hareven, pp. 84-110. Philadelphia: University of Pennsyl-
        vania Press, 1980.

01272. Cauzons, Thomas de. La Magie et la sorcellerie en France.
        Paris: Dorbin-aine, [1910-11].

01273. Guilloreau, Dom Leon. "L'abbaye d'Etival-en-Charnie et ses
        abbesses, 1109-1790." Revue historique et archéologique du
        Maine 49 (1901): 113-139; 52 (1902): 121-160.

01274. Piveteau, Cecile. La pratique matrimoniale en France d'après
        les statut synodaux. Le Puy: Imp. Jeanne d'Arc, 1957.

6. SOCIAL

"Nature weeps over the means inspired by luxury to avoid
the inconvenience of a large family."   Mirabeau, 1756.

a) Generic

01275. Couturier, Marcel. Recherches sur les structures sociales
        de Chateaudun 1525-1789. Demographie et societes, no. 10.
        Paris: S.E.V.P.E.N., 1969.

01276. Forster, Robert and Ranum, Orest, eds. Deviants and the
        Abandoned in French Society. Baltimore: Johns Hopkins
        Press, 1978,

01277. Franklin, Alfred Louis Auguste. La vie privée d'autrefois;
        arts et metiers, modes, moeurs, usages des Parisiens au
        XIIᵉ au XVIIIᵉ siècle. 23 vols. Paris: E. Plon, Nourrit
        et Cie, 1887-1901.
        [See especially vols. 1, 15-18, 19 and 20.]

01278. Le Roy Ladurie, Emmanuel. The Peasants of Languedoc. Trans-
        lated and introduced by John Day. Urbana: University of
        Illinois Press, 1974.

01279. Parturier, Louis. L'assistance à Paris sous l'Ancien Régime
        et pendant la Révolution. Paris: La Rose, 1897.

01280. Tavernier, Felix. La Vie quotidienne à Marseille, de Louis
        XIV à Louis-Philippe. Paris: Hachette, 1973.

b) Demography

01281. Ariès, Philippe. Histoire des populations françaises. Paris:
        Editions de Seuil, 1971.

01282. Borne, Louis. "Natalité à Boussieres (Doubs) de 1673 à 1935."
        Procès-verbaux et mémoires de l'Academie des sciences,
        belles-lettres et arts de Besançon 172 (1958): 146-157.

01283. Bourgeois-Pichat, Jean. "De la mesure de la mortalite infan-
        tile." Population 1 (1946): 53-68.

01284. _____. "The General Development of the Popu-
        lation of France since the Eighteenth Century." In Popula-
        tion in History, edited by David V. Glass and D.E.C. Evers-
        ley, pp. 474-506. Chicago: Aldine Pub. Co., 1965. Also in
        Population 6 (1951): 635-662.

01285. Charpy, Andre. "Registres paroissiaux et démographie en Bugey
        et Valromey (1660-1860)." Visages de l'Ain 28 (1975):
        32-36.

01286.   Deniel, Raymond. "La Population d'un village du Nord de la
         France: Sainghin-en-Melantois de 1665 à 1851." Population
         20 (1965): 563-602.

01287.   Dupaquier, Jacques. Introduction à la démographie historique.
         Paris: Gamma, 1974.

01288.   Estienne, Pierre. "Démographie ancienne d'une paroisse haute-
         alpine (1629-1822)." Cahiers d'histoire 15 (1970): 215-311.

01289.   Goubert, Pierre. "Historical Demography and the Reinterpre-
         tation of Early Modern French History: A Research Review."
         Journal of Interdisciplinary History 1 (1970): 37-48.

01290.   Guillaume, Pierre, and Jean-Pierre Poussou. La démographie
         historique. Paris: A. Colin, 1970.

01291.   Henry, Louis. "Evolution de la fecondité légitime à Meulan
         de 1660 à 1860." Population 25 (1970): 875-885.

01292.   Henry, Louis. "Une richesse demographique en friche: les
         registres paroissiaux." Population 8 (1953): 281-290.

01293.   _____ and J. Houdaille. "Fecondité des mariages dans
         le quart nordouest de la France de 1670 a 1829." Population
         28 (1973): 873-924.

01294.   Houdaille, J. "La fecondité des mariages de 1670 à 1829 dans
         le quart Nord-est de la France." Annales de demographie
         historique 1976: 341-391.

01295.   Lachiver, Marcel. La population de Meulan du XVIIe au XIXe
         siècle (vers 1600-1870); étude de démographie historique.
         Paris: S.E.V.P.E.N., 1969.

01296.   Lelièvre, Jacques. La Pratique des contrats de mariage chez
         les notaires en Chatelet de Paris de 1769 à Hoy. Paris:
         Editions Cujas, 1959.

01297.   Moulin, Raymond. "Petite étude démographique: les mariages
         à Saint-Jeannet de 1667 à 1900." Annales de Haute-Provence
         41 (1971): 263-270.

01298.   Poitou, Christian. "La mortalité en Sologne Orléanaise."
         Annales de démographie historique 1978: 235-265.

01299.   Spengler, Joseph John. France Faces Depopulation.   Durham,
         N.C.: Duke University Press, 1979.

         Also refer to #1329.

c) Family

(1) Non-specific

01300. Benjamin, Roger. "De la famille traditionnelle à la famille
moderne." Recherche sociale 26 (1969): 20-23.

01301. Berkner, Lutz K. and Shaffer, John W. "The Joint Family in
the Nivernais." Journal of Family History 3 (Summer 1978):
150-162.

01302. Ceccaldi, Dominique. Histoire des prestations familiales en
France. Paris: Union nationale des caisses d'allocations
familiales, 1957.

01303. Delzons, Louis. La Famille française et son évolution.
Paris: A. Colin, 1913.

01304. Dupâquier, Jacques. "Problèmes de représentativité dans les
études fondées sur la reconstitution des familles."
Annales de démographie historique 1972: 83-91.

01305. Du Plessis de Grenédan, Joachim. Histoire de l'autorité
paternelle et de la société familiale en France avant
1789. Paris: A. Rousseau, 1900.

01306. Flandrin, Jean-Louis. Families in former times: Kinship,
household and sexuality. Cambridge: University Press, 1979.

01307. Gaudemet, Jean. Les communautés familiales. Paris: M.
Riviere, 1963.

01308. Hilaire, Jean. "Vie en commun, famille, et esprit communau-
taire." Revue historique de droit francais et etranger
4th ser. 51 (January-March 1973): 8-53.

01309. Maranda, Pierre. French Kinship: Structure and History.
The Hague: Mouton, 1974.

01310. Moreel, Léon. "La notion de famille dans le droit de l'ancien
régime." In Renouveau des idées sur la famille, edited by
Robert Prigent, pp. 20-26. Paris: Presses universitaires
de France, 1954.

01311. Pernoud, Régine. "La vie de famille du moyen age à l'ancien
régime." In Renouveau des idées sur la famille, edited by
Robert Prigent, pp. 27-32. Paris: Presses universitaires
de France, 1954.

01312. Poumarède, Jacques. "Famille et tenure dans les Pyrénées du
moyen-âge au XIXe siècle." Annales de démographie historique 1979: 347-360.

01313. Vallin, Pierre. "La famille en France, esquisse d'histoire
religieuse." Etudes 339 (August-September 1973): 283-301.

01314. Wheaton, Robert and Hareven, Tamara K. Family and Sexuality
in French History. Philadelphia: University of Pennsylvania Press, 1980.

Also refer to #1076, 1129, 1131, 1132, 1240, 1241, 1243.

(2)   Childhood

01315. Blayo, Yves. "Illegitimate births in France from 1740 to
1829 and in the 1960's." In Bastardy and its Comparative
History, edited by Peter Laslett, Karla Oosterveen and
Richard M. Smith, pp. 278-283. Cambridge, Mass.: Harvard
University Press, 1980.

01316. Charpentier, Jehanne. Le droit de l'enfance abandonnée; son
évolution sous l'influence de la psychologies (1552-1791).
Paris: Presses universitaires de France, 1967.

01317. Dupoux, Albert. Sur les pas de Monsieur Vincent: 300 ans
d'histoire parisienne de l'enfance abandonnée. Paris:
Revue de l'Assistance publique a Paris, 1958.

01318. Lallemand, Leon. Histoires des enfants abandonnés et
delaissés. Paris: A. Picard, 1885.

01319. Meyer, Jean. "Illegitimates and Foundlings in pre-industrial
France." In Bastardy and its Comparative History, edited
by Peter Laslett, Karla Oosterveen and Richard M. Smith,
pp. 249-263. Cambridge, Mass.: Harvard University Press,
1980.

Also refer to #1129, 1233, 1282.

d)   Marriage

01320. Audiat, Pierre. Vingt-cinq siècles de mariage. Paris:
Hachette, 1961.

01321. Burgues, Jean. Les garanties de restitution de la dot en
Languedoc, des invasion barbares à la fin de l'Ancien
Regime. Paris: Recueil Sirey, 1937.

01322. Burguière, André. "Le rituel du mariage en France: Pratiques ecclesiastiques et pratiques populaires (XVIe–XVIIIe
siècle)." Annales: économies, sociétés, civilisations 33
(May–June 1978): 637–649.

01323. Duplessis, Gerard. Les Mariages en France. Cahiers de la
fondation nationale des sciences politiques, no. 53.
Paris: Librairie Armand Colin, 1954.

01324. Favarger, Dominique. Le regime matrimonial dans le comté de
Neuchâtel du XVe au XIXe siècle. Neuchâtel: Editions
Ides et Calendes, 1970.

01325. Galliot, Simone. Le régime matrimonial en droit franc-comtois
de 1459 à la Revolution. Besancon: n.p., 1954.

01326. Gay, Jean-L. Les effets pécuniares au mariage en Nivernais
du XIVe au XVIIIe siècle. Paris: Domat-Montchrestien,
1953.

01327. Lebrun, Francois. La vie conjugale sous l'ancien régime.
Paris: A. Collin, 1975.

01328. Phan, Marie-Claude. "Les déclarations de grossesse en France
(XVIe – XVIIIe siècles): essai institutionnel." Revue
d'histoire moderne et contemporaine 22 (January–March 1975):
61–88.

01329. Robine, M. "Les archives notariales, complément des registres
pariossiaux: étude de la distribution statistique de delai
entre contrat de mariage et mariage aux XVIIe XVIIIe et
XIX siècles, dans un village du Bazadais." Annales de
démographie historique 1974: 59–97.

01330. Sarg, Freddy. Le mariage en Alsace: études de quelques
coutumes passees et presents. Strasbourg: Oberlin, 1975.

01331. Segalen, Martine. "Le mariage et la femme dans les proverbes
du Sud de la France." Annales du Midi 87 (1975): 265–288.

01332. Villers, Robert. "Note sur l'immutabilité des conventions
matrimoniales dans l'ancien droit français (origines de
l'article 1895 du ancien code civil)." In Droit privé et
institutions régionales, pp. 679–689. Paris: Presses
universitaires de France, 1976.

Also refer to #1237, 1274, 1296, 1342.

e) Sex Life and Morals

(1) Non-specific

01333. Epton, Nina Consuelo. Love and the French. London:
        Cassell, 1959.

01334. Flandrin, Jean Louis. Les amours paysannes: amour et
        sexualité dans les campagnes de l'ancienne France (XVIe –
        XIXe siècle). Paris: Gallimard, 1975.

01335. _____. "Repression and Change in the Sexual
        Life of Young People in Medieval and Early Modern Times."
        In Family and Society in French History, edited by Robert
        Wheaton and Tamara K. Hareven, pp. 27–48. Philadelphia:
        University of Pennsylvania Press, 1980. Also in Journal
        of Family History 2 (1977): 196–210.

01336. Guerdan, Rene. La Femme et l'amour en France à travers les
        ages. Paris: Plon, 1965.

        Also refer to #774, 1306, 1314.

(2) Prostitutes and Courtesans

01337. Isou, Isidore. Histoire philosophique illustrée de la volupté
        à Paris. Paris: Publications et éditions Alger, 1960.

01338. Journaux et canards érotiques du temps passé. Paris: Les
        Yeux Ouverts, 1970.

01339. Le Pileur, Louis. La Prostitution du XIIIe au XVIIe siècle;
        documents tirés des archives d'Avignon, du Comtat Venaissin
        de la Principauté d'Orange et de la ville libre imperiale
        de Besançon. Paris: Champion, 1908.

01340. Villefosse, Rene Heronde. Histoire et géographie galantes de
        Paris. Paris: les Editions de Paris, 1957.

f) Health/Medical

01341. Ariès, Philippe. "On the Origins of Contraception in France."
In Popular Attitudes toward Birth Control in Pre-Industrial
France and England, edited by Orest and Patricia Ranum, pp.
10-20. New York: Harper and Row, 1972. Also in Population
3 (1953): 465-472.

01342. Burguière, André. "From Malthus to Max Weber: Belated
Marriage and the Spirit of Enterprise." In Family and
Society, edited by Robert Forster and Orest Ranum, pp. 237-
240. Baltimore: Johns Hopkins Press, 1976. Also in
Annales: economies, societes, civilisations 27 (1972):
1128-1138.

01343. Carrier, Henriette. Origines de la maternité de Paris; les
maîtresses, sages-femmes et l'office des accouchées de
l'ancien Hotel-Dieu, 1378-1796. Paris: Steinheil, 1888.

01344. Dupâquier, Jacques and Lachiver, M. "Sur les débuts de la conception en France, ou les deux malthusiannes." Annales:
économies, sociétés, civilisations 24 (1969): 1391-1406.

01345. Petrelli, Richard L. "The Regulation of French Midwifery
during the Ancien Regime." Journal of the History of
Medicine and Allied Sciences 26 (July 1971): 276-292.

01346. Van de Walle, Etienne. "Motivations and Technology in the
Decline of French Fertility." In Family and Sexuality in
French History, edited by Robert Wheaton and Tamara K.
Hareven, pp. 135-178. Philadelphia: University of Pennsyl-
vania Press, 1980.

Also refer to #1186, 1328.

7. CULTURAL

"Now I am truly a man."   Christine de Pisan

a) Generic

01347. Charrier, E. L'évolution intellectuelle féminine. Paris:
Librairie du Recueil Sirey, 1931.

01348. Kahn, Gustave. La femme dans la caricature française. Paris:
        A. Mericant, 1907?.

b) Education

01349. Barnard, Howard Clive. The French Tradition in Education:
        Ramus to Mme Necker de Saussure. 1922. Reprint. Cam-
        bridge: University Press, 1970.

01350. Chabaud, Louis. Mesdames de Maintenon, de Genlis et Campan.
        Leur rôle dans l'education chretienne de la femme. Paris:
        Plon-Nourrit et cie, 1901.

01351. Rousselot, Paul. Histoire de l'éducation des femmes en
        France. 2 vols. Paris: Didier et cie, 1883.

        Also refer to #1129.

c) Literature

01352. Brée, Germaine. Women Writers of France: variations on a
        theme. New Brunswick, N.J.: Rutgers University Press,
        1973.

01353. Kavanagh, Julia. French Women of Letters: Biographical
        Sketches. London: Hurst and Blackett, 1862.

01354. Larnac, Jean. Histoire de la littérature féminine en France.
        Paris: Editions Kra, 1929.

01355. Ravenel, Florence Leftwich. Women and the French Tradition.
        New York: Macmillan, 1918.

01356. Sullerot, Evelyne. Histoire de la presse féminine en France
        des origines à 1848. Paris: Armand Colin, 1966.

        Also refer to #1331.

d) Art and Artifacts

01357. Brussells, Palais des beaux-arts. La femme dans l'art
        français. Brussells: 1953.

01358. Friedman, Adele C. "Love, Sex and Marriage in Traditional
        French Society: The Documentary Evidence of Folksongs."
        French Review 52 (December 1978): 242-254. Also in
        Proceedings of the Fifth Annual Meeting of the Western
        Society for French History 5 (November 1977): 146-154.

01359. _____. "Stereotypes of Traditional Society in
        French Folksongs and Images Populaires." Journal of Popular
        Culture 10 (1977): 769-771.

01360. Grand-Carteret, John. Le Décolleté et le retroussé. Quatre
        siècles de Gauloiserie, 1500-1870. Paris: E. Bernard &
        Co., 1902; Edition photographique, 1910.

D. THE GERMANIES

1. SURVEYS

". . . there lie chiefly in the character of the mind of
this sex peculiar strokes, which clearly distinguish it
from ours and . . . make it know by the criterion, fair."
                                    Immanuel Kant

01361. Baumer, Gertrud. Die Frauengestalt der deutschen Fruhe.
        Berlin: F. A. Herbit, 1929.

01362. Bauer, Max. Die deutsche Frau in der Vergangenheit. Berlin:
        A. Schall, 1907.

01363. _____. Deutscher Frauenspiegel Bilder aus dem Frauen-
        leben in der deutschen Vergangenheit. 2 vols. Munich:
        Georg Muller, 1917.

01364. Garbe, Ulrike. Frauenschicksal-Frauengrosse. Lebens-und
        Charakterbilder germanischer Frauen von der Fruhzeit bis
        zur Gegenwart. Stuttgart: Union, 1936.

01365. Locke, Amy. "Austria." In Women of all Nations, edited by
        T. A. Joyce, 4: 691-697. New York: Funk and Wagnalls, 1915.

01366. _____. "Germany." In Women of all Nations, edited by
        T. A. Joyce, 4: 698-703. New York: Funk and Wagnalls, 1915.

01367. Otto, Eduard. Duetsches Frauenleben im Wandel der Jahr-
        hunderte. Natur und Geisteswelt, vol. 45. Leipzig:
        B.G. Teubner, 1903.

01368. Scherr, Johannes. Geschichte der deutschen Frauenwelt. 3
        vols. Leipzig: Hesse and Becker Verlag, 1911.

01369. Schoenfeld, Hermann. <u>Women</u> <u>of</u> <u>the</u> <u>Teutonic</u> <u>Nations</u>. Phila-
        delphia: Rittenhouse Press, 1908.

01370. Wentscher, Else. <u>Deutsche</u> <u>Frauengestalten</u>. Leipzig: Koehler
        and Voigtlander, 1943.

01371. Zahn-Harnack, Agnes von. <u>Wandlungen</u> <u>des</u> <u>Frauenlebens</u> <u>Vom</u> <u>18</u>
        <u>Jahrhundert</u> <u>bis</u> <u>zur</u> <u>Gegenwart</u>. Frankfurt a.M.: Padago-
        gischer Verlag Schulz, 1951.

01372. Zapp, Eduard. <u>Geschichte</u> <u>der</u> <u>Deutschen</u> <u>Frauen</u>. Berlin: F.
        Henschel, 1870.

2. BIOGRAPHIES

"The eternal feminine drives us onward."
                              Goethe <u>Faust</u>

01373. Bäumer, Gertrud. <u>Studien</u> <u>über</u> <u>Frauen</u>. Berlin: F. A. Herbig,
        1924.

3. POLITICAL

". . . it will be found that the fundamental fault of the
female character is that it has no sense of justice."
                              Schopenhauer

a) Legal

01374. Brauneder, Wilhelm. <u>Die</u> <u>Entwicklung</u> <u>des</u> <u>Eheguterrechts</u> <u>in</u>
        <u>Österreich</u>. Salzburg: W. Fink, 1973.

01375. Brenne, Dieter. <u>Erbenfall-</u> <u>und</u> <u>Erbantrittsprinzip</u> <u>in</u> <u>der</u>
        <u>neueren</u> <u>deutschen</u> <u>Privatrechtsgeschichte</u>. Munster: M.
        Kramer, 1959.

01376. Fehr, Hans Adolph. Die Rechtsstellung der Frau und der Kinder
        in den Weistumern. Niederwalluf bei Weisbaden: M. Sandig,
        1971.

01377. Friedberg, Emil Albert. Das Recht der Eheschliessung in
        siener geschichtlichen Entwicklung. 1865. Reprint.
        Aalen: Scientia Verlag, 1965.

01378. Huebner, Rudolf. A History of Germanic Private Law. Trans-
        lated by Francis S. Philbrick. Boston: Little, Brown and
        Co., 1918.

01379. Martin, Alfred Henri. Exposé de l'ancienne legislation
        genevoise sur le mariage. Geneva: Aubert-Schuchardt, 1891.

01380. Merschberger, Gerda. Die Rechtsstellung der germanischen
        Frau. Mannus-Bucherei, vol. 57. Leipzig: Kabitzsch,
        1937.

01381. Paulsen, Friedrich. "Die Frau im Recht der Vergangenheit und
        der Zukunft." Preussisches Jahrbuch 132 (1908): 396-413.

01382. Schmelzeisen, G.K. Die Rechtsstellung der Frau in der
        deutschen Stadtwirtschaft Eine Untersuchung zur Geschichte
        des deutschen Rechts. Arbeitungen zur deutschen Rechts-
        und Verfassungsgeschichte, vol. 10. Stuttgart: Kohlhammer,
        1935.

01383. Sohm, Rudolf. Das Recht der Eheschliessung, aus dem deutschen
        und canonischen Recht geschichtlich entwickelt. 1875.
        Reprint. Aalen: Scientia Verlag, 1966.

01384. Thieme, Hans. "Die Rechtsstellung der Frau in Deutschland."
        Société Jean Bodin Recueils de la 12 (1962): 351-376.

b) Criminal

01385. Reinhard W. Nell in Bridewell: Lenchem in Zuchthause: Descrip-
        tion of the System of Corporal Punishment (Flagellation)
        in the Female Prisons of South Germany up to the Year 1848;
        a Contribution to the History of Manners. Paris: Society
        of British Bibliophiles, 1932.

c) Political Roles

01386. Aretz, Gertrude. Die Frauen der Hohenzollern. Berlin:
        Paul Aretz Verlag, 1933.

01387.   Kirchner, Earnst David Martin. Die Churfürstinnen und König-
          innen auf dem Throne der Hohenzollern. 3 vols. Berlin:
          Weigandt and Grieben, 1866-1870.

4. ECONOMIC

The wife "became the first domestic servant."   Engels

01388.   Essig, Olga. Die Frau in der Industrie. Quellenhefte zum
          Frauenleben in der Geschichte, edited by Emmy Beckmann and
          Irma Stoss, vol. 3. Berlin: F. A. Herbig, 1927-1933.

01389.   Steiger, Emma. Geschichte der Frauenarbeit in Zurich.
          Zurich: Statistisches Amt der Stadt Zurich, 1964.

5. RELIGION

"A woman must be a learner, listening quietly and with due
submission. I do not permit a woman to be a teacher, nor
must a woman domineer over a man; she should be quiet."
                                        1 Tim. 2:11-13

01390.   Buchinger, Johann Nepomuk. "Erinnerungen an die Gründung und
          erste Verbreitung des Instituts der englischen Fraulein in
          Bayern." Oberbayerisches Archiv für vaterländische Ges-
          chichte 17 (1857): 115-173.

01391.   Erasmi, Bernhard. Deutsches Frauenleben in Vergangenheit und
          Gegenwart. Ein geschichtlicher Uberblick uber die Entwicklung
          der kulturellen Stellung der deutschen Frauen unter dem
          Einfluss der katholischen Kirche. Donauwörth: Buchhandlung
          Auer, 1933.

01392.   Kirstein, Roland. Die Entwicklung der Sponsalienlehre und der
          Lehre vom Eheschluss in der deutschen protestantischen
          Eherechtslehre bis zu J.H. Bohmer Bonn: L. Rohrscheid, 1966.

01393.   Leitner, Jakob. Geschichte der englischen Fraulein und ihrer
          Institute seit ihrer Grundung bis auf unsere Zeit. Regens-
          burg: Druck und Verlag von Georg Joseph Manz, 1869.

01394.   Pechmann, M. Gonzaga Fr. von. Geschichte des englischen
          Instituts Baetae Mariae Virginis in Bayern. Munich: Im
          Selbstverlag des General Mutterhauses Nymphenburg, 1907.

01395. Taddy, Gerhard. Das Kloster Heiningen von der Grundung bis
        zur Aufhebung. Gottingen: Vandenhoeck Ruprecht, 1966.

01396. Winkler, Maria Theodolinde. Maria Ward und das Institut der
        Englischen Fraulein in Bayern von der Grundung des Hauses
        in Munchen bis zur Sakularisation desselben 1626-1810.
        Munich: Druck und Kommissionsverlag Carl August Seyfried
        and Company, 1926.

01397. Zum Gedächtnis des 300 Jährigen Bestehens des Instituts B.M.V.
        der Englischen Fraulein in Bayern 1626-1926. Edited by
        members of the Institut der Englischen Fraulein. Munich:
        Druck von Carl August Seyfried and Company, 1926.

6. SOCIAL

> "I praise matrimony. But only because it produces
> virgins."   Jerome

a) Generic

01398. Freytag, Gustav. Pictures of German Life. 2 vols. Trans-
        lated by Mrs. Malcolm. London: Chapman and Hall, 1862.
        [See especially vol. 1, chs. 2, 8, 9, and 10.]

01399. Kloos, Werner. Die Bremerin: Ein Almanach, Portraits und
        Illustrationen aus den Sammlungen des Volke-Museums.
        Bremen: Schuremann, 1965.

01400. Pollack, Herbert. Jewish Folkways in Germanic Lands, 1648-
        1809. Cambridge, Mass.: M.I.T. Press, 1971.
        [See especially ch. 2 "Birth and Marriage."]

b) Demographic

01401. Burckhardt, Albrecht. Demographie und Epidemiologie der Stadt
        Basel während der letzten drei Jahrhunderte, 1601-1900.
        Basel: n.p., 1908.

01402. Henry, Louis. Anciennes familles genevoises: Etude démo-
        graphique, XVIe - XXe siècles. Paris: Presses universi-
        taires de France, 1956.

01403. Knodel, John. "Two and a half centuries of Demographic
        History in a Bavarian Village." Population Studies 24
        (November 1970): 353-376.

01404. Mitterauer, Michael. "Familiengrosse--Familientypus--
        Familienzyklus: Probleme quantitativer Auswertung von
        österreichischem Quellenmaterial." Geschichte und
        Gesellschaft 1 (1975): 226-255.

01405. Perrenoud, Alfred. "La mortalité à Geneve de 1625 à 1825." _Annales de démographie historique_ 1978: 209-233.

01406. _____. _La population de Geneve du seizième au début du dix-neuvième siècle: Etude démographique._ Vol. I _Structures et mouvements._ Geneva: Editions Société d'histoire et d'archéologie de Geneve, 1979.

01407. Radeff, Anne. "Naissance d'une communauté agro-industrielle du Jura Suisse: Vallorbe, 1397-1614." _Etudes rurales_ 68 (October-December 1977): 107-140.

c)   Family

(1)   Non-specific

01408. Imhof, Arthur E. "Ländliche Familienstrukturen an einem hessischen Beispiel: Heuchelheim 1690-1900." In _Sozial-geschichte der Familie in der Neuzeit Europas_, edited by Werner Conze, pp. 197-230. Stuttgart: Ernst Klett Verlag, 1976.

01409. Mitterauer, Michael. "Auswirkungen von Urbanisierung und Fruhindustrialisierung auf die Familienverfassung an Bei-spielen des österreichischen Raums." In _Sozialgeschichte der Familie in der Neuzeit Europas_, edited by Werner Conze, pp. 53-146. Stuttgart: Ernst Klett Verlag, 1976.

01410. Riehl, Wilhelm, Heinrich, _Die Familie_. Stuttgart: J.G. Cotta, 1861.

01411. Sabean, David. "Verwandtschaft und Familie in einem württembergischen Dorf 1500 bis 1870: einige methodische Überlegungen." In _Sozialgeschichte der Familie in der Neuzeit Europas_, edited by Werner Conze, pp. 231-246. Stuttgart: Ernst Klett Verlag, 1976.

01412. Schrader, O. _Die Schwiegermutter und der Hagestolz. Eine Studie aus der Geschichte unserer Familie._ Braunschweig: G. Westermann, 1904.

01413. Weber-Kellermann, Ingeborg. _Die deutsche Familie: Versuch einer Sozialgeschichte._ Frankfurt a.M.: Suhrkamp, 1974.

Also refer to #1416.

(2)   Childhood

01414.   Boesch, Hans. Kinderleben in der deutschen Vergangenheit.
         Jena: Eugen Diederichs, 1924.

01415.   Gebauer, Johannes Heinrich.   "Die 'unechten' und 'unehrlichen'
         in der Stadt Hildesheim." Archiv für Kulturgeschichte 32
         (1944): 118-171.

d)   Marriage

01416.   Freidrichs, Christopher R.   "Marriage, Family and Social
         Structure in an Early Modern German Town." Canadian Histor-
         ical Papers 1975, 17-40.

         Also refer to #1374, 1377, 1379, 1383, 1392.

e)   Sex Life and Morals

(1)   Non-specific

01417.   Tomasson, Richard L.   "A millenium of sexual permissiveness
         in the North." American Scandanavian Review 60 (December
         1974): 370-378.

(2)   Prostitutes and Courtesans

01418.   Bauer, Max. Die Dirne und ihr Anhang. Ein Beitrag zur
         Geschichte des Geschlechtslebens in der deutschen
         Vergangenheit. Dresden: P. Aretz, 1924.

01419.   _____. Liebesleben in Deutscher Vergangenheit. Berlin:
         P. Langenscheidt, 1924.

01420.   _____. Weih und Sittlichkeit: die Sittengeschichte der
         deutschen Frau. Berlin: Eigenbrodler Verlag, 1927.

01421.   Brachwitz, Richard. "Die Sittlichen Verhaltnisse im Alten
         Berlin. Eine Kulturhistorische Betrachtung." Sudhoffs
         Archiv für Geschichte der Medizin 35 (February 1943):
         339-347.

01422   Entschleierte Geheimnisse der Prostitution in Hamburg. Leip-
         zig: Julius Koffka, 1847.

01423.   Montane, H. Die Prostitution in Wien. Hamburg: P. Rasch,
         1925.

01424.   Wintsch-Maleeff, Natalie. "Struggle against the venereal
         diseases and prostitution in Switzerland." Social Hygene
         6 (April 1920): 255-262.

f)   Health/Medical

01425.   Rall, Jutta. "The Female Doctor in German Medical History."
         Deutsch Aerzteblatt-Aerztliche Mitteilung 64: (21 October
         1967): 1-12.

01426.   Schelenz, Hermann. Women in the Realm of Esculapius, a study
         for a History of Women in Medicine and Pharmacy; With Con-
         sideration of the Future of the Modern Woman Doctor and
         Pharmacist. Leipzig: Ernst Gunther, 1900.

01427.   Strecker, Gabriele. "Medical Women in German." Journal of
         the American Medical Women's Association 2: (November 1947):
         506-508.

7. CULTURAL

         "I learned everything they seemed so unaccountably anxious
         for me to know as quickly as possible in order to have done
         with the learning the sooner."   Sophie of Hanover

a)   Generic

01428.   Bodmer-Gessner, Verena. Die Zürcherinnen; klein Kulturge-
         schichte der Zürcher Frauen. Zurich: Verlag Berichthaus,
         1961.

01429.   Hassel, Henriette. Geschichte der deutschen Frauenwelt in der
         Kulturbewegung der Zeiten bis zur Gegenwart. Braunschweig:
         Bock and Company, 1898.

b) Education

01430. Blochmann, Elisabeth. Das "Frauenzimmer" und die "Gelehrsam-
        keit" Eine Studie über die Anfange des Mädchenschulwesens
        in Deutschland. Heidelberg: Quelle und Meyer, 1966.

01431. Hindringer, Rudolf. Das kirchliche Schulrecht in Altbayern
        von Albrecht V. bis zum Erlass der bayerischen Verfassungs-
        urkund 1550-1818. Paderborn: Druck und Verlag von Ferdinand
        Schöningh, 1916.

01432. Maus, Anna. Vom Philanthropin zur Mädchenoberschule 1782-
        1957. Die Geschichte der Karolinenschule zu Frankenthal/
        Pfalz. Frankenthal: Mushakesche Verlagsanstalt, Franz
        Mathes Verlag, 1958.

01433. Muller, Johannes Ludolf. Die Erziehungsanstalt Schnepfenthal
        1784-1934 Festschrift aus Anlass des 150. jahrigen Bestehens
        der Anstalt. Schnepfenthal: Buchhandlung der Erziehung-
        sanstalt Schnepfenthal, 1934.

01434. Stricker, Käthe. Deutsche Frauenbildung vom 16. Jahrhundert
        bis mitte des 19. Jahrhundert. Quellenhefte zum Frauen-
        leben in der Geschichte, edited by Emmy Beckman and Irma
        Stoss, vol. 4. Berlin: F.A. Herbig, 1929.

01435. Veith, D. "Zur Schulgeschichte des Inselklosters." Studien
        und Mitteilungen zur Geschichte des Benediktinerordens und
        seiner Zweige 85 (1974): 571-585.

01436. Zinnecker, Jürgen. Emanzipation der Frau und Schulausbildung
        I. Zur schulischen Sozialisation und gesellschaftlichen
        Position der Frau. Basle-Weinheim: Beltz, 1972.

01437. _____. Sozialgeschichte der Madchenbildung: zur
        Kritik der Schulerziehung von Madchen im burgerlichen
        Patriarchalismus. Jurgen Zinnecker. Basle-Weinheim: Betzl,
        1973.

c) Literature

01438. Bovenschen, Silvia. Imaginierte Weiblichkeit und Weibliche
        Imagination. Frankfurt: Suhrkamp, 1978.

01439. Lerche, Otto. Frauenbriefe aus Zeiten deutscher Not.
        Koln: O. Schmidt, 1929.

01440. Vogel, Johannes, ed. <u>Deutsche Frauen in der Anekdoten</u>
        <u>Anekdote, Briefe und Curiosa aus funf Jahrhunderten.</u>
        Berlin: Deutsche Bibliothek, 1943.

d) Science

01441. Oelsner, Elise. <u>Die Leistungen der deutschen Frau in den</u>
        <u>letzten 400 Jahren auf wissenschaftlichem Gebiet.</u>
        Guhrau: M. Lemke, 1894.

E. IBERIA

1. SURVEYS

". . . the men . . . will not permit any stranger to come
where their wives are, much less see them, but [they] will
keep them out of sight as much as they possibly can."
British seaman's account of visiting 17th century Lisbon

01442. Alberti, A. de. "Spain and Portugal." In <u>Women of all</u>
        <u>Nations</u>, edited by T.A. Joyce, 4: 717-724. New York: Funk
        and Wagnalls, 1915.

01443. Altamira y Crevea, Rafael. "La mujer española a traves de
        la historia." <u>Cuadernos Americanos</u> 217, (1978): 117-140.

01444. Capmany, Maria Aurelia. <u>La dona a Catalunya.</u> <u>Consciencia i</u>
        <u>situacio.</u> 2nd ed. Barcelona: Edicions 62, 1971.

01445. Catalina del Amo, Severo. <u>La mujer: apuntes para un libra.</u>
        Madrid: Manuel Tello, 1888.

2. BIOGRAPHIES

01446. Madariaga, Salvador de. <u>Mujeres Españolas.</u> Madrid: Espasa
        Calpe, 1972.

01447. Sedevila Zubiru, Fernando. <u>Les dones en la nostra història.</u>
        Barcelona: R. Dalmau, 1966.

3. POLITICAL

"to avoid quarrels, homicides, insolence, violence and
many other wrongful acts that would take place on account
of women, if marriage did not exist."
            Spanish law code, on the need for lawful marriage

a) Legal

01448. Garcia Gallo, A. "L'evolution de la condition de la femme en
        droit espagnol." Annales de la Faculté de Droit de
        Toulouse 14 (1966): 73-96.

01449. Merea, Manuel Paulo. Estudos de historia do direito.
        Coimbra: Coimbra editore, 1924.

b) Political Roles

01450. Lancastre-Laboreiro, Ana de. Infantas lusitanas, reinas de
        Espana e infantas espanolas reinas de Portugal. Caceres:
        Moderna, 1931.

01451. Miron, E. L. The Queens of Aragon, Their Lives and Times.
        New York: Brentano's, 1913.

4. ECONOMIC

". . .the Portugal women are counted as the finest needle-
women in the world, doing more for a twopence than an
Englishwoman will do for a shilling."
            British seaman's account of visiting 17th century Portugal

01452. Boxer, Charles Ralph. Women in Iberian Expansion Overseas,
        1415-1815: Some Facts, Fancies, and Personalities. New
        York: Oxford University Press, 1975.

01453. Vives, Vicens J., ed. Historia social y economica de Espana
        y America. Barcelona: Teide, 1957.

5. SOCIAL

"The brothel in the city, then, is like the stable or
latrine for the house."
                    Franciscan Fantan, 16th c. Spanish cleric

a) Generic

01454. Amador de los Rios, Roddrigo. "Costumbres muselmanas. Notas
        acerca de la mujer. Su nacimiento--Su educación--Su matri-
        monio--Su vida en el harem." España moderna 10 (May 1898):
        108-153.

01455   Amezúa y Mayo, Agustin Gonzalez de. La vida privada española
        en el protoco notarial. Madrid: n.p., 1950.

01456. Pescatello, Ann M. Power and Dawn: The Female in Iberian
        Families, Societies, and Cultures. Westport, Conn.:
        Greenwood Press, 1976.

        Also refer to #1453.

b) Demography

01457. Nadal, J. La poblcaion española (siglos XVI a XX). Barce-
        lona: Ariel, 1971.

c) Family

01458. Foster, George M. "Cofradía and Compadrazgo in Spain and
        Spanish America." Southwestern Journal of Anthropology
        9 (1953): 1-28.

01459. Mintz, Sidney and Wolf, Eric R. "An Analysis of Ritual
        Co-Parenthood (compadrazgo)." Southwestern Journal of
        Anthropology 6 (1950): 341-368.

d) Sex Life and Morals

(1) Non-specific

01460. Epton, Nina Consuelo. Love and the Spanish. Cleveland: World Books, 1962.

01461. Revilla, Federico. El Sexo en la Historia de España. Barcelona: Ediciones 29, 1973.

(2) Prostitutes and Courtesans

01462. Amdel, Doctor (pseud). La Prostitucion en España. Madrid: Editorial Fénix, 1934.

01463. Carboneres, Manuel. Picaronas y alcahuetes: ó La mancebía de Valencia. Apuntes para la historia de la Prostitución desde principios de siglo XIV hasta poco antes de la abolición de los fueros, conprofusion de notas y copias de varios documentos oficiales. Valencia: Imp. del Mercantil, 1876.

6. CULTURAL

"They [17th century Iberian urban women] . . . are most witty in repartees and stories and notions in the world. They sing, but not well . . . They play of all kinds of instruments likewise, and dance with castanetas very well."

Ann Fanshawe, British
traveler in Spain

a) Literature

01464. Guzmán, Pérez de. "La mujer española en la Minerva leteraria castellana." España moderna 10 (July 1898): 111-129; (August 1898): 84-110; (September 1898): 50-80; (October 1898): 90-120.

b) Art and Artifacts

01465. Villa Pastur, Jésus. El desnudo femenino en la pintura asturiana. Gijón: Gran Enciclopedia Asturiana, 1972.

F. ITALY

1. SURVEYS

"Rightly so, because the Statutes of Venice are against
inheritance of house by women. And also because everyone
knows it is men who continue families and maintain their
honor and not women, who pass into other families."
                                        Leonardo Dona

01466. Florence. Esposizione Beatrice. La Donna italiana.
         1890. Reprint. New Haven, Conn.: Research Publications,
         1975.

01467. Grenett, Lucy M.J. "Italy." In Women of all Nations, edited
         by T.A. Joyce, vol. 4, New York: Funk & Wagnalls, 1915.

2. BIOGRAPHICAL SKETCHES

"The Greatest praise is justly bestowed upon you, illustrious Isotta, since you have . . . overcome your own
nature. For that true virtue, which is essentially male,
you have sought with singular zeal."
                                        about Isotta Nogarola

01468. Gearey, Caroline. Daughters of Italy. London: S. Marshall
         and Co., 1886.

3. POLITICAL

". . . I used to express my disapproval of bold and forward
females who try too hard to know about things outside the
house and about the concerns of their husbands and men in
general. . ."   Leon Battista Alberti

a) Legal

01469. Bellomo, Manlio. La condizione giuridica della donna in
         Italia vicende antiche e moderne. Turin: Iri, 1970.

01470.   Calisse, Carlo. A History of Italian Law. Translated by
         Layton B. Register. New York: Augustus Kelley, 1969.

01471.   Leicht, Pier Silverio. Richerche sul diritto privato nei
         documenti preierneriani. Rome: Athenaeum, 1914.

01472.   Marin-Muracciole, Madeleine-Rose. L'honneur des femmes en
         Corse, du XIIIe siècle à nos jours. Paris: Cujas, 1964.

01473.   Pertile, Antonio. Storia del diritto Italiano dalla cudata
         dell'Impero romano alla codificazione. Turin: Union
         tipografico editrice, 1892-1902.

01474.   Rossi Guido. "Statut juridique de la femme dans l'histoire
         du droit italien." Recueils de la Société Jean Bodin 12
         (1962): 115-134.

01475.   Rossi, Guido. Le Statut juridique de la femme dans l'his-
         toire du droit italien. Epoque médiévale et moderne.
         Milan: A. Giuffre, 1958.

01476.   Winterer, Hermann. Die rechtliche Stellung der Bastarde
         in Italien von 800 bis 1500. Munich: Arbeo-Gesellschaft,
         1978.

4. SOCIAL

"Such are the times then, into which your Pactula has been
born. Slaughter and death are the toys of her childhood.
She will know tears before laughter."

                                                  Jerome

a) Generic

01477.   Dalla Costa, Mariarosa. Potere femminile e sovversione
         sociale. Padua: Marsilio, 1972.

01478.   Frati, Ludovico. La vita privata in Bologna dal secolo XIII
         al XVII. Bologna: N. Zanichelli, 1928.

01479.   Maraspini, A. L. The Study of an Italian Village. Paris:
         Mouton, 1968.
         [See especially ch. 5, "Home and Marriage," pp. 135-168, and
         ch. 6, "The Family," pp. 169-196.]

b) Demography

01480. Bachi, Roberto. "The Demographic Development of Italian
Jewry from the 17th Century." Jewish Journal of Sociology
4 (December 1962): 172-191.

01481. Beloch, Karl Julius. Bevölkerungsgeschichte Italiens. 3 vols.
Berlin: De Gruyter, 1937-61.

01482. Beltrami, Daniele. Storia della populazione di Venezia dalla
fine del secolo XVI alla caduta della Repubblica. Padua:
Cedam, 1954.

01483. Fiumi, Enrico. Demografia, movimento urbanistico e classi sociali in Prato dall'eta communale ai tempi moderni. Biblioteca storica toscana, no. 14, Florence: L.S. Olschki, 1968.

01484. Litchfield, R. Burr. "Demographic Characteristics of Florentine Patrician Families, Sixteenth to Nineteenth Centuries."
Journal of Economic History 29 (June 1969): 191-205.

c) Family

01485. Bellomo, Manlio. Profili della famiglia italiana nell'eta dei
communi. Catania: Ciannotta, 1966.

01486. Besta, Enrico. La famiglia nella storia del diritto italiano.
Milan: A. Giuffre, 1962.

01487. Davis, James C. A Venetian Family and its Fortune, 1500-1900,
The Dona and the Conversion of their Wealth. Philadelphia:
American Philosophical Society, 1975.

01488. Litta, Pompeo, ed. Le famiglie celebri italiane. 11 vols.
Milan: Typ. del dottore G. Ferrario, 1856-1885.

5. CULTURAL

"An eloquent woman is never chaste."
Maxim

01489.   Boulting, William. Women in Italy, from the Introduction of
         the Chivalrous Service of Love to the Appearance of the
         Professional Actress. New York: Bretano's, 1910.

01490,   Catanzaro, Carlo. Il progresso feminile in Italia; Manuale
         illustrato biografico delle scrittrici ed artiste viventi.
         Florence: Bibl. ed. della Rivista italiana, 1894.

01491.   Rodocanachi, E. "L'Education des femmes en italie." Revue
         des questions historiques 78 (October 1905): 460-490.

G. THE LOW COUNTRIES

1. SURVEYS

". . . women have not by nature equal right with men but
that they necessarily give way to men, and . . . it cannot
happen, that both sexes should rule alike, much less that
men should be ruled by women."

> Baruch de Spinoza
> 17th century Dutch Jew

01492.   Holland, Clive. "Belgium." In Women of all Nations, edited
         by T.A.Joyce, 4: pp. 735-39. New York: Funk & Wagnalls,
         1915.

01493.   Peacock, N. "Holland." In Women of all Nations, edited by
         T.A.Joyce,4: 704-10. New York: Funk & Wagnalls, 1915.

2. POLITICAL

"Are we shut out of counsailes, privacies,
and onely lymitted our household business?
No, certain, Lady, we partakes with all,
Or our good men pertake no rest."

> Dutch women to an English woman
> Fletcher's Tragedy of Sir John
> van Olden Barnavelt

01494.   Hogeweg-de Haart, H.P. "The History of the Women's Movement
         in the Netherlands." Netherlands Journal of Sociology 14
         (1978): 19-40.

01495. Van Buuren, Hanneke. "Le Mouvement d'emancipation de la
        femme aux Pays-Bax." Septentrion: Revue de Culture
        Neerlandaise 1 (1972): 46-65.

Also refer to #1235, 1236.

3. RELIGION

"They [Antwerp women] have very free manners, and spend
their leisure in dancing, singing and making music, being
bent on nothing but pleasure; and they run their households
without any supervision by their husbands."
                    Quirini, 16th century Italian ambassador

a) Witchcraft

01496. Dupont-Bouchat, Marie Sylvie; Frijhoff, Willem; and Muchem-
        bled, Robert. Prophètes et sorciers dans les Pay Bas
        XVIe - XVIIIe siècle. Paris: Hachette, 1978.

4. SOCIAL

"Give me other mothers and I will give you another world."
                    St. Augustine

a) Demography

01497. Slicher van Bath, B. H. "Historical Demography and the
        Social and Economic Development of the Netherlands." In
        Population and Social Change, edited by D.V. Glass and
        Roger Reville, pp. 331-346. New York: Russak, 1972. Also
        in Daedalus 97 (Spring 1968): 604-621.

01498. Vandebroeke, C. "Caracteristiques de la nuptialité et de
        la fecondité en Flandre et au Brabant aux XVIIe-XIXe
        siècles." Annales de démographie historique 1977: 7-20.

b) Health/Medical

01499. Potter, Ada. "The History of Dutch Medical Women." Medical
        Women's Journal 30 (January 1923): 5-6.

II. ANTIQUITY

A. GENERAL

1. BIBLIOGRAPHIES

"It may be suitable that the women should have their
turn on the stage when the men have quite finished
their performance." Plato, The Republic, Bk. V.

01500. Arthur, Marylin B. "Classics: A Review Essay."
Signs 2 (Winter 1976): 382-403.

01501. Goodwater, Leanna. Women in Antiquity: An Annotated
Bibliography. Metuchen, New Jersey: The Scarecrow
Press, Inc. 1975.

01502. Pomeroy, Sarah B. "Selected Bibliography on Women in
Antiquity." Arethusa 6 (Spring 1973): 125-57.

2. SURVEYS

"No trust is to be placed in women."
Odyssey

a) Generic

01503. Ehrenberg, Victor I. Aspects of the Ancient World. New
York: William Sallock, 1946.

01504. Fustel de Coulanges, Numa Denis. The Ancient City: A
Study on the Religion, Laws and Institutions of Greece
and Rome. Garden City, N.Y.: Doubleday, 1956.

01505.   Malinowski, Bronislaw. Sex and Repression in Savage
          Society. 1927. Reprint. Cleveland: Meridian, 1955.

01506.   Weigall, Arthur. Personalities of Antiquity. Garden
          City, N.Y.: Doubleday, Doran & Co., 1928.

b) Women

(1) Contemporary

01507.   Lefkowitz, Mary R. and Fant, Maureen B., ed. Women in
          Greece and Rome. Toronto: Samuel Stevens, 1977.

(2) Secondary

01508.   Baldwin, Barry. "The Women of Greece and Rome." Helikon
          15-16 (1975-1976): 130-145.

01509.   Birt, T. Frauen der Antike. Leipzig: Quelle and
          Meyer, 1932.

01510.   Burck, Erich. Die Frau in der griechisch-römischen
          Antike. Tusculum Schriften. Munich: Heimeran, 1969.

01511.   Donaldson, James. Woman: Her Position and Influence in
          Ancient Greece and Rome, and Among the Early Christians.
          New York: Gordon Press, 1973.

01512.   Evans-Pritchard, Edward. The Position of Women in
          Primitive Societies. New York: Free Press, 1965.
          [See especially ch. 2.]

01513.   Friedl, Ernestine. "The Position of Women: Appearance and
          Reality." Anthropological Quarterly 40 (1967): 97-108.

01514.   Gamble, Eliza Burt. The Evolution of Woman: An Inquiry
          into the Dogma of Her Inferiority to Man. New York:
          G.P. Putnam's Sons, 1893.

01515.   Grimal, Pierre, ed. Préhistoire et antiquité. Vol. 1
          of Histoire mondiale de la femme. Paris: Nouvelle
          Librairie de France, 1965.

01516.   Hawkes, Jacquetta. "Men, Women and Children." In The
          First Great Civilization, pp. 176-185. New York:
          Alfred A. Knopf, 1973.

01517. Kornemann, Ernst. Grosse Frauen des Altertums, im Rahmen
        Zweitausendjährigen Weltgeschehens. Bremen: C.
        Schunemann, 1958.

01518. Leipoldt. Johannes. Die Frau in der antiken Welt und im
        Urchristentum. 2nd ed. Leipzig: Kohler and Amelang, 1955.

01519. Marygrove College. Into Her Own: The Status of Women from
        Ancient Times to the End of the Middle Ages. 1946.
        Reprint. New York: Arno Press, 1972.

01520. Mason, Otis T. Woman's Share in Primitive Culture.
        New York: D. Appleton and Co., 1911.

01521. Morgan, Sydney Owenson, Lady. Woman and Her Master.
        1840. Reprint (2 vols. in 1). Westport, Conn.:
        Hyperion Press, 1976.

01522. Pomeroy, Sarah B. Goddesses, Whores, Wives, and Slaves:
        Women in Classical Antiquity. New York: Schocken
        Books, 1975.

01523. Raineville, Joseph de. La Femme dans l'antiquité. Paris:
        Charpentier, 1876.

01524. Schaible, Karl Heinrich. Die Frau im Altertum: Ein
        Kulturgeschichtliches Bild. Karlsruhe: Braun, 1898.

01525. Seltman, Charles Theodore. Women in Antiquity. New
        York: Collier, 1962.

01526. Sonnet-Altenburg, Helene. Hetären, Mütter, Amazonen:
        Frauencharaktere aus der Antiken Welt. Heidenheim:
        Hoffmann, 1963.

01527. Sumner, W.G. "Status of Women in Chaldea, Egypt, India,
        Judea and Greece to the Time of Christ." Forum 42
        (August 1909): 113-136. Also in War and Other Essays, pp.
        65-102. Freeport, N.Y.: Books for Libraries Press, 1970.

01528. Zinserling, Verena. Women in Greece and Rome. Trans-
        lated by L.A. Jones. New York: Abner Schram, 1973.

3. MATRIARCHY AND MATRILINY

"Man, born of woman, has found it a hard thing to
forgive her for giving him birth. The patriarchal
protest against the ancient matriarch has borne
strange fruit through the years."
                    Lillian Smith, Killers of the Dream

01529. Bachofen, Johan J. Myth, Religion and Mother Right:
        Selected Writings of J.J. Bachofen. Translated by
        Ralph Manheim. 1861. Reprint. Princeton, N.J.:
        Princeton University Press, 1967.

01530. Besterman, Theodore. Men against Women. London:
        Methuen, 1934.

01531. Bleibtreu-Ehrenberg, C. "Matriarchat und Patriarchat bei
        Ernest Bornemann." Anthropos 1-2 (1980): 250-257.

01532. Briffault, Robert. The Mothers: A Study of the Origins
        of Sentiments and Institutions. 7 vols. New York:
        1927. Reprint.

01533. Crawley, Ernest. The Mystic Rose. Revised and enlarged
        by Theodore Besterman. 2nd ed. London: Methuen, 1927.

01534. Eaubonne, Francois d'. Les femmes avant le patriarcat.
        Paris: Payot, 1976.

01535. Eliade, Mercea. Myths, Dreams and Mysteries. New York:
        Harper and Row, 1957.

01536. Fluehr-Lobban, C. "Marxist Reappraisals of the Matri-
        archate." Current Anthropology 20 (June 1979): 341-360.

01537. Fromm, Erich. The Forgotten Language. New York: Grove
        Press, 1951.

01538. Gallichan, Catherine Gasquoine. The Position of Women
        in Primitive Society: a Study of Matriarchy. London:
        E. Nash, 1914.

01539. Graves, Robert. The White Goddess: a Historical Grammar of
        Poetic Myth. New York: Farrar, Straus, and Giroux, 1966.

01540. Harris, Marvin. The Rise of Anthropological Theory.
        New York: Thomas Crowell, 1968.

01541. Hawkes, Jacquetta and Wooley, Sir Leonard. Prehistory
        and the Beginning of Civilization. New York: Harper
        and Row, 1963.

01542. Heinrichs, Hans-Jurgen, ed. Materialien zu Bachofens
        'Das Mutterrecht.' Frankfurt am Main: Suhrkamp, 1975.

01543. James, Edwin Oliver. The Cult of the Mother Goddess.
        London: Thames and Hudson, 1959.

01544. James, Edwin Oliver. The Worship of the Sky-God. New
        York: Athlone Press, 1963.

01545. Jensen, A.E. "Gab es eine mutterrechtliche Kultur?"
        Studium Generale 3 (1950): 418-433.

01546. Jolly, Margaret. "Matriarchy: myth and history."
Refractory Girl 11 (June 1976): 3-8.

01547. Jung, C.G. "Die psychologischen Aspekte des Mutterar-
chetypus." Eranos-Jahrbuch 1938, edited by Olga
Fröbe-Kapteyn, pp. 403-443. Zurich: Rhein-Verlag,
1939.

01548. Kluckhorn, C. Anthropology and the Classics. Providence:
Brown University Press, 1961

01549. MacLennan, John Ferguson. The Patriarchal Theory. New
York: Macmillan Co., 1885.

01550. Magli, Ida. Matriarcato e potere delle donne. Milan:
Feltrinelli, 1978.

01551. Malinowski, Bronislaw. Mutterrechtliche Familie und
Oedipus-Komplex. Vienna: International psychoanaly-
tischer Verlag, 1924.

01552. _____. The Sexual Life of the Savages.
New York: Harcourt, Brace and World, 1929.

01553. Morgan, Lewis Henry. Ancient Society. 1877. Reprint.
New York: Labor News, 1976.

01554. Neumann, Erich. The Great Mother: An Analysis of the
Archetype. 1952. Reprint. New York: Pantheon
Books, 1963.

01555. Newton, Esther and Webster, Paula. "Matriarchy: as
women see it." Aphra 4 (Summer 1973): 6-22.

01556. Pembroke, Simon. "Last of the Matriarchs: A Study in
the Inscriptions of Lycia." Journal of the Economic
and Social History of the Orient 8 (1965): 217-47.

01557. Pestalozza, U. "Le matriarcat mediterranée. Son
caractère primordial dans l'ambiance religieuse du
paléolithique." Diogène 12 (October 1955): 58-71.

01558. Pomeroy, Sarah B. "A Classical Scholar's Perspective on
Matriarchy." In Liberating Women's History, edited by
Bernice Carroll, pp. 217-223. Urbana: University of
Illinois Press, 1975.

01559. Reich, Wilhelm. The Invasion of Compulsory Sex-Morality.
New York: Farrar, Straus and Giroux, 1971.

01560. Ronhaar, J.H. Women in Primitive Mother-right Societies.
The Hague: J.B. Wolters, 1931.

01561. Schmidt, Wilhelm. Das Mutterrecht. Studia Instituti
        Anthropos, no. 10. Vienna–Modling: Verlag der
        Missions-drückerei St. Gabriel, 1955.

01562. _____. "The Position of Women with Regard to
        Private Property in Primitive Society." American
        Anthropologist n.s. 37 (1935): 244–256.

01563. Schneider, David M. and Gough, Kathleen, eds. Matrilineal
        Kinship. Los Angeles: University of California Press,
        1961.

01564. Webster, Paula. "Matriarchy: A Vision of Power." In
        Toward an Anthropology of Women, edited by Rayna R.
        Reiter, pp. 141–156. New York: Monthly Review Press,
        1975.

01565. Zahler, Leah. "Matriarchy and Myth." Aphra 4 (Summer
        1973): 25–32.

4. POLITICAL

"That a man should consort with his wife not less than
three times a month--not for pleasure surely, but as
cities renew their agreements from time to time."
Plutarch discussing Solon.

a) Legal

(1) Non-specific

01566. Daube, David. Civil Disobedience in Antiquity. Edin-
        burgh: Edinburgh University Press, 1972.

01567. Maine, Henry J.S. Ancient Law. London: Oxford Univer-
        sity Press, 1946.

01568. Schaeffer, Henry. The Social Legislation of the
        Primitive Societies. London: Humphrey Milford, 1915.

(2) Women

01569. Adams, Henry. "The Primitive Rights of Women." In
        Historical Essays, pp. 1-41. New York: Charles
        Scribner's Sons, 1891.

01570. Baecker, Louis de. Le droit de la femme dans l'antiquité,
        son devoir au moyen âge, d'après des manuscrits de la
        Bibliothèque nationale. Paris: A. Claudin, 1880.

01571. Poirier, Jean. "Le statut de la femme dans les sociétés
        archaiques." Recueils de la Société Jean Bodin 11 (1959):
        11-22.

b) Feminism

01572. Daube, David. Gewaltloser Frauenwiderstand im Altertum.
        Constance: Universitatsverlag, 1971

01573. Nevinson, Margaret Wynne (Jones). Ancient Suffragettes.
        London: Women's Freedom League, 1911.

01574. Yvelin, Cleyre. Etude sur le féminisme dans l'antiquité.
        Paris: V. Giard et E. Brière, 1908.

5. RELIGION/MYTHOLOGY

"Their priestesses with a sword in their hand, met
the prisoners of war . . . she cut the throat of
each prisoner as he was handed up to her. With
the blood that gushed into the basin, they made a
prophecy."
                        Strabo VII, 2 on the Cimbri

a) Goddesses

01575. Gimbutas, Marija. The gods and goddesses of old Europe,
        7000-3500 B.C.: myths, legends and cult images.
        Berkeley, Calif.: University of California Press, 1974.

01576. Grant, Michael. Myths of Greeks and Romans. London:
        Weidenfeld and Nicholson, 1962.

01577. Lefkowitz, Mary. "Classical Mythology and the Role of Women
        in Modern Literature." In A Sampler of Womens Studies,
        pp. 77-84. Ann Arbor: University of Michigan, 1973.

01578. Przyluski, Jean. "Die Mutter-Göttin als Verbindung
        zwischen den Lokal-Göttern und dem Universal Gott."
        Eranos-Jahrbuch 1938, edited by Olga Fröbe-Kapteyn,
        pp. 35-57. Zurich: Rhein-Verlag, 1939.

01579. _____. "Ursprünge und Entwicklung des Kultes
        der Mutter-Göttin." In Eranos-Jahrbuch 1938, edited by
        Olga Frobe-Kapteyn, pp. 11-34. Zurich: Rhein Verlag, 1939.

01580. Sanders, J.T. "Dionysus, Cybele and the 'Madness of
        Women'." In Beyond Androcentrism: New Essays on
        Women and Religion, edited by Rita M. Gross, pp. 125-
        137. Missoula, Montana: American Academy of Religion
        and Scholars' Press, 1977.

01581. Stone, Merlin. When God was a Woman. New York: Harvest,
        HBJ Book, 1978.

01582. _____. "When God was a Woman." In Womanspirit
        Rising, edited by Carol P. Christ and Judith Plaskow,
        pp. 120-130. New York: Harper and Row, 1979.

01583. Virolleaud, Charles. "Die grosse Göttin in Babylonien,
        Ägypten und Phöniken." Eranos-Jahrbuch 1938, edited
        by Olga Fröbe-Kapteyn, pp. 121-160. Zurich: Rhein-
        Verlag, 1939.

01584. Witt, R.E. Isis in the Graeco-Roman World. Ithaca,
        New York: Cornell University Press, 1971.

b) Priestesses

01585. Hardy, E. R. "Priestess in the Greco-Roman World."
        The Churchman 84 (Winter 1970): 264-270.

01586. Maringer, Johannes. "Priests and Priestesses in Pre-
        historic Europe." History of Religions 17 (November
        1977):   101-120.

c) Witchcraft

01587. Burris, Eli. "The Terminology of Witchcraft."
        Classical Philology 31 (1936): 137-145.

6. SOCIAL

"Courage and intelligence are more appropriately male
qualities because of the strength of men's bodies
and the power of their minds. Chastity is more
appropriately female."
                    Thesleff, Treatise by Members
                    of a Pythagorean Community

a) Generic

01588. Gleichen-Russwurm, Alexander von. Elegantiae Geschichte
        der vornehmen Welt in klassischen Altertum. Stuttgart:
        Julius Hoffmann, 1921.

b) Demography

01589. Angel, J. Lawrence. "Ecology and Population in the
        Eastern Mediterranean." World Archaeology 4 (1972):
        88-105.

01590. Beloch, Julius. Die Bevölkerung der griechisch-römischen
        Welt. Leipzig: Duncker and Humbolt, 1886.

01591. Biezunska-Malowist, I., and Malowist, M. "La procréation
        des esclaves comme source de l'esclavage." In Mélanges
        K. Michalowski, pp. 275-80. Warsaw: Panstowe
        Wydawnictwo Naukowe, 1966.

01592. Le Gall, Joël. "Un critère de différenciation sociale." In
        Recherches sur les structures sociales dans l'antiquité
        classique, pp. 275-286. Paris: Centre national de la
        recherche scientifique, 1970.

01593. Russell, Josiah Cox. "The Ecclesiastical Age: A Demo-
        graphic Interpretation of the Period A.D. 200-900."
        Review of Religion 5 (1941): 137-147.

01594. _____. "Late Ancient and Medieval Popula-
        tions." Transactions of the American Philosophical
        Society n.s. 48 (June 1958): 3-152.

c) Family

(1) Non-specific

01595. Bethe, Erich. Ahnenbild und Familiengeschichte bei
        Römern und Griechen. Munich: C.H. Beck, 1935.

01596. Gough, Kathleen. "The Origin of the Family." Journal
        of Marriage and the Family 33 (November 1971): 760-771.

01597. Hittel, John S. "Social Life." In A History of the
        Mental Growth of Mankind 1: 121-152. New York: Henry
        Holt and Co., 1893.

01598. Hartland, Edwin Sidney. Primitive Society, the Beginnings
        of the Family and the Reckoning of Descent. New York:
        Dutton, 1921.

01599. Samter, Ernst. Familienfeste der Griechen und Römer.
        Berlin: G. Reimer, 1901.

01600. Smith, Rockwell. "Hebrew, Greco-Roman, and Early Chris-
        tian Family Patterns." In Marriage and the Family,
        edited by Howard Becker and Reuben Hill, pp. 59-71.
        Boston: Heath, 1942.

(2) Childhood

01601. Belmont, Nicole. "Levana: or, How to Raise up Children."
        In The Family in History, edited by Robert Forster and
        Orest Ranum, pp. 1-15. Baltimore: Johns Hopkins Uni-
        versity Press, 1976.

01602. Etienne, Robert. "La conscience médicale antique et la
        vie des enfants." Annales de démographie historique
        1973 : 15-46.

01603. Eyben, Emiel. "Antiquity's View of Puberty." Latomus
        31 (1972): 677-697.

d) Marriage

01604. Ember, M. "Warfare, Sex Ratio, and Polygyny." Ethnology
        13 (April 1974): 197-206.

01605. Kornemann, Ernst. "Zur Geschwisterehe im Altertum."
        Klio 19 (1925): 355-361.

01606. MacLennan, John Ferguson. Primitive Marriage, An Inquiry
        into the Origins of the form of capture in marriage
        ceremonies. Edinburgh: Adam and Charles Black, 1865.

01607. _____. "Primitive Marriage: An Inquiry
        into the origin of the form of captive in marriage
        ceremonies." History of the Behavioral Sciences 8
        (January 1972): 147-151.

e) Sex Life and Morals

(1) Non-specific

01608. Boer, W. den. Private Morality in Greece and Rome:
        some historical aspects. Leiden: Brill, 1979.

01609. Hopfner, Theodor. Das Sexualleben der Griechen und
        Römer von den Anfangen bis ins 6. Jahrhundert nach
        Christus. 1938. Reprint. New York: AMS Press,
        1975.

(2)   Prostitutes and Courtesans

01610.   Dupouy, Edmond. La Prostitution dans l'antiquite. 5th
         ed. Paris: Librairie Meurillon, 1906.

01611.   Frichet, Henry. Fleshpots of Antiquity: The Lives and
         Loves of Ancient Courtesans. Translated and introduced
         by A.F. Niemoeller. New York: Panurge, 1934.

01612.   Herter, H. "Die Soziologie der antiken Prostitution im
         Lichte des heidnischen und christlichen Schrifttums."
         Jahrbuch für Antike und Christentum 3 (1960): 70-111.

01613.   Quivogne de Montifaud, Marie Amelie. Die Courtisanen des
         Alterthums. 3rd ed. Budapest: Grimm, 1902.

         Also refer to #1635.

f)   Fashion

01614.   Beaulieu, Michele. Le Costume antique et mediéval.
         Paris: Presses Universitaires de France, 1967.

01615.   Walton, F.T. "My Lady's Toilet," Greece and Rome
         15 (May 1946): 68-73.

g)   Recreation

01616.   Boslooper, Thomas. "The image of woman in classical
         antiquity." Women Sports 2 (September 1975): 18-22.

h)   Health/Medical

01617.   Amundsen, Darrel W., and Diers, Carol Jean. "The Age
         of Menarche in Classical Greece and Rome." Human
         Biology 41 (1969): 125-32.

01618. Amundsen, Darrel W., and Diers, Carol Jean. "The Age
        of Menopause in Classical Greece and Rome." Human
        Biology 42 (1970): 79-86.

01619. Crahay, R. "Les mortalistes anciens et l'avortement."
        L'antiquité classique 10 (1941): 9-23.

01620   Hähnel, Ruth. "Der künstliche Abortus im Altertum."
        Sudhoffs Archiv für Geschichte der Medizin 29 (1937):
        224-255.

01621. Krenkel, W.A. "Erotica 1: Der Abortus in der Antike."
        Wissenschaftliche Zeitschrift der Universität Rostock
        20 (1971): 443-452.

01622. Nardi, Enzo. Procurato aborto nel mondo greco romano.
        Milan: Giuffre editore, 1971.

01623. Noonan, John T., Jr. "An Absolute Value in History."
        In The Morality of Abortion, pp. 1-59. Cambridge, Mass.:
        Harvard University Press, 1970.

01624. Pundel, J.P. Histoire de l'opération césarienne. Etude
        historique de la césarienne dans la médicine, l'art et
        la littérature, les religions et la législation. La
        prodigieuse évolution de la césarienne depuis l'antiquité
        jusqu'aux temps moderns. Brussels: Presse Académie
        Européennes, 1969.

01625. Roussier, Jules. "Opinions anciennes sur les grossesses
        prolongées (antiquité, moyen âge)." In Etudes d'histoire
        du droit privé offerts à Pierre Petot, edited by Pierre-
        Clément Timbal, pp. 473-480. Paris: Recueil Sirey, 1959.

7. CULTURAL

"Natural gifts are to be found here and there in both
creatures alike; and every occupation is open to both,
so far as their natures are concerned, though woman
is for all purposes the weaker."
                     Plato, The Republic, Book V

a) Education

01626. Castle, E.B. Ancient Education and Today. Harmondsworth:
        Penguin Books, 1961.

01627. Marrou, H.I. A History of Education in Antiquity.
        London: Sheed and Ward, 1956.

01628. Pomeroy, Sarah B. "Technikai kai Mousikai: The Educa-
        tion of Women in the Fourth Century and in the Hellen-
        istic Period." American Journal of Ancient History 2
        (1977): 51-68.

b) Literature

01629. Ghougassian, Joseph P. Toward Women: A Study of the
        Origins of Western Attitudes Through Greco-Roman
        Philosophy. San Diego: Lukas and Sons Pubs., 1977.

01630. Joël, Karl. Die Frauen in der Philosophie. 1896.
        Reprint. New Haven, Conn.: Research Publications,
        Inc., 1977.

01631. Jones, R. The Theme of Love in the Romans d'Antiquité.
        London: The Modern Humanities Research Association,
        1972.

c) Art and Artifacts

(1) Women in Art

01632. Ahrem, Maximilian. Das Weib in der Antiken Kunst.
        Jena: E. Diederichs, 1924.

01633. Brendel, Otto J. "The Scope and Temperament of Erotic
        Art in the Greco-Roman World." In Studies in Erotic
        Art, edited by Theodore Bowie and Cornelia V. Christ-
        ensen, pp. 3-107. New York: Basic Books, 1970.

01634. Kahrstedt, Ulrich. "Frauen auf Antiken Münzen." Klio
        10 (1910): 261-314.

(2) Women Artists

01635. Gilder, Rosamond. "From Priestess to Prostitute--the
        Greek and Roman Stage." In Enter the Actress The
        First Women in the Theatre, pp. 1-17. Boston:
        Houghton Mifflin Company, 1931.

B. GREECE

1. SURVEYS

"It is thy place woman to hold thy peace and keep
within doors."

Aeschylus, Seven Against Thebes

a) Generic

(1) Non-specific

01636. Alsop, Joseph. From the Silent Earth: A Report of the
Greek Bronze Age. New York: Simon and Schuster, 1964.

01637. Bonnard, André. Greek Civilization I: From the Iliad
to the Parthenon. Translated by R.C. Knight. London:
George Allen & Unwin, 1961.

01638. Dickinson, G. Lowes. The Greek View of Life. 7th ed.
Garden City, New York: Doubleday, Doran & Co., 1925.

01639. Finley, Moses I. The Ancient Greeks. New York: The
Viking Press, 1968.

01640. _____ . The World of Odysseus. 1954. Reprint.
New York: Viking Press, 1965.

01641. Gernet, Louis. Anthropologie de la Grèce antique. Paris:
Maspero, 1968.

01642. Glotz, Gustave. The Aegean Civilization. New York:
Alfred A. Knopf, 1925.

01643. Gouldner, Alvin W. The Hellenic World: A Sociological
Analysis [part 1 of Enter Plato: Classical Greece and
the Origins of Social Theory]. New York: Harper and
Row, 1969.

01644. Kitto, H.D.F. The Greeks. Harmondsworth: Penguin
Books, 1951.
[See especially pp. 219-236.]

01645. Mahaffy, Sir John Pentland. _Social Life in Greece from Homer to Menander_. London: Macmillan and Co., Ltd., 1925.

01646. Mireaux, Emile. _Daily Life in the Time of Homer_. New York: Macmillan Co., 1959.

01647. Mylonas, George E. _Mycenae and the Mycenaean Age_. Princeton: University Press, 1966.

01648. Padgug, Robert A. "Classes and Society in Classical Greece." _Arethusa_ 8 (1975): 85–117.

01649. Pope, Maurice. _The Ancient Greeks: How They Lived and Worked_. Chester, Pa.: Dufour Editions, 1976.

01650. Robinson, C.E. _Everyday Life in Ancient Greece_. Oxford: Clarendon Press, 1933.

01651. Rose, Herbert J. _Primitive Culture in Greece_. London: Methuen & Co., Ltd., 1925.
        [See especially chs. 6 and 8.]

01652. Rostovtsev, M. _A History of the Ancient World I: The Orient and Greece_. London: Oxford University Press, 1930.

01653. _____. _Social and Economic History of the Hellenistic World_. 3 vols. Oxford: Clarendon Press, 1941.

01654. Seymour, Thomas Day. _Life in the Homeric Age_. 1908. Reprint. New York: Biblio and Tannen, 1963.

01655. Snodgrass, Anthony McElrea. _The Dark Age of Greece: an archaeological survey of the 11th to the 8th centuries B.C._ Edinburgh: The University Press, 1971.

01656. Tarn, W.W. _Hellenistic Civilization_. 1930. Rev. ed. New York: New American Library, 1961.

01657. Thomson, George Derwent. _Studies of Ancient Greek Society: The Prehistoric Aegean_. 1949. Reprint. London: Lawrence and Wishart, 1972.

01658. Walcot, Peter. _Greek Peasants, Ancient and Modern: A Comparison of Social and Moral Values_. Manchester: Manchester University Press, 1970.

01659. Zimmern, Alfred. _The Greek Commonwealth_. Oxford: Clarendon Press, 1924.
        [See especially part 2, chs. 2 and 12.]

(2) Women

01660. Arthur, Marylin B. "Early Greece: The Origins of the
        Western Attitude Toward Women." Arethusa 6 (Spring
        1973): 7-58.

01661. Bader, Clarisse. La femme grecque: étude de la vie
        antique. 2 vols. Paris: Didier et Cie., 1872.

01662. Bieber-Lux, Dora. Die Frau in der griechischen Sage und
        Geschichte. Quellenhefte zum Frauenleben in der
        Geschichte, edited by Emmy Beckman and Irma Stoss,
        vol. 1. Berlin: F.A. Herbig, 1927-1933.

01663. Braunstein, O. Die politische Wirksamkeit der griechischen
        Frau. Leipzig: August Hoffman, 1911.

01664. Burger, Franz. Die Griechischen Frauen. Tusculum
        Schriften, no. 2. Munich: E. Heimeran, 1924.

01665. Carroll, Mitchell. Greek Women. Vol. 1 of Woman: In
        All Ages and in All Countries. Philadelphia: George
        Barrie and Sons, 1907.

01666. Cartledge, Paul. "Spartan Wives: Liberalism or License?"
        Classical Quarterly n.s. 31 (1981): 84-105.

01667. Cornish, F. Warre, and Janet Bacon. "The Position of
        Women." In A Companion to Greek Studies, edited by
        Leonard Whibley, pp. 610-617. 4th ed. Cambridge:
        The University Press, 1931.

01668. Dickinson, G. Lowes. "The Greek View of Women." In
        The Woman Question, edited by Thomas Robert Smith,
        pp. 1-11. New York: Boni and Liveright Inc., 1918.

01669. Flacelière, Robert. "Histoire de la Femme Antique en
        Crete et en Grece." Prehistoire et Antiquité.
        Vol 1. of Histoire mondiale de la femme, edited by
        Pierre Grimal. Paris: Nouveau Librairie de France,
        1965.

01670. Kornemann, Ernst. Die Stellung der Frau in der Vorgriechischen
        Mittelmeer-Kultur. Orient und Antike, No. 4. Heidel-
        berg: Winter, 1927.

01671. Lenz, Carl Gotthold. Geschichte der Weiber im heroischen
        Zeitalter. Hannover: Verlage der Helwingschen
        Hofbuchhandlung, 1790.

01672.   Loraux, Nicole. "Sure la race des femmes et quelques-
          unes de ses tribus." Arethusa 11 (Spring and Fall
          1978): 43-87.

01673.   Navarre, Octave Lucien Louis. Les femmes dans la
          société grecque; étude de moeurs antiques. Paris:
          Editions Universitaires, 1937.

01674.   Nietzsche, Friedrich. "The Greek Woman." In Early
          Greek Philosophy and Other Essays. The Complete Works
          of Friedrich Nietzsche, edited by Oscar Levy, 2:
          19-26. New York: Russell and Russell, Inc., 1964.

01675.   Notor, G. La Femme dans l'antiquité grecque. Paris:
          Librairie Renouard, 1901.

01676.   Paoli, U.E. La donna greca nell'antichità. Florence:
          Le Monnier, 1953.

01677.   Putnam, Emily James. "The Greek Lady." Putnam's
          Magazine 7 (March 1910): 681-689; (April 1910): 809-817.

01678.   Whibley, Leonard. "The Position of Women." In A Com-
          panion to Greek Studies, 3rd ed. Cambridge, England:
          Cambridge University Press, 1916.

b) Athens

01679.   Gomme, A.W. "The Position of Women in Athens in the
          Fifth and Fourth Centuries B.C." Classical Philology
          20 (1925): 1-25. Reprinted in Essays in Greek History
          and Literature, pp. 89-115. Oxford: Blackwell, 1937.

01680.   Hadas, Moses. "Observations on Athenian Women."
          Classical Weekly 39 (1936): 97-100.

01681.   Richter, Donald C. "The Position of Women in Classical
          Athens." Classical Journal 67 (Oct.-Nov. 1971): 1-8.

01682.   Seltman, Charles. "The Status of Women in Athens."
          Greece and Rome 2d ser. 2 (1955): 119-24.

01683.   Shear, T.L. "Koisyra: Three Women of Athens."
          Phoenix 17 (Summer 1963): 99-112.

c) Sparta

(1) Non-specific

01684. Forrest, W.G. A History of Sparta. London: Hutchinson, 1968.

01685. Michell, H. Sparta. Cambridge: University Press, 1964. [See especially pp. 45-61.]

01686. Oliva, P. Sparta and Her Social Problems. Prague: Academia, 1971.

(2) Women

01687. Redfield, James. "The Women of Sparta." Classical Journal 73 (Dec.-Jan. 1977-78): 146-161.

d) Amazons

01688. Anderson, Florence Mary. Religious Cults Associated with the Amazons. 1912. Reprint. New York: AMS Press, 1967.

01689. Bisset, K.A. "Who were the Amazons?" Greece and Rome 18 (October 1971): 150-151.

01690. Engle, Bernice Schultz. "The Amazons in Ancient Greece." Psychoanalytic Quarterly 11 (1942): 512-554.

01691. Guyon, C.M. Histoire des amazones anciennes et modernes. Brussels: Jean Leonard, 1741.

01692. Kanter, Emanuel. The Amazons: A Marxian Study. Chicago: Kerr, 1926.

01693. Reinach, S. "L'Origine des amazones." Revue de l'histoire des religions 67 (May-June 1913): 277-307.

01694. Renault, Mary. "Amazons." Greek Heritage 1 (Spring 1964): 18-23.

01695. Rothery, G.C. The Amazons in Antiquity and Modern Times. London: Francis Griffiths, 1910.

01696. Sobol, D.J. The Amazons of Greek Mythology. South Brunswick: A.S. Barnes and Co., 1972.

01697. Von Bothmer, Dietrich. Amazons in Greek Art. Oxford Monographs on Classical Archaeology. Oxford: Clarendon Press, 1957.

01698. Zografou, Mina. Amazons in Homer and Hesiod (A Historical Reconstruction). Athens: n.p. 1972.

Also refer to #1822, 1977.

e) Other

(1) Non-specific

01699. Glasgow, G. The Minoans. London: Jonathan Cape, 1923.

01700. Hutchinson, R.W. Prehistoric Crete. Baltimore: Penguin Books, 1962.

(2) Women

01701. Kapetanopoulos, Elias. "Klea and Leontis: Two Ladies from Delphi." Bulletin de Correspondence Hellenique 90 (1966): 119-130.

01702. Tritsch, F.F.J. "The Women of Pylos." In Minoica: Festschrift zum 80: Gebartstag von J. Sundwall, edited by Ernst Grumach, pp. 406-45. Deutsche Akademie der Wissenschaften zu Berlin, Schriften der Sektion fur Altertumswissenschaft, no. 12. Berlin: Akademie Verlag, 1958.

2. MATRIARCHY AND MATRILINY

"The Lycians show the women more honor than the men; they take their names from their mothers and leave their estates to their daughters, not to their sons."
                                            Nicolaus of Damascus,
                                            Universal History

01703. Hirvonen, Kaarle. Matriarchal Survivals and Certain
        Trends in Homer's Female Characters. Annales
        Academiae Scientiarum Fennicae, Series B, vol. 152.
        Helsinki: Suomalainen Tiedeakatemia, 1968.

01704. Naquet-Vidal, Pierre. "Esclavage et gynécocratie dans la
        tradition, le mythe, l'utopie ." In Recherches sur les
        structures sociales dans l'antiquité classique, pp. 63-80.
        Paris: Centre national de la recherche scientifique, 1970.

01705. Pembroke, Simon. "Women in Charge: The Function of
        Alternatives in Early Greek Tradition and the Ancient
        Idea of Matriarchy." Journal of the Warburg and
        Courtauld Institute 30 (1967): 1-35.

01706. Pomeroy, Sarah B. "Andromaque: Un Exemple méconnu de
        matriarcat." Revue des études grecques 88 (1975):
        16-19.

01707. Rose, Herbert J. "On the Alleged Evidence for Mother-
        Right in Early Greece." Folklore 22 (September 1911):
        277-291.

01708. Thiel, J.H. "De Feminarum apud Dores Condicione."
        Mnemosyne 57 (1929): 193-205.

01709. Thomas, C.G. "Matriarchy in Early Greece: The Bronze
        and Dark Ages." Arethusa 6 (Fall 1973): 173-195.

3. POLITICAL

"Furthermore the indiscipline of the women undercuts
the organising principle of the constitution and the
happiness of the state. . . . In constitutions where
the women are handled badly, one must think of half
of the city as lawless."
                        Aristotle, Politics, on Spartans

a) Legal

(1) Non-specific

01710. Gernet, Louis. Droit et société dans la Grèce ancienne.
        Paris: Recueil Sirey, 1955.

01711. _____ . "Sur l'epiclerat." Revue des études Grecques.
        34 (1921): 337-79.

01712.   Glotz, Gustave.   Etudes sociales et juridiques sur
          l'antiquité grecque.   Paris: Hachette, 1906.

01713.   _____.   La solidarité de la famille dans le
          droit criminel en Grece.   1904. Reprint. New York:
          Arno Press, 1973.

01714.   Lewy, Henricus.   De Civili Condicione Mulierum Graecarum:
          Commentatio ad Theodorum Thalheim.   Breslau: Grassus,
          Barthius et Soc., 1885.

01715.   Smith, Gertrude.   "Early Greek Codes." Classical Philology
          17 (July 1922): 187-201.

          Also refer to #1834.

                         (2) Women

01716.   Schaps, David.   "Women in Greek Inheritance Law".
          Classical Quarterly 25 (May 1975):   53-57.

                         (3) Athens

                      (a) Non-specific

                   [1] CONTEMPORARY

10717.   Aeschines.   The Speeches of Aeschines.   Edited by
          Charles D. Adams.   Loeb Classical Library.   London:
          William Heinemann, Ltd., 1919.
          [See especially Against Timarchus.]

01718.   Isaeus.   Isaeus.   Edited by Edward Seymour Forster.
          Loeb Classic Library.   London: William Heinemann, 1927.
          [See especially On the Estate of Aristarchus and On
          the Estate of Pyrrhus.]

01719.   Isaeus.   The Speeches of Isaeus.   Edited by W. Wyse.
          Cambridge: Cambridge University Press, 1904.

01720.   Lysias.   "On the Killing of Eratosthenes, the Seducer."
          In The Murder of Herodes and Other Trials from the
          Athenian Law, edited by Kathleen Freeman, pp. 43-53.
          London: MacDonald and Co., Ltd., 1946.

[2] SECONDARY

01721. Beauchet, Ludovic. *Histoire du droit privé de la république athénienne.* New York: Arno Press. 1976.

01722. Harrison, Alick R.W. *The Law of Athens: The Family and Property.* Oxford: Clarendon Press, 1968.

01723. Lipsius, J.H. *Das attische Recht und Rechtsverfahren.* 1905-1915. Reissued. Amsterdam: Rodopi, 1969.

01724. Wolff, Hans Julius. "Marriage Law and Family Organization in Ancient Athens: A Study in the Interrelation of Public and Private Law in the Greek City." *Traditio* 2 (1944): 43-95.

(b) Women

[1] CONTEMPORARY

01725. Antiphon. "Against a Step-Mother on a charge of poisoning." In *The Murder of Herodes and Other Trials from the Athenian Law,* edited by Kathleen Freemen, pp. 86-94. London: MacDonald and Co., Ltd., 1946.

01726. Demosthenes. "An Illegal Union: Against Neaera." In *The Murder of Herodes and Other Trials from the Athenian Law Courts,* edited by Kathleen Freeman, pp. 191-226. London: MacDonald & Co., 1946.

[2] SECONDARY

01727. Bonner, Robert John. "Did Women Testify in Homicide Cases at Athens?" *Classical Philology* 1 (April 1906), 127-132.

01728. Harvey, David. "Those Epirote Women Again (SEG, XV, 384)." *Classical Philology* 64 (October 1969): 226-229.

01729. Kuenen-Janssens, L.J.T. "Some Notes Upon the Competence of the Athenian Woman to Conduct a Transaction." *Mnemosyne* 3rd ser. 9 (1941): 199-241.

01730. Larsen, J.A.O. "Epirote Grants of Citizenship to Women." *Classical Philology* 59 (April 1964): 106-107.

01731. Larsen, J.A.O. "Epirote Grants of Citizenship to Women
        Once More." Classical Philology 62 (October 1967):
        255-256.

01732. Ste. Croix, G.E.M. de. "Some Observations on the
        Property Rights of Athenian Women." Classical Review
        20 (1970): 273-278.

        Also refer to #1802.

b) Feminism

(1) Non-specific

01733. Flacelière, Robert. "D'un certain féminisme grec."
        Revue des études anciennes 64 (1962): 109-116.

01734. Vogt, Joseph. Von der Gleichwertigkeit der Geschlechter
        in der bürgerlichen Gesellschaft der Griechen. Akademie
        der Wissenschaften und der Literatur in Mainz, no. 2.
        Wiesbaden: Steiner, 1960.
        [See especially pp. 211-255.]

(2) Athens

01735. Bruns, Ivo. Frauenemancipation in Athens   Ein Beitrag
        zur attischen Kulturgeschichte des fünften und vierten
        Jahrhunderts. Kiel: Schmidtii & Klaunigii, 1900.

01736. Flacelière, Robert. Le Féminisme dans l'ancienne Athènes.
        Paris: L'Institut de France, 1971.

01737. _____. "Le féminisme dans l'ancienne Athenes."
        Comptes rendus de l'academie des Inscriptions et belles-
        lettres (1971): 698-706.

c) Political Roles

01738. Lindsay, Jack. Helen of Troy: Woman and Goddess. Totowa,
        N.J.: Rowman and Littlefield, 1974.

01739. Macurdy, Grace Harriet. Hellenistic Queens: A Study of
        Woman-Power in Macedonia, Seleucid Syria, and Ptolemaic
        Egypt. New York: AMS Press, 1976.

01740.   Macurdy, Grace Harriet. "The Political Activities and
         the Name of Cratesipolis." American Journal of
         Philology 50 (1929): 273-278.

01741.   _____. "Queen Eurydice and the Evidence
         for Woman Power in Early Macedonia." American Journal
         of Philology 48 (1927): 201-214.

01742.   _____. "Roxane and Alexander IV in
         Epirus." Journal of Hellenic Studies 52 (1932):
         256-261.

01743.   Rostovtsev, M. "Queen Dynamis of Bosporus." Journal of
         Hellenic Studies 39 (1919): 88-109.

01744.   Tritsch, Walther. Olympias, Die Mutter Alexanders des
         Grossen: Das Schicksal eines Weltreiches. Frankfurt:
         Societäts Verlag, 1936.

01745.   Wehrli, C. "Phila, fille d'Antipater et epouse de
         Demetrius, roi des Macedoniens." Historia 13 (April 1964):
         140-146.

4. ECONOMIC

"Even a poor man will bring up a son, but even a rich
man will expose a daughter."
                              Posidippus

a) Generic

01746.   Herfst, P. Le travail de la femme dans la Grece
         ancienne. Utrecht: Oostheok, 1922.

01747.   Pembroke, Simon. "Locres et Tarente: Le rôle des
         femmes dans la fondation de deux colonies grecques."
         Annales: économies, sociétés, civilisations 25 (1970):
         1240-1270.

01748.   Piper, Linda J. "Wealthy Spartan Women." Classical
         Bulletin 56 (November 1979): 5-8.

01749.   Rougé, Jean. "La colonisation grecque et les femmes."
         Cahiers d'histoire 15 (1970): 307-317.

01750.   Schaps, D.M. Economic Rights of Women in Ancient Greece.
         New York: Columbia University Press, 1979.

b) Household

01751.   Shero, L.R.   "Xenophon's Portrait of a Young Wife."
         Classical Weekly 26 (17 October 1932):   17-21.

01752.   Xenophon. Memorabilia and Oeconomicus. Translated by
         E.C. Marchant. The Loeb Classical Library.   London:
         William Heinemann, 1923.

5. RELIGION/MYTHOLOGY

          "The intensity of the orgiastic passion compounded of
          religion and sensuality shows how the woman, though
          weaker than the man, is able at times to rise to
          greater heights than he."
                              Bachofen, Mother Right

a) Generic

(1) Non-specific

01753.   Bouché-Leclercq, Auguste. Histoire de la divination dans
         l'antiquité. Paris: E. Levoux, 1880.

01754.   Cook, Arthur Bernard. Zeus: A Study in Ancient Religion.
         Cambridge: The University Press, 1940.

01755.   Delcourt, Marie. Hermaphrodite: Myths and Rites of the
         Bisexual Figure in Classical Antiquity. Translated by
         Jennifer Nicolson. London: Studio Books, 1961.

01756.   Fehrle, Eugene. Die kultische Keuschheit im Altertum.
         Religionsgeschichtliche Versuche und Vorarbeiten,
         no. 6. Giessen: A. Topelmann, 1910.

01757. Foucart, Paul. Les mystères d'Eleusis. Paris: A.
        Picard, 1914.

01758. Guthrie, W. The Greeks and Their Gods. London: Methuen
        and Company, 1950.

01759. Halliday, W.R. "The Religion and Mythology of the
        Greeks." In The Cambridge Ancient History, edited by
        J.B. Bury et. al., 2: 602-642. New York: Macmillan,
        1924.

01760. Harrison, Jane. Prolegomena to the Study of Greek
        Religion. 1903. Reprint. New York: Meridian
        Press, 1955.
        [See especially chs. 6 and 7.]

01761. Herington, C.J. Athena Parthenos and Athena Polias: A
        Study in the Religion of Periclean Athens. Manchester,
        England: Manchester University Press, 1955.

01762. Kerényi, Károly. The Gods of the Greeks. New York:
        Thames and Hudson, 1951.

01763. Lawson, J.C. Modern Greek Folklore and Ancient Greek
        Religion. Cambridge: University Press, 1910.

01764. Nilsson, M.P. Greek Popular Religion. New York:
        Columbia University Press, 1940.

01765. _____. The Minoan-Mycenaean Religion and its
        Survival in Greek Religion. Lund: C.W.K. Gleerup,
        1950.

01766. Persson, Axel W. "Der Ursprung der eleusinischen
        Mysterien." Archiv für Religionswissenschaft 21 (1922):
        287-309.

01767. Vernant, Jean-Pierre. "Hestia-Hermes: sur l'expression
        religieuse de l'espace et du mouvement chez les Grecs."
        In Mythe et pensée chez les Grecs, pp. 124-170. Paris:
        Maspero, 1971.

01768. Wehrli, Fritz. "Die Mysterien von Eleusis." Archiv für
        Religionswissenschaft 31 (1934): 77-104.

Also refer to #1810, 1811.

(2) Women

01769.   Farnell, Lewis R. "Sociological Hypothesis Concerning
         the Position of Women in Ancient Religion." Archiv für
         Religionswissenschaft 7 (1904): 70-94.

b) Goddesses

01770.   Arthur, Marylin. "Politics and Pomegranates: An Inter-
         pretation of the Homeric Hymn to Demeter." Arethusa
         10 (Spring 1977) 7-47.

01771.   Burkert, Walter. "Das Lied von Ares und Aphrodite."
         Rheinische Museum fur Philologie n.s. 103 (1960):
         130-144.

01772.   Dieterich, Albrecht. "Mutter Erde." Archiv für
         Religionswissenschaft 8 (1905): 1-50.

01773.   Heckscher, W. S. "Aphrodite as Nun." Phoenix 7
         (Autumn 1953): 105-117.

01774.   Katz, Phyllis B. "The Myth of Psyche: a Definition of
         the Nature of the Feminine." Arethusa 9 (Spring 1976):
         111-118.

01775.   Kerényi, Károly. Die Jungfrau und Mutter der griechischen
         Religion. Eine Studie über Pallas Athene. Zurich:
         Rhein-Verlag, 1952.

01776.   Lehmann-Hartleben, K. "Athena als Geburtsgöttin." Archiv
         für Religionswissenschaft 24 (1926): 19-28.

01777.   Picard, Charles. "Die Ephesia von Anatolien." In Eranos-
         Jahrbuch 1938, edited by Olga Fröbe-Kapteyn, pp. 59-90.
         Zurich: Rhein-Verlag, 1939.

01778.   _____. "Die grosse Mutter von Kreta bis
         Eleusis." In Eranos-Jahrbuch 1938, edited by Olga
         Fröbe-Kapteyn, pp. 91-119. Zurich: Rhein-Verlag, 1939.

01779.   Robert, Louis. "Les femmes théores à Ephèse." Comptes
         rendus academie inscriptions & belles-lettres (1974):
         176-181.

01780. Sourvinou-Inwood, Christiane. "Persephone and Aphrodite at
        Locri: A Model for Personality Definitions in Greek Reli-
        gion." Journal of Hellenic Studies 98 (1978): 101-121.

01781. Terrien, Samuel. "The Omphalos Myth and Hebrew Religion."
        Vetus Testamentum 20 (1970): 315-338.

01782. Vanderlip, Vera Frederika, ed. The Four Greek Hymns
        of Isidorus and the Cult of Isis. American Studies in
        Papyrology, no. 12. Toronto: Hakkert, 1972.

01783. Van Leuven, Jon C. "Mycenaean Goddesses called Potnia."
        Kadmos 18 (1979): 112-129.

c) Priestesses and Oracles

01784. Bragdon, Claude. Delphic Woman. New York: Knopf, 1936.

01785. Holderman, Elizabeth S. A Study of the Greek Priestess.
        Chicago: University of Chicago Press, 1913.

01786. Legner, A. "Sibyllen" In Lexikon für Theologie und
        Kirche 9: pp. 726-728. Freiburg: Herder, 1964.

01787. Oppe, A.I. "The Chasm at Delphi." Journal of Hellenic
        Studies 24 (1904): 214-240.

01788. Parke, H.W. and D.E.W. Wormell. The Delphic Oracle.
        2 vols. Oxford: Basil Blackwell, 1956.
        [See especially vol. 1, chs. 2 and 3.]

01789. Rohde, Erwin. Psyche, Seelenkult und Unsterblichkeitsglaube
        der Griechen. Tübingen: J.C.B. Mohr, 1921.

01790. Stengel, Paul. Die griechische Kultusaltertümer. Handbuch
        der klassischen Altertumswissenschaft, no. 5. Munich:
        C.H. Becksche Verlagshandlung, 1920.

01791. Witton, W.F. "The Priestess Eritha." American Journal of
        Philology 81 (1960): 415-421.

6. SOCIAL

"Marry a virgin, so you can teach her good habits. The
best one to marry is the girl who lives near you; look
over her in detail, so you don't marry one who'll bring
joy to your neighbors."
                          Hesiod, Works and Days

a) Generic

(1) Non-specific

01792. Becker, Wilhelm Adolf. <u>Charicles: or, Illustrations of</u>
<u>the Private Life of the Ancient Greeks</u>. Translated by
Frederick Metcalfe. London: Longmans, Green, and Co.,
1880.

01793. Blümner, Hugo. <u>The Home Life of the Ancient Greeks</u>. Translated by Alice Zimmern. New York: Funk and Wagnalls
Co., 1910.

01794. Boulter, Patricia Neils. "<u>Sophia</u> and <u>Sophrosyne</u> in
Euripides' <u>Andromache</u>." <u>Phoenix</u> 20 (Spring 1966):
51-58.

01795. Dover, K.J. <u>Greek Popular Morality in the Time of Plato</u>
<u>and Aristotle</u>. Berkeley: University of California
Press, 1974.

01796. Ehrenberg, Victor. <u>The People of Aristophanes</u>. 1943.
Reprint. New York: Barnes and Noble, 1974.

01797. Flacelière, Robert. <u>Daily Life in Ancient Greece at the</u>
<u>Time of Pericles</u>. New York: Macmillan, 1964.

01798. St. John, J.A. <u>The History of the Manners and Customs of</u>
<u>Ancient Greece</u>. 3 vols. Port Washington, N.Y.: Kennikat
Press, 1974.

01799. Winter, John Garrett. <u>Life and Letters in the Papyri</u>.
Ann Arbor: University of Michigan Press, 1933.

01800. Wright, Frederick Adam. <u>Greek Social Life</u>. London:
J.M. Dent and Sons Ltd., 1925.

Also refer to #1712.

(2) Women

01801. Hill, Dorothy Kent. "What the Women Did." <u>Classical</u>
<u>Journal</u> 42 (January 1947): 202-205.

(3) Athens

01802. Gould, J. P. "Law, Custom, and Myth: Aspects of the
         social position of women in classical Athens."
         Journal of Hellenic Studies 100 (1980): 38–59.

01803. Tucker, T.G. Life in Ancient Athens. Chautauqua, N.Y.:
         The Chautauqua Press, 1917.
         [See especially ch. 8.]

(4) Others

01804. Willett, R.F. Aristocratic Society in Ancient Crete.
         London: Routledge & Kegan Paul, 1955.

b) Family

(1) Non-specific

01805. Cameron, A. "The Exposure of Children and Greek Ethics."
         Classical Review 46 (1932): 105–14.

01806. Lacey, W.K. The Family in Classical Greece. Ithaca, N.Y.:
         Cornell University Press, 1968.

01807. Montevecchi, Orsolina. "Contributi per una storia sociale
         ed economica della famiglia nell'Egitto greco-romano."
         Aegyptus 17 (1937): 338–348.

01808. Raepsaet, G. "A propos de l'utilisation de statistiques
         en démographie grecque. Le nombre d'enfants par famille."
         L'Antiquité classique 42 (1973): 536–543.

01809. Sijpesteijn, P.J. "A Happy Family?" Zeitschrift für
         Papyrologie und Epigraphik 21 (1976): 169–81.

01810. Slater, Philip E. The Glory of Hera: Greek Mythology
         and the Greek Family. Boston: Beacon Press, 1971.

01811. _____. "The Greek Family in History and Myth."
         Arethusa 7 (Spring 1974): 9–44.

         Also refer to #713.

(2) Athens

01812. Brindesi, Fausto. La famiglia attica: il matrimonio e
        l'adozione. Firenze: La nuova Italia, 1961.

01813. Charlier, Marie-Thérèse and Raepset, Georges. "Etude d'un
        comportement social: les relations entre parents et
        enfants dans la société athénienne à l'époque classique."
        L'Antiquite classique 40 (1970): 589-606.

01814. Davies, J.K. Athenian Propertied Familes 600-300 B.C.
        Oxford: Clarendon Press, 1971.

01815. Humphreys, S. C. "Family Tombs and Tomb Cult in ancient
        Athens." Journal of Hellenic Studies 100 (1980): 96-126.

01816. Lallier, R. De la Condition de la femme dans la famille
        athénienne au Ve et au IVe siècle. Paris: E. Thorin,
        1875.

01817. Nagy, Blaise. "The Naming of Athenian Girls: A Case in
        Point." Classical Journal 74 (1979): 360-364.

01818. Roussel, Pierre. "La famille athénienne." Lettres
        d'humanité 9 (1950): 5-59.

01819. Savage, Charles Albert. The Athenian Family. Baltimore:
        Johns Hopkins University Press, 1907.

01820. Wick, Terry E. "The Importance of the Family as a De-
        terminer of Sexual Mores in Classical Athens." Societas
        5 (Spring 1975): 133-145.

        Also refer to #1722, 1724.

c) Marriage

(1) Non-specific

01821. Asheri, David. "Tyrannie et mariage forcé. Essaie
        d'histoire sociale Grecque." Annales: économies,
        sociétés, civilisations 32 (1977): 21-48.

01822. DuBois, Page. "One Horse/Men, Amazons, and Endogamy."
        Arethusa 12 (Spring 1979): 35-49.

01823. Erdmann, Walter. Die Ehe im alten Griechenland. Münchener
        Beitrage zur Papyrusforschung und antiken Rechtsgeschichte,
        vol. 20. Munich: Beck, 1934.

01824. _____ . "Die Rolle der Mutter bei der Verheiratung
        der Tochter nach griechischen Recht." Zeitschrift der
        Savigny-Stiftung fur Rechtsgeschichte Romanistische
        Abteilung 59 (1939): 544-546.

01825. Finley, Moses I. "Marriage, Sale and Gift in the Homeric
        World." Revue internationale des droits de l'antiquité
        2 (1955): 167-194.

01826. Friedl, Ernestine. "Some Aspects of Dowry and Inheritance
        in Boeotia." In Mediterranean Countrymen, edited by Julian
        Pitt-Rivers, pp. 113-136. Paris: Mouton and Company, 1958.

01827. Koestler, R. "Raub-und Kaufehe bei den Hellenen."
        Zeitschrift der Savigny-Stiftung fur Rechtsgeschichte
        Romanistische Abteilung 64 (1944): 206-232.

01828. Lacey, W.K. "Homeric Hedna and Penelope's Kurios."
        Journal of Hellenic Studies 86 (1966): 55-68.

01829. Scheid, Evelyne. "Il matrimonio omerico." Dialoghi di
        Archeologia n.s.1 (1979): 60-73.

01830. Scott, J.A. "Hebe the Maiden and Hebe the Wife."
        Classical Journal 25 (1930): 465-466.

01831. Seibert, Jakob. Historische Beiträge zu den dynastischen
        Verbindungen in hellenistischer Zeit. Historia
        Einzelschriften, no. 10. Wiesbaden: F. Steiner, 1967.

01832. Vatin, Claude. Recherches sur le mariage et la condition
        de la femme mariée à l'époque hellénistique. Paris:
        Editions de Boccard, 1970.

01833. Vernant, Jean-Pierre. "Le mariage en Grèce archaique."
        La Parola del Passato 148-49 (1973): 51-74.

01834. Wolff, Hans Julius. "Die Grundlagen des griechischen
        Eherechts." Tijdschrift voor Rechtsgeschiedenis 20
        (1972): 1-29 and 157-181.

01835. _____ . Written and Unwritten Marriages in
        Hellenistic and Post-classical Roman Law. Haverford:
        American Philological Association, 1939.

(2) Athens

01836. Fitton, J.W. "That Was No Lady, That Was . . ."
        Classical Quarterly 64 (1970): 56-66.

01837. Levy, Harry F. "Inheritance and Dowry in Classical
        Athens." In Mediterranean Countrymen, edited by Julian
        Pitt-Rivers, pp. 137-143. Paris: Mouton and Company,
        1958.

01838. Mulder, J.J.B. Quaestiones Nonullae ad Atheniensium
        Matrimonium Vitamque Coniugalem Pertinentes. Utrecht:
        Bosch, 1920.

01839. Raepsaet, G. "Les motivations de la natalité à Athènes
        aux Ve et IVe siècles." L'Antiquité classique 40 (1971):
        80-110.

01840. Schmitt, Pauline. "Athéna Apatouria et la ceinture: les
        aspects féminins des Apatouries à Athènes." Annales:
        économies, sociétés et civilisations 32 (November-
        December 1977): 1059-1073.

01841. Thompson, W.E. "Athenian Marriage Patterns: Remarriage."
        California Studies in Classical Antiquity 5 (1972):
        211-225.

01842. _____. "The Marriage of First Cousins in Athenian
        Society." Phoenix 21 (Winter 1967): 273-282.

        Also refer to #1724, 1726.

d) Sex Life and Morals

(1) Non-specific

01843. Brandt, Paul. [Hans Licht.] Sexual Life in Ancient Greece.
        Translated by J.H. Freese. New York: Barnes & Noble, 1963.

01844. Connor, Walter Robert. Theopompus and Fifth Century
        Athens. Washington: Center for Hellenic Studies.
        Distributed by Harvard University Press, Cambridge,
        Massachusetts, 1968.

01845. Devereaux, G. "Greek pseudohomosexuality and the 'Greek
        Miracle'." Symbolae Osloenes 42 (1967): 69-92.

01846. Dover, K.J. "Classical Greek Attitudes to Sexual Be-
        havior." Arethusa 6 (Spring 1973): 59-73.

01847. Flacelière, Robert. Love in Ancient Greece. New York:
        MacFadden-Bartell, 1964.

(2)   Prostitutes and Courtesans

01848.   Alciphron. The Letters of Alciphron, Aelian and Philostratus.
Translated by Allen Rogers Benner and Francis H. Fobes. The
Loeb Classical Library. Cambridge, Mass.: Harvard Univer-
sity Press, 1949.

01849.   Kowalski, G. "De Phrynes Pectore Nudato." Eos 42 (1947):
50-62.

01850.   Lacroix, Paul. Les courtisanes de la Grèce. Nice: J. Gay,
1872.

01851.   Lucian. "Dialogues of the Courtesans." Lucian, Vol. VII., pp.
355-467. Translated by M.D. Macleod. 8 vols. The Loeb
Classical Library. Cambridge, Mass.: Harvard University
Press, 1961.

01852.   Nau, A.F., ed. Histoire de Thaïs: Publication des textes
grecs et de divers autres textes et versions. Paris:
Paris: E. Leroux, 1903.

01853.   Wells, Wendy. "Mercenary Prostitution in Ancient Greece."
Quest 5 (Summer 1979): 76-80.

e) Fashion

01854.   Barker, Albert W. "Domestic Costumes of the Athenian
Woman in the Fifth and Fourth Centuries B.C." American
Journal of Archaeology 26 (October 1922): 410-425.

01855.   Galt, C.M. "Veiled Ladies." American Journal of
Archeology. 35 (1931): 373-393.

01856.   Smith, John Moyr, ed. Ancient Greek Female Costume.
London: Low, Marston, Searle, and Rivington, 1883.

f) Recreation

01857.   Box, H. "Aristophanes: Birds 785-96, and Thesmophorizussae
450-451. Were Women Admitted to the Tragic Theatre?"
Classical Review n.s. 14 (December 1964): 241-242.

01858.   Navarre, Octave L.L. Utrum Mulieres Athenienses Scaenicos
         Ludos Spectaverint Necne. Toulouse: E. Privat Bibliopola,
         1900.

                        g)   Health/Medical

                    (1)   Abortion/Birth Control

01859.   Ilberg, Johannes. "Zur gynäkologischen Ethik der
         Griechen." Archiv für Religionswissenschaft 13
         (1910): 1-19.

                    (2)   Women in Medicine

01860.   Caldwell, Ruth. "Women in Medicine: Chapter I. The
         First Women in Medicine." Medical Woman's Journal
         37 (February 1930): 40-42.

                    (3)   Women and Health

01861.   Ellinger, T. V. H. Hippocrates on Intercourse and Pregnancy.
         New York: Abelard-Schuman, 1952.

01862.   Hanson, Ann Ellis. "Hippocrates: Diseases of Women."
         Signs 1 (Winter 1975): 567-584.

01863.   Hippocrates. "Reproduction: The Dancer Lost Her Baby."
         In Hippocratic Wisdom, edited by William F. Peterson,
         pp. 23-38. Springfield, Illinois: Charles C. Thomas,
         1946.

01864.   _____. Des maladies des femmes. In Oeuvres com-
         plètes d'Hippocrates. Translated by E. Littre. 1839-
         1861. Reprint. Amsterdam: A.M. Hakkert, 1962-1978.

01865.   Rousselle, A. "Observation féminine et idéologie mascu-
         line, le corps de la femme d'après les médecins grecs."
         Annales: économies, sociétés, civilisations 35 (1980):
         1089-1115.

01866.   Welcker, F.G. Medea und die Krauterkunde bei den Frauen.
         Kleine Schriften zu den Alterthümern der Heilkunde bei
         den Griechen. Bonn: Weber, 1850.

h) Burial Customs

01867. Alexiou, Margaret. The Ritual Lament in Greek Tradition.
        London: Cambridge University Press, 1974.

01868. Kurtz, Donna C. and Boardman, John. Greek Burial Customs.
        Ithaca, N.Y.: Cornell University Press, 1971.

01869. Lattimore, Richmond. Themes in Greek and Latin Epitaphs.
        Illinois Studies in Language and Literature 28, 1 and
        2. 1943. Reprint. Urbana: University of Illinois
        Press, 1962.

01870. Pircher, J. Das Lob der Frau im vorchristlichen Grab-
        epigramm der Griechen. Innsbruck: Wagner, 1979.

01871. Smithson, Evelyn Lord. "The Tomb of a Rich Athenian Lady,
        ca. 850 B.C." Hesperia 37 (1968): 98-103.

        Also refer to #1987.

7. CULTURAL

        "I myself reproach Myrtis, lovely-voiced though she is,
        because she entered into rivalry with Pindar, though
        she was born a woman."
                            Corinna of Boeotia

a) Education

01872. Beck, F.A.G. Greek Education, 450-350 B.C. New York:
        Barnes & Noble, 1966.

01873. Jeanmaire, Henri. Couri et Courètes: essai sur l'educa-
        tion spartiate et sur les rites d'adolescence dans
        l'antiquite hellenique. Lille: Bibliotheque universi-
        taire, 1939.

b) Literature

(1) Non-specific

01874.   Gerber, Douglas E.   "The Female Breast in Greek Erotic
         Literature."   <u>Arethusa</u> 11 (Spring and Fall 1978):
         203-212.

01875.   Wright, Frederick Adam.   <u>Feminism in Greek Literature:</u>
         <u>From Homer to Aristotle</u>.   1923.   Reprint.   Port Wash-
         ington, N.Y.:   Kennikat, 1969.

01876.   Zweig, Paul.   "Man on the Run."   <u>Columbia Forum</u> 14
         (Winter 1971):   54-55; 15 (Spring 1972): 40-43.

(2) Philosophy

(a) General

01877.   Cumming, Alan.   "Pauline Christianity and Greek Philosophy:
         a Study of the Status of Women."   <u>Journal of the History</u>
         <u>of Ideas</u> 34 (Oct.-Dec. 1973):   517-528.

(b) Individuals

[1] ARISTOTLE

01878.   Aristotle.   <u>The Basic Works of Aristotle</u>.   Edited by
         Richard McKeon.   New York: Random House, 1941.
         [See especially Politics, book 1, chs. 1, 2, 12, 13
         and book 2, ch. 4.]

01879.   Aristotle.   <u>The Generation of Animals</u>.   Loeb Classical
         Library.   London: William Heinemann Ltd., 1943.
         [See especially book 2, ch. 1.]

[2] PLATO

[a] Contemporary

01880. Plato. The Republic and Other Works. Translated by
        B. Jowett. 5 vols. New York: Oxford University Press,
        1954.
        [See especially book 5.]

[b] Secondary

(i) Philosophy

01881. Levinson, Ronald B. In Defense of Plato. Cambridge:
        Harvard University Press, 1953.

01882. Lodge, Rupert. The Philosophy of Plato. London:
        Routledge and Kegan Paul, 1956.
        [See especially pp. 270-271.]

01883. Mazzeo, Joseph Anthony. "Plato's Eros and Dante's Amore."
        Traditio 12 (1956): 315-337.

01884. Shorey, Paul. What Plato Said. Chicago: University of
        Chicago Press, 1933.

01885. Taylor, A.E. Plato The Man and his Work. New York:
        Meridian, 1956.

01886. Winspear, A.D. The Genesis of Plato's Thought. New
        York: Dryden, 1940.
        [See especially pp. 241ff.]

(ii) Ideas on Women

01887. Allen, Christine Allen. "Plato on Women," Feminist
        Studies 2 (1975): 131-138.

01888. Annas, Julia. "Plato's Republic and Feminism." Philosophy
        51 (July 1976): 307-321.

01889. Calvert, Brian. "Plato and the Equality of Women."
        Phoenix 29 (1975): 231-243.

01890. Dickason, Anne. "Anatomy and destiny: the role of biology in Plato's views of women." Philosphical Forum 5 (Fall-Winter 1973-1974): 45-53.

01891. Ithurriague, Jean. Les idées de Plato sur la condition de la femme au regard des traditions antiques. Paris: J. Gamber, 1931.

01892. MacGuigan, Maryellen. "Is Woman a Question?" International Philosophy Quarterly 13 (December 1973): 485-506.

01893. Okin, Susan Moller. "Philosopher Queens and Private Wives: Plato on Women and the Family." Philosophy and Public Affairs 6 (Summer 1977): 345-369.

01894. Pierce, Christine. "Equality: Republic V." The Monist 57 (January 1973): 1-11.

01895. Pomeroy, Sarah B. "Feminism in Book V of Plato's Republic." Apeiron 8 (1974): 32-35.

01896. _____. "Plato and the Female Physician." American Journal of Philology 99 (Winter 1978): 496-500.

01897. Saxonhouse, Arlene W. "The Philosopher and the Female in the Political Thought of Plato." Political Theory 4 (May 1976): 195-212.

01898. Wender, Dorothea. "Plato: Misogynist, Paedophile, and Feminist." Arethusa 6 (Spring 1973): 75-90.

[3] SOCRATIC WOMEN

01899. Godel, Roger. Socrate et Diotime. Paris: Societe d'Edition "Les Belles Lettres", 1955.

01900. Möbius, H. "Diotima." Deutsches Archäologisches Institut Jahrbuch 49 (1934): 45-60.

01901. Natorp, P. "Aischines' Aspasia." Philologus 51 (1892): 489-500.

01902. Neumann, H. "Diotima's Concept of Love." American Journal of Philology 86 (1965): 33-59.

01903. Vermeule, C. C. "Socrates and Aspasia: New Portrait of Late Antiquity." Classical Journal 54 (November 1958): 49-55.

01904. Woodbury, Leonard. "Socrates and the Daughter of Aristides." Phoenix 27 (Spring 1973): 7-25.

[4] PYTHAGOREAN WOMEN

01905. Meunier, Mario, translator. Femmes pythagoriciennes:
        fragments et lettres de Theano, Perictione, Phintys,
        Melissa et Myia. Paris: L'Artisan du livre, 1932.

01906. Wieland, Christoph Martin. Die pythagorischen Frauen.
        n.p. 1791.

[5] OTHERS

01907. Athenaeus. The Deipnosophists or Banquet of the Learned
        of Naucratis. Translated by C. D. Yonge. 3 vols.
        London: H. G. Bohn, 1854.

01908. Bentley, Richard. A Dissertation upon the Epistles of
        Phallaris. London: G. Auld, 1817.

01909. Kenber, Owen. "Anaxagoras' theory of sex differentiation
        and heredity." Phronesis 18 (1973): 1-14.

(3) Drama

(a) General

01910. Fantham, Elaine. "Sex, Status and Survival in Hellenistic
        Athens: A Study of Women in New Comedy." Phoenix 29
        (Spring 1975): 44-74.

01911. Jenzer, Annemarie. Wandlungen in der Auffassung der Frau
        im ionischen Epos und in der attischen Tragödie bis auf
        Sophokles. Zurich: Leeman, 1933.

01912. Malkin, Michael R. "The dramatic function of matricide
        in the Greek Electra plays." Studies in the Humanities
        3 (October 1972): 22-24.

01913. Young, Sherman Plato. The Women of Greek Drama. New
        York: Exposition Press, 1953.

(b) Individuals

[1] AESCHYLUS

[a] Drama

01914. Thomson, George Derwent.   Aeschylus and Athens: A Study
of the Social Origins of Drama. London: Lawrence &
Wishart, 1966.

[b] Ideas on Women

01915. Caldwell, Richard S. "The Misogyny of Eteocles."
Arethusa 6 (Fall 1973): 197–231.

01916. _____. "The Psychology of Aeschylus'
Supplices." Arethusa 7 (Spring 1974): 59–70.

01917. Riele, G.J.M.J. Les Femmes chez Aeschyle. Gröningen:
Wolters, 1955.

01918. Winnington-Ingram, R.P. "Clytemnestra and the Vote of
Athena." Journal of Hellenic Studies 68 (1948): 130–147.

01919. Zeitlin, Froma I. "The Dynamics of Misogyny Myth and
Mythmaking in the Oresteia." Arethusa 11 (Spring and
Fall 1978): 149–184.

[2] ARISTOPHANES

01920. Haley, Herman W. "Social and Domestic Position of Women
in Aristophanes." Harvard Studies in Classical Philology
1 (1890): 159–186.

[3] EURIPIDES

01921. Dale, Amy Marjorie. Euripides' Helen. Oxford: Clarendon
Press, 1967.

01922. Daugherty, Margaret. "Women in Euripides' Moral Quest."
San Jose Studies 4 (February 1978): 73–81.

01923.   Segal, Charles. "The Menace of Dionysius. Sex Roles and
          Reversals in Euripides' Bacchae." Arethusa 11 (Spring
          and Fall 1978): 185-202.

          Also refer to #1794.

                           [4] MENANDER

01924.   Post, L.A. "The Feminism of Menander." Classical Weekly
          19 (3 May 1926): 198-202.

01925.   _____. "Women's Place in Menander's Athens." Trans-
          actions and Proceedings of the American Philological
          Association 71 (1940): 420-459.

                           [5] SOPHOCLES

01926.   Bacon, Helen H. "Woman's Two Faces: Sophocles' View of
          the Tragedy of Oedipus and his Family." In Science
          and Psychoanalysis, edited by Jules Masserman, 10:
          10-27. New York: Grune and Stratton, 1966.

01927.   Segal, Charles. "Sophocles' Praise of Man and the Con-
          flicts of the Antigone." In Sophocles, edited by T.
          Woodard, pp. 62-85. Englewood Cliffs, N.J.: Prentice-
          Hall, 1966.

01928.   Weissman, Philip. "Sophocles' Antigone: The psychology
          of the Old Maid." In Creativity in the Theater: A
          Psychoanalytical Study, pp. 190-203. New York: Basic
          Books, Inc., Publishers, 1965.

01929.   Wiltshire, Susan Ford. "Antigone's Disobedience."
          Arethusa 9 (Spring 1976): 29-36.

                           (4) Poetry

                         (a) Individuals

                         [1] ANTIMACHUS

01930.   Benecke, E.F.M. Antimachus of Colophon and the Position
          of Women in Greek Poetry. London: Swan Sonnenschein
          & Co., 1896.

[2] HESIOD

01931. Brenk, Frederick, S.J. "Hesiod: How Much a Male
        Chauvinist?" Classical Bulletin 49 (1973): 73-76.

01932. Sussman, Linda S. "Workers and Drones: Labor, Idleness
        and Gender Definition in Hesiod's Beehive." Arethusa
        11 (Spring and Fall 1978): 27-41.

[3] HOMER

01933. Amory, Anne. "The Reunion of Odysseus and Penelope." In
        Essays on the Odyssey, edited by Charles Henry Taylor,
        pp. 100-121. Bloomington, Indiana: Indiana University
        Press, 1963.

01934. Campbell, J.M. "Homer and Chastity." Philological
        Quarterly 28 (July 1949): 333-359.

01935. Foley, Helen P. "'Reverse Similes' and Sex Roles in the
        Odyssey." Arethusa 11 (Spring and Fall 1978): 7-26.

01936. Hirsch, M. "Frauenkundliche Quellen in Ilias und Odyssee."
        Archiv für Frauenkunde und Konstitutionsforschung 15
        (1929): 350-353.

01937. Kakridis, Johannes Thomas. "Meleagria." Philologus 90
        (1935): 1-25.

01938. _____. "The Role of the Woman in
        the Iliad." Eranos 54 (1956): 21-27.

01939. Perry, W.C. The Women of Homer. London: William
        Heinemann, 1898.

[4] SEMONIDES

01940. Lloyd-Jones, Hugh. "Females of the Species; on 118 Lines
        of Semonides." Encounter 44 (May 1975): 48.

01941. _____. Female of the Species: Semonides on
        Women. London: Duckworth, 1975.

[5] THEOCRITUS

01942. Swigart, Robert. "Theocritus' pastoral response to city
women." Bucknell Review 21 (Spring 1973): 145-174.

(b) Poetesses

[1] GENERAL

01943. Barnard, Sylvia. "Hellenistic Women Poets." Classical
Journal 73 (February-March 1978): 204-213.

01944. Lisi, Umbertina. Poetesse Greche: Saffo, Corinna,
Telesilla, Prassilla, Erinna, Anite, Miro, Nosside,
Edila, Melinno. Catania: Studio Editoriale Moderno, 1933.

01945. Wright, Frederick Adam. "The Women Poets of Greece."
Fortnightly Review 113 (February 1923): 323-333.

[2] INDIVIDUALS

[a] Aspasia Minore

01946. Fogazza, G. "Aspasia Minore." La Parola del Passato 25:
(1970) 420-422.

[b] Corinna

01947. Bolling, George Melville. "Notes on Corinna." American
Journal of Philology 77   (1956): 282-287.

01948. Cupaiuolo, Nice. Poetesse Greche: Corinna. Naples:
Rondinella, 1939.

01949. Guillon, Pierre. "Corinne et les Oracles Beotiens: La
Consultation d'Asopos." Bulletin de correspondence
hellenique 82 (1958): 47-60.

01950. Page, Denys L. Corinna. London: Society for the Promotion of Hellenic Studies, 1953.

[c] Erinna

01951.   Collart, Paul. "La Poétesse Erinna." Comptes rendus de
          l'Academie des inscriptions et belles-lettres (April-
          June 1944): 183-199.

01952.   Latte, Kurt. "Erinna." Nachrichten der Akademie der
          Wissenschaften in Göttingen, Philologisch-Historische
          Klasse 3 (1953): 79-94.

[d] Sappho

01953.   Bagg, Robert. "Love, Ceremony and Daydream in Sappho's
          Lyrics." Arion 3 (Autumn 1964): 44-82.

01954.   Bascoul, J.M.F. 'Hayva Eatpw: La Chaste Sappho de Lesbos
          et le mouvement feministe a Athenes au IVe siècle avant
          J.-C. Paris: Librairie universitaire, 1911.

01955.   _____. La Chaste Sappho de Lesbos et Stesichore,
          dont la concurrence et les pretentions lui inspirerent
          l'ode II: les trois dernières strophes, manquant a ce
          poeme sont reconstituées ici, pour la première fois, au
          moyen de deux fragments dont voice le plus mutile...les
          pretendues amies de Sappho. Paris: H. Welter, 1913.

01956.   Courtney, William Leonard. "Sappho and Aspasia." Fort-
          nightly Review 97 (March 1912): 488-495.

01957.   DuBois, Page. "Sappho and Helen." Arethusa 11 (Spring
          and Fall 1978): 89-99.

01958.   Goldsmith, Margaret Leland. Sappho of Lesbos, a Phycho-
          logical Reconstruction of Her Life. London: Rich and
          Cowan, 1938.

01959.   Green, Peter. "In Search of Sappho." Horizon 7 (Spring
          1966): 105-111.

01960.   Hallett, Judith P. "Sappho and her social Context:
          Sense and Sensuality." Signs 4 (Spring 1979): 447-464.

01961.   Heintze, Helga von. Das Bildnis der Sappho. Mainz:
          Kupferberg, 1966.

01962.   Lefkowitz, Mary. "Critical Stereotypes and the Poetry of
          Sappho." Greek, Roman and Byzantine Studies 14 (1973):
          113-123.

01963. McEvilley, Thomas. "Sappho, Fragment Ninety-four."
        Phoenix 25 (Spring 1971): 1-11.

01964. _____. "Sappho, Fragment Thirty-one: The
        Face Behind the Mask." Phoenix 32 (Spring 1978): 1-18.

01965. _____. "Sappho, Fragment Two." Phoenix
        26 (Winter 1972): 323-333.

01966. Prentice, William K. "Sappho." Classical Philology 13
        (October 1918): 347-360.

01967. Robinson, David M. Sappho and Her Influence. New York:
        Cooper Square Publishers, 1963.

01968. Roche, Paul. "Sappho." Greek Heritage 1 (Winter 1963): 9-15.

01969. Weigall, Arthur. Sappho of Lesbos: Her Life and Times.
        New York: Frederick A. Stokes Co., 1932.

01970. Wharton, H.T. Sappho. London, 1898. Chicago: A.C.
        McClurg and Co., 1898.

[3] WOMEN IN POETRY

01971. Jax, Karl. Die weibliche Schönheit in der griechischen
        Dichtung. Innsbruck: Universitäts Verlag Wagner, 1933.

(5) Other Works

(a) Individuals

[1] HERODOTUS

01972. Walcot, Peter. "Herodotus on Rape." Arethusa 11 (Spring
        and Fall 1978): 137-147.

[2] PLUTARCH

[a] Contemporary

01973. Plutarch. Moralia. Translated by Frank Cole Babbit. 15 vols.
        The Loeb Classical Library. London: William Heinemann
        Ltd., 1927-69.
        [See especially Advice to Married Couples, Love Stories,
        Sayings of Spartan Women, Bravery of Women.]

[b] Secondary

01974. Bowersock, G.W. "Some Persons in Plutarch's Moralia."
        Classical Quarterly n.s. 15 (November 1965):
        267-270.

01975. Stadter, Philip Austin. Plutarch's Historical Methods:
        An Analysis of the Mulierum Virtutes. Cambridge, Mass.:
        Harvard University Press, 1965.

c) Intellectuals

01976. Panayotatou, A. "Sur Quelques Femmes Intellectuelles
        de la Période Hellenistique." Festschrift zum 80.
        Geburtstag Max Neuburgers. Vienna: W. Maudrich, 1948.

d) Art and Artifacts

(1) Women in Art

01977. Bothmer, D. von. Amazons in Greek Art. Oxford: Clarendon
        Press, 1957.

01978. Forrer, L. Portraits of Royal Ladies on Greek Coins.
        Chicago: Argonaut, 1969.

01979. Gardner, P. "A Female Figure in the Early Style of
        Pheidias." Journal of Hellenic Studies 38 (1918): 1-26.

01980. Harrison, Evelyn B. "Athena and Athens in the East
        Pediment of the Parthenon." American Journal of
        Archaeology 71 (1967): 27-58.

01981. Hoffmann, H. Sexual and Asexual Pursuit a structuralist
        approach to Greek vase painting. London: Royal Anthro-
        pological Institute, 1977.

01982. Klimowsky, Ernst Werner. Das Mann-weibliche Leitbild in
        der Antike. Munich: Verlag Uni-Druck, 1972.

01983. McClees, Helen. A Study of Women in Attic Inscriptions.
        New York: Columbia University Press, 1920.

01984. McNally, Sheila. "The Maenad in Early Greek Art."
        Arethusa 11 (Spring and Fall 1978): 101-135.

01985. Palmer, Hazel. "A Lord and Lady from Olympia." Bulletin
        of the Boston Museum of Fine Arts 56 (Summer 1958):
        64-68.

01986. Panofsky, D. and E. Pandora's Box: The Changing Aspects
        of a Mythical Symbol. Bollingen Series, vol. 52. New
        York: Pantheon, 1956.

01987. Richter, G.M.A. The Archaic Gravestones of Attica. London:
        Phaidon, 1961.

01988. Salis, Arnold von. Theseus und Ariadne. Berlin and
        Leipzig: de Gruyter, 1930.

01989. Swerdlow, Amy. "The Greek citizen woman in Attic Vase
        Painting: new views and new questions." Women's
        Studies 5 (1978): 267-284.

                    (2)   Women Artists

01990. Starr, Chester G. "An Evening with the Flute Girls."
        La Parola del Passato 183 (1978): 401-410.

                    e)   Science

01991. Codellas, P.S. "Ancient Greek Woman Leaders in Science."
        In Actes du Ve congres international d'histoire des
        sciences, Lausanne, 1947, pp. 226-230. Paris: Académie
        Internationale d'histoire des sciences, 1948.

C. ROME

1. SURVEYS

"Remember the laws through which our ancestors limited
the liberation of women, through which they bent them
to the will of the men. . . . As soon as they become
equal to us, they will be our superiors."
                                        Cato

a) Generic

01992. Abbott, Frank F. Society and Politics in Ancient Rome.
        New York: Biblo and Tannen, 1963.

01993. Alfoldi, A. Early Rome and the Latins. Ann Arbor:
        University of Michigan Press, 1965.

01994. Arnott, Peter D. The Romans and their World. New York:
        St. Martin's Press, 1970.

01995. Becker, W.A. Gallus: or, Roman Scenes of the Times of
        Augustus. London: Longmans, Green and Co., 1920.

01996. Boren, Henry C. Roman Society: A Social Economic, and
        Cultural History. Lexington, Mass.: D.C. Heath, 1977.

01997. Ferrero, Gugliemo. Characters and Events of Roman History
        from Caesar to Nero. New York: G.P. Putnam's Sons, 1909.

01998. Harris, William Vernon. Rome in Etruria and Umbria.
        Oxford: Clarendon Press, 1971.

01999. McDermott, William C. and Orentzel, Anne E. Roman Portraits.
        Columbia, Mo.: University of Missouri Press, 1979.

02000. Mills, Dorothy. The Book of the Ancient Romans. New York:
        G.P. Putnam's Sons, 1937.

02001. Paoli, Ugo Enrico. Rome, its People, Life and Customs.
        Translated by R. D. McNaghten. New York: D. McKay and
        Co., 1963.

02002. Syme, Ronald. The Roman Revolution. Oxford: Clarendon
        Press, 1939.

b) Women

02003. Appleton, C. Trois épisodes de l'histoire ancienne de
        Rome: les Sabines, Lucrèce, Virginie. Paris: Librairie
        du Recueil Sirey, 1924.

02004. Bader, Clarisse. La Femme romaine: étude de la vie
        antique. Paris: Didier et Cie., 1877.

02005. Balsdon, John Percy Vyvian Dacre. Roman Women: Their
        History and Habits. New York: John Day, 1963.

02006. _____. "Women in Imperial Rome."
        History Today 10 (January 1960): 24-31.

02007. Bringmann, Lea. Die Frau im ptolemäischkaiserlichen Agypten.
        Bonn: Scheur, 1939.

02008. Brittain, A. Roman Women. Vol. II of Woman: In All Ages and
        in All Countries. Philadelphia: George Barrie & Sons, 1907.

02009. Bruder, Reinhold. Die germanische Frau im Lichte der
        Runeninschriften und der antiken Historiographie. New
        York: De Gruyter, 1974.

02010. Buck, J. T. "Pre-Feudal Women." Journal of the Rutgers Uni-
        versity Library 34 (1971): 46-51.

02011. Dale, M. "The Women of Imperial Rome and English Women
        of Today." Westminster Review 141 (May 1894): 490-502.

02012. D'Avino, Michele. The Women of Pompeii. Translated by
        Monica Hope Jones & Luigi Nusco. Naples: Loffredo, 1967.

02013. Finley, Moses I. "The Silent Women of Rome." Horizon 7
        (Winter 1965): 56-64. Reprinted in Aspects of
        Antiquity: Discoveries and Controversies, pp. 129-142.
        London: Charro and Windus, 1968.

02014. Fischl, Hans. Die Frau im alten Rom. Munich: E. Heimeran,
        1935.

02015. Grimal, Pierre. "La Femme à Rome et dans la civilisation
        romaine." In Prehistoire et antiquité. Vol. I of
        Histoire mondiale de la femme, pp. 375-485. Paris:
        Nouveau libraire de France, 1965.

02016. Macurdy, Grace Harriet. Vassal-Queens and Some Contemporary
        Women in the Roman Empire. Baltimore: Johns Hopkins
        University Press, 1937.

02017.   Marshall, Anthony J.   "Roman Women and the Provinces."
         Ancient Society 6 (1975):   109–127.

02018.   Marshall, F.H.   "The Position of Women."   In A Companion
         to Latin Studies, edited by John Edwin Sandys, pp. 184–
         190.   3rd ed.   New York: Hafner Publishing Co., 1963.

02019.   Masiello, T.   La donna tutrice: Modelli culturali e prassi
         guiridica fra gli Antonini e i Severi.   Naples: Jovene,
         1979.

02020.   Naumann, Ida.   Die altgermanische Frau der Vorzeit.   Quellen-
         hefte zum Frauenleben in der Geschichte, edited by Emmy Beck-
         mann and Irma Stoss, vol. 1.   Berlin: F. A. Herbig, 1927.

02021.   _____.   Germanische Frauen der Volkerwanderungszeit.
         Quellenhefte zum Frauenleben in der Geschichte, edited by
         Emmy Beckmann and Irma Stoss, vol. 1.   Berlin: F. A. Herbig,
         1930.

02022.   Putnam, Emily James.   "The Roman Lady."   Atlantic Monthly,
         105 (June 1910):   758–794.

02023.   Warren, Larissa Bonfante.   "Etruscan Women: A Question of
         Interpretation."   Archaeology 26 (October 1973):   242–249.

02024.   _____.   "The Women of Etruria."
         Arethusa 6 (Spring 1973):   91–101.

02025.   Wieand, Helen E.   "Position of Women in the Late Roman
         Republic."   Classical Journal 12 (March 1917):   378–392;
         (April 1917):   423–437.

02026.   Wulff, E.   Die Frau in der Römischen Sage und Geschichte.
         Quellenhefte zum Frauenleben in der Geschichte, edited by
         Emmy Beckmann and Irma Stoss, vol. 1.   Berlin: F. A. Herbig
         Verlagsbuchhandlung, 1927–1933.

2.   MATRIARCHY AND MATRILINY

Drances, a friend and counselor of King Latinus, "was
proud of the nobility derived from his mother, as to
his father he was uncertain."
                              Vergil, Aeneid

02027.   Adler, Rachel.   "A Mother in Israel: Aspects of the Mother
         Rule in Jewish Myth."   In Beyond Androcentrism, edited by
         Rita Gross, pp. 237–255.   Missoula, Mt.:   Scholars Press
         for the American Academy of Religion, 1977.

02028. Aron, Albert William. Traces of Matriarchy in Germanic Hero-
        Lore. University of Wisconsin Studies in Language and
        Literature, no. 9. Madison: University of Wisconsin, 1920.

02029. Bachofen, Johan Jacob. Die Sage von Tanaquil: eine Untersuch-
        ung über den Orientalismus in Rom und Italien. Basel: B.
        Schwabe, 1951.

02030. Gagé, Jean. "Matrones ou mères de famille? Sur des
        formes arcaiques d'encadrement feminin dans les sociétés
        primitives de Rome et du Latium." Cahiers internationaux
        de sociologie n.s. 29 (1960): 45-74.

02031. Rose, Herbert J. "Mother-Right in Ancient Italy." Folk-
        Lore 31 (June 1920): 93-108.

02032. Slotty, F. "Zur Frage des Matriarchates bei den Etruskern."
        Archiv Orientalni 18 (1950): 262-285.

3. POLITICAL

"And yet, it is not fitting even at home for you
[women] to concern yourselves with what laws are
passed or repealed here."
                    Livy, History of Rome

a) Generic

(1) Non-specific

02033. Carcopino, Jerome. Passion et politique chez les Césars.
        Paris: Hachette, 1958.

02034. Mommsen, Theodore. Römische Staatsrecht. Leipzig: S. Hirzel,
        1888.

(2) Women

02035   Abbott, Frank F. "Women and Public Affairs Under the Roman
        Republic." Scribner's Magazine 46 (September 1909):
        357-366.

02036. Balsdon, John Percy Dacre. "Women in Republican Rome."
        History Today 9 (July 1959): 455-461.

02037. Flannery, H.W. "Roman Women and the Vote." Classical
        Journal 16 (November 1920): 103-107.

02038. Förtsch, Barbara. Die politische Rolle der Frau in der
        römischen Republik. Würzburger Studien zur Altertumswis-
        senschaft, vol. 5. Stuttgart: Kohlhammer, 1935.

02039. Sandels, Friedrich. Die Stellung der kaiserlichen Frauen aus
        dem julisch-claudischen Hause. Darmstadt: K. F. Bender,
        1912.

                        b) Legal

                    (1) Non-Specific

02040. Bennecke, Hans. Die strafrechtliche Lehre vom Ehebruch in
        ihrer historisch-dogmatischen Entwicklung. 1884. Reprint.
        Aalen: Scientia Verlag, 1971.

02041. Berger, Adolf. Encyclopedic Dictionary of Roman Law.
        Philadelphia: American Philosophical Society, 1953.

02042. Castello, Carlo. Il Tema de matrimonio e concubinato nel
        mondo romano. Milan: Guiffre, 1940.

02043. Corbett, Percy Ellwood. The Augustan Divorce. London:
        Stevens & Sons, Ltd., 1929.

02044. _____. The Roman Law of Marriage. Oxford:
        Claredon Press, 1930.

02045. Crook, J.A. Law and Life of Rome: Aspects of Greek &
        Roman Life. Ithaca: Cornell University Press, 1967.

02046. Cuq, Edouard. Manuel des institutions juridiques des
        Romains. Paris: Plon-Nourrit, 1917.

02047. Daube, David. Roman Law: Linguistic, Social and Philo-
        sophical Aspects. (The Gray Lectures, 1966). Edinburgh:
        The University Press, 1969.

02048. Durry, Marcel. "Sur le mariage romain. Autocritique et
        mise au point." Revue internationale des droits de
        l'antiquité 3rd ser. 3 (1956): 227-243.

02049. Garrido García, Manuel. Ius uxorium. Rome: Sucs de Riva-
        deneyra, 1958.

02050. Ihering, Rudolph von. Der Geist des römischen Rechts auf
        den verschiedenen Stufen seiner Entwicklung. Leipzig:
        Breitkopf and Hartel, 1921-1924.

02051. Jolowicz, H.F. An Historical Introduction to Roman Law.
        New York: Cambridge University Press, 1972.

02052. Kaser, Max. Roman Private Law. 2nd ed. London: Butterworths,
        1968.

02053. LeBras, Gabriel. "Observations sur le mariage dans le
        corpus Justinien et dans le droit classique de l'église."
        In Etudes offertes à Jean Macqueron, pp. 425-429. Aix-
        en-Provence: n.p., 1970.

02054. Levy, Ernst. Der Hergang der römischen Ehescheidung. Weimar:
        H. Bohlaus Nachfolger, 1925.

02055. _____. West Roman Vulgar Law: The Law of Property.
        Philadelphia: American Philosophical Society, 1951.

02056. Medicus, Dieter. Zur Geschichte des Senatus consultum
        Velleianum. Cologne: Bohlau, 1957.

02057. Pasquier, Etienne. L'Interpretation des instituts de
        Justinien avec la conference de chasque paragraphe aux
        ordonnances royaux arrestz de parlements et coutumes
        générales de la France. Paris: Videcoq aine, 1847.

02058. Pharr, Mary Brown. "The Kiss in Roman Law." Classical
        Journal 42 (1946-1947): 393-397.

02059. Roby, Henry J. Roman Private Law in the Times of Cicero
        and of the Antonines. Cambridge: Cambridge University
        Press, 1902.

02060. Sandars, T.C. The Institutes of Justinian. London:
        Longmans, Green & Co., 1948.

02061. Van de Wiel, C. "La légitimation par mariage subsequent,
        de Constantin à Justinien. Sa réception sporadique dans
        le droit byzantin." Revue internationale des droits
        antiquité 25 (1978): 307-350.

02062. Vogt, Heinrich. Studien zum senatus consultum Velleianum.
        Bonn: L. Rohrscheid, 1952

02063. Volterra, Edoardo. "La conception du mariage à Rome."
       Revue internationale des droits de l'antiquité 3rd ser.
       2 (1955): 365-379.

02064 _____. La conception du mariage d'après les jur-
       istes romains. Paris: Tip editrice "La Garangola", 1940.

       Also refer to #1835, 2303, 2379, 2436, 2438, 2439, 2442.

                        (2) Women

02065. Bagnani, G. "The Case of the Poisoned Mushrooms."
       Phoenix 1 (June 1946): 15-20.

02066. Castillo Alvarez, A. del. La Emancipacion de la mujer
       romana en el siglo l.d.c. Granada: Universidad de
       Granada, 1976.

02067. Cicero. "For Caelius." In The Basic Works of Cicero,
       translated by Richard Y. Hathorne and edited by Moses
       Hadas, pp. 295-336. New York: The Modern Library, 1951.

02068. Crook, J.A. "Patria Potestas." Classical Quarterly 17
       (1967): 113-122.

02069. Durry, Marcel. "Le mariage des filles impuberes dans la
       Rome antique." Revue internationale des droits de
       l'antiquité 3rd ser. 2 (1955): 263-273.

02070. Gaudemet, Jean. "Le Statut de la femme dans l'empire romain."
       Recueils de la société Jean Bodin 11 (1959): 191-222.

02071. Hermann, Claudine. Le rôle judiciare et politique des femmes
       sous le république romaine. Berchem, Brussels: Latomus,
       1964.

02072. Kattenhorn, L. Über Intercessionen der Frauen nach
       römischen Rechten. Frankfurt a.M.: Kelp, 1970.

02073. Noailles, Pierre. "Le Procès de Virginia." Revue des
       études latines 20 (1942): 106-138.

02074. Pierret, Paul. Le Senatus consulte Velleien: étude sur
       l'incapacité civile de la femme à Rome. Thuillies: Les
       Editions Ramgal, 1947.

02075. Pomeroy, Sarah B. "The Relationship of the Married Woman
       to Her Blood Relatives in Rome." Ancient Society 7
       (1976): 215-227.

02076. Townsend, G.B. "The Trial of Aemilia Lepida in A.D. 20."
        Latomus 21 (July-September 1962): 484-493.

02077. Villers, Robert. "Le Statut de la femme à Rome jusqu'à la
        fin de la république." Recueils de la Société Jean Bodin
        11 (1959): 117-189.

c) Feminism

02078. Fau, Guy. L'Emancipation féminine dans la Rome antique.
        Paris: Société d'édition, 1978.

02079. Lewis, Naphtali. "On Paternal Authority in Roman Egypt."
        Revue internationale des droits de l'antiquité 17 (1970):
        251-258.

02080. Teufer, Johannes. Zur Geschichte der Frauenemanzipation
        im Alten Rom: Eine Studie zu Livius 34, 1-8. Leipzig:
        B.G. Teubner, 1913.

d) Political Roles

(1) Women

02081. Austin, L. "The Caerellia of Cicero's Correspondence."
        Classical Journal 41 (April 1946): 305-309.

02082. Babcock, Charles L. "The Early Career of Fulvia."
        American Journal of Philology 86 (January 1965): 1-32.

02083. Babelon, J. Les Impératrices syriennes. Paris: Editions
        Albin Michel, 1957.

02084. Bartels, H. Studien zum Frauenportrat der Augusteischen
        Zeit: Fulvia, Octavia, Livia, Julia. Munich: Feder,
        1963.

02085. Bellezza, A. "Cecilia Paolina." In Tetraonyma: Miscellanea
        Graeco-Romana, pp. 75-83. Genoa: Instituto di Filologia
        Classica e Medioevale, 1966.

02086. Boyance, P. "L'Apothéose de Tullia." Revue des études
        anciennes 46 (1944): 179-184.

02087. Boyé, A.J. "Pro Petronia Iusta." In Mélanges Henri Levy-
        Bruhl, pp. 29-48. Paris: Sirey, 1959.

02088. Buckler, Georgina Grenfell. Anna Comnena. A Study. London:
        Oxford University Press, 1929.

02089. Bury, J.B. "Justa Grata Honoria." Journal of Roman
        Studies 9 (1919): 1-13.

02090. Calderini, Aristide. Le Donne dei Severi. Rome: Instituto di
        Studi Romani, 1945.

02091. Cameron, A. "The Empress Sophia." Byzantion 45 (1975):
        5-21.

02092. Carandini, Andrea. Vibia Sabina: Funzione politica,
        inconografia, e il problema del classicismo Adrianeo.
        Florence: Leo S. Olschki, 1969.

02093. Chastagnol, Andre. "Les femmes dans l'ordre senatorial:
        titulature et rang social à Rome." Revue historique
        (Paris) 104 (July-September 1979): 3-28.

02094. Corradi, Giuseppi. Cornelia e Sempronia. Rome: Instituto
        di Studi Romani, 1946.

02095. Daltrop, George; Hausmann, Ulrich; and Wegner, Max. Die
        Flavier: Vespasian, Titus, Domitia, Nerva, Julia Titi,
        Domitilla, Domitia. Berlin: Mann, 1966.

02096. Dalven, Rae. Anna Comnena. New York: Twayne Publishers,
        1972.

02097. Deutsch, Monroe E. "Caesar's First Wife." Classical
        Philology 12 (January 1917): 93-96.

02098. _____. "The Women of Caesar's Family."
        Classical Journal 13 (April 1918): 502-514.

02099. Diehl, Charles. Byzantine Empresses. Translated by
        Harold Bell and Theresa de Kerpely. New York: Knopf,
        1963.

02100. Diener, Bertha. Imperial Byzantium. Boston: Little,
        Brown, 1938.

02101. Dorey, T.A. "Cicero, Clodia and the Pro Caelio." Greece
        and Rome 2nd ser. 5 (1958): 175-180.

02102. Ferrero, Guglielmo. Women of the Caesars. Translated by
        Christian Gauss. New York: Century Co., 1911.

02103. _____. "The Women of the Caesars." Century
        Magazine 82 (May-October 1911): 3-14, 225-239, 399-414,
        610-623, 651-665, 806-823.

02104. Giacosa, Giorgio. Portraits of the Women of the Caesars.
       Translated by R. Ross Holloway. Montclair, N.J.: Abner
       Schram, 1977.

02105. Gobl, Robert. Regalianus und Dryantilla: Dokumentation,
       Münzen, Texte, Epigraphisches. Cologne: Bohlau, 1970.

02106. Hamilton, Gail. "The Ladies of the Last Caesars." North
       American Review 151 (November 1890): 548-566.

02107. Hayne, L. "M. Lepidus and his Wife." Latomus 33 (1974):
       76-79.

02108. Hillard, T.W. "The Sisters of Clodius again." Latomus 32
       (1973): 505-514.

02109. Johnson, W.H. "The Sister-in-Law of Cicero." Classical
       Journal 8 (January 1913): 160-165.

02110. Leon, Ernestine F. "Notes on Caecilia Attica." Classical
       Bulletin 38 (January 1962): 35-36.

02111. _____. "Scribonia and Her Daughters." Trans-
       actions and Proceedings of the American Philological
       Association 82 (1951): 168-175.

02112. McCabe, Joseph. The Empresses of Rome. New York: H.
       Holt and Co., 1911.

02113. McDermott, William C. "The Sisters of P. Clodius."
       Phoenix 24 (Spring 1970): 39-47.

02114. Macurdy, Grace Harriet. "Iotape." Journal of Roman
       Studies 26 (1936): 40-42.

02115. Malcovati, Enrica. Clodia, Fulvia, Marzia, Terenzia.
       Donne di Roma Antica, No. 1. Rome: Instituto di Studi
       Romani, 1944.

02116. Marshall, Anthony J. "Tacitus and the Governor's Lady."
       Greece and Rome 2nd ser. 22 (April 1975): 11-18.

02117. Mattingly, Harold. "The Consecration of Faustina the
       Elder and Her Daughter." Harvard Theological Review
       41 (April 1948): 147-151.

02118. Mazzarino, Santo. Serena e le Due Eudossie. Donne di
       Roma Antica, no. 7. Rome: Instituto di Studi Romani,
       1946.

02119. Mommsen, Theodor. "Porcia." Hermes 15 (1880): 99-102.

02120. Mullens, H.G. "The Women of the Caesars." Greece and
       Rome 11 (February 1942): 59-67.

02121. Oliver, James H. "The Empress Plotina and the Sacred
        Thymelic Synod. Historia 24 (1975): 125-128.

02122. _____. "Lollia Paulina, Memmius Regulus and
        Caligula." Hesperia 35 (April-June 1966): 150-153.

02123. Paratore, Ettore. Plotina, Sabina e le Due Faustine.
        Donne di Roma Antica, no. 2. Rome: Instituto di Studi
        Romani, 1945.

02124. Paris, Pierre. Quatenus Feminae Res Publicas in Asia
        Minore, Romanis Imperantibus, Attigerint. Paris: E.
        Thorin, 1891.

02125. Pastorino, A. "La Sempronia della Congiura di Catilina."
        Giornale italiano di filologia 3 (1950), 358-363.

02126. Perowne, Stewart. The Caesars' Wives: Above Suspicion?
        London: Hodder and Stoughton, 1974.

02127. Pfister, Kurt. Die Frauen der Casaren. Berlin: A. Nauck,
        1951.

02128. Rankin, H.D. "Clodia II." L'Antiquité classique 38 (1969):
        501-506.

02129. Richmond, I.A. "Queen Cartimandus." Journal of Roman
        Studies 44 (1954): 43-52.

02130. Rogers, Robert Samuel. "Fulvia Paulina C. Sentii Saturnini."
        American Journal of Philology 53 (July 1932): 252-256.

02131. _____. "An Incident of the Opposition to
        Tiberius." Classical Journal 47 (December 1951): 114-115.

02132. Rouge, Jean. "Justine, la belle Sicilienne." Latomus 33
        (1974): 676-679.

02133. Rowland, Robert G. "Sallust's Wife." Classical World 62
        (December 1968): 134.

02134. Rumpf, Andreas. Antonia Augusta. Berlin: W. de Gruyter,
        1941.

02135. Rutland, Linda W. "Women as Makers of Kings in Tacitus'
        Annals." Classical World 72 (September 1978): 15-29.

02136. Scheid, J. "Scribonia Caesaris et les Cornelii Lentuli."
        Bulletin de correspondance hellenique 100 (1976): 485-491.

02137. Schmidt, Otto Eduard. Cicero und Terentia. Leipzig:
        B.G. Teubner, 1898.

02138. Scott, R.D. "The Death of Nero's Mother. (Tacitus.
        Annals XIV: 1-13.)." Latomus 33 (1974): 105-115.

02139. Serviez, Jacques Roergas de. Lives of the Roman Empresses:
        The History of the Lives and Secret Intrigues of the
        Wives, Sisters and Mothers of the Caesars. New York:
        Wm. H. Wise & Co., 1935.

02140. Small, Jocelyn Penny. "The Death of Lucretia." American
        Journal of Archaeology 80 (Fall 1976): 349-360.

02141. Smallwood, E. Mary. "The Alleged Jewish Tendencies of
        Poppaea Sabina." Journal of Theological Studies n.s. 10
        (October 1959): 329-335.

02142. Stadelmann, Heinrich. Messalina: A Picture of Life in
        Imperial Rome. Translated by H.F. Angold. New York:
        E.P. Dutton & Co., 1930.

02143. Suolahti, Jaakko. "Claudia Insons. Why Was a Fine Imposed
        on Claudia Ap.f. in 246 BC?" Arctos 11 (1977): 133-151.

02144. Syme, Ronald. "Sallust's Wife." Classical Quarterly 28
        (1978): 292-295.

02145. Temporini, Hildegard. Die Frauen am Hofe Trajans: Ein
        Beitrag zur Stellung der Augustae im Principat. Berlin:
        DeGruyter, 1978.

02146. Turton, Godfrey Edmund. The Syrian Princesses: The Women
        Who Ruled Rome. London: Cassell, 1974.

02147. Van Buren, A.W. "Pompeii--Nero--Poppaea." In Studies
        Presented to David Moore Robinson, edited by George E.
        Mylonas and Doris Raymond, 2: 970-974. St. Louis,
        Mo.: Washington University, 1953.

02148. Wegner, Max. Hadrian, Plotina, Marciana, Matidia, Sabina.
        Berlin: Mann, 1956.

02149. Weil, Bruno. Clodia: Roms Grosse Dame und Kurtisane.
        Zurich: W. Classen, 1960.

02150. Wiggers, Heinz Bernhard. Caracalla, Geta, Plautilla;
        bound with Max Wegner, Macrinus bis Balbinus. West
        Berlin: Gebrüder Mann, 1971.

02151. Williams, Richard S. "The Role of Amicitia in the Career
        of A. Gavinius (Cox. 58.)." Phoenix 32 (1978): 195-210.

02152. Wiseman, Carl. "Clodia: Some Imaginary Lives." Arion
        n.s.2(1975): 96-115.

        Also refer to #2016.

(2) Individuals

(a) Agrippina

02153. Alexander W. H. "The Communiqué to the Senate on Agrippina's
Death." Classical Philology 49 (April 1954): 94-97.

02154. Charlesworth, Martin P.   "The Banishment of the Elder
Agrippina." Classical Philology 17 (July 1922): 260-261.

02155. Dawson, A. "Whatever Happened to Lady Agrippina?"
Classical Journal 64 (March 1969): 253-267.

02156. Godolphin, Francis Richard Borroum. "A Note on the
Marriage of Claudius and Agrippina." Classical Philology
29 (April 1934): 143-145.

02157. Katzoff, Ranon. "Where was Agrippina Murdered?" Historia
22 (1973): 72-78.

02158. McDaniel, Walton Brooks. "Bauli the Scene of the Murder
of Agrippina." Classical Quarterly 4 (April 1910):
96-102.

02159. Paratore, Ettore. "Un Evento Clamoroso nella Roma di
Millenovecento Anni Fa." Studi Romani 7 (September-
October 1959): 497-510.

02160. Rogers, Robert Samuel. "The Conspiracy of Agrippina."
Transactions and Proceedings of the American Philological
Association 62 (1931): 141-168.

02161. Stahr, Adolph. Agrippina, die Mutter Neros. Berlin: J.
Guttentag, 1880.

02162. Tacitus. Agrippina: A Story of Imperial Rome. Edited
by J.B.E. Garstang. London: G. Bell & Sons, 1938.

(b) Berenice

02163   Crook, J.A. "Titus and Berenice." American Journal of
Philology 72 (April 1951): 162-175.

02164. Jordan, Ruth. Berenice. New York: Barnes and Noble, 1974.

02165. Macurdy, Grace Harriet. "Julia Berenice." American
Journal of Philology 56 (July 1935): 246-253.

02166. Mireaux, Emile. La Reine Berenice. Paris: Albin Michel,
        1951.

02167. Sullivan, Philip B. "A Note on the Flavian Accession."
        Classical Journal 49 (November 1953): 67-70, 78.

                        (c) Boudicca

02168. Bulst, Christoph M. "The Revolt of Queen Boudicca in
        A.D. 60." Historia 10 (1961): 497-509.

02169. Dudley, Donald Reynolds. "The Rebellion of Boudicca."
        History Today 10 (June 1960): 387-394.

02170. _____, and Webster, Graham. The Re-
        bellion of Boudicca. New York: Barnes and Noble, 1962.

02171. Du Toit, L. A. "Tacitus and the Rebellion of Boudicca."
        Acta Classica 20 (1977): 149-158.

02172. Pitt, John. "Boudicca's Rebellion." British History
        Illustrated 3 (1976): 46-55.

02173. Scott, James Maurice. Boadicea. London: Constable, 1975.

02174. Scott, M.A. "The Rebellion of Boudicca: The Burnt Layer
        and the Narrative of Tacitus." Pegasus 8 (1967): 12-14.

02175. Spence, Lewis. Boadicea, Warrior Queen of the Britons.
        London: Robert Hale, Ltd., 1937.

02176. Webster, Graham. Boudica, the British Revolt Against
        Rome, A.D. 60. Totowa, N.J.: Rowman and Littlefield, 1978.

                        (d) Cleopatra

02177. Bailly, August. Cleopatre. Paris: J. Tallandier, 1939.

02178. Bradford, Ernie D.S. Cleopatra. New York: Harcourt,
        Brace, Jovanovich, 1972.

02179. Grant, Michael. Cleopatra. London: Weidenfeld and
        Nicolson, 1972.

02180. Johnson, W. R. "A Quean, a Great Queen? Cleopatra and the
        Politics of Misrepresentation." Arion 6 (Autumn 1967):
        387-402.

02181. Levi, Mario Attilio. "Cleopatra e l'apside." La Parola del
        Passato 9 (1954): 293-295.

02182. Lindsay, Jack. Cleopatra. New York: Coward-McCann, 1970.

02183. Ludwig, Emil. Cleopatra: The Story of a Queen. New
        York: Viking Press, 1937.

02184. Scott, Kenneth. "The Political Propaganda of 44-30 B.C."
        Memoirs of The American Academy in Rome 11 (1933): 7-49.

02185. Tarn, William and Charlesworth, Martin P. Octavian,
        Antony and Cleopatra. Rev. ed. New Rochelle, N.Y.:
        Cambridge University Press, 1965.

02186. Volkmann, Hans. Cleopatra: A Study in Politics and
        Propaganda. Translated by T.J. Cadoux. New York:
        Sagamore Press Inc., 1958.

02187. Weigall, Arthur. The Life and Times of Cleopatra, Queen
        of Egypt. Rev. ed. New York: G.P. Putnam's Sons, 1924.

                    (e)   Galla Placidia

02188. Nagi, Maria Assunta. Galla Placidia. Studien zur Geschichte
        und Kultur des Altertums, vol. 2, no. 3. Paderborn:
        F. Schoningh, 1908.

02189. Oost, Stewart Irvin. "Galla Placidia and the Law."
        Classical Philology 63 (April 1968): 114-121.

02190. Oost, Stewart Irvin. Galla Placidia Augusta: A Biographi-
        cal Essay. Chicago: University of Chicago Press, 1968.

02191. _____. "Some Problems in the History of
        Galla Placidia." Classical Philology 60 (January 1965):
        1-10.

02192. Sirago, Vito Antonio. Galla Placidia e la trasformazione
        Politica dell' occidente. Recueil de Travaux d'histoire
        et de philologie, ser. 4, no. 25. Louvain: Bibliotheque
        de l'université catholique, 1961.

                    (f)   Julias

02193. Avery, W. "Julia and Lucius Vinicius." Classical
        Philology 30 (April 1935): 170-171.

02194. Benario, Herbert W. "Julia Domna--Mater Senatus et Patriae."
        Phoenix 12 (Summer 1958): 67-70.

02195. _____. "The Titulature of Julia Soaemias and
        Julia Mamaea: Two Notes." Transactions and Proceedings
        of the American Philological Association 90 (1959): 9-14.

02196.   Carcopino, Jerome. "La Véritable Julie." La Revue de
         Paris 65 (January 1958): 17-31 and 65 (February 1958):
         66-80.

02197.   Giannelli, Giulio. Giulia e Servilia. Donne di Roma
         Antica, no. 3. Rome: Instituto di Studi Romani, 1945.

02198.   Gross, Walter Hatto. Iulia Augusta: Untersuchungen zur
         Grundlegung einer Livia-Ikonographie. Göttingen:
         Vandenhoeck & Ruprecht, 1962.

02199.   Levick, Barbara. "The Fall of Julia the Younger."
         Latomus 35 (1976): 301-339.

02200.   Olson, H. "The Five Julias of the Severan Emperors."
         The Voice of the Turtle 4 (1965): 197.

02201.   Ritter, Hans-Werner. "Livias Erhebung zur Augusta." Chiron
         2 (1972): 313-338.

02202.   Rogers, Robert Samuel. "The Deaths of Julia and Gracchus,
         A.D. 14." Transactions and Proceedings of the American
         Philological Association 98 (1967): 383-390.

02203.   Wild, Payson S. "Two Julias." Classical Journal 13
         (October 1917): 14-24.

02204.   Williams, Mary Gilmore. "Studies in the Lives of Roman
         Empresses, I: Julia Domna." American Journal of
         Archaeology 6 (1902): 259-305.

02205.   _____. "Studies in the Lives of Roman
         Empresses, II: Julia Mamaea." In Roman Historical
         Sources and Institutions, edited by Henry A. Sanders,
         pp. 67-100. 1904. Reprint. New York: Johnson Reprint
         Corp., 1967.

         Also refer to #2084, 2095, 2497.

(g) Livias

02206.   Alexander, C. "A Portrait of Livia." The Metropolitan
         Museum of Art Bulletin 11 (February 1953): 168-171.

02207.   Charlesworth, Martin P. "Livia and Tanaquil." Classical
         Review 41 (May 1927): 55-57.

02208.   Deckman, A.A. "Livia Augusta." Classical Weekly 19
         (19 October 1925): 21-25.

02209.   Esdaile, K.A. "The Aged Livia." Journal of Roman
         Studies 4 (1914): 139-141.

02210. Gardner, Percy. "A New Portrait of Livia." Journal of
        Roman Studies 12 (1922): 32-34.

02211. Grether, Gertrude E. "Livia and the Roman Imperial Cult."
        American Journal of Philology 67 (July 1946): 222-252.

02212. Oliver, James H. "Livia as Artemis Boulaia at Athens."
        Classical Philology 60 (July 1965): 179.

02213. Willrich, Hugo. Livia. Leipzig: B.G. Teubner, 1911.

02214. Wiseman, T.P. "The Mother of Livia Augusta." Historia
        14 (July 1965): 333-334.

        Also refer to #2084, 2496, 2498, 2503.

                        (h)   Octavia

02215. Doer, Bruno. "Octavia: Eine Aussergewöhnliche Frau des
        alten Rom." Das Altertum 14 (1968): 20-31.

02216. Raubitschek, Antony E. "Octavia's Deification at Athens."
        Transactions of the American Philological Association
        77 (1946): 146-150.

02217. Singer, Mary White. "Octavia's Mediation at Tarentum."
        Classical Journal 43 (December 1947): 173-177.

02218. _____. "The Problem of Octavia Minor and
        Octavia Major." Transactions and Proceedings of the
        American Philological Association 79 (1948): 268-274.

        Also refer to #2084.

                        (i)   Theodora

02219. Bridge, A. Theodora: Portrait of a Byzantine Landscape.
        London: Cassell, 1978.

02220. Browning, Robert. Justinian and Theodora. New York:
        Praeger Publishers, 1971.

02221. Diehl, Charles. Theodora. Translated by Samuel Rosenbaum.
        New York: F. Unger Publishing Co., 1972.

02222. Fisher, Elizabeth A. "Theodora and Antonina in the
        Historia Arcana: History and/or Fiction?" Arethusa 11
        (Spring and Fall 1978): 253-279.

02223. Fitton, James. "The Death of Theodora." <u>Byzantion</u> 46
          (1976): 119.

02224. Holmes, William Gordon. <u>The Age of Justinian and
          Theodora</u>. 2 vols. London: G. Bell and Sons, 1912.

02225. Lamb, Harold. <u>Theodora and the Emperor: The Drama of
          Justinian</u>. Garden City, N.Y.: Doubleday, 1952.

02226. Mallett, C.E. "The Empress Theodora." <u>English Historical
          Review</u> 2 (January 1887): 1-20.

02227. Schubart, Wilhelm. <u>Justinian and Theodora</u>. Munich:
          F. Bruckmann, 1943.

                    (j) Zenobia

02228. Downey, G. "Aurelian's Victory over Zenobia at Immae,
          A.D. 272." <u>Transactions and Proceedings of the American
          Philological Association</u> 81 (1950): 57-68.

02229. Gay, Stewart Irwin. "The Beautiful Queen Zenobia."
          <u>Transactions and Proceedings of the American Philological
          Association</u> 71 (1940): xxxv-xxxvi.

02230. Vaughan, Agnes Carr. <u>Zenobia of Palmyra</u>. New York:
          Doubleday and Co., 1967.

02231. Wright, William. <u>An Account of Palmyra and Zenobia, with
          Travels and Adventures in Bashan and the Desert</u>. New
          York: Thomas Nelson and Sons, 1895.

4. RELIGION/MYTHOLOGY

            "Mother of the Roman race, delight of men and gods"
                        Lucretius' address to Venus
                        <u>On the Nature of the Universe</u>

                    a) Generic

                    (1) Non-specific

02232. Altheim, F. <u>A History of Roman Religion</u>. Translated by H.
          Mattingly. London: Methuen and Co., Ltd., 1938.

02233. Bailey, Cyril. Phases in the Religion of Ancient Rome. 1932.
        Reprint. Westport, Conn.: Greenwood Press, 1972.

02234. Tran Tam Tinh, V. Le culte des divinites orientales à
        Herculaneum. Leiden: Brill, 1971.

02235. _____. Le culte des divinites orientales
        en Campanie. Leiden: Brill, 1972.

02236. Wissowa, Georg. Religion und Kultus der Römer. Handbuch der
        klassischen Altertumswissenschaft, vol. 5. Munich: C. H.
        Beck'sche Verlagshandlung, 1912.

        Also refer to #2388.

                        (2) Women

02237. Gagé, Jean. Matronalia: Essai sur les devotions et les
        organisations cultuelles des femmes dans l'ancienne
        Rome. Collection Latomus, no. 60. Brussels: Latomus,
        Revue d'etudes latines, 1963.

02238. Pichon, Rene. "Le Rôle religieux des femmes dans l'ancienne
        Rome." Annales du Musee Guimet, bibliothèque de vul-
        garisation 39 (1912): 77-135.

                     b) Goddesses

                    (1) Individuals

                      (a) Isis

02239. Grandjean, Yves. Une nouvelle aretalogie d'Isis à Maronee.
        Etudes preliminaires aux religions orientales dans l'Empire
        Romain, vol. 49. Leiden: E. J. Brill, 1975.

02240. Heybob, Sharon Kelly. The Cult of Isis among Women in the
        Graeco-Roman World. Etudes preliminaires aux religions
        orientales dans l'Empire Romain, vol. 51. Leiden: E. J.
        Brill, 1975.

02241. Tran Tam Tinh, V. Le culte d'Isis à Pompei. Paris: Editions
        J. De Boccard, 1964.

(b) Tanaquil

02242. Euing, Ludwig. Die Sage von Tanaquil. Frankfurt a.M.:
         V. Klostermann, 1933.

02243. Gage, J. "Tanaquil et les Rites Etrusques de la 'Fortune
         Oiseleuse'; de l'   Magique au Fuseau de Gaia Caecilia."
         Studi Etruschi 22 (1952-1953): 79-102.

(2) Others

02244. Fliedner, H. Amor und Cupid. Untersuchungen über römischen
         Liebesgott. Meisenheim am Glan: Hain, 1974.

02245. Le Bonniec, Henri. Le culte de Ceres à Rome. Paris:
         Klincksieck, 1958.

c) Sibyls

02246. Bigonzo, Guiseppe. Le Sibille e i Libri Sibillini di Roma:
         Cenni Critico-Storici. 2nd ed. Geneva: Sordomuti, 1885.

02247. Bousset, Wilhelm. "Sibyllen und Sybillinische Bücher."
         Realencyclopadie für protestantischen Theologie und
         Kirche, edited by Albert Hauck, 18: 265-280. Leipzig:
         J. C. Hinrich's Verlag, 1903-1906.

02248. The Sibylline Oracles. Translated by Milton S. Terry. New
         York: Hunt & Eaton, 1890.

02249. Wolff, Max J. "Sibyllen und Sibyllinen." Archiv für
         Kulturgeschichte 24 (1934): 312-325.

d) Vestal Virgins

02250. Beard, Mary J. "The Sexual Status of Vestal Virgins."
         Journal of Roman Studies 70 (1980): 12-127.

02251. Bowen, E. "The Virgins and the Empress." Harper's
         Magazine 219 (November 1959): 50-55.

02252. Hadas, Moses. "Vestal Virgins and Runaway Slaves."
        Classical Weekly 24 (2 February 1931): 108.

02253. Howard, Albert Andrew. "The Institution of the Vestal
        Virgins at Rome." Overland Monthly 2nd ser. 16
        (August 1890): 136-149.

02254. Jordan, E. Der Tempel der Vesta und das Haus der
        Vestalinnen. Berlin: Weidmann, 1886.

02255. Meeker, Arthur. Vestal Virgin. New York: G.P. Putnam's
        Sons, 1934.

02256. Preuner, August. Hestia-Vesta: Ein Zyklus Religions-
        geschichtlicher Forschungen. Tübingen: Laupp, 1864.

02257. Rose, Herbert J. "De Virginibus Vestalibus." Mnemosyne
        2nd ser. 54 (1926): 440-448.

02258. _____. "Iterum de Virginibus Vestalibus."
        Mnemosyne 2nd ser. 56 (1928): 79-80.

02259. Schilling, Robert. "Vestales et vierges chrétiennes dans
        la Rome antique." Revue des sciences religieuses 35
        (April 1961): 113-129.

02260. Wissowa, Georg. "Vestalinnenfrevel." Archiv für
        Religionsgeschichte 22 (1923-1924): 201-214.

02261. Worsfold, Sir Thomas Cato. The History of the Vestal
        Virgins of Rome. London: Rider and Co., 1934.

e) Jews

02262   Leon, Harry J. "The Daughters of Gadias." Transactions of
        the American Philological Association 84 (1953): 67-72.

f) Early Christianity

(1) Non-specific

02263. Aubert, Jean Marie. La Femme antiféminisme et christianisme
        Paris: Cerf./Desclee, 1975.

02264. Augar, Friedrich. Die Frau im römischen Christenprozess.
        Leipzig: J.C. Hinrichs, 1905.

02265. Bardis, Panos D. "Early Christianity and the Family."
        Sociological Bulletin 13 (1964): 1-23.

02266. Blum, Georg. "Das Amt der Frau im Neuen Testament." Novum
        Testamentum 7 (March 1964): 142-161.

02267. Campbell, J.A. "Virgins Consecrated to God in Rome during
        the First Centuries." American Catholic Quarterly Review
        25 (1900): 766-799.

02268. Crouzel, Henri. L'eglise primitive face au divorce, du
        premier au cinquième siècle. Théologie historique,
        no. 13. Paris: Beauchesne, 1971.

02269. Davies, Steven L. The Revolt of the Widows: The Social
        World of the Apocryphal Acts. Carbonsdale, Ill.:
        Southern Illinois University Press, 1980.

02270. Eckenstein, Lina. The Women of Early Christianity. Mil-
        waukee: Morehouse Publishing Co., 1935.

02271. Falk, Ze'ev. "Über die Ehe in den biblischen Prophetien."
        Zeitschrift der Savigny Stiftung für Rechtgeschichte
        (Romanistische Abteilung) 90 (1973): 36-44.

02272. Fiorenza, Elisabeth Schussler. "Women in the Early Christian
        Movement." In Womanspirit Rising, edited by Carol P. Christ
        and Judith Plaskow, pp. 84-92. New York: Harper and Row,
        1979.

02273. _____. "You are not to be called
        Father: early Christian History in a Feminist Perspective."
        Cross Currents 29 (Fall 1979): 301-333.

02274. Julicher, A. "Die geistlichen Ehe in der alten Kirche."
        Archiv für Religionswissenschaft 7 (1904): 373-386.

02275. Kirsch, Johann Peter. Die Frauen des kirchlichen Altertums.
        Paderborn: Ferdinand Schoningh, 1920.

02276. Klauser, Theodor. "Studien zur Entstehungsgeschichte der
        christlichen Kunst." Jahrbuch für Antike und Christentum
        2 (1959): 115-145; 3 (1960): 112-133.

02277. Klawiter, Frederick C. "The Role of Martyrdom and Persecution
        in Developing the Priestly Authority of Women in Early
        Christianity: A Case Study of Montanism." Church History
        49 (September 1980): 251-261.

02278. Knudsen, Johannes. "The Lady and the Emperor A Study in
        the Domitian Persecution." Church History 14 (March 1945):
        17-32.

02279. Kretschmar, Georg. "Ein Beitrag zur Frage nach den Ursprung
        des frühchristlicher Askese." Zeitschrift für Theologie
        und Kirche 61 (April 1964): 27-67.

02280. La Bonnardière, Anne Marie. Chrétiennes des premiers
        siècles. Paris: Editions Ouvrières, 1957.

02281. Laland, Erling. "Die Martha-Maria-Peri Kope Lukas 10. 38-42."
        Studia Theologica 13 (1959): 70-85.

02282. Lanslots, Ildephonse. The Primitive Church; or the Church in
        the Days of the Apostles. St. Louis: Herder, 1926.

02283. Leclercq, Henri. "Femme." In Dictionnaire d'archéologie
        chretienne et de liturgie V, pp. 1300-1353. Paris:
        Librairie Letouzey et Ane, 1922.

02284. Lord, Mary Louise. "Dido as an Example of Chastity."
        Harvard Library Bulletin 17 (1969): 22-44.

02285. McLoughlin, Eleanor L. "The Christian Past: Does it Hold a
        Future for Women?" In Womanspirit Rising, edited by Carol
        P. Christ and Judith Plaskow, pp. 93-106. New York: Harper
        and Row, 1979.

02286. McNamara, JoAnn. "Wives and Widows in Early Christian
        Thought." International Journal of Women's Studies 2
        (1979): 575-592.

02287. Meeks, Wayne. "The Image of the Androgyne: Some Uses of a
        Symbol in Earliest Christianity." History of Religion 13
        (1973-1974): 165-208.

02288. Meyer, Charles. Ordained Women in the Early Christian
        Church. Chicago: Chicago Studies, 1965.

02289. Milman, Henry Hart. The history of Christianity, from the
        birth of Christ to the abolition of paganism in the Roman
        Empire. 1863. Reprint. New York: AMS Press, 1978.

02290. Pagels, Elaine H. "What Became of God the Mother? Conflict-
        ing Images of God in Early Christianity." Signs 2 (Winter
        1976): 293-303. Also in Womanspirit Rising, edited by
        Carol P. Christ and Judith Plaskow, pp. 107-119. New York:
        Harper and Row, 1979.

02291. Palmer, Robert E.A. "Roman Shrines of Female Chastity
        from the Caste Struggle to the Papacy of Innocent I."
        Revista storica dell'antichita 4 (1974): 294-309.

02292. Parvey, Constance. "The Theology and Leadership of Women in
        the New Testament." In Religion and Sexism, edited by Rose-
        mary Ruether, pp. 117-149. New York: Simon and Schuster,
        1974.

02293. Preisker, Herbert. Christentum und Ehe in den ersten drei
        Jahrhunderten. Berlin: Trowitzsch & Sohn, 1927.

02294. Stocker, Lydia. Die Frau in der alten Kirche. Tübingen: Mohr, 1907.

02295. Thomas, W. Derek. "The Place of Women in the Church at Philippi." Expository Times 83 (1971-1972): 117-120.

02296. Thraede, K. "Frau." In Reallexikon für Antike und Christentum VIII, pp. 227-268. Stuttgart: Anton Hiersemann, 1972.

02297. Wilpert, Joseph. Die gottgeweihten Jungfrauen in den ersten Jahrhunderten der Kirche. Freiburg-im-Breisgau: Herder, 1892.

02298. Yarbrough, Anne. "Christianization in the Fourth Century: The Example of Roman Women." Church History 45 (June 1976): 149-165.

02299. Zscharnack, Leopold. Der Dienst der Frau in den ersten Jahrhunderten der christlichen Kirche. Gottingen: Vandenhoeck & Ruprecht, 1902.

Also refer to #2396, 2415.

(2) St. Paul

02300. Allmen, Daniel van. "L'homme et la femme dans les textes pauliniens." Foi et Vie 70 Supplement (1970): 157-181.

02301. Baltensweiler, H. Die Ehe im Neuen Testament. Zurich: Zwingli Verlag, 1967.

02302. Caird, G. B. "Paul and Women's Liberty." Bulletin of the John Rylands Library 54 (Spring 1972): 268-281.

02303. Dauvillier, Jean. "Le droit du mariage dans les cités grecques et hellénistiques d'après les écrits de Saint Paul." Revue internationale des droits de l'antique 3rd ser. 7 (1960): 149-164.

02304. Delling, Gerhard. Paulus' Stellung zu Frau und Ehe. Stuttgart: Kohlhammer, 1931.

02305. Hall, Barbara. "Paul and Women." Theology Today 31 (April 1974): 50-55.

02306. Kahler, Else. Die Frau in den Paulinischen Briefen unter besonderer Berucksichtigung des Begriffs der Unterordnung. Zurich: Gotthelf-Verlag, 1960.

02307. Kahler, Else. "Zur 'Unterordnung' der Frau im Neuen Testament." Zeitschrift für Evangelische Ethik 3 (1959): 1-13.

02308. Munro, Winsome. "Patriarchy and Charismatic Community in
        'Paul.'" In Women and Religion, edited by Judith Plaskow
        and Joan Arnold Romero, pp. 189-198. Missoula, Mt.:
        American Academy of Religion and Scholar's Press, 1974.

02309. Scroggs, Robin. "Paul and the Eschatological Woman."
        Journal of the American Academy of Religion 40 (September
        1972): 283-303.

02310. _____. "Paul: Chauvinist or Liberationist?" The
        Christian Century 89 (15 March 1972): 307-309.

02311. Smith, Derwood C. "Paul and Non-Eschatological Women."
        Ohio Journal of Religious Studies 4 (March 1976): 11-18.

02312. Trompf, G. "On Attitudes toward Women in Paul and Paulinist
        Literature: 1 Corinthians 11:3-16 and Its Context."
        Catholic Biblical Quarterly 42 (1980): 196-215.

02313. Williams, Don. The Apostle Paul and Women in the Church.
        Glendale, Ca.: Regal Books, 1979.

                    (3)   Fathers of the Church

                        (a)   General

02314. Crouzel, Henri. "Separation ou remariage selon les Pères
        anciens." Gregorianum 47 (1966): 472-494.

02315. Ruether, Rosemary. "Misogynism and Virginal Feminism in
        the Fathers of the Church." In Religion and Sexism,
        edited by Rosemary Ruether, pp. 150-183. New York:
        Simon and Schuster, 1974.

                        (b)   Individuals

                    [1] ST. AMBROSE

02316. Ambrosius, Saint, Bishop of Milan. Letters. Vol. 26 in
        Fathers of the Church, edited by R.J. Defferari. New
        York: Fathers of the Church Inc., 1954.
        [See especially letter 44, pp. 225-230 on virginity.]

02317. Dooley, William Joseph. Marriage according to St. Ambrose.
        Studies in Christian Antiquity, no. 11. Washington, D.C:
        The Catholic University Press, 1948.

[2] ST. AUGUSTINE

02318.   Augustinus Aurelius, saint, bishop of Hippo. <u>Treatises</u>
          <u>on Marriage and Other Subjects</u>. Vol. 27 in <u>Fathers of</u>
          <u>the Church</u> edited by R.J. Deferrari. New York: Fathers
          of the Church Inc., 1955.
          [See especially The Good of Marriage, pp. 9-51; Adulterous
          Marriages, pp. 55-132; Holy Virginity, pp. 135-212.]

02319.   _____. <u>Treatises on</u>
          <u>Various Subjects</u>. Vol. 16 in <u>Fathers of the Church</u>,
          edited by R.J. Deferrari. New York: Fathers of the
          Church Inc., 1952.
          [See especially On Widows, pp. 41-43, 267-319.]

02320.   Borreson, Kari-Elisabeth. <u>Subordination et équivalence</u>.
          <u>Nature et role de la femme d'après Augustin et Thomas</u>
          <u>d'Aquin</u>. Oslo: Universitets Forlaget, 1968.

02321.   O'Meara, John J. "St. Augustine's Attitude to Love in
          the Context of His Influence on Christian Ethics."
          <u>Arethusa</u> 2 (Spring 1969): 46-60.

[3] ST. BASIL

02322.   Basilius, saint, the great, archbishop of Caesarea.
          <u>Letters</u>. Vol. 13 in <u>Fathers of the Church</u>, edited by
          R.J. Deferrari. New York: Fathers of the Church, Inc.,
          1951.
          [See especially letter 46, To a Fallen Virgin, pp.
          118-128.]

02323.   _____.
          <u>Letters</u>. Vol. 28 in <u>Fathers of the Church</u>, edited by
          R.J. Deferrari. New York: Fathers of the Church, Inc.,
          1955.
          [See especially letter 199, To Amphilochius (re: marriage),
          pp. 47-62.]

[4] ST. JOHN CHRYSOSTOM

02324.   Dacier, Henriette. <u>Saint Jean Chrysostome et la femme</u>
          <u>chretienne au IVe siècle de l'église grecque</u>. Paris:
          H. Falque, 1907.

02325. Dumortier, J. "Le mariage chrétien dans les milieux
        d'Antioche et de Byzance d'après saint Jean Chrysostome."
        Lettres d'humanité 6 (1947): 102-166.

        Also refer to #2328.

[5] ST. CYPRIAN

02326. Cyprianus, saint, bishop of Carthage. Treatises Vol. 36
        in Fathers of the Church, edited by R.J. Deferrari.
        New York: Fathers of the Church, 1958.
        [See especially The Dress of Virgins, pp. 25-52.]

[6] ST. JEROME

02327. Campbell, Gerald J. "St. Jerome's Attitude Toward
        Marriage and Women." American Ecclesiastical Review
        143 (1960): 310-320, 384-394.

02328. Clark, Elizabeth, ed. Jerome, Chrysostom, and Friends:
        Essays and Translations. Studies in Women and Religion,
        vol. 2. Lewiston, N.Y.: Edwin Mellen Press, 1979.

02329. Kelly, J.N.D. Jerome: His Life, Writings and Con-
        troversies. New York: Harper and Row, 1976.
        [See especially ch. 10, Jerome and early christian
        women.]

02330. St. Jerome. Select Letters of St. Jerome. Translated
        by F.A. Wright. New York: G.P. Putnam's Sons, 1933.
        [See especially letters 22, 38, 54, 107, 128.]

02331. Turcan, M. "Saint Jerome et les femmes." Bulletin de
        l'association Guillaume Budé 4th ser. (1968): 259-272.

[7] ST. TERTULLIAN

02332. Church, F. F. "Sex and Salvation in Tertullian." Harvard
        Theological Review 68 (April 1975): 83-101.

02333. Stücklin, Christoph. Tertullian de virginibus velandis.
        Übersetzung, Einleitung, Kommentar. Ein Betrag zur
        altkirchlichen Frauenfrage. Frankfurt: Peter Lang,
        1974.

02334.   Tertullianus, Quintus Septimius Florens. Disciplinary,
         Moral and Ascetical Works. Vol. 40 in Fathers of the
         Church, edited by R.J. Deferrari. New York: Fathers
         of the Church, 1959.
         [See especially The Apparel of Women, pp. 111-149.]

02335.   _____. "On Exhortation to Chastity." In The Ante-
         Nicene Fathers 4: 50-58. New York: Charles Scribner's
         Sons, 1905.

02336.   _____. "On Modesty." In The Ante-Nicene Fathers
         4: 74-101. New York: Charles Scribner's Sons, 1905.

02337.   _____. "On Monogamy." In The Ante-Nicene Fathers
         4: 59-73. New York: Charles Scribner's Sons, 1905.

02338.   _____. "On the Veiling of Virgins." In The Ante-
         Nicene Fathers 4: 27-38. New York: Charles Scribner's
         Sons, 1905.

02339.   _____. La Toilette des femmes (de cultu feminarum).
         Translated by Marie Turcan. Paris: Les Editions du Cerf,
         1971.

02340.   _____. Treatises on Marriage and Remarriage.
         Translated by William P. LeSaint. Westminster, Md.:
         Newman Press, 1956.
         [See especially, To His Wife.]

                    (4) Saints/Religious Women

                        (a) Individuals

                    [1] ST. AGNES

02341.   Denomy, Alexander J. "An Anglo-French Life of Saint
         Agnes." Harvard Studies and Notes in Philology and
         Literature 16 (1934): 51-68.

02342.   _____. The Old French Lives of St. Agnes and
         Other Vernacular Versions of the Middle Ages. Cambridge,
         Mass.: Harvard University Press, 1938.

                    [2] ST. ANNE

02343.   Charland, Paul V. Madame Saincte Anne et son culte au
         Moyen Age. Paris: Picard, 1911.

02344. Emminghaus, Johann H. **Anna**. Heilige in Bild und Legende,
        no. 25. Recklinghausen: Verlag Aurel Bongers, 1968.

02345. Forster, Max. "Die Legende vom Trinubium der heiligen
        Anna." In Probleme der englischen Sprache und Kultur
        Festschrift Johannes Hoops zum 60. Geburtstag, pp. 105-
        130. Heidelberg: C. Winter, 1925.

[3] ST. CATHERINE OF ALEXANDRIA

02346. Knust, Hermann. Geschichte der Legenden der heiligen
        Katherina von Alexandrien und der heiligen Maria
        Aegyptiaca. Halle a.S.: Max Niemeyer, 1880.

02347. Roberts, Phyllis B. "Stephen Langton and St. Catherine
        of Alexandria: A Paris Master's Sermon on the Patron
        Saint of Scholars." Manuscripta 20 (July 1976): 96-104.

02348. Sudhof, Siegfried, ed. Die Legende der heiligen Katharina
        von Alexandrien. Texte des späten Mittelalters, no. 10.
        Berlin: Schmidt, 1959.

02349. Varnhagen, Hermann. Zur Geschichte der Legende der Katharina
        von Alexandrien. Erlangen: Verlag von Freidrich Junge,
        1891.

[4] ST. MARY MAGDALENE

02350. Garth, Helen Meredeth. Saint Mary Magdalene in Medieval Lit-
        erature. The Johns Hopkins University Studies in Historical
        and Political Science, no. 67. Baltimore: Johns Hopkins
        Press, 1950.

02351. Hengel, Martin. "Maria Magdalena und die Frauen als Zeugen."
        In Abraham unser Vater: Festschrift für O. Michel, Arbeiten
        zur Geschichte des Spätjudentums und Urchristentums 5,
        edited by Otto Betz, Martin Hengel and Peter Schmidt, pp.
        243-256. Leiden: E. J. Brill, 1963.

02352. Quivogne de Montifaud, Marie Amelie (Chartroule de Montifaud).
        Les Courtesanes de l'antiquité, Marie Magdaleine. Paris:
        Libraire internationale, 1870.

(b) Others

02353. Hunt, E.D. "St. Silvia of Aquitaine. The Role of a Theo-
dosian Pilgrim in the Society of East and West." Journal
of Theological Studies n.s. 23 (October 1972): 351-373.

02354. Lefkowitz, Mary R. "The Motivations for St. Perpetua's Martyrdom." Journal of American Academy of Religion 44 (1976):
417-421.

02355. Tervarent, Guy de. La Legende de Sainte Ursule dans la littérature et l'art du moyen âge. Paris: Les Editions G. van
Oest, 1931.

02356. Tout, Mary. "The Legend of St. Ursula and the Eleven Thousand
Virgins." In Historical Essays First published in 1902 in
commemoration of the Jubilee of the Owens College, Manchester, pp. 17-56. Manchester: University Press, 1903.

(5) Mariology

02357. Buonaiuti, Ernesto. "Die heilige Maria Immaculata in der
christlichen Überlieferung." In Eranos-Jahrbuch 1938,
edited by Olga Frobe-Kapteyn, pp. 364-402. Zurich:
Rhein-Verlag, 1939.

02358. _____. "Maria und die jungfrauliche Geburt
Jesu." In Eranos-Jahrbuch 1938, edited by Olga Frobe-
Kapteyn, pp. 325-363. Zurich: Rhein-Verlag, 1939.

02359. Conybeare, F. C. "Die jungfrauliche Kirche und die jungfrauliche Mutter Eine Studie über den Ursprung des
Mariendiensts." Archiv für Religionswissenschaft 8
(1905): 373-389 and 9 (1906): 73-86.

02360. Murray, Robert. "Mary, the second Eve in the early Syriac
Fathers." Eastern Churches Review 3 (1971): 372-384.

g) Celtic and Germanic Practices

02361. Collum, V.C.C. "Die schöpferische Mutter-Göttin der Volker
keltischer Sprache, ihr Werkzeug, das mystische 'Wort', ihr
Kult und ihre Kult-Symbole." In Eranos-Jahrbuch 1938, edited
by Olga Frobe-Kapteyn, pp. 221-324. Zurich: Rhein-Verlag,
1939.

02362. Helm, K. Waluburg die Wahrsagerin. Beiträge zur Geschichte
der deutschen Sprache und Literatur, edited by Wilhelm
Braune, vol. 43. Halle: M. Niemeyer, 1918.

02363. Herrmann, Paul. Das altgermanische Priesterwesen. Jena:
E. Diedrichs, 1929.

02364. Kendrick, Thomas Downing. The Druids: A Study in Keltic
Prehistory. London: Metheun & Co. Ltd., 1927.

02365. Schröder, Edward. "Walburg, die Sibylle." Archiv für
Religionswissenschaft 19 (1916-1919): 196-200.

02366. Vries, Jan de. Altgermanische Religionsgeschichte. 2 vols.
Berlin: de Gruyter, 1936-1937.
[See especially vol. 2, p. 123ff.]

5. SOCIAL

"I know the ways of women: they won't when thou wilt,
and when thou won't they are passionately fond."
                            Terence, Eunuchus

a) Generic

(1) Non-specific

02367. Alfoldy, Geza. Römische Sozialgeschichte. 2nd rev. ed.
Wiesbaden: Steiner, 1979.

02368. Arnold, Ralph. A Social History of England 55 B.C. to A.D.
1215. New York: Barnes and Noble, 1967.

02369. Balsdon, John Percy Vyvian Dacre. Life and Leisure in Ancient
Rome. New York: McGraw-Hill Book Co., 1969.

02370. Birley, Anthony R. Life in Roman Britain. New York: Putnam,
1964.
[See especially ch. 6, "Home Life," pp. 100-119.]

02371. Brunt, P.A. Social Conflicts in the Roman Republic. New
York: Norton, 1971.

02372. Carcopino, Jerome. Daily Life in Ancient Rome: The
People and the City at the Height of the Empire. New
Haven, Conn.: Yale University Press, 1960.
[See especially section 4.]

02373. Davis, W.S. A Day in Old Rome: A Picture of Roman Life.
        Boston: Allyn and Bacon, 1925.

02374. Dill, Samuel. Roman Society from Nero to Marcus Aurelius.
        London: Macmillan and Co., 1925.

02375. Etienne Robert. La vie quotidienne à Pompei. Paris:
        Hachette, 1966.

02376. Fowler, W. Warde. Social Life at Rome in the Age of Cicero.
        New York: Macmillan Co., 1933.
        [See especially ch. 5.]

02377. Frank, Tenney. Aspects of Social Behavior in Ancient
        Rome. Martin Classical Lectures, vol. 2. Cambridge,
        Mass.: Harvard University Press, 1932.

02378. Friedlander, Ludwig. Roman Life and Manners Under the
        Early Empire. Translated by Leonard A. Magnus. 4 vols.
        New York: Barnes & Noble, Inc., 1965.
        [See especially vol. 1, ch. 5.]

02379. Garnsey, Peter. Social Status and Legal Privilege in the
        Roman Empire. Oxford: Clarendon Press, 1970.

02380. Heurgon, Jacques. Daily Life of the Etruscans. Trans-
        lated by James Kirkup. New York: The Macmillan Co.,
        1964.
        [See especially ch. 4.]

02381. _____. "Valeurs féminines et masculines dans la
        civilisation étrusque." Mélanges d'archéologie et d'his-
        toire de l'école française de Rome 73 (1961): 139-160.

02382. Johnston, Harold Whetstone. The Private Lives of the
        Romans. Chicago: Scott, Foresman and Co., 1903.

02383. Johnston, Mary. Roman Life. Glenview, Ill.: Scott,
        Foresman and Company, 1957.

02384. Leffingwell, Georgia W. Social and Private Life at Rome
        in the Time of Plautus and Terrence. New York: Columbia
        University Press, 1918.

02385. McDaniel, Walton Brooks. Roman Private Life and its Survivals.
        Boston: Marshall Jones Company, 1924.

02386. Mau, August. Pompeii, Its Life and Art. New York: Mac-
        millan, 1902.

02387. Pfiffig, A.J. "Zur Sittengeschichte der Etrusker."
        Gymnasium 71 (1964): 17-36.

02388. Rogers, H.L. and Harley, T.R. Roman Home Life and
        Religion. Oxford: Clarendon Press, 1923.

02389.   Treggiari, Susan. "Domestic Staff at Rome in the
          Julio-Claudian Period, 27 B.C. to A.D. 68." Histoire
          sociale; revue canadienne 6 (1973): 241-255.

02390.   _____. Roman Freedmen during the Late Republic.
          Oxford: Clarendon Press, 1969.

02391.   Tucker, T.G. Life in the Roman World of Nero and St.
          Paul. New York: Macmillan Co., 1911.

02392.   Weaver, P.R.C. Familia Caesaris: A Social Study of the
          Emperor's Freedmen and Slaves. London: Cambridge
          University Press, 1972.

                        (2) Women

02393.   Assa, Janine. The Great Roman Ladies. New York: Grove
          Press, 1960.

02394.   Colin, Jean. "Sobriquets de femmes dans la Rome alexan-
          drine (d'après Ciceron et Lucrece.)" Revue belge de
          philologie et d'histoire 33 (1955): 853-876.

02395.   Dalby, Andrew. "On Female Slaves in Roman Egypt." Arethusa
          12 (Fall 1979): 255-259. Also see Arethusa 12 (Fall 1979):
          259-263.

02396.   Gottlieb, Elfriede. Die Frau in der fruhchristlichen
          Gemeinde. Quellenhefte zum Frauenleben in der Geschichte
          edited by Emmy Beckmann and Irma Stoss, vol. 1. Berlin:
          F. A. Herbig, 1928.

02397.   Hamilton, Gail. "Society Women Before Christ." North
          American Review 151 (August 1890): 146-159.

02398.   _____. "Society Women of the Time of Christ."
          North American Review 151 (September 1890): 274-288.

02399.   Kajanto, Iiro. "Women's Praenomina Reconsidered." Arctos
          n.s. 7 (1972): 13-30.

02400.   Mohler, S.L. "Feminism in the Corpus Inscriptionum
          Latinarum." Classical Weekly 25 (15 February 1932):
          113-117.

02401.   Will, Elizabeth Lyding. "Women in Pompeii." Archaeology
          32 (1979): 34-43.

          Also refer to #2466.

b) Demography

02402. Boer, W. den. "Demography in Roman History." Mnemosyne 4th ser. 26 (1973): 29-46.

02403. Bradley, Keith R. "The Age at Time of Sale of Female Slaves." Arethusa 11 (Spring and Fall 1978): 243-252.

02404. Hopkins, Keith. "The Age of Roman Girls at Marriage." Population Studies 18 (March 1965): 309-327.

02405. _____. "On the Probable Structure of the Roman Population." Population Studies 20 (1966): 245-264.

02406. Kajanto, Iiro. "On the Problem of the Average Duration of Life in the Roman Empire." Annales Academiae Scientiarum Fennicae, ser. B, 153, 2. Helsinki: Suomalainen Tiedeakatemia, 1968.

c) Family

02407. Baudrillart, André. Moeurs paiennes, moeurs chrétiennes I: La famille dans l'antiquité et aux premiers siècles du christianisme. Paris: Bloud and Gay, 1929.

02408. Borda, Maurizio. Lares. La vita familare romana nei documenti archeologici et letterari. Vatican City: Società amici catacombe presso Pontifico istituto di archeologia, 1947.

02409. Calderini, Aristide. La composizione della famiglia secondo el schede di censimento dell'Egitto Romano. Milan: Societa editrice "vita e pensiero", 1923?

02410 Flory, Marleen Bourdreau. "Family in Familia: Kinship and Community in Slavery." American Journal of Ancient History 3 (1978): 78-95.

02411. Last, Hugh. "Family and Social Life." In The Legacy of Rome, edited by Cyril Bailey, pp. 209-236: Oxford: Clarendon Press, 1923.

02412. McDaniel, Walton Brooks. Conception, Birth and Infancy in Ancient Rome and Modern Italy. Lancaster, Pa.: Business Press Inc., 1948.

02413. Paribeni, Roberto. La Famiglia Romana. 4th ed. Bologna:
        Capelli, 1943.

02414. Queen, Stuart V.; Habenstein, Robert W.; and Adams, John B.
        "The Ancient Romans--Continuity and Change." In The
        Family in Various Cultures, pp. 159-180. New York:
        J.B. Lippincott Company, 1961.

02415. _____ .
        "The Legacy of the Early Christian Family." In The
        Family in Various Cultures, pp. 181-201. New York:
        J.B. Lippincott Company, 1961.

02416. Rawson, Beryl. "Family Life Among the Lower Classes at
        Rome in the First Two Centuries of the Empire." Classical
        Philology 61 (April 1966): 71-83.

02417. Treggiari, Susan. "Family Life Among the Staff of the
        Volusii." Transactions of the American Philological
        Association 105 (1975): 393-401.

02418. Trillmich, W. Familienpropaganda der Kaiser Caligula und
        Claudius. Agrippina Maior und Antonia Augusta auf
        Münzen. Berlin: De Gruyter, 1978.

02419. Veyne, Paul. "La Famille et l'amour sous le haut-empire
        romain." Annales: économies, societes et civilisations
        33 (January-February 1978): 35-63.

02420. Volterra, Edoardo. "Sui mores della familia romana."
        Atti della Accademia Nazionale dei Lincei, Rendiconti
        8th ser. 4 (1949): 516-534.

02421. Zajac, Jozef. "Einige vermögende Familien aus Celeia in
        der römischen Provinz Noricum (1. -- 3. Jh. u. Z.)"
        Rivista storiche dell'antichità 8 (1978): 63-88.

        Also refer to #2265, 2421.

                              d) Marriage

02422. Bayer, E. "Die Ehen der Jungeren Claudia Marcella."
        Historia 17 (January 1968): 118-123.

02423. Campbell, Brian. "The Marriage of Soldiers under the
        Empire." Journal of Roman Studies 68 (1978): 153-166.

02424. Collins, J.H. "Tullia's Engagement and Marriage to
        Dolabella." Classical Journal 47 (February 1952):
        164-168, 186.

02425. Daube, David. "Licinia's Dowry." Studi in Onore di
        B. Biondi I. Milan: Giuffre, 1965.

02426. Dorey, T.A. "Adultery and Propaganda in the Early Roman
        Empire." University of Birmingham Historical Journal 8
        (1961): 1-6.

02427. Fowler, W. Warde. "Marriage: and the Roman Lady." In
        The Woman Question, edited by Thomas Robert Smith,
        pp. 12-32. New York: Boni and Liveright, 1918.

02428. _____. "On the New Fragment of the So-Called
        Laudatio Turiae (C.I.L. VI. 1527)." Classical Review
        19 (June 1905): 261-266.

02429. Frey, J.B. "Signification des termes 'monandros' et
        'univirae'." Recherches de science religeuse 20 (1930):
        48-60.

02430. Gordon, Hattie L. "The Eternal Triangle, First Century B.C."
        Classical Journal 28 (1933): 574-578.

02431. Hopkins, Keith. "Brother-Sister Marriage in Roman Egypt."
        Comparative Studies in Society and History 22 (1980):
        303-354.

02432. Humbert, Michel. Le Remariage à Rome. Etude d'histoire
        juridique et sociale. Milan: Dott A. Dioffre Editore,
        1972.

02433. Johnston, Mary. "Widows in the First and the Seventeenth
        Centuries." Classical Weekly 25 (16 November 1931): 48.

02434. Kajanto, Iiro. "On Divorce Among the Common People of
        Rome." Revue des etudes latines 47 (1970): 99-113.

02435. Lightman, Marjorie and Zeisel, William. "Univira: An
        Example of Continuity and Change in Roman Society."
        Church History 46 (1977): 19-32.

02436. Pearce, T.E.V. "The Role of the Wife as CUSTOS in Ancient
        Rome." Eranos 72 (1974): 16-33.

02437. Rawson, Beryl. "Roman Concubinage and Other de facto
        Marriages." Transactions of American Philological
        Association 104 (1974): 279-305.

02438. Robleda, Olis. "Il consenso matrimoniale presso i romani."
        Gregorianum 60 (1979): 249-284.

02439. Sanders, H.A. "A Latin Marriage Contract." Transactions
        of the American Philological Association 69 (1938):
        104-116.

02440. Toynbee, Jocelyn. "The Villa Item and a Bride's Ordeal."
        Journal of Roman Studies 19 (1929): 67-88.

02441. Treggiari, Susan. "Libertine Ladies." Classical World
        64 (1971): 196-198.

02442. Visky, Karoly. "Le divorce dans la législation de
        Justinien." Revue internationale des droits de
        l'antiquité 23 (1976): 239-264.

02443. Williams, Gordon. "Some Aspects of Roman Marriage Cere-
        monies and Ideals." Journal of Roman Studies 48 (1958):
        16-29.

        Also refer to #2040, 2042-2044, 2048, 2049, 2053-2055, 2062,
        2064, 2065, 2069, 2075, 2269, 2275, 2279, 2286, 2292, 2293,
        2303, 2304, 2314, 2317, 2318, 2323, 2325, 2336, 2339, 2404,
        2492.

                    e)   Sex Life and Morals

                    (1)   Non-specific

                    (a)   Contemporary

02444. Ovid. The Art of Love and Other Poems. Translated by
        J.H. Mozley. The Loeb Classical Library. Cambridge,
        Mass.: Harvard University Press, 1947.

02445. _____ . The Loves, the Art of Beauty, the Remedies for
        Love, and the Art of Love. Translated by Rolfe Humphries.
        Bloomington: Indiana University Press, 1957.

02446. _____ . Ovid's Heroides. Translated by Harold C. Cannon.
        New York: Dutton, 1971.

                    (b)   Secondary

02447. Corte, M. della. Loves and Lovers in Ancient Pompeii: A
        Pompeian Erotic Anthology. Rome: E. di Mauro, 1960.

02448. Curran, Leo C. "Rape and Rape Victims in the Metamorphoses."
        Arethusa 11 (Spring and Fall 1978): 213-241.

02449. Grimal, Pierre. Love in Ancient Rome. Translated by
        Arthur Train, Jr. New York: Crown Publishers, 1967.

02450. Kiefer, O. Sexual Life in Ancient Rome. 1934. Reprint.
        London: Abbey Library, 1971.

02451. Pike, Edgar Royston. Love in Ancient Rome. London: F.
        Muller, 1965.

        Also refer to #2250, 2264, 2419.

(2)   Prostitutes and Courtesans

02452. Bassani, F. Commodo e Marcia: Una Concubina Augusta.
        Venice: Emiliana, 1905.

02453. Fontenrose, Joseph E. "Propertius and the Roman Career."
        University of California Publications in Classical
        Philology 13 (1949): 371-388.

02454. Lacroix, Paul. Les Courtisanes de l'ancienne Rome.
        Brussels: Brancart, 1884.

02455   Meyer, Paul. Der römische Konkubinat nach den Rechtsquellen
        und den Inschriften. Leipzig: B.G. Teubner, 1895.

02456. Wedeck, Harry E. "Synonyms for Meretrix." Classical
        Weekly 37 (3 January 1944): 116-117.

        Also refer to #2130, 2149.

f)   Fashion

02457. Barini, C. Ornatus Muliebris: I Gioielli e le Antiche
        Romane. Torino: Loescher, 1958.

02458. Bonfante, Larissa. Etruscan Dress. Baltimore: Johns
        Hopkins University Press, 1976.

02459. Leon, Ernestine F. "Bobs vs. Knobs in Imperial Rome."
        Art and Archaeology 24 (November 1927): 170-175.

02460. _____. "'Miss Roma'--200 B.C." The Mentor
        16 (October 1928): 49-51.

02461. Palmerlee, Grace. "The Coiffure of Roman Women as Shown
        on Portrait Busts and Statues." Records of the Past 9
        (May-June 1910): 166-176.

        Also refer to #2333, 2337, 2338.

g)   Recreation

02462.   Duke, T.T.   "Women and Pygmies in the Roman Arena."
         Classical Journal 50 (February 1955):   223-224.

h)   Health/Medical

02463.   Hopkins, Keith.   "Contraception in the Roman Empire."   Com-
         parative Studies in Society and History 8 (1965): 124-151.

02464.   Le Gall, Joel.   "Métiers de femmes au Corpus inscriptorum
         Latinarum."   Revue des études latines 47 (1970):   123-130.

i)   Burial Customs

02465.   Durry, Marcel, ed.   Eloge funèbre d'une matrone romaine.
         Paris: Société d'édition "Les Belles-lettres," 1950.

6. CULTURAL

"Let me have a wife not too lettered."
                Martial, Epigrams

a)   Generic

02466.   Adcock, F.E.   "Women in Roman Life and Letters."   Greece
         and Rome 14 (January 1945):   1-11.

02467.   Poulsen, Frederik.   Glimpses of Roman Culture.   Translated
         by J. Dahlmann-Hansen.   Leiden: E.J. Brill, 1950.

02468.   Quartana, M.   La donna romana nella letteratura latina del
         I° secolo.   Milan: R. Sandron, 1921.

b) Literature

(1) Philosophy

02469. Favez, Ch. "Les opinions de Seneque sur la femme."
        Revue des etudes latines 16 (1937): 335-345.

02470. Manning, C.E. "Seneca and the Stoics on the Equality
        of the Sexes." Mnemosyne 26 (1973): 170-177.

02471. Motto, Anna Lydia. "Seneca on Women's Liberation."
        Classical World 65 (January 1972): 155-157.

(2) Drama

(a) Plautus

02472. Forehand, Walter F. "Plautus' Casina: An Explication."
        Arethusa 6 (Fall 1973): 233-256.

02473. MacCary, W. Thomas. "Patterns of Myth, Ritual and Comedy
        in Plautus' Casina." Texas Studies in Literature and
        Language 15 (1974): 881-889.

02474. Schumann, Elisabeth. "Ehescheidung in den Komodien von
        Plautus." Zeitschrift der Savigny Stiftung fur Rechtsge-
        schichte (Romanistische Abteilung) 93 (1976): 19-32.

(b) Others

02475. Konstan, David. "Terence's Hecyra." Far Western Forum 1
        (1974): 23-34.

(3) Poetry

02476. Bruno, Lidia. Le donne nella poesia di Marziale. Salerno:
        D. Giaumo, 1965.

02477. Cloonan, William. "Women in Horace." Romance Notes 16
        (Spring 1975): 647-652.

02478. Grant, John N. "Dido Melessa." Phoenix 23 (Winter 1969):
        380-391.

02479. Jax, Karl. Der Frauentypus der römischen Dichtung. Inns-
        bruck: Rauch, 1938.

                        (4) Elegy

02480. Betensky, Aya. "Woman in Roman Elegy." Arethusa 6 (1973):
        267-269.

02481. Hallett, Judith P. "The Role of Women in Roman elegy:
        Counter-cultural Feminism." Arethusa 6 (1973): 103-124
        and 7 (1974): 211-219.

02482. Lilja, Sara. The Roman Elegists' Attitude to Women.
        Annales Academiae Scientiarum Fennicae, series B., vol.
        135, 1. Helsinki: Suomalainen Tiedeakatemia, 1965.

                        (5) Satire

                        (a) Juvenal

02483. Juvenal. The Satires of Juvenal. Translated by Peter Green.
        Baltimore: Penguin, 1967.
        [See especially Satire 6.]

02484. Labriolle, Pierre de. "La sixième satire de Juvenal. Les
        femmes romaines." Revue des cours et conférences 32
        (June 1931): 385-398; 531-545; 32 (July 1931): 690-706.

                        (b) Petronius

02485. Petronius. The Satyricon and the Fragments. Translated
        by John Sullivan. Baltimore: Penguin Books, 1965.

(6)   Prose

(a)   *Individuals*

[1]   APULEIUS

02486.   Boberg, Inger Margrethe.   "The Tale of Cupid and Psyche."
         Classica et Mediaevalia 1 (1938):   177-216.

02487.   Neumann, Erich.   Amor and Psyche: The Psychic Development
         of the Feminine, A Commentary on the Tale by Apuleius.
         Translated by Ralph Manheim.   Bollingen ser., vol. 54.
         New York: Pantheon Books, 1956.

[2]   CICERO

02488.   Best, E.E.   "Cicero, Livy and Educated Roman Women."
         Classical Journal 65 (1970):   199-204.

[3]   LIVY

02489.   Piper, Linda J.   "Livy's Portrayal of Early Roman Women."
         Classical Bulletin 48 (December 1971):   26-28.

02490.   Smethurst, S.E.   "Women in Livy's History."   Greece and
         Rome 19 (June 1950):   80-87.

         Also refer to #2488.

[4]   PLINY

02491.   Maniet, A.   "Pline le Jeune et Calpurnia: Etude semantique
         et psychologique."   L'Antiquité classique 35 (1966):
         149-185.

[5]   TACITUS

02492.   Königer, Hans.   Gestalt und Welt der Frauen bei Tacitus.
         Erlangen-Nuremberg: Universität Erlangen-Nuremberg, 1966.

(7)   Other Works

02493.   Bonjour, M.   "Les personnages féminins et la terre natale
dans l'épisode de Coriolan."   Revue des études latines
53 (1975): 157-181.

02494.   Hoffsten, Ruth.   Roman Women of Rank of the Early Empire
as Portrayed by Dio, Paterculus, Suetonius, and Tacitus.
Philadelphia: University of Pennsylvania Press, 1939.

c)   Art and Artifacts

(1)   Women in Art

02495.   Calza, Guido.   "Some Portraits of Roman Empresses."   Art
and Archaeology 19 (February 1925):   93-99.

02496.   Gabriel, Mabel M.   Livia's Garden Room at Prima Porta.
New York: New York University Press, 1955.

02497.   Hiesinger, Ulrich S.   "Julia Domna: Two Portraits in
Bronze."   American Journal of Archaeology 73 (January
1969):   39-44.

02498.   Maiuri, Amedeo.   "The Statue of Livia from the Villa of
the Mysteries."   Translated by Arthur Stanley Riggs.
Art and Archaeology 33 (July-August 1932):   170-174, 222.

02499.   Pink, K.   "Magnia Urbica."   Numismatische Zeitschrift 79
(1961):   5-9.

02500.   Polaschek, Karin.   Studien zur Ikonographie der Antonia
Minor.   Rome: "L'Erma" di Bretschneider, 1973.

02501.   Traversari, Gustavo.   Statue iconiche femminili cirenaiche.
Rome: "L'Erma" di Bretschneider, 1960.

02502.   Trillmich, Walter.   Das Torlonia-Mädchen Zu Herkunft und
Entstehung der kaiserzeitlichen Frauenporträts.   Göttingen:
Vandehoeck and Ruprecht, 1976.

02503.   Waldhauer, Oscar.   "A Note on Another Portrait-Head of
Livia."   Journal of Roman Studies 13 (1923):   190.

Also refer to #2277.

(2) Women Artists

02504. Garton, Charles. "A Republican Mime--Actress?" Classical
        Review n.s. 14 (December 1964): 238-239.

d) Science

(1) Non-specific

02505. Coolidge, J.L. "Six Female Mathematicians." Scripta
        Mathematica 17 (March-June 1951): 20-31.

02506. Iacobacci, Rora F. "Women of Mathematics." Arithmetic
        Teacher 17 (April 1970): 316-324.

02507. _____. "Women of Mathematics." Mathematics
        Teacher 63 (April 1970): 329-337.

(2) Hypatia

02508. McCabe, Joseph. "Hypatia." Critic 43 (September 1903):
        267-272.

02509. Richeson, A.W. "Hypatia of Alexandria." National
        Mathematics Magazine 15 (November 1940): 74-82.

02510. Rist, J.M. "Hypatia." Phoenix 19 (Autumn 1965): 214-225.

02511. Schrek, D.J.E. "Hypatia von Alexandrie." Euclides 21
        (1945-46): 164-173.

02512. Socrates Scholasticus. "The Murder of Hypatia." In A
        Treasury of Early Christianity, edited by Anne Fremantle,
        pp. 379-380. New York: The Viking Press, 1953.

02513. Wolf, Stephan. Hypatia, die Philosophin von Alexandrien:
        Ihr Leben, Wirken und Lebensende nach den Quellenschriften
        dargestellt. Vienna: Holder, 1879.

III. MIDDLE AGES

A. GENERAL

1. BIBLIOGRAPHIES

"If a woman keeps her body intact, all her other defects
are hidden and she can hold her head high."
                    Philippe de Navarre

02514. Erickson, Carolly, and Casey, Kathleen, eds. "Women in the
        Middle Ages: A Working Bibliography." Medieval Studies
        37 (1975): 340-359.

02515. Verdon, Jean. "Les sources de l'histoire de la femme en
        Occident aux Xe-XIIIe siècles." Cahiers de civilisation
        médiévale 20 (1977): 219-251.

2. SURVEYS

"A woman is just like melting wax, which is always ready to
take a new form and to receive the impress of anybody's
seal."
                    Andreas Capellanus

a) Generic

02516. Bessinger, Jess B. and Raymo, Robert R., eds. Medieval
        Studies in Honor of Lillian Herlands Hornstein. New York:
        New York University Press, 1976.

02517. Bloch, Marc. Feudal Society. Translated by L.A. Manyon.
        Chicago: University of Chicago Press, 1968.

02518. Bühler, Johannes. Die Kultur Mittelalters. Leipzig:
        A. Kroner, 1931.
        [See especially ch. "Vom mittelalterlichen Leben," pp.
        289-335.]

02519. Crump, C.G., and Jacob, E.F., eds. The Legacy of the Middle
        Ages. Oxford: Clarendon Press, 1926.

02520. Eicken, Henrich von. Geschichte und System der mit-
        telalterlichen Weltanschauung. 4th ed. Stuttgart: Cotta,
        1923.

02521. Gies, Joseph and Gies, Frances. Life in a Medieval Castle.
        New York: Harper and Row, 1974.

02522. _____. Life in a Medieval City. New York:
        Apollo Edition, 1969.

02523. Hastings, M. Medieval European Society. New York: Random
        House, 1971.

02524. Heer, Friedrich. The Medieval World, Europe 1100-1350. New
        York: World Publishing Co., 1961.
        [See especially ch. 13, Jews and Women.]

02525. Huizinga, J. The Waning of the Middle Ages. 1924. Reprint.
        New York: Doubleday Anchor Books, 1954.

02526. Matthew, Donald. The Medieval European Community. New York:
        St. Martin's Press, 1977.

02527. Morrall, John B. The Medieval Imprint: The Founding of the
        Western European Tradition. Harmondsworth: Penguin, 1970.

02528. Thrupp, Sylvia, ed. Early Medieval Society. New York:
        Appleton-Century-Crofts, 1967.

                              b) Women

02529. Baker, Derek, ed. Medieval Women. Oxford: Basil Blackwell,
        1978.

02530. Bennett, Henry Stanley. Six Medieval Men and Women. New
        York: Atheneum, 1962.
        [Includes Margaret Paston and Margery Kempe.]

02531. Bücher, Karl. Die Frauenfrage im Mittelalter. 2nd ed.
        Tübingen: Laupp, 1910.

02532. Casey, Kathleen. "The Cheshire Cat: Recon-
        structing the Experience of Medieval Woman".
        In Liberating Women's History, edited by
        Bernice Carroll, pp. 224-249. Urbana: Uni-
        versity of Illinois Press, 1976.

02533. Duckett, Eleanor. Medieval Portraits from East
        and West. Ann Arbor: University of Michigan
        Press, 1972.

02534. Finke, Heinrich. Die Frau im Mittelalter.
        Sammlung Kösel, vol. 62. Kempten: J. Kösel,
        1913.

02535. Gies, Frances and Gies, Joseph. Women in the
        Middle Ages. New York: Thomas Y. Crowell
        Company, 1978.

02536. Hanawalt, Barbara A. "Women's rights in the Middle
        Ages and after." The Center Magazine 7 (March-
        April 1974): 56.

02537. Harksen, Sibylle. Women in the Middle Ages.
        Translated by Marianne Herzfeld. New York:
        Abner Schram, 1975.

02538. Kemp-Welch, Alice. Of Six Medieval Women. 1913.
        Reprint. Williamstown, Ma.: Corner House, 1972.

02539. Morewedge, Rosmarie Thee, ed. The Role of
        Women in the Middle Ages. Albany, New
        York: State University of New York   Press, 1975

02540. Portmann, Marie-Louise. Die Darstellung der
        Frau in der Geschichtsschreibung des fruhreren
        Mittelalters. Basler Beitrage zur Geschichts-
        wissenschaft, no. 69. Basle: Helbing and
        Lichtenhahn, 1958.

02541. Power, Eileen. Medieval People. New York: Univer-
        sity Paperbacks, 1966.
        [See especially chs. 4 and 5.]

02542. _____. Medieval Women. Edited by M. M. Postan.
        New York: Cambridge University Press, 1975.

02543. _____. "The Position of Women." In Legacy of
        the Middle Ages, edited by G.C. Crump and E. F.
        Jacob, pp. 401-433. Oxford: Claredon Press, 1926.

02544. Stuard, Susan Mosher, ed. Women in Medieval
        Society. Philadelphia: University of
        Pennsylvania Press, 1976.

        Also refer to #1518, 1519.

3. MATRIARCHY AND MATRILINY

"Although King Ailill was the ruler, his queen
always had the final word in the land of Connacht,
for she could order what she liked, take as lover
whomever she desired . . . ."
                    about Maeve in Irish Saga

02545. Farnsworth, William Oliver. Uncle and Nephew
        in the Old Chansons de Geste: a study in
        the survival of matriarchy. New York: AMS
        Press, 1913.

4. POLITICAL

"We know that everything a woman says is
said with the intention of deceiving,
because she always has one thing in her
heart and another on her lips."
                    Andreas Capellanus

a) Legal

02546. Beaucamp, Joelle. "Le vocabulaire de la faiblesse féminine
        dans les textes juridiques romaines du IIIe au Vi^e siècle."
        Revue historique de droit français et etranger 54 (1976):
        485-508.

02547. Bellomo, Manlio. Richerche sui rapporti patrimoniali fra
        coniugi. Contributo alla storia della famiglia medievale.
        Milan: Giuffrè, 1961.

02548. Champeaux, Ernest. "Jus sanguinis, trois façons, de calcular
        la parenté au Moyen âge." Revue historique de droit fran-
        çais et étranger 4th ser. 12 (1933): 241-290.

02549. Delpini, Francesco. Divorzio e separazione dei coniugi nel
        diritto romano e nella dottrina della chiesa fino al secolo
        V. Scrinium theologicum no. 5. Turin: Marietti, 1956.

02550. Donahue, Charles, Jr. "The Case of the Man who Fell into the
        Tiber. The Roman Law of Marriage at the Time of the
        Glossators." American Journal of Legal History 22 (January
        1978): 1-53.

02551.   Drew, Katherin Fischer, trans. The Lombard
         Laws. Philadelphia: University of Philadelphia
         Press, 1973.

02552.   Falk, Ze'ev W. Jewish Matrimonial Law in
         the Middle Ages. Scripta Judaica, no. 6.
         London: Oxford University Press, 1966.

02553.   Fransen, Gerard. "Le mariage simulé. Deux
         questions disputées du XII siècle." In Etudes
         de droit et d'histoire. Mélanges Mgr. H.
         Wagnon, pp. 531-541. Louvain: University
         of Louvain, 1976.

02554.   Gaudemet, Jean. "Le Legs du droit romain en
         matière matrimoniale." In Il matrimonio
         nella società altomedievale 1: 139-189.
         Spoleto, Centro Italiano di Studi sull'
         Alto Medioevo, 1977.

02555.   _____. "Sur trois 'dicta Gratiani' relatifs
         au 'matrimonium ratum'." In Etudes de droit et
         d'histoire. Melanges Mgr. H. Wagnon, pp. 543-555.
         Louvain: University of Louvain, 1976.

02556.   Goody, Jack. "Inheritance, property, and women: some
         comparative considerations." In Family and Inheri-
         tance, edited by Jack Goody et. al., pp. 10-36. New
         York: Cambridge University Press, 1976.

02557.   Goria, Fausto. "Ricerche su impedimento da adulterio
         e obligo di repudio da Guistiniano a Leone VI."
         Studia et documenta historiae et juris 39 (1973):
         281-384.

02558.   Howarth, W. D. "Droit du Seigneur: Fact or Fantasy?
         Journal of European Studies 1 (1971): 291-312.

02559.   Lefebvre, Charles. "Interférences de la juris prudence
         matrimoniale et de l'anthropologie au cours de
         l'histoire." Revue de droit canonique 27 (1977):
         84-102.

02560.   Leisching, Peter. "Eheschliessung vor dem Notar im 13.
         Jahrhundert." Zeitschrift der Savigny Stiftung
         für Rechtsgeschichte (Kanonistische Abteilung) 94
         (1977): 20-46.

02561.   Lepointe, Gabriel. Droit romaine et ancien droit
         français. Regimes matrimoniaux, liberalités,
         successions. Paris: Monchristien, 1958.

02562.   Lingenthal, K.E. Zachariae von. "A Medieval Procedural
         Form for Marriage Annulment Cases." The American
         Journal of Legal History 10 (January 1966): 76-81.

02563. Pesendorfer, Marianne. "Das Ehehindernis in der
       gesetzlichen Verwandtschaft (c. 1059 und c. 1080).
       Zur Frage der Anknüpfung an die staatliche Rechtsord-
       nung und einiger damit im Zusammenhang stehenden
       Probleme des kanonischen Rechts." Österreichisches
       Archiv für Kirchenrecht 20 (1969): 199-225.

02564. Richard, Jean. "Le statut de la femme dans l'Orient
       latin." Reprint from Recueils de la société Jean
       Bodin 12 (1962): 377-388. In Orient et occident au
       moyen âge: contacts et relations (XII-XVe siècles).
       A Collection of Essays by Jean Richard, pp. 377-388.
       London: Variorum Reprints, 1976.

02565. Ritzer, Korbinian. "Secular Law and the Western
       Church's Concept of Marriage." Concilium 55 (1970):
       67-75.

02566. Smith, Charles E. Papal Enforcement of Some Medieval
       Marriage Laws. 1940. Reprint. Port Washington, New
       York: Kennikat Press, 1972.

02567. Stein, Simon. "Lex Salica." Speculum 22 (1947): 113-
       134, 395-418.

02568. Tabacco, Giovanni. "Il tema della famiglia e del suo
       funzionamento nella societa medievale." Quaderni
       Storici 33 (September-December 1976): 892-928.

02569. Trusen, Winfried. "Zur Urkundenlehre der mittelalter-
       lichen Jurisprudenz." Vortrage und Forschungen 23
       (1977): 197-219.

02570. Wojnar, M.M. "Legal Relationship and Guardianship as
       Matrimonial Impediments." The Jurist 30 (1970):
       343-355 and 456-498.

       Also refer to #2745.

b) Criminal

02571. Lanhers, Yvonne. "Crimes et criminels aux 14 ème
       siecle." Revue historique 240 (October-December
       1968): 325-338.

02572. Pollack, Otto. The Criminality of Women. Philadelphia:
       University of Pennsylvania Press, 1950.

c)   Political Roles

02573.   Dahmus, Joseph. Seven Medieval Queens. Garden City,
         N.Y.: Doubleday and Company, 1972.

02574.   Gentzkow, Liane von. Königliche Frauen der Wanderungs-
         zeit und des frühen Mittelalters. Freiburg im
         Breisgau: Herder and Co., 1936.

02575.   Laboulaye, Edouard de. Recherches sur la condition civile
         et politique des femmes. Paris: A. Durand, 1843.

02576.   Vogelsang, Thilo. Die Frau als Herrscherin im hohen
         Mittelalter. Studien zur "consors regni" Formel.
         Göttingen Bausteine zur Geschichtswissenschaft, no. 7.
         Göttingen: Musterschmidt, Wissenschaftlicher Verlag,
         1954.

02577.   Wemple, Suzanne F. and McNamara, JoAnn. "Medieval
         Women: Their Gain and Loss of Power." Barnard Alumnae
         63 (Winter 1974): 8-11.

         Also refer to #2755.

5. ECONOMIC

"Just as [the husband] has the power over her, also he
is to have it over all her possessions."
Leges Burgundionum

a)   Generic

02578.   Duby, Georges. The Early Growth of the European Economy:
         Warriors and Peasants from the Seventh to the Twelfth
         Century. Ithaca, N.Y.: Columbia University Press, 1976.

02579.   _____ . Rural Economy and Country Life in
         Medieval West. Translated by Cynthia Postman.
         Columbia, S.C.: University of South Carolina Press,
         1968.

02580.   Pirenne, Henri. Economic and Social History of Medieval
         Europe. London: Routledge and Kegan, 1936.

b)   Women

02581.   Jehel, Georges.   "Le rôle des femmes et du milieu
familial à Gênes dans les activités commerciales au
cours de la premier moitié du XIIIe siècle," Revue
d'histoire économique et sociale 53 (1975): 193-215.

6.   RELIGION

"There is no place which monks should dread more than
women, the soul's death."
Carmen de Mundi contemptu

a)   Generic

(1)   Non-specific

02582.   Cadoux, Cecil J.   The Early Church and the World.
Edinburgh: T. & T. Clark, 1925.

02583.   Coulton, G. G.   Ten Medieval Studies.   Boston: Beacon
Press, 1959.

02584.   Dawson, C.   Medieval Religion.   New York: Sheed and
Ward, 1933.

02585.   Heaney, Seamus P.   The Development of the Sacramentality
of Marriage from Anselm of Laon to Thomas Aquinas.
Washington, D.C.:   Catholic University of America
Press, 1963.

02586.   Lea, Henry Charles.   A History of the Inquisition of
Middle Ages.   New York: The Macmillan Co., 1922.

02587.   Southern, Richard William.   Western Society and the
Church in the Middle Ages.   Grand Rapids, Michigan:
Eerdmans, 1970.
[See especially pp. 309-352.]

Also refer to #2789, 2290.

(2) Women

02588. Alverny, Marie-Thérèse d'. "Comment les théologiens et
        les philosophes voient la femme." Cahiers de civili-
        sation médiévale 20 (1977): 105-129.

02589. Bernards, Matthäus. "Die Frau in der Welt und die
        Kirche während des 11. Jahrhunderts." Sacris Erudiri
        20 (1971): 39-100.

02590. _____. Speculum Virginum: Geistigkeit und
        Seelenleben der Frau im Hochmittelalter. Koln-Graz:
        Böhlau-Verlag, 1955.

02591. Brittain, Alfred, and Carroll, Mitchell. Women of
        Early Christianity. Philadelphia: Rittenhouse Press,
        1908.

02592. Cabane, Abbé Auguste. Essais d'études religieuses. La
        femme avant et depuis l'Evangile. Origines de la
        bienfaisance chrétienne. Montpellier: Grollier et
        fils, 1884.

02593. Danielou, Jean. The Ministry of Women in the Early
        Church. London: Faith, 1961.

02594. Dietrick, Ellen B. Women in the Early Christian Ministry.
        Philadelphia: Alfred J. Ferris, 1897.

02595. Dumas, André. Biblical Anthropology and the Participa-
        tion of Women in the Ministry of the Early Church.
        Geneva: World Council of Churches, 1963.

02596. Gottlieb, Elfriede. Die Frau im frühen Christentum.
        Leipzig: A. Klein, 1930.

02597. Gout, Raoul. Le miroir des dames chrétiennes, pages
        féminines du moyen âge. Paris: Editions "Je Sers", 1935.

02598. Goyau, Lucie Faure. Christianisme et culture féminine.
        Paris: Perrin Cie, 1918.

02599. Grevy-Pons, N. Célebat et nature. Une controverse
        médiévale. Paris: C.N.R.S.., 1975.

02600.   Gryson, R. "L'attitude de l'église ancienne vis-à-vis
          du ministère des femmes." Collectanea Mechliniensia
          53 (1958): 352-363.

02601.   _____. Le ministère de femmes dans l'église ancienne.
          Recherches et syntheses. Section d'histoire, no. 4.
          Gembloux: Duculot, 1972.

02602.   Leclercq-Kadaner, Jacqueline. "De la Terre-Mère à la
          Luxure. A propos de 'La migration des symboles.'"
          Cahiers de civilisation médiévale 18 (January-March
          1975): 37-43.

02603.   McLaughlin, Eleanor Commo. "Equality of Souls,
          Inequality of Sexes: Women in Medieval Theology."
          In Religion and Sexism, edited by Rosemary Ruether,
          pp. 213-266. New York: Simon and Schuster, 1974.

02604.   McNamara, Jo Ann. "Sexual Equality and the Cult of
          Virginity in Early Christian Thought." Feminist Studies
          3 (Spring-Summer 1976): 145-158.

02605.   Payer, Pierre. "Eve's Sin, Woman's fault: a medieval
          view." Atlantis 2 (Spring 1977): 2-15.

02606.   Pykare, Nina Coombs. "The Sin of Eve and the Christian
          Conduct Book." Ohio Journal of Religious Studies 4
          (March 1976): 34-43.

02607.   Quasten, Johannes. "The Liturgical Singing of Women in
          Christian Antiquity." Catholic Historical Review 27
          (July 1941): 149-165.

02608.   Range, Joan A. "Legal Exclusion of Women from Church
          Office." The Jurist 34 (Winter-Spring 1974): 112-127.

02609.   Watson, Arthur. "Speculum Virginium with special
          reference to the tree of Jesse." Speculum 3 (1928):
          445-469.

02610.   Zerbst, Fritz. The Office of Woman in the Church.
          Translated by A.G. Merkens. St. Louis: Concordia, 1955.

          Also refer to #2876.

                    b) Saints/Religious Women

02611.   Bolton, Brenda M. "Mulieres Sanctae." In Women in
          Medieval Society, edited by Susan Mosher Stuard,
          pp. 141-158. Philadelphia: University of Pennsylvania
          Press, 1976. Also in Studies in Church History 10
          (1973): 77-95.

02612. Bourdon, Mathilde. <u>Marcia</u> <u>et</u> <u>les</u> <u>femmes</u> <u>aux</u> <u>premiers</u>
        <u>temps</u> <u>du</u> <u>Christianisme</u>. Paris: Delhome et Briquet, 18--.

02613. Dunbar, Agnes. <u>A</u> <u>Dictionary</u> <u>of</u> <u>Saintly</u> <u>Women</u>. London:
        G. Bell and Sons, 1905.

02614. Goodich, Michael. "The Contours of Female Piety in Later
        Medieval Hagiography." <u>Church</u> <u>History</u> 50 (March 1981):
        pp. 20-32.

02615. Jacobus de Voragine. <u>The</u> <u>Golden</u> <u>Legend</u>. Translated by
        Granger Ryan and Helmut Ripperger. New York:
        Longmans, Green, 1948.

02616. Noble, Schlomo. "The Jewish Woman in Medieval Martyr-
        ology." In <u>Studies</u> <u>in</u> <u>Jewish</u> <u>Bibliography</u>, edited by
        Charles Berlin, pp. 347-355. New York: Ktav, 1971.

02617. Schulenberg, Jane Tibbetts. "Sexism and the celestial
        gynaeceum - from 500 to 1200." <u>Journal</u> <u>of</u> <u>Medieval</u>
        <u>History</u> 4 (March 1978): 117-133.

02618. Taylor, H.O. "Mystic Visions of Ascetic Women." In
        <u>The</u> <u>Medieval</u> <u>Mind</u>, pp. 458-486. New York: The
        Macmillan Co., 1919.

02619. Werner, Ernst. "Zur Frauenfrage und zum Frauenkult im
        Mittelalter." <u>Forschungen</u> <u>und</u> <u>Fortschritte</u> 29
        (September 1955): 269-276.

                         c) Mariology

02620. Adams, Henry. <u>Mont</u> <u>Saint-Michel</u> <u>and</u> <u>Chartres</u>. New York:
        Putnam, 1980.

02621. Beumer, Johannes. "Der mariologische Gehalt der Predigten
        Gottfrieds von Admont (d1165)." <u>Scholastik</u> 35 (1960):
        40-56.

02622. Borchgrave d'Altena, J. de. "Madones en majesté. A
        propos de Notre-Dame, d'Eprave." <u>Revue</u> <u>belge</u>
        <u>d'archéologie</u> <u>et</u> <u>d'histoire</u> <u>de</u> <u>l'art</u> 30 (1961): 3-114.

02623. Corbin, Solange. "Miracula beatae Mariae semper virginis."
        <u>Cahiers</u> <u>de</u> <u>civilisation</u> <u>médiévale</u> 10 (1967): 409-433.

02624.   Dal Pino, A.M.   Iconografia mariana da secolo VI al XIII.
          Rome: Marianum, 1963.

02625.   Delius, W. and Kolping, A. Texte zur Mariologie und
          Marienverehrung der mittelalterlichen Kirche. Kleine
          Texte fur Vorlesungen und Übungen, no. 184. Berlin:
          De Gryter, 1961.

02626.   Doheny, William and Kelly, Joseph P. Papal Documents
          on Mary. Milwaukee: The Bruce Publishing Company,
          1954.

02627.   Emminghaus, Johannes H. "Marienbild." Lexikon für
          Theologie und Kirche 7 (1957): 58-62.

02628.   Fournée, Jean. "Les orientations doctrinales de
          l'iconographie Mariale à la fin de l'époque romane."
          Centre international d'études romanes 1 (1971): 23-60.

02629.   Frank, Hardy Long. "Virginal Politics." Frontiers 3
          (Spring 1978): 46-50.

02630.   Graef, Hilda C. Mary. A History of Doctrine and De-
          votion. I: From the Beginnings to the Eve of the
          Reformation. London: Sheed Ward, 1963.

02631.   Gripkey, Mary Vincentine. The Blessed Virgin Mary as
          Mediatrix. New York: AMS Press, 1938.

02632.   _____. "Mary Legends in Italian
          Manuscripts in the Major Libraries of Italy.
          Groups I-III." Medieval Studies 14 (1952): 9-47.

02633.   _____. "Mary Legends in Italian
          Manuscripts in the Major Libraries of Italy.
          Part II. Groups IV-V." Medieval Studies 15 (1953):
          47-94.

02634.   Heiler, Friedrich. "Die Hauptmotive des Madonnenkultes."
          Zeitschrift für Theologie und Kirche n.s. 1 (1920):
          417-447.

02635.   _____. "Die Madonna als religiöses Symbol."
          In Eranos-Jahrbuch 1934, edited by Olga Fröbe-Kapteyn,
          pp. 263-303. Zurich: Rhein-Verlag, 1934.

02636.   Jameson, Anna Brownell, ed. Legends of the Madonna.
          New York: Houghton, Mifflin & Co., 1911.

02637.   Kesting, Peter. Maria-Frouwe. Über den Einfluss der
          Marienverehrung auf den Minnesang bis Walther von der
          Vogelweide. Munich: Fink, 1965.

02638. Küppers, Leonhard. Mary. The Saints in Legend and Art,
        no. 14. Translated by Hans Hermann Rosenwald.
        Recklinghausen: Verlag Aurel Bongers, 1967.

02639. Lange, Reinhold. Das Marienbild der frühen Jahrhunderte.
        Recklinghausen: Verlag Aurel Bongers, 1969.

02640. Laurentin, René. "Bulletin sur la Vierge Marie." Revue
        des sciences philosophiques et theologiques 56 (July
        1972): 433-491.

02641. Levi D'Ancona, Mirella. The Iconography of the Immaculate
        Conception in the Middle Ages and the Early Renaissance.
        Monographs on Archaeology and Fine Arts, no. 7. New
        York: College Art Association of America, 1957.

02642. Liell, Joseph. Die Darstellungen der allerseligsten
        Jungfrau und Gottesgebärerin Maria auf den Kunstdenk-
        malem der Katakomben. Freiburg: Herder, 1887.

02643. McKenzie, A. Dean. "The Virgin Mary as the Throne of
        Salomon in Medieval Art." Marsyas 12 (1964-65):
        972-73.

02644. Meier, Theodor. Die Gestalt Marias im geistlichen
        Schauspiel des deutschen Mittelalters. Bielefeld:
        Schmidt, 1959.

02645. Miegge, Giovanni. The Virgin Mary. London: Butterworth,
        1955.

02646. Mussafia, Adolf. Studien zu den mittelalterlichen
        Marienlegenden. I-III. Vienna: Tempsky, 1887-1889.

02647. Palmer, Paul. Mary in the Documents of the Church.
        Westminster, Maryland: The Newman Press, 1952.

02748. Pohle, Joseph. Mariology. London: B. Herder, 1953.

02649. Sabbe, E. "Le culte marial et la Genese de sculpture
        médiévale." Revue Belge d'archeologie et d'histoire
        de l'art 20 1951): 101-125.

02650. Salvat, Joseph. "La sainte Vierge dans la littérature
        occitaine du moyen âge. In Mélanges de linguistique et
        de littérature romanes à la memoire d'Istvan Frank,
        pp. 614-656. Saarbrücken: Universitat des Saarlandes,
        1957.

02651. Seidel, Max. "Die Berliner Madonna des Giovanni Pisano."
        Pantheon 30 (1972): 181-192.

02652.   Spicq, Ceslas. Ce que Jésus doit a sa mère selon la
         théologie biblique et d'après les théologiens médiévaux.
         Paris: Vrin, 1959.

         Also refer to #2969.

                    d)   Monastic Life

02653.   Anson, John. "The Female Transvestite in Early Monas-
         ticism: Origin and Development of a Motif." Viator 5
         (1974): 1-32.

02654.   Bangerter, Otto. Frauen im Aufbruch. Die Geschichte
         einer Frauenbewegung in der alten Kirche. Neukirchen-
         Vluyn: Neukirchener Verlag, 1971.

02655.   Bateson, Mary. "The Origin and Early History of the
         Double Monastery." Transactions of the Royal Historical
         Society n.s. 13 (1899): 137-198.

02656.   Berlière, Ursmer. Les monasteres doubles aux XIIe et
         XIII siècles. Academie de Belgique classe de lettres
         et des sciences morales et politiques, no. 18. Brussels:
         M. Lamertin, 1923.

02657.   Bernards, Matthäus. "Zur Seelsorge in den Frauenklostern
         des Hochmittelalters." Revue benedictine 66 (1956):
         256-268.

02658.   Dubay, Thomas. Ecclesial Women. New York: Alba House,
         1970.

02659.   Eckenstein, Lina. Woman under Monasticism. Cambridge:
         Cambridge University Press, 1896.

02660.   Fontette, Micheline de. Les religieuses à l'âge classique
         du droit canon. Bibliotheque de las société d'histoire
         ecclesiastique de la France. Paris: Librairie
         philologique J. Vrin, 1967.

02661.   Jameson, Anna. Legends of the Monastic Orders. Boston:
         Houghton, Mifflin and Company, 1895.

02662.   McLaughlin, T.P. "Abelard's Rules for Religious Women."
         Medieval Studies 18 (1956): 241-292.

02663.   Shahar, Shulamith. "De quelques aspects de la femme dans
         la pensée et la communaté religieuses au XIIe et XIIIe
         siècles." Revue de l'histoire des religions 185
         (January 1974): 29-77.

02664. Thompson, Sally. "The Problem of the Cister an Nuns in
        the Twelfth and early Thirteenth Centuries." In
        Medieval Women, edited by Derek Baker, pp. 227-252.
        Oxford: Basil Blackwell, 1978.

02665. Workman, Herbert B. The Evolution of the Monastic Ideal.
        London: C.H. Kelly, 1913.

e) Canon Law

02666. Borsinger, Hildegard. Rechtsstellung der Frau in der
        katholischen Kirche. Leipzig: Universitats Verlag
        R. Noske. 1930.

02667. Brundage, James A. "Concubinage and Marriage in Medieval
        Canon Law." Journal of Medieval History 1 (April 1975):
        1-17.

02668. _____. "The Crusader's Wife: a Canonistic
        Quandary." Studia Gratiana 12 (1967): 425-442 and
        14 (1967): 241-252.

02669. _____. "Prostitution in the Medieval Canon
        Law." Signs 1 (Summer 1976): 825-845 and 2 (Summer
        1977): 922-924.

02670. _____. "Rape and Marriage in the Medieval
        Canon Law." Revue de droit canonique 28 (1978): 62-75.

02671. Burr, David. "Olivi on Marriage: The Conservative as
        Prophet." Journal of Medieval and Renaissance Studies
        2 (Fall 1972): 183-204.

02672. Catchpole, David R. "The Synoptic Divorce Material as a
        Tradition-Historical Problem." Bulletin of the John
        Rylands Library 57 (Autumn 1974): 92-127.

02673. Dauvillier, Jean. Le mariage dans le droit classique de
        l'église, depuis le décret de Gratien (1140) jusqu'a
        la mort de Clement V (1314). Paris: Recueil Sirey,
        1933.

02674. _____. "Pierre le Chantre et la dispense de
        mariage non consommé." In Etudes d'histoire du droit
        privé offertes à Pierre Petot, edited by Pierre-Clement
        Timbal, pp. 97-106. Paris: Recueil Sirey, 1959.

02675. Decker, Raymond G. "Institutional Authority versus
        Personal Responsibility in the Marriage Section of
        Gratian's 'A Concordance of Discordant Canon'."
        The Jurist 32 (Fall 1972): 51-65.

02676. Delhaye, Philippe. "The Development of the Medieval
        Church's Teaching on Marriage." Concilium 55 (1970):
        83-88.

02677. Donahue, Charles Jr. "The Policy of Alexander the Third's
        consent Theory of marriage." In Proceedings of the
        Fourth International Congress of Medieval Canon Law,
        edited by Stephan Kuttner, pp. 251-281. Vatican City:
        Biblioteca Apostolica Vaticana, 1976.

02678. Esmein, Adhémar. Le mariage en droit canonique. 2 vols.
        1891. Reprint. New York: B. Franklin, 1968.

02679. Fahrner, Ignatz. Geschichte der Ehescheidung im kanonischen
        Recht. I. Geschichte des Unaufloslichkeitsprinzips und
        der vollkommenen Scheidung. Freiburg: Herder, 1903.

02680. Feghali, Joseph. "La Formation du mariage dans le droit
        des églises orientales, comparée avec celle du droit
        de l'Eglise occidentale." In Etudes de droit et
        d'histoire Mélanges Mgr. H. Wagnon, pp. 515-530.
        Louvain: University of Louvain, 1976.

02681. Gaudemet, Jean. "Droit canonique et droit romain. A
        propos de l'erreur sur la personne en matière de
        mariage." Studia Gratiana 9 (1966): 45-64.

02682. _____. "Le lien matrimonial: les incertitude
        du haut Moyen Age." Revue de droit canonique 21
        (1971): 81-105.

02683. Gy, Pierre-Marie. "Le sacrement de mariage exige-t-il
        la foi? La position médiévale." Revue des sciences
        philosophiques et théologiques 61 (1977): 437-442.

02684. Kottje, Raymund. "Konkubinat und Kommunionswürdigkeit im
        vorgratianischen Kirchenrecht. Xu c. 12 der römischen
        Ostersynod von 1059." Annuarium historiae conciliorum
        7 (1975): 159-165.

02685. Laeuchli, Samuel. Power and Sexuality: The Emergence
        of Canon Law at the Synod of Elvira. Philadelphia:
        Temple University Press, 1972.

02686. LeBras, Gabriel. "Le mariage dans la théologie
        et le droit de l'église du XIe au XIIIe siècle."
        Cahiers de civilisation médiévale 11 (April-
        June 1968): 191-202.

02687. Lettmann, Reinhard. Die Diskussion über die klan-
        destinen Ehen und die Einführung einer zur
        Gültigkeit Verpflichtenden Eheschliessungsform
        auf dem Konzil von Trient: eine kanonistische
        Untersuchung. Munsterische Beiträge zur Theologie,
        no. 31. Munster in Westfalen: Aschendorff, 1967.

02688. Lynch, John E. "Marriage and Celibacy of the Clergy:
        The Discipline of the Western Church. An Historico-
        Canonical Synopsis." The Jurist 32 (Fall-Winter
        1972): 14-38.

02689. _____. "Marriage and Celibacy of the Clergy.
        The Discipline of the Western Church: An Historico-
        Canonical Synopsis, Part II." The Jurist 32 (Spring
        1972): 189-212.

02690. McLaughlin, T.P. "The Prohibition of Marriage against
        Canons in the Early Twelfth Century." Medieval
        Studies 3 (1941): 94-100.

02691. Makowski, Elizabeth M. "The Conjugal debt and
        medieval canon law." Journal of Medieval History 3
        (June 1977): 99-114.

02692. Merzbacher, Friedrich. "Die Eheschliessung durch
        Stellvertreter nach altem und geltendem kanonischen
        Recht." In Ecclesia et ius. Festgabe für Audomar
        Scheuermann zur 60. Geburtstag, edited by Karl
        Sieper et. al., pp. 455-466. Munich: F. Schöningh,
        1968.

02693. Metz, Rene. "Recherches sur la condition de la femme
        selon Gratien." Studia Gratiana 12 (1967): 380-396.

02694. _____. "Recherches sur le statut de la femme en
        droit canonique: bilan historique et perspectives
        d'avenir: problèmes de méthodes." L'année
        canonique 12 (1968): 85-113.

02695. _____. "Le statut de las femme en droit canonique
        médiéval." Recueils de la Société Jean Bodin 12 (1962):
        59-113.

02696. Noonan, John T., Jr. "Abortion and the Catholic
        Church: A Summary History." Natural Law Forum 12
        (1967): 85-131.

02697. _____. "Freedom, Experimentation and
        Permanence in the Canon Law on Marriage." In Law
        for Liberty, edited by James E. Biechler, pp. 52-68.
        Baltimore: Helicon, 1967.

02698. _____. "Marriage in the Middle Ages:
        Power to Choose." Viator 4 (1973): 419-434.

02699.   Onclin, W. "L'âge requis pour le mariage dans le doctrine
          canonique médiévale." In Proceedings of the Second Interna-
          tional Congress of Medieval Canon Law, Boston College, 12-16
          August 1963, edited by Stephan Kuttner and J. Joseph Ryan,
          pp. 1237-1247. Vatican City: S. Congregatio de Seminariis et
          Studiorum Universitatibus, 1965. Also see Monumenta iuris
          canonici Series C 1 (1965): 237-247.

02700.   Pfaff, Volkert. "Das kirchliche Eherecht em Ende des 12.
          Jahrhunderts." Zeitschrift der Savigny Stiftung für Rechts-
          geschichte (Kanonistische Abteilung) 94 (1977): 73-117.

02701.   Picasso, Giorgio. "Il fondamenti del matrimonio nelle Colle-
          zioni canoniche." In Il Matrimonio nella società altomed-
          ievale. Centro Italiano di Studi sull'Alto Medioevo, 1977.

02702.   Ritzer, Korbinan. Le mariage dans les églises chrétiennes
          du Ier au XIe siècle. Paris: Cerf, 1970.

02703.   Rondet, H. Introduction a l'étude de la théologie du
          mariage. Theologie, pastorale, et spiritualité,
          no. 6. Paris: Lethilleux, 1960.

02704.   Rordorf, Willy. "Marriage in the New Testament and in the
          Early Church." Journal of Ecclesiastical History 20
          (October 1969): 193-210.

02705.   Rosambert, André. La Veuve en droit canonique jusqu'au
          XVIe siècle. Paris: Dalloz, 1923.

02706.   Rossetti, Gabriella. "Il matrimonio del clero nella società
          alto medievale." In Il matrimonio nella società alto med-
          ievale, 1: 473-567. Spoleto: Centro Italiano di Studi
          Sull Alto Medioevo, 1977.

02707.   Rudt de Collenberg, Wipertus H. "Les dispenses matrimoniales
          accordées à l'Orient Latin selon les registres du Vatican
          d'Honorius III à Clément VII (1223-1385)." Mélanges de l'
          école Francaise de Rome, moyen âge et temps modernes 89
          (1977): 11-93.

02708.   Russ, Joanna. "Comment on 'Prostitution in Medieval Canon
          Law', by James Brundage." Signs 2 (Summer 1977): 922-924.

02709.   Stockmeier, P. "Scheidung und Wiederverheiratung in der alten
          Kirche." Theologische Quartalschrift 151 (1971): 39-51.

02710.   Taviani, Huguette. "Le mariage dans l'hérésie de l'an mil."
          Annales: économies, sociétés, et civilisations 32 (November-
          December 1977): 1074-1089.

02711.   Thomas Aquinas. Basic Writings. 2 vols. Edited by
          Anton C. Pegis. New York: Random House, 1945.
          [See especially vol. I, Summa Theologica, Q 92, The
          Production of Women, pp. 879-884.]

02712.   Vogel, Cyrille. "L'âge des époux chrétiens au moment
          de contracter mariage, d'après les inscriptions
          paléochrétiennes." _Revue de droit canonique_ 16
          1966): 355-366.

02713.   Weigand, Rudolf. "Kanonistische Ehetraktate aus dem
          12. Jahrhundert." In _Proceedings of the 3rd
          International Congress of Medieval Canon Law,
          Strasbourg, 3-6 September 1968_, pp. 59-79. Vatican
          City: Biblioteca Apostolica Vaticani, 1971.

02714.   _____. "Das Scheidungsproblem in der mittelalter-
          lichen Kanonistik." _Theologische Quartalschrift_ 151
          (1971): 52-60.

          Also refer to #2320, 2549, 2555, 2559, 2566.

                          f) Heresy

                        (1) Non-specific

02715.   Lambert, M.D. "The Motives of the Cathars: Some Re-
          flections." _Studies in Church History_ 16 (1979):
          49-59.

02716.   Lerner, Robert. _The Heresy of the Free Spirit in the
          Later Middle Ages_. Berkeley: University of
          California Press, 1972.

02717.   McDonnell, Ernest W. _The Beguines and Beghards in
          Medieval Culture_. 1955. Reprint. New York: Octagon Books,
          Books, 1969.
          [See especially part 2, ch. 1 and part 3, chs. 1 and 2.]

02718.   Mens, A. "Les béguines et béghards dans le cadre de
          la culture médiévale. _Moyen âge_ 64 (1958): 305-315.

02719.   Ridder, C.B. de. "Quelques mots sur l'origine des
          béguines." _Annales d'histoire ecclesiastique belgique_
          12 (1875): 5-21.

02720.   Turberville, Arthur Stanley. _Medieval Heresy and the
          Inquisition_. London: C. Lockwood, 1920.

          Also refer to #2710.

(2) Women

02721. Clark, Gracia. "The Beguines: A Medieval Women's
        Community." Quest 1 (1975): 72-80.

02722. Koch, Gottfried. "Die Frau im mittelalterlichen
        Katharismus und Waldensertum." Studi medievali
        3rd ser. 5 (1964): 741-774.

02723. _____. Frauenfrage und Ketzertum im Mittel-
        alter. Die Frauenbewegung im Rahmen des Katharismus
        und des Waldensertums und ihre sozialen Würzeln.
        Forschungen zur mittelalterlichen Geschichte, vol. 9.
        Berlin: Akademie Verlag, 1962.

02724. _____. "Waldensertum und Frauenfrage im
        Mittelalter." Forschungen und Fortschritte 36
        (1962): 22-26.

02725. McLaughlin, Eleanor. "Les femmes et l'héresie médiévale.
        Un problème dans l'histoire de la spiritualité.
        Concilium Nijmegen 111 (1976): 73-90.

02726. Werner, Ernst. "Die Stellung der Katharer zur Frau."
        Studi Medievali 3rd ser. 2 (1961): 295-301.

g) Witchcraft

02727. Brown, Peter. "Sorcery, Demons and the Rise of
        Christianity from Late Antiquity into the Middle
        Ages." In Witchcraft Confessions and Accusations,
        edited by Mary Douglas, pp. 17-45. New York:
        Tavistock Publications, 1970.

02728. Clark, S. "Inversion, Misrule and the Meaning of
        Witchcraft." Past and Present 87 (May 1980):
        98-127.

02729. Eliade, Mircea. "Some Observarions on European
        Witchcraft." History of Religions 14 (1975):
        149-172.

02730. Haan, Jean. Von Hexen und wildem Gejäg. Luxembourg:
        Edi-Centre, 1971.

02731. Hansen, Joseph. Quellen und Untersuchungen zur
        Geschichte des Hexenwahns und der Hexenverfolgung im
        Mittelalter. Bonn: C. Georgi, 1901.

02732. Hansen, Joseph. Zauberwahn, Inquisition und Hexenprozesse
        im Mittelalter und die Entstehung der grossen
        Hexenverfolgung. Historische Bibliothek, no. 12.
        Munich: R. Oldenbourg, 1900.

02733. Jones, William R. "Political Uses of Sorcery in
        Medieval Europe." The Historian 34 (August 1972):
        670-687.

02734. Kieckhefer, Richard. European Witch Trials: Their
        Foundation in Popular and Learned Culture, 1300-1500.
        Berkeley: University of California Press, 1976.

02735. Kors, Alan C. and Peters, Edward, ed. Witchcraft in
        Europe, 1100-1700: A Documentary History. Phila-
        delphia: University of Pennsylvania Press, 1972.

02736. Leutenbauer, Siegfried. Hexerei und Zaubereidelikt in
        der Literatur von 1450 bis 1550. Berlin: Verlag
        J. Schweitzer, 1972.

02737. McCall, Andrew. "Sorcerers and Witches." In The
        Medieval Underworld, pp. 238-258. London: Hamish
        Hamilton, 1979.

02738. Mayer, Anton. Erdmutter und Hexe: Eine Untersuchung
        zur Geschichte des Hexenglaubens und zur Vorgeschichte
        der Hexenprozesse. Munich-Freising: Datterer, 1936.

02739. Michelet, Jules. Satanism and Witchcraft: A Study in
        Medieval Superstition. 1958. Reprint. Secaucus,
        N.J.: Citadel Press, 1974.

02740. _____. The Witch of the Middle Ages. Trans-
        lated by L.J. Trotter. London: Simpkin, Marshall,
        and Co., 1863.

02741. Midelfort, Eric. "Recent Witch Hunting Research, or
        where do we go from here?" Papers of the Biblio-
        graphical Society of America 62 (1968): 373-420.

02742. Miller, B.D.H. "She who hath Drunk any Potion." Medium
        Aevum 31 (1962): 188-193.

02743. Monter, E. William. "The Pedestal and the Stake:
        courtly love and witchcraft." In Becoming Visible:
        Women in European History, edited by Renate Bridenthal
        and Claudia Koonz, pp. 119-36. Boston: Houghton
        Mifflin, 1978.

02744. Orr, L. "Sort of History: Michelet's La sorcière."
        Yale French Studies 58 (1980): 119-126.

02745. Peters, Edward. The Magician, the Witch, and the Law.
        Philadelphia: University of Pennsylvania Press, 1978.

02746. Reinhard, J.R. "Burning at the stake in Medieval Law
        and Literature." Speculum 16 (April 1941): 186-209.

02747. Richardson, Herbert. Nun, Witch, Playmate. New York:
        Harper and Row, 1974.

02748. Ruether, Rosemary. "The persecution of witches: a
        case of sexism and ageism?" Christianity and Crisis
        34 (December 1974): 291-295.

02749. Russell, Jeffrey Burton. Witchcraft in the Middle Ages.
        Ithaca, N.Y.: Cornell University Press, 1972.

02750. Tucker, Elizabeth. "Antecedents of Contemporary Witch-
        craft in the Middle Ages." Journal of Popular Culture
        14 (Summer 1980): 70-78.

02751. "Women Doctors in the Viking Age." Boston Medical and
        Surgical Journal 176 (24 May 1917): 746-747.

7. SOCIAL

"The young nobleman followed his father to camp and
court, where he tasted of the experiences of life;
the young noblewoman stayed at home, cut off from
intercourse with those of her age and standing and
from every possibility of widening her mental horizon."
                            Lina Eckenstein, Women
                            under Monasticism, 1896.

a) Generic

(1) Non-specific

02752. Abrahams, Israel. Jewish Life in the Middle Ages.
        Rev. ed. London: E. Goldston, Ltd., 1932.

02753. Davis, William, Sterns. Life in a Medieval Barony.
        1923. New York: Harper Brothers, 1951.
        [See especially ch. 5.]

02754. Duby, Georges. The Chivalrous Society. Berkeley:
        University of California Press, 1977.

02755. Duckett, Eleanor Shipley. Death and Life in the Tenth
        Century. Ann Arbor, Mich.: University of Michigan Press,
        1967.

02756. Fossier, Robert. Histoire sociale de l'occident médiéval.
        Paris: Colin, 1970.

02757. Gleichen-Russwurm, Alexander von. Die gotische Welt
        Sitten und Gebräuche im späten Mittelalter. Stutt-
        gart: Julius Hoffmann, 1922.

02758. _____. Der Ritterspiegel
        Geschichte der vornehmen Welt im romanischen Mittel-
        alter. Stuttgart: Julius Hoffmann, 1923.

02759. Haucourt, Genevieve d'. La vie au moyen âge. 3rd ed.
        Paris: Presses universitaires de France, 1952.

02760. Jarrett, Bede. Social Theories of the Middle Ages
        1200-1500. Westminster, Maryland: The Newman Book
        Shop, 1942.

02761. Marcus, Jacob R. The Jew in the Medieval World A
        Source Book. New York: Atheneum, 1969.

02762. Neumann, E. Der Streit um das ritterliche Tugendsystem.
        Erbe der Vergangenheit Festgabe fur Karl Helm zum 80.
        Geburtstag. Tubingen: Niemeyer, 1951.

02763. Riche, Pierre. Daily Life in the World of Charlemagne.
        Translated by JoAnn McNamara. Philadelphia:
        University of Pennsylvania Press, 1978.

02764. Rörig, Fritz. Die europäische Stadt und die Kultur des
        Bürgertums im Mittelalter. Edited by Luise Rorig.
        Kleine Vandenhoeck, Reihe, nos. 12-13. Gottingen:
        Vandenhoeck and Ruprecht, 1955.

02765. Rosenthal, Joel T. Nobles and the Noble Life 1295-1500.
        New York: Barnes and Noble, 1976.

02766. Rowling, Marjorie. Life in Medieval Times. New York:
        G.P. Putnam's Sons, Capricorn Books, 1973.
        [See especially ch. 4, Women and Wives.]

                        (2) Women

02767. Bezzola, Reto R. "La transformation des moeurs et le
        rôle de la femme dans la classe féodale du XIe au
        XIIe siècle." In Les origines et la formation de la
        littérature courtoise en Occident (500-1200),
        edited by Reto R. Bezzola, Part 2, Vol. 2, pp. 461-484.
        Bibliothèque de l'école des hautes études. Sciences
        historiques et philologiques, no. 313. Paris:
        Champion, 1960.

02768.   Brooke, Christopher N.L.   "'Both small and great
          beasts:'   an introductory study." In Medieval Women,
          edited by Derek Baker, pp. 1-13. Studies in Church
          History, Subsidia, I. Oxford: Blackwell, 1978.

02769.   Erickson, Carolly. "The View of Women". In The
          Medieval Vision, pp. 181-212. New York: Oxford
          University Press, 1975.

02770.   Fossier, Robert. "La femme dans les sociétés occi-
          dentales." Cahiers de civilisation médiévale 20
          (1977): 93-104.

02771.   Fries, Maureen. "Popular Images of Women in
          Medieval Literature." Journal of Popular Culture
          14 (Summer 1980): 79-86.

02772.   Herlihy, David. "Land, Family, and Women in Continental
          Europe, 701-1200." In Women in Medieval Society,
          edited by Susan Mosher Stuard, pp. 13-46. Philadel-
          phia: University of Pennsylvania Press, 1976. Also in
          Social History of Italy and Western Europe, pp. 89-120,
          edited by David Herlihy. London: Valorium Reprints, 1978.

02773.   _____. Women in Medieval Society. Houston,
          Texas: University of St. Thomas, 1971. Reprinted
          in The Social History of Italy and Western Europe,
          700-1500, edited by David Herlihy,   pp. 3-17.
          London: Valorium Reprints, 1978.

02774.   Kaufman, Michael W. "Spare Ribs: The Conception of
          Woman in the Middle Ages and the Renaissance."
          Soundings 56 (Summer 1973): 139-163.

02775.   Labande, Edmond-René. "Conclusions of the Colloquium
          'La Femme dans les civilisatins des Xe-XIIIe siecles.'"
          Cahiers de civilisation médiévale 20 (1977): 253-260.

02776.   Leclercq, Jacqueline. "Un temoin de l'antifeminisme au
          moyen âge." Revue bénédictine 80 (1970): 304-309.

02777.   McNamara, JoAnn and Wemple, Suzanne F. "Sanctity and
          power: the dual pursuit of medieval women." In
          Becoming Visible: Women in European History, edited
          by Renate Bridenthal and Claudia Koonz, pp. 90-118.
          Boston: Houghton Mifflin, 1977.

02778.   Marchalonis, Shirley. "Above Rubies: Popular Views of
          Medieval Women." Journal of Popular Culture 14
          (Summer 1980): 87-93.

02779.   Pascal, Carlo. "Misoginia medievale (duc carmi medievali
          control le donne). Studi Medievali 2 (1906-1907):
          242-248.

02780. Radcliff-Umstead, Douglas. The Roles and Images of
        Women in the Middle Ages and Renaissance. Pittsburgh:
        University of Pittsburgh Publications on the Middle
        Ages and Renaissance, 1975.

b) Demography

02781. Amundsen, Darrel W. and Diers, Carol Jean. "The Age of
        Menarche in Medieval Europe." Human Biology 45
        (1973): 363-368.

02782. Fregier, Honoré Antoine. Des Classes dangereuses de la
        population dans les grandes villes et des moyens de
        les rendre meilleures. 2 vols. Paris: J.B. Bailliere,
        1840.

02783. Green, V.H.H. "Population and Health." In Medieval
        Civilization in Western Europe, pp. 15-32. London:
        Edward Arnold, 1971.

02784. Hallam, H.E. "Some Thirteenth-Centurh Censuses."
        Economic History Review 2nd ser. 10 (April 1958):
        340-361.

02785. Herlihy, David. "Life Expectancies for Women in
        Medieval Society." In The Role of Women in the
        Middle Ages, edited by Rosmarie Thee Morewedge,
        pp. 1-22. Albany, New York: State University
        of New York Press, 1975.

02786. _____. "The natural history of medieval women."
        Natural History 87 (March 1978): 56-67.

02787. Post, J.B. "Age at Menopause and Menarche: Some
        Medieval Authorities." Population Studies 25 (1971):
        83-87.

02788. Riche, Pierre. "Problemes de démographie historique du
        Haut Moyen Age (Ve-VIIIe siècles)." Annales de démo-
        graphie historique (1966): 37-55.

02789. Riquet, Michel. "Christianisme et population." Popula-
        tion 4 (October-December 1949): 615-630.

02790   Russell, Josiah Cox. "Late Medieval Population Pat-
        terns." Speculum 20 (1945): 157-171.

02791. _____. "Population in Europe 500-1500."
        In Fontana Economic History of Europe, edited by
        Carlo Cipolla, pp. 25-70. London: Collins-Fontana
        Books, 1972.

02792. Russell, Josiah Cox. "Recent Advances in Medieval
        Demography." Speculum 40 (January 1965): 84–101.

        Also refer to #1593, 1594.

                        c) Family

                    (1) Non-specific

02793. Bullough, D.A. "Early Medieval Social Groupings:
        The Terminology of Kinship." Past and Present 45
        (November 1969): 3–18.

02794. Duby, Georges. "Présentation de l'enquête sur 'Famille
        et sexualité au moyen âge.'" In Famille et parenté
        dans l'occident médiéval, edited by Georges Duby and
        Jacques Le Goff, pp. 9–11. Collection de l'école
        française de Rome, no. 30. Rome: Collection de
        l'école française de Rome, 1977.

02795. _____. "Structures familiales dans le moyen
        age occidental." XIII congres international des
        sciences historiques 16–23 août, 1970 1 (1973):
        152–161.

02796. Hareven, Tamara K. "Household and Family in Past Time."
        History and Theory 14 (1975): 242–251.

02797. Hughes, Diane Owen. "Struttura familiare e sistemi
        di successione ereditaria nei testamenti dell'Europa
        medievale." Quaderni storici 33 (September–December
        1976): 929–952.

02798. _____. "Toward Historical Ethnography:
        Notarial Records and Family History in the Middle
        Ages." Historical Methods Newsletter 7 (1974):
        61–71.

02798. McNamara, JoAnn and Wemple, Suzanne. "The power of
        women through the Family in Medieval Europe." In
        Clio's Consciousness Raised, edited by Mary Hartman
        and Louise Banner, pp. 103–118. New York: Harper
        and Row, 1974. Also in Feminist Studies 1 (Winter–
        Spring 1973): 126–155.

02799. Manselli, Raoul. "Vie familiale et ethique sexuelle dans
        les penitentiels." In Famille et parenté dans l'Occident
        médiéval, Actes du Colloque de Paris (6-8 Juin 1974)
        organisée par l'Ecole Pratique des haut études (VI e
        section) en collaboration avec le College de France et
        l'école française de Rome, edited by George Duby and
        Jacques le Goff, pp. 363-378. Rome: Collection de
        l'école française de Rome, 1977.

02800. Trani, G. "Le 'Retour a la table,' une tentative
        coutumière pour maintenir le patrimomoine familial."
        Revue historique de droit française et étranger 4th
        ser. 49 (1971): 65-94.

        Also refer to #2547, 2568, 2581, 2772, 2831.

                        (2) Childhood

02801. Biraben, Jean-Noel. "La médecine et l'enfant au Moyen
        Age." Annales de démographie historique (1973): 73-75.

02802. Brissaud, Y.-B. "L'infanticide à la fin du moyen âge,
        ses motivations psychologiques et sa repression."
        Revue historique de droit francais et étranger. 4th
        ser. 50 (1972): 229-256.

02803. Coleman, Emily. "Infanticide in the Early Middle Ages."
        In Women in Medieval Society, edited by Susan Mosher
        Stuard, pp. 47-70. Philadelphia: University of
        Pennsylvania Press, 1976. Also in Annales: économies,
        sociétés, et civilisations 29 (March-April 1974): 315-
        335.

02804. Demaître, Luke. "The Idea of Childhood and Childcare in the
        Medical Writings of the Middle Ages." Journal of Psycho-
        History 4 (Spring 1977): 461-490.

02805. Etienne, Robert. "La conscience médicale antique et la
        vie des enfants." Annales de démographie historique
        (1973): 15-46.

02806. Feilzer, Heinrich. Jugend in der mittelalterlichen
        Ständegesellschaft. Vienna: Herder, 1971.

02807. Lyman, Richard B., Jr. "Barbarism and Religion: Late
        Roman and Early Medieval Childhood." In The History
        of Childhood, edited by Lloyd deMause, pp. 75-100.
        New York: Harper Torchbook, Harper and Row, 1975.

02808.   McLaughlin, Mary Martin. "Survivors and Surogates:
         Children and Parents from the Ninth to the Thirteenth
         Centuries." In The History of Childhood, edited by
         Lloyd deMause, pp. 101-182. New York: Harper Torch-
         book, Harper and Row, 1975.

                          d) Marriage

02809.   Albertario, Emilio. "Di alcuni riferimenti al
         matrimonio e al possesso in S. Agostono." In Studi
         di diritto romano, edited by Emilio Albertario,
         1: 229-248. Milan: A. Giuffrè, 1933.

02810.   Blundell, James. "Husbands galore." The Coat of Arms
         n.s. 3, 105 (1978): 11-16.

02811.   Bullough, Vern L. "Marriage in the Middle Ages: Five
         Medical and Scientific Views of Women." Viator 4
         (1973): 485-501.

02812.   Crouzel, Henri. Virginité et mariage selon origène.
         Breslauer Studien zur historischen Theologie, no. 23.
         Paris: Desclée de Brouwer, 1963.

02813.   Delhaye, Philippe. "Le dossier antimatrimonial de
         l'Adversus Jovinianum et son influence sur quelques
         écrits latins du XIIᵉ siècle." Medieval Studies 13
         (1951): 65-86.

02814.   Duby, Georges. "Le mariage dans la société du haut
         moyen âge." In Il Matrimonio nella società alto-
         medievale 1: 13-39. Spoleto: Centro Italiano di Studi
         sull'Alto Medioevo, 1977.

02815.   Emmen, A. "Verginità e matrimonio nella valutazione
         dell'Olivi." Studi francescani 64 (1967): 11-57.

02816.   Fransen, Gerard. "La rupture du mariage." In Il matri-
         monio nella società alto medievale 2: 603-632.
         Spoleto: Centro Italiano di Studi sull'Alto Medioevo,
         1977.

02817.   Gregoire, Reginald. "Il matrimonio mistico." In Il
         matrimonio nella società alto medievale 2: 701-817.
         Spoleto: Centro Italiano di Studi sull'Alto Medioevo, 1977.

02818.   Guillet-Rydell, Mireille. "Nature et rôle du mariage
         dans les lais anonymes bretons." Romania 96 (1975):
         91-104.

02819. Hamelin, Leonce. "Le mariage. Hier. Aujourd 'hui. Demain." In S. Bonaventure 1274-1974, edited by Jacques Guy Bougerol, 4: 461-502. Rome: Collegio S. Bonaventura, 1974.

02820. Herlihy, David. "The Medieval Marriage Market." Medieval and Renaissance Studies 6 (1976): 3-27.

02821. Hillman, Eugene. "The Development of Christian Marriage Structures." Concilium 55 (1970): 25-38.

02822. Leyerle, John et al. "Marriage in the Middle Ages: An Introduction." Viator 4 (1973): 413-448.

02823. McLaughlin, T.P. "The Formation of the Marriage Bond According to the Summa Parisiensis." Medieval Studies 15 (1953): 208-212.

02824. Manselli, Raoul. "Il matrimonio nei Penitenziali." In Il matrimonio nella società altomedievale, 1: 287-319. Spoleto: Centro Italiano di Studi sull'Alto Medioevo, 1977.

02825. Mueller, Hermann. L'Influence considerable des mariages princiers, et des femmes en général, au moyen âge. Heidelberg: n.p., 1880.

02826. Noonan, John T., Jr. "Marital Affection in the Canonists." Studia Gratiana 12 (1967): 479-509.

02827. Parmisano, Fabian. "Love and Marriage in the Middle Ages." New Blackfriars 50 (1969): 599-608 and 649-660.

02828. Paulus, Niklaus. "Mittelalterliche Stimmen über den Eheorden." Historisch- politische Blätter für das katholische Deutschland 141 (1908): 1008-1024.

02829. Pellegrini, Giovan Battista. "Terminologia matrimoniale." In Il matrimonio nella società altomedievale, 1:43-102. Spoleto: Centro Italiano di Studi sull'Alto Medioevo, 1977.

02830. Rosenthal, Joel T. "Marriage and the Blood Feud in 'Heroic' Europe." British Journal of Sociology 17 (1966): 133-144.

02831. Schmid, Karl. "Heirat, Familienfolge, Geschlechterbe- wusstsein." In Il Matrimonio nella società alto- medievale, 1:103-138. Spoleto: Centro Italiano di Studi sull'Alto Medioevo, 1977.

02832. Sheehan, Michael M. "Choice of Marriage Partner in the Middle Ages: Development and Mode of Application of a Theory of Marriage. Studies in Medieval and Renaissance History n.s. 1 (1978): 1-33.

02833. Soggin, Jan Alberto. "Il matrimonio presso i Valdesi
        prima della Riforma (1170-1532)." Il diritto
        ecclesiastico 64 (1953): 31-95.

02834. _____. "Uno scritto sul matrimonio dei
        Valdesi prima della Riforma." Atti della Accademia
        Nazionale dei Lincei, Rendiconti, Classe di scienze,
        morali, storiche e filologiche 8th ser. 6 (July-Octo-
        ber 1951): 400-404.

02835. _____. "Uno scritto sul matrimonio dei
        Valdesi prima della Riforma; Epilegomena." Atti della
        Accademia Nazionale dei Lincei, Rendiconti, Classe di
        scienze, morali, storiche e filologiche 8th ser. 14
        (May-June 1959): 259-262.

02836. Thurston, H. "Mediaeval Matrimony." Dublin Review 17
        (1922): 44-57.

02837. Turlan, Juliette M. "Recherches sur le mariage dans
        la pratique coutumière." Revue d'histoire de droit
        français et étranger 35 (1957): 477-528.

02838. Verlinden, Charles. "Le mariage des esclaves". In
        Il matrimonio nella società altomedievale, 2:569-602.
        Spoleto: Centro Italiano di Studi sull'Alto Medioevo,
        1977.

02839. Violante, Cinzio. "Discorso di chiusura." In Il
        matrimonio nella societa altomedievale, 2:967-996.
        Spoleto: Centro Italiano di Studi sull'Alto Medioevo,
        1977.

02840. Vismara, Guilio. "I rapporti patrimoniali tra coniugi
        nell'alto medioevo." In Il Matrimonio nella societa
        altomedievale, 2:633-700. Spoleto: Centro Italiano
        di studi sull'Alto Medioevo, 1977.

02841. Vogel, Cyrille. "Les rites de la célébration du
        mariage: leur signification dans la formation du
        lien durant le haut moyen âge." In Il matrimonio
        nella società altomedievale, 1:379-472. Spoleto:
        Centro Italiano di Studi sull'Alto Medioevo, 1977.

        Also refer to #2547, 2549-2551, 2553-2555, 2557, 2559-2563,
        2565, 2566, 2570, 2584, 2667, 2668, 2670-2684, 2687-2693,
        2698-2707, 2709-2714, 4622, 4623.

                    e) Sex Life and Morals

                    (1) Non-specific

02842. Browe, Peter. Beiträge zur Sexualethik des Mittel-
        alters. Breslau: Müller and Seifert, 1932.

02843. Bugge, John M. Virginitas: An Essay in the History of
        a Medieval Ideal. The Hague: Martinus Nijhoff, 1975.

02844. Bullough, Vern L. "Transvestites in the Middle Ages."
        American Journal of Sociology 79 (May 1974): 1381-
        1394.

02845. Cleugh, James. Love Locked Out: An Examination of the
        Irrepressible Sexuality of the Middle Ages. New York:
        Spring Books, 1963.

02846. Dervieu. "Le lit et le berceau au moyen âge." Bulletin
        monumental 81 (1912): 387-415.

02847. Dingwall, Eric John. The Girdle of Chastity. A Medico-
        Historical Study. London: G. Routledge and Sons,
        1931.

02848. Lemay, Helen Rodnite. "Some thirteenth and fourteenth
        century lectures on female sexuality." International
        Journal of Women's Studies 1 (July-August 1978): 391-
        400.

02849. _____. "The Stars and Human Sexuality:
        Some Medieval Scientific Views." Isis 71 (March 1980):
        127-137.

02850. Löffler, J. Die Störungen des geschlechtlichen Vermögens
        in der Literatur der autoritativen Theologie des
        Mittelalters. Wiesbaden: Steiner, 1958.

02851. Menager, Leon-Robert. "Sesso e repressione: quando,
        perchè?" Quaderni medievali 4 (1977): 44-68.

02852. Radcliff-Umstead, Douglas, ed. Human Sexuality in the
        Middle Ages and Renaissance. University of Pittsburgh
        Publications on the Middle Ages and Renaissance, no. 4.
        Pittsburgh: Center for Medieval and Renaissance Studies,
        1978.

        Also refer to #2794, 2800, 2831.

                    (2) Prostitutes

02853. McCall, Andrew. "Prostitutes." In The Medieval Under-
        world, pp. 179-198. London: Hamish Hamilton, 1979.

02854. Markun, Leo. Prostitution in the Medieval World.
        Girard, Kansas: Haldeman-Julius Co., 1926.

02855. Veze, Raoul (Jean Hervez). Ruffians et ribaudes au moyen âge;
        d'après l'histoire de la prostitution de Pierre Dufour, les
        chroniques du temps les romans de chevalerie et recueils
        poétiques. Paris: Bibliotheque des curieux, 1913.

        Also refer to #2669.

f) Fashion/Manners

02856. Lacroix, Paul. Manners, Customs and Dress during the Middle
        Ages and Renaissance. London: Chapman and Hall, 1874.

02857. Taylor, G.S., ed. The Book of the Knight of La Tour
        Landry. London: The Verona Society, 1930.

        Also refer to #1614.

g) Health/Medical

(1) Non-specific

02858. Fort, George F. History of Medical Economy during the
        Middle Ages. New York: J.W. Bouton, 1883.

02859. Walsh, James Joseph. Medieval Medicine. London:
        A. and C. Black, Ltd., 1920.

(2) Abortion/Birth Control

02860. Lio, Ermenegildo. "Alessandro di Hales e la contra-
        ccezione." Antonianum 52 (1977): 289-308.

        Also refer to #2697.

(3) Women in Medicine

02861. Benedek, Thomas G. "The Roles of Medieval Women in the Healing
        Arts." In The Roles and Images of Women in the Middle Ages
        and Renaissance, pp. 145-159. Pittsburgh: University of
        Pittsburgh Center for Medieval and Renaissance Studies, 1975.

02862.   Bolton, H. Carrington.   "The Early Practice of Medicine
         by Women." Journal of Science 18 (February 1881):
         57-70.

02863.   Caldwell, Ruth.   "Women in Medicine: Chapter II.
         Medieval Women Physicians." Medical Woman's Journal
         37 (March 1930): 72-75.

02864.   Diepgen, Paul. Frau und Frauenheilkunde in der Kultur
         des Mittelalters. Stuttgart: G. Thieme, 1963.

02865.   Hughes, Muriel J. Women Healers in Medieval Life and
         Literature. 1943. Reprint. New York: Arno, 1978.

02866.   Huppert, M.P. "Women Doctors in the Middle Ages."
         History of Medicine 5 (Autumn 1973): 25-26.

02867.   Hurd-Mead, Kate Campbell. "Concerning Certain Medical
         Women of the Late Middle Ages." Medical Life 42
         (March 1935): 110-128.

02868.   Power, Eileen. "Some Women Practitioners of Medicine
         in the Middle Ages." Proceedings of the Royal
         Society of Medicine 14 (21 December 1921): 20-23.

02869.   Schoenfeld, Walther. Frauen in der abendlandischen
         Heilkunde. Stuttgart: Enke, 1947.

02870.   Segre, Marcello. "Jewish Female Doctors in the Middle
         Ages." Pagina di Storia della Medicina 14 (1970):
         98-106.

         Also refer to #2751, 2811.

8. CULTURAL

"Everybody knows that love can have no place between
husband and wife."

                               Andreas Capellanus

a) Education

02871.   Campbell, Jane. "Women Scholars of the Middle Ages."
         American Catholic Quarterly Review 43 (April 1938):
         237-240.

02872. Duckett, Eleanor Shipley. Women and their Letters in
        the Early Middle Ages. Northampton, Mass.: Smith
        College, 1965.

02873. Ferrante, Joan M. "The Education of Women in the Middle
        Ages in Theory, Fact, and Fantasy." In Beyond their
        Sex, Learned Women of the European Past, edited by
        Patricia Labalme, pp. 9-42. New York: New York
        University Press, 1980.

02874. Grundmann, Herbert. "Litteratus-illiteratus." Archiv
        für Kulturgeschichte 40 (1958): 1-65.
        [See especially pp. 58-59.]

02875. Guadier, M. "De l'éducation des femmes au XIVe siècle, étude
        historique." Annale de l'académie de Macon 9 (1870): 30-42.

02876. Heinrich, Sister Mary Pia. The Canonesses and Educa-
        tion in the Early Middle Ages. Washington D.C.:
        Catholic University Press, 1924.

02877. Hentsch, Alice A. De la littérature didactique du
        moyen âge s'adressant spécialement aux femmes.
        Cahors: A. Coueslant, 1903.

02878. Jourdain, Charles. "Memoire sur l'éducation des femmes
        au moyen âge." Mémoires de l'académie des inscriptions
        et belles-lettres 2nd ser. 28 (1874): 79-133.
        Also in Excursions Historiques et Philosophiques,
        pp. 464-509. Paris: Firmin-Didot, 1888.

02879. Kösterus, Friedrich. Frauenbildung im Mittelalter:
        eine kulturhistorische Studie. Wurzburg: Woerl, 1877.

02880. Lehrman, Sara. "The Education of Women in the Middle
        Ages." In The Roles and Images of Women in the
        Middle Ages and Renaissance, pp. 133-144. Pittsburgh:
        University of Pittsburgh Center for Medieval and
        Renaissance Studies, 1975.

02881. Meyn-von Westenholz, Elisabeth. Frauenbildung im
        Mittelalter. Quellenhefte zum Frauenleben in der
        Geschichte, edited by Emmy Beckmann and Irma Stoss,
        vol. 2. Berlin: F. A. Herbig, 1927-1933.

b) Literature

(1) Non-specific

02882. Brewer, Derek S. "The Ideal of Feminine Beauty in
        Medieval Literature." Modern Language Review 50
        (1955): 257-269.

02883. Bruckner, Albert. "Zum Problem der Frauenhandschriften
        im Mittelalter." In Aus Mittelalter und Neuzeit:
        Gerhard Kallen zum 70. Geburtstag, edited by Josef
        Engel and Hans Martin Klinkenberg, pp. 171-183. Bonn:
        P. Hanstein, 1957.

02884. Burton, T.L. "The crocodile as the symbol of an
        evil woman: a medieval interpretation of the croco-
        dile relationship." Parergon 20 (1978): 25-34.

02885. Combridge, Rosemary. "Ladies, Queens and Decorum."
        Reading Medieval Studies 1 (1975): 71-83.

02886. Demers, Jeanne. "La quête de l'anti-Graal ou un
        récit fantastique: 'Le Paradis de la Reine Sibylle'."
        Moyen âge 83 (1977): 469-492.

02887. Dronke, Peter. Medieval Latin and the Rise of
        European Love-Lyric. 2 vols. Oxford: Clarendon
        Press, 1968.

02888. Economou, George D. The Goddess Natura in medieval
        literature. Cambridge, Mass.: Harvard University
        Press, 1972.

02889. Ferrante, Joan M. Woman as Image in Medieval Literature
        from the Twelfth Century to Dante. New York:
        Columbia University Press, 1975.

02890. Grundmann, Herbert. "Die Frauen und die Literatur im
        Mittelalter." Archiv für Kulturgeschichte 25 (1935):
        129-161.

02891. Knapp, Peggy Ann. "Nature is a Woman." In The Roles
        and Images of Women in the Middle Ages and Renaissance,
        pp. 59-71. Pittsburgh: University of Pittsburgh
        Center for Medieval and Renaissance Studies, 1975.

02892. Krayer, Rudolf. Frauenlob und die Natur-Allegorese.
        Motivgeschichtliche Untersuchungen. Ein Beitrag
        zur Geschichte des antiken Traditionsgutes. Heidel-
        berg: Winter, 1960.

02893. Lot-Borodine, Myrrha. De l'amour profane à l'amour
        sacré. Etudes de psychologie sentimentale au moyen
        âge. Paris: Nizet, 1961.

02894. Moser-Rath, Elfriede." Frauenfeindliche Tendenzen im
        Witz." Zeitschrift für Volkskunde 74 (1978): 40-57.

02895. Schibanoff, Susan. "Images of Women in Medieval
        Literature: A Selected Bibliography of Scholarship."
        Women's Studies Newsletter 4 (Fall 1976): 10-11.

02896. Schreiber, Earl G. "Venus in the Medieval Mythographic
        Tradition." Journal of English and Germanic Philology
        74 (October 1975): 519-535.

02897. Verdier, Philippe. "Woman in the Marginalia of Gothic
        Manuscripts and Related Works." In The Role of Women
        in the Middle Ages, edited by Rosmarie Thee Morewedge,
        pp. 121-187. Albany, New York: State University of
        New York Press, 1975.

02898. Wulff, August. Die frauenfeindlichen Dichtungen in
        den romanistischen Literature des Mittelalters bis
        zum Ende des XIII Jahrhunderts. Romanistische
        Arbeiten, edited by Carl Voretzoch, vol. 4. Halle:
        M. Niemeyer, 1914.

                    (2)   Philosophy

02899. Camus, Pierre. "Le mythe de la femme chez saint
        Thomas d'Aquin." Revue Thomiste 76 (1976):
        243-265, 394-409.

                    (3)   Poetry

02900. Harris, Joseph. "'Maiden in the Mor Lay' and the
        Medieval Magdalene Tradition." The Journal of
        Medieval and Renaissance Studies 1 (1971): 58-87.

02901. Suttina, Luigi. "Una cantilena medievale contro le
        donne." Studi Medievali 2 (1906-1907): 457-460.

                    (4)   Troubadours, Trouvères

02902. Belperron, Pierre. "La Joie d'Amour," contribution
        a l'étude des troubadours et de l'amour courtois.
        Paris: Plon, 1948.

02903. Bogin, Meg. The Women Troubadours. New York:
        Paddington Press, 1976.

02904. Briffault, Robert. The Troubadours. Translated by
        Lawrence F. Koons. Bloomington: Indiana University
        Press, 1965.

02905. Camproux, Charles. Le "joy d'amour" des troubadours
        jeu et joie d'amour. Montpellier: Causse/Castelnau,
        1965.

02906.   Chaytor, H.J. Rev. The Troubadours. Cambridge: The
           University Press, 1912.

02907.   Davenson, Henri. Les Troubadours. Paris: Edition du
           Seuil, 1961.

02908.   Diez, Friedrich. Leben und Werke der Troubadours. Ein
           Beitrag zur nähren Kenntniss des Mittelalters. 1882.
           Reprint. Amsterdam: Rodopi, 1965.

02909.   Hoepffner, Ernest. Les troubadours dans leurs vies et
           dans leurs oeuvres. Paris: A. Colin, 1955.

02910.   Holznecht, Karl Julius. Literary Patronage in the
           Middle Ages. Philadelphia: Collegiate Press, 1923.
             [See especially ch. 3, Troubadours, Trouveres,
             and Minnesingers.]

02911.   Igly, France and Rime, William. Troubadours et
           trouvères. La musique médiévale. Paris: Seghers,
           1960.

02912.   Köhler, Erich. "Der Frauendienst des Trobadors
           dargestellt an ihren Streitgedichten." Germanisch-
           Romanische Monatsschrift 41 (1960): 201-231.

02913.   _____. "Observations historiques et sociologiques
           sur la poésie des troubadours." Cahiers de civilisation
           médiévale 7 (Jan.-March 1964): 27-51.

02914.   _____. Troubadourlyrik und höfischer Roman.
           Aufsätze zur französischen und provenzalischen
           Literatur des Mittelalters. Berlin: Rütter and
           Loening, 1962.

02915.   Lafitte-Houssat, Jacques. Troubadours et cours d'amour.
           Paris: P.U.F., 1960.

02916.   Lemay, Richard. "A propos de l'origine arabe de l'art
           des troubadours." Annales: économies, sociétés,
           civilisations 21 (Sept.-Oct. 1966): 990-1011.

02917.   Lindsay, Jack. The Troubadours and their World of the
           Twelfth and Thirteenth Centuries. London: Frederick
           Muller, 1976.

02918.   Marrou, Henri Irenee. Les Troubadours. Paris: Edition
           du Seuil, 1961.

02919.   Paden, William D., Jr. et. al. "The Troubadour's Lady:
           Her Marital Status and Social Rank." Studies in
           Philology 72 (January 1975): 28-50.

02920.   Rowbotham, John F. The Troubadours and the Courts of
           Love. London: S. Sonnenshein and Co., 1895.

02921.   Schultz, Alwin. Das höfische Leben zur Zeit der
         Minnesinger. 2 vols. Leipzig: Hirzel, 1879, 1880.

02922.   Smythe, Barbara, trans. Troubadour Poets. New York:
         Duffield, 1911.

02923.   Sutherland, D. R. "The Language of the Troubadours."
         French Studies 10 (1956): 199-215.

02924.   Topsfield, L. T. Troubadours and Love. Cambridge:
         University Press, 1975.

02925.   Wechssler, E. Das Kulturproblem des Minnesangs.
         Studien zur Vorgeschichte der Renaissance, vol. 1.
         Halle: M. Niemeyer, 1909.

                         c)   Chivalry

                    (1)   Non-specific

02926.   Barber, Richard. The Knight and Chivalry. New York:
         Scribners, 1970.

02927.   Batty, J. The Spirit and Influence of Chivalry.
         London: Elliot Stock, 1890.

02928.   Cline, Ruth H. "The influence of romances on tournaments
         of the Middle Ages" Speculum 20 (1945): 204-211.

02929.   Curtius, Ernst Robert. "Das ritterliche Tugendsystem."
         Deutsche Vierteljahresschrift für Literaturwissenschaft
         21 (1943): 343-368.

02930.   Flori, Jean. "La notion de chevalerie dans les Chansons
         de Geste du XIIe siècle. Etude historique de voca-
         bulaire." Moyen âge 81 (1975): 211-244, 407-445.

02931.   Gautier, Leon. La Chevalerie. Paris: Arthaud, 1959.

02932.   Kohn, Anna. Das weibliche Schönheitsideal in der
         ritterlichen Dichtung. Form und Geist Arbeiten zur
         germanischen Philologie, vol. 14. Leipzig: Hermann
         Eichblatt Verlag, 1930.

02933.   Prestage, Edgar, ed. Chivalry. New York: Alfred A.
         Knopf, 1928.

(2)   Courtly Love

02934.   Benton, John F.   "Clio and Venus: An Historical View of
          Medieval Love."   In The Meaning of Courtly Love, edited
          by F.X. Newman, pp. 19–42.   Albany: State University
          of New York Press, 1968.

02935.   Bezzola, Reto R.   Les origines et la formation de la
          littérature courtoise en Occident (500–1200).   Vol. 1.
          Paris: Champion, 1960.

02936.   _____.   La société féodale et la transformation
          de la litterature de cour.   Vol. 2.   Paris: Champion,
          1960.

02937.   Boase, Roger.   The Origin and Meaning of Courtly Love:
          A Critical Study of the Scholarship.   Manchester:
          Manchester University Press, 1977.

02938.   Bowden, Betsy.   "The Art of Courtly Copulation."
          Medievalia et Humanistica 9 (1979):   67–85.

02939.   Denomy, Alexander Joseph.   "Courtly love and courtliness."
          Speculum 28 (1953):   44–63.

02940.   _____.   The Heresy of Courtly Love.
          Gloucester, Mass.:   Peter Smith, 1965.

02941.   Donaldson, E. T.   "The Myth of Courtly Love."   Venture
          5 (1965):   16–23.

02942.   Dupin, Henri.   La courtoisie au moyen âge.   Paris:
          A. Picard, 1931.

02943.   Ferrante, Joan and Economou, George, eds.   In Pursuit of
          Perfection.   Port Washington, N.Y.:   Kennikat Press, 1975.

02944.   Frappier, Jean.   Amour courtois et table ronde.   Paris:
          Droz, 1973.

02945.   Huby, M.   "Adaptation courtoise et société ou 'la realité
          depasse la fiction'."   Etudes germaniques 29 (July–
          Sept. 1974):   289–301.

02946.   Jonin, Pierre.   "Les types féminins dans les chansons de
          toite."   Romania 91 (1970):   433–466.

02947.   Lawlord, John, ed.   Patterns of Love and Courtesy.
          Evanston: Northwestern University Press, 1966.

02948. Lazar, Moshé. Amour courtois et "fin amors" dans la littérature du XIIe siecle. Paris: Klincksieck, 1964.

02949. Lefay-Toury, Marie Noëlle. "Roman breton et mythes courtois: L'evolution du personnage féminin dans les roman de Chrétien de Troyes." Cahiers de civilisation médiévale 15 (July-September 1972): 193-204, 283-293.

02950. Lewis, C.S. The Allegory of Love: A Study in Medieval Tradition. London: Oxford University Press, 1936.

02951. McRobbie, Kenneth. "Women and Love: some Aspects of Competition in Late Medieval Society." Mosaic 5 (Winter 1972): 139-168.

02952. Mahler, Herbert. "The Social Causation of Courtly Love Complex." Comparative Studies in Society and History 1 (1958-59): 7-63.

02953. Moller, Herbert. "The Meaning of Courtly Love." Journal of American Folklore 73 (1960): 39-52.

02954. _____. "The social causation of the courtly love complex." Comparative Studies in Society and History 1 (January 1959): 137-163.

02955. Moore, John C. "'Courtly Love': A Problem of Terminology." Journal of the History of Ideas 40 (Oct.-Dec. 1979): 621-632.

02956. Mott, Lewis Freeman. The System of Courtly Love Studied as an Introduction to the Vita Nuova of Dante. New York: Haskell House, 1965.

02957. Newman, Francis X., ed. The Meaning of Courtly Love. Albany, N.Y.: State University of New York Press, 1968.

02958. Press, A.R. "Amour courtois, amour adultère." In Actes du VIeme congres international de langue et littérature d'Oc et études Franco-Provençales, 2: 435-442. Montpellier: University of Montpellier, 1971.

02959. Robertson, D.W. "The Concept of Courtly Love as an Impediment to Understanding of Medieval Texts." In The Meaning of Courtly Love, edited by F.X. Newman, pp. 1-18. Albany: State University of New York Press, 1968.

02960. Rougement, Denis de. Love Declared: Essays on the Myth of Love. Translated by Richard Howard. Boston: Beacon, 1964.

02961. Rousselot, Pierre. Pour l'histoire du problème de l'amour au moyen âge. Paris: J. Vrin, 1933.

02962.   Silverstein, Theodore. "Guenevere, or the Uses of Courtly
          Love." In The Meaning of Courtly Love, edited by F.X.
          Newman, pp. 77-102. Albany: State University of New
          York Press, 1968.

02963.   Sutherland, D. R. "The Love Meditation in Courtly
          Literature." In Studies in Medieval French presented to
          A. Ewert, pp. 165-193. Oxford: Claredon Press, 1961.

02964.   Utley, Francis L. "Must we Abandon the Concept of Courtly
          Love?" Medievalia et Humanistica 2nd ser. 3 (1972):
          299-324.

          Also refer to #2743, 2893, 2902.

d)   Art

(1)   Women in Art

02965.   Evans, Michael. "Allegorical women and practical men:
          the iconography of the artes reconsidered." In Medieval
          Women, edited by Derek Baker, pp. 305-329. Studies in
          Church History, Subsidia, I. Oxford: Blackwell, 1978.

02966.   Frugoni, Chiara. "L'iconographie de la femme au cours des
          Xe-XIIIe siècles." Cahiers de civilisation médiévale
          20 (1977): 177-188.

02967.   _____. "L'iconografia del matrimonio e della
          coppia nel medioevo." In Il matrimonio nella società
          alto medievale 2: 901-966. Spoleto: Centro Italiano di
          Studi sull'Alto Medioevo, 1977.

02968.   Kahr, Madlyn. "'Delilah': Representations of Delilah in
          European painting from the 13th to the 17th century."
          Art Bulletin 54 (1972): 282-299.

02969.   Kraus, Henry. "Eve and Mary: Conflicting Images of
          Medieval Women." In The Living Theatre of Medieval Art.
          pp. 41-62. Bloomington: University of Indiana Press,
          1967.

02970.   Lyons, Lisa. "Sugar and Vice: Images of Women in Late
          Medieval Art." Feminist Art Journal 3 (Winter 1974-75):
          8-10.

02971.   Pijoan, Joseph. "The Parable of the Virgins from Dura-
          Europas." Art Bulletin 19 (1937): 592-595.

02972.   Renier, Rodolfo. Il tipo estetico della donna nel medio-
          evo. Ancona: A.G. Morelli, 1885.

(2)   Women Artists

(a)   Musicians

02973.   Meyer, Kathi. <u>Der chorische Gesang der Frauen</u>. Leipzig: Breitkopf and Hartel, 1917.

02974.   Rokseth, Yvonne. "Les femme musiciennes du XIIe au XIVe siecle." <u>Romania</u> 61 (October 1935): 464-480.

(b)   Painters/Sculptors

02975   Carr, Annemarie Weyl. "Women as artists in the Middle Ages." <u>Feminist Art Journal</u> 5 (Spring 1976): 5-9.

02976.   Miner, Dorothy E. <u>Anastaise and Her Sisters: Women Artists of the Middle Ages</u>. Baltimore: Walters Art Gallery, 1974.

02977.   Wilkins, David. "Women as Artist and Patron in the Middle Ages and the Renaissance." In <u>The Roles and Images of Women in the Middle Ages and Renaissance</u>, pp. 107-131. Pittsburgh: University of Pittsburgh Center for Medieval and Renaissance Studies, 1975.

B.   BRITISH ISLES

1.   BIBLIOGRAPHIES

"Lies, tears, and spinning are the things God gives by nature to a woman while she lives."
                                                    Chaucer

02978.   Casey, Kathleen. "Woman in Norman and Plantagenet England." In <u>The Women of England from Anglo-Saxon Times to the Present</u>, edited by Barbara Kanner, pp. 83-123. Hamden, Conn.: Archon Books, 1979.

02979.   Dietrich, Shiela. "An Introduction to Women in Anglo-
         Saxon Society (c. 600-1066)." In The Women of England
         from Anglo-Saxon Times to the Present, edited by Barbara
         Kanner, pp. 32-56. Hamden, Conn.: Archon Books, 1979.

2. SURVEYS

"It is seldom, almost never that a married woman can
have any action to use her wit only in her own name:
her husband is her stern, her prime mover, without whom
she cannot do much at home, and less abroad."
                    The Lawes Resolution of Women's Rights

02980.   Browne, George Forrest. The Importance of Women in Anglo-
         Saxon Times. New York: Macmillan Co., 1919.

02981.   Coulton, George Gordon. Life in the Middle Ages. Cam-
         bridge: University Press, 1967.

02982.   Herm, Gerhard. The Celts: The People who came out of
         darkness. New York: St. Martin's, 1975.

02983.   Hilton, Rodney Howard. The English Peasantry in the
         Later Middle Ages. Oxford: Clarendon Press, 1975.
         [See especially ch. 6, "Women in the Village."]

02984.   _____. A Medieval Society: The West
         Midlands at the End of the Thirteenth Century. London:
         Weidenfeld and Nicholson, 1966.

02985.   Homans, George. English Villages of the Thirteenth
         Century. Cambridge, Mass.: Harvard University Press, 1941.

02986.   Hunt, Percival. Fifteenth Century England. Pittsburgh:
         University of Pittsburgh Press, 1962.

02987.   Stuart, Dorothy Margaret. Men and Women of Plantagenet
         England. London: George G. Harrap and Co., Ltd., 1932.

3. MATRIARCHY AND MATRILINY

"Now the Picts had no wives, and asked them of the Scots
who would not consent to grant them upon any other terms
than that when any difficulty should arise, they should
choose a king from the female royal race rather than
from the male."   Bede, Ecclesiastical History

02988.   Boyle, Alexander. "Matrilineal Succession in the Pictish
          Monarchy." Scottish Historical Review 56 (April 1977):
          1-10.

02989.   Fraser, J. "The Alleged Matriarchy of the Picts." In
          Medieval Studies in Memory of Gertrude Schoepperle
          Loomis, edited by Roger Loomis, pp. 407-412. New York:
          Columbia University Press, 1927.

4. POLITICAL

"Salic law is no inheritance for women; rather, all the
land goes to the male sex--the brothers."
                                        Pactus Legis Salicae

a) Legal

(1) Non-specific

02990.   Barton, J.L. "Nullity of Marriage and Illegitimacy in
          the England of the Middle Ages." In Legal History
          Studies. Papers Presented to the Legal History Con-
          ference, Aberystwyth, 18-21 July 1972, edited by Dafydd
          Jenkins, pp. 28-49. Cardiff: University of Wales
          Press, 1975.

02991.   Engdahl, David E. "Medieval Metaphysics and English
          Marriage Laws." Journal of Family Law 8 (1968):
          381-397.

02992.   Hazeltine, Harold Dexter. Zur Geschichte der Eheschlies-
          sung nach angel-sächsischen Recht. Berlin: Franz Vahlen,
          1905.

02993.   Helmholz, Richard H. "Bastardy Litigation in Medieval
          England." American Journal of Legal History 13 (1969):
          360-383.

02994.   _____. Marriage Litigation in Medieval England.
          Cambridge Studies in English Legal History. New York:
          Cambridge University Press, 1975.

02995.   Maitland, Frederic William. "The Laws of Wales, the Kindred
          and the Blood Feud." Collected Papers 1 (1911): 202-229.

02996.   Mason, Emma. "Maritagium and the Changing Law." Bulletin
          of the Institute of Historical Research 49 (November 1976):
          286-289.

02997. Pollock, Frederick and Maitland, F.W. History of English
        Law Before the Time of Edward I. London: Cambridge
        University Press, 1968.

02998. Schultze, Alfred. Das Eherecht in den älteren angel-
        sächsischen Königsgesetzen. Leipzig: Hirzel, 1942.

02999. Sheehan, Michael M. The Will in Medieval England.
        Pontifical Institute of Mediaeval Studies, Studies and
        Texts, no. 6. Toronto: Pontifical Institute of
        Mediaeval Studies, 1963.

03000. Whitelock, Dorothy, ed. and trans. Anglo-Saxon Wills.
        Cambridge: The University Press, 1930.

03001. Woodbine, George E., ed. Bracton on the Laws and Custom
        of England. Translated by Samuel E. Thonne. 2 vols.
        Cambridge, Mass.: Harvard University Press, 1968.

03002. Young, Ernest. "The Anglo-Saxon Family Law." In Essays
        in Anglo-Saxon Law, pp. 121-182. Boston: Little,
        Brown and Co., 1905.

                        (2) Women

03003. Buckstaff, Florence. "Married Woman's Property in Anglo
        Norman Law and Origin of the Common Law Power." Annals
        of the American Academy of Political and Social Science
        4 (1894): 233-264.

03004. Hand, Geoffrey. "The King's widow and the King's widows."
        Law Quarterly Review 93 (1977): 506-507.

03005. Ives, E.W. "'Against taking away of women:' the
        inception and operation of the Abduction Act of 1487."
        In Wealth and Power in Tudor England. Essays presented
        to S.T. Bindoff, edited by E.W. Ives, R.J. Knecht, and
        J.J. Scarisbrick, pp. 21-44. London: Athlone Press,
        1978.

03006. Jouon de Longrais, F. "Le statut de la femme en Angle-
        terre." Recueils de la Société Jean Bodin 12 (1962):
        135-241.

03007. Kittel, Ruth. "Women under the law in Medieval England:
        1066-1485." In The Women of England from Anglo-
        Saxon Times to the Present, edited by Barbara Kanner,
        pp. 124-137. Hamden, Conn.: Archon Books, 1979.

03008. Margulies, Cecile Stoller. "The Marriages and the Wealth
        of the Wife of Bath." Medieval Studies 24 (1962):
        210-216.

03009. Meyer, Marc Anthony. "Land Charter and the Legal Position
        of Anglo-Saxon Women." In The Women of England from
        Anglo-Saxon Times to the Present, edited by Barbara
        Kanner, pp. 57-82. Hamden, Conn.: Archon Books, 1979.

03010. O'Corrain, Donncha. "Women in Early Irish Society." In
        Women in Irish Society: The Historical Dimension, edited
        by Margaret Maccurtain and Donncha O'Corrain, pp. 1-13.
        Westport, Conn.: Greenwood Press, 1979.

03011. Post, J.B. "Ravishment of women and the Statue of
        Westminster." In Legal Records and the Historian, edited
        by J.H. Baker, pp. 150-164.   Royal Historical Society
        Studies in History. London: Royal Historical Society
        1978.

03012. Rivers, Theodore John. "'Widows' rights in Anglo-Saxon
        law." American Journal of Legal History 19 (1975):
        208-215.

03013. Simms, Katherine. "The Legal Position of Irishwomen in the
        later Middle Ages." Irish Jurist n.s. 9 (1975):   96-111.

03014. Walker, Sue Sheridan. "Widow and Ward: The Feudal Law of
        Child Custody in Medieval England," Feminist Studies 3
        (Spring-Summer 1976): 104-116. Also in Women in Medieval
        Society, edited by Susan Mosher Stuard, pp. 159-172.
        Philadelphia: University of Pennsylvania Press, 1976.

                            b)   Criminal

                        (1) Non-specific

03015. Given, James Buchanan. Society and Homicide in Thirteenth
        Century England. Stanford, California: Stanford Univer-
        sity Press, 1977.
        [See especially chs. 3 and 7.]

03016. Hanawalt, Barbara A. Crime and Conflict in English
        Communities 1300-1348. Cambridge, Mass.: Harvard,
        1979.
        [See especially ch. 5, "The Relationship between Victim
        and the Accused," pp. 151-183.]

03017. _____. "The Peasant Family and Crime in
        Fourteenth Century England." Journal of British Studies
        13 (1974): 1-18.

03018.   _____. "Violent Death in Fourteenth and
          Fifteenth Century England." Comparative Studies in
          Society and History 18 (1976): 297-320.

(2) Women

03019.   Griffiths, Ralph A. "The Trial of Eleanor Cobham: An
          Episode in the Fall of Duke Humphrey of Gloucester."
          Bulletin of the John Rylands Library 51 (Spring 1969):
          381-399.

03020.   Hanawalt, Barbara A. "The Female Felon in fourteenth
          century England." Viator 5 (1974): 253-268. Reprinted
          in Women in Medieval Society, edited by Susan Mosher
          Stuart, pp. 125-140. Philadelphia: University of
          Pennsylvania Press, 1976.

c) Political Roles

(1) Women

03021.   Abbott, Jacob. History of Margaret of Anjou, Queen of
          Henry VI of England. New York: Harper and Bros., 1861.

03022.   Anderson, Marjorie. "Blanche, Duchess of Lancaster."
          Modern Philology 45 (February 1948): 152-159.

03023.   Bailey, S. J. "The Countess Gundred's Lands." Cambridge
          Law Journal 10 (1948): 84-103.

03024.   Bootes, Alfred. "Famous Women of Kent, no. 2. Ethelburga,
          wife of King Edwin of Northunbria." Kent 209 (1977): 13.

03025.   Braddy, Haldeen. "Chaucer and Dame Alice Perrers."
          Speculum 21 (April 1946): 222-228.

03026.   Butler, Mildred Allen. "Katherine the Fair." British
          History Illustrated 4 (Jan. 1978): 16-29.

03027.   Craig, Malcolm A. "A Second Daughter of Geoffrey of
          Brittany." Bulletin of the Institute of Historical
          Research 50 (May 1977): 112-15.

03028.   Cutler, Kenneth E. "Edith, Queen of England, 1045-1066."
          Medieval Studies 35 (1973): 222-231.

03029. Erlanger, Philippe. Margaret of Anjou, Queen of England.
        Coral Gables, Florida: University of Miami Press, 1971.

03030. Fahy, Conor. "The Marriage of Edward IV and Elizabeth
        Woodville: A New Italian Source." English Historical
        Review 76 (October 1961): 660-667.

03031. Galway, Margaret. "Joan of Kent and the Order of the
        Garter." University of Birmingham Historical Journal
        1 (1947): 13-50.

03032. Hardy, Blanche Christable. Philippa of Hainault and her
        Times. London: J. Long, 1910.

03033. Hookham, Mary Ann. The Life and Times of Margaret of
        Anjou, Queen of England and France. London: Tinsley
        Bros., 1872.

03034. Kay, Frederick George. Lady of the Sun: The Life and
        Times of Alice Perrers. New York: Barnes & Noble, 1966.

03035. Lander, J.R. "Marriage and Politics in the Fifteenth
        Century: the Nevilles and Wydevilles." In Crown and
        Nobility 1450-1509, Collected Essays of J. R. Lander,
        pp. 94-126. London: Edward Arnold, 1976. Also in
        Bulletin of the Institute of Historical Research 36
        (1963): 119-152.

03036. Lewis, F.R. "Beatrice of Falkenburg, the third wife of
        Richard of Cornwall." English Historical Review 51
        (1937): 279-282.

03037. Lucas, H.S. "A Document related to the Marriage of
        Philippa of Hainault (1327)." In Etudes d'histoire
        dédicées à la mémoire de Henri Pirenne par ses anciens
        élèves, pp. 199-207. Brussels: Nouvelle societe
        d'éditions, 1937.

03038. Morel-Fatio, A. "Marguerite d'York et Perkin Warbeck."
        In Mélanges d'histoire offerts à M. Charles Bemont,
        pp. 411-416. Paris: F. Alcan, 1913.

03039. Painter, Sidney. "Who was the Mother of Oliver Fitz Roy?"
        In Feudalism and Liberty, Articles and Addresses of
        Sidney Painter, edited by Fred Cazel, pp. 240-243.
        Baltimore: John Hopkins Press, 1961. Also in
        Medievalia and Humanistica 8 (1954): 17-19.

03040. Parsons, John Carmi, ed. The Court and Household of
        Eleanor of Castille in 1290. Toronto: Pontifical
        Institute of Mediaeval Studies, 1977.

03041. Poole, Astin Lane. "Loretta, Countess of Leicester."
        In Historical Essays in Honor of James Tait, pp. 247-
        272. Manchester: Printed for the Subscribers, 1933.

03042.   Prestwich, Michael. "Isabella de Vescy and the Custody
          of Bamburgh Castle." Bulletin of the Institute of
          Historical Research 44 (November 1971): 148-152.

03043.   Stafford, Pauline. "Sons and Mothers: Family politics
          in the early Middle Ages." In Medieval Women, edited
          by Derek Baker, pp. 79-100. Studies in Church History,
          Subsidia, I. Oxford: Blackwell, 1978.

03044.   Stephens, George R. "The Early Life of Joan Makepiece."
          Speculum 20 (July 1945): 300-309.

03045.   Wainwright, F. T. "Aethelflaed, Lady of the Mercians."
          In The Anglo-Saxons, edited by Peter Clemoes, pp. 53-69.
          London: Bowes and Bowes, 1959.

                     (2)   Individuals

                     (a)   Emma

03046.   Barlow, Frank. "Two Notes: Cnut's Second Pilgrimage and
          Queen Emma's Disgrace in 1043." English Historical
          Review 73 (Oct. 1958): 649-656.

03047.   Campbell, Miles W. "Emma, reine d'Angleterre mère dénaturée
          ou femme vindicative?" Annales de Normandie 23 (1973):
          99-114.

03048.   _____. "Queen Emma and Aelfgifu of Northampton:
          Canute the Great's Women." Medieval Scandanavia 4 (1971):
          66-79.

                     (b)   Isabella of Angoulême

03049.   Blackey, F. D. and Hermansen, G. "A Household Book of
          Queen Isabella of England, 1311-1312." Canadian
          Historical Association.Historical Papers 1968: 140-151.

03050.   _____. "Isabella and the Bishop of Exeter." In
          Essays in Medieval History presented to Bertie Wilkinson,
          pp. 220-235. Toronto: University of Toronto Press, 1969.

03051.   _____. "Isabella of France, Queen of England
          1308-1358 and the Late Medieval Cult of the Dead."
          Canadian Journal of History 15 (April 1980): 23-47.

03052.   Cazel, F. A. Jr. "The Marriage of Isabelle of Angouleme."
          English Historical Review 63 (January 1948): 83-89.

03053.   Doherty, P.C.   "The Date of the Birth of Isabella, Queen
         of England (1308-58), "Bulletin of the Institute of
         Historical Research 48 (November 1975):   246-248.

03054.   Hunter, J.   "Journal of the Mission of Queen Isabella for
         the Court of France and of her Long Residence in that
         Country." Archaeologica 36 (1855):   242-257.

03055.   Mirot, L.   Isabelle de France, reine d'Angleterre, comtesse
         d'Angouleme, duchesse d'Orléans.   (1389-1409.) Paris:
         Plon et Nourrit, 1905.

03056.   Painter, Sidney.   "The Marriage of Isabella of Angoulême."
         In Feudalism and Liberty, Articles and Addresses of
         Sidney Painter, edited by Fred Cazel, pp. 165-177. Balti-
         more: Johns Hopkins Press, 1961. Also in English Histori-
         cal Review 63 (Jan. 1948):   83-89.

03057.   Richardson, Henry G.   "King John and Isabelle of Angoulême."
         English Historical Review 65 (July 1950): 360-371.

03058.   _____. "The Marriage and Coronation of Isabella
         of Angouleme." English Historical Review 61 (1946):
         289-314.

03059.   _____. "The Marriage of Isabelle of
         Angouleme. A Problem of Canon Law." Studia Gratiana
         12 (1967):   397-423.

                    (c)   Margaret of Scotland

03060.   Baker, Derek.   "A Nursery of Saints: St. Margaret of Scot-
         land Reconsidered." In Medieval Women, edited by Derek
         Baker, pp. 119-141. Oxford: Basil Blackwell, 1978.

03061.   Barnett, Thomas Ratcliffe. Margaret of Scotland, Queen
         and Saint. London: Oliver and Boyd, 1926.

03062.   Henderson-Howat, A.M.D. Royal Pearl, the Life and Times
         of Margaret, Queen of Scotland. London: S.P.C.K., 1948.

03063.   Menzies, Lucy. St. Margaret, Queen of Scotland. New York:
         E. P. Dutton and Co., 1925.

         Also refer to #3214.

                    (d)   Queen Matilda

03064.   Leve, A. La Tapisserie de la reine Mathilde, dite la
         Tapisserie de Bayeux. Paris: H. Laurens, 1919.

03065.   Pain, Nesta. _Empress Matilda. Uncrowned Queen of England._
          London: Weidenfeld and Nicholson, 1978.

03066.   Rössler, Oskar. _Kaiserin Mathilde. Mutter Heinrichs von_
          Anjou und das Zeitalter der Anarchie in England. His-
          torische Studien, no. 7. Berlin: E. Ebering, 1897.

03067.   Schnith, Karl. "'Kaiserin' Mathilde." In _Grossbritannien_
          und Deutschland Festschrift für John W.P. Bourke, pp.
          166–182. Munich: Goldmann, 1974.

03068.   _____. "_Regni et pacis inquietatrix_: zur Rolle
          der Kaiserin Mathilde in der 'Anarchie.'" _Journal of_
          Medieval History 2 (June 1976): 135–187.

03069.   Schramm, Percy Ernest. "Ein bisher unbeachtetes Bildnis
          der Kaiserin Mathilde, Königin von England († 1167), in
          2. Ehe verheiratet mit Gottfried von Anjou." In _Mélanges_
          offerts à René Crozet, edited by Pierre Gallais and Yves-
          Jean Riou, 2: 863–867. Poitiers: Société d'études
          médiévales, 1966.

5. ECONOMIC

          We reconciled our differences we two
          He let me have the bridle in my hand
          For management of both our house and land.
                         Chaucer, Wife of Bath

a) Generic

03070.   Bennett, Henry Stanley. _Life on the English Manor, A Study_
          of Peasant Conditions, 1150–1400. New York: Macmillan
          Co., 1937.

          Also refer to #3155.

b) Household

03071.   Faulkner, P.A. "Domestic Planning from the Twelfth to
          the Fourteenth Century." _Archeological Journal_ 115
          (1958): 150–183.

03072. Fowler, G. H. "A Household Expense Roll, 1328."   <u>English</u>
        <u>Historical</u> <u>Review</u> 55 (October 1940): 630-632.

03073. Krause, John T. "The medieval household, large or small?"
        <u>Economic</u> <u>History</u> <u>Review</u> 2nd ser. 9 (1956-57):   420-432.

03074. Myers, A. R. "The Household of Queen Elizabeth Woodville,
        1466-7." <u>Bulletin</u> <u>of</u> <u>John</u> <u>Rylands</u> <u>Library</u> 50 (Autumn
        1967 and Spring 1968):   207-235 and 443-481.

03075. Turner, H. T., ed. <u>Manners</u> <u>and</u> <u>Household</u> <u>Expenses</u> <u>of</u>
        <u>England</u> <u>in</u> <u>the</u> <u>Thirteenth</u> <u>and</u> <u>Fourteenth</u> <u>Centuries.</u>
        London: W. Nicol, 1841.

                         c) Women

03076. Abram, Annie. "Women Traders in Medieval London." <u>Economic</u>
        <u>Journal</u> 26 (June 1916):   276-185.

03077. Mate, Mavis. "Profit and Productivity on the Estates of
        Isabella de Forz (1260-1292)." <u>Economic</u> <u>History</u> <u>Review</u>
        33 (August 1980):   326-334.

        Also refer to #3008.

                      ## 6. RELIGION

        "--damp convent where it's rumored that at least one
        nun, 'Dame Purnell', a priest's concubine . . . had a
        child in cherry time.
                              Piers Plowman, <u>The</u> <u>Vision</u>

                         a) Generic

03078. Godfrey, John. <u>The</u> <u>Church</u> <u>in</u> <u>Anglo-Saxon</u> <u>England.</u> Cam-
        bridge: University Press, 1962.
        [See especially ch. 10, Monks and Nuns in Early England.]

03079. MacCulloch, John Arnott. <u>The</u> <u>Religion</u> <u>of</u> <u>the</u> <u>Ancient</u>
        <u>Celts.</u> Edinburgh: T. and T. Clark, 1911.

03080. Moorman, John R. H.   "The Medieval Parsonage and Its
        Occupants." Bulletin of the John Rylands Library 28
        (March 1944): 137-153.

03081. Owst, G.R. Literature of the Pulpit of Medieval England.
        1933. Reprint. New York: Barnes & Noble, 1961.

03082. Reynolds, Roger E. "Virgines subintroductae in Celtic
        Christianity." Harvard Theological Review 61 (October
        1968): 547-566.

03083. Thomas, Keith. Religion and the Decline of Magic. New
        York: Scribners, 1971.

03084. Winandy, Jacques. "La femme: un homme manque?" Nouvelle
        revue théologique 109 (1977): 865-70.

                    b) Goddesses/Mythology

03085. Donahue, Charles. "The Valkyries and the Irish War
        Goddesses." Publications of the Modern Language Associ-
        ation 56 (March 1941): 1-12.

03086. Helbig, Althea K. "Women in Ireland: three heroic
        figures." University of Michigan Papers in Women's
        Studies 1 (June 1974): 73-88.

03087. Hennessy, W.M. "The Ancient Irish Goddesses of War."
        Revue celtique 1 (1870): 32-55

                    c) Saints/Religious Women

                        (1) Women

03088. Bowen, E.G. "The Cult of St. Brigit." Studia Celtica
        8-9 (1973-74): 33-47.

03089   Braswell, Laurel. "Saint Edburga of Winchester: a study
        of her cult, a.d. 950-1500, with an edition of the
        fourteenth-century Middle English and Latin lives."
        Medieval Studies 33 (1971): 292-333.

03090. Esposito, M. "La Vie de Ste. Vulfhide par Goscelin de
        Cantorbery." Analecta Bollandiana 32 (1913): 10-26.

03091.   Goodman, A.E.   "The Piety of John Brunham's Daughter of
         Lynn."   In Medieval Women, edited by Derek Baker, pp.
         347-358.   Oxford: Basil Blackwell, 1978.

03092.   Holdsworth, Christopher J.   "Christina of Markyate."   In
         Medieval Women, edited by Derek Baker, pp. 185-204.
         Oxford: Basil Blackwell, 1978.

03093.   Schmid, Toni.   "Le culte en Suède de Ste. Brigide
         l'Irlandaise."   Analectica Bollandiana 61 (1943):
         108-115.

03094.   Stephens, George R.   "The Burial Place of St. Lewinna."
         Medieval Studies 21 (1959):   303-312.

03095.   Talbot, C. H., ed. and trans.   The Life of Christina of
         Markyate: A Twelfth Century Recluse.   New York: Oxford
         University Press, 1959.

         Also refer to #3060-3063.

                        (2)   Individuals

                    (a)   Juliana of Norwich

03096.   Berschin, Walter.   "Zur lateinischen und deutschen Juliana-
         Legende."   Studi Medievali 3rd ser. 14 (1973): 1003-1012.

03097.   Chambers, Percy Franklin, ed., Juliana of Norwich: An
         Introductory Appreciation and an Interpretative Antho-
         logy.   New York: Harper and Row, 1955.

03098.   Colledge, Edmund and Walsh, James.   "Editing Julian of
         Norwich's Revelations: A Progress Report."   Medieval
         Studies 38 (1976):   404-427.

03099.   Molinari, P.   Julian of Norwich, the Teachings of a Fourteenth
         Century Mystic.   London: Longmans, Green and Co., 1958.

03100.   Windeatt, B.A.   "Julia of Norwich and her audience."   Re-
         view of English Studies 28 (February 1977):   1-17.

         Also refer to #3103.

                    (b)   Margery Kempe

03101.   Cholmeley, Katherine.   Margery Kempe, Genius and Mystic.
         London: Longmans, Green and Co., 1947.

03102.   Collis, Louise. Memoirs of a Medieval Woman: The Life
          and Times of Margery Kempe. New York: Apollo Editions,
          1964.

03103.   Stone, Robert K. Middle English prose style: Margery
          Kempe and Julian of Norwich. The Hague: Mouton, 1970.

                    d) Monastic Life

03104.   Bourdillon, A. F. C. The Order of Minoresses in England.
          Manchester: University Press, 1926.

03105.   Bullock-Davies, Constance. "Marie, Abbess of Shaftesbury,
          and her Brothers." English Historical Review 80 (April
          1965): 314-322.

03106.   Byrne, Mary. The Tradition of the Nun in Medieval England.
          Washington, D.C.: Catholic University of America, 1932.

03107.   Constable, Giles. Aelred of Rievaulx and the nun of Watton:
          an episode in the early history of the Gilbertine Order."
          In Medieval Women, edited by Derek Baker, pp. 205-226.
          Oxford: Basil Blackwell, 1978.

03108.   Floyd, J. Arthur. "An Extinct Religious Order. Its Founder."
          The Catholic World 63 (1896): 343-353.

03109.   Godfrey, John. "The Double Monastery in Early English
          History." Ampleforth Journal 79 (1974): 19-32.

03110.   _____. "The Place of the Double Monastery in the
          Anglo-Saxon Minister System." In Famulus Christi:
          Essays in Commemoration of the Thirteenth Century of
          the Birth of the Venerable Bede, edited by Gerald Bonner,
          pp. 344-350. London: S.P.C.K., 1976.

03111.   Graves, Coburn V. "English Cistercian Nuns in Lincoln-
          shire." Speculum 54 (July 1979): 492-499.

03112.   Hugo, Thomas. The Medieval Nunneries of the County of
          Somerset, and Diocese of Bath and Wells; Together with
          the Annals of Their Impropriated Benefices, from the
          Earliest Times to the Death of Queen Mary. London:
          Taunton, 1867.

03113.   Kälsmann, Hans. "Zur Frage der ursprünglichen Fassung
          der 'Ancrene rewle.'" Anglia 75 (1957): 134-156.

03114.   Knowles, David. The Religious Orders in England.
          Cambridge: University Press, 1959.

03115. Meyer, Marc Anthony. "Women and the Tenth Century English
        Monastic Reform." Revue Benedictine 87 (1977): 34-61.

03116. Murray-Davey, D. "Anglo-Saxon Nuns of the Golden Age."
        Dublin Review (1928): 282-292.

03117. Power, Eileen. Medieval English Nunneries, 1275-1535.
        Cambridge: Cambridge University Press, 1922.

03118. Sims-Williams, Patrick. "Cuthswith, seventh-century abbess
        of Inkberros." Anglo-Saxon England 5 (1976): 1-21.

e) Canon Law

03119. Brooke, Christopher N.L. "Gregorian Reform in Action:
        Clerical Marriage in England, 1050-1200." Cambridge
        Historical Journal 12 (1956): 1-21.

03120. Kelly, Henry Ansgar. "Canonical Implications of Richard
        III's Plan to Marry His Niece." Traditio 23 (1967):
        269-311.

03121. Sheehan, Michael M. "The Influence of Canon Law on the
        Property Rights of Married Women in England." Medieval
        Studies 25 (1963): 109-124.

03122. _____. "Marriage Theory and Practice in the
        Conciliar Legislation and Diocesan Statutes of Medieval
        England." Medieval Studies 40 (1978): 408-460.

f) Heresy

03123. Cross, Claire. "'Great reasoners in scripture,' the
        activities of women Lollards 1380-1530." In Medieval
        Women, edited by Derek Baker, pp. 359-380.   Studies
        in Church History, Subsidia, I . Oxford: Basil
        Blackwell, 1978.

g) Witchcraft

03124. Crawford, Jane. "Evidences for Witchcraft in Anglo-Saxon
        England." Medium Aevum 32 (1963): 99-116.

03125. Hole, Christina. "Some Instances of Image-Magic in Great Britain." In The Witch Figure, edited by Venetia Newall, pp. 80-94. Boston: Routledge and Kegan Paul, 1973.

03126. Kelly, Henry A. "English Kings and the Fear of Sorcery." Medieval Studies 39 (1977): 206-238.

03127. Ross, Anne. "The Divine Hag of the Pagan Celts." In The Witch Figure, edited by Venetia Newall, pp. 139-164. Boston: Routledge and Kegan Paul, 1973.

03128. Yoshioka, Barbara. "Whoring after strange gods: a narrative of women and witches." Radical Religion 1 (Spring 1974): 6-11.

7. SOCIAL

"[Experience] . . . goes to show that Marriage is a misery and a woe."

                              wife of Bath, Chaucer

a) Generic

(1) Non-specific

03129. Abram, Annie. English Life and Manners in the Later Middle Ages. London: George Routledge and Sons, Ltd., 1913. [See especially "Position of Women," pp. 31-45; and "Family Life," pp. 113-133.]

03130. _____. Social Life in England in the Fifteenth Century. London: G. Routledge & Sons, 1909.

03131. Bennett, Henry Stanley. The Pastons and their England; Studies in an Age of Transition. Cambridge: University Press, 1970.

03132. Britton, Edward. The Community of the Vill: A Study in the History of the Family and Village Life in Fourteenth Century England. Toronto: Macmillan of Canada, 1977.

03133. Brown, Jennifer W., ed. Scottish Society in the Fifteenth Century. New York: St. Martin's Press, 1978.

03134. Chadwock, Dorothy. Social Life in the Days of Piers Plowman. New York: Russell and Russell, 1969.

03135. Contamine, Philippe. La Vie quotidienne pendant la guerre
        de Cent Ans: France et Angleterre, XIV siècle. Paris:
        Hachette, 1976.

03136. Coulton, George Gordon. Medieval Panorama: The English
        Scene from Conquest to Reformation. Cambridge: Uni-
        versity Press, 1970.

03137. _____. Social Life in Britain from the
        Conquest to the Reformation. New York: Barnes and Noble,
        1968.
        [See especially sect. 12 "Women's Life."]

03138. Du Boulay, F. R. H. An Age of Ambition: English Society in
        the Late Middle Ages. New York: Viking Press, 1970.
        [See especially ch. 5 "Marriage and Sex," pp. 80-108, and
        ch. 6 "Household and Family," pp. 109-127.]

03139. Duckett, Eleanor Shipley. The Gateway to the Middle Ages,
        II. France and Britain. Ann Arbor, Mich.: University
        of Michigan Press, 1961.

03140. Holmes, Urban Tigner. Daily Living in the Twelfth Century,
        based on the Observations of Alexander Neckam in London
        and Paris. Madison: University of Wisconsin Press, 1952.

03141. Joyce, P.W. A Social History of Ancient Ireland. 2 vols.
        New York: Benjamin Blom, 1968.
        [See especially ch. 19, "The Family."]

03142. Kendall, Paul Murray. The Yorkist Age: Daily Life during
        the War of the Roses. New York: W. W. Norton and Co.,
        1962.
        [See especially section III.]

03143. La Barge, Margaret Wade. A Baronial Household of the
        Thirteenth Century. New York: Barnes and Noble,
        1965.
        [See especially "Lady of the House," pp. 38-52.]

03144. Lester, G.A. The Anglo-Saxons: how they lived and worked.
        London: David and Charles, 1976.

03145. Page, R.I. Life in Anglo-Saxon England. London: B.T.
        Batsford, 1970.
        [See especially "A Woman's Place," pp. 66-77.]

03146. Pastoureau, Michel. La Vie quotidienne en France et en
        Angleterre au temps des chevaliers de la table ronde:
        XIIe-XIIIe siècles. Paris: Hachette, 1976.

03147. Raftis, J. Ambrose. Tenure and Mobility: Studies in the
        Social History of the Medieval English Village. Toronto:
        Pontifical Institute of Medieval Studies, 1964.

03148. Razi, Zvi. Life, Marriage and Death in a Medieval Parish: Economy, Society and Demography in Halesowen 1270-1400. New York: Cambridge University Press, 1980.

03149. Rickert, Edith, ed. Chaucer's World. New York: Columbia University Press, 1948.
[See especially chs. "Family Life," pp. 71-83; and "Bringing Up Children," pp. 94-100.]

03150. Salusbury, G.T. Street Life in Medieval England. Oxford: Pen-in-Hand, 1948.

03151. Salzman, Louis Francis. English Life in the Middle Ages. London: Humphrey Milford, 1927.
[See especially ch. 12 "Women," pp. 249-265.]

03152. Snell, F.J. The Customs of Old England. London: Methuen and Co., 1911.

03153. Stenton, D.M. English Society in the Early Middle Ages. Reprint. 1951. Harmondsworth: Penguin, 1969.

03154. Thrupp, John. The Anglo-Saxon Home: A History of the Domestic Institutions and Customs of England from the Fifth to the Eleventh Century. London: Longman, Green, Longman and Roberts, 1862.

03155. Thrupp, Sylvia. The Merchant Class of Medieval London, 1300-1500. Chicago: University of Chicago Press, 1948.

03156. Tomkeieff, O.G. Life in Norman England. London: B.T. Batsford Ltd., 1966.

03157. Vinogradov, P.G. English Society in the Eleventh Century. Oxford: Clarendon Press, 1908.

03158. Wood, Margaret. The English Medieval House. London: Phoenix House, 1965.

(2) Women

03159. Bandel, Betty. "The English Chroniclers' Attitude toward Women." Journal of the History of Ideas 16 (1955): 113-118.

03160. Boehler, M. Die altenglischen Frauennamen. Berlin: E. Ebering, 1930.

03161. Clark, Cecily. "Women's names in post-Conquest England: Observations and Speculations." Speculum 53 (1978): 223-251.

03162. Markale, Jean. <u>Women of the Celts</u>. Translated by A.
    Mygind, C. Hauch, and P. Henry. London: Gordon
    Cremonesi, 1980.

03163. Nicholson, Joan. "<u>Feminae gloriosae</u>: women in the age
    of Bede." In <u>Medieval Women</u>, edited by Derek Baker,
    pp. 15-29. (Studies in Church History, Subsidia, I)
    Oxford: Blackwell, 1978.

03164. Simms, Katharine. "Women in Norman Ireland." In <u>Women</u>
    <u>in Irish Society: The Historical Dimension</u>, edited by
    Margaret Maccurtain and Donncha O'Corrain, pp. 14-25.
    Westport, Conn.: Greenwood Press, 1979.

03165. Stenton, F.M. "The Place of Women in Anglo-Saxon Society."
    <u>Transactions of the Royal Historical Society</u> 4th ser. 25
    (1943): 1-13.

03166. Woolf, Henry. "The Naming of Women in Old English Times."
    <u>Modern Philology</u> 36 (1938): 113-120.

Also refer to #2010.

b) *Demography*

03167. Postan, M. "Some Economic Evidence of Declining Population
    in the Later Middle Ages." <u>Economic History Review</u> 2nd
    ser. 2 (1950): 247-265.

03168. Russell, Josiah Cox. <u>British Medieval Population</u>.
    Albuquerque: University of New Mexico Press, 1948.

03169. _____. "Late Thirteenth-Century Ireland as
    a Region." <u>Demography</u> 3 (1966): 500-512.

Also refer to #4310.

c) *Family*

(1) Non-specific

03170. Britton, Edward. "The Peasant Family in Fourteenth-
    Century England." <u>Peasant Studies</u> 5 (1976): 2-7.

03171. Faith, Rosamund J. "Peasant Families and Inheritance
        Customs in Medieval England." Agriculture History Re-
        view 14 (1966): 77-95.

03172. Lancaster, Lorraine. "Kinship in Anglo-Saxon Society."
        In Early Medieval Society, edited by Sylvia Thrupp,
        pp. 17-41. New York: Appleton-Century-Crofts, 1967.
        Also in British Journal of Sociology 9 (1958): 230-250
        and 359-377.

03173. Loyn, H. R. "Kinship in Anglo-Saxon England." Anglo-
        Saxon England 3 (1974): 197-210.

03174. Painter, Sydney. "The Family and the Feudal System in
        Twelfth-Century England." Speculum 35 (January 1960):
        1-16. Also in Feudalism and Liberty, edited by
        Fred A. Cazel Jr., pp. 195-219. Baltimore: Johns
        Hopkins University Press, 1961.

03175. Queen, Stuart A.; Habenstein, Robert W.; and Adams, John B.
        "The Anglo-Saxon Family--Folkways in Transition." In
        The Family in Various Cultures, pp. 202-223. New York:
        J. B. Lippincott Company, 1961.

03176. _____.
        "The Medieval English Family--Values in Conflict." In
        The Family in Various Cultures, pp. 224-246. New York:
        J.B. Lippincott Company, 1961.

03177. Smith, R.M. "Kin and Neighbors in a Thirteenth Century
        Suffolk Community." Journal of Family History 4 (Fall
        1977): 219-256.

        Also refer to #2995, 3002, 3132, 3199.

                        (2) Childhood

03178. Francois, Martha Ellis. "Adults and Children: Against
        Evil or against Each Other." History of Childhood
        Quarterly 1 (1973-74): 164-177.

03179. Hanawalt, Barbara A. "Childrearing among the Lower Classes
        of Late Medieval England." Journal of Interdisciplinary
        History 8 (Summer 1977): 1-22. Also in Marriage and
        Fertility, edited by R. Rotberg and T. Rabb, pp. 19-40.
        Princeton, N.J.: Princeton University Press, 1980.

03180. Helmholz, R.H. "Infanticide in the Province of Canterbury
        during the Fifteenth Century." History of Childhood
        Quarterly 2 (Winter 1975): 379-390.

03181.   Kellum, Barbara A. "Infanticide in England in the later
          Middle Ages." History of Childhood Quarterly 1 (Winter
          1974): 367-388.

d) Marriage

03182.   Brundage, James A. "The Treatment of Marriage in the
          Questiones Londinenses (MS Royal 9.E.VII)," Manuscripta
          19 (July 1975): 86-97.

03183.   Chadwick, N.K. "Pictish and Celtic Marriage in Early
          Literary Tradition." Scottish Gaelic Studies 8 (1958):
          56-155.

03184.   Gougaud, L. "Mulierum Consortia: Etude sur le syneisak-
          tisme chez les ascètes celtiques." Eriu: Journal of the
          School of Irish Learning 9 (1921-1923): 147-156.

03185.   Hair, P.E.H. "Bridal Pregnancy in Rural England in
          Earlier Centuries." Population Studies 20 (November
          1966): 233-243.

03186.   Haskell, Ann S. "The Paston Women on Marriage in
          Fifteenth-Century England." Viator 4 (1973): 459-471.

03187.   Kelly, Henry A. Love and Marriage in the Age of
          Chaucer. Ithaca, N.Y.: Cornell University Press,
          1975.

03188.   Mathew, Gervase. "Marriage and Amour Courtois in Late
          Fourteenth-Century England." In Essays Presented to
          Charles Williams, pp. 128-135. New York: Oxford
          University Press, 1947.

03189.   Owen, Dorothy M. "White Annays and others." In Medieval
          Women, edited by Derek Baker, pp. 331-346. Studies in
          Church History, Subsidia, I . Oxford: Blackwell, 1978.

03190.   Pope, John C. "An Unsuspected Lacuna in the Exeter Book:
          Divorce Proceedings for an Ill-Matched Couple in the
          Old English Riddles." Speculum 49 (October 1974):
          615-622.

03191.   Power, Patrick. Sex and Marriage in Ancient Ireland.
          Dublin: Mercier Press, 1976.

03192.   Pratt, Robert A. "Jankyn's Book of Wikked Wyves: Medieval
          Antimatrimonial Propaganda in the Universities." Annuale
          Mediaevale 3 (1962): 5-27.

03193. Roderick, A.J. "Marriage and politics in Wales, 1066-1282."
        The Welsh History Review 4 (June 1968): 3-20.

03194. Scammell, Jean. "Freedom and Marriage in Medieval England."
        Economic History Review 27 (November 1974): 523-537.

03195. _____. "Wife Rents and Merchet." Economic History
        Review 29 (August 1976): 487-490.

03196. Searle, Eleanor. "Freedom and Marriage in Medieval England:
        An Alternative Hypothesis." Economic History Review 2nd
        ser. 29 (August 1976): 482-486.

03197. _____. "Seigneurial Control of Women's Marriage:
        The Antecedents and Functions of the Merchet in England."
        Past and Present 82 (February 1979): 3-43.

03198. Sheehan, Michael M. "The Formation and Stability of
        Marriage in Fourteenth-Century England: Evidence of an
        Ely Register." Medieval Studies 33 (1971): 228-263.

03199. _____. "Marriage and family in English
        conciliar and synodal legislation. In Essays in Honour
        of Anton Charles Pegis, edited by J. Reginald O'Donnell,
        pp. 205-214. Toronto: Pontifical Institute of
        Medieval Studies, 1974.

03200. Walker, Sue Sheridan. "Feudal Constraint and Free Consent
        in the making of Marriages in Medieval England: Widows
        on the King's Gift." Canadian Historical Association.
        Historical Papers 1978: 97-110.

03201. Wentersdorf, Karl P. "The Clandestine Marriages of the
        Fair Maid of Kent." Journal of Medieval History 5
        (September 1979): 203-231.

        Also refer to #2990-2996, 2998, 3008, 3010, 3119-3122, 3330,
        3331, 3335, 3345.

                    e) Sex Life and Morals

03202. Williams, Edith Whitehurst. "What's So New about the
        Sexual Revolution? Some Comments on Anglo-Saxon
        Attitudes towards Sexuality in Women Based on Four
        Exeter Book Riddles." Texas Quarterly 18 (1975):
        46-55.

f) Fashion/Manners

03203. Cunnington, C. Willett. Handbook of English Mediaeval
        Costume. London: Faber and Faber, 1952.

03204. Houston, Mary Galway. Medieval Costume in England and
        France. London: A. and C. Black, 1950.

03205. Wright, Thomas. A History of Domestic Manners and
        Sentiments in England during the Middle Ages. London:
        Chapman and Hall, 1862.

g) Health/Medical

(1) Non-specific

03206. Rowland, Beryl, ed. Medieval Woman's Guide to Health.
        Kent, Ohio: Kent State University Press, 1980.

03207. Rubin, Stanley. Medieval English Medicine A.D. 500-1300.
        New York: Barnes-Noble, 1974.

(2) Abortion/Birth Control

03208. Ariès, Philippe. "Deux contributions à l'histoire des
        pratiques contraceptives. II. Chaucer et Mme de
        Sévigné." Population 9 (October-December 1954): 692-698.

03209. Honings, Bonifacio. "L'aborto nei libri penitenziali
        Convergenza morale e divergenze pastorali." Appolinaris
        48 (1975): 501-523.

(3) Women and Health

03210. Hawkes, Sonia C. and Wells, Calvin. "An Anglo-Saxon
        Obstetric Calamity from Kingsworthy, Hampshire." Medical
        and Biological Illustration 25 (1975): 47-51.

8. CULTURAL

"There is not on the earth so bold a man who can
swear false or lie as a woman can."
                        Chaucer, Wife of Bath

a) Education

03211. Leach, Arthur F. "The Medieval Education of Women in
        England." Journal of Education 42 (December 1910):
        838-841.

03212. Sorley, Janetta C. Kings' Daughters. New York: Macmillan,
        1937.

b) Literature

(1) Non-specific

03213. Dove, Mary. "Gawain and the Blasme de Femmes Tradition."
        Medium aevum 41 (1972): 20-26.

03214. Earl, James. "Saint Margaret and the Pearl Maiden."
        Modern Philology 70 (1972): 1-8.

03215. Eckhardt, Caroline D. "Women as Mediator in the Middle
        English Romances." Journal of Popular Cultures 14
        (Summer 1980): 94-107.

03216. Gist, Margaret Adlum. Love and War in the Middle
        English Romances. Philadelphia: University of
        Pennyslvania Press, 1947.

03217. Hansen, Elaine Tuttle. "Women in Old English Poetry
        Reconsidered." Michigan Academician 9 (Summer 1976):
        109-117.

03218. Harris, Adelaide E. Heroine of the Middle English
        Romances. Folcroft, Pa.: Folcroft Press, 1928.

03219.   Holbrook, S.E. "Nymue, the Chief Lady of the Lake, in
          Malory's 'Le Morte D'arthur'." Speculum 53 (October
          1978): 761-777.

03220.   Judd, Elizabeth. "Influential Women in Anglo-Saxon
          England." In New Research on Women at the University
          of Michigan, edited by Dorothy G. McGuigan, pp. 50-57.
          Ann Arbor, Mich.: University of Michigan, Center for
          Continuing Education of Women, 1974.

03221.   Kliman, Bernice W. "Women in early English literature."
          Nottingham Medieval Studies 21 (1977): 32-49.

03222.   Lods, Jeanne. "Symbolisme Chrétien tradition celtique
          et verité psychologique dans les personnages feminins
          de Perlesvaus." In Mélanges de langue et de littera-
          ture médiévales offerts à Pierre Le Gentil, pp. 505-
          522. Paris: SEDES, 1973.

03223.   Lucas, Peter J. "Gawain's Anti-Feminism." Notes and
          Queries n.s. 15 (1968): 324-325.

03224.   Monfrin, J. "Poeme Anglo-Normand sur le mariage, les
          vices et les vertus, par Henri (XIIIe siecle)." In
          Melanges offerts à Jean Frappier de langue et littera-
          ture du moyen âge et de la renaissance, 2: 845-866.
          Publications romanes et française, no. 112. Geneva:
          Librairie Droz, 1970.

03225.   Newstead, Helaine. "The Beseiged Ladies in Arthurian
          Romance." Publications of the Modern Language Asso-
          ciation 63 (September 1948): 803-830.

03226.   Perrine, L. "Morris's 'Guenevere': An Interpretation."
          Philological Quarterly 39 (April 1960): 234-241.

03227.   Stiller, Nikki. Eve's Orphans. Mothers and Daughters in
          Medieval English Literature. Contributions in Women's
          Studies, no. 16. Westport, Conn.: Greenwood Press, 1980.

03228.   Thompson, Raymond H. "'For quenys I myght have inow . . .'"
          the Knight Errant's Treatment of Women in the English
          Arthurian Verse Romances." Atlantis 4 (Spring 1979):
          34-47.

03229.   Wenzel, Siegfried. "The Moor Maiden: A Contemporary
          View." Speculum 49 (January 1974): 69-74.

Also refer to #3606.

(2)   Chaucer

03330. Bolton, W.F. "The Wife's Lament and The Husband's
        Message: A Reconsideration Revisited." Archiv fur
        das Studium der neueren Sprachen und Literaturen 205
        (February 1969): 337-351.

03331. Brewer, D.S. "Love and Marriage in Chaucer's Poetry."
        Modern Language Review 49 (1954): 461-464.

03332. Brown, Emerson, Jr. "Biblical Women in the Merchant's
        Tale: Feminism, Antifeminism and Beyond." Viator 5
        (1974): 387-412.

03333. Chaucer, Geoffrey. The Canterbury Tales. Translated
        by Neville Coghill. Baltimore: Penguin Books, 1952.
        [See especially "The Wife of Bath" and "The Prioress."]

03334. Corrigan, Matthew. "Chaucer's Failure with Women. The
        Inadequacy of Criseyde." Western Humanities Review 23
        (Spring 1969): 107-120.

03335. Cotter, James Finn. "The Wife of Bath and the Conjugal
        Debt." English Language Notes 6 (March 1969): 169-172.

03336. Delaney, Sheila. "Womanliness in the Man of Law's Tale."
        Chaucer Review 9 (1974): 63-72.

03337. Doane, A.N. "Heathen Form and Christian Function in
        'The Wife's Lament'." Medieval Studies 28 (1966):
        77-91.

03338. Frank, Robert Worth. Chaucer and the Legend of Good
        Women. Cambridge, Mass.: Harvard University Press, 1972.

03339. _____. "The legend of the 'Legend of Good
        Women'." Chaucer Review 1 (1966-1967): 110-133.

03340. Haller, Robert S. "The Wife of Bath and the Three
        Estates." Annuale Mediaevale 6 (1965): 47-64.

03341. Hanning, Robert W. "From Eva and Ave to Eglentyne and
        Alisoun: Chaucer's Insight into the Roles Women Play."
        Signs 2 (Winter 1976): 580-599.

03342. Haskell, Ann S. "The Portrayal of Women by Chaucer and
        His Age." In What Manner Woman, edited by Marlene
        Springer, pp. 1-13. New York: New York University
        Press, 1977.

03343. Hawkins, Harriet. "The Victims Side: Chaucer's Clerk
        Tale and Webster's Duchess of Malfi." Signs 1 (Winter
        1975): 339-361.

03344. Hoffmann, Richard I. "Jephthah's Daughter and Chaucer's
        Virginia." Chaucer Review 2 (1967): 20-31.

03345. Kelly, Henry A. "Clandestine Marriage and Chaucer's
        Troilus." Viator 4 (1973): 435-458.

03346. Mariella, Sister. "The Parson's Tale and Marriage Group."
        Modern Language Notes 53 (April 1938): 251-256.

03347. Mathewson, Jeanne T. "For love and not for hate: the
        value of virginity in Chaucer's Physician's Tale."
        Annuale Mediaevale 14 (1973): 35-42.

03348. Matthews, William. "The Wife of Bath and all her Sect."
        Viator 5 (1974): 413-443.

03349. Murtaugh, Daniel M. "Women and Geoffrey Chaucer." English
        Literary History 38 (December 1971): 473-492.

03350. Overbeck, Pat Trefzger. "Chaucer's good woman." Chaucer
        Review 2 (1967): 75-94.

03351. Palomo, Dolores. "The Fate of the Wife of Bath's 'Bad
        Husbands.'" Chaucer Review 9 (Spring 1975): 303-319.

03352. Poteet, Daniel P. "Avoiding Women in Times of Afflic-
        tion: An Analogue for 'The Miller's Tale,' A33589-91."
        Notes and Queries n.s. 19 (1972): 89-90.

03353. Renoir, Alain. "A Reading Context for 'The Wife's Lament.'"
        In Anglo-Saxon Poetry: Essays in Appreciation for John
        C. McGalliard, edited by Lewis E. Nicholson and Dolores
        Warwick Frese, pp. 224-241. Notre Dame: University Press,
        1975.

03354. Reisner, Thomas Andrew. "The Wife of Bath's Dower: A
        Legal Interpretation." Modern Philology 71 (1974):
        301-302.

03355. Richmond, Velma. "Pacience in Adversitee: Chaucer's
        Presentation of Marriage." Viator 10 (1979): 323-354.

03356. Ridley, Florence H. The Prioress and the Critics.
        University of California Publications in English
        Studies, no. 30. Berkeley: University of California
        Press, 1965.

03357. Rowland, Beryl. "Chaucer's Dame Alys." Neuphilologische
        Mitteilungen 73 (1972): 381-395.

03358.   Shapiro, Gloria K.   "Dame Alice as Deceptive Narrator."
         Chaucer Review 6 (1972):   130-142.

03359.   Young, Karl.   "The Maidenly Virtues of Chaucer's Virginia."
         Speculum 16 (July 1941):   340-349.

         Also refer to #3360-3362.

c) Chivalry

(1) Courtly Love

03360.   Coffman, George R.   "Chaucer and Courtly Love Once
         More--'The Wife of Bath's Tale'." Speculum 20
         (January 1945):   43-50.

03361.   Dodd, W.G. Courtly Love in Chaucer and Gower. Gloucester,
         Mass.: P. Smith, 1913.

03362.   Donaldson, E. Talbot.   "The Myth of Courtly Love."   In
         Speaking of Chaucer, by E. Talbot Donaldson, pp. 154-163.
         New York: W. W. Norton and Co., 1972.

03363.   Evans, W.O.   "Cortaysye in Middle England." Mediaeval
         Studies 29 (1967):   143-157.

03364.   Miller, Robert P.   "The Wounded Heart: Courtly Love and
         the Medieval Antifeminist Tradition." Women's Studies 2
         (1974):   335-350.

         Also refer to #3188.

d) Art and Artifacts

03365.   Andersen, Jorgen. The Witch on the Wall: Medieval Erotic
         Sculpture in the British Isles. Copenhagen: Rosenkilde,
         1977.

03366.   Davidson, Clifford.   "Erotic Women's Songs in Anglo-
         Saxon England." Neophilologus 59 (1975):   451-462.

03367.   Markale, Jean.   "The Three Faces of Celtic Women." UNESCO
         Courier 28 (December 1975):   18-22, 31.

C. FRANCE

1. SURVEYS

"All inhabitants of Villefranche have the right to beat
their wives, provided they do not kill them thereby."
Customary law and practice,
13th statute, city of Gascony

a) Generic

03368. Evans, Joan. Life in Medieval France. London: Phaidon
Press, 1925.

03369. Lacroix, Paul. France in the Middle Ages; customs, classes
and conditions. New York: Frederick Unger Publishing
Co., 1963.

b) Women

03370. Butler, Pierce. Women of Medieval France. Vol. 5 of
Women in All Ages and in All Countries. 1908. Reprint.
NewYork: Gordon Press, 1975.

03371. Lehmann, André. Le Role de la femme dans l'histoire de
France au moyen âge. Paris: Berger-Levrault, 1952.

2. POLITICAL

"A girl of sixteen (isn't it an unnatural thing?) who
doesn't find her armor heavy; it seems that her up-
bringing is responsible for that, she is so strong and
hardy; and before her flees the enemy, no one stands
up to her."
Christine de Pisan
on Joan of Arc, 1429

a) Legal

(1) Non-specific

03372. Aubenas, Roger. "La famille dans l'ancienne Provence."
Annales d'histoire économique et sociale 8 (1936):
523-541.

03373. Carbasse, Jean-Marie. "La répression de l'adultère
dans les coutumes du Rouergue." In Etudes sur le
Rouergue pp. 107-113. Rodez: Société des lettres,
sciences, et arts de l'Aveyron, 1974.

03374. Dumas, Auguste. Etude sur le droit romain en pays de
droit écrit. La condition des gens mariés dans la
famille périgourdine au XVe et au XVIe siècles.
Paris: L. Larose and L. Tenin, 1908.

03375. Frank, Roslyn M.; Laxalt, Monique; and Vosburg, Nancy.
"Inheritance, Marriage, and Dowry Rights in the
Navarrese and French Basque Law Codes." Proceedings of
the Western Society for French History 4 (1976): 22-31.

03376. Imbert, Jean. "Le Regime matrimonial de la coutume de
la cité de Metz." In Etudes d'histoire du droit privé
offertes à Pierre Petot, edited by Pierre-Clement
Timbal, pp. 289-300. Paris: Recueil Sirey, 1959.

03377. Lafon, Jacques. Les époux bordelais (1450-1550):
regimes matrimoniaux et mutations sociales. Paris:
S.E.V.P.E.N., 1972.

03378. Petot, Pierre. "Les meubles des epoux au moyen age d'apres
les coutumes française." Revue internationale des
de l'antiquité 3 (1949): 213-230.

03379. Poumarède, Jacques. Les successions dans le sud-ouest
de la France au moyen âge. Publications de l'Universite
des sciences sociales de Toulouse. Centre d'histoire
juridique. Serie historique, no. 1. Paris: Presses
universitaires de France, 1972.

Also refer to #2049, 3549.

(2) Women

03380. Ganshof, François Louis. "Le statut de la femme dans la
monarchie franque." Recueils de la Société Jean Bodin
12 (1962): 5-58.

03381. Ganshcf, François-Louis. "Note sur quelques textes invoqués
        en faveur de l'existence d'une tutelle de la femme en droit
        franc." In Etudes d'histoire du droit privé offertes à
        Pierre Petot, edited by Pierre-Clement Timbali. Paris:
        Recueil Sirey, 1959.

03382. Guilhiermoz, Paul. "Le droit de renonciation de la femme
        noble, lors de la dissolution de la communauté, dans
        l'ancienne coutume de Paris." Bibliothèque de l'école
        des chartes 44 (1883): 489-500.

                    b) Political Roles

                       (1) Women

03383. Collas, Emile. Valentine de Milan, duchesse d'Orleans.
        Paris: Plon, 1911.

03384. Dhondt, Jean. "Sept femmes et un trio de rois." Con-
        tributions à l'histoire economique et sociale 3 (1964-
        1965): 37-70.

03385. Facinger, Marion F. "A Study of Medieval Queenship:
        Capetian France, 987-1237." Studies in Medieval and
        Renaissance History 5 (1968): 1-47.

03386. Frager, Marcel. Marie d'Anjou, femme de Charles VII.
        Paris: Editions de Paris, 1948.

03387. Geraud, Hercule. "Ingeburge de Danemark, reine de
        France, 1193-1236." Bibliothèque de l'école des
        chartes 6 (1844): 3-27, 93-118.

03388. Griffiths, Ralph A. "Queen Katherine of Valois and a
        missing statute of the realm." Law Quarterly Review
        93 (1977): 248-258.

03389. Konechy, Silvia. Die Frauen des karolgischen Konigshauses.
        Vienna: Verlag des Verbandes des wissenschaftlichen
        Gesellschaften Osterreichs, 1976.

03390. Lacarra, J.M., and Gonzales Anton, L. "Les testaments
        de la reine Marie de Montpellier." Annales du Midi 90
        (April-June 1978): 105-120.

03391. Levis-Mirepoix, Antoine François Joseph Pierre Marie,
        duc de. Philippe Auguste et ses trois femmes. Paris:
        Libraire A. Fayard, 1957.

03392. Maulde la Clavière, R. Jeanne de France, duchesse
        d'Orléans. Paris: Champion, 1883.

03393. Richard, Jules-Marie. Une petite-niece de saint Louis:
        Mahaut Comtesse d'Artois et de Bourgogne (1302-1329),
        etude sur la vie privee, les arts et l'industrie en
        Artois et a Paris a commencement du XIVe siècle.
        1887. Reprint. Geneva: Slatkine, 1975-1976.

03394. Sade, Donatien Alphonse François, marquis de. Histoire
        secrète d'Isabelle de Bavière, reine de France. Paris:
        Gallimard, 1953.

03395. Vallet de Viriville, Auguste. Isabeau de Bavière. Paris:
        Techener, 1859.

03396. Vajay, Szabolcs de. "Mathilde, reine de France inconnue.
        Contribution à l'histoire politique et sociale du
        royaume de France au XIe siècle." Journal des savants
        1971 (October-December 1971): 241-260.

        Also refer to #3064-3069.

                    (2)   Individuals

                    (a)   Blanche of Castile

03397. Berger, Elie. Histoire de Blanche de Castille, reine
        de France. 1895. Reprint. Geneva: Slatkine, 1975-1976.

03398. Bertrand, Rene. La France de Blanche de Castille.
        Paris: R. Laffont, 1977.

03399. Brion, Marcel. Blanche de Castile, femme de Louis VIII,
        mère de Saint Louis. Paris: Les Editions de France, 1939.

03400. González Ruiz, Nicolas. Blanca de Castilla: María de
        Molina. Barcelona: Ed. Cervantes, 1954.

03401. Germiny, Maxime de. "Blanche de Castille, reine de France."
        Revue des questions historiques 59 (April 1896): 506-511.

03402. Orliac, Jehanne d'. Blanche de Castille, mère de saint
        Louis et de Sainte Isabelle. Paris: Cambrai, 1861.

03403. Pernoud, Regine. Blanche of Castile. New York: Barnes and
        Noble, 1975.

(b)   Eleanor of Aquitaine

03404.   Brown, Elizabeth A. R. "Eleanor of Aquitaine: Parent, Queen and Duchess." In Eleanor of Aquitaine, Patron and Politician, edited by William W. Kibler, pp. 9-34. Austin, Texas: University of Texas Press, 1976.

03405.   Chambers, Frank McMann. "Some Legends Concerning Eleanor of Aquitaine." Speculum 16 (October 1941): 459-468.

03406.   Chapman, Robert L. "Notes on the Demon Queen Eleanor." Modern Language Notes 70 (June 1955): 393-396.

03407.   Greenhill, Eleanor S. "Eleanor, Abbot Suger, and Saint-Denis." In Eleanor of Aquitaine, Patron and Politician, edited by William W. Kibler, pp. 81-113. Austin, Texas: University of Texas Press, 1976.

03408.   Kelly, Amy. "Eleanor of Aquitaine and Her Courts of Love." Speculum 12 (January 1937): 3-19.

03409.   _____. Eleanor of Aquitaine and the Four Kings. Cambridge, Mass.: Harvard University Press, 1950.

03410.   Kibler, William W., ed. Eleanor of Aquitaine: Patron and Politician. Symposia in the Arts and the Humanities, No. 3. Austin: University of Texas Press, 1976.

03411.   Lejeune, Rita. "Rôle littéraire de la famille d'Aliénor d'Aquitain." Cahiers de civilisation médiévale 1 (July-September 1958): 319-337.

03412.   McCash, June Hall Martin. "Marie de Champagne and Eleanor of Aquitaine: A Relationship Re-examined." Speculum 54 (October 1979): 698-711.

03413.   Markale, Jean. Aliénor d'Aquitaine reine de France, puis d'Angleterre, dame des troubadours et des bardes bretons. Paris: Payot, 1979.

03414.   Meade, Marion. Eleanor of Aquitaine: A Biography. New York: Hawthorn Books, 1977.

03415.   Pernoud, Regine. Eleanor of Aquitaine. Translated by P. Wiles. New York: Coward-McCann, 1968.

03416.   Richardson, Henry G. "The Letters and Charters of Eleanor of Aquitaine." English Historical Review 74 (April 1959): 193-213.

03417.   Rosenberg, Melrich V. Eleanor of Aquitaine: Queen of
         the Troubadours and of the Courts of Love. Boston:
         Houghton Mifflin, 1937.

03418.   Seward, Desmond. Eleanor of Aquitaine. New York: Times
         Books, 1979.

03419.   Spens, Willy de. Eléonore d'Aquitaine et ses troubadours.
         Paris: Editions de Pars, 1957.

03420.   Walker, Curtis H. Eleanor of Aquitaine. Chapel Hill:
         University of North Carolina Press, 1950.

03421.   _____. "Eleanor of Aquitaine and the disaster
         at Cadmos mountain on the second crusade." American
         Historical Review 55 (1949-1950): 857-861.

         Also refer to #3605, 3610, 3687.

                        (c)   Joan of Arc

03422.   Bourassin, Emmanuel. Jeanne d'Arc. Paris: Perrin, 1977.

03423.   Champion, Pierre. "Notes sur Jeanne d'Arc." Le Moyen
         âge 20 (1907): 193-201; 22 (1909): 370-377; 23 (1910):
         175-197.

03424.   Chavigny, Jean. Jeanne d'Arc au coeur de la France.
         Blois: Imp. Alleaume, 1975.

03425.   Christiani, Leon. St. Joan of Arc, Virgin Soldier.
         Translated by M. Angeline Bouchard. Boston: St.
         Paul Editions, 1977.

03426   Cordier, Jacques. Jeanne d'Arc: sa personnalité, son
         role. Paris: Editions de la table ronde, 1948.

03427.   Desama, Claude. "Jeanne d'Arc et Charles VII. L'entrevue
         du signe (Mars-Avril 1429)." Revue de l'histoire des
         religions 170 (July-Sept. 1966): 29-46.

03428.   Destefanis, Abel. Louis XII et Jeanne de France: Etude
         historique et juridique sur une cause en nullite de
         mariage a la fin du XVe siècle (1498). Avignon: Les
         Presses universelles, 1975.

03429.   Duby, Andre and Duby, Georges. Les Procès de Jeanne
         d'Arc. Paris: Gallimard, 1975.

03430.   Enklaar, Diederik and Post, R.R. La Fille au grand
         coeur: Etudes sur Jeanne d'Arc. Groningen: J.B.
         Wolters, 1955.

03431. Fabre, Lucien. Jeanne d'Arc. 1947. Reprint. Paris:
        J. Tallandier, 1977.

03432. Ferreira, Christine. Jeanne d'Arc: Hier et aujourd'hui.
        Paris: Hachette, 1972.

03433. Gérard, André-Marie. Jeanne la mal jugée. Paris:
        Bloud et Gay, 1964.

03434. Grandeau, Yann. Jeanne insultée: Procès en diffamation.
        Preface by Régine Pernoud. Paris: Albin Michel, 1973.

03435. Grayeff, Felix. Joan of Arc: Legends and Truth.
        London: Philip Goodall, 1978.

03436. Guitton, Jean. Problème et mystère de Jeanne d'Arc.
        Paris: Libraire Artheme Fayard, 1961.

03437. Hartemann, Jean. Une Jeanne d'Arc possible. Paris: La
        Pensée universelle, 1978.

03438. Joly, Henri. "La Psychologie de Jeanne d'Arc. Etudes
        119 (April 1909): 158-183.

03439. Kyle, Elizabeth. Maid of Orleans: The Story of Joan
        of Arc. London: Thomas Nelson and Sons, 1957.

03440. LaMartinière, Jules de. "Frère Richard et Jeanne d'Arc
        à Orleans, Mars-Juillet 1430." Le Moyen âge 44
        (1934): 184-198.

03441. Lancesseur, Pierre de. Jeanne d'Arc, Chef de Guerre.
        Paris: Nouvelles éditions Debresse, 1961.

03442. Lavater-Sloman, Mary. Jeanne d'Arc. Munich: Heyne,
        1977.

03443. Leroy, Olivier. Sainte Jeanne d'Arc. Paris: Alsatia,
        1958.

03444. Lightbody, Charles W. The Judgements of Joan: Joan of
        Arc, A Study in Cultural History. Cambridge, Mass.:
        Harvard University Press, 1961.

03445. Luce, Simeon. Jeanne d'Arc à Domremy. Recherches
        critiques sur les origines de la mission de la Pucelle,
        acompagnees de pieces justificatives. 1886. Reprint.
        Geneva: Slatkine, 1975-1976.

03446. Lucie-Smith, Edward A. Joan of Arc. New York: Norton,
        1977.

03447. Lynn, Therese B. "The Ditie de Jeanne d'Arc: its
        political, feminist and aesthetic significance."
        15th Century Studies 1 (1978): 149-156.

03448. Lyonne, René. Jeanne d'Arc, legende et histoire.
        Nancy: Cour d'Appel de Nancy, 1973.

03449. Michelet, Jules. Jeanne d'Arc. Translated by Albert
        Guerard. Ann Arbor, Mich.: University of Michigan
        Press, 1967.

03450. Paine, Albert Bigelow. Joan of Arc, Maid of France.
        New York: Macmillan Co., 1925.

03451. Pernoud, Régine. Joan of Arc. Translated by Jeanne
        Unger Duell. New York: Grove Press, 1961.

03452. Scott, Walter Sidney. Jeanne d'Arc: Her Life, Her
        Death and the Myth. New York: Harper & Row, 1974.

03453. Sermoise, Pierre de. Joan of Arc and her Secret Missions.
        Translated by Jennifer Taylor. London: R. Hale, 1973.

03454. Smith, John Holland. Joan of Arc. New York: Charles
        Scribner's Sons, 1973.

03455. Steinbach, Hartmut. Jeanne d'Arc. Gottingen: Muster-
        schmidt Verlag, 1973.

03456. Thomas, Edith. Jeanne d'Arc. Paris: Editions "Hier et
        aujourd'hui", 1947.

03457. Tisset, Pierre. Procès de condamnation de Jeanne d'Arc.
        Vol. II. Traduction et Notes. Paris: Klincksieck,
        1970.

03458. Waldman, Milton. Joan of Arc. New York: Longmans
        Green and Co., 1935.

03459. Xerri, Jean-Francois. Jeanne d'Arc n'a pas existé.
        Paris: La Pensee universelle, 1973.

3. ECONOMIC

"Women have so much avarice that generous gifts break
down all the barriers of their virtue."
                                    Andreas Capellanus

a) Generic

03460. Emery, Richard Wilder. The Jews of Perpignan in the 13th
        Century. New York: Columbia University Press, 1959.

03461. Fagniez, Gustave. Etudes sur l'industrie et la classe
        industrielle à Paris, au XIIIe siècle. Bibliothèque
        de l'école des hautes études. Sciences philologiques
        et historiques, no. 33. Paris: F. Vieweg, 1877.

03462. Franklin, Alfred. Les corporations ouvrières de Paris,
        du XIIe au XVIIIe siècle, histoire, statuts, armoiries,
        d'après des documents originaux ou inédits. Paris:
        Firmin-Didot, 1884.

03463. Geremek, Bronislav. Le salariat dans l'artisanat
        parisien du XIIIeme au XVeme siècle. Etude sur le
        marche de la main-d'oeuvre au moyen âge. Paris:
        Mouton, 1968.

        Also refer to #3495.

b) Household

03464. Le Menagier de Paris, traité de morale et d'économie
        domestique compose vers 1393, par un bourgeois
        parisien. Paris: Impr. de Crapelet, 1846.

03465. Myers, A.R. "The Captivity of a Royal Witch: The
        Household Accounts of Queen Joan of Navarre, 1419-1421."
        Bulletin of the John Rylands Library 24 (October 1940):
        263-284.

c) Women

03466. Dixon, E. "Craftswomen in the Livre des metiers."
        Economic Journal 5 (1895): 209-228.

03467. Jordan, William Chester. "Jews on Top: Women and the
        Availability of Consumption Loans in Northern France
        in the Mid-Thirteenth Century." Journal of Jewish
        Studies 29 (Spring 1978): 39-56.

4. RELIGION

"Woman, sweet evil, honey and poison alike, annointing
with balm the sword with which thou piercest even wise
men's hearts. Who persuaded our first parent to taste
the forbidden thing? A woman."

Marbode, Bishop of Rennes,
11th century

a) Generic

03468. Huyghebaert, Nicolas-Norbert. "Les femmes laiques dans la
vie religieuse des XIe et XIIe siècles dans la province
ecclesiastique de Reims." In I laici nella "Societas
christiana" dei secoli XIe XII, pp. 346-389. Publica-
zioni dell'Università Cattolica del Sacro Cuore, Serie
Terza, 5. Miscellanea del Centro di studie medioevali,
no. 5. Milan: Società editrice Vita e Pensiero, 1968.

03469. Smith, Jacqueline. "Robert of Arbrissel's relations with
women." In Medieval Women, edited by Derek Baker,
pp. 175-84. Studies in Church History, Subsidia, I .
Oxford: Blackwell, 1978.

b) Goddesses/Mythology

03470. Lecouteaux, Claude. "La structure des légendes Mélusin-
iennes." Annales: économies, sociétés, civilisations 33
(March-April 1978): 294-306.

03471. LeGoff, Jacques. "Mélusine maternelle et défricheuse."
Annales: économies, sociétés, civilisations 26 (May-August
1971): 587-603.

c) Saints/Religious Women

03472.   Auriol, A. "Sainte Cécile et la Cathedrale d'Albi."
          In Mélanges de littérature et d'histoire religieuse
          publiés à l'occasion du jubilé épiscopal de Mgr. de
          Cabrières, pp. 329-342. Paris: A. Picard, 1899.

03473.   Briand, Abbe Emile. Histoire de Sainte Radegonde, reine
          de France, et des sanctuaires et pèlerinages en son
          honneur. Paris: Oudin, 1898.

03474.   Gad, Tue. "Die Marienlegende von Beatrix als Katharinen-
          legende." Classica et Mediaevalia 14 (1953): 205-225.

03475.   Geary, Patrick J. "Saint Helen of Athyra and the
          Cathedral of Troyes in the 13th Century." Journal of
          Medieval and Renaissance Studies 7 (1977): 149-168.

03476.   Jullian, Camille. "Sainte Genevieve à Nanterre." In
          Melanges offertes à M. Gustave Schlumberger 2: 372-375.
          Paris: P. Geuthner, 1924.

03477.   Laurent, Theis. "Saint sans famille? Quelques remarques
          sur la famille dans le monde franc à travers les
          sources hagiographiques." Revue historique 255 (1976):
          3-20.

03478.   Saxer, Victor. Le culte de Marie-Madeleine en Occident,
          des origines à la fin du moyen âge. 2 vols. Paris:
          Clavreuil, 1959.

d) Mariology

03479.   Durliat, Marcel. "Marie dans l'art du sud-Ouest de la
          France et de la Catalogne aux XIe siècles." In Le Livre
          des miracles de Notre Dame de Rocamandour, pp. 157-175.
          Luzech: Impr. Boissor, 1973.

03480.   Forsyth, William H. "Madonnas of the Rhone-Meuse Valley."
          Metropolitan Museum of Art, Bulletin n.s. 28 (1969-1970):
          252-261.

03481.   Gaborit-Chopin, Danielle. "La Vierge à l'Enfant d'ivoire
          de la Sainte-Chapelle." Bulletin Monumental 130 (1972):
          213-224.

03482.   Lodolo, Gabriela. "Il segno della donna nel Medioevo."
          Aevum 50 (1976):   348-356.

03483.   Therel, M-L. "Etude inconographique des vaussures du
          portail de la Vierge-Mere à la cathedrale de Laon."
          Cahiers de civilisation médiévale 15 (1972):   41-51.

03484.   Vegas, Liana Castelfranchi. "A new French Madonna
          dating from about 1400." The Burlington Magazine 114
          (1972):   396-399.

e) *Monastic Life*

(1) Non-specific

03485.   Iogna-Prat, Dominique. "La femme dans la perspective
          pénitentielle des ermites du Bas-Maine (fin XIe -
          debut XIIe siècle)." Revue d'histoire de la spiritualite
          53 (1977):   47-64.

03486.   Krenig, Ernst G. "Mittelalterliche Frauenklöster nach
          den Konstitutionen von Citeaux, unter besonderer
          Berücksichtigung fränkischer Nonnenkonvente." Analecta
          sacri ordinis cisterciensis 10 (1954):   1-105.

03487.   Leclercq, Jean. Monks and Love in Twelfth-Century France.
          New York: Oxford University Press, 1979.

03488.   Levillain, Leon. "Etudes mérovingiennes: la charte de
          Clotilde (10 mars, 673)." Bibliothèque de l'école des
          chartes 105 (1944):   5-63.

03489.   Lorcin, Marie-Thérèse. "Retraite des veuves et filles
          au couvent: quelques aspects de la condition féminine
          à la fin du moyen âge." Annales de démographie
          historique(1975):   187-204.

03490.   Maillé, Geneviève Aliette (de Rohan-Chabot), marquise de.
          Les Cryptes de Jouarre. Paris: A. and J. Picard, 1971.

03491.   Prinz, F. Frühes Mönchtum im Frankreich. Kultur und
          Gesellschaft in Gallien, den Rheinlanden und Bayern am
          Beispiel der monastischen Entwicklung. Vienna:
          Oldenbourg, 1965.

03492.   Roisin, Simone. "L'efflorescence cistercienne et le courant
          féminin de piété au xiii siècle." Revue d'histoire
          ecclesiastique 39 (1943):   342-378.

03493. Scheiblreiter, G. "Königtöchter im Kloster: Radegund (587)
        und der Nonnenaufstand von Poitiers." Mitteilungen des
        Instituts für österreichische Geschichtsforschung 87
        (1979): 1-37.

03494. Verdon, Jean. "Les moniales dans la France de l'Ouest
        aux XIe et XIIe siècles. Etude d'histoire sociale."
        Cahiers de civilisation médiévale 19 (July-Sept. 1976):
        247-264.

03495. _____. "Notes sur le rôle économique des
        monastères féminins en France dans la seconde moitié
        du IXe et au debut du Xe siècle." Revue Mabillon 58
        (April-Sept. 1975): 329-343.

03496. _____. "Recherches sur les monasteres féminins
        dans la France du Sud aux IXe-XIe siècles." Annales
        du Midi 88 (April-June 1976): 117-138.

                          (2) Héloïse

03497. Archambault, Paul. "The Silencing of Cornelia: Heloise,
        Abelard, and their Classics." Papers on Language and
        Literature 6 (Winter 1970): 3-17.

03498. Beggiato, Fabrizio. "La prima lettera di Eloisa ad
        Abelardo nella traduzione di Jean de Meun." Cultura
        neolatina 32 (1972): 211-229.

03499. Dronke, Peter. Abelard and Heloise in Medieval Testi-
        monies. Glasgow: University Press, 1976.

03500. _____. "Heloise and Marianne: Some Reconsidera-
        tions." Romanische Forschung 72 (1960): 223-256.

03501. Gilson, Etienne. Heloise and Abelard. Ann Arbor, Mich.:
        University of Michigan, 1960.

03502. Hamilton, Elizabeth. Heloise. New York: Doubleday, 1967.

03503. Jeandet, Yette. Héloïse. L'amour et l'absolu. Lausanne:
        Editions Rencontre, 1966.

03504. McLeod, Enid. Heloise: A Biography. London: Chatto
        and Windus, 1938.

03505. Melling, Leonard. Abelard and Heloise. London: Regency
        Press Ltd., 1970.

03506. Moos, Peter von. "Die Bekehrung Heloise."
        Mittellateinisches Jahrbuch 11 (1976): 95-125.

03507. Moos, Peter von. "Cornelia und Helois." Latomus 34
        (October-December 1975): 1024-1059.

03508. Muckle, J.T. "The Letter of Heloise on Religious Life
        and Abelard's First Reply." Medieval Studies 17
        (1955): 240-281.

03509. _____. "The Personal Letters Between Abelard and
        Heloise: Introduction, Authenticity and Text."
        Medieval Studies 15 (1953): 47-94.

03510. Pernoud, Regine. Heloise and Abelard. Translated by
        Peter Wiles. London: Collins, 1973.

03511. Robertson, D.W., Jr. Abelard and Heloise. New York:
        Dial Press, 1972.

03512. Truc, Gonzague. Abélard avec ou sans Héloïse. Paris:
        Foyard, 1956.

03513. Waddell, Helen. Peter Abelard. New York: Penguin
        Paperbacks, 1978.

03514. Zumthor, Paul. "Héloïse et Abelard." Revue des
        sciences humaines n.s. 91 (July-Sept. 1958): 313-332.

                    f) Canon Law

03515. Daudet, Pierre. L'établissement de la compétance de
        l'église en matière de divorce et consanguinite.
        France-Xe-XII siècles Etudes sur l'histoire de la
        jurisdiction matrimoniale. Paris: Recueil Sirey,
        1941.

03516. _____. Les origines carolingiennes de la com-
        petence exclusive de l'église (France et Germanie).
        Etudes sur l'histoire de la jurisdiction matrimoniale.
        Paris: Recueil Sirey, 1933.

03517. Lefebvre-Teillard, Anne. "Ad matrimonium contrahere
        compellitur." Revue de droit canonique 28 (1978):
        210-217.

g) Heresy

(1) Non-specific

03518. Manselli, Raoul. _Spirituali e Beghini in Provenza._
Instituto storico italiano per il medio evo. Studi
storici, nos. 31-34. Rome: Nella sede dell'Instituto,
1959.

03519. Oldenburg, Zoe. _Massacre at Montsegur._ London:
Weidenfield and Nicolson, 1961.

(2) Women

03520. Abels, Richard and Harrison, Ellen. "The Participation
of Women in Languedocian Catharism." _Medieval Studies_
41 (1979): 215-251.

03521. Barber, Malcolm C. "Women and Catharism." _Reading
Medieval Studies_ 3 (1977): 45-62.

03522. Langlois, C. V. "Marguerite Porete." _Revue historique_
54 (1894): 295-299.

h) Witchcraft

03523. Nelli, Rene. "Magie et contraception. L'herbe
ensorcelée du cure de Montaillou (Ariège) (Pierre
Clergue)." _Folklore_ (Carcassonne) 38 (1975): 2-8.

5. SOCIAL

"Here is an example to every good woman that she suffer
and endure patiently, nor strive with her husband nor
answer him before strangers, as did once a woman who
did answer her husband before strangers with short
words and he smote her in her visage and broke her
nose, and all her life she had her nose crooked.
_The Book of the Knight of the
Tower_, 1371.

a) Generic

(1) Non-specific

03524. Bezard, Yvonne. La Vie rurale dans le sud de la region
        parisienne de 1450 a 1560. Paris: Firmin-Didot, 1929.

03525. Chamberlin, R. Life in Mediaeval France. London:
        B.T. Batsford Ltd., 1967.

03526. Defourneaux, Marcelin. La Vie quotidienne au temps de
        Jeanne d'Arc. Paris: Hachette, 1952.
        [See especially pp. 140–158.]

03527. Demolon, Pierre. Le Village mérovingien de Brebières (VIe
        VIIe siècles). Arras: Commission departementale des
        monuments historiques du Pas-du-Calais, 1972.

03528. Duby, Georges. La société aux XIe et XIIe siècles dans
        la région Mâconnaise. Paris: S.E.V.P.E.N., 1971.

03529. Duval, Paul-Marie. La Vie quotidienne en Gaule pendant
        la paix romaine. Paris: Hachette, 1953.

03530. Faral, Edmond. La Vie quotidienne au temps de Saint
        Louis. Paris: Hachette, 1950.

03531. Franklin, Alfred. La Vie privée au temps des premiers
        Capetiens. Paris: Emile Paul, 1911.

03532. Langlois, Charles. La vie en France au moyen âge d'après
        quelque moralistes du temps. Paris: Hachette, 1908.

03533. Lelong, Charles. La Vie quotidienne en Gaule a l'époque
        mérovingienne. Paris: Hachette, 1963.

03534. LeRoy Ladurie, Emmanuel. Montaillou: The Promised Land
        of Error. Translated by Barbara Bray. New York:
        George Brazillier, 1978.

03535. Patault, A. M. Hommes et femmes de corps en Champagne
        méridionale à la fin du moyen âge. Nancy: Annales
        de l'université, 1978.

03536. Ribbe, Charles. La Société provençale à la fin du moyen
        âge. Paris: Perrin et Cie., 1898.

        Also refer to #3135, 3139, 3140, 3146.

(2) Women

03537. Lehmann, André. Le rôle de la femme dans l'histoire de
        la Gaule. Paris: Presses universitaires de France,
        1944.

03538. Verdon, Jean. "La femme vers le milieu du IXe siècle
        d'après la polyptique de l'abbye de Saint-Rémi de
        Reims." Mémoires de la Société d'agriculture, commerce,
        sciences et arts du department de la Marne 91 (1976):
        111-134.

03539. _____. "Notes sur la femme en Limousin vers 1300."
        Annales du Midi 90 (July-Dec. 1978): 319-329.

        b) Demography

03540. Aries, Philippe. "Sur les origines de la contraception
        en France." Population 8 (July-Sept. 1953): 465-472.

03541. Baratier, Edouard. La démographie provençale du XIIIe au
        XVIe siècle. Paris: S.E.V.P.E.N., 1961.

03542. Biraben, Jean-Noël. "La population de Toulouse au XIVe
        et au XVe siècles." Journal des Savants (1964): 284-300.

03543. Bocquet, Andre. Recherches sur la population rurale de
        l'Artois et du Boulonnais pendant la période bour-
        guignonne (1384-1477). Arras: Commission departmentale
        des monuments historiques, 1969.

03544. Houdaille, Jacques. "Fécondité des familles souveraines
        du XVIe au XVIIIe siècle, influence de l'âge du père
        sur la fecondité." Population 31 (1976): 1- 70.

03545. Le Mené, Michel. "La population nantaise à la fin du
        XVe siècle." Annales de Bretagne 71 (1964): 189-220.

03546. Pounds, Norman J.G. "Overpopulation in France and the
        Low Countries in the Later Middle Ages." Journal of
        Social History 3 (Spring 1970): 225-247.

03547. _____. "Population and Settlement in the Low
        Countries and Northern France in the Later Middle Ages."
        Revue belge de philologie et d'histoire 49 (1971): 403-
        481; 1119-1174.

c) Family

(1) Non-specific

03548. Aubenas, Roger. "L'adoption en Provence au moyen âge." Revue historique de droit français et étranger 4th ser. 13 (1934): 700-726.

03549. _____. "Note sur quelques aspects de la recherche de la paternité naturelle en pays de droit écrit à la fin du Moyen Age." Recueil de mémoires et travaux publiés par la Société d'histoire du droit et des institutions des anciens pays du droit écrit 3 (1955): 1-3.

03550. Bouchard, Constance B. "The Structure of a Twelfth-Century French Family: The Lords of Seignelay." Viator 10 (1979): 39-56.

03551. Chérel, Albert. La famille française. Pages choisies de nos bons écrivains de 825 à 1924. I:Le moyen âge et le XVIe siècle. Paris: Spes, 1925.

03552. Chevrier, Georges. "Autorité communale et vie familiale à Dijon aux XIVe et XVe siècles." Annales de Bourgogne 16 (1944): 7-14; 17 (1945): 131-138; 18 (1946): 251-257.

03553. Duby, Georges. "Lineage, nobility and chivalry in the region of the Macon in the Twelfth Century." In Family and Society, edited by Robert Forster and Orest Ranum, pp. 16-40. Baltimore: Johns Hopkins Press, 1976. Also in Annales: économies, sociétés, civilisations 27 (1972): 803-823.

03554. _____. "Structures de parente et noblesse, France du Nord X^e-XIIe siècles." In Miscellanea Mediaevalia in memoriam Jan Frederik Niermeyer, pp. 149-165. Groningen: J.B. Wolters, 1967.

03555. _____. "Structures familiales aristocratiques en France du XIe siècle en rapport avec les structures de l'état." In L'Europe aux IXe-XIe siècles, aux origines des états nationaux, edited by T. Manteuffel et A. Gieysztor, pp. 57-62. Warsaw: Institut d'Histoire de l'Academie Polonaise des Sciences, 1968.

03556. Fedou, Rene. "Une famille aux XIVe et XVe siècles: les Jossard de Lyon." Annales: économies, sociétés, civilisations 9 (1954): 461-480.

03557. Flandrin, Jean-Louis. Families in Former Times, Kinship,
        Household and Sexuality in Early Modern France.
        Translated by Richard Southern. New York: Cambridge
        University Press, 1979.

03558. Gonon, Marguerite. La vie familiale en Forez au XIVe
        siecle et son vocabulaire d'apres les testaments. Paris:
        Societe d'edition "Les Belles lettres," 1961.

03559. Haidu, Robert. "Family and Feudal Ties in Poitou, 1100-
        1300." Journal of Interdisciplinary History 8 (Summer
        1977): 117-139.

03560. Jeay, Madeleine. "Sexuality and Family in 15th Century
        France: Are Literary Sources a Mask or a Mirror?"
        Journal of Family History 4 (Winter 1979): 328-345.

03561. Levy, J.P. "L'officialité de Paris et les questions
        familiales à la fin du XIVe siècle." Etudes d'histoire
        de droit canonique dediées à Gabriel Le Bras 2 (1965):
        1265-1294.

03562. Ourliac, Paul. "La famille pyrénéenne au Moyen Age."
        In Recueil d'études sociales publié à la mémoire de
        Frederic Le Play, pp. 257-263. Paris: A. et J.
        Picard, 1956.

03563. Weinberger, Stephen. "Peasant households in Provence:
        ca. 800-1100." Speculum 48 (April 1973): 247-257.

03564. Werner, K. F. "Bedeutende Aldelsfamilien im Reich Karls
        des Grossen." In Karl der Grosse 1: 83-142. Düsseldorf:
        Pädagogischer Verlag Schwan, 1965.

03565. Wolff, Philippe. "Une famille, du XIIIe au XVIe siècle:
        les Ysalquier de Toulouse." Mélanges d'histoire
        sociale 1 (1942): 35-58.

03566. _____. "Quelques actes notariés concernant
        famille et mariage (XIVe - XVe siècles)." Annales
        du Midi 78 (1966): 115-123.

        Also refer to #3372, 3374.

                        (2) Childhood

03567. Beitscher, Jane K. "'As the twig is bent . . .'" Children
        and their Parents in an Aristocratic Society." Journal
        of Medieval History 2 (September 1976): 181-191.

03568. Bellot, Claudine. "Les enfants abandonnées à Chartres à
        la fin du Moyen Age." Annales de demographie historique
        (1975): 167-186.

03569. Richardot, H. "Tutelle, curatelle et émancipation des
        enfants legitimes en Forez au XIIIe siècle." Revue
        historique de droit français et étranger 4th ser. 24
        (1945): 29-79.

                        d) Marriage

03570. Bonnecorse de Lubières, Gabriel de. La condition des gens
        mariés en Provence aux XIVe, et XVIe siècles. Paris:
        Recueil, 1929.

03571. Coleman, Emily R. "Medieval Marriage Characteristics:
        A Neglected Factor in the History of Medieval Serfdom."
        Journal of Interdisciplinary History 2 (Autumn 1971):
        205-219. Also in The Family in History, edited by T.
        Rabb and R. Rotberg, pp. 1-15. New York: Harper and Row
        Torchbooks, 1973. Also in Marriage and Fertility,
        edited by R. Rotberg and T. Rabb, pp. 3-17. Princeton,
        N.J.: Princeton University Press, 1980.

03572. Comet, Georges. "Quelques remarques sur la dot et les
        droits de l'épouse dans la région d'Arles au XIIe et
        XIIIe siècles." Melanges offerts à René Crozet, edited
        by Pierre Gallais and Yves-Jean Riou, 2: 1031-1034.
        Poitiers: Société d'etudes médiévales, 1966.

03573. Duby, Georges. Medieval Marriage, Two Models from Twelfth-
        Century France. Baltimore: Johns Hopkins University
        Press, 1978.

03574. Fransen, Gerard. "La formation du lien matrimonial au
        moyen âge." In Le Lien matrimonial, colloque de Cerdic,
        Strasbourg 21-23 Mai, 1970, edited by Rene Metz and
        Jean Schlick, pp. 106-126. Strasbourg: C.E.R.D.I.C.,
        1970.

03575. Girard, René. "Marriage in Avignon in the Second Half
        of the Fifteenth Century." Speculum 28 (July 1953):
        485-498.

03576. Gonon, Marguerite. "Les dots en Forez au XVe siècle, d'après
        les testaments enregistrés en la chancellerie de Forez."
        Mélanges Pierre Tisset: Recueil de memoires et travaux
        publiés par la Société d'histoire du droit et des insti-
        tutions des anciens pays de droit ecrit 7 (1970): 247-265.

03577.   Gottlieb, Beatrice. "The Meaning of Clandestine Marriage."
         In Family and Sexuality in French History, edited by
         Robert Wheaton and Tamara K. Hareven, pp. 49-83. Phila-
         delphia: University of Pennsylvania Press, 1980.

03578.   Hilaire, Jean. Le régime des biens entre époux dans la
         région de Montpellier du debut XIIIe siècle à la fin
         du XVIe siècle. Montpellier: Causse, Graille et
         Costelnau, 1957.

03579.   _____. "Les régimes matrimoniaux aux XIe et
         XIIe siècles dans la région de Montpellier." Recueil
         des mémoires et travaux publiés par la Société
         d'histoire du droit et des institutions des anciens
         pays du droit écrit 3 (1955): 15-37.

03580.   Laribière, Geneviève. "Le mariage a Toulouse aux XIVe et
         XVe siècles." Annales du Midi 79 (1967): 335-361.

03581.   Lefebvre, Charles. La coutume française du mariage au
         temps de Saint Louis. Paris: L. Larose, 1901.

03582.   Mestayer, Monique. "Les contrats de mariage à Douai
         du XIIIeme au XVeme siècle reflets du droit et de la
         vie d'une société urbaine." Revue du Nord 61 (April-
         June 1979): 353-380.

03583.   Molin, Jean Baptiste and Mutembe, Protais. Le rituel du
         mariage en France du XIIe au XVIe siècle. Paris:
         Beauchesne, 1974.

03584.   Ourliac, Paul. "Le mariage à Avignon au XVe siècle."
         Recueil de mémoires et travaux publiés par la Société
         d'histoire du droit et des institutions des anciens
         pays de droit ecrit 1 (1948): 55-61.

03585.   Payen, Jean-Charles. "La crise du mariage à la fin du
         XIIIe siècle d'après la littérature au temps." In
         Famille et parenté dans l'Occident médiéval, edited
         by Georges Duby and Jacques Le Goff, pp. 413-26.
         (Collection de l'école française de Rome, 30.) Rome:
         Collection de l'école française de Rome, 1977.

03586.   Petot, Pierre. "Licence de mariage et formariage des
         serfs dans les coutumes françaises au moyen âge."
         Czasopismo prawno-historyczne. Annales d'histoire du
         droit 2 (1949): 199-208.

03587.   _____. "Le mariage des vassales." Revue
         historique de droit française et étranger 56 (1978):
         29-47.

03588.   Ribbe, Charles. Les fiançailles et les mariages en
         Provence à la fin du moyen âge. Montpellier: G.
         Firmin et Montane, 1896.

03589. Timbal, Pierre-Clement. "La belle-mère, le gendre et le facteur; un mariage parisien au XIVe siècle." In _Etudes d'histoire du droit prive offertes à Pierre Petot_, edited by Pierre-Clement Timbal, pp. 543-552. Paris: Recueil Sirey, 1959.

03590. Turlan, Juliette-M. "Une licence du mariage au XIVe siecle. Survivance ou exaction?" _Etudes d'histoire du droit canonique dediées à Gabriel Le Bras_ 2 (1965): 1447-1457.

Also refer to #2049, 3374-3378, 3515-3517, 3566.

e) Sex Life and Morals

(1) Non-specific

03591. Moore, John C. _Love in Twelfth-Century France_. Philadelphia: University of Pennsylvania Press, 1972.

03592. _____. "Love in Twelfth-Century France: A Failure in Synthesis." _Traditio_ 24 (1968): 429-443.

03593. Shapiro, Norman R. and Wadsworth, James. _The Comedy of Eros: Medieval French Guides to the Art of Love_. Urbana: University of Illinois Press, 1971.

Also refer to #3557, 3560.

(2) Prostitutes

03594. Le Pileur, Louis. _La prostitution du XIIIe au XVIIe siècle; documents tires des archives d'Avignon, du Comtat Venaissin de la principauté d'Orange et de la ville libre imperiale de Besancon_. Paris: Champion, 1908.

03595. Rossiaud, Jacques. "Prostitution, youth and society in the towns of southeastern France in the Fifteenth Century." In _Deviants and the Abandoned in French Society_, edited by Robert Forster and Orest Ranum, pp. 1-46. Baltimore: Johns Hopkins Press, 1978. Also in _Annales: economies, sociétés, civilisations_ 31 (March-April 1976): 289-325.

03596. Terroine, Anne. "Le roi des ribauds de l'Hotel du roi et les prostitutes parisiennes." _Revue historique de droit français et étranger_ 56 (1978): 253-267.

f) Fashion/Manners

03597.   Crozet, René. "Sur un détail vestimentaire féminin du
          XIIe siècle." Cahiers de civilisation médiévale 4
          (January–March 1961): 55–56.

03598.   Evans, Joan. Dress in Medieval France. Oxford:
          Clarendon Press, 1952.

03599.   Piponnier, Françoise. Costume et vie sociale: la cour
          d'Anjou XIVe–XVe siècle. Paris: Mouton, 1970.

g) Health/Medical

03600.   Pinto, Lucille. "The Folk Practice of Gynecology and
          Obstetrics in the Middle Ages." Bulletin of the
          History of Medicine 47 (1973): 513–523.

          Also refer to #3523, 3540.

6. CULTURAL

". . . for her beautiful bearing
And her beautiful, charming looks.
A Man would have to be more than a hundred
Who could not seize the joy of love [of Eleanor]. . ."
                    Duke William IX of Aquitaine
                    12th Century

a) Education

03601.   Beauvais, Vincent de. De Eruditione Filiorum Nobilium,
          edited by Arpad Steiner. Cambridge, Mass.: The Medi-
          cal Academy of America, 1938.

03602. Jacobius, Helene. Die Erziehung des Edelfräuleins im
        alten Frankreich nach Dichtungen des XII, XIII und
        XIV Jahrhunderts. Beiheft zur Zeitschrift für
        romanische Philologie, no. 16. Halle: M. Niemeyer,
        1908.

03603. Tobin, Rosemary Barton. "Vincent of Beauvais' double
        stand in the education of girls." History of Education
        7 (1978): 1-5.

03604. _____. "Vincent of Beauvais on the
        education of women." Journal of the History of Ideas
        35 (July-September 1974): 485-489.

b) Literature

(1) Non-specific

03605. Benton, John F. "The Court of Champagne as a Literary
        Center." Speculum 36 (October 1961): 551-591.

03606. Brault, Gerard J. "Isolt and Guenevere: Two Twelfth-
        Century Views of Women." In The Role of Women in the
        Middle Ages, edited by Rosmarie Thee Morewedge, pp. 41-
        64. Albany, N.Y.: State University of New York Press,
        1975.

03607. Crow, Joan. "The Art of the Medieval Conteur : A Study
        of 'La Fille du Comte de Pontieu.'" French Studies 30
        (January 1976): 1-18.

03608. Grisay, Auguste, et. al. Les dénominations de la femme
        dans les anciens texte littéraires français. Gembloux:
        Duculot, 1969.

03609. Jonin, Pierre. Les personnages féminins dans les romans
        français de Tristan au XIIe siècle. Etude des in-
        fluences contemporaines. Publication des annales de la
        faculté des lettres, Aix-en-Provence, n.s., no. 22.
        Gap: Ophrys, 1958.

03610. Lazar, Moshé. "Cupid, the Lady and the Poet." In Eleanor
        of Aquitaine, Patron and Politician, edited by William
        W. Kibler, pp. 35-59. Austin, Texas: University of
        Texas Press, 1976.

03611. Lejeune, Rita. "La femme dans les littératures française
        et occitaine du XIe et XIIIe siècle." Cahiers de
        civilisation médiévale X^e-XIIe siècles 20 (1977):
        201-217.

03612. Norman, F. "Eleanor of Poitou in the Twelfth Century
        German Lyric." German Life and Letters n.s. 16
        (April–July 1963): 248–255.

03613. Pickens, Rupert T. "The Concept of Feminine Ideal in
        Villon's Testament: Huitain LXXXIX." Studies in
        Philology 70 (January 1973): 42–50.

03614. Pollmann, Leo. Die Liebe in der hochmittelalterlichen
        Literatur Frankreichs. Frankfurt a.M.: Vittorio
        Klostermann, 1966.

03615. Richardson, Lula. The Forerunners of Feminism in French
        Literature of the Renaissance from Christine de Pisan to
        Marie de Gournay. 1929. Reprint. New York: Johnson
        Reprint Co., 1973.

        Also refer to #3404–3421.

                              (2) Poetry

                           (a) Women

03616. Santy, Sernin. La Comtesse de Die, sa vie, ses oeuvres
        complètes, les fetes données en son honneur, avec tous
        les documents. Paris: Picard, 1893.

03617. Schultz, Oscar. Die provenzalischen Dichterinnen.
        Leipzig: Gustav Fock, 1888.

                         (b) Individuals

                    [1] CHRETIEN DE TROYES

03618. Bezzola, Reto R. Liebe und Abenteur im höfischen Roman
        Chrétien de Troyes. Hamburg: Rowohlt, 1961.

03619. Borodine, Myrrha (Mme. F. Lot). La Femme et l'amour au
        XIIe siècle, d'après les poèmes de Chrétien de Troyes.
        Paris: Picard, 1909.

03620. Duplat, Andre. "Etude stylistique des apostrophes
        adressées aux personnages féminins dans les romans de
        Chrétien de Troyes." Cahiers de civilisation médiévale
        17 (April–June 1974): 129–152.

03621.   Noble, Peter. "The Character of Guinevere in the
         Arthurian Romances of Chrétien de Troyes." The
         Modern Language Review 67 (1972): 524-535.

                    [2] CHRISTINE DE PISAN

03622.   Bell, Susan Groag. "Christine de Pizan (1364-1430):
         Humanism and the Problem of a Studious Woman."
         Feminist Studies 3 (Spring-Summer 1976): 173-184.

03623.   Davis, Judith M. "Christine de Pisan and Chauvinist
         Diplomacy." Female Studies 6 (1972): 116-122.

03624.   Du Castel, Françoise. Damoiselle Christine de Pizan.
         Paris: Editions A. et J. Picard, 1973.

03625.   Dulac, Liliane. "Christine de Pisan et le malheur der
         Vrais Amans." In Melanges de langue et de littérature
         médiévales offerts a Pierre Le Gentil, pp. 223-234.
         Paris: SEDES, 1973.

03626.   Favier, Marguerite. Christine de Pisan, muse des cours
         souveraineo. Lausanne: Ed. Recontre, 1967.

03627.   Gauvard, Claude. "Christine de Pisan a-t-elle eu une
         pensée politique?" Revue historique 250 (Oct.-Dec.
         1973): 417-430.

03628.   Kennedy, Angus J. and Varty, Kenneth. "Christine de
         Pisan's 'Ditie de Jehanne d'Arc'. Nottingham
         Medieval Studies 18 (1974): 29-55 and 19 (1975):
         53-76.

03629.   Laigle, Mathilde. Le "Livre des Trois Vertus" de
         Christine de Pisan et son milieu historique et
         litteraire. Bibliothèque du XVe siècle, no. 16.
         Paris: H. Champion, 1912.

03630.   Le Gentil, Pierre. "Christine de Pisan, poète méconnu."
         In Mélanges d'histoire littéraire offerts à Daniel
         Mornet, pp. 1-10. Paris: Nizet, 1951.

03631.   McLeod, Enid. The Order of the Rose, the Life and Ideas
         of Christine de Pizan. Totowa, N.J.: Rowman and
         Littlefield, 1976.

03632.   Margolis, Nadia. "The Human Prison: The Metamorphosis
         of Misery in the Poetry of Christine de Pizan, Charles
         d'Orleans and François Villon." 15th Century Studies
         1 (1978): 185-192.

03633.   Nys, Ernest. Christine de Pisan et ses principales
          oeuvres. Brussels: Société anonyme M. Weissenbruch,
          1914.

03634.   Pinet, Marie Josephe. Christine de Pisan, 1364-1430. Etude
          biographique et littéraire. Paris: H. Champion, 1927.

03635.   Pisan, Christine de. The Book of the Duke of True
          Lovers. London: Chatto and Windus, 1908.

03636.   _____. Christine de Pisan. Edited and intro-
          duced by Jeanine Moulin. Paris: Seghers, 1962.

03637.   _____. L'Epitre au dieu d'Amours. In
          Oeuvres poétiques. Paris: Firmin Didot et Cie.,
          1886-1896.

03638.   _____. Oeuvres poétiques de Christine de
          Pisan. 3 vols. Paris: Firmin Didot et Cie., 1889-
          1896.
          [See especially "Cent ballades d'amante de de dame."]

03639.   Rigaud, R. Les Idées féministes de Christine de Pisan.
          1911. Reprint. Geneva: Slatkine Reprints, 1973.

03640.   Solente, Suzanne. Christine de Pisan. Paris: Imprimerie
          National/C. Klincksieck, 1969.

03641.   Willard, Charity Cannon. "A Fifteenth-Century View of
          Women's Role in Medieval Society: Christine de Pizan's
          Livre des Trois Vertus." In The Role of Women in the
          Middle Ages, edited by Rosmarie Thee Morewedge, pp.
          90-120. Albany, N.Y.: State University of New York
          Press, 1975.

03642.   _____. "The Manuscript Tradition of
          the Livre des Trois Vertus and Christine de Pizan's
          Audience." Journal of the History of Ideas 27 (1966):
          433-444.

03643.   Wisman, Josette A. "L'éveil du sentiment national au
          moyen âge: La pensee politique de Christine de Pisan."
          Revue histoire 522 (April-June 1977): 289-297.

[3] MARIE DE FRANCE

03644.   Caluwé, Jacques de. "La conception de l'amour dans le
          lai d'Eliduc· de Marie de France." Le Moyen âge 77
          (1971): 53-77.

03645.   Green, Robert B. "Fin'amors dans deux lais de Marie de
          France. Equitan et Chaitivel."Le Moyen âge 81 (1975):
          265-272.

03646.   Hoepffner, Ernest. "Marie de France et l',,Eneas,,."
          Studi Medievali n.s. 5 (1932): 272-308.

03647.   _____. "Marie de France et les lais anonyme."
          Studi Medievali n.s. 4 (1931): 1-31.

03648.   _____. "Thomas d'Angleterre et Marie de
          France." Studi Medievali n.s. 7 (1934): 8-23.

03649.   Levi, Ezio. "Sulla Cronologia delle opere di Maria di
          Francia." Nuovi Studi Medievali 1 (1923-24): 41-72.

03650.   Mickel, Emmanuel J., Jr. Marie de France. Boston:
          G.K. Hall, Twayne, 1974.

03651.   Salviati, Jean. "Marie de France ou la poésie courtoise."
          Medecine de France 247 (1973): 43-50.

03652.   Sienaert, E. Les lais de Marie de France. Paris: Champion,
          1978.

03653.   Spitzer, Leo. "Marie de France, Dichterin von Problem-
          Marchen." Zeitschrift für Romanische Philologie 50
          (1930): 29-67.

03654.   Stevens, John. "The granz biens of Marie de France."
          In Patterns of Love and Courtesy, edited by John
          Lawlord, pp. 1-25. Evanston: Northwestern University
          Press, 1966.

03655.   Wathelet-Willem, Jeanne. "Equitan dans l'oeuvre de
          Marie de France." Le Moyen âge 69 (1963): 325-345.

                    (3) Troubadours, Trouveres

03656.   Bec, Pierre. "Trobairitz et chansons de femme. Contri-
          bution à la connaissance du lyrisme féminin au moyen
          âge." Cahiers de civilisation medievale 22 (July-
          September 1979): 235-262.

03657.   Bizet. J. A. Suso et le Minnesang: ou, la morale de
          l'amour courtois. Paris: Aubier, 1947.

03658   Crawford, Jane. "The Troubadours of Southern France and
          their Ethic of Love: A Hypothesis." Proceedings of
          the First Annual Meeting of the Western Society for
          French History 1 (1974): 1-14.

03659.   Denomy, Alexander Joseph. "Finamors: the Pure Love of the
          Troubadours, Its Amorality and Possible Source." Medieval
          Studies 7 (1945): 139-207.

03660. Frank, Grance. "The Distant Love of Jaufre Rudel."
        Modern Language Notes 57 (November 1942): 24-28.

03661. Jansen, Rudolf D. "Randbemerkungen zum ersten Troubadour
        und ersten Minnesanger." Deutsche Vierteljahresschrift
        für Literaturwissenschaft und Geistesgeschichte 48
        (1974): 767-771.

03662. Nelli, René. L'Erotique des troubadours. Toulouse:
        E. Privat, 1963.

03663. Shapiro, Marianne. "The provencal Trobairitz and the
        limits of courtly love." Signs 3 (Spring 1978):
        560-571.

                        (4) Satire

03664. Keidel, George C., ed. The Evangile aux femmes--An Old
        French Satire on Women. Baltimore: Friedenwald, 1895.

03665. Neff, Theodore Lee. La Satire des femmes dans la poésie
        lyrique française du moyen âge. Paris: V. Giard and
        E. Brière, 1900.

                    c) Chivalry

                (1) Non-specific

03666. Painter, Sidney. French Chivalry. 1940. Reprint.
        Ithaca, N.Y.: Great Seal Books, 1957.
        [See especially ch. 4.]

                (2) Courtly Love

                (a) General

03667. Coppin, Joseph. Amour et mariage dans la littérature
        francaise du Nord au moyen âge. Paris: D'Argences,
        1961.

03668. Crosland, J. "Ovid's Contribution to Courtly Love,"
        Modern Language Review 42 (April 1947): 199-206.

03669. Denomy, Alexander Joseph. "An Inquiry into the Origins of
        Courtly Love." Medieval Studies 6 (1944): 175-260.

03670. Duby, Georges. "La femme, l'amour, et le chevalier."
        Histoire 1 (1978): 6-13.

03671. Frappier, Jean. "Vues sur les conceptions courtoises dans les litteratures d'oc et d'oil au XIIe siècle." Cahiers de civilisation medievale 2 (April-June 1959): 135-156.

03672. Marks, Claude. Pilgrims, Heretics and Lovers: A Medieval Journey. New York: Macmillan Publishing Co., 1975.

03673. Vitti, Earl D. "Remarks on old French narrative: courtly love and poetic form." Romance Philology 26 (1972): 77-93.

03674. Wiegand, Hermann J. Three Chapters on Courtly Love in Arthurian France and Germany: Lancelot, Andreas Capellanus, Wolfram von Eschenbach's Parzival. Chapel Hill, N.C.: University of North Carolina Press, 1956.

Also refer to #3591-3593, 3618.

(b) Individuals

[1] ANDREAS CAPELLANUS

03675. Andreas, Capellanus. The Art of Courtly Love. Translated by John Jay Parry. 1941. Reprint. New York: Frederick Ungar Publishing Co., 1959.

03676. Benton, John F. "The Evidence for Andreas Capellanus Re-Examined Again." Studies in Philology 59 (July 1962): 471-478.

03677. Denomy, Alexander Joseph. "The De Amore of Andreas Cappelanus and the Condemnation of 1227." Medieval Studies 8 (1948): 107-149.

03678. Jackson, W. T. H. "The 'De amore' of Andreas Cappelanus and the Practice of Love at Court." Romanic Review 49 (December 1958): 243-251.

03679. Kelly, Douglas. "Courtly Love in Perspective: The Hierarchy of Love in Andreas Cappelanus." Traditio 24 (1968): 119-147.

03680. Schlosser, Felix. "Die Minneauffassung des Andreas Capellanus und die zeitgenössiche Ehelehre." Zeitschrift für deutsche Philologie 79 (1960): 266-284.

03681. Wiegand, Hermann John. Three Chapters on Courtly Love in Arthurian France and Germany: Lancelot, Andreas Cappelanus and Wolfram von Eschenbach's Parzival. Chapel Hill: University of North Carolina Press.

[2]   JEAN DE MEUN

03682.   Baird, Joseph L. and Kane, John R.   "La Querelle de la Rose:
in defense of the opponents." The French Review 48 (1974):
298-307.

03683.   Dahlberg, Charles. "Love and the Roman de la Rose."
Speculum 44 (October 1969):   567-584.

03684.   Friedman, Lionel J.   "'Jean de Meun,' Antifeminism and
'Bourgeois Realism'." Modern Philology 57 (August 1959):
13-23.

03685.   Meun, Jean de and Lorris, Guillaume de. Romance of the
Rose. Translated by Charles Dahlberg.   Princeton:
University Press, 1971.

03686.   Payen, Jean-Charles. La Rose et l'utopie. Révolution
sexuelle et communisme nostalgique chez Jean de Meung.
Paris: Ed. sociales, 1976.

03687.   Ward, Charles F. "The Epistles on the Romance of the
Rose and Other Documents in the Debate." Transactions
of the Royal Society of Canada 3rd ser. 4.2 (1910):
191-204.

d)   Art

03688.   Baltzer, Rebecca A. "Music in the Life and Times of
Eleanor of Aquitaine."   In Eleanor of Aquitaine,
Patron and Politician, edited by William W. Kibler,
pp. 61-80. Austin, Tx.:   University of Texas Press,
1976.

D. THE GERMANIES

1. SURVEYS

"So much he loved his wedded wife,
No wife of man's selection,
E'er knew so much affection,
I mean so faithfully and true."
                    Wolfram von Eschenbach, Parzival

03689. Knieriem, Pauline von. Die deutsche Frau und Furstin im
        Mittelalter Historische und Literarische Quellen.
        Quellenhefte zum Frauenleben in der Geschichte, edited
        by Emmy Beckmann and Irma Stoss, vol. 2. Berlin:
        F.A. Herbig, 1927.

03691. Kranz, E. and Meyn-von Westenholz, E. Die mittel-
        alterliche Hausfrau. Quellenhefte zum Frauenleben
        in der Geschichte, edited by Emmy Beckmann and Irma
        Stoss, vol. 2. Berlin: F. A. Herbig Verlags-
        buchhandlung, 1931.

03691. Reinsch, Gustav. Stellung und Leben der deutschen Frau
        im Mittelalter. Berlin: C. Habel, 1882.

        Also refer to #2009.

2. POLITICAL

"When a man takes a wife, he also takes all her goods
into his power by right of guardianship."
                    Der Sachsenspiegel

a) Legal

(1) Non-specific

03692. Demelius, Heinrich. Eheliches Gütterecht im spätmittel-
        alterlichen Wien. Vienna: H. Bohlau, 1970.

03693. Drew, Katherine Fischer. "The Germanic Family of the
        Leges Burgundionum." Medievalia et humanistica 15
        (1963): 5-14.

03694. Eisenmann, Hartmut. Konstanzer Institutionen des Familien-
        und Erbrechts von 1370-1521. Constance: Kommissions-
        Verlag J. Thorbecke, 1964.

03695. Frolich, Karl. "Die Eheschliessung des deutschen Fruh-
        mittelalters im Lichte Forschung." Hessische Blatter fur
        Volkskunde 27 (1928): 144-194.

03696. Kalifa, Simon. "Singularités matrimoniales chez les
        anciens Germains: le rapt et le droit de la femme a
        disposer d'elle-même." Revue historique de droit
        francais et etranger 4th ser. 48 (1970): 199-225.

03697. Mezger, F. "Did the Institution of Marriage by Purchase
        Exist in Old Germanic Law?" Speculum 18 (July 1943):
        369-371.

03698. Weigand, Rudolf. "Die Rechtspechung des Regensburger
        Gerichts in Ehesachen unter besonderer Berucksichtigung
        der Bedingten Eheschliessung nach Gerichtsbüchern aus
        dem Ende des 15. Jahrhunderts." Archiv fur katholisches
        Kirchenrecht 137 (1968): 403-463.

03699. Zallinger, Otto. Die Ringgaben bei der Heirat und das
        Zusammengeben im mittelalterlich-deutschen Recht.
        Vienna: Holder-Pichler-Tempsky, A. G., 1931.

        Also refer to #3708, 3783.

                        (2) Women

03700. Bechstein, Susanne. "Die Frauen in Hohenlohe im mittel-
        alterlichen Vormundschaftsrecht." Württembergisch
        Franken 50 (1966): 268-275.

03701. Espinas, Georges. "Le femme au moyen âge dans les villes
        allemands." Annales d'Histoire Economique et Sociale
        8 (1936): 390-393.

03702. Rivers, Theodore John. "The Legal Status of Free-women
        in the Lex Alamannorum." Zeitschrift der Savigny-
        Stiftung für Rechtsgeschichte Germanistische Abteilung
        91 (1974): 175-179.

03703. Rullkoetter, William. The Legal Protection of Woman among
        the Ancient Germans. Chicago: University of Chicago Press,
        1900.

03704. Senn, Noel. Le contrat de vente de la femme en droit
        matrimonial germanique. Portentruy: Imprimerie deu
        "Jura", 1946.

03705. Stammler, Rudolf. Ueber die Stellung der Frauen im alten
        deutschen Recht. Berlin: C. Habel, 1877.

        Also refer to #2040.

            b) Political Roles

                (1) Women

03706. Couturier, Mathieu J. Sainte Bathilde, reine des
        Francs. Paris: Pierre Téqui, 1909.

03707. Klewitz, Hans-Walter. "Die Abstammung der Kaiserin
        Beatrix." Deutsches Archiv für Erforschung des
        Mittelalters 7 (1944): 204-212.

03708. Konechy, Silvia. "Eherecht und Ehepolitik unter Ludwig
        dem Frommen." Mitteilungen des Instituts fur oster-
        reichische Geschichtsforschung 85 (1977): 1-21.

03709. Lintzel, Martin. "Die Mathilden-Viten und das Wahrheits-
        problem in der Überlieferung der Ottonen-Zeit." Archiv
        für Kulturgeschichte 38 (1956): 152-166.

03710. Schreiner, Klaus. "'Hildegardis regina.' Wirklichkeit
        und Legende einer karolingischen Herrscherin." Archiv
        für Kulturgeschichte 57 (1975): 1-70.

        Also refer to #3064-3069.

                (2) Individuals

                (a) Adelheid

03711. Bäumer, Gertrud. Adelheid, Mutter der Königreiche.
        Tübingen: R. Wunderlich, 1949.

03712. _____. Otto I und Adelheid. Tübingen:
        R. Wunderlich, 1951.

03713. Paulhart, Herbert, ed. Die Lebensbeschreibung der
        Kaiserin Adelheid von Abt Odile von Cluny. Cologne:
        Bohlau, 1962.

03714. _____. "Zur Heiligsprechung der Kaiserin
        Adelheid." Mitteilungen des Instituts für öster-
        reichische Geschichtsforschung 64 (1956): 65-67.

03715. Wollasch, Joachim. "Das Grabkloster der Kaiserin
        Adelheid in Selz am Rhein." Frühmittelalterliche
        Studien 2 (1968): 135-143.

                        (b) Brunhilde

03716. Boggs, Ray A. "The Popular Image of Brunhilde." In
        The Roles and Images of Women in the Middle Ages and
        Renaissance, edited by Douglas Radcliff Umstead,
        pp. 23-39. Pittsburgh: University of Pittsburgh,
        Center for Medieval and Renaissance Studies, 1975.

03717. Heusler, Andreas. "Die Quelle der Brunhildsage in
        Thidreks Saga und Niebelungenlied." In Aufsatze zur
        Sprach-und Literaturgeschichte Wilhelm Braun zum 20.
        Februar 1920, pp. 47-84. Dortmund: Friedrich Wilhelm
        Ruhfus, 1920.

03718. Nelson, Janet L. "Queens as Jezebels: The Careers of
        Brunhild and Bathild in Merovingian History." In
        Medieval Women, edited by Derek Baker, pp. 31-77.
        Oxford: Basil Blackwell, 1978.

                        3. ECONOMIC

            "Even the peasant women who brought fowls or eggs
            from the neighboring villages to the castles were
            given for their trouble . . . a plate of soup with
            two pieces of bread."
                            E. Belfort Bax, German Society
                            at the Close of the Middle Ages

03719. Barchewitz, Jutta. Beiträge zur Wirtschaftstätigkeit
        der Frau. Breslau: Piebatsch's Buchhandlung, 1937.

03720. Behaghel, Wilhelm. Die gewerbliche Stellung der Frau im
        mittelalterlichen Köln. Berlin: W. Rothschild, 1910.

03721. Hess, Luisa. Die deutschen Frauenberufe des Mittelalters.
        Munich: Neuer Filser-Verlag, 1940.

03722. Schuster, Dora. Die Stellung der Frau in der Zunftver-
        fassung. Quellenhefte zum Frauenleben in der Geschichte,
        edited by Emmy Beckmann and Irma Stoss, vol. 2. Berlin:
        F. A. Herbig, 1927.

4. RELIGION

A maiden Veleda of the Bructei, "held a wide sovereignty
in accordance with the ancient custom of the Germani,
which makes them regard most women as endowed with the
gift of prophecy and, as their devotion grows, even as
goddesses."

Tacitus, Histories

a) Goddesses/Mythology

03723. Davidson, H.R. Ellis. "The Smith and the Goddess."
        Frühmittelalterliche Studien 3 (1969): 216-226.

b) Saints/Religious Women

(1) Women

03724. Ancelet-Hustache, Jeanne. "Ascétique et mystique
        féminine du haut moyen âge." Etudes germaniques 15
        (April-June 1960): 152-160.

03725. _____ . Mechtilde de Magdebourg (1207-
        1282). Paris: Champion, 1926.

03726. Bäumer, Gertrud. Manner und Frauen im geistigen Werden
        des deutschen Volkes. Tübingen: Rainer Wunderlich
        Verlag, 1934.

03727. Bihlmeyer, Karl. "Die schwäbische Mystikerin Elsbeth
        Achler von Reute († 1420) und die Uberlieferung ihrer
        Vita." In Festgabe Philipp Strauch zum 80. Geburtstag,
        pp. 88-109. Halle: M. Niemeyer, 1932.

03728.   Didier, J.C. "Elisabeth de Schonau." Dictionaire d'histoire
          et de géographique ecclésiastiques 15 (1963): 221-224.

03729.   Dietz, Josef. "St. Helena in der rheinischen Überlieferung."
          In Festschrift Matthias Zender: Studien zu Volkskultur,
          Sprache und Landesgeschichte, edited by Edith Ennen,
          Gunter Wiegelmann et. al., 1: 356-383. Bonn: Röhrscheid
          Verlag, 1972.

03730.   Emminghaus, Johann H. Ursula. Heilige in Bild und Legende,
          no. 26. Recklinghausen: Verlag Aurel Bongers, 1967.

03731.   Jeremy, Sister Mary. "'Similitudes' in the Writing of
          St. Gertrude of Helfte." Medieval Studies 19 (1957):
          48-54.

03732.   Klauser, Renate. Der Heinrichs-und Kunigundenkult im
          mittelalterlichen Bistum Bamberg. Bamberg: Historischer
          Verein, 1957.

03733.   Krebs, Engelbert. "Die Mystik in Adelhausen. Eine
          vergleichende Studie über die 'Chronik' der Anna von
          Munzingen und die Thaumatographische Literatur des 13.
          und 14. Jahrhunderts als Beitrag zur Geschichte der
          Mystik im Predigerorden." In Festgabe Heinrich Finke,
          pp. 43-105. Munster: Aschendorff, 1904.

03734.   Krogmann, Willy. "Die heilige Ursula auf Helgoland."
          Classica et Mediaevalia 19 (1958): 177-211.

03735.   Kurth, G. Sainte Clotide. Paris: Lecoffre, 1897.

03736.   Meyn von Westenholz, Elisabeth. Nonne und Heilige im
          deutschen Mittelalter. Quellenhefte zum Frauenleben
          in der Geschichte, edited by Emmy Beckmann and Irma
          Stoss, vol. 1. Berlin: F. A. Herbig, 1927.

          Also refer to #3706.

                    (2) Saint Elizabeth of Hungary

03737.   Justi, Karl Wilhelm. Elisabeth die heilige Landgrafin von
          Thüringen. Marburg: Garthe, 1835.

03738.   Maresch, Maria. Elisabeth Landgräfin v. Thüringen.
          Bonn: Verlag der Buchgemeinde, 1931.

03739.   Montalemberg, Charles Forbes René de Tryon, comte de.
          L'Histoire de Elisabeth de Hongrie, duchesse de
          Thuringe. Paris: P. Tequi, 1930.

03740. Nigg, Walter. Elisabeth von Thüringen. Translated by
        Otto Krage. Dusseldorf: Patmos-Verlag, 1963.

03741. Saubin, Antoine F. Sainte Elisabeth de Hongrie. Paris:
        C. Poussielgue, 1902.

03742. Schmidt-Paul, Elisabeth von. Saint Elisabeth, Sister of
        Saint Francis. New York: Henry Holt and Co., 1932.

03743. Seesholtz, Anne. Saint Elizabeth, Her Brother's Keeper.
        New York: Philosophical Library, 1948.

03744. Vauchez, Andre. "Charité et Pauvreté chez sainte Elisabeth
        de Thuringe, d'après les actes des procès du canonisation."
        In Etudes sur l'Histoire de la Pauvreté, edited by Michel
        Mollat, vol. 1, pp. 163-173. Paris: Publications de la
        Sorbonne, 1974.

                    c) Monastic Life

                    (1) Non-specific

03745. Bruckner, Albert. "Weiblicher Schreibtatigkeit im
        schweizerischen Spätmittelalter." Festschrift Bernhard
        Bischoff zu seinem 65. Geburtstag, pp. 441-448. Stutt-
        gart: Anton Hiersemann, 1971.

03746. Buhler, Johannes. Klosterleben im deutschen Mittelalter,
        nach zeitgenössischen Aufzeichnungen. Leipzig: Insel-
        Verlag, 1921.

03747. Lipphardt, W. "Die liturgische Funktion deutscher
        Kirchenlieder in den Klöstern niedersachsischer Zister-
        zienserinnen des Mittelalters." Zeitschrift für
        Katholische Theologie 94 (1972): 158-198.

03748. Lobbedey, Uwe. "Zur archäologischen Erforschung
        westfälischer Frauenkloster des 9. Jahrhunderts
        (Freckenhorst, Vreden, Meschede, Herford)." Frühmittel-
        alterliche Studien 4 (1970): 320-340.

03749. Perst, O. "Die kaisertochter Sophie, Äbtissin von
        Gandersheim und Essen (975-1039)." Braunschweigisches
        Jahrbuch 38 (1957): 5-46.

03750. Young, Bonnie. "Needlework by Nuns: a Medieval Religious
        Embroidery." Metropolitan Museum of Art, Bulletin n.s.
        28 (1969-1970): 263-277.

        Also refer to #3491, 3736, 3792, 3812-3825.

                        (2) Individuals

                  (a) Herrade de Landsberg

03751. Cames, Gerard. Allegories et symboles dans l'Hortus
        Deliciarum. Leiden: E.J. Brill, 1971.

03752. Straub, A., and Keller, G. Herrade de Landsberg, Hortus
        Deliciarum. Strasbourg: n.p., 1901.

                  (b) Hildegard von Bingen

03753. Battandier, Albert. "Sainte Hildegarde, sa vie et ses
        oeuvres." Revue des questions historiques 33 (April
        1883): 395-425.

03754. Bernhart, Joseph. "Hildegard von Bingen." Archiv für
        Kulturgeschichte 20 (1930): 249-260.

03755. Eltz, Monika zu. Hildegard. Freiburg: Herder, 1963.

03756. Fischer, Hermann. Die heilige Hildegard von Bingen, die
        erste deutsche Naturforscherin und Arztin, ihr Leben und
        Werk. Münchener Beitrage zur Geschichte und Literatur
        der Naturwissenschaften und Medizin, nos. 7-8. Munich:
        Münchener Drucke, 1927.

03757. Führkötter, Adelgundis. Hildegard von Bingen. Salzburg:
        Otto Müller Verlag, 1972.

03758. _____. "Hildegard von Bingen 1098-1179."
        Die grossen Deutschen 5 (1957): 39-47.

03759. Graber, Georg. "Hildegard von Stein. Zur Kritik der Sage
        und des Brauches." In Festschrift Eugen Mogk zum 70.
        Geburtstag, pp. 525-535. Halle: M. Niemeyer, 1924.

03760. Graef, Hilda C. "Hildegard von Bingen." Lexikon für
        Theologie und Kirchengeschichte 5 (1957): 341-342.

03761. Koch, Josef. "Der heutige Stand der Hildegard-Forschung."
        Historische Zeitschrift 186 (1958): 558-572.

03762. Lampen, W. Hildegard von Bingen (1098-1179). Utrecht:
        Spectrum, 1956.

03763. Liebeschutz, Hans. Das allegorische Weltbild der heiligen
        Hildegard von Bingen. Leipzig: Teubner, 1930.

03764. Pereira, Michela. "Maternita' e sessualita'd femminile in
        Ildegarda di Bingen: Proposte di Letturs." Quaderni
        Storici 44 (August 1980): 564-574.

03765. Quentin, E. "Hildegard von Bingen: A Modern Woman
        Physician--800 Years Ago." Munchener Medizinische
        Wochenschrift 109-147 (24 November 1967): 2509-2510.

03766. Roth, F.W.E. "Beiträge zur Biographie der Hildegarde von
        Bingen, O.S.B., sowie zur Beurtheilung ihrer Visionen."
        Zeitschrift für kirchliche Wissenschaft und kirchliches
        Leben 9 (1888): 453-471.

03767. Schipperges, H., ed. Hildegard von Bingen "Heilkunde"
        das Buch von dem Grund und Wesen und der Heilung der
        Krankheiten. Salzburg: Müller, 1957.

03768. Schmelzeis, Johan Philipp. Das Leben und Wirken der
        Heiligen Hildegardis. Freiburg: Herder'sche Verlag,
        1879.

03769. Singer, Charles. "The Scientific Views and Visions of
        Saint Hildegard (1098-1180)." In Studies in the
        History and Method of Science, edited by Charles Singer,
        pp. 1-55. London: Oxford University Press, 1917.

03770. _____. "The Visions of Hildegard of Bingen."
        In From Magic to Science, pp. 199-239. New York: Dover
        Publications, Inc., 1958.

03771. Strubing, E. "Nährung und Ernährung bei Hildegard von
        Bingen, Aebtissin, Aerztin und Naturforscherin (1098-
        1179)." Centaurus 9 (1963): 73-124.

                    d) Mariology

03772. Bindschedler, Maria. "Gedanken zur Marienlyrik des
        Mittelalters und der Romantik." In Geschichte, Deutung,
        Kritik, Literaturwissenschaftliche Beitrage dargebracht
        zum 65. Geburtstag Werner Kohlschmidts, edited by
        Maria Bindschedler and Paul Zinsli, pp. 79-90. Bern:
        Francke Verlag, 1969.

03773. Engelen, Ulrich. "Die Edelsteine im Rheinischen Marienlob."
        Frühmittelalterliche Studien 7 (1973): 353-376.

03774. Hilger, Hans Peter. "Eine Statue der Muttergottes aus dem
        Prager Parler-Kreis im Dom zu Koln." Pantheon 30 (1972):
        95-114.

03775. Kern, Peter. Trinität, Maria, Inkarnation. Studien zur
        Thematik der deutschen Dichtung des spateren Mittelalters.
        Philologische Studien und Quellen, no. 55. Berlin:
        E. Schmidt, 1971.

03776. Meier, Eugen A. Marienverehrung und Mariengebete im
        mittelalterlichen Basel. Basle: Helbing und Lichtenhahn,
        1967.

03777. Scheffczyk, Leo. Das Mariengeheimnis in Frommigkeit und
        Lehre der Karolingerzeit. Leipzig: Benno-Verlag, 1959.

e) Heresy

03778. Grundmann, Herbert. Religiöse Bewegungen im Mittelalter.
        Untersuchungen über die geschichtlichen Zusammenhänge
        zwischen der Ketzerei, den Bettelorden, und der religiösen
        Frauenbewegung im 12. und 13. Jahrhundert und über die
        geschichtlichen Grundlagen der deutschen Mystik. 1935.
        Reprint. Vaduz: Kraus, 1965.

03779. Neumann, Eva G. Rheinisches Beginen-und Begardenwesen.
        Mainzer Abhandlungen zur mittleren und neueren
        Geschichte, no. 4. Meisenheim: Anton Hain K.G., 1960.

03780. Phillips, Dayton. Beguines in Medieval Strasburg. Ann
        Arbor, Mich.: Edwards Brothers, Inc., 1941.

03781. Wemter, Ernst M. "Die Beginen im mittelalterlichen
        Preussenlande." Zeitschrift für die Geschichte und
        Altertumskunde Ermlands 33 (1969): 41-52.

f) Witchcraft

03782. Caro Baroja, Julio. "Witchcraft Among the German and
        Slavonic Peoples." In Witchcraft and Sorcery, edited
        by Max Marwick, pp. 88-100. Baltimore: Penguin
        Books, 1970.

03783. Kiessling, Edith. Zauberei in den germanischen Volksrecht.
        Beiträge zur mittelalterlichen, neueren und allgemeinen
        Geschichte, no. 17. Jena: Verlag von Gustav Fischer,
        1941.

03784. Kunstmann, Hartmut. <u>Zauberwahn</u> <u>und</u> <u>Hexenprozess</u> <u>in</u> <u>der</u> <u>Reich</u>-
       <u>stadt</u> <u>Nürnberg</u>. Nürnberg: Schriftenreihe des Stadtarchivs
       Nürnberg, 1970.

03785. Lipowsky, Felix Joseph. <u>Agnes</u> <u>Bernauerin</u> <u>historisch</u>
       <u>geschildert</u>. Munich: Lentner, 1800.

03786. Merzbacher, Friedrich. <u>Die</u> <u>Hexenprozesse</u> <u>in</u> <u>Franken</u>.
       Munich: Verlag C.H. Beck, 1970.

03787. Ziegler, Wolfgang. <u>Möglichkeiten</u> <u>der</u> <u>Kritik</u> <u>am</u> <u>Hexen</u>-
       <u>und</u> <u>Zauberwesen</u> <u>im</u> <u>ausgehenden</u> <u>Mittelalter</u>. <u>Zeit</u>-
       <u>genössische</u> <u>Stimmen</u> <u>und</u> <u>ihre</u> <u>soziale</u> <u>Zugehörigkeit</u>.
       Cologne: Bohlau, 1973.

5. SOCIAL

"The loves of dress, which thou does hate and despise
in the women of the world who come to thee, has grown
apace on earth, and has become a madness, and brings
down the wrath of God."
St. Elizabeth of Schönau

a) Generic

(1) Non-specific

03788. Maschek, H. <u>Vom</u> <u>Alltag</u> <u>des</u> <u>deutschen</u> <u>Mittelalters</u>. Die
       kleine Bücherei, vol. 22. Munich: Langen/Muller, 1938.

(2) Women

03789. Buschan, Georg Hermann Theodor. <u>Leben</u> <u>und</u> <u>Treiben</u> <u>der</u>
       <u>deutschen</u> <u>Frau</u> <u>in</u> <u>der</u> <u>Urzeit</u>. 1893. Reprint. New
       Haven, Conn.: Research Publications, Inc., 1975.

03790. Strauss und Torney, Lulu von. <u>Die</u> <u>deutschen</u> <u>Frauenleben</u> <u>in</u>
       <u>der</u> <u>Zeit</u> <u>der</u> <u>Sachsenkaiser</u> <u>und</u> <u>Hohenstaufen</u>. Jena:
       E. Diederichs, 1927.

03791. Weinhold, Karl. <u>Die</u> <u>deutschen</u> <u>Frauen</u> <u>in</u> <u>dem</u> <u>Mittelalter</u>.
       <u>Ein</u> <u>Beitrag</u> <u>zu</u> <u>den</u> <u>Haushalterthumern</u> <u>der</u> <u>Germanen</u>. 2
       vols. 1882. Reprint. Englewood Cliffs, N.J.: Scholastic
       Book Services, 1968.

03792. Wemple, Suzanne F. Women in Frankish Society: Marriage and
        the Cloister, 500-900. Philadelphia: University of
        Pennsylvania Press, 1981.

b) Family

03793. Galy, Charles. La famille à l'epoque mérovingienne étude
        faite principalement d'après les recits de Grégoire de
        Tours. Paris: L. Larose, 1901.

03794. Leyser, K. "Debate: Maternal Kin in Early Medieval Germany.
        A Reply." Past and Present 49 (November 1970): 126-134.

03795. _____. "The German Aristocracy from the 9th to the Early
        12th century." Past and Present 41 (December 1968): 25-53.

03796. Phillpotts, Berthe. "The Germanic Kindreds." In Early
        Medieval Society, compiled by Sylvia Thrupp, pp. 3-16.
        New York: Appleton Century Crofts, 1967.

        Also refer to #3693, 3694.

c) Marriage

03797. Gellinek, Christian. "Marriage by Consent in Literary
        Sources of Medieval Germany." Studia Gratiana 12
        (1967): 555-579.

03798. Koebner, Richard. "Die Eheauffassung des ausgehenden
        deutschen Mittelalters." Archiv für Kulturgeschichte
        9 (1911): 136-198; 279-318.

03799. McNamara, JoAnn and Wemple, Suzanne F. "Marriage and
        Divorce in the Frankish Kingdom." In Women in Medieval
        Society, edited by Susan Mosher Stuard, pp. 95-124.
        Philadelphia: University of Pennsylvania Press, 1976.

03800. Neckel, Gustav. Liebe und Ehe bei den vorchristlichen
        Germanen. Leipzig: Teubner, 1934.

03801. Roller, Otto Konrad. "Die Kinderehen im ausgehenden deutschen
        Mittelalter." Sozialhygienische Mitteilungen 9 (1925): 3-29.

03802. Schroder, Edward. "Brautlauf und Tanz." Zeitschrift für
        deutsches Altertum 61 (1924): 17-34.

03803. Toubert, Pierre. "La théorie du mariage chez les
        moralistes carolingiens." In Il Matrimonio nella
        società altomedievale, 1:233-285. Spoleto: Centro
        Italiano di Studi sull'Alto Medioevo, 1977.

        Also refer to #2040, 3516, 3692, 3695-3699, 3704, 3792.

d)   Sex Life and Morals

03804. Jung, Gustav. Die Geschlechtsmoral des deutschen Weibes
        im Mittelalter. Leipzig: Ethnologischer Verlag, 1921.

03805. Wustmann, Gustav. "Frauenhäuser und freie Frauen in
        Leipzig im Mittelalter." Archiv fur Kulturgeschichte
        5 (1907): 469-482.

e)   Fashion/Manners

03806. Sronkova, Olga. Gothic Woman's Fashion. Prague:
        Artia, 1954.

03807. Thevenin, André. "La parure féminine à l'époque
        merovingienne, Ve-Vii^e siècle." Saisons d'Alsace
        (Strasbourg) 14 (1969): 183-201.

6. CULTURAL

". . . You, who have been trained in the study of
philosophy and have perfected yourselves in the pursuit of knowledge, have held my writings, those of a
lowly woman, worthy of admiration . . ."
                        Hrotswitha of Gandersheim, poet-
                        dramatist-historian, 10th century

a)   Literature

(1)   Non-specific

03808.   Bindschedler, Maria.   "Weiblich Leitbilder in der alten
Literatur."   Reformatio 18 (1969): 102-113.

03809.   Brietzmann, Franz.   Die böse Frau in der deutschen
Literatur des Mittelalters.   1912.   Reprint.   New
York: Johnson Reprint, 1967.

03810.   Kaiser, Elsbet.   Frauendienst im mittelhochdeutschen
Volksepos.   Breslau: M. and H. Marcus, 1921.

03811.   Schneider, Annerose.   "Zum Bild von der Frau in der
Chronistik des fruhen Mittelalters."   Forschungen und
Fortschritte 35 (1961):   112-114.

03812.   Ziegler, Matthes.   Die Frau im Marchen.   Leipzig: Koehler,
1937.

(2)   Drama

(a)   Hrotswitha of Gandersheim

03813.   Aschbach, Joseph von.   "Roswitha und Conrad Celtes."
Kaiserlichen Akademie der Wissenschaften, Sitzungs-
berichte 56 (1867):   3-62.

03814.   Frankforter, A. Daniel.   "Hroswitha von Gandersheim and
the Destiny of Women."   The Historian 41 (February 1979):
295-314.

03815.   Gilder, Rosamond.   "Hrotsvitha, a Tenth-Century Nun
The First Woman Playwright."   In Enter the Actress
The First Women in the Theatre, pp. 18-45.   Boston:
Houghton Mifflin Company, 1931.

03816.   Haight, Anne L.   Hroswitha of Gandersheim.   New York:
Hroswitha Club, 1965.

03817.   Hozeski, Bruce W.   "The Parallel Patterns in Hrotsvitha
of Gandersheim, a Tenth Century German Playwright, and
in Hildegard of Bingen, a Twelfth Century German Playwright."   Annuale Mediaevale 18 (1977):   42-53.

03818. Hudson, William Henry. "Hrotsvitha of Gandersheim."
        English Historical Review 3 (July 1888): 431-457.

03819. Klose-Greger, H. Roswitha von Gandersheim. Berlin:
        Union Verlag, 1961.

03820. Kronenberg, K. Roswitha von Gandersheim Leben und Werk.
        Aus Gandersheims grosser Vergangenheit, no. 4. Bad
        Gandersheim: Hertel, 1962.

03821. Nagel, Bert. Hrotsvit von Gandersheim. Stuttgart: J.B.
        Metzler, 1965.

03822. Neumann, Friedrich. "Der Denkstil Hrotsvits von Gandersheim."
        In Festschrift fur Hermann Heimpel zum 70. Geburtstag,
        3: 37-60. Gottingen: Vandenhoeck and Ruprecht, 1971-1972.

03823. Sticca, Sandro. "Sin and Salvation: The Dramatic Context
        of Hrotswitha's Women." In The Roles and Images of
        Women in the Middle Ages and Renaissance, edited by
        Doublas Radcliff Umstead, pp. 3-22. Pittsburgh:
        University of Pittsburgh, Center for Medieval and
        Renaissance Studies, 1975.

03824. Trumper, Bernarda. Hrotsvithas Frauengestalten. Munster:
        Schöningh, 1908.

03825. Zeydel, Edwin H. "Were Hrotsvitha's Dramas Performed
        During her Lifetime?" Speculum 20 (October 1945):
        443-456.

                        (3) Poetry

                        (a) General

03826. Bäuml, Franz H. "Transformations of the Heroine: From
        Epic Heard to Epic Read." In The Role of Women in the
        Middle Ages, edited by Rosmarie Thee Morewedge, pp. 23-
        40. Albany, N.Y.: State University of New York Press,
        1975.

03827. Bell, Clair Hayden. "The Sister's Son in the Medieval
        German Epic: A Study in the Survival of Matriliny."
        University of California Publications in Modern Philology
        10 (1922): 37-182.

03828. Jackson, W. T. H. The Anatomy of Love. The Tristan of
        Gottfried von Strassburg. New York: Columbia University
        Press, 1971.

03829. Murdoch, Brian. "Eve's Anger: Literary Secularisation
        in Lutwin's Adam und Eve." Archiv fur das Studium der
        neueren Sprachen und Literaturen 215 (1978): 256-271.

03830. Valous, Guy de. "La poesie amoureuse en langue latine au
        moyen âge." Classica et Mediaevalia 13 (1952): 285-
        345; 14 (1953): 156-204; 15 (1954): 146-197.

                    (b) Wolfram von Eschenbach

03831. Gibbs, Marion E. "The Role of Woman in Wolfram's
        'Parzival'." German Life and Letters n.s. 21 (July
        1968): 296-308.

03832. _____. Wiplîchez wîbes reht: A Study of the
        Women Characters in the Works of Wolfram von Eschenbach.
        Pittsburgh: Duquesne University Press, 1972.

03833. Heise, Ursula. "Frauengestalten im 'Parzival' Wolframs
        von Eschenbach." Deutschunterricht 9 (1957): 37-62.

        Also refer to #3681.

                    (c) Gudrun/Kudrun

03834. Loerzer, Eckart. Eheschliessung und Werbung in der "Kudrun"
        Munich: Beck, 1971.

03835. Ward, Donald J. "The Rescue of Kudrun: A Dioscuric Myth."
        Classica et Mediaevalia 26 (1965): 334-353.

03836. Zallinger, Otto. Die Eheschliessung im Nibelungenlied und in
        der Gudrun. Vienna: Hölder-Pichler-Tempsky, A. G., 1923.

03837. _____. Heirat ohne Trauung im Nibelunglied und
        in der Gudrun. Innsbruck: Wagner, 1928.

                    (4) Troubadours and Minnesingers

03838. McLintock, D.R. "Walther's Mädchenlieder." Oxford German
        Studies 3 (1968): 30-43.

03839. Mohr, Wolfgang. "Die 'Vrouwe' Walthers von der Vogelweide."
        Zeitschrift für deutsche Philologie 86 (1967): 1-10.

b) Chivalry

(1) Courtly Love

03840. Hatto, A.T. "Vrouwen Schowen." Modern Language Review
34 (January 1939): 40-49.

03841. Jackson, T.R. "Religion and Love in Flore und Blanscheflur."
Oxford German Studies 4 (1969): 12-25.

03842. Jackson, W.T.H. "Faith Unfaithful--The German Reaction to
Courtly Love." In The Meaning of Courtly Love, edited by F.
X. Newman, pp. 55-76. Albany, N.Y.: State University of
New York Press, 1968.

03843. Wenzel, Horst. Frauendienst und Gottesdienst Studien zur
Minneideologie. Philologische Studien und Quellen,
no. 74. Berlin: Erich Schmidt Verlag, 1974.

Also refer to #3674.

E. IBERIA

1. POLITICAL

"Married women . . . cannot sell any personal possessions . . . without the express consent of the
husband."
Land Charter of Sepulveda

a) Legal

(1) Non-specific

03844. Cordier, E. "Le droit de famille aux Pyrénées." Revue historique de droit français et étranger 1st ser. 5 (1859):
257-396.

03845. Gibert Sánchez, R. "El consentimiento familiar en el
matrimonio en el derecho medieval español." Anuario
de Historia del Derecho Español 18 (1947): 706-761.

03846. Merêa, Manuel Paulo. Estudio de direito hispánico
medieval. Coimbra: n.p., 1952-1953.

03847.   Merêa, Manuel Paulo. Estudio de direito visigótico.
         Coimbra: n.p., 1948.

03848.   _____. "Da minha gaveta (Silva Historico-
         Juridica), II: Sinopse historica da adopcao (perfilhamen-
         to)." Boletim da Faculdade de Direito 32 (1956): 182-194.

03849.   _____. "Notas sobre o poder paternal no direito
         hispanico ocidental: Em torno do CCVI do Foro de Cuenca."
         Estudios de Direito Hispânico Medieval 2 (1953): 83-112.

03850.   _____. "Notulas Historico-Juridicas, II:
         Sobre a adopcao no seculo, II." Boletim da Faculdade
         de Direito 31 (1955): 372-376.

03851.   _____. "Un problema filogico-juridico: A
         Palavra 'arras'." Novos Estudos de Historia do Direito
         (1937): 139-149.

03852.   _____. "Sobre o Casamento de Juras." Soletim
         da Faculdade de Direito 14 (1937-1938): 12-20.

03853.   _____. "Enq torno do Casamento de Juras."
         Estudios de Direito Hispanico Medieval 1 (1952): 151-171.

03854.   Schultze, Alfred. Über westgotischspanisches Eherecht.
         Leipzig: Hirzel, 1943.

         Also refer to #3880, 3896.

                            (2) Women

03855.   Dillard, Heath. "Women in Reconquest Castile: The
         Fueros of Sepulveda and Cuenca." In Women in Medieval
         Society, edited by Susan Mosher Stuard, pp. 71-94.
         Philadelphia: University of Pennsylvania Press, 1976.

03856.   Merêa, Manuel Paulo. "Mulher recabdada." Novos Estudos
         do Historia do Direito (1937): 75-82.

         Also refer to #3885.

                         b) Political Roles

03857.   Agapito y Revilla, Juan. "Casamiento de dona Juana de
         Navarra, hija natural de don Carlos III el Noble, con Inigo
         Ortiz, hijo de Diego Lopez de Estuniga, justica mayor del
         Rey de Castilla." Boletin de la Real Academia de la Histo-
         ria Madrid 81 (November 1922): 383-414.

03858.   Armistead, M.G. "An Unnoticed Epic Reference to Doña
          Elvira, sister of Alphonso VI." Romance Philology 12
          (November 1958): 143-146.

03859.   Bague, Enric. "Notes sobre la reine Elionor de Xipre,
          des del seu retorn a Catalunya fins a la seva mort."
          In Homenatge a Antoni Rubio i Lluch 3: 547-554.
          Barcelona: n.p., 1936.

03860.   Ballesteros-Beretta, Antonia. "Doña Leonor de Guzmán a la
          muerte de Alfonson XI." Boletin de la Real Academia
          de la Historia Madrid 100 (April-June 1932): 624-636.

03861.   Chalon, Louis. "A propos des filles du Cid." Le Moyen
          âge 73 (1967): 217-237.

03862.   Domingues, Mario. D. Dinis e Santa Isabel. Lisbon:
          Romano Torres, 1967.

03863.   Hernández-Léon de Sanchez, Francisca. Doña María de Castilla,
          esposa de Alfonso V el magnánimo. Valencia: Univer-
          sidad de Valencia, 1959.

03864.   Huarte y Echenique, Amalio. "Pedro I de Castilla y la
          infanta Beatriz de Portugal." Boletin de la Real Academia
          de la Historia Madrid 105 (July-December 1934): 515-546.

03865.   Javierre Mur, Aurea L. "Matha de Armanyach, Duquesa de
          Gerona (1373-1378)." Boletin de la Real Academia de la
          Historia Madrid 96 (January-March 1930): 107-247.

03866.   Laplane, Gabriel. "La morte de Blanche de Bourbon."
          Bulletin Hispanique 6 (January-June 1964): 5-16.

03867.   LeBrun, I. Vida de santa Isabel. Madrid: n.p., 1913.

03868.   Lozoya, Marques de. "Doña Angelina de Grecia (Segunda
          versión.)" Boletin de la Real Academia de la
          Historia Madrid 126 (January-March 1950): 37-78.

03869.   Sanahuja, (Pere). "El mobiliari de la infanta Joana, filla
          de Pere III." In Homenatge a Antoni Rubio i Lluch,
          2: 165-172. Barcelona: n.p., 1936.

03870.   Sarrablo, Eugenio. "La Reine que vino de Oriente: Maria
          de Chipre, esposa de Jaime II, Rey de Aragon." Boletín
          de la Real Academia de la Historia 148 (January-March
          1961): 13-160.

03871.   Sturcken, H. T. "The Unconsummated Marriage of Jaime of
          Aragon and Leonor of Castile (October 1319)." Journal
          of Medieval History 5 (September 1979): 185-201.

          Also refer to #3400, 3875.

2. RELIGION

"Of all the possible crimes a woman can commit inter-
racial [more accurately interfaith] sexual intercourse
is the most severely punished."
                          Land Charter of Sepulveda

a) Saints/Religious Women

03872. Barnett, F.J. "'Virginity' in the Old French Sequence of
        Saint Eulalia." French Studies 13 (July 1959):   252-256.

03873. Fábrega Grau, Ángel. Santa Eulalia de Barcelona. Publi-
        caciones del Institut Española de Estudios Eclesiásticos,
        no. 4. Rome: Iglesia nacional española, 1958.

03874. Lede, Marqués de. "Ensayo de una bibliografia de publi-
        caciones dedica a Santa Barbara La devocion a Santa
        Barbara en España." Boletin de la Real Academia de la
        Historia Madrid 140 (January-March 1957):   177-282.

        Also refer to #3682.

b) Monastic Life

03875. Maur Cocheril, P. "Les infantes Teresa, Sancha, Mafalda
        et l'Ordre de Cîteaux au Portugal." Revista Portuguesa
        de Historia 16 (1976):   33-49.

03876. Piquer I Jover, Josep-Joan. "L'expansió monàstica femenia
        a Catalunya durant els segles XII i XIII." Analecta
        sacra tarraconensia 45 (Jan.-June 1972):   3-25.

c) Canon Law

03877. Finke, Heinrich and Jaffe, Elsbet. "Die gefälschte Ehedispens
fur Konig Sancho IV. von Kastilien und Maria de Molina."
<u>Archiv</u> <u>fur</u> <u>Kulturgeschichte</u> 19 (1929): 139-157.

d) Witchcraft

03878. Alvarez Blazquez, José Maria. "A mulher na lírica
medieval galegoportuguesa." In <u>Actas</u> <u>congresso</u> <u>de</u>
<u>Braga</u>, pp. 86-102. Braga: Camara municipal, 1963.

3. SOCIAL

"If her husband kill her for this [adultery] although he
had not actually caught her in the adultery, the husband
will not die for the crime, nor should there be any
penalty of justice imposed."
Alfonso IV

a) Generic

(1) Non-specific

03879. Guichard, Pierre. <u>Structures</u> <u>sociales</u> <u>"orientales"</u> <u>et</u>
<u>"occidentales"</u> <u>dans</u> <u>l'Espagne</u> <u>musulmane</u>. Civilisations
et sociétés, no. 60. Paris: Mouton, 1977.

03880. King, P.D. <u>Law</u> <u>and</u> <u>Society</u> <u>in</u> <u>the</u> <u>Visigothic</u> <u>Kingdom</u>.
Cambridge Studies in Medieval Life and Thought, 3rd
ser., no. 5. New York: Cambridge University Press,
1972.

03881. Marques, Antonia Henrique R. de Oliveira. <u>Daily</u> <u>Life</u> <u>in</u>
<u>Portugal</u> <u>in</u> <u>the</u> <u>Late</u> <u>Middle</u> <u>Ages</u>. Translated by S.S. Wyatt.
Madison: University of Wisconsin Press, 1971.

03882. Naveros, E. de Hinojosa y. "La communidad domestica en
        Espana durante la edad media." Obras 2 (1955): 329-341.

(2) Women

03883. Errazuriz, Helena. "La mujer en tiempos de Fray Luis de
        Leon." Cuadernos Americanos 225 (March-April 1975):
        153-160.

03884. Frank, Roslyn M., and Lowenberg, Shelley. "The Role of
        the Basque Woman as 'Etxeko-andrea', the Mistress of
        the House." Proceedings of the Western Society for
        French History 4 (1976): 14-21.

03885. Naveros, E. de Hinojosa y. "Sobre la condicíon de la
        mujer casada ne la esfera del derecho civil." Obras
        2 (1955): 345-388.

b) Family

03886. Belmartino, Susana M. "Estructura de la familia y 'edades
        sociales' en la aristocracia de Leon y Castilla segun
        las fuentas literarias y historiograficas (siglos X-XIII)."
        Cuadernos de historia de España 47-48 (1968): 256-328.

03887. Bonnaissie, Pierre. "A family of the Barcelona Countryside
        and its Economic Activities around the Year 1000." In
        Early Medieval Society, edited by Sylvia Thrupp, pp. 103-
        123. New York: Appleton-Century-Crofts, 1967.

03888. Cuvillier, Jean-Pierre. "Famille et société en Méditerranée
        occidentale chrétienne. Analyse comparative des modeles
        sicilien et catalan. Constats d'un médiéviste." Mélanges
        de la Casa de Valasquez 15 (1979): 187-205.

03889. Fuertes, J. La familia visigoda. Rome: Apud custodiam
        libranam Port. Instituti Utriusque Iuris, 1951.

03890. Ruiz Doménec, José E. "Las estructuras familiares catalanes
        en la alta Edad Media." Cuaderno de arquelogia e historia
        de la cuidad 16 (1975): 69-123

03891. _____. "Solidaridad familiar y organización
        de classes en la cuidad de Barcelona en los ss.XI y XII."
        Miscellanea Barcinonensia 15 (November 1976): 7-26.

        Also refer to #3844, 3849.

c) Marriage

03892. Bertrand, Rafael O. "Un capítulo de la política matrimonial
        de los Papas." Cuadernos de historia de España 18 (1952):
        71-129.

03893. Cabral de Moncada, Luis. "O Casamento em Portugal na Idade
        Media." Estudos de História do Direito 1 (1948): 37-82.

03894. Crawford, J. P. Wickersham. "Early Spanish Wedding Plays."
        Romanic Review 12 (October-December 1921): 370-384.

03895. Gonzalez de Fauve, Maria Estela. "El nuptio en los reinos
        occidentales de Espana (siglos X-XIV)." Cuader nos de
        historia de Espana 57-58 (1973): 280-330.

03896. Herculano de Carvalho e Arauja, Alexandre. Estudos sobre o
        Casamento Civil: Por ocasião do Opsculo do sr. Visconde
        de Seabra sobre este assumpto. Lisbon: L. Vraria Bertrand,
        192-.

        Also refer to #3845, 3852-3854, 3877.

4. CULTURAL

"The singing of the Princess is praised a great deal and
so is her playing of the virginal and dancing according
to her personal style."   Said of Leonore

a) Literature

(1) Poetry

03897. Deyermond, Alan. "'El Convento de Dolencias': The Works
        of Ter esa de Cartagena." Journal of Hispanic Philology
        1 (Autumn 1976): 19-29.

03898. Sponsler, Lucy A. "Women in Spain: Medieval Law versus
        Epic Literature." Revista de estudios hispanicos 7
        (October 1973): 427-448.

03899. Sponsler, Lucy A. Women in the Medieval Spanish Epic
        and Lyric Traditions. Lexington: University Press of
        Kentucky, 1975.

                        (2) Troubadours

03900. Boase, Roger. The Troubadour Revival: A Study of Social
        Change and Traditionalism in Late Medieval Spain. Boston:
        Routledge & Kegan Paul, 1979.

03901. Nunes, José Joaquim. Cantigas di amigo dos trovadores
        galego-portugueses. Vol. I Ciombra: Imprensa da
        Universidade, 1928.

03902. Pelegrin, Benito. "Vierge, épouse, catin: l'archétype
        fatal de la femme espagnole de la chanson épique à la
        chanson typique." Etudes Corses 4 (1976): 241-279.

                        b) Chivalry

                        (1) Courtly Love

03903. Ruiz, Juan. The Book of Good Love. Translated by Rigo
        Mignani and Mario di Cesare. Albany: State University
        of New York Press, 1970.

F. ITALY

1. POLITICAL

        "But the sister may ask for no share of her father's
        inheritance if her brother procures a decent match
        for her and gives her a dowry."
                        Milan law, 1216

a) Legal

(1) Non-specific

03904.   Motta, Giuseppi. "'In primo coniugio' . . . Une falsa
         attribuzione Milanese di Burcado (9.8)." Richerche
         storiche sulla Chiese Ambrosiana 6 (1976): 137-141.

(2) Women

03905.   Mistruzzi de Frisinga, Charles. "La succession nobiliaire
         feminine en Italie dans le droit et dans l'histoire."
         Appendix to Ida Auda-Gioanet. Une randonnée à travers
         l'histoire d'Orient: les Comnenes eet les Anges. Rome:
         F. Ferrari, 1953.

b) Political Roles

(1) Women

03906.   Camobreco, Fortunato. "Il matrimonio del Duca d'Atene
         con Beatrice principesse di Taranto." In Nozze Federle
         De Fabritiis, pp. 303-307. Naples: R. Ricciardi, 1908.

03907.   Columbo, Alessandro. "Il 'Grido di dolore' di Isabella
         d'Aragona duchessa di Milano." In Studi di storia
         napoletana in more di Michelangel Schipa, pp. 331-346.
         Naples: ITEA, 1926.

03908.   Fasola, Livia. "Una famiglia di sostenetori milaneso di
         Federico I. Per la storia con le forze sociali e
         politiche della Lombardia." Quellen und Forschungen
         aus italenischen Archiven und Bibliotheken 48 (1968):
         64-79 and 52 (1972): 116-218.

03909.   Mor, Carol Guido. "Intorno ad una lettera di Berta di
         Toscana al Califfo di Bagdad." Archivio Storico
         Italiano 112 (1954): 299-312.

03910.   Odegaard, Charles E.   "The Empress Engelberge."   Speculum
         26 (January 1951):   77-103.

03911.   Schwarzmaier, Hans Martin. "Zur Familie-Viktor IV in der
         Sabina." Quellen und Forschungen aus Italienischen
         Archiven und Bibliotheken 48 (1958):   64-79.

(2)   Matilda of Tuscany

03912.   Briey, Renaud Marie Charles Eugene de.   Mathilde, duchesse
         de Toscane.   Genbloux: n.p., 1934.

03913.   Duff, Nora.   Matilda of Tuscany.   New York: E. P. Dutton,
         1910.

03914.   Gillis, Florance M.   "Mathilda, countess of Tuscany."
         Catholic Historical Review 10 (1924):   234-245.

03915.   Grimaldi, Natale.   La Contessa Matilde e la sua stirpe
         feudale.   Florence: Vallecchi, 1928.

03916.   Overmann, Alfred.   Gräfin Mathilde von Tuscien.   Innsbruck:
         Wagner, 1895.

03917.   Pannenborg, A.   Studien zur Geschichte der Herzogin Matilde
         von Canosa.   Göttingen: Vandehoeck und Ruprecht, 1872.

03918.   Tondell, Leone.   Matilde di Canossa.   Bizzocchi: Reggio
         Emilia, 1926.

2. ECONOMIC

> "But she [Matilda of Tuscany] did not lose sight of
> economic strength in Tuscany and she was both adept
> in winning cooperation from the merchant guilds and
> sagacious in guarding the security of craft guilds."
> Mary Beard, Women as a Force in History

a)   Generic

03919.   Origo, Iris.   The Merchant of Prato.   Bedford Historical
         Series, no. 16.   London: Jonathan Cape, 1960.

b) Women

03920.   Bonds, William N.   "Genoese Noble Women and Gold Thread
         Manufacturing." <u>Medievalia et Humanistica</u> 17 (1966):
         79-81.

03921.   Briganti, Antonio. <u>La Donna e il diritto statutario in</u>
         <u>Perugia.</u> <u>La donna commerciante</u> (<u>secoli XII e XIV.</u>)
         Perugia: Guerra, 1911.

3. RELIGION

"It is a great grace to be a woman because more women
are saved than men."
                              St. Bernardino

a) Generic

(1) Non-specific

03922.   Moorman, John Richard Humpidge. <u>A History of the Franciscan</u>
         <u>Order from its Origins to the year 1517.</u> Oxford: Clare-
         don Press, 1968.

03923.   Quinn, John Francis. "Saint Bonaventure and the sacrament
         of Matrimony." <u>Franciscan Studies</u> 34 (1974): 101-143.

03924.   Trexler, Richard C. "Le célibat à la fin du Moyen âge:
         les religeuses de Florence." <u>Annales: economies,</u>
         <u>sociétés, civilisations</u> 27 (November-December 1972):
         1329-1350.

(2) Women

03925.   Bartoli, Marie-Claude. "La femme à Bonifacio à la fin du
         Moyen âge." <u>Etudes Corses</u> 4 (1975): 310-322.

03926.   Gagnan, Dominique. "Le symbole de la femme chez Saint
         Francois d'Assise." <u>Laurentianum</u> 18 (1977): 256-291.

03927. Healy, Sister Emma Therese. Woman According to Saint
        Bonaventure. New York: Georgian Press, 1956.

03928. Origo, Iris. "Eve or Mary? The Tuscan Women of the
        Fifteenth Century, as seen by San Bernadino of Sienna."
        Cornhill Magazine 173 (Winter 1962-1963): 65-84.

03929. Rezette, Jean. "Le Sacerdoce et la femme chez Saint
        Bonaventure." Antonianum 51 (1976): 520-527.

b) Saints/Religious Women

(1) Women

03930. Cusack, Pearse Ardan. "Saint Scholastica: Myth or Real
        Person?" The Downside Review 92 (1974): 145-159.

03931. Papa, Pasquale. "La leggenda di S. Caterina d'Alessandria
        in decima rima." In Miscellanea nuziale Rossi-Teiss,
        pp. 453-509. Bergamo: n.p., 1897.

03932. Petroff, Elizabeth. "Medieval Women Visionaries: Seven
        stages to power." Frontiers 3 (Spring 1978): 34-45.

(2) Individuals

(a) St. Clare

03933. Brooke, Rosalind B. and Brooke, Christopher N. L. "St.
        Claire." In Medieval Women, edited by Derek Baker, pp.
        275-287. Oxford: Basil Blackwell, 1978.

03934. Gilliat-Smith, Ernest. Saint Claire of Assisi: her Life
        and Legislation. New York: E. P. Dutton and Co., 1914.

03935. Thomas of Celano. The Life of Saint Clare. Translated and
        edited by Fr. Paschal Robinson. Philadelphia: Dolphin
        Press, 1910.

(b) St. Margaret of Cortona

03936. Cuthbert, R.P. A Tuscan Penitent. The Life and Legend of
        St. Margaret of Cortona. London: Burns and Oates, 1907.

03937. Mauriac, Francois. St. Margaret of Cortona. New York:
        Philosophical Library, 1948.

c) Mariology

03938.   Herzmer, Volker. "Donatellos Madonna vom Paduaner
Hochaltar--eine 'Schwarze Madonna'?" <u>Mitteilungen des</u>
<u>Kunsthistorischen</u> <u>Institutes</u> <u>in</u> <u>Florenz</u> 16 (1972):
142-152.

d) Monastic Life

03939.   Boyd, Catherine. <u>A</u> <u>Cistercian</u> <u>Nunnery</u> <u>in</u> <u>Mediaeval</u> <u>Italy:</u>
<u>The</u> <u>Story</u> <u>of</u> <u>Rifreddo</u> <u>in</u> <u>Saluzzo,</u> <u>1220-1300.</u> Cambridge,
Mass.: Harvard University Press, 1943.

e) Heresy

03940.   Volpe, G. <u>Movimenti</u> <u>Religioso</u> <u>e</u> <u>sette</u> <u>Ereticali</u> <u>nella</u>
<u>Società</u> <u>Medievale</u> <u>Italiana.</u> Florence: n.p., 1922.

03941.   Wessley, Stephen. "The thirteenth-century Guglielmites:
salvation through women." In <u>Medieval</u> <u>Women</u>, edited
by Derek Baker, pp. 289-303.   Studies in Church History,
Subsidia, I . Oxford: Blackwell, 1978.

4. SOCIAL

"So by such a kind of subjection woman is naturally
subject to man, because in man the discretion of
reason predominates."
                        St. Thomas Aquinas
                        <u>Summa</u> <u>Theologica</u>

a) Generic

(1) Non-specific

03942. Duckett, Eleanor Shipley. The Gateway to the Middle
        Ages, I. Italy. Ann Arbor, Mich.: University of
        Michigan Press, 1961.

03943. Herlihy, David. Medieval and Renaissance Pistoia: The
        Social History of an Italian Town, 1200-1430. New
        Haven: Yale University Press, 1967.

03944. _____. "Some Psychological and Social Roots of
        Violence in the Tuscan Cities." In Violence and Civil
        Disorder in Italian Cities, 1200-1500, edited by
        Lauro Martines, pp. 129-154. Berkeley: University of
        California Press, 1972.

(2) Women

03945. Cecchetti, Bartolomeo. "La Donna nel medioevo a Venezia."
        Archivio Veneto 31 (1886): 33-69, 307-349.

03946. Savi-Lopez, Maria. La Donna Italiana del Trecento.
        Napoli: n.p., 1891.

b) Demography

03947. Herlihy, David. "Deaths, Marriages, Births, and the
        Tuscan Economy (ca. 1300-1550)." In Population Patterns
        in the Past, edited by Ronald Demos Lee, pp. 135-164.
        New York: Academic Press, 1977.

03948. _____. "Mapping Households in Medieval Italy."
        The Catholic Historical Review 58 (April 1972): 1-24.

03949. _____. "Population, Plague, and Social Change
        in Rural Pistoia, 1201-1430." Economic History Review
        2nd ser. 18 (August 1965): 225-244.

03950. Klapisch, Christiane. "L'enfance en Toscane au début
        du XVe siècle." Annales de demographie historique
        (1973): 99-122.

03951.   Ring, Richard R.   "Early Medieval Peasant Households in
         Central Italy." Journal of Family History 4 (Spring
         1979): 2-25.

                        c) Family

                        (1) Non-specific

03952.   Cammarosano, Paolo. La famiglia dei Berardenghi. Con-
         tributo alla storia della società senese nei secolo
         XI-XIII. Spolete: Centro itali. di Studi sull'
         alto medioevo, 1974.

03953.   Heers, Jacques. Family Clans in the Middle Ages:
         A Study of Political and Social Structures in Urban
         Areas. New York: North Holland, 1977.

03954.   Herlihy, David. "Family Solidarity in Medieval Italian
         History." In Economy, Society, and Government: Essays
         in Memory of Robert L. Reynolds, edited by David Herlihy,
         Robert S. Lopez and Vsevolod Slessarev, pp. 173-184.
         Kent, Ohio: Kent State University Press, 1969.
         Also in Explorations in Economic History 7 (Fall-Winter
         1969-1970): 173-184.

03955.   Hughes, Diane Owen. "Domestic Ideals and Social Behavior:
         Evidence from Medieval Genoa." In The Family in History,
         edited by Charles E. Rosenberg, pp. 115-143. Philadelphia:
         University of Pennsylvania Press, 1975.

03956.   _____. "Urban Growth and Family Structures
         in Medieval Genoa." Past and Present 66 (February 1975):
         3-28.

03957.   Marongiu, Antonia. La famiglia nell'Italia Meridionale
         (sec. VIII-XII). Milan: Societa Editorice Vita e
         Pensiero, 1944.

03958.   Moresco, Mattia. "Parente e querre civli in Genova nel
         secolo XII." In Scritti di Mattia Moresco. Milan:
         Guiffrè, 1959.

03959.   Vismara, Giulio. "L'unità della famiglia nella storia
         del diritto in Italia." Studia et documenta historiae
         et iuris 22 (1956): 228-265.

         Also refer to #3888, 3908, 3911, 3951.

(2)   Childhood

03960.   Tabacco, Giovanni.   "Le rapport de parenté comme instrument
de domination consortiale: quelques exemples piémontais."
In Famille et parenté dans l'occident médiéval, edited
by Georges Duby and Jacques Le Goff, pp. 153-158.
(Collection de l'école française de Rome, 30).   Rome:
Collection de l'école française de Rome, 1977.

03961.   Winterer, Hermann.   "Die Stellung des unehelichen Kindes in
der langobardischen Gesetzgebung."   Zeitschrift der Savigny
Stiftung für Rechtsgeschichte 87 (1970): 32-56.

d)   Marriage

03962.   Bronzini, Giovanni B.   "Bernal Frances e 'Il marito
guistiziere.'"   In Studi in Onore di Angelo Monteverdi,
1:   109-137.   Modena: Società Tipografica Editrice
Modenese, 1959.

03963.   Cattaneo, Enrico.   "La celebrazione delle nozze e Milano."
Ricerche storiche sulla Chiesa Ambrosiana 6 (1976):
142-180.

03964.   Cherubino da Siena.   Regole della vita matrimonale.
Bologna: Romagnoli-dell'Acqua, 1888.

03965.   Ercole, Francesco.   "L'istituto dotale nella pratica
e nella legislazione statutaria dell'Italia superiore."
Rivista italiana per le scienze giuridiche 45 (1908):
191-302;   46 (1910):   167-257.

03966.   Forchieri, Giovanni. "I rapporti matrimonali fra coniugi
a Genova nel secolo XII."   Bollettino Ligustico per la
storia e la cultura regionale 22 (1970):   3-20.

03967.   Grignaschi, M.   "Il matrimonio di Margarite Maultasch et
il 'Tractato de matrimonio di Marsilio da Padova."
Rivista di storia el diritto italiano 25 (1952):   195-
204.

03968.   Guillou, Andre.   "Il matrimonio nell' Italia bizantina nei
secoli X et XI."   In Il Matrimonio nella societa altomedievale 2:869-86.   Spoleto: Centro Italiano di   Studi
sull'Alto Medioevo, 1977.

03969. Klapisch-Zuber, Christine. "The Medieval Latin Mattinata."
        Journal of Family History 5 (Spring 1980): 2-27.

03970. Sanfillipo, Mario. "Spoleto: il matrimonio nella
        società altomedievale." Quaderni medievali 2 (1976):
        212-218.

03971. Vaccari, Pietro. "Aspetti singolari dell'istituto del
        matrimonio nell'Italia meridionale." Archivio storico
        publiese 6 (1953): 43-49.

        Also refer to #3904.

                    e) Sex Life and Morals

03972. Pavan, Elisabeth. "Police des moeurs, société et politique
        à Venise à la fin du Moyen Âge." Revue historique 536
        (October-December 1980): 241-288.

                    f) Health/Medical

03973. Bayon, H.P. "Trotula and the Ladies of Salerno: A Con-
        tribution to the Knowledge of the Transition between
        Ancient and Mediaeval Physick." Proceedings of the
        Royal Society of Medicine 33 (10 January 1940):
        471-475.

03974. Halbot, C. H. "Dame Trot and her Progency." In English
        Association Essays and Studies n.s. (1972): 1-14.

03975. Mason-Hohl, Elizabeth. "Trotula: Eleventh Century
        Gynecologist." Medical Woman's Journal 47 (December
        1940): 349-356.

03976. Stuard, Susan Mosher. "Dame Trot." Signs 1 (Winter 1975):
        537-542.

03977. Trotula of Salerno. The Diseases of Women. Translated
        by Elizabeth Mason-Hohl. Los Angeles: Ward Ritchie
        Press, 1940.

03978. Tuttle, Edward F. "The Trotula and Old Dame Trot: A Note
        on the Lady of Salerno." Bulletin of the History of
        Medicine 50 (1976): 61-72.

5. CULTURAL

"The female is an empty thing and easily swayed, she
runs great risks when she is away from her husband."
                    Libro di buoni costumi

a) Literature

(1) Non-specific

03979. Zingarelli, Nicola. "Bel Cavalier e Beatrice di Monferrat."
        In Studi letterari e linguistici dedicati a Pio Pajna,
        pp. 557-575. Florence: E. Ariani, 1911.

(2) Troubadours

03980. Torraca, Francesco. "Donne italiane e trovatori provenzali."
        Studi Medievali n.s 1 (1928): 487-491.

G. LOW COUNTRIES

1. SURVEYS

". . . Margaret [of Flanders] regarded herself as a vassal
of the French King and of the German Emperor . . . did
all in her power to promote urban independence."
                    Friedrich Heer, The Medieval World

03981. Nicholas, David. Town and Countryside: Social Economic,
        and Political Tensions in Fourteenth-Century Flanders.
        Bruges: De Tempel, 1971.

2. POLITICAL

"Weary, grieving, I am left to wonder why God summoned
my father to his company so early, leaving such a noble
heritage to me his daughter, once a happy child, and
now condemned to lose my all through default of justice."
Jacqueline, countess of Holland

a) Legal

03982.   Bart, Jean. Recherches sur l'histoire des successions
ab intestat dans le droit du duché de Bourgogne du
XIIIe siècle à la fin du XVIe siècle (coutume et
pratique). Paris: les Belles lettres, 1966.

03983.   Bosch, Jan Willem. "Le statut de la femme dans les
anciens Pays-Bas septentrionaux." Recueils de la Société
Jean Bodin 12 (1962): 323-350.

03984.   Gilissen, John. "Le statut de la femme dans l'ancien
droit belge." Recueils de la Societe Jean Bodin 12 (1962):
255-321.

b) Political Roles

03985.   Gastout, Marguerite. Béatrix de Brabant. Landgravine
de Thuringe, Reine des Romains, Comtesse de Flandre
Dame De Courtrai (1225?-1288.) Louvain: Bibliothèque
de l'Université, 1943.

03986.   Glaesener, Henri. "Un mariage fertile en conséquences
(Godefroid de Barbu et Béatrice de Toscane.)" Revue
d'histoire ecclésiastique 42 (1947): 379-416.

03987.   Putnam, Ruth. A Mediaeval Princess; being a true record
of the changing fortunes which brought divers titles to
Jacqueline, Countess of Holland . . . New York: G.P.
Putnam's Sons, 1904

03988.   Sproemberg, Heinrich. "Clementia, Grafin von Flandern."
Revue belge de philologie et d'histoire 42 (1964):
1203-1241.

03989. Vercauteren, F. "La Princesse captive. Note sur les
        négociations entre le pape Jean XXII et le comte
        Guillaume Ier de Hainaut en 1322-1323." Moyen age 83
        (1977): 89-101.

3. RELIGION

"They who are cared for obey."   St. Augustine

a) Generic

03990. Bolton, Brenda M. "Vitae Matrum: a further aspect of the
        Frauenfrage." In Medieval Women, edited by Derek Baker,
        pp. 253-273.   Studies in Church History, Subsidia, I .
        Oxford: Blackwell, 1978.

b) Saints/Religious Women

03991. Coens, Maurice. "Geneviève de Brabant, une sainte? Le
        terroir de sa legende." Academie royale de Belgique
        bulletin de classe des lettres et des sciences morales
        et politiques 5th ser. 46 (May 1960): 345-363.

c) Mariology

03992. Smith, Graham. "The Betrothal of the Virgin by the
        Master of Flémalle." Pantheon 30 (1972): 115-132.

d) Monastic Life

03993. Denuit, Désiré. "Les grandes abbesses d'Aywiers." <u>Revue</u>
        <u>generale</u> 4 (Summer 1976): 13-24.

03994. Huyghebaert, N. "L'abbesse Frisilde et les debuts de
        l'abbaye de Messines." <u>Revue d'histoire ecclesiastique</u>
        50 (1955): 141-157.

4. SOCIAL

"These facts 'certainly do not show that the women of
the Middle Ages were all on the side of civilization--
or all against it.'"   Mary Beard

a) Marriage

03995. Arkem, Hans. "Le mariage et les conventions matrimoniales
        des mineurs. Etudes sur le status juridique des infant
        mineurs dans l'histoire du droit privé neerlandais à
        partir du 13e siècle." <u>Revue d'histoire du droit</u> 46
        (1978): 203-249.

        Also refer to #3546, 3547.

b) Sex Life and Morals

03996. De Waha, M. "Note sur l'usage de moyens contraceptifs à
        Bruxelles au debut du XVe siècle." <u>Annales de la</u>
        <u>société belge d'histoire des hôpitaux</u> 13 (1977): 3-28.

IV. RENAISSANCE/ REFORMATION

A. GENERAL

1. BIBLIOGRAPHIES

"I say that women can understand all the things men can
understand and that the intellect of a woman can penetrate
wherever a man's can."

Castiglione

03997. Davis, Natalie Zemon and Conway, Jill K., eds. Society and
the Sexes. A Bibliography of Women's History in Early
Modern Europe, Colonial America and the United States.
New York: Garland Publishing, 1981.

03998. Hageman, Elizabeth H. "Images of Women in Renaissance
Literature: a Selected Bibliography of Scholarship."
Women's Studies Newsletter 5 (Winter/Spring 1977): 15-17.

2. SURVEYS

"Women and men were equally endowed with the gifts of
spirit, reason, and the use of words; they were created for
the same end, and the sexual difference between them will
not confer a different destiny."

Agrippa d'Aubigné

a) Women

(1) Contemporary

03999.   Bornstein, Diane, intro. Distaves and Dames: Renaissance
          Treatises For and About Women. Delmar, New York: Scholars'
          Facsimiles & Reprints, 1978.

04000.   Bouchot, Henri Francois. Les Femmes de Brantome. Paris:
          Maison Quantin, 1890.

04001.   Brantôme, Pierre de Bourdeille, seigneur de. Tales of Fair
          and Gallant Ladies. Translated by Lowell Bair. New York:
          Bantam Books, 1958.

04002.   Fahy, Conor. "Three Early Renaissance Treatises on Women."
          Italian Studies 11 (1956): 30-55.

04003.   Wright, Celeste Turner. "Something More About Eve." Studies
          in Philology 41 (1944): 156-163.

(2) Secondary

04004.   Anderson, James. Ladies of the Reformation and Ladies of the
          Covenant. Edinburgh: Blackie and Son, 1855.

04005.   Blei, Franz. Frauen und Manner der Renaissance. Hellerau:
          Avalun, 1930.

04006.   Floerke, Hanns. Das Weib in der Renaissance. Munich:
          G. Müller, 1929.

04007.   Kelly-Gadol, Joan. "Did Women have a Renaissance?" In Be-
          coming Visible: Women in European History, edited by
          Renate Bridenthal and Claudia Koonz, pp. 137-164. Boston:
          Houghton Mifflin, 1978.

04008.   _____. "Notes on Women in the Renaissance." In
          Conceptual Frameworks for Studying Women's History, Part II,
          pp. 1-11. Bronxville: Sarah Lawrence Publications, 1976.

04009.   Maulde la Clavière, R. de. The Women of the Renaissance. 1905.
          Reprint. Folcroft, Pa.: Folcroft Library Editions, 1978.

04010.   Portigliotti, Giuseppe. Some Fascinating Women of the Renais-
          sance. Translated by Bernard Miall. New York: Brentano's,
          1929.

04011. Putnam, Emily James. "The Lady of the Renaissance." Con-
        temporary Review 98 (1910): 157-173.

04012. Radcliff-Umstead, Douglas. The Roles and Images of Women in
        the Middle Ages and Renaissance. Pittsburgh: University of
        Pittsburgh Publications on the Middle Ages and Renaissance,
        1975.

04013. Sachs, Hannelore. The Renaissance Woman. New York: McGraw-
        Hill, 1971.

04014. Savoye-Ferreras, Jacqueline. La Situation ambigue de la femme
        au xve siècle. Paris: Ediciones Hispano Americanas, 1966.

3. POLITICAL

"She listened to the people, heard their pleas, and was
accepted by the Ferrarese people. And the duke devoted
himself to having a good time and playing."
about Eleonora of Aragon

a) Feminism

04015. Bornstein, Diane, intro. The Feminist Controversy of the
        Renaissance. Delmar, N.Y.: Scholars' Facsimiles and
        Reprints, 1980.

04016. Doumic, R. "Le féminisme au temps de la Renaissance." Revue
        des deux mondes 149 (1898): 921-932.

04017. Wellington, James E. "Renaissance Anti-Feminism and the
        Classical Tradition." In Sweet Smoke of Rhetoric, edited
        by H.G. Lawrence and J.A. Reynolds, pp. 1-18. Coral Gables,
        Fla.: University of Miami Press, 1964.

4. RELIGION

"As for the question, why a greater number of witches is
found among the fragile sex than among men. . . they are
more credulous . . . and naturally more impression-
able . . . "
The Hammer of Witches

a) Generic

(1) Non-specific

04018. Bainton, Roland H.   The Reformation of the Sixteenth Century.
        Boston: Beacon Press, 1952.
        [See especially pp. 252-261.]

04019. Fremantle, Anne. The Protestant Mystics.   Boston: Little,
        Brown & Co., 1964.

04020. Williams, George Hunston. The Radical Reformation.   Phila-
        delphia: Westminster Press, 1962.
        [See especially ch. 20, "Marriage in the Radical Refor-
        mation."]

(2) Women

04021. Douglas, Jane Dempsey. "Women and the Continental Reformation."
        In Religion and Sexism, edited by Rosemary Ruether, pp. 292-
        318. New York: Simon and Schuster, 1974.

04022. Good, J.I. Famous Women of the Reformed Church.   Philadelphia:
        Heidelberg Press, 1901.

04023. Steinmetz, David C.   "Theological Reflections on the Reformation
        and the Status of Women." Duke Divinity School Review 41
        (Fall 1976): 197-207.

b) Saints/Religious Women

04024. Bokenham, Osbern. Legendys of Hooly Wummen, edited by Mary
        Sidney Serjeantson. Oxford: University Press, 1938.

c) Mariology

04025. Beissel, Stephan. Geschichte der Verehrung Marias im 16. und
        17. Jahrhundert. Ein Beitrag zur Religionswissenschaft und
        Kunstgeschichte. 1910. Reprint. Nieuwkoop: Graaf, 1970.

04026. Tappolet, Walter. Das Marienlob der Reformatoren. Tubingen:
        Katzmann-Verlag, 1962.

        Also refer to #2641.

d) Canon Law

04027. Conrad, Hermann. "Das tridentinische Konzil und die
        Entwicklung des kirchlichen und weltlichen Eherechts."
        das Weltkonzil von Trient, edited by G. Schrieber
        (Freiberg Nerder, 1951), 1, 297-324.

04028. Fransen, Piet. "Divorce on the Ground of Adultery—The Council
        of Trent (1563)." Concilium 55 (1970): 89-100.

04029. Franzen, August. Zolibat und Priesterehe in der Auseinander-
        setzung der Reformationzeit und der katholischen Reform des
        16. Jahrhunderts. Munster: Aschendorff, 1970.

e) Witchcraft

(1) Contemporary

04030. Institoris, Henricus. Malleus Maleficarum. Translated by
        Rev. Montague Summers. New York: Dover, 1971.

(2) Secondary

04031. Anglo, S. "Melancholia and Witchcraft: The Debate between
        Wier, Bodin and Scot." In Folie et déraison à la
        Renaissance, edited by A. Gerlo, pp. 209-222. Brussels:
        Editions de l'université de Bruxelles, 1976.

04032. Boguet, Henry. An Examen of Witches. 1st ed. ca 1590.
        Suffolk: Richard Clay and Sons, 1929.

04033. Curie, E. P. "The Control of Witchcraft in Renaissance
        Europe." In The Social Organization of Law, edited by
        Donald Black and Maureen Mileski, pp. 344-367. New York:
        Seminar Press, 1973.

04034. Döbler, Hannsferdinand. Hexenwahn. Munich: Bertelsmann,
        1977.

04035. Kittredge, George Lyman. <u>Notes</u> <u>on</u> <u>Witchcraft</u>. Worcester,
        Mass.: Davis Press, 1907.

04036. Muchembled, Robert. "Sorcellerie, culture populaire et
        christianisme au XVIe siècle." <u>Annales: économies, socié-</u>
        <u>tes, civilisations</u> 28 (1973): 264-284.

04037. Nugent, Donald. "The Renaissance and/or Witchcraft." <u>Church</u>
        <u>History</u> 40 (March 1971): 69-78.

04038. Paulus, Nikolaus. <u>Hexenwahn</u> <u>und</u> <u>Hexenprozess</u> <u>vornehmlich</u> <u>im</u>
        <u>16.</u> <u>Jahrhundert</u>. Freiburg: Herder, 1910.

04039. Schumaker, Wayne. <u>The</u> <u>Occult</u> <u>Sciences</u> <u>in</u> <u>the</u> <u>Renaissance</u>.
        New York, Berkeley: University of California Press, 1972.

04040. Trevor-Roper, Hugh. <u>The</u> <u>European</u> <u>Witch</u> <u>Craze</u> <u>of</u> <u>the</u> <u>Six-</u>
        <u>teenth</u> <u>and</u> <u>Seventeenth</u> <u>Centuries</u>. New York: Harper and
        Row, 1969.

04041. _____. "Witches and Witchcraft: An Historical
        Essay." <u>Encounter</u> 28 (May 1967): 3-25; (June 1967): 13-34.

04042. Zilboorg, Gregory, M.D. <u>The</u> <u>Medical</u> <u>Man</u> <u>and</u> <u>the</u> <u>Witch</u> <u>during</u>
        <u>the</u> <u>Renaissance</u>. 1935. Reprint. New York: Cooper Square
        Pub., Inc., 1969.

        Also refer to #2728, 2729, 2733, 2734, 2735, 2740, 2742.

5. SOCIAL

"I think that in her ways, manners, words, gestures, and
bearing, a woman ought to be very unlike a man." Castiglione

a) Generic

04043. Checksfield, M.M. <u>Portraits</u> <u>of</u> <u>Renaissance</u> <u>Life</u> <u>and</u> <u>Thought</u>.
        New York: Barnes and Noble, 1965.

04044. Gail, Marzieh. <u>Life</u> <u>in</u> <u>the</u> <u>Renaissance</u>. New York: Random
        House, 1968.

04045. Gleichen-Russwurm, Alexander von. <u>Die</u> <u>Sonne</u> <u>der</u> <u>Renaissance</u>
        <u>Sitten</u> <u>und</u> <u>Gebrauche</u> <u>der</u> <u>europäischen</u> <u>Welt</u> <u>1450-1600</u>.
        Stuttgart: Julius Hoffmann, 1921.

04046. Kamen, Henry. <u>The</u> <u>Iron</u> <u>Century</u>: <u>Social</u> <u>Change</u> <u>in</u> <u>Europe</u>
        <u>1550-1660</u>. New York: Praeger Publishers, Inc., 1972.

04047. Lefranc, Abel. La Vie quotidienne au temps de la renaissance.
        Paris: Hachette, 1938.

04048. Loesch, Ilse. So war es Sitte in der Renaissance. Hanau:
        M. Dausien, 1965.

        Also refer to #2774, 2880.

b) Demography

04049. Spengler, Joseph J. "Demographic Factors in Early Modern
        Economic Development." Daedalus 97 (Spring 1968):
        433-446.

c) Marriage

(1) Contemporary

04050. Eyb, Albrecht von. Ehebüchlein. Ob einem manne sey zunemen
        ein eelichr weyb oder nicht. Reprint. 1472. Wiesbaden:
        Pressler, 1966.

04051. La Sale, Antoine de. Les quinze joyes de mariage. Paris:
        E. de Boccard, 1929

(2) Secondary

04052. Kawerau, Waldemar. Die Reformation und die Ehe. Schriften des
        Vereins für Reformationsgeshichte, no. 39. Halle: Max
        Niemeyer, 1892.

        Also refer to #4027-4029.

d) Fashion/Manners

04053. Laver, James. Costume of the Western World: The Tudors to
        Louis XIII. London: George C. Harrup, 1952.

04054.   Vecellio, Cesare. <u>Vecellio's Renaissance Costume Book</u>. 1598.
          New York: Dover Publications, 1977.

e) Health/Medical

04055.   Benedek, Thomas G. "The Changing Relationship between Mid-
          wives and Physicians during the Renaissance." <u>Bulletin of
          the History of Medicine</u> 51 (Winter 1977): 550-564.

04056.   Bloch, Iwan. <u>Das erste Auftreten des Syphilis (Lustseuche) in
          der europäische Kulturwelt</u>. Jena: G. Fischer, 1904.

04057.   Crosby, Alfred W. <u>The Columbian Exchange: Biological and
          Cultural Consequences of 1492</u>. Westport, Conn.: Greenwood
          Publishing Co., 1972.

04058.   Eshleman, Michael K. "Diet during Pregnancy in the Sixteenth
          and Seventeenth Centuries." <u>Journal of the History of
          Medicine and Allied Sciences</u> 30 (January 1975): 23-39.

04059.   Niccoli, Ottavia. "Menstrum quasi Monstruum.': Parti Mostru-
          osi e Tabu' Menstruale nel '500." <u>Quaderni Storici</u> 44
          (August 1980): 402-428.

          Also refer to #4042, 4066.

6. CULTURAL

          "I would that even the lowliest women read the gospels."
                                                        Erasmus

a) Education

04060.   Bainton, Roland H. "Learned Women of the Sixteenth Century."
          In <u>Beyond their Sex, Learned Women of the European Past</u>,
          edited by Patricia Labalme, pp. 117-128. New York: New
          York University Press, 1980.

04061.   Cannon, Mary A. <u>Education of Women during the Renaissance</u>.
          Washington, D.C.: National Capital Press, 1916.

04062.   Rousselot, Paul. <u>La Pédagogie féminine: Extraite des princi-
          paux écrivains qui on traité de l'education des femmes depuis
          le XVI siècle</u>. Paris: C. Delagrave, 1881.

04063. Woodward, William Harrison. Studies in Education during the
        Renaissance. London: Macmillan Co., 1906

b) Literature

(1) Non-specific

04064. Bruyn, Lucy De. Woman and the Devil in Sixteenth Century
        Literature. Tisbury, England: Compton Press, 1979.

04065. Houdoy, Jules. La Beauté des Femmes dans la Littérature et
        dans l'Art du XIIe au XVIe siècle. Paris: A. Aubry, 1876.

04066. Maclean, I. The Renaissance Notion of Women: A Study in the
        Fortunes of Scholasticism and Medical Science in European
        Intellectual Life. New York: Cambridge University Press,
        1980.

04067. Valency, Maurice. In Praise of Love: An Introduction to the
        Love-Poetry of the Renaissance. New York: Macmillan, 1961.
        [See especially ch. "The Ladies," pp. 59–85.]

B. BRITISH ISLES

1. BIBLIOGRAPHIES

        "A woman [is] as variable as wind, being of her love
        unstable and fickle."   Proverb, 1509

04068. Gartenberg, Patricia and Whittemore, Nena Thames. "A check-
        list of English women in print, 1475–1650." Bulletin of
        Bibliography and Magazine Notes 34 (January–March 1977):
        1–13.

04069. Greco, Norma and Novothny, Ronaele. "Bibliography of women in
        the English Renaissance." University of Michigan Papers in
        Women's Studies 1 (June 1974): 30–57.

04070. Masek, Rosemary. "Women in an Age of Transition: 1485–1714."
        In The Women of England from Anglo-Saxon Times to the Present,
        edited by Barbara Kanner, pp. 138–182. Hamden, Conn.: Archon
        Books, 1979.

2. SURVEYS

"Thy husband is thy lord, thy life, thy keeper, thy head,
thy sovereign."   Shakespeare

a) Women

(1) Contemporary

04071. Barker (Bercher), William. The Nobility of Women. Edited by
R. Warick Bond. London: Roxburghe Club, 1904.

04072. Stein, Harold. "Six Tracts about Women: A Volume in the
British Museum." Library 4th ser. 15 (1934): 38-48.

(2) Secondary

04073. Bainton, Roland H. Women of the Reformation: From Spain to
Scandinavia. Minneapolis: Augsburg Publishing House, 1977.

04074. _____. Women of the Reformation in France and
England. Minneapolis: Augsburg Publishing House, 1973.

04075. Bradford, Gamaliel. Elizabethan Women. 1936. Reprint.
Freeport, N.Y.: Books for Libraries, 1969.

04076. Camden, Charles Carrol. The Elizabethan Woman. New York:
Appel, 1978.

04077. Hoffmann, Ann, comp. Lives of the Tudor Age. New York:
Barnes and Noble, 1977.

04078. Hogrefe, Pearl. Tudor Women: Commoners and Queens. Ames,
Iowa: Iowa State University, 1975.

04079. _____. Women of Action in Tudor England: Nine
Biographical Sketches. Ames, Iowa: Iowa State University
Press, 1977.

04080. Marienstras, Richard. "La femme de la Renaissance. L'Anglaise
sous le règne d'Elizabeth." In Histoire mondiale de la femme.
Edited by Pierre Grimal, 2: 397-454. Paris: Nouvelle
Librairie de France, 1966.

04081. Notestein, Wallace. "The English Woman 1580–1650." In Studies
        in Social History Presented to G.M. Trevelyan, edited by
        J.H. Plumb, pp. 69–107. New York: Longmans, Green and Co.,
        1955.

04082. Plowden, Alison. Tudor Women, Queen and Commoners. New York:
        Atheneum, 1979.

04083. Putnam, Maxine. "A Glimpse into the Lives of English Women
        during the Renaissance." Florida State University Studies
        5 (1952): 67–78.

04084. Weinstein, Minna F. "Reconstructing Our Past: Reflections
        on Tudor Women." International Journal of Women's Studies
        1 (March–April 1978): 133–140.

04085. Wright, Celeste Turner. "The Elizabethan Female Worthies."
        Studies in Philology 43 (1946): 628–643.

3. POLITICAL

"I know I have the body of a weak and feeble woman; but I
have the heart and stomach of a king."   Elizabeth I

a) Legal

04086. Hogrefe, Pearl. "Legal Rights of Tudor Women and Their
        Circumvention." The Sixteenth Century Journal 3 (1972):
        97–105.

04087. Wiener, Carol Z. "Is a Spinster an Unmarried Woman?" American
        Journal of Legal History 20 (January 1976): 27–31.

b) Criminal

04088. Meadows, Denis. Elizabethan Quintet. New York: Longmans,
        Green, 1956.

04089. Weiner, Carol Z. "Sex-roles and crime in late Elizabethan
        Hertfordshire." Journal of Social History 8 (Summer 1975):
        38–60.

c) *Feminism*

04090. Garanderie, M.W. de la. "La Féminisme de Thomas More et
        d'Erasme." Moreana 10 (May 1966): 23-29.

04091. Jones, Judith P. and Seibel, Sherianne Sellers. "Thomas More's
        Feminism: To Reform or Re-Form." Albion 10 (Supplement
        1978): 67-77.

04092. Mackerness, E.D. "Margaret Tyler: An Elizabethan Feminist."
        Notes and Queries 190 (1946): 112-113.

04093. Shapiro, Susan C. "Feminists in Elizabethan England."
        History Today 27 (November 1977): 299-316.

d) *Political Roles*

(1) Women

04094. Adlard, George. Amy Robsart and Leicester. London: J. R.
        Smith, 1870.

04095. Bradford, Charles Agnell. Helena: Marchioness of North-
        ampton. London: Allen and Unwin, 1936.

04096. Brewster, Eleanor. Oxford and his Elizabethan Ladies.
        Philadelphia: Dorrance and Co., 1972.

04097. Brooks, Janice Young. Kings and Queens, the Plantagenets of
        England. Nashville, Tenn.: Thomas Nelson Inc., 1975.

04098. Chapman, Hester W. Two Tudor Portraits: Henry Howard, Earl
        of Surrey and Lady Katherine Grey. Boston: Little Brown,
        1963.

04099. Cooper, Charles Henry. Memoir of Margaret, Countess of
        Richmond and Derby. Cambridge: University Press, 1874.

04100. Cowan, Maurice. The six wives of Henry VIII: The King seen
        through the eyes of each of his ill-fated wives. London:
        Frewin, 1968.

04101. Foss, Michael. Tudor Portraits: Success and Failure of an
        Age. New York: Barnes and Noble, 1974.

04102. Frere, Bartley Henry Temple. Amy Robsart of Wymondham; the Story of her Life and the Mystery of her Death. Norwich: Jarrold and Sons, Ltd., 1937.

04103. Goff, Cecilie. A Woman of the Tudor Age: Katherine Willoughby, Duchess of Suffolk. London: J. Murray, 1930.

04104. Halstead, Caroline. Life of Margaret Beaufort. London: n.p., 1839.

04105. Harvey, Nancy Lenz. Elizabeth of York: The Mother of Henry VIII. New York: Macmillan Publishing Co., 1973.

04106. Hume, A. S. Martin. The Wives of Henry VIII. New York: McClure, Phillips and Co., 1905.

04107. Jerrold, Walter. Henry VIII and His Wives. New York: George H. Doran Co., 1926.

04108. Kelly, Henry Ansgar. Matrimonial Trials of Henry the Eighth. Stanford, Calif.: Stanford University Press, 1976.

04109. Krück von Poturzyn, Maria Josepha. Die Frauen Heinrichs VIII. Hamburg: Hoffman and Campe, 1937.

04110. Lloyd, J. E. "The Mysterious Death of Amy Robsart." Contemp Review 175 (January 1949): 49-52.

04111. Loomie, Albert J. "A Grandniece of Thomas More: Catherine Bentley, ca 1565-ca. 1625." Moreana 29 (March 1971): 13-15.

04112. _____. The Spanish Elizabethans: The English Exiles at the Court of Philip II. New York: Fordham University Press, 1963.

04113. McCann, Timothy J. "Catherine Bentley, Great Grand-Daughter of St. Thomas More, and Her Catholic Connections in Sussex." Moreana 11 (November 1974): 41-45.

04114. McInnes, Ian. Arabella: The Life and Times of Lady Arabella Seymour 1575-1615. London: W.H. Allen, 1968.

04115. McKerlie, Emmeline Marianne H. Mary of Guise-Lorraine, Queen of Scotland. London: Sands, 1932.

04116. Mirot, Lein. "Isabelle de France Reine d'Angleterre (1389-1409)." Revue d'histoire diplomatique 19 (1905): 60-95; 161-191; 481-522.

04117. Oyley, Elizabeth D' "The Death of Amye Robsart." History Today 6 (April 1956): 252-260.

04118. Putzel, Rosamond. "Queen Gertrude's Crime." Renaissance Papers 1961: 37-46.

04119. Rait, Robert. *Five Stuart Princesses*. London: A. Constable and Co., Ltd., 1908.

04120. Read, Evelyn. *My Lady Suffolk: A Portrait of Catherine Willoughby, Duchess of Suffolk*. New York: Knopf, 1963.

04121. Reynolds, Ernest Edwin. *Margaret Roper, Eldest Daughter of Saint Thomas More*. New York: P.J. Kenedy, 1960.

04122. Rival, Paul. *The Six Wives of Henry VIII*. New York: Putnam's, 1936.

04123. Routh, Enid M.G. *Lady Margaret*. London: Oxford University Press, 1924.

04124. Rye, Walter. *The Murder of Amy Robsart*. London: E. Stock, 1885.

04125. Sitwell, Edith. *The Queen and the Hive*. London: Macmillan, 1962.

04126. Sjogren, Gunnar. "Helena, Marchioness, of Northampton." *History Today* 28 (September 1978): 597-604.

04127. Strickland, Agnes. *Lives of the Tudor and Stuart Princesses*. London: G. Bell, 1902.

04128. _____. *Memoirs of the Queens of Henry VIII and of his Mother Elizabeth of York*. Philadelphia: Blanchard and Lea, 1853.

04129. Tabor, Margaret Emma. *Four Margarets*. New York: The Macmillan Co., 1929.

04130. Taylor, M.A. "Queen Elizabeth and Women Pages." *Shakespeare Association Bulletin* 11 (1936): 122-123.

04131. Wilson, Violet. *Queen Elizabeth's Maids of Honour and Ladies of the Privy Chamber*. London: John Lane, 1922.

04132. Young, Francis Berkeley. *Mary Sidney, Countess of Pembroke*. London: David Nutt, 1912.

(2) Individuals

(a) *Catherine of Aragon*

04133. Behrens, Betty. "A Note on Henry VIII's Divorce Project of 1514". *Bulletin of the Institute of Historical Research* 11 (February 1934): 163-164.

04134. DuBoys, Albert. *Catherine of Aragon*. 1881. Reprint. New York: Burt Franklin, 1968.

04135. Froude, J.A. The Divorce of Catherine of Aragon. 1891. Re-
        print. New York: AMS Press, 1970.

04136. Harrison, K. P. "Katharine of Aragon's Pomegranate."
        Transactions of the Cambridge Bibliographical Society 2
        (1954): 88-92.

04137. Hope, Anne (Fulton). The First Divorce of Henry VIII. London:
        Kegan Paul, Trench, Trubner and Co., Ltd., 1894.

04138. Luke, Mary M. Catherine the Queen. New York: Coward, McCann
        and Geoghegan, 1967.

04139. Mattingly, Garrett. Catherine of Aragon. New York: Knopf,
        1960.

04140. Merry del Val, Alfonso. "Enteriamiento de la Reine de
        Inglaterre doña Catalina de Aragon, mujer de Enrique VIII,
        en la Catedral de Peterborough." Boletin de la Real
        Academia de la Historia Madrid 85 (July 1924): 17-20.

04141. Paul, John E. Catherine of Aragon and Her Friends. New York:
        Fordham University Press, 1966.

04142. Plaidy, Jean. Katherine of Aragon. London: Hale, 1968.

04143. Thurston, Herbert. "Clement VII, Campeggio and the Divorce [of
        Henry VIII]. American Catholic Quarterly Review 29 (April
        1904): 288-306.

(b) Anne Boleyn

04144. Anthony, Evelyn. Anne Boleyn. New York: Thomas Y. Crowell,
        1957.

04145. Benger, E. Memoirs of the Life of Ann Boleyn. Philadel-
        phia: A. Small, 1822.

04146. Bruce, Marie Louise. Anne Boleyn. New York: Coward, McCann
        and Geoghegan, 1972.

04147. Chapman, Hester W. The Challenge of Anne Boleyn. New York:
        Coward, McCann and Geoghegan, 1974.

04148. Fitzpatrick, Benedict. Frail Anne Boleyn. New York: Dial
        Press, 1931.

04149. Friedmann, Paul. Anne Boleyn: A Chapter in English History
        1527-1536. London: Macmillan, 1884.

04150. Harrier, Richard C. "Note on Wyatt and Anne Boleyn." Journal
        of English and Germanic Philology 53 (1954): 581-584.

04151. Lofts, Norah. <u>Anne Boleyn</u>. New York: Coward, McCann, and
Geoghegan, 1979.

04152. Momigliano, E. <u>Anne Bolena</u>. Milan: Corbaccio, 1933.

04153. Sergeant, Philip Walsingham. <u>Life of Anne Boleyn</u>. New York:
D. Appleton and Co., 1924.

(c)   Elizabeth I

04154. Giffin, Frederick C. "'Good Queen Bess': The Monarch as
Master Politician." <u>International Review of History and
Political Science</u> 10 (February 1973): 104-128.

04155. Heisch, Allison. "Queen Elizabeth I: Parliamentary Rhetoric
and the Exercise of Power." <u>Signs</u> 1 (Fall 1975): 31-55.

04156. Jenkins, Elizabeth. <u>Elizabeth the Great</u>. New York: Coward,
McCann, 1959.

04157. Johnson, Paul. <u>Elizabeth I: A Biography</u>. New York: Holt,
Rinehart and Winston, 1974.

04158. Luke, Mary M. <u>Gloriana: The Years of Elizabeth I</u>. New York:
Coward, McCann & Geoghegan, Inc., 1973.

04159. Neale, John E. <u>Elizabeth I and her Parliaments</u>, 2 vols.
1957. Reprint. New York: Norton, 1966.

04160. _____. <u>Queen Elizabeth I</u>. New York: St. Martin's
Inc., 1958.

04161. Plowden, Alison. <u>Marriage With My Kingdom: The Courtships
of Elizabeth I</u>. London: Macmillan, 1977.

04162. _____. <u>The Young Elizabeth</u>. New York: Stein and
Day, 1971.

04163. Read, Conyers. <u>Lord Burghley and Queen Elizabeth</u>. New York:
Knopf, 1961.

04164. Rowse, Alfred Leslie. <u>Queen Elizabeth and Her Subjects</u>.
Freeport, N.Y.: Books for Libraries, 1970.

04165. Smith, Lacey Baldwin. <u>Elizabeth Tudor, Portrait of a Queen</u>.
Boston: Little, Brown, 1975.

04166. Strong, Roy. <u>The Cult of Elizabeth: Elizabethan Portraiture
and Pagentry</u>. London: Thames and Hudson, 1977.

04167. Waldman, Milton. <u>Queen Elizabeth I</u>. 1952. Reprint.
Hamden, Conn.: Archon Books, 1966.

04168. Williams, Neville. The Life and Times of Elizabeth I.
        Introduced by Antonia Fraser. New York: Doubleday, 1972.

        Also refer to #4793.

(d) Jane Grey

04169. Chapman, Hester W. Lady Jane Grey. London: J. Cape, 1962.

04170. Dargaud, J.M. Histoire de Jane Grey. Paris: Libraire
        Hachette, 1863.

04171. Davey, Richard Patrick Boyle. The Nine Days' Queen, Lady Jane
        Grey and Her Times. London: Methuen and Co., 1909.

04172. Howard, George. Lady Jane Grey and Her Times. London: Sher-
        wood, Neely, and Jones, 1822.

04173. Laird, Francis Charles. Lady Jane Grey and Her Times. London:
        Sherwood, Neely, and Jones, 1822.

04174. Mathew, David. Lady Jane Grey: The Setting of the Reign. New
        York: Barnes and Noble Books, 1972.

(e) Bess of Hardwick

04175. Durant, David. Bess of Hardwick: Portrait of an Elizabethan
        Dynasty. London: Weidenfeld and Nicolson, 1977.

04176. Rawson, Maud Stepney. Bess of Hardwick and Her Circle. London:
        Hutchinson and Co., 1910.

04177. Williams, Ethel Carleton. Bess of Hardwick. New York: Long-
        mans, Green, 1959.

(f) Catherine Howard

04178. Glenne, Michael. Henry VIII's Fifth Wife: The Story of
        Catherine Howard. New York: Robert M. McBridge and Co.,
        1948.

04179. Smith, Lacey Baldwin. A Tudor Tragedy: The Life and Times
        of Catherine Howard. New York: Pantheon, 1961.

(g) Mary I

04180.   Erickson, Carolly. Bloody Mary. Garden City, N.Y.: Doubleday and Co., 1978.

04181.   Henderson, Daniel. The Crimson Queen, Mary Tudor. New York:
Duffield and Green, 1933.

04182.   Hume, A.S. Martin. Two English Queens and Philip. New York:
G.P. Putnam's Sons, 1908.

04183.   Lewis, Hilda. I am Mary Tudor. New York: Warner Books,
1973.

04184.   Llanos y Torriglia, Felix de. Maria I de Inglaterra, "la
sanguinaria"? reina de Espana. Madrid: Espasa-Calpe, 1946.

04185.   Loades, D.M. The Reign of Mary Tudor. New York: St.
Martin's, 1979.

04186.   Maynard, Theodore. Bloody Mary. Milwaukee, Wisc.: Bruce,
1955.

04187.   Prescott, Hilda Francess Margaret. Mary Tudor. New York:
Macmillan Co., 1962.

04188.   Ridley, Jasper. The Life and Times of Mary Tudor. London:
Weidenfeld and Nicolson, 1973.

04189.   Simon, Eric. The Queen and the Rebel: Mary Tudor and Wyatt
the Younger. London: Muller, 1964.

04190.   Simpson, Helen. The Spanish Marriage. New York: G.P. Putnam's
Sons, 1933.

04191.   Stone, J.M. The History of Mary Queen of England. London:
Sands, 1901.

04192.   Waldman, Milton. The Lady Mary: A Biography of Mary Tudor,
1516-1558. New York: Charles Scribner's Sons, 1972.

04193.   White, Beatrice. Mary Tudor. New York: Macmillan, 1935.

Also refer to #4778.

(h) Mary Queen of Scots

04194.   Bordeaux, Paule Henry. Marie Stuart. Paris: Librairie Plon,
1944.

04195. Buchanan, George. The Tyrannous Reign of Mary Stewart (1582).
        Translated and edited by W. A. Gutherer. 1958. Reprint.
        Westport, Conn.: Greenwood Press, 1978.

04196. Cowan, Ian B. The Enigma of Mary Stuart. London: Gollancz,
        1971.

04197. Davison, M.H. Armstrong. The Casket Letters: A Solution to
        the Mystery of Mary Queen of Scots and the Murder of Lord
        Darnley. Seattle: University of Washington Press, 1965.

04198. Edwards, Francis. The Dangerous Queen. New York: Hilary
        House, 1966.

04199. Francis, Grant R. Mary of Scotland, 1561-1568. London:
        Murray, 1930.

04200. Fraser, Antonia. Mary, Queen of Scots. New York: Delacorte
        Press, 1970.

04201. Gorman, Herbert. The Scottish Queen. New York: Farrar and
        Rinehart, 1932.

04202. Heritier, Jean. Marie Stuart et le meurte de Darnley.
        Paris: Felix Alcan, 1934.

04203. MacNalty, Arthur Salisbury, Sir. Mary Queen of Scots: The
        Daughter of Debate. London: Johnson, 1971.

04204. Morrison, Nancy Brysson. Mary Queen of Scots. London: Vista
        Books, 1960.

04205. Phillips, James Emerson. Images of a Queen: Mary Stuart in
        16th Century Literature. Berkeley: University of California
        Press, 1964.

04206. Rat, Maurice. Marie Stuart. Brussels: Brepols, 1959.

04207. Saint-Lambert, Patrick. Marie Stuart. Verviers: Gerard, 1965.

04208. Thomson, George Malcolm. The Crime of Mary Stuart. New York:
        E.P. Dutton and Co., 1967.

04209.· Zweig, Stephan. Maria Stuart. Frankfurt A.M.: Fischer
        Bucherei, 1959.

(i) Catherine Parr

04210. Gordon, Marian A. Life of Queen Katharine Parr. Kendal,
        England: Wilson, 1951.

04211. Haugaard, William P. "Katharine Parr: The Religious Convic-
        tions of a Renaissance Queen." Renaissance Quarterly 22
        (Winter 1969): 346-359.

04212. Hoffman, G. Fenno, Jr. "Catherine Parr as a Woman of Letters."
        Huntington Library Quarterly 23 (August 1960): 349-367.

04213. McConica, J.K. "The Last Years of the Reign: the Role of
        Catherine Parr." In English Humanists and Reformation
        Politics under Henry the VIII and Edward VI, pp. 200-234.
        Oxford: Clarendon Press, 1965.

04214. Martienssen, Anthony. Queen Katherine Parr: A Biography.
        New York: McGraw Hill, 1974.

04215. Weinstein, Minora. "Queen's Power: The Case of Katherine
        Parr." History Today 26 (1976): 788-795.

(j) Arbella Stuart

04216. Durant, David N. Arbella Stuart: A Rival to the Queen.
        London: Weidenfeld and Nicolson, 1978.

04217. Handover, P.M. Arbella Stuart, Royal Lady of Hardwick and
        Cousin to King James. London: Eyre Spottiswoode, 1957.

04218. Hardy, Blanche Christabel. Arbella Stuart: A Biography. New
        York: Dutton, 1913.

(k) Margaret and Mary Tudor

04219. Chapman, Hester W. The Sisters of Henry VIII: Margaret Tudor,
        Queen of Scotland (November 1489-October 1541), Mary Tudor,
        Queen of France and Duchess of Suffolk (March 1496-June 1533).
        Bath: Chivers, 1974.

04220. Harvey, Nancy Lenz. The Rose and the Thorn: The Lives of Mary
        and Margaret Tudor. New York: Macmillan Publishing Co., 1975.

e) Gynecocratic Controversy

(1) Contemporary

04221. Aylmer, John. An Harborowe for Faithfull Treuve Subjects.
        1559. Reprint. New York: Da Capo Press, 1972.

04222. Elyot, Sir Thomas. The Defence of Good Women. 1545.
        Reprint.   In The Feminist Controversy in the Renaissance.
        Delmar, N.Y.: Scholars' Facsimiles and Reprints, 1980.

04223. Goodman, Christopher. How the Superior Powers Ought to be
        Obeyed. 1558. Reprint. New York: Columbia University
        Press, 1931.

04224. Knox, John. The First Blast of the Trumpet Against the
        Monstrous Regiment of Women. 1558. Reprint. New York:
        De Capo Press, 1972.

                    (2) Secondary

04225. Neill, Kerby. "Spenser on the Regiment of Women: a Note on
        'The Faerie Queene'. 5, 5, 25." Studies in Philology 34
        (1937): 134-137.

04226. Northrup, Douglas A. "Spenser's Defense of Elizabeth." Uni-
        versity of Toronto Quarterly 38 (1969): 277-294.

04227. Phillips, James Emerson. "The Background of Spenser's Atti-
        tude Toward Women Rulers." Huntington Library Quarterly 5
        (October 1941): 5-32.

04228. _____. "The Woman Ruler in Spencer's
        Fairie Queene." Huntington Library Quarterly 5 (1942):
        211-234.

04229. Reynolds, Ernest Edwin. "St. John Fisher and Lady Margaret
        Beaufort." Moreana 23 (1969): 32-33.

04230. Scalingi, Paula Louise. "The Scepter or the Distaff: The
        Question of Female Sovereignty, 1516-1607." The Historian
        41 (November 1978): 59-75.

4. ECONOMIC

        "Megge lets her husband boast of Rule and Riches. But she
        rules all the roost and wears the breeches."
                            John Taylor, A Juniper Lecture

04231. Dale, Marian K. "The London Silkwomen of the Fifteenth
        Century." Economic History Review 4 (October 1933):
        324-335.

04232.   Mann, J. de L.   "A Wiltshire Family of Clothiers: George
          and Hester Wansey, 1683-1714."   Economic History Review
          2nd ser. 9 (December 1956):   241-253.

5. RELIGION

"To promote a woman, to bear rule, superiority, dominion, or
empire above any realm, nation, or city, is repugnant to
nature: contumely to God."   John Knox

a) Generic

(1) Non-specific

04233.   Dickens, A. G.   The English Reformation.   London: B. T. Batsford,
          1966.

(2) Women

04234.   Collinson, Patrick.   "The Role of Women in the English Refor-
          mation Illustrated by the Life and Friendships of Ann Locke."
          Studies in Church History 2 (1965):   258-272.

04235.   Cranmer, Thomas.   "Letter to Crumwell 1536."   In The Works of
          Thomas Cranmer, edited by G. E. Duffield, pp. 255-257.
          Appleford, Berkshire, England: Sutton Courtenay Press, 1964.

04236.   Irwin, Joyce L., ed.   Womanhood in Radical Protestantism:
          1525-1675.   Studies in Women and Religion, vol. 1.   Lewis-
          ton, N.Y.:   Edwin Mellen Press, 1979.

04237.   Thomson, D. P.   Women of the Scottish Reformation, their Con-
          tribution to the Protestant Cause.   Crieff, Perthshire: St.
          Ninian's, 1960.

b)   Saints/Religious Women

(1)   Women

(a)   General

04238. Claridge, Mary. Margaret Clitherow 1556-1586. New York:
        Fordham University Press, 1966.

04239. Norman, Marion. "Dame Gertrude More and the English Mystical
        Tradition." Recusant History 13 (April 1976): 196-211.

04240. White, Helen C. Tudor Book of Saints and Martyrs. Madison:
        University of Wisconsin Press, 1967.

04241. Williams, J.A. "Katherine Gaven, papist." The Month 215 n.s.
        29 (1963): 169-175.

(b)   Elizabeth Barton

04242. Devereux, E. J. "Elizabeth Barton and Tudor Censorship."
        Bulletin of the John Rylands Library 49 (1966-1967):
        91-106.

04243. Neame, Alan. The Holy Maid of Kent. The life of Elizabeth
        Barton, 1506-1534. London: Hodder and Stoughton Ltd.,
        1971.

04244. Whatmore, L. E. "The Sermon against the Holy Maid of
        Kent and Her Adherents, delivered at Paul's Cross,
        Nov. the 23rd, 1533, and at Canterbury." English Histor-
        ical Review 53 (October 1943): 462-475.

(2)   John Foxe

04245. Bainton, Roland H. "John Foxe and the Ladies." In The Social
        History of the Reformation, edited by Lawrence P. Buck and
        Jon Zophy, pp. 208-222. Columbus, Ohio: Ohio State Univer-
        sity Press, 1972.

04246. Foxe, John. Acts and Monuments, 1570. Reprint. 8 vols. New
        York: AMS Press, 1965.

04247. Haller, William. Foxe's Book of Martyrs. London: Jonathan Cape, 1963.

c) Religious Orders

04248. Butler, Audrey. "Anne Boroeghe of Clerkenwell and Dingley." Northamptonshire Past and Present 5 (1977): 407-411.

d) Recusants

04249. Aveling, Dom Hugh. "The Marriage of Catholic Recusants, 1559-1642." Journal of Ecclesiastical History 14 (1963): 68-83.

04250. Hanlon, Sister Joseph Damien. "These Be But Women." From the Renaissance to the Counter-Reformation, edited by Charles H. Carter, pp. 371-400. New York: Random House, 1965.

e) Puritans

04251. Cannon, Charles D. "A Warning for Fair Women and the Puritan Controversy." Studies in English 9 (1968): 85-99.

04252. Frye, Roland M. "The Teaching of Classical Puritanism on Conjugal Love." Studies in the Renaissance 2 (1955): 148-159.

04253. Schnucker, Robert V. "La Position puritaine à l'égard de l'adultere." Annales: économies, sociétés, civilisations 27 (November-December 1972): 1379-1388.

04254. Sensabaugh, G.F. "Platonic Love and the Puritan Rebellion." Studies in Philology 37 (1940): 457-481.

04255. Todd, Margaret. "Humanists Puritans and the spiritualized Household." 49 (March 1980): 18-34.

f)   John Knox

04256.   Stevenson, Robert Louis.   "John Knox and his Relations to
         Women."   In Familiar Studies of Men and Books, pp. 224-225.
         New York: G. Scribner's Sons, 1907.

         Also refer to #4244.

g)   Witchcraft

(1)   Contemporary

04257.   Scot, Reginald.   The Discoverie of Witchcraft.   1584.   Reprint.
         New York: Dover Publications, 1972.

(2)   Secondary

04258.   Anderson, Alan, and Gordon, Raymond.   "Witchcraft and the
         Status of Women--The Case of England."   British Journal of
         Sociology 29 (June 1978):   171-84.

04259.   Briggs, Katherine Mary.   Pale Hecate's Team: an Examination
         of the Beliefs on Witchcraft and Magic among Shakespeare's
         Contemporaries and His Immediate Successors.   New York:
         Humanities Press, 1962.

04260.   MacFarlane, Alan.   Witchcraft in Tudor and Stuart England.
         New York: Harper and Row, 1970.

04261.   _____.   "Witchcraft in Tudor and Stuart Essex."
         In Crime in England, 1550-1800, edited by J.S. Cockburn,
         pp. 72-89.   Princeton: Princeton University Press, 1977.
         Also in Witchcraft Confessions and Accusations, edited by
         Mary Douglas, pp. 81-99.   New York: Tavistock Publishers,
         1970.

04262.   Marshburn, Joseph H.   Murder & Witchcraft in England, 1550-1640.
         Norman: University of Oklahoma Press, 1971.

04263.   Menefee, S.P.   "The 'Merry Maidens' and the 'Noce de Pierre'."
         Folklore 85 (Spring 1974):   23-42.

04264.   Seth, Ronald. _Children against Witches_. London: Robert
          Hale, 1969.

04265.   Stuart, Clark and Morgan, P.T.J. "Religion and Magic in
          Elizabethan Wales: Robert Holland's Dialogue on Witchcraft."
          Journal of Ecclesiastical History 27 (1976): 31-46.

04266.   Teall, John L. "Witchcraft and Calvinism in Elizabethan
          England: Divine Power and Human Agency." _Journal of the
          History of Ideas_ 23 (1962): 21-36.

04267.   Thomas, Keith. "The Making of a Witch." In _Religion and the
          Decline of Magic_, pp. 502-534. New York: Charles Scribner's
          Sons, 1971.

04268.   _____. "The Relevance of Social Anthropology to the
          Historical Study of English Witchcraft." In _Witchcraft
          Confessions and Accusations_, edited by Mary Douglas, pp.
          47-81. New York: Tavistock Publications, 1970.

04269.   _____. "Witchcraft and Religion." In _Religion and
          the Decline of Magic_, pp. 469-501. New York: Charles
          Scribner's Sons, 1971.

04270.   Walker, D. P. _Unclean Spirits: Possession and Exorcism in
          France and England in the Late Sixteenth and Early Seven-
          teenth Centuries_. Philadelphia: University of Pennsylvania
          Press, 1981.

04271.   Young, Alan R. "Elizabeth Lowrys: Witch and Social Victim,
          1564." _History Today_ 22 (December 1972): 833-842.

6. SOCIAL

"The woman is a weak creature not endowed with like strength
and constancy of mind."   Homily on Matrimony

a) Generic

(1) Non-specific

04272.   Beier, A. L. "Social Problems in Elizabethan London."
          Journal of Interdisciplinary History 9 (Autumn 1978):
          203-222.

04273. Bingham, Madeleine. Scotland under Mary Stuart. An Account
        of Everyday Life. New York: St. Martin's Press, 1973.
        [See especially ch. 4, "Family Life," pp. 71-89.]

04274. Burton, Elizabeth. The Early Tudors at Home, 1485-1558.
        London: Allen Lane, 1976.

04275. _____. The Elizabethans at Home. London:
        Secker and Warburg, 1963.

04276. _____. The Pageant of Early Tudor England 1485-
        1558. New York: Scribner, 1976.

04277. Byrne, Muriel St. Clare. Elizabethan Life in Town and Country.
        New York: Barnes and Noble, 1961.

04278. Davis, William Stearn. Life in Elizabethan Days. New York:
        Harper and Brothers, 1930.
        [See especially ch. 7, "Concerning Maids, Matrons, and
        Matrimony," pp. 90-106.]

04279. Dodd, Arthur Herbert. Life in Elizabethan England. London:
        B.T. Batsford, 1961.

04280. Dominiac, Sister Mary Rose. "Some Social Aspects of the Renais-
        sance in England as Reflected in Diaries of the Period."
        Renaissance Papers 1 (1954): 4-10.

04281. Emmisar, Frederick George. Elizabethan Life. Colchester,
        Essex: Cullingford and Co., 1970.

04282. Emmison, F. G. Tudor Food and Pasttimes. London: Ernest
        Benn Ltd., 1964.

04283. Garside, B. People and Homes in Hampton-on-Thames in the
        Sixteenth and Seventeenth Centuries. Hampton: n.p., 1956.

04284. Goodman, William. The Social History of Great Britain during
        the Reigns of the Stuarts. 2 vols. New York: William H.
        Colyer, 1843.

04285. Green, Alice Sophia Amelia (Stopford, Mrs. J.R.). Town Life in
        the Fifteenth Century. New York: Macmillan and Co., 1895.

04286. Hall, Hubert. Court Life Under the Plantagenets. London:
        S. Sonnenschein & Co., 1899.

04287. Hardy, E. "Life on a Suffolk Manor in the 16th and 17th
        Centuries." Suffolk Review 3 (1965-1970): 225-237.

04288. Heal, Felicity, and O'Day, Rosemary, eds. Church and Society
        in England: Henry VIII to James I. Hamden, Conn.: Archon
        Books, 1977.

04289. Hole, Christina. English Home-Life, 1500-1800. 2nd ed. New
        York: Batsford, 1949.

04290. Holmes, Martin. Elizabethan London. New York: F.A. Praeger, 1969.

04291. Lemonnier, Léon. La Vie quotidienne en Angleterre sous
        Elizabeth. Paris: Libraire Hachette, 1950.

04292. Pearson, Lu Emily. Elizabethans at Home. Stanford: Stanford
        University Press, 1957.

04293. Rowse, Alfred Leslie. The Elizabethan Renaissance: The Life
        of the Society. New York: Charles Scribner's Sons, 1971.

04294. _____. Sex and Society in Shakespeare's Age:
        Simon Forman the Astrologer. New York: Scribners, 1974.

04295. Salgado, Gamini. The Elizabethan Underworld. Totowa,
        N.J.: Rowman and Littlefield, 1977.

04296. Salzman, L.F. England in Tudor Times: An Account of its
        Social Life and Industries. London: B.T. Batsford Ltd., 1926.

04297. Spufford, Margaret. Contrasting Communities, English
        Villages in the Sixteenth and Seventeenth Centuries.
        New York: Cambridge University Press, 1974.

04298. Steer, Francis W. "The Inventory of Anne, Viscountess Dor-
        chester." Notes and Queries 198 (1953): 94-96, 155-158,
        379-381, 414-417, 469-473, 515-559; also in Die Neuer
        Sprachen I (1954): 21-24.

04299. Williams, Penry. Life in Tudor England. New York: G.P.
        Putnam's Sons, 1964.

04300. Wilson, Derek. A Tudor Tapestry: Men, Women and Society in
        Reformation England. Pittsburgh: University of Pittsburgh
        Press, 1972.

04301. Wright, Louis B. Middle Class Culture in Elizabethan England.
        New York: Cornell University Press, 1958.
        [See especially ch. 7, "Instructions in Domestic Relations,"
        and ch. 13, "The Popular Controversy over Women."]

04302. Wrightson, Keith and Levine, David. Poverty and Piety in
        an English Village: Terling, 1525-1700. New York:
        Academic Press, 1979.

(2)   Women

(a)   Contemporary

04303.   Alexis, Guillaume.   An Argument betwyxt man and woman.
(1525).   In The Feminist Controversy in the Renaissance.
Delmar, N.Y.:   Scholars' Facsimilies and Reprints, 1980.

04304.   Bansley, Charles.   A Tretyse Shrewing and Declaring the Pryde
and Abuse of Women Now a Dayes by Charles Bansley.   Reprint.
London: Percy Society, 1942.

04305.   More, Edward.   "A Lytle and Bryefe Treatyse, Called the Defence
of Women."   In Select Pieces of Early Popular Poetry, edited
by E.V. Utterson, 2:   95-140.   London: Longman, Hurst, Rees,
Orme and Brown, 1817.

(b)   Secondary

04306.   Dunn, Catherine M.   "The Changing Image of Woman in Renaissance
Society and Literature."   In What Manner Woman, edited by
Marlene Springer, pp. 15-38.   New York: New York University
Press, 1977.

04307.   Einstein, Lewis.   "The Evolution of Woman."   In Tudor
Ideals, pp. 124-131.   New York: Russell and Russell Inc.
1962.

04308.   Murray, Lucy Hunter.   The Ideal of the Court Lady, 1561-1625.
Chicago: University Libraries, 1938.

04309.   Wilson, Violet.   Society Women of Shakespeare's Time.   1924.
Reprint.   Port Washington, N.Y.:   Kennikat Press, 1970.

b)   Demography

04310.   Campbell, B.M.S.   "Population Change and the Genesis of
common fields on a Norfolk Manor."   Economic History
Review 33 (May 1980): 174-192.

04311. Cornwall, Julian. "English Population in the Early Sixteenth
        Century." Economic History Review 2nd ser. 23 (April 1970):
        32-44.

04312. Finlay, Roger A. P. "Gateways to Death? London Child Morta-
        lity Experience 1570-1653." Annales de demographie
        historique (1978): 104-134.

04313. _____. "Population and Fertility in London, 1580-
        1650." Journal of Family History 4 (Spring 1979): 26-38.

04314. Jones, R. E. "Further Evidence on the decline of Infant
        Mortality in Pre-Industrial England: North Shropshire,
        1561-1810." Population Studies 34 (July 1980): 239-250.

04315. Rich, E. "The population of Elizabethan England." Economic
        History Review 2d ser. 2 (1950): 247-265.

04316. Sutherland, Ian. "When was the Great Plague? Mortality in
        London, 1563 to 1665." In Population and Social Change,
        edited by D. V. Glass and Roger Reville, pp. 287-320. New
        York: Crane, Russak, 1972.

        Also refer to #4603.

                        c) Family

                    (1) Non-specific

04317. Bacquet, P. "Le concept de 'famille' à l'époque de la
        Renaissance." Recherches anglaises et americaines 8 (1975):
        7-12.

04318. Berlatsky, Joel. "Marriage and Family in a Tudor Elite:
        Familial Patterns of Elizabethan Bishops." Journal of Family
        History 3 (Spring 1978): 6-22.

04319. Chaytor, Miranda. "Household and Kinship: Ryton in the
        Late Sixteenth and Early Seventeenth Centuries." History
        Workshop 10 (Autumn 1980): 25-60.

04320. Einstein, Lewis. "The Family." In Tudor Ideals, pp. 244-
        251. New York: Russell Russell, 1962.

04321. Knappen, Marshall Mason. Tudor Puritanism. Chicago: Univer-
        sity of Chicago Press, 1939.
        [See especially ch. 5, "Domestic Life," pp. 451-466.]

04322   Lacassagne, C. "La famille dans l'oeuvre de l'évêque Hall
          (1574-1656)." Recherches anglaises et americaines 8 (1975):
          41-53.

04323.   Powell, Chilton Latham. English Domestic Relations, 1487-1653;
          A Study of Matrimony and Family Life. New York: Columbia
          University Press, 1917.

04324.   Schofield, R. S. "La reconstitution de la famille par ordinateur."
          Annales: Economies, Societes, Civilisations 27 (1972):
          1071-1082.

04325.   Stone, Lawrence. The Crisis of the Aristocracy, 1558-1641.
          New York: Oxford University Press, 1965.
          [See especially ch. 11, "Marriage and the Family,"
          pp. 269-302.]

04326.   Willan, T. S. "Wealth and Family." In Elizabethan Man-
          chester, pp. 81-105. Manchester: Printed for the
          Chetham Society, 1980.

04327.   Winchester, Barbara. Tudor Family Portrait. London: Jonathan
          Cape, 1955.

          Also refer to #4603.

                         (2) Childhood

04328.   Berry, B.M. "The First English Pediatricians and Tudor Atti-
          tudes Toward Childhood." Journal of the History of Ideas
          25 (1974): 561-577.

04329.   Hair, P.E.H. "Homicide, Infanticide, and Child Assault in
          Late Tudor Middlesex." Local Population Studies 9 (1972):
          43-46.

04330.   Levine, David and Wrightson, Keith. "The social context of
          illegitimacy in early modern England." In Bastardy and its
          Comparative History, edited by Peter Laslett, Karla Ooster-
          veen, and Richard M. Smith, pp. 158-175. Cambridge, Mass.:
          Harvard University Press, 1980.

04331.   Macfarlane, Alan. "Illegitimacy and illegitimates in
          English history." In Bastardy and its Comparative History,
          edited by Peter Laslett, Karla Oosterveen, and Richard M.
          Smith, pp. 71-85. Cambridge, Mass.: Harvard University
          Press, 1980.

04332.   Pinchbeck, Ivy. "The State and the Child in Sixteenth Century
          England." British Journal of Sociology 7 (1956): 273-385;
          8 (1957): 59-74.

04333.   _____, and Hewitt, Margaret. Children in English
            Society from Tudor Times to the Eighteenth Century. London:
            Routledge and Kegan Paul, 1969.

04334.   Tucker, M.J. "The Child as Beginning and End: Fifteenth and
            Sixteenth Century English Childhood." In The History of
            Childhood, edited by Lloyd de Mause, pp. 229-258. New York:
            Harper Torchbooks, Harper and Row, 1975.

            Also refer to #4264, 4603.

                            d) Marriage

04335.   Ashley, Maurice. The Stuarts in Love with Some Reflections on
            Love and Marriage in the Sixteenth and Seventeenth Centuries.
            London: Hodder and Stoughton, 1963.

04336.   Burgess, Anthony. "Shakespeare's Marriage." Prose 1 (1970):
            45-62.

04337.   Carlton, Charles. "The Widow's Tale: Male Myths and Female
            Reality in Sixteenth and Seventeenth Century England."
            Albion 10 (Summer 1978): 118-129.

04338.   Furnivall, F.J., ed. Child-Marriages, Divorces, and Ratifi-
            cations (and etc.) in the Diocese of Chester, A.D. 1561-1566.
            Early English Text Society, Original Series, no. 108. London:
            Kegan Paul, Trench, Trubner and Co., 1897.

04339.   Goode, William J. "Marriage Among the English Nobility in the
            Sixteenth and Seventeenth Centuries: A Comment." Comparative
            Studies in Society and History 3 (1960-1961): 207-214.

04340.   Harding, Davis P. "Elizabethan Betrothals and 'Measure for
            Measure'." Journal of English and Germanic Philology 49
            (1950): 139-158.

04341.   Hay, William. William Hay's Lectures on Marriage. Trans-
            lated and edited by John C. Barry. Edinburgh: Stair
            Society, 1967.

04342.   Hurstfield, Joel. The Queen's Wards: Wardship and Marriage
            under Elizabeth I. Cambridge, Mass.: Harvard University
            Press, 1958.

04343.   _____. "Wardship and Marriage under Elizabeth I."
            History Today 4 (September 1954): 605-612.

04344.   Jackson, Donald. Intermarriage in Ireland, 1550-1650. Minnea-
            polis: Cultural and Educational Productions, 1970.

04345.   Morell, C.C.   "Tudor Marriages and Infantile Mortality."
         Journal of State Medicine 43 (1935):   173-181.

04346.   Saffady, William.   "The Effects of Childhood Bereavement and
         Parental Remarriage in Sixteenth-Century England: The Case
         of Thomas More."   History of Childhood Quarterly 1 (1973-
         1974):   310-336.

04347.   Stone, Lawrence.   "Marriage among the English Nobility in the
         16th and 17th Centuries."   Comparative Studies in Society and
         History 2 (January 1961):   182-206.   Also in The Family: Its
         Structure and Functions, edited by Rose Laub Coser, pp. 153-
         183.   New York: St. Martin's, 1964.

04348.   Yost, John K. "Changing Attitudes toward Married Life in Civic
         and Christian Humanism."   Occasional Papers of the American
         Society for Reformation Research 1 (1977):   151-166.

04349.   _____. "The Value of Married Life for the Social Order
         in the Early English Renaissance."   Societas 6 (Winter 1976):
         25-39.

         Also refer to #4235, 4249, 4318, 4323.

e)   Sex Life and Morals

04350.   Greene, Robert.   "A Disputation between a He-Cony-Catcher and
         a She-Cony-Catcher, 1592."   In The Elizabethan Underworld,
         edited by A.V. Judges, pp. 206-247.   New York: E.P. Dutton
         and Company, 1930.

04351.   Guerra, F.   "Sex and Drugs in the Sixteenth Century."   British
         Journal of Addiction 18 (September 1974):   273-287.

04352.   Judges, A.V., ed.   The Elizabethan Underworld.   New York: E.P.
         Dutton and Co., 1930

         Also refer to #4090, 4295, 4335.

f)   Fashion/Manners

04353.   Cunnington, Cecil Willett.   Handbook of English Costume in
         the Sixteenth Century.   London: Faber and Faber, 1954.

04354.   Gosson, Stephen.   Pleasant Quippes for Vpstart Newfangled
         Gentlewomen.   1596.   Reprint.   Oxford, Ohio: Anchor Press,
         1942.

04355.   LaMar, Virginia A. English Dress in the Age of Shakespeare.
          Washington, D.C.: Folger Shakespeare Library, 1958.

04356.   Weigall, Rachel. "An Elizabethan Gentlewoman." Quarterly
          Review 215 (July 1911): 119-138.

g) Health/Medical

04357.   Forbes, Thomas Rogers. "The Regulation of English Midwives
          in the Sixteenth and Seventeenth Centuries." Medical History
          8 (July 1964): 235-244.

04358.   Hitchcock, James. "A Sixteenth Century Midwife's License."
          Bulletin of the History of Medicine 41 (January-February
          1967): 75-76.

04359.   Maclennan, Hector. "A Gynaecologist Looks at the Tudors."
          Medical History 11 (1967): 66-74.

04360.   Schnucker, Robert V. "Elizabethan Birth Control and Puritan
          Attitudes." Journal of Interdisciplinary History 5 (Spring
          1975): 655-668. Also in Marriage and Fertility, edited
          by Robert I. Rotberg and Theodore K. Rabb, pp. 71-83.
          Princeton, N.J.: Princeton University Press, 1980.

7. CULTURAL

"Great things by reason of my sexe, I may not doe."
                    Anne Locke

a) Education

(1) Contemporary

04361.   Ascham, Roger. The Scholemaster. Edited by Edward Arber.
          1570. Reprint. London: Constable, 1927.

04362.   Hyrde, Richard. "On the Education of Women." In Vives and
          the Renaiscence Education of Women, edited by Foster Watson,
          pp. 159-173. New York: Longmans, Green and Co., 1912.

04363.   _____. "A Plea for Learned Women." Moreana 13
          (February 1967): 5-24.

04364.   More, Sir Thomas.   "The School of Sir Thomas More."   In <u>Vives</u>
         <u>and the Renaiscence Education of Women</u>, edited by Foster
         Watson, pp. 175-194.   New York: Longmans, Green and Co., 1912.

                        (2)   Secondary

04365.   Axon, William E.A.   "The Lady Margaret as a Lover of Litera-
         ture."   <u>Library</u> n.s. 8 (1907):   34-41.

04366.   Bayne, Diane Valeri.   "The Instruction of a Christian Woman:
         Richard Hyrde and the Thomas More Circle."   <u>Moreana</u> 45
         (February 1975):   5-15.

04367.   Charlton, Kenneth.   <u>Education in Renaissance England</u>.   Toronto:
         University of Toronto Press, 1965.
         [See especially pp. 205-214.]

04368.   Goldsmith, Robert Hillis.   "My Lady Tongue: The Witty Women
         of the Renaissance."   <u>Illinois English Quarterly</u> 34 (Fall
         1972):   52-64.

04369.   Murray, Francis G.   "Feminine Spirituality in the More House-
         hold."   <u>Moreana</u> 27-28 (1957-1958):   92-102.

04370.   Wright, Louis B.   "The Reading of Renaissance English Women."
         <u>Studies in Philology</u> 28 (1931):   671-688.

                        b)   Literature

                        (1)   Non-specific

04371.   Blackburn, William.   "Lady Magdalene Herbert and her Son George."
         <u>South Atlantic Quarterly</u> 50 (1951):   378-388.

04372.   Fritz, Angela McCourt.   "The Novel Women: Origins of the
         Feminist Literary Tradition in England and France."   In
         <u>New Research on Women at the University of Michigan</u>,
         edited by Dorothy G. McGuigan, pp. 20-46.   Ann Arbor,
         Mich.: University of Michigan, Center for Continuing
         Education of Women, 1974.

04373.   Nathan, Norman.   "Portia, Nerissa, and Female Friendship."
         <u>Topic</u> 7 (1964):   56-60.

04374.   Pearson, Lu Emily.   <u>Elizabethan Love Conventions</u>.   Berkeley:
         University of California Press, 1933.

04375. Pratt, Samuel. "Jane Shore and the Elizabethan: Some Facts
        and Speculation." Texas Studies in Literature and Language
        11 (1970): 1293-1306.

04376. Rawson, Maud Stepney. Penelope Rich and Her Circle. London:
        Hutchinson and Co., 1911.

04377. Smith, Malcolm C. "Ronsard and Queen Elizabeth I." Biblio-
        theque d'humanisme et renaissance 29 (1967): 93-119.

04378. Travitsky, Betty, ed. The Paradise of Women. Writings by
        Englishwomen of the Renaissance. Contributions in
        Women's Studies, no. 22. Westport, Conn.: Greenwood
        Press, 1981.

04379. Wood, James O. "Woman with a Horn." Huntington Library
        Quarterly 29 (1966): 295-300.

04380. Wright, Celeste Turner. "The Amazons in Elizabethan Litera-
        ture." Studies in Philology 37 (1940): 433-456.

        Also refer to #3344.

(2) Drama

(a) Women

04381. Binns, J.W. "Women or Transvestites on the Elizabethan Stage?:
        An Oxford Controversy." Sixteenth Century Journal 5 (October
        1974): 95-120.

04382. Bradford, Gamaliel. "The Women of Middleton and Webster."
        Sewanee Review 29 (1921): 14-29.

04383. Brustein, Robert. "The Monstrous Regiment of Women: Sources
        for the Satiric View of the Court Lady in English Drama."
        Renaissance and Modern Essays 48 (1966): 35-50.

04384. Fletcher, John. The Woman's Prize or the Tamer Tamed. Edited
        by George B. Ferguson. The Hague: Mouton, 1966.

04385. Gagen, Jean Elizabeth. The New Women: Her Emergence in En-
        glish Drama 1600-1730. New York: Twayne Publishers, 1954.

04386. Greene, David H. "Lady Lumley and Greek Tragedy". Classical
        Journal 36 (1941): 537-547.

04387. Levin, Richard, "Nuns and 'nunnery' in Elizabethan Drama."
        Notes and Queries 213 (1968): 248-249.

04388. Mason, Eudo C. "Satire on Women and Sex in Elizabethan Tragedy."
        English Studies 31 (1950): 1-10.

04389. Schoenbaum, Samuel. "'The Widow's Tears' and the Other Chap-
        man." Huntington Library Quarterly 23 (1960): 321-338.

04390. Thorp, Willard. The Triumph of Realism in Elizabethan Drama,
        1558-1612. Princeton: University Press, 1928.
        [See especially ch. 1, pt. 2, "The Position of Women in
        Elizabethan Drama."]

04391. Ure, Peter. "Marriage and Domestic Drama in Heywood and
        Ford." English Studies 32 (1951): 200-216.

                        (b) Shakespeare

04392. Acheson, Arthur. Mistress Davenant: The Dark Lady of the
        Sonnets. New York: W.M. Hill, 1913.

04393. Beckman, M. B. "The Figure of Rosalind in As You Like It."
        Shakespeare Quarterly 29 (Winter 1978): 44-51.

04394. Brown, Ivor. The Women in Shakespeare's Life. London: Bodley
        Head Ltd., 1968.

04395. Dusinberre, Juliet. Shakespeare and the Nature of Woman. New
        York: Barnes and Noble, 1975.

04396. Gerwig, George W. Shakespeare's Ideals of Womanhood. New
        York: Joycroft, 1929.

04397. Gilbert, Sandra M. and Gubar, Susan. Shakespeare's Sisters:
        Feminist Essays on Women Poets. Bloomington, Ind.:
        Indiana University Press, 1979.

04398. Giles, Henry. Human Life in Shakespeare. Boston: Lee and
        Shepard, 1887.
        [See especially "Women in Shakespeare," pp. 134-171.]

04399. Harris, Frank. Women of Shakespeare. New York: Horizon
        Press, 1970.

04400. Heine, Heinrich. Shakespeare's Maidens and Women. Translated
        by Charles Godfrey Leland. New York: E.P. Dutton, 1906.

04401. Herford, Charles H. Shakespeare's Treatment of Love and
        Marriage and Other Essays. London: T.F. Unwin, 1921.

04402. Horne, Herman Harrell. Shakespeare's Philosophy of Love.
        Raleigh, N.C.: Edwards-Broughton Co., 1945.

04403. Hutcheson, W.J. Fraser. Shakespeare's Other Anne: A Short
        Account of the Life and Works of Anne Whateley of Beck, A
        Sister of the Order of St. Clare, Who Nearly Married William
        Shakespeare in November 1582 A.D. Glasgow: MacLellan, 1950.

04404. Jameson, Anna Brownell (Murphy). Shakespeare's Heroines:
        Characteristics of Women, Moral, Poetical and Historical.
        London: G. Bell and Sons, 1924.

04405. Lenz, Carolyn Ruth; Green, Gayle; and, Neely, Carol Thomas,
        eds. The Woman's Part: Feminist Criticism of Shakespeare.
        Urbana: University of Illinois Press, 1980.

04406. Mackenzie, Agnes Mure. The Women in Shakespeare's Plays: A
        Critical Study from the Dramatic and the Psychological Point
        of View and in Relation to the Development of Shakespeare's
        Art. New York: Doubleday, 1924.

04407. Pitt, Angela. Shakespeare's Women. Totowa, N.J.: Barnes
        and Noble, 1981.

04408. Ross, William. The Story of Anne Whateley and William
        Shaxpere. London: Holmes, 1940.

04409. Steensma, Robert C. "Shakespeare and Women: A Bibliography."
        Shakespeare Newsletter 11 (1962): 12.

04410. Stoll, E.E. Shakespeare's Young Lovers. New York: Oxford
        University Press, 1937.
        [See especially "Shakespeare's Maidens," pp. 45-118.]

        Also refer to #4414.

                          (3) Poetry

                          (a) Women

04411. Bradford, Gamaliel. "Elizabethan Women." Poet Lore 12 (1900):
        392-405.

04412. Falks, Cyril. "Penelope Rich and the Poets." In Essays by
        Divers Hands, edited by Angela Thirhell, 28: 123-137.
        Oxford: University Press, 1956.

04413. Freer, Coburn. "The Countess of Pembroke in a World of Words."
        Style 5 (1971): 37-56.

04414. Leech, Clifford. "Venus and Her Nun: Portraits of Women in
        Love by Shakespeare and Marlowe." Studies in English Litera-
        ture 5 (1965): 247-268.

04415. Oakshott, Walter. The Queen and the Poet. London: Faber, 1960.

04416. Tucker, M. J. "The Ladies in Skeleton's 'Garland of Laurel.'"
        Renaissance Quarterly 22 (Winter 1969): 333-345.

(b) Individuals

[1] JOHN DONNE

04417. Hughes, Richard E. "The Woman in Donne's Anniversaires."
Journal of English Literary History 34 (1967): 307-326.

04418. Yoklavich, J. "Donne and the Countess of Huntington."
Philological Quarterly 43 (1964): 283-288.

[2] PHILIP SIDNEY

04419. Hudson, Hoyt H. "Penelope Devereux as Sidney's Stella."
Huntington Library Bulletin 7 (1935): 89-129.

04420. Robertson, Jean. "Sir Philip Sidney and Lady Penelope Rich."
Review of English Studies 15 (1964): 296-297.

[3] EDMUND SPENSER

04421. Hamer, Douglas. "Spenser's Marriage." Review of English
Studies 7 (1931): 271-290.

04422. McLane, Paul E. "The Death of a Queen: Spenser's Dido as
Elizabeth." Huntington Library Quarterly 18 (1954): 1-11.

04423. _____. "Spenser's Chloris: The Countess of Derby."
Huntington Library Quarterly 24 (1961): 145-150.

04424. Neill, Kerby. "Spenser's Acrasia and Mary Queen of Scots."
Publications of the Modern Language Association 60 (1945):
682-688.

(4) Prose

(a) Thomas More

[1] CONTEMPORARY

04425. More, Sir Thomas. Utopia. Translated and edited by Robert M.
Adams. New York: Norton and Co., 1975.

[2] SECONDARY

04426.   Khanna, Lee Cullen. "Images of Women in Thomas More's Poetry."
Albion 10 Supplement (1978): 78-88.

04427.   _____. "No Less Real than Ideal: Images of Women
in More's Work." Moreana 14 (December 1977): 35-51.

Also refer to #4091, 4092, 4364, 4366, 4369.

(b) Others

04428.   Rowe, Kenneth T. "The Countess of Pembroke's Editorship of
the Arcadia." Publications of the Modern Language Association
54 (1939): 122-138.

04429.   Schlaugh, Margaret. "Mary of Nijmeghen (The Female Faust) in
an English Prose Version of the Early Tudor Period." Philo-
logica Pragensia 6 (1963): 4-11.

C. FRANCE

1. SURVEYS

"Men have larger heads and therefore more brains and sense
than woman."   Jean Bodin

a) Women

(1) Contemporary

04430.   Billon, François de. Le Fort inexpugnable de l'honneur du sexe
féminin, 1555. Reprint. New York: Johnson Reprint, 1970.

04431.   Postel, Guillaume. Les Tres merveilleuses victories des femmes
du nouveau-monde. Geneva: Slatkine Reprints, 1970.

(2) Secondary

04432. Mandach, Laure de. Portraits de Femmes: Renaissance et Ré-
        forme. Geneva: Labor et Filles, 1952.

04433. Mettra, Claude. "La femme de la renaissance. La française au
        XVIe siècle." In Histoire mondiale de la femme, edited by
        Pierre Grimal, vol. 2: 305-341. Paris: Nouvelle librairie
        de France, 1966.

04434. Sichel, Edith. Women and Men of the French Renaissance. 1901.
        Reprint. Port Washington, N.Y.: Kennikat Press, 1970.

04435. Wiley, W.L. The Gentleman of Renaissance France. Cambridge:
        Harvard University Press, 1954.
        [See especially ch. 11, "The Question of Women," pp. 195-
        213.]

Also refer to #4074.

2. POLITICAL

"It might seem bad enough that she is a woman, but one has
to add quickly that she is a foreigner, and what is more a
Florentine and a commoner."
                                    Michele Suriana, 1562
                                    of Catherine de Medici

a) Legal

04436. Portemer, Jean. "Le Statut de la femme en France depuis la
        reformation des coutumes jusqu'à la rédaction la code civil."
        Recueils de la Société Jean Bodin 12 (1962): 447-497.

Also refer to #4621, 4624, 3374, 3377.

b) Feminism

04437. Bascou-Vance, P. "Les conditions des femmes en France et le
        progrès des idées féministes du XVIe au XVIIIe siècle."
        L'Information historique 28 (1966): 139-144.

04438. Ivanoff, Nicola. "Le Roland furieux et la querelle des femmes
        au XVIe siècle." Revue du XVIe siècle 9 (1932-1933): 262-
        272.

04439. Screech, Michael A. "The Illusion of Postel's Feminism."
        Journal of the Warburg and Courtauld Institutes 16 (1953):
        162-170.

c) Political Roles

(1) Women

04440. Armaillé, Marie Celestine Amelie (de Segur), comtesse d'.
        Catherine de Bourbon. Paris: Didier et c^{ie}, 1872.

04441. Chabot, Comte de. "Une Cour huguenote en Bas-Poitou Catherine
        de Parthenay, Duchesse de Rohan." Revue de la renaissance
        5 (1905): 63-71, 97-107. Reprint. Geneva: Slatkine Re-
        prints, 1968.

04442. Champion, Pierre. La dauphine mélancolique. Paris: M.
        Lesage, 1927.

04443. Delaborde, Jules, Comte. Charlotte de Bourbon, Princesse
        d'Orange. Paris: Fischbacher, 1888.

04444. _____. Eleonore de Royé, Princesse de Conde,
        1535-1564. Paris: Sandon et Fischbacher, 1876.

04445. _____. Louise de Coligny, Princesse d'Orange.
        Paris: Fischbacher, 1890.

04446. Derblay, Claude. Une Héroïne de Brantôme: Renée de Bussy
        d'Amboise, maréchale de Balagney, princesse de Cambrai.
        Paris: Plon, 1935.

04447. Fawcett, Millicent Garrett. Five Famous French Women.
        London: Cassell and Co., Ltd., 1905.

04448. Fonda, Jean. "L'infortunee Catherine de Bourbon, soeur unique
        d'Henri IV." Revue de l'Agenais 93 (1967): 137-150.

04449. Forster, Ann M.C. The Good Duchess: Joan of France (1464-
        1505). New York: P.J. Kennedy and Sons, 1950.

04450. Heim, Maurice. François Ier et les femmes. Paris: Gallimard,
        1956.

04451. Henrard, P. Henri IV et la princesse de Conde. Brussels:
        Merzbach & Falk, 1885.

04452. Imbert de Saint Armand, Arthur Leon. Women of the Valois Court. Translated by Elizabeth Martin. New York: C. Scribner's Sons, 1909.

04453. La Batut, Guy de. Les Amours des rois de France: Henri IV. Paris: Editions Montaigne, 1928.

04454. La Garanderie, Paul de. "Marie d'Anjou, Reine de France (1404-1433)." Mémoires de l'académie des sciences, belles-lettres et arts d'arts d'angers 9 (1965) 1966: 27-41.

04455. Lescure, Mathurin Francois Adolphe de. Les amours de François I. Paris: n.p., 1865.

04456. _____. Les Amours de Henri IV. Paris: A. Fauve, 1864.

04457. Levis Mirepoix, Duc de. "François Ier entre trois femmes." Historia 335 (October 1974): 66-73.

04458. Marshall, Rosalind K. Mary of Guise. London: Collins, 1977.

04459. Moeller, Charles Clemente Auguste. Eleonore d'Autriche et de Bourgogne, reine de France. Paris: Thorin, 1895.

04460. Orliac, Jehanne d'. Anne de Beaujeu, roi de France. Paris: Plon Nourrit et Cie, 1926.

04461. _____. The Lady of Beauty, Agnes Sorel, First Royal Favourite of France. Philadelphia: J.B. Lippincott, 1931.

04462. _____. Yolande d'Anjou, la reine des quatres royaumes. Paris: Plon, 1933.

04463. Pelicier, Paul. Essai sur le gouvernement de la dame de Beaujeu, 1483-1491. 1882. Reprint. Geneva: Slatkine, 1975-1976.

04464. Pimodan, Gabriel de. La Mere des Guise: Antoinette de Bourbon 1494-1583. 1925. Reprint. Geneva: Slatkine, 1976.

04465. Rat, Maurice. "La vicomtesse d'Auchy, le grand amour de M. de Malherbe." Revue des deux mondes (October 1965): 445-450.

04466. Ritter, Raymond. Une Dame de chevalerie, Corisande d'Andoins, Comtesse de Guiche. 1936. Paris: A. Michel, 1959.

04467. Sherman, Claire Richter. "The Queen in Charles V's 'Coronation Book': Jeanne de Bourbon and the 'Ordo ad reginam benedicendam'." Viator 8 (1977): 255-298.

Also refer to #3385, 4614, 4774.

(2) Individuals

(a) Jeanne d'Albret

04468. Castries, Duc de. "Jeanne d'Albret." Nouvelle revue de deux
mondes (April 1974): 32-46.

04469. Cazaux, Yves. Jeanne d'Albret. Paris: Editions Albin Michel,
1973.

04470. _____. "Pour un nouveau portrait de Jeanne d'Albret."
Bulletin de la société de l'histoire du protestantisme
français 119 (October-November-December 1973): 503-528.

04471. Freer, Martha. The Life of Jeanne d'Albret, Queen of Navarre.
London: Hurst and Blackett, 1862.

04472. Nabonne, Bernard. Jeanne d'Albret. Paris: Hachette, 1945.

04473. Roelker, Nancy Lyman. Queen of Navarre: Jeanne d'Albret,
1528-1572. Cambridge, Mass.: Belknap Press of Harvard
University, 1968.

04474. Ruble, Alphonse de. Antoine de Bourbon et Jeanne d'Albret.
1881-1886. Reprint. Geneva: Slatkine, 1975-1976.

04475. _____. Jeanne d'Albret et la guerre civile. 1897.
Reprint. Geneva: Slatkine, 1975-1976.

04476. _____. Le Mariage de Jeanne d'Albret. 1877.
Reprint. Geneva: Slatkine, 1975-1976.

(b) Anne de Bretagne

04477. Bailly, Auguste. Anne de Bretagne, femme de Charles VIII et
de Louis XII. Paris: Les Editions de France, 1940.

04478. Brie, Germain de. "Les epitaphes latines d'Anne de Bretagne."
Annales de Bretagne 74 (1967): 377-396.

04479. Butler, Mildred Allen. Twice a Queen of France. Anne of
Brittany. New York: Funk and Wagnalls Co., 1967.

04480. Costello, Louise Stuart. Memoirs of Anne, Duchess of Brittany,
Twice Queen of France. London: W. and F.C. Cash, 1855.

04481. Gabory, Emile. L'Union de la Bretagne et de la France, Anne
de Bretagne, duchess et reine. Paris: Plon et Nourrit,
1941.

04482. La Croix, Paul. Louis XII et Anne de Bretagne. Paris:
        G. Hurtrel, 1882.

04483. Le Boterf, Hervé. Anne de Bretagne. Paris: Editions France-
        Empire, 1976.

04484. Leroux de Lincy, Antoine Jean Victor. Vie de la reine Anne
        de Bretagne. Paris: L. Curmer, 1861.

04485. Mauny, Michel de. Anne de Bretagne. Rennes: Editions
        Kanevedenn, 1976.

04486. Salmon, J. H. M. "The Regent and the Duchesse; Anne de
        Beaujeu and Anne de Bretagne." History Today 16 (April
        1960): 341-348.

04487. Segalen, A. P. "Anne de Bretagne dans les lettres françaises
        au XVIIe siècle." Annales de Bretagne 84 (July 1977):
        369-390.

04488. Toudouze, George G. Anne de Bretagne, duchess de Bretagne et
        reine de France. Paris: Andre Bonne, 1959.

                    (c)   Gabrielle d'Estrées

04489. Desclozeaux, A. Gabrielle d'Estrées. Paris: H. Champion,
        1889.

04490. Erlanger, Phillippe. Gabrielle d'Estrées, femme fatale.
        Paris: J. Dullis, 1975.

04491. Gerson, Noel Bertram. Lady of France, A Biography of Gabrielle
        d'Estrées, Mistress of Henry the Great. London: Redman, 1964.

04492. Ritter, Raymond. La Vie de Gabrielle d'Estrées. Paris: Le
        Cercle Historia, 1964.

        Also refer to #4456.

                    (d)   Catherine de Medici

04493. Bouchot, Henri François. Catherine de Médicis. Paris: Goupil
        et Cie, 1899.

04494. Boulé, Alphonse. Catherine de Médicis et Coligny. Paris:
        H. Champion, 1913.

04495. Castelnau, Jacques Thomas de. Catherine de Médicis. Paris:
        Hachette, 1954.

04496.   Dodu, Gaston. "Le Drame conjugal de Catherine de Médicis."
          Revue des études historiques 96 (April-June 1930): 89-128.

04497.   Erlanger, Philippe. "Catherine de Medicis." Historia 340
          (March 1975): 98-109.

04498.   Galzy, Jeanne. Catherine de Medicis. Paris: Gallimard, 1936.

04499.   Héritier, Jean. Catherine de Medici. 1959 ed. Translated by
          Charlotte Haldane. New York: St. Martin's Press, 1963.

04500.   Jensen, DeLamar. "Catherine de Medici and her Florentine
          Friends." Sixteenth Century Journal 9 (July 1978): 57-74.

04501.   Luzzatti, Ivo. Catherine de Medici (1519-1589). Milan:
          A. Garzanti editore, 1939.

04502.   Mahoney, Irene. Madame Catherine. New York: Coward McCann
          and Geoghegan, 1975.

04503.   Mariejol, Jean Hippolyte. Catherine de Médici, 1519-1589.
          Paris: Hachette, 1920.

04504.   Remy, Jean-Charles. Catherine de Medicis ou la mere de trois
          rois. Lausanne: Editions Rencontre, 1965.

04505.   Roeder, Ralph. Catherine de Medici and the Lost Revolution.
          1937. Reprint. New York: Vintage Books, 1964.

04506.   Romier, Lucien. Le Royaume de Catherine de Medicis. La
          France à la veille des guerres de religion. 1925. Reprint.
          Geneva: Slatkine, 1975-1976.

04507.   Ross Williamson, Hugh. Catherine de Medici. New York: Viking
          Press, 1973.

04508.   Sichel, Edith. Catherine de Medici and the French Refor-
          mation. 1905. Reprint. London: Dawsons, 1969.

04509.   _____. The Later Years of Catherine de Medici. 1908.
          Reprint. London: Dawsons of Pall Mall, 1969.

04510.   Strage, Mark. Woman of Power, the Life and Times of Catherine
          de Medici. New York: Harcourt, Brace, Jovanovich, 1976.

04511.   Sutherland, N.M. Catherine de Medici and the Ancien Regime.
          London: Historical Association, 1966.

04512.   _____. "Catherine de Medici - Legend of the Wicked
          Italian Queen." Sixteenth Century Journal 9 (July 1978):
          45-56.

04513.   Van Dyke, Paul. Catherine de Medicis. 2 vols. New York:
          Scribners, 1924.

04514. Waldman, Milton. <u>Biography of a Family, Catherine de Medici and her Children</u>. Boston: Houghton-Mifflin, 1936.

04515. Watson, Francis. <u>The Life and Times of Catherine de Medici</u>. New York: D. Appleton-Century Co., 1935.

(e)   Marguerite of Navarre

04516. Angoulême, Marguerite de. <u>The Heptameron. Tales and Novels of Marguerite de Navarre</u>. Translated by Arthur Macheu. New York: Knopf, 1929.

04517. Atance, Félix R. "Les comédies profanes de Marguerite de Navarre: Aspects de la satire religieuse en France au XVI siècle." <u>Revue d'histoire et de philosophie religieuses</u> 56 (July 1976): 289-313.

04518. _____. "Les Religieux de l'Heptameron Marguerite de Navarre et les Novateurs." <u>Archiv für Reformationsgeschichte</u> 65 (1974): 185-210.

04519. Bambeck, Manfred. "Religiöse Skepsis bei Margarete von Navarra?" <u>Zeitschrift für französische Sprache und Literatur</u> 77 (1967): 12-22.

04520. Benson, Edward. "Marriage Ancestral and Conjugal in the <u>Heptameron</u>." <u>Journal of Medieval and Renaissance Studies</u> 9 (Fall 1979): 261-275.

04521. Castelnau, Jacques Thomas de. <u>Marguerite de Navarre</u>. Paris: le Cercle historia, 1969.

04522. Chamberlin, E.R. <u>Marguerite of Navarre</u>. New York: Dial Press, 1974.

04523. Febvre, Lucien. <u>Amour Sacre, Amour Profane. Autour de l'Heptameron</u>. Paris: Gallimard, 1971.

04524. Ferrière, Hector de la. <u>Marguerite d'Angoulême soeur de Francois I</u>^{er}. Paris: Aubry, 1862.

04525. _____. <u>Marguerite d'Angoulême une veritable abbesse de Jouarre</u>. Paris: C. Levy, 1891.

04526. Freer, Martha. <u>The Life of Marguerite d'Angouleme</u>. London: Hurst and Blackett, 1854.

04527. Gelernt, Jules. <u>World of Many Loves: The Heptameron of Marguerite de Navarre</u>. Chapel Hill: University of North Carolina Press, 1966.

04528. Heller, Henry. "Marguerite of Navarre and the Reformers of
       Meaux." Bibliotheque d'humanisme et renaissance 33 (1971):
       271-310.

04529. Jourda, Pierre. Marguerite d'Angoulême: Duchesse d'Alencon,
       Reine de Navarre (1493-1549): Etude biographie et litteraire.
       1930. Reprint. Geneva: Slatkine, 1978.

04530. Lebègue, Raymond. "Marguerite de Navarre et le theatre."
       Humanisme et renaissance 5 (1938): 330-333.

04531. Lefranc, Abel. Les Idées religieuses de Marguerite de Navarre.
       1898. Reprint. Geneva: Slatkine, 1969.

04532. _____. Marguerite de Navarre et le Platonisme de la
       Renaissance. Paris: E. Champion, 1914.

04533. _____. "Marguerite de Navarre et le Platonisme de la
       Renaissance." Bibliotheque de l'Ecole des Chartres 43 (1897):
       712-757; 59 (1898): 712-757.

04534. Mercieux, Pierre. La Reine de Navarre, Marguerite d'Angouleme.
       Paris: Calmann-Levy, 1900.

04535. Parturier, E. "Les sources du mysticisme de Marguerite de
       Navarre." Revue de la Renaissance 5 (1905): 1-16, 49-62.
       Reprint. Geneva: Slatkine Reprints, 1968.

04536. Phillips, M. Mann. "Marguerite de Navarre et Erasme: une
       reconsideration." Revue de litterature comparee 52
       (April-December 1978): 194-201.

04537. Putnam, Samuel. Marguerite of Navarre. New York: Coward-
       McCann, 1935.

04538. Ritter, Raymond. Les Solitudes de Marguerite de Navarre, 1527-
       1549. Paris: H. Champion, 1953.

04539. Rival, Paul. The Madcap Queen: The Story of Marguerite of
       Navarre. New York: G.P. Putnam's Sons, 1930.

04540. Sage, Pierre. "Le platonisme de Marguerite de Navarre."
       Travaux de linguistique et de littérature romanes de l'uni-
       versité de Strasbourg 7 (1969): 65-82.

04541. Telle, Emile Villemeur. L'Oeuvre de Marguerite d'Angoulême,
       reine de Navarre, et la querelle des femmes. Toulouse:
       Imprimerie toulousaine Lion et Fils, 1937.

(f) Diane de Poitiers

04542. Bardon, Françoise. Diane de Poitiers et le mythe de Diane.
Paris: Presses universitaires de France, 1963.

04543. Capefigue, J.B.H.R. Diane de Poitiers. Paris: Amyot, 1960.

04544. Erlanger, Philippe. Diane de Poitiers: Déesse de la
renaissance. Paris: Perrin, 1976.

04545. _____. "Diane de Poitiers, the Myth." Connoisseur 163 (1966): 83-87.

04546. Hay, Marie. Madame Dame Diane de Poitiers. London: J. and E.
Bumpus, 1900.

04547. Henderson, Helen W. The Enchantress. Boston: Houghton-
Mifflin Co., 1928.

04548. Orliac, Jehanne d'. The Moon Mistress, Diane de Poitiers,
grant senechalle de Normandy. Translated by F.M. Atkinson.
London: G.G. Harrap, 1931.

04549. Seely, Grace Hart. Diane the Huntress: the Life and Times
of Diane de Poitiers. New York: D. Appleton Century Co.,
1936.

(g) Louise de Savoy

04550. Arici, Zelmira. Luisa di Savoia Reggente di Francia 1476-1531.
Turin: G.B. Paravia and C., 1930.

04551. Bordeaux, Paule Henry. Louise de Savoye, "Roi" de France.
Paris: Perrin, 1971.

04552. Freeman, John F. "Louise of Savoy: A Case of Maternal Oppor-
tunism." Sixteenth Century Journal 3 (October 1972): 77-98.

04553. Griffiths, Gordon. "Louise of Savoy and Reform of the Church."
Sixteenth Century Journal 10 (Fall 1979): 29-36.

04554. Henry-Bordeaux, Paule. Louise de Savoie, regente et roi de
France. Paris: Plon, 1954.

04555. Jacqueton, Gilbert. La Politique extérieure de Louise de
Savoie. Relations diplomatiques de la France et de l'Angle-
terre pendant la captivite de Francois Ier, 1525-1526. 1892.
Reprint. Geneva: Slatkine, 1975-1976.

04556. Luzzatti, Ivo. <u>Luisa di Savoia, 1476-1531</u>. Bologna: Cappelli, 1951.

04557. Maulde de Claviere, R. de. <u>Louise de Savoy et Francois I</u>. Paris: n.p., 1895.

04558. Mayer, Lady Dorothy Moulton (Piper). <u>The Great Regent</u>. <u>The mother of Francois I</u>. New York: Funk and Wagnalls, 1967.

(h) Mary Tudor

04559. Brown, Mary Croom. <u>Mary Tudor, Queen of France</u>. New York: G. P. Putnam's Sons, 1911.

04560. Richardson, Walter Cecil. <u>Mary Tudor: The White Queen</u>. Seattle, Wash.: University of Washington Press, 1970.

Also refer to #4219-4220.

(i) Marguerite de Valois

04561. Babelon, Jean. <u>La Reine Margot</u>. Paris: 1965. Berger-Levrault, 1965.

04562. Delpech, Jeanine. "L'inoubliable reine Margot." <u>Nouvelles litteraires</u> (21 May 1953): 1-2.

04563. Donnay, Maurice Charles. <u>La Regina Margot</u>. Paris: Artheme Fayard, 1954.

04564. Ferrière, Hector de la. <u>Trois Amoureuses au seizième siècle: Francois de Rohan, Isabelle de Limeuil, la Reine Margot</u>. Paris: Calmann-Levy, 1885.

04565. Haldane, Charlotte. <u>The Queen of Hearts, Margaret of Valois, 'La Reine Margot,' 1553-1615</u>. Indianapolis: Bobbs-Merrill, 1968.

04566. Holban, Maria. "Autour du Livre d'Heures de Marguerite de Valios." In <u>Memoria lui Vasile Pârvan</u>, pp. 168-180. Bucharest: n.p., 1934.

04567. Mariéjol, Jean Hippolyte. <u>A Daughter of the Medicis</u>. New York: Harper and Bros., 1929.

04568. Merki, Charles. <u>La Reine Margot et la fin des Valois (1553-1615)</u>. Paris: Plon-Nourrit et Cie., 1905.

04569. Polignac, Hedwige de Chabannes, Princesse François de. <u>Marguerite de Valois, grande princesse, grand écrivain</u>. Paris: La Pensée universelle, 1973.

04570. Saint-Poncy, Léo. Histoire de Marguerite de Valois, reine de
        France et de Navarre. Paris: Gaume et Cie, 1887.

04571. Taylor, William Cooke, ed. Romantic Biography of the Age of
        Elizabeth. 1842. Reprint. New York: Arno Press, 1979.
        [Includes Margaret de Valois.]

04572. Tilley, Arthur Augustus. "The Literary Circle of Margaret
        of Navarre." In A Miscellany of Studies in Romantic Lang-
        uages and Literature Presented to Leon E. Kastner, edited
        by Mary Williams and James A. de Rothschild, pp. 518-531.
        Cambridge: W. Heffer & Sons, 1932.

04573. Vaissiere, Pierre de. "La jeunesse de la reine Margot."
        Humanisme et renaissance 7 (1940): 7-44 and 190-212.

04574. _____. "Reine sans couronne: la reine Margot
        a Paris." Revue des études historiques 105 (January-March
        1938): 17-44.

3. RELIGION

"Churches I saw rich, beautiful and old. And Altars deck'd
with images of silver and of gold. My heart was fil'd with
pleasure . . ."   Margaret of Navarre

a) Generic

04575. Bainton, Roland H. "The Role of Women in the Reformation."
        Archiv für Reformationsgeschichte 63 (1972): 141-142.

04576. Bremond, Henri. A Literary History of Religious Thought in
        France. 2 vols. New York: Macmillan Co., 1928.
        [See especially chs. 2, 4, 6 and 7.]

04577. Davis, Natalie Zemon. "City Women and Religious Change in
        Sixteenth-Century France." In A Sampler of Women's Studies,
        edited by Dorothy McGuigan, pp. 17-45. Ann Arbor, Mich.:
        University of Michigan Center for Continuing Education of
        Women, 1973. Also in Society and Culture in Early Modern
        France, edited by Natalie Zemon Davis, pp. 65-96. Stanford:
        University Press, 1975.

04578. Francis de Sales, Saint. Saint François de Sales et les
        femmes mariées. Edited by Marcelle Georges-Thomas. Intro-
        duction by Olivier de la Brosse et Henri Caffarel. Paris:
        Les Éditions du Cerf, 1967.

04579. Roelker, Nancy Lyman. "The Role of Noble Women in the French Reformation." Archiv für Reformationsgeschichte 63 (1972): 168-195.

04580. Schueller, Th. La femme et le saint. La femme et ses problemes d'après François de Sales. Paris: Les Editions Ouvrières, 1970.

b) Saints/Religious Women

04581. Broglie, Emmanuel, Prince de. La Bienheuruese Marie de l'Incarnation, Madame Acarie, 1566-1618. Paris: J. Gabalda, 1921.

04582. Richomme, Agnes. Sainte Germaine de Pibrac. Paris: Editions Fleurus, 1967.

04583. Sheppard, L.C. Barbe Acarie, Wife and Mystic. London: Burns Oates, 1953.

c) Monastic Life/Religious Orders

04584. Balde, Jean. Les dames de la Miséricorde. Paris: Editions Bernard Grasset, 1932.

04585. Martin, Herve. "Religieux mendicants et classes sociales en Bretagne aux XIVe et XVe siècles. Annales de Bretagne 82 (1975): 19-46.

04586. Ruutz-Rees, Caroline. "Renee, a sixteenth century nun." Romanic Review 13 (January-March 1922): 28-36.

d) Calvinism

04587. Bieler, Andre. L'Homme et la femme dans la morale calviniste. La Doctrine réformée sur l'amour, le marriage, le célibat, le divorce, l'adultère et la prostitution, considerée dans son cadre historique. Geneva: Labor et Fides, 1963.

04588. Roelker, Nancy Lyman. "The Appeal of Calvinism to French Noble Women in the Sixteenth Century." The Journal of Interdisciplinary History 2 (Spring 1972): 391-418.

e) Witchcraft

04589. Bouteiller, Marcelle. Sorciers et jeteurs de sort. Paris:
Libraire Plon, 1958.

04590. Delcambre, Etienne. Le concept de la sorcellerie dans le
duché de Lorraine au XVIe et au XVIIe siècles. 3 vols.
Nancy: Societe d'archéologie Lorraine, 1951.

04591. _____. Les Jeteurs de sort notamment dans
l'ancienne Lorraine. Nancy: Societe d'archaelogie Lorraine,
1950.

04592. Garrett, Clarke W. "Witches, Werewolves and Henry Boguet."
Proceedings of the Western Society for French History 4
(1976): 126-134.

04593. Monter, E. William. "French and Italian Witchcraft."
History Today 30 (November 1980): 31-35.

04594. _____. "Inflation and Witchcraft: the Case of
Jean Bodin." In Action and Conviction in Early Modern
Europe, edited by Theodore K. Rabb and Jerrold E. Seigel,
pp. 371-389. Princeton, N.J.: Princeton University Press,
1969.

04595. _____. Witchcraft in France and Switzerland:
The Borderlands during the Reformation. Ithaca, N.Y.:
Cornell University Press, 1976.

04596. Soman, Alfred. "The Parlement of Paris and the Great Witch
Hunt (1565-1640)." Sixteenth Century Journal 9 (July
1978): 31-44.

04597. Villette, Abbé Pierre. La Sorcellerie et sa repression dans
le nord de la France. Paris: La Pensée universelle, 1976.

Also refer to #4271.

4. SOCIAL

"Even though the dignity of marriage hides the shame of
incontinence, this is not to say that marriage is an invita-
tion to sensuality."   Calvin

a) Generic

04598. Bodin, Jean. The Six Books of a Commonweale. 1606. Reprint. Edited and translated by Kenneth Douglas McRae. Cambridge, Mass.: Harvard University Press, 1962.

04599. Erlanger, Philippe. La Vie quotidienne sous Henri IV. Paris: Hachette, 1958.

04600. Febvre, Lucien. Life in Renaissance France. Translated by Marian Rothsteinn. Cambridge, Mass.: Harvard University Press, 1977.

04601. Rat, Maurice. Dames et bourgeoises amoureuses et galantes du XVIe siècle. Paris: Plon, 1955.

04602. Tenenti, Alberto. Il senso della morte e l'amore della vita nel Rinascimento. Turin: G. Einaudi, 1957.

Also refer to #3524.

b) Demography

04603. Armengaud, Andre. La Famille et l'enfant en France et en Angleterre du XVIe au XVIIIe siècle: aspects démographiques. Paris: Société d'édition d'enseignement supérieur, 1975.

04604. Challamel, Jean Bernard. La Population d'Annecy du XVIe siecle. Grenoble: Diplome d'Etudes Supérieures, 1967.

04605. Croix, Alain. "La démographie du pays nantais au XVIe siècle." Annales de démographie historique(1967): 63-90.

04606. _____. Nantes et le pays nantais au XVIe siècle: étude démographique. Paris: S.E.V.P.E.N., 1974.

04607. Gascon, Richard. "Immigration et croissance urbaine au XVIe siècle: l'exemple de Lyon." Annales: économies, sociétés, civilisations 25 (July-August 1970): 988-1001.

04608. Goubert, Pierre. "Recent Theories and Research in French Population between 1500 and 1700." In Population in History, edited by David V. Glass and D.E.C. Eversley, pp. 457-473. Chicago: Aldine Publishing Co., 1965.

c) Family

04609.   Davis, Natalie Zemon. "Ghosts, Kin, and Progeny: Some Features
         of Family Life in Early Modern France." Daedalus 106 (Spring
         1977): 87-114.

04610.   Le Roy Ladurie, Emmanuel. "Family structures and inheritance
         customs in sixteenth century France." In Family and Society,
         edited by Robert Forster and Orest Ranum, pp. 75-103.
         Baltimore: Johns Hopkins University Press, 1976. Also in
         Family and Inheritance Rural Society in Western Europe,
         1200-1800, edited by Jack Goody, Joan Thirsk, and E. P.
         Thompson, pp. 37-70. Cambridge, Mass.: University Press,
         1976. Also in Annales: économies, sociétés, civilisations
         27 (1972): 825-846.

04611.   Mandrou, Robert. "Basic forces for solidarity: the married
         couple and the family." In Introduction to Modern France,
         1500-1640. An Essay in Historical Psychology, pp. 83-89.
         New York: Harper and Row, 1977.

04612.   Muchembled, Robert. "Famille, amour et mariage: mentalités
         et comportements des nobles artesiens à l'époque de Philippe
         II." Revue d'histoire moderne et contemporaine 22 (April-
         June 1975):   233-261.

04613.   Ribbe, Charles. Une Famille au XVIe siècle. Tours: A. Mame
         et Fils, 1879.

         Also refer to #3551, 3557, 3563, 3374. 4321, 4603.

d) Marriage

04614.   Armstrong, C.A.J. "La politique matrimoniale des ducs de
         Bourgogne de la maison de Valois." Annales de Bourgogne
         40.1 (1968): 5-58; 40.2 (1968): 1-139.

04615.   Bels, Pierre. "La formation du lien de mariage dans l'église
         protestante française (XVIe et XVIIe siècle)." Le Droit des
         gens mariés 27 (1966): 331-344.

04616.   _____. Le Mariage des protestants français jusqu'en
         1685. Paris: Librairie générale de droit et de jurisprudence,
         1968.

04617. Canestrier, Paul. "La dot en Provence au XVIe siècle d'après des documents dialectaux." Bulletin philologique et historique du comité des travaux historiques et scientifiques 1955 (1953-1954): 279-292.

04618. Coudert, J. "Le mariage dans le diocèse de Toul au XVIe siècle." Annales de l'Est 5th ser. 3 (1952): 61-92.

04619. Dumas, Auguste. La condition des gens mariés dans la famille périgourdine au XVe et au XVIe siecles. Paris: n.p., 1908.

04620. Estienne, Nicole. "Les misères de la femme mariée." In Variétés historiques et littéraires, III, by Edouard Fournier, pp. 321-331. Paris: P. Jannet, 1855.

04621. Hilaire, Jean. "Les aspects communautaires du droit matrimonial des régions situées autour du Massif Central à la fin du XVe siècle et au début du XVIe." Recueil des mémoires et travaux publiés par la société d'histoire du droit et des institutions des anciens pays du droit ecrit 4 (1958-1960): 99-109.

04622. Lafon, J. Regimes matrimoniaux et mutations sociales: les époux bordelais (1450-1550). Paris: S.E.V.P.E.N., 1972.

04623. Montaigne, Michel de. "Of Three Good Women." In Complete Works, 35th Essay, Book 2, pp. 563-569. Stanford: University Press, 1948.

04624. Screech, Michael A. The Rabelaisian Marriage. London: Arnold and Co., 1958.
        [See especially chs. 1 and 6.]

04625. Wood, James B. "Demographic Pressure and Social Mobility among the Nobility of Early Modern France." Sixteenth Century Journal 8 (1977): 3-16.

04626. _____. "Endogamy and Mesalliance, the Marriage Patterns of the Nobility of the Election of Bayeux, 1430-1669." French Historical Studies 10 (Spring 1978): 375-392.

        Also refer to #3374, 3377, 4611, 4612.

                    e)   Sex Life and Morals

                        (1)   Non-specific

04627. Davis, Natalie Zemon. "Women on Top." In Society and Culture in Early Modern France, pp. 124-151. Stanford: University Press, 1975.

04628. Desjardins, Albert. Les Sentiments moraux au XVIe siècle.
        Paris: A. Durand et Pedone-Lauriel, 1887.

04629. Levi, Anthony. French moralists: The Theory of the Passions,
        1585-1649. Oxford: Claredon Press, 1964.

04630. Montaigne, Michel de. "That our Desire is increased by Diffi-
        culty." In Complete Works, 15th Essay, Book 2, pp. 463-468.
        Stanford: University Press, 1948.

                        (2)   Prostitutes

04631. Rossiaud, Jacques. "Prostitution, Youth and Society in the
        Towns of Southeastern France in the Fifteenth Century." In
        Deviants and the Abandoned in French Society, edited by
        Robert Forster and Orest Ranum, pp. 1-46. Baltimore:
        Johns Hopkins Press, 1978. Also in Annales: économies,
        sociétés, civilisations 31 (March-April 1976): 289-325.

                    f)   Fashion/Manners

04632. Racinet, Albert Charles Auguste. Geschichte der Kostüms in
        chronologischer Entwicklung. Vol. 4. Paris: n.p., 1888.

                    g)   Health/Medical

04633. Damour, Felix. Louise Bourgeois: Sa Vie, Son Oeuvre. Paris:
        Jouve and Boyer, 1900.

04634. Goodell, William. A Sketch of the Life and Writings of Louyse
        Bourgeois, Midwife to Marie de Medici, the Queen of Henry IV
        of France. Philadelphia: Collins, 1876.

04635. Strassman, P. "Louis Bourgeois as Midwife (1601-1610) to
        Queen Marie de Medici, Wife of Henry IV of France."
        Allgemeine Deutsche Hebammen-Zeitung 19:13 (June 19, 1904):
        203-207, 226-229.

5. CULTURAL

". . . a disproportionate elevation of the mind is apt to
breed pride. I have seen two bad effects from this: con-
tempt for housekeeping, for poverty and for a husband less
clever than oneself and discord."   Agrippa d'Aubigne

a) Literature

(1) Non-specific

04636.   Dow, Blanch H. The Varying Attitude Towards Women in French
         Literature in the 15th Century. New York: Publications of
         the Institute of French Studies, 1936.

04637.   Françon, Marcel. Notes sur l'esthétique de la femme au XVIe
         siècle. Cambridge, Mass.: Harvard University Press, 1939.

04638.   Potez, Henri. "Denys Lambin et les femmes." Revue de la
         Renaissance 8 (1908): 141-189. Reprint. Geneva: Slatkine
         Reprints, 1968.

04639.   Quentin-Bauchard, Ernest. Les Femmes bibliophiles de France.
         Paris: D. Morgand, 1886.

04640.   Saint-Ange, Louis de. Le Secret de triompher des femmes et de
         les Fixer. Brussels: F. Sacre, 1871.

         Also refer to #3615, 4516-4541, 4640.

(2) Poetry

(a) Women

04641.   Feugère, Léon Jacques. Les femmes poètes au XVIe siècle.
         Paris: Didier et Cie, 1860.

04642.   Montmorand, Maxime de. Une femme poète du XVIe siècle,
         Anne de Graville, sa Famille, sa vie, son oeuvre, sa
         posterité. Paris: Picard: 1917.

04643.   Rat, Maurice. "Hélène de Surger." Revue des deux mondes
         (August 1965): 379-389.

04644. Zezula, Jindrich and Clemens, Robert J. "'La Troisième Lyon-
        naise': Georgette de Montenay (1540-1581)." In The Pere-
        grine Muse, edited by Robert J. Clemens, pp. 198-210. Stu-
        dies in Romance Languages and Literature, no. 82. Chapel
        Hill, N.C.: University of North Carolina Press, 1969.

(b) Louise Labé

04645. Healy, Elliott D. "Louise Labé and the Comtessa de Dia." In
        Studies in Comparative Literature, edited by Waldo F. McNeir,
        pp. 47-68. Baton Rouge, La.: Louisiana State University
        Press, 1962.

04646. Larnac, Jean. Louise Labé, la belle cordière de Lyon (1522?-
        1566). Paris: Firmin-Didot et C^{Ie}, 1934.

04647. O'Connor, D. Louise Labé, sa vie et son oeuvre. Paris:
        Presses Françaises, 1926.

04648. Tricou, Georges. "Louise Labé et sa famille." Bibliothèque
        d'humanisme et renaissance 5 (1944): 67-74.

04649. Varty, Kenneth. "The Life and Legend of Louise Labé." Not-
        tingham Mediaeval Studies 3 (1959): 78-108.

04650. Wheatley, Katherine E. "A Woman of the Renaissance (Louise
        Labé)." Forum 9 (Spring 1971): 55-63.

04651. Zamaron, Fernand. Louise Labé, dame de francaise. Paris:
        Nizet, 1968.

(3) Prose

(a) Hélène de Crenne

04652. Baker, M.J. "France's first sentimental novel and novels of
        chivalry." Bibliothèque d'humanisme et renaissance 36
        (1974): 33-45.

04653. Neubert, Fritz. "Hélisenne de Crenne und ihr Werk." Zeitschrift
        für französische Sprache und Literatur 80 (December 1970):
        291-322.

(b) Marie de Gournay and Montaigne

(c) Rabelais

04654. Breusson, Jean Jacques. "Une suffragette au temps de Montaigne,
        Mlle. de Gournay." Nouvelles Littéraires 12 (22 April 1933):
        3.

04655. Casevitz, Therese. "Mlle. de Gournay et le féminisme." Revue
        bleue 63 (December 1925): 768-771

04656. Chénot, Anna Adele. "Marie de Gournay, feminist and friend of
        Montaigne." Poet Lore 34 (1923): 63-71.

04657. Ilsley, M.H. A Daughter of the Renaissance, Marie le Jars de
        Gournay: Her Life and Works. The Hague: Mouton and Co.,
        1963.

04658. Insdorf, Cecile. Montaigne and Feminism. Studies in the
        Roman Languages and Literature, no. 194. Chapel Hill,
        N.C.: University of North Carolina Press, 1977.

04659. Schiff, M. La Fille d'alliance de Montaigne, Marie de Gournay.
        Paris: H. Champion, 1910.

                    (c) Rabelais

04660. Aronson, Nicole. "Les reines et le 'Cinquième Livre' de
        Rabelais." Studi francesi 47-48 (1972): 324-329.

04661. Lefranc, Abel. "Le Tiers Livre de Pantagruel et la querelle
        des femmes." In Grand écrivains francais de la renaissance,
        pp. 252-260. Paris: H. Champion, 1914.

                    b) Literary Salons

04662. Diller, George E. Les Dames des Roches: Etude sur la vie
        littéraire à Poitiers dans la deuxieme moitié du XVIe
        siècle. Paris: E. Droz, 1936.

04663. Keating, Louis Clark. Studies on the Literary Salon in France,
        1550-1615. Cambridge, Mass.: Harvard University Press, 1941.

04664. Schutz, A.H. "The Group of the Dames des Roches in 16th Cen-
        tury Poitiers." Publications of the Modern Language Associ-
        ation 48 (1933): 648-654.

                    c) Art

04665. Dain, A. "La fille d'Ange Vergèce." Humanisme et renaissance
        1 (1934): 133-144.

04666. Gilder, Rosamond. "From Saltimbanque to Tragedienne: The
        Pioneer Actresses of France." In Enter the Actress: The
        First Women in the Theatre, pp. 82–99. Boston: Houghton-
        Mifflin Co., 1931.

D. THE GERMANIES

1. SURVEYS

"Women should remain at home, sit still, keep house and bear
and bring up children."
                                        Martin Luther

04667. Bainton, Ronald H. Women of the Reformation in Germany and
        Italy. Minneapolis, Minn.: Augsburg Publishing House, 1971.

04668. Diethoff, Ernestine Dietsch. Edle Frauen der Reformation und
        der Zeit der Glaubenskämpfe. Leipzig: O. Spamer, 1892.

04669. Havemann, Elisabeth. Die Frau der Renaissance. Quellenhefte
        zum Frauenleben in der Geschichte, edited by Emmy Beckmann
        and Irma Stoss, vol. 2. Berlin: F. A. Herbig Verlags-
        buchhandlung, 1927–1933.

04670. Heinsius, Maria. Frauen der Reformationszeit am Oberrhein.
        Karlsruhe: Hans-Thoma-Verlag, 1964.

04671. Stallman, Heinz and Stallman, Marianne. "La femme de la
        renaissance. L'allemande au temps de la réforme." Trans-
        lated by Thomas Aron. In Histoire mondiale de la femme,
        edited by Pierre Grimal, 2: 342–396. Paris: Nouvelle
        Librairie de France, 1966.

2. POLITICAL

"Our most dear and very well beloved wife, possesses ex-
cellent virtues, prudence and great qualities. The love
which she has for these kingdoms and their subjects is the
same as We have: and she is, as a consequence, beloved by
them, revered, and obeyed."
                                  Charles V of wife Isabella

a) Legal

04672. Hess, Rolf-Dieter. Familien- und Erbrecht im württembergi-
        schen Landrecht von 1555, unter besonderer Berücksichtigung
        des alteren wurttembergischen Rechts. Stuttgart: W.
        Kohlhammer, 1968.

        Also refer to #4761, 4762.

b) Political Roles

(1) Women

04673. Buchner, Anton. "Klara Dettin aus Augsburg, Stammutter der
        Fürsten von Löwenstein-Wertheim. Die Gefangene von Linden-
        fels?" Archiv für Hessische Geschichte und Altertumskunde
        33 (1975): 391-402.

04674. Calvi, Felice. Bianca Maria Sforza Visconti, regini dei romani,
        imperatrice germanica. Milan: n.p., 1888.

04675. Ermisch, Hubert. "Herzogin Ursula von Munsterberg." Neues
        Archiv fur Sachische Geschichte und Alterthumskunde 3 (1882):
        290-333.

04676. Fichtner, Paula Sutter. "Dynastic Marriage in Sixteenth-
        Century Habsburg Diplomacy and Statecraft: An Interdis-
        ciplinary Approach." American Historical Review 81 (April
        1976): 243-265.

04677. Hesse, A. (Kurs). Elisabeth, Herzogin von Braunschweig-Calen-
        berg. Halle: Verein fur Reformationsgeschichte, 1891.

04678. Scheller, Rita. Die Frau am preussischen Herzogshof. Berlin:
        Grote'sche Verlagsbuchhandlung, 1966.

(2)   Individuals

(a)   Barbara Blomberg

04679.   Herre, Paul.   Barbara Blomberg, die Geliebte Kaiser Karls V.
          und Mutter Don Juans de Austria: Ein Kulturbild des 16.
          Jahrhunderts.   Leipzig: Quelle und Meyer, 1909.

04680.   Redonet, Luis.   "Barbara de Blomberg." Boletin de la Real
          Academia de la Historia Madrid 158 (April–June 1966): 121–
          145.

(b)   Mary of Burgundy

04681.   Cazaux, Yves.   Marie de Bourgogne.   Paris: Albin Michel, 1967.

04862.   Dumont, Georges Henri.   Marie de Bourgogne, imperatrice d'Alle-
          magne.   Brussells: C. Dessart, 1945.

04863.   Hommel, Luc.   Marie de Bourgogne ou le grand heritage.
          Brussels: A. Goemaere, 1951.

04864.   Linden, Herman van der.   Itinéraires de Marie de Bourgogne et
          de Maximilien d'Autriche (1477–1482).   Brussels: M. Lamer-
          tini, 1934.

04685.   Munch, Ernst Hermann Joseph.   Maria von Burgund, nebst dem
          Leben ihrer Stiefmutter von Margaretha von York, Gemahlin
          Karls des Kuhnen.   Leipzig: F. A. Brockhaus, 1832.

04686.   Ussel, Paul van.   Maria van Bourgondië.   Bruges: De Kink-
          horen, 1944.

04687.   Van der Haegen, Victor.   "La charte donnée auz Gantois par
          Marie de Bourgogne en 1477."   In Melanges Paul Fredericq,
          pp. 273–278.   Brussels: H. Lambertin, 1904.

3. RELIGION

"All witchcraft comes from carnal lust, which is in woman
insatiable..."   The Hammer of Witches

a) Generic

04688.   Chrisman, Miriam U. "Women and the Reformation in Strasbourg, 1490–1530." Archiv für Reformationsgeschichte 63 (1972): 143–168.

04689.   Gundermann, Iselin. "Zu einem Gebetbuch der preussischen Herzogin Dorothea von 1534." Archiv für Kulturgeschichte 48 (1966): 234–241.

04690.   Heinsius, Maria. Das Unüberwindliche Wort: Frauen der Reformationzeit. Munich: C. Kaiser, 1951.

04691.   Rothkrug, Lionel. "Mariology and the Struggle Against the German Inquisition." In Religious Practices and Collective Perceptions Hidden Homologies in the Renaissance and Reformation, pp. 85–101. Historical Reflections 7 (Spring 1980).

04692.   Stricker, Kathe. Die Frau in der Reformation. Quellenhefte zum Frauenleben in der Geschichte, edited by Emmy Beckmann and Irma Stoss, vol. 2. Berlin: F. A. Herbig, 1927–1933.

Also refer to #4575.

b) Saints/Religious Women

(1) Women

04693.   Farner, Oskar. "Anna Reinhart." Zwingliana 3 (1920): 229–245.

04694.   Krezdorn, Siegfried. "Gräfin Rosamunde zu Ortenburg, Gemahlin des Grafen Karl von Hohenzollern-Haigerloch. Ein Frauenschicksal aus dem Dreissigjährigen Krieg." Zeitschrift für Hohenzollerische Geschichte 7–8 (1971–72): 50–76.

04695.   Loesche, Georg. "Die evangelischen Furstinnen im Hause Habsburg." Jahrbuch der Gesellschaft fur Geschichte des Protestantismus in Osterreich 15 (1904): 5–21.

04696.   Tschackert, Paul. "Herzogin Elisabeth von Münden." Hohenzollern Jahrbuch 3 (1899): 49–65.

04697.   Weber, Karl von. "Zur Lebensgeschichte der Herzogin Katharina von Sachsen, Gemahlin Herzog Heinrichs des Frommen." Archiv fur die sachsische Geschichte 6 (1868): 1–35.

04698. Wolters, Maria Agnes. "Prinzessin Charitas Wasa, Konventualin
        in Lichtenthal." Freiburger Diozesan-Archiv 82-83 (1962-63):
        287-298.

(2) Individuals

(a) Elizabeth of Brandenburg

04699. Berbig, G. "Ein Gutachten über die Flucht der Kurfürstin
        Elisabeth von Brandenburg aus dem Schlosse zu Berlin."
        Archiv für Reformations Geschichte 8 (1910-1911): 380-394.

04700. Jakobi, Rudolf. "Die Flucht der Kurfürstin Elisabeth von
        Brandenburg." Hohenzollern Jahrbuch 13 (1909): 155-196.

04701. Riedel, Adolf Friedrich. "Die Kurfürstin Elisabeth von Brand-
        enburg in Beziehung auf die Reformation." Zeitschrift fur
        preussische Geschichte und Landeskunde 2 (1865): 66-100,
        354-355.

(b) Argula von Grumbach

04702. Engelhardt, E. Argula von Grumbach. Nuremberg: J. Phil.-
        Rair, 1860.

04703. Kolde, Th. "Arsacius Seehofer und Argula von Grumbach."
        Beitrage zur bayerischen Kirchengeschichte 11 (1905): 49-77,
        97-124, 148-188.

04704. Lipowsky, Felix Joseph. Argula von Grumbach. Munich: J.
        Lindauer, 1801.

(c) Katherine Zell

04705. Bainton, Roland H. "Katherine of Zell." Medievalia et
        Humanistica 2nd ser. 1 (1970): 3-28.

04706. Roehrich, Timotheus Wilhelm. Kathrina Zell. Strasbourg:
        n.p., 1853.

c) Monastic Life

04707. Vierling, Josef Fridolin. Das Ringen um die letzten dem
        Katholicismus treuen Kloster Strassburgs. Strasbourg:
        Herdersche Buchhandlung, 1914.

d) Lutheranism

(1) Theological Views

(a) *Contemporary*

04708. Luther, Martin. <u>The Babylonian Captivity of the Church</u>. In
<u>Luther's Works</u>, edited and translated by A. R. Wentz.
Philadelphia: Fortress Press, 1959.
[See especially pp. 92-106.]

04709. _____. "The Estate of Marriage." In <u>Luther's Works</u>,
edited by Walther Brandt, 45: 13-49. Philadelphia:
Muhlenberg Press, 1962.

04710. _____. <u>Luther's Works</u>. Edited and translated by
Theodore G. Tappert. Philadelphia: Fortress Press, 1972.
[See especially vol. 49, letters 154, 157, and 158.]

(b) *Secondary*

04711. Beckman, J. "Luther and Celibacy." <u>Priest</u> 34 (1978): 14-16.

04712. Cocke, Emmett W., Jr. "Luther's view of marriage and family."
<u>Religion in Life</u> 42 (Spring 1973): 103-116.

04713. Lähteenmäki, Olavi. <u>Sexus und Ehe bei Luther</u>. Turku: n.p.,
1955.

04714. Ludolphy, Ingetraut. "Die Frau in der Sicht Martin Luthers."
In <u>Vierhundertfünfzig Jahre lutherische Reformation 1517-1967:
Festschrift für Franz Lau zum 60. Geburtstag</u>, pp. 204-221.
Berlin: Evangelische Verlagsanstalt, 1967.

04715. Suppan, Klaus. <u>Die Ehelehre Martin Luthers.</u> Salzburg:
Pustet, 1971.

04716. Zarncke, Lilly. "Die naturhafte Eheanschauung des jungen
Luthers." <u>Archiv für Kulturgeschichte</u> 25 (1935): 281-305.

(2) Katherine von Bora

04717. Boehmer, Heinrich. "Luther's Ehe." <u>Lutherjahrbuch</u> 7 (1925):
40-69.

04718. Brittain, Virginia J. "While Katy did the dishes." <u>Dialog</u> 11
(1972): 222-224.

04719. Davy, Yvonne. <u>Frau Luther</u>. Mountain View, Calif.: Pacific
Press, 1979.

04720. Dentler, Clara Louise. <u>Katherine Luther of Wittenberg Parsonage</u>.
Philadelphia: The United Lutheran Publication House, 1924.

04721. Hesselbacher, Karl. <u>Luthers Käthe</u>. <u>Das Leben der Katharina
von Bora unserem Volk erzählt</u>. Stuttgart: Quell-Verlag, 1934.

04722. Kroker, Ernst. <u>Katharina von Bora</u>. Berlin: Evangelische
Verlangsanstalt, 1964.

04723. Morris, John Gottlieb. <u>Catherine de Bora; or, Social and
Domestic Scenes in the Home of Luther</u>. Philadelphia:
Lindsay and Blakiston, 1856.

04724. Schmidt-Konig, Fritz. <u>Frau Käthe Luther</u>. Giessen: Brunnen-
Verlag, 1963.

04725. Schreiber, Clara Seuel. <u>Katherine Wife of Luther</u>. Philadelphia: Muhlenberg Press, 1954.

04726. Thoma, Albrecht. <u>Katharina von Bora</u>. Berlin: G. Reimer,
1900.

(3)   Margaret Luther

04727. Bainton, Roland H. "Luther und seine mutter." <u>Lutherjahrbuch</u>
44 (1973): 123-130.

04728. Siggins, Ian D. K. "Luther's Mother Margarethe." <u>Harvard
Theological Review</u> 71 (January-April 1978): 125-150.

e)   Other Protestant Sects

04729. Clasen, Claus Peter. <u>Anabaptism: A Social History, 1525-
1618: Switzerland, Austria, Moravia, South and Central
Germany</u>. Ithaca, N.Y.: Cornell University Press, 1972.

04730. Wenger, John C., ed. "Concerning Divorce: A Swiss Brethren
Tract on the Primacy of Loyalty to Christ and the Right to
Divorce and Remarriage." <u>Mennonite Quarterly Review</u> 21
(April 1947): 114-119.
[Tract attributed to Michael Sattler, 1527.]

f) Witchcraft

04731. Bader, Guido. Die Hexenprozesse in der Schweiz. Affoltern:
        Weiss, 1945.

04732. Christinger, R. and Genequand, J.E. "Un procès genevois de
        sorcellerie inédit." Geneva n.s. 17 (1969): 113-138.

04733. Diefenbach, Johann. Der Hexenwahn vor und nach der Glauben-
        spaltung in Deutschland. Mainz: F. Kirchheim, 1886.

04734. Leutenbauer, Siegfried. Hexerei und Zaubereidelikt in der
        Literatur von 1450 bis 1550. Mit Hinweisen auf die Praxis
        im Herzogtum Bayern. Berlin: Schweitzer, 1972.

04735. Mahlknecht, Bruno. "Barbara Pächlerin, die Sarntaler Hexe auf
        dem Scheiterhaufen hingericht an 28 August 1540." Der
        Schlern 50 (1976): 511-530.

04736. Midelfort, Eric. "Witchcraft and Religion in 16th Century
        Germany: The Formation and Consequences of an Orthodoxy."
        Archiv für Reformationsgeschichte 62 (1971): 266-278.

04737. _____. Witchhunting in Southwestern Germany 1562-
        1684: The Social and Intellectual Foundations. Stanford,
        Calif.: Stanford University Press, 1972.

04738. Monter, E. William. "Patterns of Witchcraft in the Jura."
        Journal of Social History 5 (Fall 1971): 1-25.

04739. _____. "Witchcraft in Geneva, 1537-1662." Journal
        of Modern History 43 (1971): 179-204.

04740. Neumaier, Helmut. "Hexenwahn im badischen Frankenland."
        Würtembergisch Franken 60 (1976): 264-277.

04741. Reiss, Wolfgang. "Die Hexenprozesse in der Stadt Baden-Baden."
        Freiburger Diözesan-Archiv 91 (1971): 202-266.

04742. Riezler, Sigmund. Geschichte der Hexenprozesse in Bayern.
        Stuttgart: Verlag der Cotta'schen Buchhandlung, 1896.

04743. Rosen, Edward. "Kepler and Witchcraft Trials." The Historian
        28 (May 1966): 447-450.

04744. Rothkrug, Lionel. "Witches and Peasant Insurgents. Prelude
        to Religious Reform and Rural Revolution." In Religious
        Practices and Collective Perceptions. Hidden Homologies in
        the Renaissance and Reformation, pp. 103-123. Historical
        Reflections 7 (Spring 1980).

04745.   Schormann, G. Hexenprozesse in Nordwestdeutschland.
         Hildescheim: Lax, 1977.

04746.   Veverka, Georgina. "Meinem Fluch entgehst du Nicht, und das
         Urteil ist der Tod!" Wiener Geschichte Blatter 32 (1977):
         161-166.

04747.   Wilbertz, Gisela. "Hexenprozesse und Zauberglaube im Hochstift
         Osnabrück." Osnabruck Mitteilungen 84 (1978): 33-50.

04748.   Wulz, Gustav. "Die Nördlinger Hexen und ihre Richter."
         Rieser Heimatbote 142-145 and 147 (1939).

04749.   _____. "Nordlinger Hexenprozesse." Jahrbuch des
         historischen Vereins für Nordlingen und das Ries 20 (1937):
         42-72; 21 (1938-1939): 95-120.

         Also refer to #3784, 3786, 4595.

4. SOCIAL

"To have peace and love in marriage is a gift which is next
to the knowledge of the Gospel."   Luther

a) Generic

04750.   Agrippa von Nettesheim, Henricus Cornelius. Female Pre-
         eminence. In the Feminist Controversy in the Renaissance.
         Delmar, N.Y.: Scholars' Facsimiles and Reprints, 1980.

04751.   Allen, Richard M. "Rebellion within the Household: Hans
         Sachs' Conception of Women and Marriage." Essays in History
         19 (1975): 43-74.

04752.   Guerdan, Rene. La Vie quotidienne à Genève au temps de Calvin.
         Paris: Hachette, 1973.

04753.   Guttenberg, Erich, Freiherrn von. "Einblicke in das Leben
         frankischer Landesedelfrauen des 16. Jahrhunderts." Archiv
         für Kulturgeschichte 14 (1919): 60-80.

04754.   Kingdon, Robert M. "The control of morals in Calvin's Geneva."
         In The Social History of the Reformation, edited by Lawrence
         P. Buck and Jonathan W. Zophy, pp. 3-16. Columbus: Ohio
         State University Press, 1972.

04755.   MacIlquham, Harriet. "Cornelius Agrippa: his appreciation
         of women." The Westminster Review 154 (1900): 303-313.

04756.   Winckelmann, Otto. "Strassburger Frauenbriefe des 16. Jahr-
         hunderts." Archiv für Kulturgeschichte 2 (1904): 172-195.

b) Demography

04757. Monter, E. William. "Historical Demography and Religious
History in Sixteenth-Century Geneva." Journal of Interdisciplinary History 9 (Winter 1979): 399-428.

c) Family

04758. Adam, Paul. "Une famille bourgeoise à Seléstat aux XVe au
XVIe siècles: les Ergersheims." In La Bourgeoisie
alsacienne, pp. 197-202. Strasbourg: F. X. Le Poux, 1954.

04759. Sabean, David. "Famille et tenure paysanne: aux origines de
la guerre des paysans en Allemagne (1525)." Annales:
économies sociétés, civilisations 27 (July-September 1972):
903-922.

04760. Schwarz, Ingeborg. Die Bedeutung der Sippe fur die Öffent-
lichkeit der Eheschliessung im 15. und 16. Jahrhundert.
Tübingen: n.p., 1959.

Also refer to #4712.

d) Marriage

04761. Dieterich, Hartwig. Das protestantische Eherecht in Deutschland bis zur Mitte des 17. Jahrhunderts. Munich: Claudius
Verlag, 1970.

04762. Jegel, August. "Altnürnberger Hochzeitsbrauch und Eherecht,
besonders bis zum Ausgang des 16. Jahrhunderts." Mitteilungen des Vereins für die Geschichte der Stadt Nürnberg 44
(1953): 238-274.

04763. Wendel, Francois. Le Mariage à Strasbourg a l'époque de la
réforme. Strasbourg: Imprimerie Alsacienne, 1928.

Also refer to #4676, 4708-4713, 4715, 4716, 4730, 4751, 4760.

e)   Sex Life and Morals

04764.   Hashagen, Justus.   "Aus Kölner Prozessakten.   Beiträge zur
         Geschichte der Sittenzustande in Köln im 15. und 16. Jahr-
         hundert."   Archiv für Kulturgeschichte 3 (1905):   301-321.

5. CULTURAL

"Let sweet girls vie with the males, As I see it, your
glory will not be light."   Melanchthon

a)   Education

04765.   Green, Lowell C.   "The Education of Women in Reformation."
         History of Education Quarterly 19 (Spring 1979):   93-116.

04766.   Mayr, M.   "Magdalena Haymair Schulmeisterin und Dichterin in
         der Reformationszeit."   Die Oberpfalz 3 (1965):   39-44.

b)   Literature

04767.   Berent, Eberhart.   "Frauenverehrung und Frauenverachtung in
         der Dichtung des frühen Barock."   Studies in Germanic
         Languages and Literature, edited by Robert W. Fowkes and
         Volkmar Sander, pp. 21-34. Reutlingen: Hutzler, 1967.

04768.   Coupe, W. A.   "Ungleiche Liebe, A 16th century Topos."   Modern
         Language Review 62 (1967):   661-671.

04769   Stupperich, Robert.   "Die Frau in der Publizistik der Refor-
         mation."   Archiv für Kulturgeschichte 37 (1955):   204-233.

c)   Art

04770.   Wirth, Jean.   La jeunne fille et la mort: recherches sur les
         themes macabres dans l'art germanique de la Renaissance.
         Geneva: Droz, 1979.

E. IBERIA

1. SURVEYS

"If the husband be the woman's head, the mind, the father,
the Christ, he ought to execute the office of such a
man . . . and to teach the woman."   Juan Luis Vives

04771.   Bomli, Petronella Wilhelmina. La Femme dans l'espagne du
siecle d'or. The Hague: M. Nijhoff, 1950.

Also refer to #4073.

2. POLITICAL

"Isabella must bear her full share of whatever blame attaches
to one who acts from a false sense of values. Piety was an
obsession with her."
R. Merton, Cardinal Ximenes and the Making of Spain

a) Feminism

04772.   Matulka, Barbara. "An Anti-Feminist Treatise of Fifteenth
Century Spain: Lucena's Repeticion de Amores." Romanic
Review 22 (April-June 1931): 99-116.

b) Political Roles

(1) Women

04773.   Alba, Duque de. "Biografía de doña María Enriquez, mujer de
gran Duque de Alba." Boletin de la Real Academia de la
Historia Madrid 121 (July-September 1947): 7-39.

04774. Boom, Ghislaine de. Eléonore d'Autriche, reine de Portugal
        et de France. Brussels: C. Dessart, 1943.

04775. Cerro, Jose de le Torres y del. Beatriz Enriques de Harana y
        Cristobal Colon. Madrid: Compania Ibero-Americana de
        Publicaciones, 1933.

04776. Cloulas, Annie. "Les portraits de l'impératrice de Portugal."
        Gazette des Beaux Arts 121 (February 1979): 58-68.

04777. Costes, R. "Le mariage de Philippe II et de l'infante
        Maria de Portugal." Bulletin Hispanique 17 (January 1915):
        151-35.

04778. Dhanys, Marcel. Les Quatre femmes de Philippe II. Paris:
        Alcan, 1933.

04779. Gutierez Lasanta, Francisco. La Santa Peninsular, Isabel,
        infanta de Aragon y reine de Portugal. Zaragoza: El
        Noticiero, 1967.

04780. Hume, A.S. Martin. Queens of Old Spain. New York: McClure,
        Phillips & Co., 1906.

04781. Llanos y Torriglia, Félix de. Una consejera del Estadodo:
        Doña Beatrix Galendo. Madrid: Editorial Reus, 1920.

04782. López de Toro, Jose. "El casemiento de la Infanta Catalina."
        Boletin de la Real Academia de la Historia Madrid 162
        (April-June 1968): 113-169.

04783. Muro, Gaspar. La Princesa de Eboli. Paris: Charpentier,
        1878.

04784. Vales y Failde, Francisco Javier. La emperatriz Isabel.
        Madrid: M. Aguilar, 1944.

04785. Wencker-Wildberg, Friedrich. Die Spanische Salome. Der Roman
        der Fürstin Eboli und des Staatssekretars Antonio Perez.
        Leipzig: Payne, 1937.

(2) Individuals

(a) Isabella I

04786. Azcona, P. de. Isabel la Católica. Madrid: la Editorial
        Catolica, 1965.

04787. Bouissounouse, Janine. Isabelle la Catholique. Paris:
        Hachette, 1949.

04788. Del Val, Isabel. Isabel la Catolica, princesa (1468-1474).
        Valladolid: Instituto Isabel la Catolica de historia
        eclesiastica, 1974.

04789. Dieulafoy, Jane Paule Henriete Rachel (Magre). Isabelle la
        Grande, reine de Castille, 1451-1504. Paris: Hachette,
        1920.

04790. Fernandez, Luis Juarez. Politica internacionale de Isabel
        la Catolica estudio y documentos. I 1468-1481. II. 1481-
        1488. Valladolid: n.p., 1965 and 1966.

04791. Fernandez-Armesto, Felipe. Ferdinand and Isabella. New York:
        Taplinger, 1975.

04792. Foronda, Marques de. "Dónde y cuándo nació Isabel la
        Catolica?" Boletin de la Real Academia de la Historia
        Madrid 75 (April 1920): 308-329.

04793. Gonzales Ruiz, Nicolas. Isabel de España, Isabel de Ingla-
        terra. Barcelona: Editorial Cervantes, 1955.

04794. Llanos y Torriglia, Felix de. "De dónde murió Isabel la
        Católica: Errores notarios y dudas que subsisten." Boletin
        de la Real Academia de la Historia Madrid 110 (January-
        March 1942): 45-84; (April-June 1942): 245-291.

04795. _____ . "Isabel la Católica no murió
        en la Mota." Boletin de la Real Academia de la Historia
        Madrid 111 (July-December 1942): 201-215.

04796. López Prudencio, J. Isabel la Cátolica, reina del mundo.
        Plasencia: Sanchez Rodrigo, 1967.

04797. Lunenfeld, Marvin. "Isabella I of Castile and the Company of
        Women in Power." Historical Reflections 4 (Winter 1977):
        207-229.

04798. Marina, Luis Santa. Vida de Isabel la Catolica. Barcelona:
        Seix y Barral Hermano, 1941.

04799. Nervo, Baron de. Isabel la Católica. Madrid: Biblioteca
        neuva, 1941.

04800. Perez-Bustamante, Ciriaco. "Isabel la Católica. La feminidad
        y la realeza." Boletin de la real academia de la historia
        171 (September-December 1974): 443-451.

04801. Plunket, Irene Arthur Lifford. Isabel of Castile and the
        Making of the Spanish Nation. New York: AMS Press, 1974.

04802. Prescott, William H. History of the Reign of Ferdinand and
        Isabella, the Catholic. 3 vols. London: Phillips, Sampson,
        and Co., 1858.

04803. "La Reina que Amandrino un Mondo." _Abside_ 30 (1974): 232-236.

04804. Rodrigues Valencia, Vincente, comp. _Isabel la Católica en la
        opinion de Españoles y extranjeros, siglos XV al XX._
        Valladolid: Instituto Isabel la Católica de historia
        eclesiastica, 1970.

04805. Silío Cortés, Cesar. _Isabel la Catolica, fundadora de España.
        Su vida, su tiemp, su reinado (1451-1504)._ 4th ed. Madrid:
        Espasa-Calpe, 1967.

04806. Val Valdivielso, María Isabel de. "Isabel la Católica o el
        triunfo de la intriga." _Historia_ 16 (August 1979): 47-51.

04807. Walsh, William Thomas. _Isabella of Spain: The Last Crusader._
        New York: McBride, 1930.

04808. Wittlin, Alma. _Myself a Goddess. A New Biography of Isabella
        of Spain._ London: Nicholson and Watson, Ltd., 1936.

(b) Isabel (Elizabeth) de Valois

04809. Amezúa y Mayo, Agustin González de. _Isabel de Valois, reina
        de España (1546-1568)._ Madrid: Gráficas Ultra, 1949.

04810. DuPrat, Antoine Théodore, marquis. _Elizabeth de Valois._
        Paris: Techener, 1850.

04811. Freer, Martha. _Elizabeth de Valios, queen of Spain and the
        court of Philip II._ London: Hurst and Blackett, 1857.

        Also refer to 4778.

(c) Joanna the Mad

04812. Bergström, Magnus. "Doña Joana, Princesa de Portugal e
        Rainha de Castela." _Revista de historia_ 3 (July-September
        1951): 49-56.

04813. Llanos y Torrigla, Félix de. "Sobra la fuga frustrada de
        doña Juana la Loca." _Boletin de la Real Academia de la
        Historia Madrid_ 102 (January-March 1933): 97-114.

04814. _____. "Más sobre la fuga frustrada de
        doña la Loca." _Boletin de la Real Academia de la Historia
        Madrid_ 102 (April-June 1933): 324-326.

04815. Prast, Antonia. "El Castillo de la Mota, de Medina del Campo.
        Intento de 'huída' de doña Juana la Loca." Boletin de la
        Real Academia de la Historia Madrid 101 (October–December
        1932): 508–522.

04816. Prawdin, Michael. Mad Queen of Spain. London: Allen and
        Unwin, 1938.

04817. Tighe, Harry. A Queen of Unrest. London: S. Sonnenschein
        and Co., Ltd., 1905.

04818. Rösler, E. Robert. Johanna die Wahnsinnige. Vienna:
        Faesy und Erick, 1870.

3. RELIGION

"Since they [women] are feebler both in mind and body, it
is not surprising that they should come more under the spell
of witchcraft."   Malleus Maleficarum

a) Saints/Religious Women

(1) Women

04819. Boehmer, Eduard. Franzisca Hernandez und Frau Franzisco Ortiz.
        Leipzig: H. Haessel, 1865.

04820. Bruno, P.F. L'Espagne mystique au XVIe siècle. Paris: AMG,
        1946.

04821. Longhurst, John. "La Beata Isabel de la Cruz ante la Inquisi-
        tion, 1524–1529." Cuadernos de historia de España 15–16
        (1957): 279–303.

(2) Saint Theresa of Avila

04822. Albarran, A. de Castro. The Dust of Her Sandals. New York:
        Benziger Bros., 1936.

04823. Auclair, Marcelle. La Vie de Sainte Thérèse d'Avila. Paris:
        Editions du Seuil, 1967.

04824. Beever, John Leonard. St. Teresa of Avila. New York: Hanover
        House, 1961.

04825. Dicken, E.W. Trueman. The Crucible of Love: A Study of the
        Mysticism of Terese of Jesus and St. John of the Cross. New
        York: Sheed and Ward, 1963.

04826. Hamilton, Elizabeth. Saint Theresa. New York: Charles
        Scribner's Sons, 1959.

04827. Isasi Garcia, Alfredo. Santa Teresa de Jesus. Madrid: Publi-
        caciones Españolas, 1959.

04828. Lopez, Rubio, José. Santa Teresa de Jesús. Madrid: Prensa
        espanola, 1971.

04829. Olmedo, Felix G. "Santa Teresa de Jesus y los predicatores
        del siglo de oro." Boletin de la Real Academia de la
        Historia Madrid 84 (January 1924): 165-175: (February
        1924): 280-295.

04830. Ontanon, Juana de. Santa Teresa de Jesús. Las Moradas. Libro
        de su vida. Mexico: Porrua, 1966.

04831. Peers, E. Allison. "St. Teresa." In Studies of the Spanish
        Mystics 1: 107-181. New York: The Macmillan Co., 1951.

04832. Peterson, Robert T. The Art of Ecstacy: Teresa, Bernini and
        Crashaw. New York: Atheneum, 1970.

04833. Revesz, Andrés. Teresa de Jesús. La Santa siempre joven.
        Plasencia: Sánchez Rodrigo, 1967.

04834. Salvador de la Virgen del Carmen. Teresa de Jesús. Alava:
        Consejo de cultura, 1968.

04835. Walsh, William Thomas. St. Teresa of Avila: A Biography.
        Milwaukee: Bruce Pub. Co., 1944.

04836. Werrie, Paul. Thérèse d'Avila. Paris: Mercure de France,
        1971.

04837. West, Victoria Mary Sackville. The Eagle and the Dove: A
        Study in Contrasts St. Teresa of Avila and St. Therese of
        Lisieux. New York: Doubleday-Doran, and Co., Inc., 1944.

                        b) Mariology

04838. Ulloa Barrenechea, Ricardo. La Virgen Maria en el Museo del
        Prado. Madrid: Editora Nacional, 1967.

c)   Monastic Life

04839.   Casas I Homs, Josep Maria.   "Elecció d'una abadessa de Vall-
         donzella l'any 1476."   In I Colloqui d'Historia del Monaquisme
         català, Santes Creus, 1966, pp. 63-84.   Santes Creus:
         l'Arxiu bibliografic, 1967.

04840.   Cocheril, Maur.   "Les abbesses de Lorvão au XVIe siècle."
         Revue d'histoire ecclésiastique 55.1 (1960): 916-935.

d)   Saint Ignatius Loyola

04841.   Ignatius of Loyla, Saint.   Letters to Women.   Edited by Hugo
         Rahner.   New York: Herder and Herder, 1960.

4. SOCIAL

"There is no load heavier than a light woman."
                              Cervantes

a)   Generic

(1)   Non-specific

04842.   Caro Baroja, Julio.   Los moriscos del reino de Granada.
         Madrid: Instituto de Estudio Politicos, 1957.

04843.   Carriazo, J. de M.   "Amor y moralidad bajo los Reyes
         Catolicos."   Revista de archivos, bibliotecas y museos
         5th ser. 60 (January-June 1954): 53-76.

04844.   Defourneaux, Marcelin.   Daily Life in Spain in the Golden Age.
         Translated by Newton Branch.   New York: Praeger, 1971.
         [See especially ch. 8.]

04845. Pike, Ruth. Aristocrats and Traders: Sevillia Society in the
        Sixteenth Century. Ithaca, N.Y.: Cornell University Press,
        1972.

                            (2)   Women

04846. Espinosa, Juan de. Dialogo en laude de las muyeres, ed.
        Angela Gonzalez Simon. Madrid: Consejo Superior de
        Investigaciones Genitificas, Instituto Nicolas Antonio,
        1946.

04847. Fitzmaurice-Kelly, Julia. "Woman in sixteenth century
        Spain." Revue hispanique 70 (1927): 557-632.

04848. McKendrick, Melveena. Woman and Society in the Spanish
        Drama of the Golden Age. New York: Cambridge University
        Press, 1974.

04849. Roth, Cecil. The House of Nasi: Dona Gracia. Philadelphia:
        Jewish Publication Society of America, 1948.

        Also refer to #4864.

                        b)   Demography

04850. Sentaurens, Jean. "Seville dans le seconde moitié du XVIe
        siècle: population et structures sociales. Le recensement
        de 1561." Bulletin Hispanique 77 (July-December 1975):
        321-390.

                    c)   Sex Life and Morals

04851. Perry, Mary Elizabeth. "'Lost Women' in early modern Seville:
        the politics of prostitution." Feminist Studies 4 (February
        1978): 195-214. Also in Crime and Society in Early Modern
        Seville, pp. 212-234. Hanover, N.H.: University Press of
        New England, 1980.

04852. Rodrigues-Solis, E. Historia de la prostitucion en España y
        America. 1890. Reprint. Madrid: Biblioteca Nueva, 1931.

5. CULTURAL

"The study of wisdom . . . teacheth them the way of good
and holy life."   Juan Luis Vives

a) Education

(1) Non-specific

04853. Oettel, Therese. "Una catedrática en el siglo de Isabel la
        Catolica: Luisa (Lucía) de Medrano." Boletin de la Real
        Academia de la Historia Madrid 107 (July-September 1935):
        289-368.

(2) Juan Luis Vives

04854. Vives, Juan Luis. "Instruction of a Christian Woman." In
        Vives and the Renascence Education of Women, edited by
        Foster Watson, pp. 29-136. 1912. Reprint. New York:
        Kelly, 1972.

04855. _____. "The Learning of Women." (From the Duty of
        Husbands). In Vives and the Renascence Education of Women,
        edited by Foster Watson, pp. 195-210. 1912. Reprint.
        New York: Kelly, 1972.

04856. _____. "Plan of Girls' Studies." In Vives and the
        Renascence Education of Women, edited by Foster Watson,
        pp. 137-149. 1912. Reprint. New York: Kelly, 1972.

04857. _____. "Satellitium or Symbola." In Vives and the
        Renascence Education of Women, edited by Foster Watson,
        pp. 151-158. 1912. Reprint. New York: Kelly, 1972.

04858. Watson, Foster. Vives and the Renascence Education of
        Women. 1912. Reprint. New York: Kelly, 1972.

b) Literature

(1) Non-specific

04859. Rumeau, A. "Isabel de Basilea et Alexandre de Canova Le
conflit de 1565-1566." Bulletin hispanique 73 (July-
December 1971): 248-262.

04860. _____. "Isabel de Basilea 'mujer impresora?'" Bulletin
hispanique 73 (July-December 1971): 231-247.

04861. Sigée, Louise. Dialogue de deux jeunes filles sur la vie
de cour et la vie de retraite (1552). Translated, edited
and introduced by Odette Sauvage. Paris: Presses Universitaires de France, 1970.

04862. Sims, Edna N. "Resumen de la imagen negativa de la mujer en
la literatura española hasta midiados del siglo XVI."
Revista de estudios hispanicos 11 (October 1977): 433-449.

(2) Cervantes

04863. Arco, Ricardo del. "La vida privada en las obras de Cervantes." Revista de Archivos Bibliotecas y Museos 4th ser.
56 (1950): 577-616.

04864. Bataillon, Marcel. "Cervantes et le 'mariage chrétien.'"
Bulletin hispanique 49 (1947): 129-144.

04865. Iventosch, Herman. "Cervantes and courtly love: the
Grisostomo-Marcela episode of Don Quixote." Publication
of the Modern Language Association 89 (January 1974): 64-77.

F. ITALY

1. SURVEYS

"Husbands who take counsel with their wives . . . are
mad-men if they think true prudence or good counsel lies in
the female brain."   Alberti

a) Generic

04866. Burckhardt, Jacob. The Civilization of the Renaissance in
        Italy. New York: Harper and Row, 1978

        Also refer to #3943, 3944.

b) Women

04867. Andrews, Marian. Men and Women of the Italian Reformation.
        London: S. Paul & Co., 1914.

04868. _____. The Most Illustrious Ladies of the Italian
        Renaissance. 1907. Reprint. Williamstown, Mass.: Cornet
        House Pub., 1972.

04869. Boulting, William. Women in Italy. London: Methuen and Co.,
        1910.

04870. Chojnacki, Stanley. "Patrician women in early Renaissance
        Venice." Studies in the Renaissance 21 (1974): 176-203.

04871. De Filipis, Felice. "Dame napoletane del Rinascimento." In
        Cronache e profili napoletani, pp. 83-92. Naples: Berisio,
        1968.

04872. Inguanti, Maria. Le Donne Della Riforma in Italia. Roma:
        Casa ed. Battista dell' unione cristiana evangelica
        battista d'Italia, 1968.

04873. Kelso, Ruth. Doctrine for the Lady of the Renaissance.
Urbana, Ill.: University of Illinois Press, 1956.

04874. Lagno, Isadora. Women of Florence. London: Chatto and
Windus, 1907.

04875. La Sizeranne, Robert de. Celebrities of the Italian Renais-
sance in Florence and Louvre. Translated by Jeffery E.
Jefferey. 1926. Reprint. Freeport, N.Y.: Books for
Librairies, 1969.

04876. Lungo, Isidoro del. Women of Florence. Translated by Mary
C. Steagmann. London: Chatto & Windus, 1907.

04877. Marchesi, G.B. "Le polemiche sul sesso femminile nei secoli
XVI et XVII." Giornale Storico della letteratura italiana
25 (1895): 362-369.

04878. Martines, Lauro. "A Way of Looking at Women in Renaissance
Florence." Journal of Medieval and Renaissance Studies 4
(Spring 1974): 15-28.

04879. Pecchiai, Pio. Donne del Rinascimento in Roma: Imperia,
Lucrezia, figlia d'imperia, lamisteriosa Flammetta. Padua:
CEDAM, 1958.

04880. Rochon, André. "La femme de la Renaissance. l'italienne."
In Histoire Mondiale de la Femme, edited by Pierre Grimal,
2: 213-304. Paris: Nouvelle librairie de France, 1966.

04881. Rodocanachi, Emmanuel Pierre. La Femme italienne avant, pendant
et après la renaissance: sa vie privee et mondaine, son
influence sociale. Paris: Hachette, 1922.

04882. Staley, John Edgcumbe. Famous Women of Florence. New York:
C. Scribner's Sons, 1909.

04883. _____. Heroines of Genoa and the Rivieras.
New York: C. Scribner's Sons, 1912.

04884. _____. Lords and Ladies of the Italian Lakes.
Boston: Little, Brown and Co., 1912.

04885. Zonta, Giuseppe. Trattati del cinquecento sulla donna. Bari:
Gius. Laterza & Figli, 1913.

Also refer to #4667, 4669.

2. POLITICAL

"We also prayed that he might grant us the grace to live together in peace and harmony for many happy years and with many male children . . ."   Leon Battista Alberti

a) Criminal

04886. Ruggiero, Guido. "Sexual Criminality in the early Renaissance: Venice 1338-1358." Journal of Social History 8 (Summer 1975): 18-37.

Also refer to #4901.

b) Feminism

04887. Gundersheimer, Werner L. "Bartolomeo Goggio: A Feminist in Renaissance Ferrara." Renaissance Quarterly 33 (Summer 1980): 175-200.

c) Political Roles

(1) Women

04888. Bax, Clifford. Bianca Capello. 1927. Reprint. Norwood, Pa.: Norwood Editions, 1975.

04889. Brion, Marcel. Catherine Cornaro, reine de Chypre. Paris: A. Michel, 1945.

04890. Brown, Horatio F. "Caterina Cornaro, Queen of Cyprus." In Studies in the History of Venice, 1: 255-292. 1907. Reprint. New York: Burt Franklin, 1973.

04891. Chiappini, Luciano. Eleonora d'Aragona, prima Duchessa di Ferrara. Rivigo: S.T.E.R., 1956.

04892. Corvisieri, C. "Il trionfo romano di Eleonora d'Aragona nel giugno del 1473." Archivo della società romana di storia patria 1 (1878): 475-491.

04893. Davari, Stefano. Il Matrimonio di Dorotea Gonzaga con Galeazzo
        Maria Sforza. Genoa: n.p. 1890.

04894. Faraglia, Nunzio Federigo. Storia della regina Giovanna Il
        d'Angio. Lanciano: R. Carabba, 1904.

04895. Giachetti, Cipriano. Bianca Cappello, la leggenda e la storia.
        Florence: Bemporad, 1936.

04896. Gundersheimer, Werner L. "Women, Learning and Power: Eleonora
        of Aragon and the Court of Ferrara." In Beyond their Sex,
        Learned Women of the European Past, edited by Patricia
        Labalme, pp. 43-65. New York: University of New York Press,
        1980.

04897. Lazzari, Alfonso. Le ultime tre Duchesse di Ferrara e la corte
        estense a' tempi di Torquato Tasso. Florence: Ufficio della
        Rassenga Nazionale, 1913.

04898. Maguire, Yvonne. The Women of the Medici. London: G. Rout-
        ledge and Sons, 1927.

04899. Peyre, Roger Raymond. Une princesse de la renaissance,
        Marguerite de France, duchesse de Berry, duchesse de Savoie.
        Paris: E. Paul, 1902.

04900. Randi, Luigi. Caterina Ginori. Storia di un salotto fiorentino
        nel secolo XVI. Modigliana: Tipogra fia sociale, 1905.

04901. Ricci, Corrado. Beatrice Cenci. Translated by Morris Bishop.
        2 vols. New York: Boni and Liveright, 1925.

04902. Staley, John Edgcumbe. The Dogaressas of Venice. New York:
        Charles Scribner's Sons, 1910.

04903. Whale, Winifred (Stephens). Margaret of France, Duchess of
        Savoy, 1523-1574. New York: John Lane, 1912.

                          (2) Individuals

                        (a) Lucretia Borgia

04904. Bellonci, Maria. The Life and Times of Lucretia Borgia.
        Translated by Bernard and Barbara Wall. 1939. New York:
        Grosset and Dunlap, 1953.

04905. Berence, Frederic. Lucrece Borgia, 1480-1519. Paris: Payot,
        1937.

04906. Catalano, Michele. Lucrezia Borgia duchessa di Ferrara.
        Ferrara: A. Taddei e figli editori, 1921.

04907.   Erlanger, Rachel. Lucrezia Borgia: A Biography. New York:
         Hawthorn, 1978.

04908.   Funck-Bretano, F. Lucrèce Borgia. Paris: Nouvelle revue
         critique, 1931.

04909.   Gilbert, William. Lucrezia Borgia, Duchess of Ferrara. 2
         vols. London: Hurst and Blackett, 1869.

04910.   Gregorovius, Ferdinand Adolf. Lucrezia Borgia: A Chapter
         from the Morals of the Italian Renaissance. London: New
         English Library, 1969.

04911.   Haslip, Joan. Lucrezia Borgia. Indianapolis: Bobbs-Merrill,
         1954.

04912.   Mancini, Franco. "Lucrezia Borgia governatrice di Spoleto."
         Archivio storico italiano 115 (1957): 182-187.

04913.   Martini, Magda. Lucrece Borgia ou la passive victime.
         Lausanne: Editions Rencontre, 1965.

04914.   Schirokauer, Alfred. Lucretia Borgia. London: Jarrolds, 1937.

04915.   X. "La garde-robe de Lucrece Borgia." Revue de la renaissance
         4 (1904): 221-228. Reprint. Geneva: Slatkine Reprints,
         1968.

                          (b)   Beatrice d'Este

04916.   Cartwright, Julia. Beatrice d'Este. 8th ed. New York:
         E.P. Dutton and Co., 1920.

04917.   La Sizeranne, Robert de. Beatrice d'Este and her Court.
         New York: Brentano's, 1923.

                          (c)   Isabella d'Este

04918.   Bonati Savorgnan d'Osopo, F. "Isabella d'Este, nei rapporti
         dei Gonzaga con l'Estero." Archivio storico lombardo 95
         (1969): 171-192.

04919.   Bongiovanni, Giannetto. Isabella d'Este marchesa di Mantova.
         Rome: Edizioni moderne Canesi, 1960.

04920.   Boujassy, Jeanne. Isabelle d'Este, grande dame de la
         renaissance. Paris: A. Fayard, 1960.

04921.   Capilupi, Giuliano. Isabella d'Este fidanzata e sposa.
         Verona: Nova Historia, 1950.

04922. Cartwright, Julia. Isabella d'Este, Marchioness of Mantua:
        A Study of the Renaissance. 1903. New York: E.P. Dutton
        and Co., 1923.

04923. Lauts, Jan. Isabella d'Este, Fürstin der Renaissance, 1474-
        1539. Hamburg: M. von Schroder, 1952.

04924. Luzio, Alessando and Renier, Rodolfo. "La coltura e le
        relazioni letterarie di Isabella d'Este Gonzaga." Gior-
        nale storico della letteratura italiana 33 (1899): 1-62;
        34 (1899): 1-97; 35 (1900): 193-257; 36 (1900): 325-349;
        37 (1901): 201-245; 38 (1901): 41-268; 39 (1902): 193-251;
        40 (1902): 289-334; and, 42 (1903): 75-111.

04925. _____. Isabella d'Este e i Borgia. Milan: L.F.
        Cogliati, 1915.

04926. _____. Isabella d'Este e il sacco di Roma. Milan:
        Tipografia editrice L.F. Cogliati, 1908.

04927. _____. "Isabella d'Este e Leone X dal Congresso
        di Bologna alla presa di Milano (1515-1521). Archivio
        storico italiano 5th ser. 40 (1907): 18-97; 44 (1909):
        72-128; 45 (1910): 245-302.

04928. _____. Mantova e Urbino. Isabella d'Este e
        Elisabetta Gonzaga nelle relazione famigliari e nelle vicende
        politiche. Rome: L. Roux, 1893.

04929. Marek, George R. The Bed and the Throne: The Life of
        Isabella d'Este. New York: Harper & Row, 1976.

04930. Martindale, Andrew. "The Patronage of Isabella d'Este at
        Mantua." Apollo 79 (March 1964): 183-191.

04931. Meyer, Edith Patterson. First Lady of the Renaissance: A
        Biography of Isabella d'Este. Boston: Little, Brown Co.,
        1970.

04932. Strano, Titina. Isabella d'Este. Milan: Ceshina, 1938.

                        (d) Julia Gonzaga

04933. Amante, Brutto. Giula Gonzaga, contessa di Fondi, e il
        movimento religioso feminile nel secolo XVI. Bologna:
        N. Zanichelli, 1896.

04934. Andrews, Marian. A Princess of the Italian Renaissance:
        Giulia Gonzaga. New York: Charles Scribner's Sons, 1912.

04935. Benrath, Karl. Julia Gonzaga. Ein Lebensbild aus der Gesch-
        ichte der Reformation in Italien. Halle: H. Neimeyer, 1900.

04936. Nicolini, Benedetto. "Giulia Gonzaga e la crisi del valde-
        sianesimo." In Studi cinquecenteschi I. ideali e passioni
        nell'Italia religiosa del cinquecento, pp. 119-153. Bologna:
        Tamari Editori, 1968.

04937. Nulli, S.A. Giulia Gonzaga. Milan: Treves, 1938.

04938. Paladino, Giuseppe. Giulia Gonzaga e il movimento valdesiano.
        Naples: F. Sangio Vanni & Figlo, 191?.

                        (e) Joanna I

04939. Crivelli, Domenico. Della prima e della seconda Giovanna,
        regime di Napoli. Padua: Co. tipi della Minerva, 1832.

04940. Scarpetta, Domenico. Giovanna I di Napoli. Naples: G.
        Gioffi, 1903.

04941. Steele, Francesca Mana. The Beautiful Queen Joanna I of
        Naples. New York: Dodd, Mead and Company, 1910.

                        (f) Renée de France

04942. Blumner, F. Renata von Ferrara, ein Lebensbild aus der Zeit
        der Reformation. Frankfurt: n. p., 1870.

04943. Fontana, Bartolomeo. Renata di Francia. 3 vols. Rome:
        Forzani e y tipografi del Senato, 1893-1899.

04944. Jenkins-Blaisdell, Charmarie. "Renée de France Between
        Reform and Counter-Reform." Archiv für Reformations-
        geschichte 63 (1972): 196-226.

04945. Rodocanachi, Ernest Pierre. Une protectrice de la Reforme
        en Italie et en France, Renée de France. 1896. Reprint.
        New Haven, Conn.: Research Publications, Inc., 1976.

                        (g) Catherine Sforza

04946. Braschi, Angelo. Caterina Sforza. Rocca da Casciano:
        Capelli, 1965.

04947. Breisach, Ernst. Caterina Sforza: A Renaissance Virago.
        Chicago: University of Chicago Press, 1967.

04948. Cerato, Margherita. Caterina Sforza. Rome: n.p., 1903.

04949. Cian V. Caterina Sforza. Turin: Fratelli Bocca editori, 1893.

04950. Kühner, Hans. Caterina Sforza, Fürstin, Tyrennin Busserin.
        Zurich: Werner Classen, 1957.

04951. Oliva Fabio. Vita di Caterina Sforza, Visconti. Forli: n.p.,
        1821.

04952. Pasolini, Pier Desiderio. Caterine Sforza. 4 vols. Rome:
        ELA, 1968.

04953. Randi, Aldo. Caterina Sforza. Milan: Ceshina, 1951.

(h) Lucretia Tornabuoni

04954. Felice, B. "Donne medicee avanti il principato: Il Lucrezia
        Tornabuoni moglie di Piero di Cosimo." Rassegna nazionale
        146 (1905): 645-660.

04955. Parducci, A. "La ystoria della devota Susanna di Lucrezia
        Tornabuoni." Annali delle universita toscane n.s. 10
        (1925-26): 177-201.

04956. Pieraccini, Gaetano. "Lucrezia Tornabuoni." Archivio storico
        italiano 107 (1949): 212-215.

3. ECONOMIC

        "Unless there were no male heirs, they never allowed girls
        to share in the division of the estate."   James Davis

04957. Caroselli, M.R. "L'abbigliamento femminile nel rinascimento
        italiano." Economia e storia 12 (1965): 590-601.

04958. Goldthwaite, Richard. Private Wealth in Renaissance Florence.
        Princeton, N.J.: Princeton University Press, 1968.

04959. Kirschner, Julius, and Molho, Anthony. "The Dowry Fund and
        the Marriage Market in Early Quattrocento Florence." Journal
        of Modern History 50 (September 1978): 403-438.

04960. Mancarella, A. "I depositi di Agnese e Giovanna di Durazzo
        presso it Monte Comune di Firenze." Archivio Storico
        Italiano 71.2 (1913): 373-381.

04961.   Staley, John Edgcumbe. Guilds of Florence. London: Methuen
          and Co., 1906.

4. RELIGION

"With a cable of love and fidelity, welded together I
fasten my barque to a never-yielding rock, to Christ."
                                        Vittoria Colonna

a)   Generic

04962.   Doherty, Dennis. The Sexual Doctrine of Cardinal Cajetan.
          Regensburg: Friedrich Pustet, 1966.

04963.   Nicolini, Benedetto. "A proposito di un trattato sulla
          verginità." In Studi cinquecenteschi I. Ideal e passioni
          nell'Italia religiosa del cinquecento, pp. 157-174. Bologna:
          Tamari Editori, 1968.

b)   Saints/Religious Women

(1)   Women

04964.   Agresti, Guglielmo di. Santa Caterina de Ricci. Bibliografia
          ragionata con appendice savonaroliana. Florence: L.S.
          Olschki, 1973.

04965.   Ancilli, Ermanno. "La passione di Santa Maria Maddalena de
          Pazzi per la Chiesa." Ephemerides Carmeliticae 7 (1966):
          405-446.

04966.   Casadei, Alfredo. "Donne della Riforma Italiana: Isabella
          Bresegha." Religio 12 (1937): 6-63.

04967.   Hugel, Friedrich Freiherr von. The Mystical Element in
          Religion as Studied in Saint Catherine of Genoa and her
          Friends. New York: E.P. Dutton and Co., 1927.

04968.   Izard, Georges. Saint Catherine de Gênes. Paris: Ed. du
          Seuil, 1969.

04969.   Misciattelli, Piero. The Mystics of Siena. Cambridge: W.
          Heffer and Sons, Ltd., 1929.

04970. Nicolini, Benedetto. "Una calvinista Isabella Bresenga." In
        Studi cinquecenteschi I. Ideal e passioni nell'Italia re-
        ligiosa del cinquecento, pp. 1-33. Bologna: Tamari Editori,
        1968.

04971. Paganelli Ferrari, Paolina. Caterina Fieschi Adorno, santa
        dell'affocato amore, 1447-1510. Turin: Marietti editori,
        1965.

04972. Puccini, Vincenzio. The Life of Suor Maria Maddalena de'
        Parsi. 1619. Reprint. Menston: Scholar Press, 1970.

04973. Soranzo, Giovanni. "Orisine Orsino, Adriana di Mila sua madre,
        e Giulia Farnese sua moglie, nei loro rapporti con Papa
        Alessandro VI." Archivi 2nd ser. 26 (1959): 119-150.

(2) Individuals

(a) Catherine of Sienna

04974. Bizziccari, Alvaro. "Stile e personalita di S. Caterina da
        Siena." Italica 43 (1966): 43-56.

04975. Chiminelli, Piero. S. Caterina da Siena 1347-1380. Rome:
        Sales, 1941.

04976. Curtayne, Alice. Saint Caterina of Siena. New York: Mac-
        millan Co., 1929.

04977. De la Bedoyère, Michael. Catherine Saint of Siena. London:
        Hollis and Carter, 1947.

04978. Fawtier, Robert and Canet, Louis. La Double experience de
        Catherine Benincasa. Paris: Gallimard, 1948.

04979. Gardner, Edmund Garratt. Saint Catherine of Siena: A Study
        in the Religion, Literature, and History of the Fourteenth
        Century in Italy. New York: E.P. Dutton and Co., 1907.

04980. Gauthiez, Pierre. Sainte Catherine de Sienne, 1347-1380.
        Paris: Bloud and Gay, 1916.

04981. Gillet, Martin Stanislas. The Mission of Saint Catherine.
        Translated by Sister M. Thomas Lopez. St. Louis: Herder
        Book Co., 1955.

04982. Giordani, Igino. Catherine of Siena. Milwaukee, Wisc.: Bruce
        Pub. Co., 1959.

04983. Grion, P. Alvaro. Santa Caterina da Siena. Cremona: Mor-
        celliana, 1953.

04984.   Jörgensen, Johannes. Saint Catherine of Siena. New York:
          Longmans, Green and Co., 1938.

04985.   Levasti, Arrigo. Katharina von Siena. Translated by Helene
          Moser. Regensburg: Friedrich Pustet, 1952.

04986.   Maresch, Maria. Katharina von Siena. Vienna: Herder, 1947.

04987.   Perrin, J.M. St. Catherine of Siena. Westminster, Md.:
          Newman Press, 1965.

04988.   Rousset, Paul. "Saint Catherine de Sienne et le probleme de
          la croisade." Schweizerische Zeitschrift fur Geschichte 25
          (1975): 499-513.

04989.   Scudder, Vida. Saint Catherine of Siena as Seen in Her Letters.
          New York: E.P. Dutton and Co., 1905.

04990.   Taurisano, Innoc. S. Caterina da Siena. Patrona d'Italia.
          Rome: F. Ferrari, 1940.

04991.   Uboldi, Leonilda. Santa Caterina da Siena. Rome: S.A.L.E.S.,
          1965.

                    (b) Vittoria Colonna

04992.   Bainton, Roland H. "Vittoria Colonna and Michelangelo."
          Forum 9 (Spring 1971): 34-41.

04993.   Bernardy, Amy. La Vita e l'opera di Vittoria Colonna.
          Florence: La Monnier, 1927.

04994.   Ennesch, Carmen. La Vie comblee de Vittoria Colonna. Paris:
          La Grande revue, 1848.

04995.   Giordano, Amalia. La Dimora di Vittoria Colonna a Napoli.
          Naples: Melfi et Joele, 1906.

04996.   Jerrold, Maud F. Vittoria Colonna: With Some Account of Her
          Friends and Her Times. 1906. Reprint. New York: Arno
          Press, 1978-1979.

04997.   Jung, Eva Maria. "Vittoria Colonna: Between Reformation and
          Counter-Reformation." Review of Religion 15 (1951):
          144-159.

04998.   Nicolini, Benedetto. "Sulla Religiosita di Vittoria Colonna."
          In Studi cinquecenteschi I. Ideali e passioni nell'Italia
          religiosa del cinquecento, pp. 37-63. Bologna: Tamari
          Editori, 1968.

04999. Pfister, Kurt. Vittoria Colonna: Werden und Gestalt der
        frühbarocken Welt. Munich: J. Bruckmann, 1950.

05000. Reumont, Alfred von. Vittoria Colonna, Marchesa di Pescara.
        Turin: E. Loescher, 1892.

05001. Therault, Suzanne. Un Cénacle humaniste de la renaissance
        autour de Vittoria Colonna châtelaine d'Ischia. Paris:
        Marcel Didier, 1968.

05002. Wyss, Johann J. Vittoria Colonna und ihr Kanzoniere. Frauen-
        feld: Huber, 1916.

(c) Angela Merici

05003. Caraman, Philip G. St. Angela. The Life of Angela Merici,
        Foundress of the Ursulines, 1474-1540. New York: Farrar,
        Strauss, 1964.

05004. Ledóchowska, Teresa. Angèle Merici et la compagnie de Ste.
        Ursula. Rome: Ancora, 1968.

05005. Monica, Sister M. Angela Merici and Her Teaching Ideas.
        1474-1540. New York: Longmans, Green and Co., 1927.

05006. Reidy, M. The First Ursuline: St. Angela Merici. London:
        Burns and Oates Ltd., 1962.

c) Mariology

05007. Fiskovic, Cvito. "La Madonna della battega di Paolo Veneziano
        nelle Bocche Cattaro." Arte Veneta 25 (1971): 248-252.

05008. Venturi. "L'image de la Madone en Italie." Revue de la
        renaissance 3 (1903): 116-127. Reprint. Geneva: Slatkine
        Reprints, 1968.

d) Witchcraft

05009. Brucker, Gene A. "Sorcery in early Renaissance Florence."
        Studies in the Renaissance 10 (1963): 7-24.

5. SOCIAL

"No one celebrated because it was wished that she [Beatrice]
might have been a male."   daughter of Elenora of Aragon

a) Generic

(1) Non-specific

05010. Bezold, Friedrich von. "Aus dem Briefwechsel der Markgrafin
Isabella von Este-Gonzaga." Archiv für Kulturgescheschte
8 (1910): 385-418.

05011. Biagi, G. La Vita italiana nel rinascimento. Milan: Treves,
1931.

05012. Brucker, Gene A. "The Florentine Popolo Minuto 1340-1440."
In Violence and Civil Disorder in Italian Cities, edited
by Lauro Martines, pp. 155-183. Berkeley: University of
California Press, 1972.

05013. _____. The Society of Renaissance Florence: A
Documentary Study. New York: Harper and Row, 1971.

05014. Gage, John. Life in Italy at the Time of the Medici. New
York: Putnam, 1968.
[See especially ch. 12.]

05015. Lucas-Dubreton, J. Daily Life in Florence in the Time of
the Medici. New York: Macmillan, 1961.

05016. Luchaire, Julien. Les Sociétés italiennes des XIVe et XVIe
siecles. Paris: A. Colin, 1933.

05017. Martines, Lauro. The Social World of the Florentine Humanists
1390-1460. London: Routledge and Paul, 1963.

05018. Molmenti, Pompeo Gherardo. La Storia di Venzi nella vita
privata dalle origini alla caduta della repubblica. Bergamo:
Instituto italiano d'arti grafiche, 1910-1912.

05019. Pullan, Brian. Rich and Poor in Renaissance Venice. Cambridge:
Mass.: Harvard University Press, 1971.
[See especially pp. 376-397 on prostitution.]

05020. Roth, Cecil. The Jews in the Renaissance. Philadelphia:
        Jewish Publication Society of America, 1959.
        [See especially ch. 3, "Jewish Women in Renaissance
        Italy."]

05021. Sheedy, Anna T. Bartolus on Social Conditions in the 14th
        Century. New York: Columbia University Press, 1942.

        Also refer to #4602.

                            (2) Women

05022. Casanova, Eugenio. La donna senese de Quattrocento, nella
        vita privata. Sienna: L. azzeri, 1901.

                        b) Demography

05023. Conti, E. I catasti agrari della republica fiorentina e il
        catasti particellare toscano. Rome: Instituto storico
        italiano per il Medio Evo, 1966.

05024. Herlihy, David. "The Population of Verona in the First
        Century of Venetian Rule." In Renaissance Venice, edited
        by J. R. Hale, pp. 91–120. Totowa, N.J.: Rowman and
        Littlefield, 1973.

05025. _____. "The Tuscan Town in the Quattrocento."
        Medievalia et humanistica 1 (1970): 81–110.

05026. _____. "Vieillir au Quattrocento." Annales:
        economies, sociétés, civilisations 24 (November–December
        1969): 1338–1352.

                        c) Family

                        (1) Non-specific

05027. Alberti, Leon Battista. The Family in Renaissance Florence.
        Translated by Renee N. Watkins. Columbia, S.C.: University
        of South Carolina Press, 1969.

05028. Chojnacki, Stanley. "Dowries and Kinsmen in Early Renaissance
        Venice." Journal of Interdisciplinary History 5 (Spring
        1975): 571-600. Also in Women in Medieval Society, edited
        by Susan Mosher Stuard, pp. 173-98. Philadelphia: Univer-
        sity of Pennsylvania Press, 1976. Also in Marriage and
        Fertility, edited by Robert I. Rotberg and Theodore K. Rabb,
        pp. 41-70. Princeton, N.J.: Princeton University Press,
        1980.

05029. _____. "In Search of the Venetian Patriciate:
        Families and Factions in the 14th Century." In Renaissance
        Venice, edited by J.R. Hale, pp. 47-90. London: Faber and
        Faber, 1973.

05030. Goldthwaite, Richard. "The Florentine Palance as Domestic
        Architecture." American Historical Review 77 (October 1972):
        977-1013.

05031. Guicciardini, Francesco. "Memorie de famiglie." In Scritti
        autobiografici e rari, edited by Roberto Palmarocchi, pp. 3-
        50. Bari: G. Laterza & figli, 1936.

05032. Herlihy, David. "Family and Property in Renaissance Florence."
        In The Medieval City, edited by Harry A. Miskimin; David
        Herlihy, and A.L. Udovitch, pp. 3-23. New Haven, Conn.:
        Yale, 1977.

05033. _____. The Family in Renaissance Italy. St. Louis:
        Forum Press, 1975.

05034. _____, and Klapisch-Zuber, Christiane. Les toscans
        et leurs familles: une étude du catasto florentin de 1427.
        Paris: Presses de la fondation nationale des sciences poli-
        tiques, 1978.

05035. Jones, P.J. "Florentine Families and Florentine Diaries in
        the Fourteenth Century." Papers of the British School at
        Rome 24 (n.s. 11) (1956): 183-205.

05036. Kent, Francis W. Household and Lineage in Renaissance Florence:
        The Family Life of the Capponi, Ginori, and Rucellai. Prince-
        ton, N.J.: Princeton University Press, 1971.

05037. King, Margaret Leah. "Caldiera and the Barbaros on Marriage
        and the Family: Humanist Reflections of Venetian Realities."
        Journal of Medieval and Renaissance Studies 6 (Spring 1976):
        19-50.

05038. Kirshner, Julius. "Pursuing Honor While Avoiding Sin, the
        Monte della Doti of Florence." Studi senesi 89 (1977):
        175-258.

05039. Klapisch, Christaine. "Genitori naturali e genitori de latte
        nella Firenze del Quattrocentro." Quaderni storici 44
        (August 1980): 543-563.

05040. Klapisch, Christianne. "Household and family in Tuscany in
        1427." In Household and Family in Past Time, edited by
        Peter Laslett and Richard Wall, pp. 267-281. Cambridge:
        The University Press, 1972.

05041. _____. "'Parenti, amici e vicini': Il terri-
        torio urbano d'una famiglia mercantile nel XV secolo."
        Quaderni storici 33 (September-December 1976): 953-982.

05042. _____ and Demonet, Michel. "A uno pane e uno
        vino: the rural Tuscan family at the beginning of the
        fifteenth century." In The Family in History, edited by
        Robert Forster and Orest Ranum, pp. 41-74. Baltimore:
        Johns Hopkins University Press, 1976.

05043. Lugli, Vittorio. I Trattatisti della famiglia nel Quattrocento.
        Biblioteca filologica e letteraria, no. 2. Bologna-Modena:
        A.F. Formiggini, 1909.

05044. Luzzati, Michelle. "Famiglie nobili e famiglia mercantili a
        Pisa e in Toscano nel Basso Medioevo." Rivista Storica
        Italiana 86 (1974): 441-459.

05045. Starn, Randolph. "Francesco Guicciardini and his Brothers."
        In Renaissance Studies in Honor of Hans Baron, edited by
        Anthony Molho and John A. Tedeschi, pp. 411-444. Dekalb,
        Ill.: Northern Illinois University Press, 1971.

05046. Tamassia, Nino. La Famiglia italiana nei secolo decimoquinto
        e decimosesto. Milan: R. Sandron, 1911.

05047. Woodward, William Harrison. "Leon Battista Alberti and La Cura
        della Famiglia." In Studies in Education during the Age of
        the Renaissance. Classics in Education, no. 32: 48-64.
        1906. Reprint. New York: Teachers' College, Columbia
        University, 1967.

                        (2) Childhood

05048. Ross, James Bruce. "The Middle-Class Child in Urban Italy,
        Fourteenth to Early Sixteenth Century." In The History of
        Childhood, edited by Lloyd de Mause, pp. 183-228. New York:
        Harper Torchbook, Harper and Row, 1975.

05049. Trexler, Richard C. "The Foundlings of Florence 1395-1455."
        History of Childhood Quarterly 1 (Fall 1973): 259-284.

05050. _____. "Infanticide in Florence: new sources
        and first results." History of Childhood Quarterly 1
        (Summer 1973): 98-116.

d) Marriage

05051. Bullard, Melissa Meriam. "Marriage Politics and the Family
in Florence: The Strozzi-Medici Alliance of 1508." American
Historical Review 84 (June 1979): 668-687.

05052. Delille, Gérard. "Classi sociali e scambi matrimoniali nel
Salernitano: 1500-1650 circa." Quaderni storici 33 (1976):
983-997.

05053. Herlihy, David. "Marriage at Pistoia in the Fifteenth
Century." Bullettino storico pistoiese 74 (1972): 3-21.

05054. Pesce, Ambrogio. "Le trattative per il matrimonio di Battistina
Fregoso con Iacopo III Appiani (1454)." Archivio Storico
Italiano 71.2 (1913): 132-141.

Also refer to #4959, 4960, 5037.

e) Sex Life and Morals

05055. Calza, Carlo. Documenti mediti sulla prostituzione, tratti
cagli archivi della republica Veneta. Milan: Società Coop,
1869.

05056. Casagrande di Villaviera, Rita. La Cortigiane veneziano nel
cinquecento. Milan: Longanesi, 1968.

05057. Giacoma, Salvatore di. La Prostitutuzione a Napoli nei secolo
XV, XVI e XVII. Naples: Marghieri, 1899.

05058. Stefanutti, Ugo. "Cortigiane in Venezia d'altritempi aspecti
medici e sociali." Rass Medica 35 (5): 158.

Also refer to #4886, 5012, 5019.

f) Fashion/Manners

05059. La Valva, Maria Providenza. "Cosmetica maschile nel Rinasci-
        mento." In Renatae Litterae Studium zum Nachleben der Antike
        und zur europäischen Renaissance. August Beck zum 60. Geburt-
        stag, edited by Klaus Heitmann and Eckhart Schroeder, pp. 95-
        105. Frankfurt a.M.: Athenaum, 1973.

05060. Newett, Mary Margaret. "The Sumptuary Laws of Venice in the
        14th and 15th Centuries." In Historical Essays First
        Published in 1902 in Commemoration of the Jubilee of the
        Owens College Manchester, pp. 245-278. Manchester: Univer-
        sity Press, 1903.

6. CULTURAL

"I, a woman, have dropped the symbols of my sex, Yarn,
shuttle, basket, thread."   Olympia Morata

a) Education

05061. Woodward, William Harrison. "The Tractate of Leonardo Bruni
        d'Arezzo, De Studiis et Literis." In Vittorino da Feltre
        and other Humanist Educators. Classics in Education, 18:
        119-133. 1897. Reprint. New York: Teachers' College,
        Columbia University, 1963.

05062. _____ . Vittorino de Feltre and Other
        Humanist Educators. 1897. Reprint. New York: Teacher's
        College, Columbia University, 1963.

b) Literature

(1) Non-specific

05063. Campenella, Tommaso. La Cité du soleil, edited by Luigi
        Firpo. Translated by Arnaud Tripet. Geneva: Droz, 1972.

05064. Lorenzetti, Paolo. La Bellezza de l'amore nei trattati del
        cinquecento. Pisa: Stab. tipografico Suco, fratelli Nistri,
        1917.

05065. Tonelli, L. L'Amore nella poesia e nel pensiero del Rinas-
        cimento. Florence: Sansoni, 1933.

05066. Woodford, Susan. "The Woman of Sestos: A Plinian Theme in
        the Renaissance." Journal of the Warburg and Courtauld
        Institute 28 (1965): 343-348.

        Also refer to #4930, 4992-5002.

                          (2) Poetry

                     (a) Dante Alighieri

05067. Alighieri, Dante. La Vita Nuova. Translated by Barbara
        Reynolds. Baltimore: Penguin Books, 1971.

05068. Grandgent, Charles H. The Ladies of Dante's Lyrics. Cam-
        bridge, Mass.: Harvard University Press, 1917.

05069. Singleton, Charles S. "Dante: Within Courtly Love and Beyond."
        In The Meaning of Courtly Love, edited by F.X. Newman,
        pp. 43-54. Albany: State University of New York Press,
        1968.

05070. Williams, Charles. The Figure of Beatrice in Dante. New York:
        Octagon Books, 1972.

        Also refer to #1883.

                     (b) Francesco Petrarch

05071. Bernardo, Aldo S. "Petrarch's Laura: The Convolutions of a
        Humanistic Mind." In The Role of Women in the Middle Ages,
        edited by Rosmarie Thee Morewedge, pp. 65-89. Albany, N.Y.:
        State University of New York Press, 1975.

05072. Siegel, Paul. "The Petrarchan Sonneteers and Neo-Platonic
        Love." Studies in Philology 42 (1945): 164-182.

        Also refer to 4954-4956, 5089, 5101-5107.

(3) Prose

(a) Pietro Aretino

05073. Aretino, Pietro. The Ragionamenti, or Dialogues. Paris: I.
Lisieux, 1889.
[See especially "Life of Nuns," "Life of Married Women,"
"Life of Courtesans."]

(b) Giovanni Boccaccio

05074. Allen, Shirley, S. "The Griselda Tale and the portrayal of
women in the Decameron." Philological Quarterly 56 (1977):
1-13.

05075. Boccaccio, Giovanni. Decameron. Translated by Mark Musa and
Peter E. Bondanella. New York: Norton, 1977.
[See especially 2nd day, 7th story; 3rd day, 1st story,
10th story.]

05076. Bonadeo, A. "Some aspects of Love and Nobility in the society
of the 'Decameron'." Philological Quarterly 47 (1968): 513-
525.

05077. Brown, Marshall. "In the Valley of the Ladies (Boccaccio's
'Decameron')." Italian Quarterly 18 (Spring 1975): 33-52.

05078. Givens, Azzurra B. La Dottrina d'amore nel Boccaccio. Biblioteca di cultura comtemporanea, no. 102. Florence: Editions
G. d'Anna, 1968.

05079. Griffin, R. "Boccaccio's Fiammetta: Pictures at an Exhibition."
Italian Quarterly 18 (Spring 1975): 75-94.

05080. Nurmela, Tauno. "La misogynie chez Boccace." In Boccaccio in
Europe, edited by Gilbert Tournoy, pp. 191-196. Louvain:
University Press, 1977.

05081. Radcliff-Umstead, Douglas. "Boccaccio's Idle Ladies." In
The Roles and Images of Women in the Middle Ages and
Renaissance, pp. 75-103. Pittsburgh: University of Pitts-
burgh Center for Medieval and Renaissance Studies, 1975.

05082. Scaglione, Aldo. Nature and Love in the Late Middle Ages.
Berkeley: University of California Press, 1963.

05083. Shapiro, Marianne. Women Earthly and Divine in the Comedy
of Dante. Studies in Romance Languages, no. 12. Lexing-
ton, Kentucky: The University Press of Kentucky, 1975.

05084.   Zaccaria, Vittorio. "La fortuna del 'de Mulieribus Claris' del
          Boccaccio nel secolo XV: Giovanni Sabbadino degli Arienti,
          Jacopo Filippo Foresti e le loro biografie femminili." In
          Il Boccaccio nelle culture e letterature nazionali. Atti
          del congresso internazionale "la Fortuna del Boccaccio nelle
          culture e nelle letterature nazionali." Firenze–Certaldo,
          22–25 maggio 1975, promoso dalle università di Firenze, Pisa
          e Siena e dall'ente nazionale "Giovanni Boccaccio," edited
          by Francesco Mazzoni, pp. 519–45. (Publicazioni dell'ente
          nazionale "Giovanni Boccaccio, 3). Florence: Leo S.
          Olschki, 1978.

(c) Giordano Bruno

05085.   Nelson, John Charles. Renaissance Theory of Love: the Context
          of Giordano Bruno's Eroici Furori. New York: Columbia Uni-
          versity Press, 1958.

(d) Baldassare Castiglione

05086.   Castiglione, Baldasar. The Book of the Courtier. Translated
          by George Ball. Baltimore, Md.: Penguin Books, 1967.
          [See especially book 3, pp. 88–100, Debate on the character
          and value of women.]

(e) Niccolo Machiavelli

05087.   Machiavelli, Niccolo. "Belfagor or the Devil Takes a Wife."
          Italian Quarterly 1 (Spring 1957): 44–52.

05088.   _____. "Belfagor: The Devil Who Married."
          In Machiavelli: The Chief Works and Others, translated by
          Allen Gilbert. 3: 776–821. Durham, N.C.: Duke University
          Press, 1965.

c) Intellectuals

(1) Women

05089.   Borzelli, Angelo. Una Poetessa italiana del secolo XVI
          (Gaspara Stampa 1523–1553). Naples: L. Chuirazzi, 1888.

05090.   Cavazzana, C. "Cassandra Fedele erudita veneziana del rinas-
          cimento." Ateneo veneto 29 (1906): 73–91, 249–275.

05091. Feliciangeli, B. "Notizie sulla vita e sugli scritti di
        Costanza Varano-Sforza. (1426-1447)." Giornale storico
        della letteratura italiana 23 (1894): 1-75.

05092. Franceschini, G. "Battista Montefeltre Malatesta, signora di
        Pesaro." Studia oliveriana 6 (1958): 7-43.

05093. King, Margaret Leah. "Book-Lined Cells: Women and Humanism in
        the Early Italian Renaissance." In Beyond their Sex:
        Learned Women of the European Past, edited by Patricia
        Labalme, pp. 66-90. New York: New York University Press,
        1980.

05094. _____. "Thwarted Ambitions: Six Learned Women
        of the Early Italian Renaissance." Soundings 76 (1976):
        280-300.

05095. Kristeller, Paul Oskar. "Learned Women of Early Modern Italy:
        Humanists and University Scholars." In Beyond their Sex:
        Learned Women of the European Past, edited by Patricia
        Labalme, pp. 91-116. New York: New York University Press,
        1980.

05096. Medin, A. "Maddalena degli Scrovegni e le discordie tra i
        Carraresi e gli Scrovegni." Atti e memorie dell'Accademia
        di Padova n.s. 12 (1895-96): 243-272.

05097. Michiel, Domenico. Elogio di Costanza da Varano. Venice:
        n.p., 1807.

05098. Pesenti, G. "Alessandra Scala, una figura della Rinascenza
        fiorentina." Giornale storico della letteratura italiana
        85 (1925): 241-267.

05099. Rabil, Albert. Laura Cereta, Quattrocento Humanist. Bing-
        hamton, N.Y.: Medieval and Renaissance Texts and Studies,
        1981.

05100. Simonsfeld, H. "Zur Geschichte der Cassandra Fedele." In
        Studien zur Litteraturgeschichte, Michael Bernays gewidmet
        pp. 97-108. Leipzig: L. Voss, 1893.

                        (2) Olympia Morata

05101. Bonnet, Jules. Vie d'Olympia Morata, episode de la renaissance
        et de la réforme en Italie. 1856. Reprint. New Haven,
        Conn.: Research Publications Inc., 1975.

05102. Bowles, Caroline. Olympia Morata. London: Smith Elder, 1834.

05103. Munch, Ernst Hermann Joseph. Olympia Fulvia Morata. Freiburg
        im Breisgau: n.p., 1827.

05104.   Smyth, Amelia Gillespie. Olympia Morata, her Times, Life and
          Writings. London: Smith, Elder, 1836.

05105.   Turnbull, Robert. Olympia Morata, Her Life and Times.
          Boston: Sabbath School Society, 1846.

05106.   Vorlander, Dorothea. "Olympia Fulvia Morata eine evangelische
          Humanistin in Schweinfurt." Zeitschrift für bayerische
          Kirchengeschichte 29 (1970): 95-113.

05107.   Walser, Hermann. Olympia Morata (1526-1555). Der Lebensweg
          einer ungewöhnlichen Frau. Stuttgart: Steinkopf, 1933.

                     (3) Isotta Nogarola

05108.   King, Margaret Leah. "The Religious Retreat of Isotta
          Nogarola (1418-1466): Sexism and its Consequences in the
          Fifteenth Century." Signs 3 (Summer 1978): 807-822.

05109.   Robathan, Dorothy. "A Fifteenth-Century Bluestocking."
          Medievalia et humanistica 2 (1944): 106-111.

05110.   Sabbadini, R. "Notizie sulla vita e gli scritti di alcuni
          dotti umanisti del secolo XV raccolte da codici italianai,
          V: Isotta Nogarola." Giornale storico della letteratura
          italiana 6 (1885): 163-165.

                     d) Art and Artifacts

                     (1) Women in Art

05111.   Allen, Virginia. "The Naked Lady: A Look at Venus in the
          Renaissance." Feminist Art Journal 6 (Spring 1977): 27-29.

05112.   Arciniegas, German. El Mundo de la Bella Simonetta. Buenos
          Aires: Editorial Sudamericana, 1962.

05113.   Jacobson-Schutte, Anne. "'Trionfo delle donne': Tematiche
          di Rovesciamento dei Ruoli nella Firenze Rinascementale."
          Quaderni storici 44 (August 1980): 474-496.

05114.   Schapiro, Meyer. "Leonardo and Freud: An Art-Historical
          Study." Journal of the History of Ideas 17 (1956): 147-178.

05115.   Steinberg, Leo. "Metaphors of Love and Birth in Michelangelo's
          Pietas." In Studies in Erotic Art, edited by T. Bowie, O.J.
          Brundel, et. al., pp. New York: Basic Books, 1970.

05116.   Tomory, P.A.   "Profane Love in Italian Early and High Baroque
         Painting. The Transmission of Emotive Experience." In
         Essays in the History of Art Presented to Rudolph Wittkower,
         edited by Douglas Fraser, Howard Hibbard and Milton J.
         Lewis, pp. 182-187. London: Phaidon Press, 1967.

                          (2)   Women Artists

                          (a)   Actresses

05117.   Gilder, Rosamond. "The Commediante Appears. The First
         Actresses in Italy." In Enter the Actress, the First
         Women in the Theatre, pp. 46-66. Boston: Houghton-
         Mifflin Company, 1931.

05118.   _____. "Isabella Andreini Europe's Prima Donna
         Innamorata." In Enter the Actress, the First Women in the
         Theatre, pp. 67-81. Boston: Houghton-Mifflin Company,
         1931.

                          (b)   Painters/Sculptors

                          [1]   SOFONISBA ANGUISSOLA

05119.   Bonetti, C. "Nel centario di Sofonisba Anguissola." Archivio
         storico lombardo 55 (1928): 285-306.

05120.   Cook, Herbert. "More Portraits by Sofonisba Anguissola."
         Burlington Magazine 26 (1914-1915): 228-236.

05121.   Fournier-Sarloveze M. "Sofonisba Anguissola et ses soeurs."
         Revue de l'art ancien et moderne 5 (1899) no. 25: 313-324
         and no. 26: 379-392.

05122.   Haraszti-Takács, Marianne. "Nouvelles donnees relatives à la
         vie et a l'oeuvre de Sofonisba Anguissola." Bulletin du
         Musée hongrois des beaux-arts 31 (1968): 53-67.

05123.   Holmes, C.J. "Sofonisba Anguissola and Philip II." Burlington
         Magazine 26 (1914-1915): 181-187.

05124.   Kühnel-Kunze, Irene. "Zur Bildniskunst der Sofonisba und
         Lucia Anguisciola." Pantheon 20 (1962): 83-96.

05125. Nicodemi, G. "Commemorazione di artisti minori -- Sofonisba
        Anguissola." Emporium 66 (1927): 222-233.

05126. Tolnay, Charles de. "Sofonisba Anguissola and her relations
        with Michelangelo." Journal of the Walters Art Gallery 4
        (1941): 115-119.

05127. Tufts, Eleanor. "Sofonisba Anguissola. Renaissance Woman."
        Art News 71 (1972): 50-53.

                        [2] OTHERS

05128. Bissell, R. Ward. "Artemisia Gentileschi--A New Documented
        Chronology." Art Bulletin 50 (June 1968): 153-168.

05129. Ragg, Laura. The Women Artists of Bologna. London: Methuen
        and Co., 1907.

05130. Vasari, Georgio. Lives of the Most Eminent Painters, Sculptors,
        and Architects. 10 vols. London: Philip Lee Warner, 1912.
        [See especially vol. 5, "Life of Madonna Properzia de'
        Rossi," pp. 123-128.]

G. LOW COUNTRIES

1. POLITICAL

"Margaret of Austria matured into a person who knew very
well what she wanted. She refused to let herself be used
any longer in the political game . . . ."
                        Jane de Iongh, Margaret of Austria

a) Political Roles

(1) Women

05131. Claikens, W. "Marie-Anne, archduchesse d'Autriche, duchesse
        de Lorraine et de Bar, gouvernante-générale éphémère des
        Pay-Bas." Folklore brabançon 210 (June 1976): 209-263.

05132. Stouff, Louis. Catherine de Bourgogne et la féodalité de
        l'Alsace autrichienne, ou un essai des ducs de Bourgogne
        pour constituer une seigneurie bourguignonne en Alsace
        (1411-1426). Paris: Librairie de la société de recueil
        Sirey, 1913.

05133.   Thelliez, C. Marie de Luxembourg, duchesse douairière de
         Vendôme, comtesse douairière de St.-Pol, comtesse douairière
         d'Enghien, dame de La Fere, et son temps. Anciens pays et
         assemblées d'états, no. 52.   Louvain: Editions Nauwelaerts,
         1970.

05134.   Willard, Charity Cannon. "Isabel of Portugal and the French
         Translation of the 'Triunfo de las donas.'" Revue belge
         de philologie et d'histoire 43 (1965): 961-969.

         Also refer to #4681-4687.

                          (2) Individuals

                     (a) Margaret of Austria

05135.   Andrews, Marian. The High and Puissant Princess Marguerite
         of Austria, Princess Dowager of Spain, Duchess Dowager of
         Savoy, Regent of the Netherlands. New York: C. Scribner's
         Sons, 1907.

05136.   Besson, André. Marguerite d'Autriche ou la Belle Marguerite.
         Paris: Nouv. ed. Latines, 1968.

05137.   Boom, Ghislaine de. Marguerite d'Autriche-Savoie et la pre-
         renaissance. Paris: Droz, 1935.

05138.   Bruchet, Max. "A propos de lettres mal datées de la Chancel-
         lerie de Marguerite d'Autriche." In Mélanges d'histoire
         offerts à Henri Pirenne, pp. 55-62. Brussels: Vromant,
         1926.

05139.   _____. Marguerite d'Autriche, duchesse de Savoie.
         Lille: Imprimerie L. Danel, 1927.

05140.   Carton de Wiart, Henry, comte. Marguerite d'Autriche.
         Paris: B. Grasset, 1935.

05141.   Chagney, A. and Girard, Fr. Marguerite d'Autriche-Bourgogne.
         Chambery: Dardet, 1929.

05142.   Iongh, Jane. Margaret of Austria. New York: Norton, 1958.

05143.   Jacquemin, Juliette. Une Princesse de jadis: Marguerite
         d'Autriche. Paris: Libraire de France, 1931.

05144.   Juste, Theodore. Charles V et Marguerite d'Autriche.
         Brussels: M. Hayes, 1858.

05145.   Munch, Ernst. Margaretha von Osterreich, Statthalterin der
         Niederlanden. Leipzig: J. Scheible, 1833.

05146. Pinchia, E. Margherita d'Austria, duchessa di Savoia (1480-1530). Ivrea: Viasonne, 1931.

05147. Thibaut, Francisque. Marguerite d'Autriche et Jehan Lemaire de Belges. Paris: E. Leroux, 1888.

05148. Tremayne, Eleanor E. The First governess of the Netherlands: Margaret of Austria. New York: G. P. Putnam's Sons, 1908.

05149. Winker, E. Margarete von Österreich: Grande dame der renaissance. Munich: Callwey, 1966.

(b) Margaret of Parma

05150. Caesari, Giovanni de. Margherita di Savoia-Farnese e la citta di Penne. Penne: Volpi, 1929.

05151. Gomez del Campillo, M. "Margarita de Austria, Duquesa de Parma." Boletin de la Real Academia de la Historia 145 (October-December 1959): 145-178; 146 (January-March 1960): 21-62.

05152. Rachfahl, Felix. Margaretha von Parma, Statthalterin der Niederlande. Munich: R. Oldenbourg, 1898.

(c) Mary of Hungary

05153. Boom, Ghislaine de. Marie de Hongrie. Brussels: La Renaissance du Livre, 1956.

05154. Heiss, Gernot. "Politik und Ratgeber der Königin Maria von Ungarn in den Jahren 1521-1531." Mitteilungen des Instituts für Österreichische Geschichtsforschung 82 (1974): 119-180.

05155. _____. "Die ungarischen, bohmischen und österreichischen Gesitzungen der Königin Maria (1505-1558) und ihre Verwaltung." Mitteilungen des österreichischen Staatsarchivs 27 (1974): 61-100.

05156. Iongh, Jane. Mary of Hungary: Second Regent of the Netherlands. London: Faber and Faber, 1959.

05157. Juste, Th. Le Pay Bas sous Charles V. Vie de Marie de Hongrie. Paris: Librairie de Decq., 1861.

2. SOCIAL

"Distaff and spindle are the proper equipment for women."
Erasmus, Colloquies

05158. Godding, Ph. "Le droit des gens mariés à Nivelles (14e - 15^e
siecles)." Revue d'histoire du droit 40 (1972): 73-117.

Also refer to #5162.

3. CULTURAL

"A woman that is truly wise does not think herself so; but
on the contrary, one that knows nothing thinks herself to be
wise, and that is being twice the fool."
Erasmus, The Colloquies

a) Desiderius Erasmus

05159. Erasmus, Desiderius. The Colloquies. Translated by Craig R.
Thompson. Chicago: University of Chicago Press, 1965.
[See especially "The Abbot and the Learned Lady," pp. 217-
223.]

05160. _____. "The Education of Girls." In Desiderius
Erasmus: Concerning the Aim and Method of Education, by
William Harrison Woodward, pp. 148-153. 1904. Reprint.
New York: Lennox Hill Publishing and Distributing Co.,
1971.

05161. _____. The Praise of Folly. Translated by
Thomas Chaloner. New York: Oxford University Press, 1965.

05162. Telle, Emile Villemeu. Erasme de Rotterdam et le septième
sacrament. Étude d'evangelisme matrimonial au VI siècle
et contribution a la biographie intellectuelle d'Erasme.
Geneva: Librarie E. Droz, 1954.

05163. Woodward, William Harrison. Desiderius, Erasmus: Concerning
the Aim and Method of Education. 1904. Reprint. New York:
Lenox Hill Publishing and Distribution Co., 1971.
[See especially pp. 148-154.]

V. SEVENTEENTH CENTURY

A. GENERAL

1. POLITICAL

"If they [women who entered convents] had been of the other
sex they would have commanded and governed the world."
Comment on ecclesiastical regulations

05164. Vincens, Cecile. <u>Princesses and court ladies</u>. New York:G.P.
Putnam's Sons, 1906.

2. RELIGION

"You know that in several parts of France . . . and in
several other parts of Europe, all one hears is of witchcraft, and that no town or hamlet is so small that it has no
one reputed to be a witch."
Pierre Bayle

05165. Pensa, Henri. <u>Sorcellerie et religion du désordre dans les
esprits et dans les moeurs aux XVIIe et XVIIIe siècles</u>.
Paris:Poinsot, 1935.

05166. Sinistrari, Ludovico Maria. <u>Demoniality</u>. Translated by
Montague Summers. London: Fortune Press, 1928.

3. SOCIAL

"A Woman is a kind of merchandise which must be carefully
protected because it is easily damaged."
                    17th century Venetian nobleman

a) Generic

05167. Gleichen-Russwurm, Alexander von. Das galante Europa.
        Geselligkeit der grossen Welt, 1600-1789. Stuttgart:
        Julius Hoffman, 1921.

b) Demography

05168. "Fertility of the XVII and XVIII centuries ruling families.
        Age of the father as a factor of fertility." Population 31
        July-October 1976): 961-969.

05169. Perrenoud, Alfred. "Malthusianisme et protestantisme, 'un modele
        démographique weberien.'" Annales: économies, sociétés,
        civilisations 29 (July-August 1974): 975-978.

        Also refer to #4049.

c) Family

05170. Flandrin, Jean-Louis. "La cellule familiale et l'oeuvre de
        procréation dans l'ancienne société." XVIIe siècle 102-103
        (1974): 3-14.

05171. Laslett, Peter. "La famille et le ménage: approches histori-
        iques." Annales: economies, sociétés, civilisations 27
        (July-September 1972): 847-872.

d) Fashion/Manners

05172. Parsons, Frank Alvah. "The Seventeenth Century in France,
        Italy and England." In The Psychology of Dress, pp. 149-
        192. New York: Doubleday, Page and Co., 1921.

05173. Payne, Blanche. "Women's Costume of the Seventeenth Century."
        In History of Costume, pp. 355-384. New York: Harper and
        Row Publishers, 1965.

4. CULTURAL

"What has poor Woman done, that she must be Debarr'd from
Sense and Sacred poetry?"

                          Aphra Behn, 1678

a) Education

05174. Babeau, Albert. "L'Enseignement professionel et ménager des
        filles aux XVIIe et XVIIIe siècles." Reforme sociale 50
        (1905): 205-217.

05175. Park, Roberta J. "Concern for the physical education of the
        female sex from 1675 to 1800 in France, England and Spain."
        Research Quarterly 45 (May 1974): 276-292.

b) Literature

05176. Richards, S. A. Feminist writers of the Seventeenth Century,
        with special reference to Francois Poulain de la Barre.
        London: D. Nutt, 1914.

B. BRITISH ISLES

1. SURVEYS

"A Woman now comes to reform the stage who once has stood the brunt of this unthinking age."

The Unnatural Mother 1697

a) Non-specific

05177. Butler, H.B. and Fletcher, C.R.L. *Historical Portraits.* 1600–1700. Oxford: Clarendon Press, 1911.

05178. Clark, George N. *The Later Stuarts,* 1660–1714. Oxford: Clarendon Press, 1949.

05179. Petherick, Maurice. *Restoration Rogues.* London: Hollis Carter, 1951.

05180. Sergeant, Philip Walsingham. *Rogues and Scandals.* New York: Brentano's, 1927.

05181. Urdang, Laurence, Associates, compilers. *Lives of the Stuart Age.* New York: Barnes & Noble, 1976.

b) Women

05182. Anderson, James. *The Ladies of the Convent, Memoirs of Distinguished Scottish Female Character.* New York: Redfield, 1853.

05183. _____ . *Memorable women of the Puritan times.* London; Blackie and Son, 1862.

05184. Fea, Alan. *Some Beauties of the Seventeenth Century.* London: Methuen and Co., 1906.

05185. Johnson, Grace. *Leading Women of the Restoration.* London: Digby, Long, 1892.

2. POLITICAL

"It is a sin for a man to come lower than God hath set him:
it is not humility, but baseness to be ruled by her, whom
he should rule."

The Bride Bush, 1619

a) Legal

05186. Edwards, Valerie S. "The Case of the Married Spinster: An
Alternative Explanation." American Journal of Legal History
21 (July 1977): 260-265.

05187. Heale, William. An Apologie For Women: or, and Opposition to
Mr. Dr.G., his Assertion . . . that is Lawful for Husbands
to Beate Their Wives. 1609. Reprint. Norwood, N.J.: W.W.
Johnson, 1974.

05188. McLaren, Dorothy. "The Marriage Act of 1653: Its Influence on
the Parish Registers." Population Studies 28 (July 1974):
319-327.

05189. Shanley, Mary Lyndon. "Marriage Contract and Social Contract
in Seventeenth Century English Political Thought." Western
Political Quarterly 32 (March 1979): 79-91.

b) Criminal

05190. Blumenthal, Walter Hart. Brides from Bridewell: Female Felons
Sent to Colonial America. Rutland, Vt.: Charles E. Tuttle
Company, 1962.

05191. D'Auvergne, Edmund B. "'The German Princess.' (Mary Carleton)."
In Adventuresses and Adventurous Ladies, pp. 45-63. New
York: J.H. Sears and Company, Inc., 1927.

05192. LeComte, Edward. The Notorious Lady Essex. New York: Dial
Press, 1969.

05193. Main, C.F. "The German Princess; or Mary Carleton in Fact
and Fiction." Harvard Library Bulletin 10 (1956): 166-85.

05194.   Matter, Joseph Allan. My Lords and Ladies of Essex: Their
         State Trials. Chicago: Henry Regnery Co., 1969.

05195.   Singleton, Robert R. "Defoe, Moll Flanders, and the Ordinary
         of Newgate." Harvard Library Bulletin 24 (October 1976):
         407-413.

c) Feminism

05196.   Baines, Barbara J., intro. Three Pamphlets on the Jacobean
         Antifeminist Controversy. New York: Scholars' Facsimiles
         and Reprints, 1978.
         [Hic Mulier:or, the Man-Woman
          Haec-Ur:or, The Womanish-Man
          Muld Sacke:or, The Apologie of Hic Mulier]

05197.   Butler, Melissa. "Early Liberal Roots of Feminism: John
         Locke and the Attack on Patriarchy." American Political
         Science Review 72 (March 1978): 135-150.

d) Political Roles

(1) Women

05198.   Bunten, Alice Chambers. Life of Alice Barnham (1592-1650)
         Wife of Sir Francis Bacon, baron Verulam, viscount St.
         Albans. London: Oliphants Ltd., 1928.

05199.   Cecil, Lord David. Two Quiet Lives. Dorothy Osborne. Thomas
         Gray. New York: Bobbs Merrill, 1948.

05200.   Evelyn, John. The Life of Mrs. Godolphin. Edited by Harriet
         Sampson. New York: Oxford University Press, 1940.

05201.   Fea, Allan. "Portraits of Nell Gwyn, Moll Davis, and others."
         Connoisseur 111 (1943): 29-33.

05202.   Fell-Smith, Charlotte. Mary Rich, countess of Warwick, (1625-
         1678): her family and friends. New York: Longmans, Green
         and Co., 1901.

05203.   Fullerton, Georgiana. Life of Elizabeth, Lady Falkland
         (1585-1639). London: Burns, 1883.

05204. Grant, Douglas. Margaret the First: A Biography of Margaret
        Cavendish, Duchess of Newcastle, 1623-1673. London:
        Hart-Davis, 1956.

05205. Hartmann, Cyril Hughes. La Belle Stuart. Memoirs of court and
        society in the times of Frances Teresa Stuart, Duchess of
        Richmond and Lennox. London: G.Routledge and Sons, 1924.

05206. Jameson, Anna Brownell (Murphy). The beauties of the court of
        King Charles the Second: a series of memoirs. Philadelphia:
        E.L. Carey and A. Hart, 1834.

05207. McArthur, Ellen A. "Women Petitioners and the Long Parlia-
        ment." English Historical Review 24 (1909): 698-709.

05208. Marshall, Rosalind. The days of Duchess Anne, Life in the
        household of the Duchess of Hamilton 1656-1716. London:
        Collins, 1973.

05209. Norsworthy, Laura. The Lady of Bleeding Heart Yard, Lady
        Elizabeth Hatton, 1576-1646. New York: Harcourt, Brace
        and Co., 1936.

05210. Senior, Dorothy Ponsonby. The king's ladies. Charles II and
        his ladies of pleasure. London: Hale, 1936.

05211. Weigall, David. "Women Militants in the English Civil War."
        History Today 22 (June 1972): 434-438.

05212. Williams, Ethel Carleton. Anne of Denmark. London: Longmans,
        1970.

05213. Witt, Henriette Elizabeth (Guizot) dame de. The Lady of
        Lathom: life and Letters of Charlotte de la Tremouille,
        Countess of Derby. London: Smith, Elder and Co., 1869.

                        (2) Individuals

                    (a) Catherine of Braganza

05214. Bevan, Bryan. "Queen Catherine of Braganza 1638-1705."
        Contemporary Review 207 (1965):308-312.

05215. Davidson, Lillias Campbell. Catherine of Braganza, Infanta
        of Portugal and queen-consort of England. London: J.
        Murray, 1908.

05216. MacKay, Janet. Catherine of Braganza. London: J. Long,
        Ltd., 1937.

(b) Lady Anne Clifford

05217. Notestein, Wallace. Four Worthies: John Chamberlain, Anne
        Clifford, John Taylor, Oliver Heywood. New Haven: Yale
        University Press, 1957.

05218. Spence, R. T. "Lady Anne Clifford, Countess of Dorset,
        Pembroke and Montgomery (1590-1676): A Reappraisal."
        Northern History 15 (1979): 43-65.

05219. Williamson, George C. Lady Anne Clifford, Countess of Dorset,
        Pembroke and Montgomery 1590-1676. 1922. Reprint.
        Buntingford, Hertfordshire: Layston Press Ltd., 1967.

(c) Nell Gwyn

05220. Bax, Clifford. Pretty Witty Nell. New York: Morrow, 1933.

05221   Bevan, Bryan. Nell Gwyn. London: Robert Hale, 1969.

05222. Cunningham, Peter, ed., The Story of Nell Gwyn and the
        the Sayings of Charles II. Edinburgh: John Grant, 1908.

05223. Dasent, Arthur Irwin. Nell Gwynne, 1650-1687. London:
        Macmillan and Co., ltd., 1924.

05224. Hoare, Joan. "The death of Nell Gwyn." History Today 27
        (June 1977): 396-399.

05225. Van Lennep, William. "Nell Gwyn's playgoing at the king's
        expense." Harvard Library Bulletin 4 (1950): 405-408.

05226. Wilson, John Harold. Nell Gwyn: Royal Mistress. New York:
        Pellegrini & Cudahy, 1952.

        Also refer to #5201.

(d) Henrietta Maria

05227. Bone, Quentin. Henrietta Maria, Queen of the Cavaliers.
        Urbana: University of Illinois Press, 1972.

05228. Carré, Henri. Henriette de France, reine d'Angleterre.
        Paris: Grasset, 1947.

05229. Hamilton, Elizabeth. *Henrietta Maria*. London: Hamish Hamilton, 1976.

05230. MacKay, Janet. *Little madam. A biography of Henrietta Maria*. London: Bell, 1939.

05231. Oliver, Jane. *Queen of Tears. The Life of Henrietta Maria*. London: Collins, 1940.

05232. Oman, Carola. *Henrietta Maria*. London: Hodder and Stoughton, 1936.

05233. Saint-André, Claude. *Henriette d'Angleterre et la cour de Louis XIV*. Paris: Plon, 1933.

05234. Smuts, R.M. "The Puritan Followers of Henrietta Maria in the 1630's." *English Historical Review* 93 (1978): 26-45.

(e) Mary II

05235. Bowen, Marjorie. *The Third Mary Stuart, Mary of York, Orange, and England*. London: John Lane, 1929.

05236. Chapman, Hester W. *Mary II, Queen of England*. 1953. Reprint. Westport, Conn.: Greenwood Press, 1976.

05237. Hamilton, Elizabeth. *William's Mary, A Biography of Mary II*. New York: Taplinger Publishing Co., 1972.

05238. Sandars, Mary F. *Princess and Queen of England, Life of Mary II*. London: Stanley Paul, 1913.

05239. Van der Zee, Henry, and Van der Zee, Barbara. *William and Mary*. New York: Knopf, 1973.

05240. Waterson, Nellie Marion. *Mary II, Queen of England, 1689-1694*. Durham, N.C.: Duke University Press, 1928.

Also refer to #4120.

(f) Mary of Modena

05241. Halle, Marie. *Queen Mary of Modena, Her Life and Letters*. New York: Dutton, 1905.

05242. Hopkirk, Mary. *Queen over the water, Mary Beatrice of Modena, Queen of James II*. London: Murray, 1953.

05243. Oman, Carola. *Mary of Modena*. London: Hodder and Stoughton, 1962.

05244.   Zuccoli, V. Capece Galeota. _Maria di Modena regina d'Inghliterra_. Milan: Ceschina, 1939.

(g) Louise de Keroualle, duchess of Portsmouth

05245.   Baldensperger, Ferdinand. "Louise de Keroualle et ses quinze ans d'Angleterre." _Revue bleue_ 73 (1935): 694-700.

05246.   Delpech, Jeanine. _Life and Times of Duchess of Portsmouth_. Translated by Ann Lindsay. New York: Rov Publishers, 1953.

05247.   Forneron, H. _Louise de Keroualle, duchesse of Portsmouth_. London: S. Sonnenschein and Co., 1891.

05248.   Grant, Colquhoun. _Louise Renée de Keroualle (Duchess of Portsmouth)_. 1909. Reprint. Philadelphia: Richard West, 1977.

(h) Barbara Villiers

05249.   Andrews, Allen. _The Royal Whore: Barbara Villiers, Countess of Castelmaine_. London: Hutchinson, 1971.

05250.   Gilmour, Margaret. _The great lady: a biography of Barbara Villiers, mistress of Charles II_. New York: Alfred A. Knopf, 1941.

05251.   Hamilton, Elizabeth. _The Illustrious Lady_. _A Biography of Barbara Villiers, Countess of Castelmaine and Duchess of Cleveland_. London: Hamish Hamilton, 1980.

05252.   Sergeant, Philip Walsingham. _My Lady Castlemaine_. London: Hutchinson and Co., 1912.

3. ECONOMIC

"In your marriage look after goodnes rather [than] goodes."
Sir Edward Montagu

05253.   Clark, Alice. _Working Life of Women in the Seventeenth Century_. Fairfield, N.J.: Augustus M. Kelley, 1978.

05254.   Fenton, A. "Farm Servant Life in the Seventeenth to Nineteenth Centuries." _Scottish Agriculture_ 44 (1965): 281-285.

05255.   Hole, Christina. The English Housewife in the Seven-
         teenth Century. London: Chatto and Windus, 1953.

4. RELIGION

"When women preach and cobblers pray, the fiends in hell
make holiday."
                                      Lucifer's Lackey, 1641

a) Saints/Religious Women

05256.   English Churchwomen of the Seventeenth Century. New York:
         J.A. Sparks, 1846.

05257.   The lives of Women Saints of our Contrie of England, also
         some of the ancient fathers (1610-1615). Edited by C.
         Horstman, 1886. Reprint. Millwood, New York: Kraus
         Reprint Co., 1973.

b) Religious Orders

(1) Women

05258.   Hardman, Sister Ann. Two English Carmelites. Mother Mary
         Xaveria Burton (1688-1714). Mother Mary Margeret Wake
         (1617-1678). London: Burns, Oates and Washbourne, 1939.

05259.   Matthew, Sir Tobie. The Life of Lady Lucy Knatchbull 1642.
         Reprint. London: Sheed and Ward, 1932.

(2) Mary Ward

05260.   Chambers, Mary Catherine Elizabeth. The Life of Mary Ward.
         (1585-1645). London: Burns, 1882.

05261.   Codenhove, Ida Goerres. Mary Ward. London: Longmans
         Green and Co., 1939.

05262. Egenter, Richard. Wagnis in Christo, Maria Ward und die
        Idee der christlichen Selbständigkeit. Regensburg:
        Verlag von Josef Habbel, 1936.

05263. Grisar, Joseph. "Die beiden ältesten Leben Maria Wards der
        Grunderin der Englischen Fraulein." Historisches Jahrbuch
        70 (1951): 154-189.

05264. Herkommer, Agnes. Mary Ward. Augsburg: Kyrios Verlag, 1947.

05265. Oliver, Sister Mary. Mary Ward, 1585-1645. New York:
        Sheed and Ward, Inc., 1959.

05266. Salome, Mother M. Mary Ward: A Foundress of the Seventeenth
        Century. New York: Benziger Bros., 1901.

c) Puritans

05267. Cohen, Alfred. "The Fifth Monarchy Mind: Mary Cary and the
        Origins of Totalitarianism." Social Research 31 (Summer
        1964): 195-213.

d) Quakers

05268. Blecki, Catherine La Courreye. "Alice Hayes and Mary Pening-
        ton: Personal Identity within the Tradition of Quaker
        Spiritual Autobiography." Quaker History 65 (Spring 1976):
        19-31.

05269. Brailsford, Mabel Richmond. Quaker Women, 1650-1690.
        London: Duckworth and Co., 1915.

05270. Crosfield, Helen G. Margaret Fell of Swarthmoor Hall.
        London: Headley Brothers, 1913.

05271. Edwards, Irene L. "The Women Friends of London." Journal
        of the Friends' Historical Society 47 (1955): 3-21.

05272. Manners, Emily. Elizabeth Hooton, first Quaker Woman
        Preacher, 1660-1672. New York: D. S. Taber, 1914.

05273. Ross, Isabel. Margaret Fell: Mother of Quakerism. London:
        Longmans, Green and Co., 1948.

05274. Vann, Richard T. The Social Development of Quakerism, 1655-
        1755. Cambridge, Mass.: Harvard University Press, 1969.

05275. "Women Writers among Friends in the Seventeenth Century and
        Later." Journal, Friends Historical Society 10 (1913):
        93-95.

e) Other Protestant Sects

05276. Thomas, Keith. "Women and the Civil War Sects." In
        Crisis in Europe, 1560-1660, edited by Trevor Aston, pp.
        332-357. New York: Basic Books, 1965. Also in Past and
        Present 13 (1958): 42-62.

05277. Williams, Ethyn Morgan. "Women Preachers in the Civil War."
        Journal of Modern History 1 (December 1929): 561-569.

        Also refer to #4236.

f) Witchcraft

05278. Bovet, Richard. Pandaemonium. 1684. Reprint. London:
        Aldington, Kent, Hand and Flower Press, 1951.

05279. Glanvill, Joseph. Sadducismus triumphatus, or A Full and
        Plain Evidence Concerning Witches and Apparitions. 1689.
        Reprint. Gainesville, Fla.: Scholars Facsimiles and
        Reprints, 1966.

05280. Harris, Anthony J. Night's Black Agents: Witchcraft and
        Magic in Seventeenth Century English Drama. Totowa,
        N.J.: Rowman and Littlefield, 1980.

05281. Harrison, G.B., ed. The Trial of the Lancaster Witches,
        A.D. MDCXII. London: Peter Davies, 1929.

05282. Hill, Christopher. Anti-Christ in 17th Century England.
        New York: Harper and Row, 1970.

05283. Kittredge, George Lyman. "English Witchcraft and James I." In
        Studies in the History of Religion presented to Crawford
        Howell Toy by pupils, colleagues and friends, edited by
        David Fout Moore, pp. 1-65. New York: Macmillan, 1912.

05284. Summers, Montague. The Discovery of Witches, A Study of
        Master Matthew Hopkins Commonly Call'd Witch Finder
        General. Includes Reprint of the Discovery of Witches.
        1647. London: Cayme Press, 1928.

05285.   Thomas, Keith. "Witchcraft: Decline." In Religion and
          the Decline of Magic, pp. 570-583. New York: Charles
          Scribner's Sons, 1971.

05286.   White, Beatrice. "Cain's Kin." In The Witch Figure,
          edited by Venetia Newall, pp. 188-199. Boston: Rout-
          ledge and Kegan Paul, 1973.

          Also refer to #4033, 4040, 4260-4262, 4264, 4267-4269, 4271.

5. SOCIAL

"One of the greatest mistakes and mischiefs of our age
is dis-esteem of wives."

                              E. Waterhouse

a) Generic

(1) Non-specific

05287.   Ashley, Maurice. Life in Stuart England. New York:
          Putnam, 1964.

05288.   Bahlmann, Dudley. The Moral Revolution of 1688. New
          Haven: Yale University Press, 1957.

05289.   Bedford, Jessie. Home Life under the Stuarts, 1603-1649.
          London: Stanley Paul and Co., 1925.

05290.   _____. Social Life under the Stuarts. New York:
          E.P. Dutton and Co., 1904.

05291.   Besant, Sir Walter. London in the Time of the Stuarts.
          London: Adam and Charles Black, 1903.

05292.   Bridenbaugh, Carl. Vexed and Troubled Englishmen 1590-1642.
          New York: Oxford University Press, 1968.

05293.   Brooke, Iris. Life under the Stuarts. London: Falcon Edu-
          cational Books, 1950.
          [See especially ch. 15.]

05294.   Burton, Elizabeth. The Jacobeans at home. London: Secker
          and Warburg, 1962.

05295. Burton, Elizabeth. The Pageant of Stuart England. New York: Scribner, 1962.

05296. Coate, Mary. Social Life in Stuart England. 1924. Reprint. Westport, Conn.: Greenwood Press, 1971.

05297. Hill, Christopher. Puritanism and Revolution Studies in Interpretation of the English Revolution of the Seventeenth Century. London: Seeker and Warburg, 1958.
        [See especially Ch. 14, pp. 367-394, Clarissa Harlowe and her Times (Puritan attitudes toward Society, Marriage, and Individual conscience), pp. 367-394.]

05298. _____. Society and Puritanism in Pre-Revolutionary England. London: Panther, 1969.

05299. _____. The World Turned Upside Down, Radical Ideas during the English Revolution. London: Temple Smith, 1972.
        [See especially ch. 15, "Base Imprudent Kisses, The Puritan Sexual Revolution and Beyond," pp. 247-260.]

05300. Laslett, Peter. "Clayworth and Cogenhoe." In Family Life and illicit love in earlier generations, pp. 50-101. New York: Cambridge University Press, 1977.

05301. Roebuck, Peter. Yorkshire Baronets, 1640-1760: Family, Estates, and Fortunes. New York: Oxford University Press, 1980.

05302. Saunders, Beatrice. The Age of Candlelight, The English Social Scene in the Seventeenth Century. London: Centaur Press, 1959.

        Also refer to #4283, 4301.

(2) Women

(a) Contemporary

05303. Drake, Judith.   An Essay in Defense of the Female Sex. 1696. Reprint. New York: Source Book Press, 1970.

05304. Halifax, George Saville, first marquis of. The Lady's New Years Gift; Advice to a Daughter. 1688. Reprint. New Haven: Research Publications Inc., 1975.

(b) Secondary

05305. Bradley, Rose M. The English Housewife in the Seventeenth and Eighteenth Century. London: Edward Arnold, 1912.

05306. Michel, Robert H. "English Attitudes Towards Women, 1640–
        1700." Canadian Journal of History 13 (April 1978): 35–60.

05307. Thompson, Roger. Women in Stuart England and America, a
        comparative study. London: Routledge and Kegan Paul, 1974.

b) Demography

05308. Glass, David Victor. "Notes on the demography of London at the
        end of the 17th century." In Population and Social Change,
        edited by D.V. Glass and Roger Reville, pp. 275–285. New
        York: Crane, Russak, 1972. Also in Daedalus 97 (Spring
        1968): 581–592.

05309. Hollingsworth, Mary and Hollingsworth, T.H. "Plague Mortality
        Rates by Age and Sex in the Parish of St. Botolph's Without,
        Bishopgate, London, 1603." Population Studies 25 (1971):
        131–146.

05310. Kuczynski, R. R. "British Demographers' Opinion on Fertility,
        1660–1760." Political Arithmetic, edited by Lancelog
        Hogben, pp. 283–327. New York: Macmillan, 1938.

05311. Lloyd, L.C., "Multiple Births in Shropshire, 1601–1800,"
        Local Population Studies 3 (1969): 29–37.

05312. McLaren, Dorothy. "Fertility, Infant Mortality and Breast
        Feeding in the Seventeenth Century." Medical History 22
        (October 1978): 378–396.

05313. Wrigley, E. Anthony. "Marital Fertility in Seventeenth–Century
        Colytn: A Note (reply to Richard B. Morrow)." Economic
        History Review 31 (August 1978): 429–436.

        Also refer to #4311, 4312, 4314.

c) Family

(1) Non-specific

05314. Bourcier, Elisabeth. "La famille anglaise dans la premier
        moitié du XVIIe siècle a travers les journaux privés du
        temps." Recherches anglaises et américaines 8 (1975): 30–40.

05315. Carrive, L. "La vision de la famille chez les moralistes
        puritains." Recherches anglaises et américaines 8 (1975):
        54-71.

05316. MacFarlane, Alan. The Family Life of Ralph Josselin,
        a Seventeenth-Century Clergyman: An Essay in Historical
        Anthropology. Cambridge: University Press, 1970.

05317. Schlatter, R. The Social Ideas of the Religious Leaders,
        1660-1688. 1940. Reprint. New York: Octagon Books, 1971.
        [See especially part 1, The Family.]

05318. Schnucker, R.V. "The English Puritans and Pregnancy,
        Delivery and Breast Feeding." History of Childhood
        Quarterly 1 (Spring 1974): 637-658.

05319. Schochet, Gordon J. "Patriarchalism, Politics and Mass
        Attitudes in Stuart England." Historical Journal 12
        (1969): 413-441.

05320. Schucking, Levin Ludwig. The Puritan Family: a social study
        from the literary sources. Translated by Brian Balter-
        shaw. 1926. Reprint. New York: Schocken Books, 1970.

05321. Thomson, Gladys Scott. Life in a Noble Household 1641-
        1700. London: J. Cape, 1950.

05322. _____. The Russells in Bloomsbury, 1669-
        1771. London: J. Cape, 1940.

05323. _____. Two Centuries of Family History.
        New York: Longmans Green and Co., 1930.

        Also refer to #4317, 4399, 4603, 5300.

                        (2) Childhood

05324. Illick, Joseph. "Child-Rearing in Seventeenth-Century
        England and America." In The History of Childhood, edited
        by Lloyd deMause, pp. 303-350. New York: Harper Torch-
        books, Harper & Row, 1975.

05325. King, Walter J. "Punishment for Bastardy in Early Seventeenth-
        Century England." Albion 10 (Summer 1978): 130-151.

05326. Laslett, Peter. "Parental deprivation in the past: A note
        on orphans and stepparenthood in English history." In
        Family life and illicit love in earlier generations, pp.
        160-173. New York: Cambridge University Press, 1977.

05327. Wrightson, Keith. "Infanticide in Earlier Seventeenth-
        Century England." Local Population Studies 15 (1975): 10-22.

05328.   Wrightson, Keith. "Infanticide in Earlier Seventeenth-
          Century England." Local Population Studies 15 (1975): 10-22.

05329.   _____. "The nadir of English illegitimacy in the
          seventeenth century." In Bastardy and its Comparative
          History, edited by Peter Laslett, Karla Oosterveen, and
          Richard M. Smith, pp. 176-191. Cambridge, Mass.: Harvard
          University Press, 1980.

          Also refer to #4333.

                              d) Marriage

05330.   Ashley, Maurice. "Love and Marriage in Seventeenth Century
          England." History Today 8 (October 1958): 667-675.

05331.   Bettey, J. H. "Marriages of Convenience by Copyholders in
          Dorset during the Seventeenth Century." Proceedings of
          the Dorset Natural History Archaeological Society 98
          (1976): 1-5.

05332.   Blackwood, B.G., "The Marriages of the Lancashire Gentry
          on the Eve of the English Civil War," Genealogists
          Magazine 16 (1970): 321-327.

05333.   Bonfield, Lloyd. Marriage Settlements and the "Rise of
          Great Estates": The Demographic Aspect [1625-1740].
          Economic History Review 32 (November 1979): 483-493.

05334.   Haller, William and Haller, Malleville. "The Puritan Art
          of Love." Huntington Library Quarterly 5 (1941-1942):
          235-272.

05335.   Johnson, James Turner. "The Covenant Idea and the Puritan
          View of Marriage." Journal of the History of Ideas 32
          (1971): 107-118.

05336.   _____. "English Puritan Thought on the
          Ends of Marriage." Church History 38 (December 1969):
          429-436.

05337.   _____. A Society Ordained by God: English
          Puritan Marriage Doctrine in the first half of the Seven-
          teenth Century. Nashville: Abingdon Press, 1970.

05338.   Mendelsohn, Sara Heller. "The Weightiest Business: Marriage
          in an Upper Gentry Family in Seventeenth-Century England."
          Past and Present 85 (November 1979): 126-135.

05339. Osmond, Rosalie E. "Body, Soul and the Marriage Relation-
        ship: The History of an Analogy." Journal of the History
        of Ideas 34 (April-June 1973): 283-290.

05340. Slater, Miriam. "The Weightiest Business: Marriage in an
        Upper Gentry Family in Seventeenth-Century England."
        Past and Present 72 (August 1976): 25-54. Also see 85
        (November 1979): 136-140.

05341. Thomas, Gertrude Z. Richer than Species, How a Royal Bride's
        Dowry Introduced Cane, Lacquer, Cottons, Tea and Porcelain
        to England. New York: Alfred A. Knopf, 1965.

05342. Thompson, C. J. S. Love, marriage, and romance in old
        London. London: Heath, Cranton, 1936.

05343. Thompson, Claude A. "The Doctrine and Discipline of
        Divorce, 1643-1645: A Bibliographical Study." Transactions
        of the Cambridge Bibliographical Society 7 (1977): 74-93.

05344. Wilkins, George. The Miseries of Enforced Marriage. 1607.
        Reprint. Oxford: University Press, 1964.

05345. Wrigley, E. Anthony, "Clandestine Marriage in Tetbury in the
        Late 17th Century," Local Population Studies 10 (1973):
        15-21.

        Also refer to #2433, 4322, 4334, 4335, 4337, 4339, 4344, 4347,
        5368, 5373, 5377, 5390, 5393, 5404.

                    e) Sex Life and Morals

05346. Bingham, Caroline. "Seventeenth Century Attitudes Toward
        Deviant Sex." Journal of Interdisciplinary History 1
        (Spring 1971): 447-472.

05347. Oaks, Bert F. "'Things fearful to name': sodomy and buggery
        in seventeenth century England." Journal of Social History
        12 (Winter 1978): 268.

05348. Pallavicino, Ferrante. The Whore's Rhetorick, calculated to
        the meridian of London and conformed to the rules of the
        art, in two dialogues. Reprint. New York: Ivan Obolen-
        sky, 1961.

05349. Quaife, G.R. "The Consenting Spinster in a Peasant Society:
        Aspects of Premarital Sex in Puritan Somerset, 1645-1660."
        Journal of Social History 11 (1977): 228-244.

05350. Quaife, G. R. Wanton Wenches and Wayward Wives Peasants and
         Illicit Sex in Early Seventeenth-Century England. New
         Brunswick, N.J.: Rutgers University Press, 1979.

05351. Thompson, Roger, "Seventeenth-Century English and Colonial
         Sex Rations: A Postscript," Population Studies 28 (1974):
         153-165.

         Also refer to #4352.

f) Fashion/Manners

05352. Brooke, Iris. Dress and Undress: The Restoration and
         Eighteenth Century. London: Methuen, 1958.

05353. _____ . English Costume of the Seventeenth
         Century. London: A & C. Black Ltd., 1947.

05354. Cunnington, Cecil W. and Cunnington, Phyllis. Handbook of
         English Costume in the 17th Century. London: Faber & Faber,
         1955.

05355. Drew-Bear, Annette. "Cosmetics and Attitudes toward Women in
         the Seventeenth Century." Journal of Popular Culture 9
         (Summer 1975): 31-37.

05356. Gourget, Brenda. "Cosmetics and Perfumes in Stuart Times."
         History Today 16 (1966): 633-639.

g) Recreation

05357. Brailsford, Dennis. Sport and Society: Elizabeth to Anne.
         Toronto: University of Toronto, 1969.
         [See especially pp. 232-241, sports at female schools.]

h) Health/Medical

05358. Blackman, Janet M. "Seventeenth-Century Midland Midwifery-
         A comment," Local Population Studies 9 (1972): 47-48.

05359. "Celebrated midwives of the 17th and beginning of the 18th
         centuries: With a short account of the present position
         of midwives." St. Thomas Hospital Gazette 5 (1895):33-36.

05360. Sadler, John. The Sicke Womans Private Looking Glasse Wherein
        Methodically Are Handled All Uterine Affects, or Diseases
        Arising from Ye Wombe. 1636. Reprint. Norwood, N.J.:
        Walter J. Johnson, Inc., 1977.

        Also refer to #3209.

6. CULTURAL

"Most in this depraved age think a women learned enough if
she can distinguish her husband's bed from another's."
                                            Hannah Wooley, 1675

a) Education

05361. Brink, J.R. "Bethsua Makin: scholar and educator of the
        seventeenth century." International Journal of Women's
        Studies 1 (July/August 1978): 417-426.

05362. Humiliata, Sister Mary. "Standards of taste advocated for
        feminine letter writing, 1640-1797." Huntington Library
        Quarterly 13 (1950): 261-277.

05363. Norman, Marion. "Eve's Daughters at School (education of 17th
        Century English Women)." Atlantis 3 (Spring 1978): 66-81.

b) Literature

(1) Non-specific

05364. Barranger, Milly S. "The Cankered Rose: A Consideration
        of the Jacobean Tragic Heroine." College Language
        Association Journal 14 (1970): 178-186.

05365. George, Margaret. "From 'Goodwife' to 'Mistress': The
        Transformation of the Female in Bourgeois Culture."
        Science and Society 37 (Summer 1973): 152-177.

05366. Jerrold, Walter and Jerrold, Clare. Five Queer Women.
        1929. Reprint. Norwood, Pa.: Norwood Editions, 1976.

05367. Latt, David J. "Praising Virtuous Ladies: The Literary Image
        and Historical Reality of Women in Seventeenth-Century
        England." In What Manner Woman, edited by Marlene Springer,
        pp. 39-64. New York: New York University Press, 1977.

05368. McClung, Ellen. "For Love and Convenience: Women on Marriage
        in Literature, 1670-1750." Atlantis 2 (Fall 1976): 67-78.

05369. Richetti, John J. "The Portrayal of Women in Restoration
        and Eighteenth-century English Literature." In What
        Manner Women, edited by Marlene Springer, pp. 65-97.
        New York: New York University Press, 1977.

        Also refer to #4372.

                        (2) Philosophy

05370. Chapman, Richard A., "Leviathan Writ Small: Thomas Hobbes on
        the Family." American Political Science Review 69 (1975):
        76-90.

05371. Hinton, R. W. K. "Husbands, Fathers and Conquerors. II.
        Patriarchalism in Hobbes and Locke." Political Studies
        16 (February 1968): 55-67.

05372. Owen, Gilbert Roy. "The Famous Case of Lady Anne Conway."
        Annals of Medical History 9 (1937): 567-571.

                          (3) Drama

                          (a) Women

05373. Alleman, G.S. Matrimonial Law and the Materials of Restor-
        ation Comedy. Wallingford, Pa.: n.p., 1942.

05374. Cohen, Derek. "The Revenger's Comedy: Female Hegemony in
        The Country Wife." Atlantis 5 (Spring 1980): 120-130.

05375. Crandall, Coryl, ed., Swetnam the Woman-Hater: The Controversy
        and the Play. Lafayette, Ind.: Purdue University Studies,
        1969.

05376. Gagen, Jean Elizabeth. The New Women: Her Emergence in
        English Drama, 1600-1730. New York: Twayne Publishers, 1954.

05377. Kenney, Shirley Strum. "Elopements, Divorce, and the Devil
        Knows What': Love and Marriage in English Comedy, 1690-
        1720." South Atlantic Quarterly 78 (Winter 1979):84-106.

05378. McDonald, Margaret Lamb. The Independent Woman in the
        Restoration Comedy of Manners. Atlantic Highlands,
        N.J.: Humanities Press, 1976.

05379. Maus, K. E. "Playhouse Flesh and Blood: Sexual Ideology and
        the Restoration Actress." EHL 46 (Winter 1979): 595-617.

05380. Novak, Maximillian E. "Margery Pinchwife's 'London Disease':
        Restoration Comedy and the Libertine Offensive of the
        1670's." Studies in Literary Imagination 10 (Spring 1977):
        1-23.

(b) Women Dramatists

[1] APHRA BEHN

05381. Baker, Herschel. "Mrs. Behn forgets." Studies in English
        4226 (1942): 121-123.

05382. Day, Robert Adams. "Aphra Behn's First Biography." Studies
        in Bibliography 22 (1969): 227-240.

05383. Duffy, Maureen. The Passionate Shepherdess: Aphra Behn,
        1640-1689. London: Jonathan Cape, 1977.

05384. Gilder, Rosamond. "Aphra Behn England's First Professional
        Woman Playwright." In Enter the Actress The First Women
        in the Theatre, pp. 173-201. Boston: Houghton Mifflin
        Company, 1931.

05385. Woodcock, George. "Founding Mother of the English Novel:
        Aphra Behn." Room of One's Own 2 (1976): 31-44.

05386. _____ . The Incomparable Aphra. New York: T.V.
        Boardman, 1948.

[2] OTHERS

05387. Pearse, Nancy Cotton. "Mary Pix, Restoration Playwright."
        Restoration and 18th Century Theatre Research 15 (May
        1976): 12-23.

(4)   Poetry

(a)   Milton

05388.   Bowers, Mary Beacom. "Milton's Conception of Woman."
Ohio Journal of Religious Studies 4 (March 1976): 19-33.

05389.   Gilbert, A. H. "Milton on the Position of Woman." Modern
Language Review 15 (1920): 7-27, 240-264.

05390.   Halkett, John G. Milton and the Idea of Matrimony: A
Study of the Divorce Tracts and Paradise Lost. New
Haven: Yale University Press, 1970.

05391.   Haller, William. "Hail Wedded Love." ELH: A Journal of
English Literary History 13 (June 1946): 79-97.

05392.   Isaak, Jo-Anne. "The Education of Eve: Milton." Atlantis
2 (Spring 1977): 114-122.

05393.   Miller, Leo. John Milton among the Polygamophiles. New
York: Loewenthal Press, 1974.

05394.   Milton, John. "The Doctrine and Disciplines of Divorce."
In The Complete Prose Works, 2: 220-356. New Haven:
Yale University Press, 1959.

05395.   Mollenkott, V.R. "Milton and Women's Liberation: A Note on
Teaching Method." Milton Quarterly 7 (December 1973): 99-103.

05396.   Owen, Evion. "Milton and Selden on Divorce." Studies in
Philology 43 (1946): 233-57.

05397.   Siegel, Paul N. "Milton and the humanist attitude toward
women." Journal of the History of Ideas 2 (1950): 42-53.

(b)   Anne Finch, countess of Winchelsea

05398.   Messenger, Ann P. "Lady Winchelsea and Twice-Fallen Women."
Atlantis 3 (Spring 1978): 82-98.

(5)   Satire

05399.   Brooks, Elmer R. "An Unpublished Restoration Satire on the
Court Ladies." English Language Notes 10 (1973): 201-208.

05400. O'Neill, John H. "Sexuality, Deviance, and Moral Character
        in the Personal Satire of the Restoration." Eighteenth-
        Century Life 2 (September 1975): 16-19.

05401. Satires on Women: Love Given o're [Robert Gould] (1682),
        The Female Advocate [Sarah Fige], (1687), The Folly of
        Love [Richard Ames], (1691). Introduction by Felicity
        A. Nussbaum. Los Angeles: Clark Library, 1976.

                        (6) Prose

                        (a) Authors

                    [1] MARY ASTELL

                    [a] Contemporary

05402. Astell, Mary. An Essay in Defense of the Female Sex. 1696.
        Reprint. New York: Source Book Press, 1970.

05403. _____. A Serious proposal to the Ladies for the Advance-
        ment of their Sex. 1701. Reprint. New York: Source Book
        Press, 1970.

05404. _____. Some Reflections upon Marriage. New York:
        Source Book Press, 1970.

                    [b] Secondary

05405. Janes, Regina. "Mary, Mary, Quite Contrary, or, Mary Astell
        and Mary Wollstonecraft Compared," Studies in Eighteenth-
        Century Culture 5 (1976): 121-139.

05406. Kinnaird, Joan K. "Mary Astell and the Conservative Contribu-
        tion to English Feminism." Journal of British Studies 19
        (Fall 1979): 53-75.

05407. Smith, Florence M. Mary Astell. New York: Columbia Univer-
        sity Press, 1916.

[2] OTHERS

05408. Horner, Joyce M. <u>The English women novelists and their connec-</u>
        <u>tion with the feminist movement,</u> 1688-1797. 1929-1930.
        Reprint. Folcroft, Pa.: Folcroft Library Editions, 1973.

05409. MacCarthy, B. G. <u>Women Writers: their contribution to the</u>
        <u>English novel, 1621-1744.</u> Cork: University Press, 1945.

(b) Periodicals

05410. Adburgham, Alison. <u>Women in Print. Writing Women and Women's</u>
        <u>Magazines from the Restoration to the Accession of Victoria.</u>
        London: George Allen and Unwin, 1972.

05411. Stearns, Bertha-Monica. "The First English Periodical for
        Women." <u>Modern Philology</u> 28 (August 1930): 45-59.

c) Intellectuals

05412. Hughes, Helen Sard. "Lady Winchilsea and her friends."
        <u>London Mercury</u> 19 (April 1929): 624-635.

05413. Reynolds, Myra. <u>The Learned Lady in England (1650-1760).</u>
        1920. Reprint. Glouchester, Mass.: Peter Smith, 1964.

05414. Upham, A. H. "English Femmes Savantes at the End of the
        Seventeenth Century." <u>Journal of English and Germanic</u>
        <u>Philology</u> 12 (1913): 262-276.

05415. Wallas, Ada. <u>Before the Bluestockings.</u> 1929. Reprint.
        Folcroft, Pa.: Folcroft Library Editions, 1977.

d) Art

(1) Actresses

05416. Gilder, Rosamond. "Enter Ianthe, Veil'd The First Actress in England." In Enter the Actress The First Women in the Theatre, pp. 132–143. Boston: Houghton Mifflin Company, 1931.

05417. _____. "Mary Betterton and the Restoration Actresses." In Enter the Actress The First Women in the Theatre, pp. 144–172. Boston: Houghton Mifflin Company, 1931.

05418. Gosse, Edmund. Life of William Congreve. London: William Heinemann, Ltd., 1924.
        [See especially ch. 4, on Anne Bracegirdle, pp. 118–163.]

05419. Highfill, Philip H., Jr.; Burnim, Kalman A.; and Langhans, Edward A. A Biographical Dictionary of Actors, Actresses, Musicians, Dancers, Managers & Other Personnel in London, (1660–1800). 2 vols. Carbondale, Ill.: Southern Illinois University Press, 1973.

05420. Hook, Lucyle. "Anne Bracegirdle's First Appearance." Theatre Notebook 13 (1959): 133–136.

05421. Lanier, Henry Wysham. The First English Actresses. New York: The Players, 1931.

05422. Wilson, John Harold. All the King's Ladies: Actresses of the Restoration. Chicago: University of Chicago Press, 1958.

05423. _____. "Lord Oxford's 'Roxalana.'" Theatre Notebook 12 (Autumn 1957): 14–16

Also refer to #5379.

e) Science

05424. Haynes, Alan. "The First Great Lady: Margaret, Duchess of Newcastle." History Today 26 (November 1976): 724–733.

05425. Meyer, Gerald Dennis. The Scientific Lady in England, 1650–
        1760: An Account of Her rise, with Emphasis on the major
        roles of the Telescope and Microscope. Berkeley: Univer-
        sity of California Press, 1955.

05426. Mintz, Samuel I. "The Duchess of Newcastle's visit to the
        Royal Society." Journal of English and Germanic Philology
        51 (1952): 168–176.

05427. Perry, Henry Ten Eyck. The First Duchess of Newcastle and
        Her Husband as Figures in Literary History. 1918. Reprint.
        New York: Johnson Reprint, 1968.

C. FRANCE

1. SURVEYS

"Sure it is not Chance, but Unavoidable Necessity that
hinders them from playing their parts."
                    François Poulain de la Barre (1647–1723)

05428. Cousin, Victor. "Les femmes illustres du XVIIe siècle." Revue
        des deux mondes 1 (1844): 193–203.

05429. Fagniez, Gustave. La femme et la société français dans la
        première moitié du XVIIe siècle. Paris: Librairie universi-
        taire J. Gamber, 1929.

05430. Reynier, Gustave. La Femme au XVII siecle. Paris: Plon, 1933.

05431. Sainte-Beuve, Charles Augustin. Portraits of the 17th
        Century, historic and literary. Translated by Katherine
        P. Wormeley. New York: G. P. Putnam's Sons, 1904.

        Also refer to #5184.

2. POLITICAL

"God keep me from being the mistress of the king."
                    Madame de Montespan

a) Legal

05432. Ghestin, Jacques. "L'action des parlements contres les
        'mesalliances' aux XVIIe et XVIIIe siècles." Revue
        historique de droit français et etranger 4th ser. 34
        (1956): 74–110, 196–224.

05433. Portemer, Jean. La Femme et la legislation royale des deux
        derniers siècles de l'Ancien Régime. Paris: Libraire
        generale de droit et de jurisprudence, 1959.

05434. Timbal, P.C. "L'ésprit du droit privé au XVIIe siècle."
        XVIIe siecle 58-59 (1963): 30-39.

        Also refer to #4436.

b) Criminal

(1) Non-specific

05435. Abbiateci, Andre; Billacois, François; Castan, Yves; Petro-
        vitch, Porphyrie; Bongert, Yvonne; and Caston, Nicole.
        Crimes et criminalite en France: 17e-18e siècles.
        Paris: Colin, 1971.

05436. Caston, Nicole. "La criminalité familiale dans le ressort du
        Parlament de Toulouse, 1690-1730." In Crimes et criminalite
        en France sous l'ancien regime, XVIIe-XVIIIe siecles, edited
        by A. Abbiateci et. al., pp. 91-107. Paris: A. Colin, 1971.

05437. Riley, Philip F. "Women and Police in Louis XIV's Paris."
        Eighteenth-Century Life 4 (December 1977): 37-42.

(2) Madame de Brinvilliers

05438. Saint-Germain, Jacques. Madame de Brinvilliers. Paris:
        Hachette, 1971.

05439. Smith, Albert. The Marchioness of Brinvilliers: The Poisoner
        of the Seventeenth Century 1886. Reprint. Darby, Pa.:
        Arden Library, 1978.

05440. Vernon, Virginia (Fox-Brooks). Enchanting Little Lady:
        The Criminal Life of the Marquise de Brinvilliers. New
        York: Abelard-Schuman, 1964.

c) Feminism

05441. Baumal, Francis. Le féminisme au temps de Moliere. Paris:
        La Renaissance du Livre, 1923.

05442. Joran, Theodore. "Féministes d'autrefois: VIII 'Le Merite
        des dames' par le sieur de Saint—Gabriel (1657)."
        Université catholique 65 (1910): 214—240.

05443. Payer, Alice de. Le feminisme au temps de la Fronde. Paris:
        n.p., 1922.

                    d) Political Roles

                    (1) Women

05444. Armaillé, Marie Celestine Amélie de Ségur, comtesse de.
        Madame Elisabeth, soeur de Louis XIV. Paris: Perrin, 1886.

05445. Birrell, Francis. La Duchesse du Maine. London: Gerald
        Howe, 1929.

05446. Boileau, Jean—Jacques. Vie inedite de la Duchesse de Luynes
        (1624—1651). Paris: P. Tamizey de Larroque, 1880.

05447. Bronne, Carlo. "L'adroite princess." Revue de Paris 74
        (June 1967): 64—67.

05448. Cousin, Victor. Madame de Hautefort. Paris: Didier, 1886.

05449. Ernemont, Madeleine. Jeanne—Marguerite de Montmorency
        (La solitaire des Pyrénées). Paris: Lethielleux, 1929.

05450. Fromageot, Paul Une cousine du grand Condé Isabelle de
        Montmorency, duchesse de Chatillon et de Mecklembourg.
        Paris: Emile—Paul freres, 1913.

05451. Hall, Geoffrey. Moths Around the Flame. 1935. Reprint.
        Freeport, N.Y.: Books for Libraries Press, 1969.

05452. Homberg, Octave. La Femme du Grand Condé, Claire Clémence
        de Maillé Brézé. Paris: Plon, 1933.

05453. Imbert, de Saint—Armand, Arthur Leon. Women of Versailles:
        The Court of Louis XIV. Translated by Elizabeth Gilbert
        Martin. New York: C. Scribner's Sons, 1893.

05454. Latour, Thérèse Louis. Princesses, Ladies and Adventur—
        esses of the Reign of Louis XIV. New York: Knopf, 1924.

05455. Lürssen, Elizabeth. Die Frauen des fürstlichen Absolutismus und
        des internationalen Adels. Quellenhefte zum Frauenleben in
        der Geschichte, edited by Emmy Beckmann and Irma Stoss, vol.
        3. Berlin: F. A. Herbig Verlagsbuchhandlung, 1927—1933.

05456. Mongrédien, Georges. <u>Marion</u> <u>de</u> <u>Lorme</u> <u>et</u> <u>ses</u> <u>amours</u>. Paris:
        Hachette, 1940.

05457. Noailles, Vicomte de. <u>La</u> <u>Mere</u> <u>du</u> <u>Grand</u> <u>Condé</u>. Paris: Emile-
        Paul, 1924.

05458. Philpin de Piépape, Léonce Marie Gabriel. <u>La</u> <u>duchesse</u> <u>du</u>
        <u>Maine,</u> <u>reine</u> <u>de</u> <u>Sceaux</u> <u>et</u> <u>conspiratrice,</u> <u>1676-1753</u>. Paris:
        Plon, 1936.

05459. Reyna, Ferdinand. "Christine de France." <u>La</u> <u>Revue</u> <u>des</u> <u>deux</u>
        <u>mondes</u> (September-October 1966): 522-535.

(2) Women and the Fronde

05460. Georges-Renard, L. "Les femmes et la politique religieuse sous
        la Fronde." <u>Revue</u> <u>politique</u> <u>et</u> <u>parlementaire</u> 45 (1905: 315-
        328.

05461. Livet, Charles Louis. "Les Femmes de la Fronde." <u>Revue</u>
        <u>europeene</u> 3 (1859): 529-551, 726-758.

05462. Pollitzer, Marcel. <u>Amazones</u> <u>de</u> <u>la</u> <u>Fronde</u> <u>et</u> <u>le</u> <u>quadrille</u>
        <u>des</u> <u>intrigants</u>. Avignon: Aubanel, 1959.

        Also refer to #5443, 5457, 5497-5500.

(3) Individuals

(a) Anne of Austria

05463. Bardon, Françoise. "Reines a la Croix." <u>XVII</u>^e <u>siecle</u> 36-37
        (July-October 1957): 414-419.

05464. Buchanan, Meriel. <u>Anne</u> <u>of</u> <u>Austria,</u> <u>The</u> <u>Infanta</u> <u>Queen</u>.
        London: Hutchinson, 1937.

05465. Darricau, Raymond. "L'action charitable d'une reine de France:
        Anne d'Autriche." <u>XVIII</u>^e <u>siècle</u> 90-91 (1971): 111-125.

05466. Freer, Martha. <u>The</u> <u>Married</u> <u>Life</u> <u>of</u> <u>Anne</u> <u>of</u> <u>Austria,</u> <u>queen</u> <u>of</u>
        <u>France,</u> <u>mother</u> <u>of</u> <u>Louis</u> <u>XIV</u>. London: Trosley Bors., 1864.

05467. _____. <u>The</u> <u>Regency</u> <u>of</u> <u>Anne</u> <u>of</u> <u>Austria</u>. London:
        Trosley Bors., 1866.

05468. La Varende, Jean de. <u>Anne</u> <u>d'Autriche</u> <u>femme</u> <u>de</u> <u>Louis</u> <u>VIII,</u>
        <u>1601-1666</u>. 1938. Reprint. Paris: Falmmarion, 1954.

05469. Robiquet, Paul. Le Coeur d'une Reine: Anne d'Autriche
        Louis XIII. et Mazarin. Paris: Felix Alcan, 1912.

(b) Adelaide of Savoy, duchess of Burgundy

05470. Carre, Henri. The King's Darling, Adelaide of Savoy, Duchess
        of Burgundy and Mother of Louis XV. London: Lane, 1936.

05471. Haussonville, M. le comte de. "Le duchesse de Bourgogne et
        l'alliance savoyard sous Louis XIV." Revue des deux mondes
        4th ser. 134 (15 April 1896): 721-756; 4th ser. 135 (1 June
        1896): 481-511; 4th ser. 136 (15 August 1896): 721-761.

05472. Norton, Lucy. First Lady of Versailles: Mary Adelaide of
        Savoy, Dauphine of France. Philadelphia: Lippincott, 1978.

(c) Madame de Rohan, duchess of Chevreuse

05473. Batiffol, Louis. The Duchesse de Chevreuse, a life of intrigue
        and adventure in the days of Louis XIII. New York: Dodd,
        Mead and Co., 1914.

05474. Campbell, Dorothy de Brissac. The Intriguing duchess, Marie de
        Rohan, Duchesse de Chevreuse. New York: Covici-Friede, 1930.

05475. Charol, Michael. Marie de Rohan, Duchesse de Chevreuse.
        London: Allen and Unwin, 1971.

05476. Cousin, Victor. Madame de Chevreuse. Paris: Didier et c^{ie},
        1886.

05477. _____. Madame de Chevreuse et Madame de Hautfort.
        Paris: Didier et c^{ie}, 1856.

05478. Prawdin, Michael. Marie de Rohan, Duchesse de Chevreuse.
        London: George Allen and Unwin, 1971.

(d) Anne of Gonzaga

05479. Acremont, Henri d'. Anne de Gonzague. Mézières-Charleville:
        Editions des Ecrivains Ardennais, 1951.

05480. Minot, Paul. "Anne de Gonzague, princesse Palatine."
        Nouvelle revue des deux mondes 1973 (July 1973): 82-91.

05481. Raffin, L. Anne de Gonzague, princesse palatine 1616-1684.
        Paris: Desclee de Brouwer, 1935.

(e)   Henrietta Anna, duchess d'Orléans

05482. Cartwright, Julia. Madame, a life of Henrietta, daughter of Charles I and duchess of Orleans. London: Seeley & Co., 1894.

05483. Derblay, Claude. Henriette d'Angleterre et sa legende. Paris: Sfelt, 1950.

05484. Engel, Claire-Elaine. "Henriette d'Angleterre et les Lettres franco-anglaises." Revue de litterature comparee 30 (1956): 305-317.

05485. Hartmann, Cyril Hughes. Charles II and Madam. London: William Heinemann, 1934.

05486. _____. The King my Brother, An Account of the mission to England of Henrietta Anna, consort of Philip, duke of Orleans. London: William Heinemann, 1954.

05487. La Fayette, Marie Madeline, comtesse de. The Secret History of Henrietta, Princess of England. New York: Dutton, 1929.

05488. Roche, T. W. E. "Minette"--Henrietta of Exeter. London/ Chichester: Phillimore, 1971.

(f)   Louise de La Vallière

05489. Lair, Jules Auguste. Louise de La Vallière and the Early Life of Louis XIV. Translated by Ethel Colburn Mayne. New York: G.P. Putnam's Sons, 1908.

05490. Trouncer, Margaret. A Courtesan of Paradise: Louise duchess de la Valliere. London: Faber and Faber, Ltd., 1936.

05491. Truc, Gonzague. Louis XIV et Mlle. de La Valliere. Paris: Editions du siecle, 1933.

05492. Vioux, Marcelle. Trois amours de Louis XIV. Vol. I. Louis de La Vallière. Paris: Fasquelle, 1939.

(g)   Ninon de Lenclos

05493. Cohen, Edgar H. Mademoiselle Libertine. Boston: Houghton Mifflin, 1971.

05494.   Day, Lilian. <u>Ninon, a courtesan</u> of <u>quality</u>. Garden City,
          N.Y.: Doubleday, 1957.

05495.   Goudal, Jean. <u>Ninon</u> <u>de</u> <u>Lenclos</u>. Paris: Hachette, 1937.

05496.   Magne, Emile. <u>Ninon</u> <u>de</u> <u>Lenclos</u>. Translated by Gertrude
          Scott Stevenson. New York: Holt and Co., 1926.

                    (h) Madame de Longueville

05497.   Cousin, Victor. <u>Madame</u> <u>de</u> <u>Longueville</u>. Paris: Perrin et
          c^{ie}, 1891.

05498.   Debu-Bridel, Jacques. <u>Anne-Geneviève</u> <u>de</u> <u>Bourbon,</u> <u>Duchesse</u>
          <u>de</u> <u>Longueville</u>. Paris: Gallimard, 1938.

05499.   Delpech, Jeanine. <u>L'ame</u> <u>de</u> <u>la</u> <u>Fronde:</u> <u>Madame</u> <u>de</u> <u>Longue-</u>
          <u>ville</u>. Paris: A. Maynard, 1957.

05500.   Erlanger, Philippe. <u>Madame</u> <u>de</u> <u>Longueville:</u> <u>de</u> <u>la</u> <u>revolte</u>
          <u>au</u> <u>mysticisme</u>. Paris: Perrin, 1977.

                    (i) Madame de Maintenon

05501.   Aragonnès, Claude. <u>Madame</u> <u>Louis</u> <u>XIV,</u> <u>Françoise</u> <u>d'Aubigne</u> <u>mar-</u>
          <u>quise</u> <u>de</u> <u>Maintenon</u>. Paris: Maison de la Bonne presse, 1938.

05502.   Bailly, Auguste. <u>Madame</u> <u>de</u> <u>Maintenon</u>. Paris: Les Editions
          de France, 1942.

05503.   Baudrillart, Alfred. "Madame de Maintenon: son rôle politique
          pendant les dernières années du règne de Louis XIV, 1700-
          1715." <u>Revue</u> <u>des</u> <u>questions</u> <u>historiques</u> 47 (1890): 101-161.

05504.   Boislisle, Arthur Andre Gabriel Michel de. <u>Paul</u> <u>Scarron</u> <u>et</u>
          <u>Françoise</u> <u>d'Aubigné,</u> <u>d'apres</u> <u>des</u> <u>documents</u> <u>nouveaux</u>.
          Paris: Bureaux de la Revere, 1894.

05505.   _____. "Paul Scarron et Françoise d'Aubigné."
          <u>Revue</u> <u>des</u> <u>questions</u> <u>historiques</u> 54 (1892): 86-144, 389-443.

05506.   _____. "Le Veuvage de Françoise d'Aubigné."
          <u>Revue</u> <u>des</u> <u>questions</u> <u>historiques</u> 56 (1894): 48-110.

05507.   Bonhomme, Honore. <u>Madame</u> <u>de</u> <u>Maintenon</u> <u>et</u> <u>sa</u> <u>famille</u>.
          Paris: Didier & Cie, 1863.

05508.   Cordelier, Jean. <u>Madame</u> <u>de</u> <u>Maintenon</u>. Paris: Club des
          éditeurs, 1959.

05509.   Cruttwell, Maude. <u>Madame</u> <u>de</u> <u>Maintenon</u>. New York: E. P.
          Dutton & Co., Inc., 1930.

05510. Girard, Georges. Madame de Maintenon, celle qui n'a jamais
        aime. Paris: Michel, 1936.

05511. Guitton, Georges. "Un conflict de direction spirituelle
        Mme. de Maintenon et le Pere de la Chaize." XVIIe siecle
        29 (October 1955): 378-395.

05512. Haldane, Charlotte F. Madame de Maintenon: Uncrowned
        Queen of France. London: Constable, 1970.

05513. Hastier, Louis. Louis XIV et Madame de Maintenon. Paris:
        Librairie A. Fayard, 1957.

05514. Langlois, Marcel. Madame de Maintenon. Paris: Plon, 1932.

05515. _____. "Les 'petits livres secrets' de Madame
        de Maintenon." Revue d'histoire litteraire de la France
        35 (1928): 354-368.

05516. Mermaz, Louis. Madame de Maintenon au l'amour devot.
        Lausanne: Editions Rencontre, 1966.

05517. Noailles, Paul, duc de. Histoire de Madame de Maintenon
        et des principaux évènements du règne de Louis XIV.
        Paris: Comptoir de imprimeurs-unis, Lacroix-Comon, 1849-1858.

05518. Pilastre, Edouard. Vie et caractère de Madame de
        Maintenon. Paris: F. Alcan, 1907.

05519. Sainte-René Taillandier, Madeleine Marie Louise (Chevri-
        llon). Madame de Maintenon. Translated by Lady Mary
        Loyd. London: W. Heinemann, 1922.

05520. Truc, Gonzague. La Vie de Madame de Maintenon. Paris:
        Gallimard, 1929.

        Also refer to #5701-5706.

(j) Mancini Family

05521. Barthelemy, Eduard Marie, comte de. Une nièce de Mazarin;
        la Princesse de Conti. Paris: Firmin Didot, 1875.

05522. Chantelauze, Francois Regis de. Louis XIV et Marie Mancini.
        Paris: Didier et c^ie, 1880.

05523. Hartmann, Cyril Hughes. The Vagabond Duchess, The Life
        of Hortense Mancini, Duchesse Mazarin. London:
        G. Routledge and Sons, 1926.

05524. Herpin, Clara Adele. (Percy, Lucian, pseud.) Le Roman du
        Grand Roi, Louis XIV et Marie Mancini. Paris: Calmann Levy,
        1894.

05525. Petit, Léon. Marie-Anne Mancini, duchesse de Bouillon.
        Paris: Editions du Cerf-Volant, 1970.

05526. Renée, Amédée. Les Nièces de Mazarin. Paris: Firmin
        Didot freres, 1856.

05527. Rival, Paul. Marie Mancini. Paris: Nouvelle revue
        francaise, 1938.

05528. Sutherland, Monica. Louis XIV and Marie Mancini. New
        York: Roy, 1956.

05529. Williams, Hugh Noel. Five Fair Sisters. London: Hutchin-
        son, 1906.

                       (k) Marie de Medici

05530. Albertis, Giulia Datta de. Maria Medici 1573-1642.
        Translated by Emma Schneider. Munich: Bruckmann, 1940.

05531. Batiffol, Louis. Marie de Medicis and the French Court
        in the XVIIth Century. Translated by Mary King. New
        York: C. Scribner's Sons, 1908.

05532. _____. La vie intime d'une reine de France 2
        vols. Paris: Calmann-Levy, 1911.

05533. Foucart, Jacques. (Jacques Thullier) Reubens' life
        of Marie de Medici. New York: Harry N. Adams, 1970.

05534. Heisner, Beverly. "Marie de Medici. Self-promotion through
        Art." Feminist Art Journal 6 (Summer 1977): 21-26.

05535. Kermina, Francoise de. "Marie de Medicis contre Richelieu."
        Historia 392 (July 1979): 66-75.

05536. _____. Marie de Medicis. Reine, regente
        et rebelle. Paris: Perrin, 1979.

05537. Mastellone, Salvo. Le Reggenza di Maria di Medici.
        Messina-Florence: Casa Editrice G. d'Anna, 1962.

05538. Thiroux d'Arconville, Marie Genevieve Charlotte. La vie de
        Marie de Médicis. Paris: Rualt, 1774.

05539. Zeller, Berthold. Henri IV et Marie de Médicis. Paris:
        Didier, 1877.

                     (l) Madame de Montespan

05540. Audiat, Pierre. Madame de Montespan. Paris: Fasquelle, 1939.

05541. Carré, L.C. Madame de Montespan. Paris: Hachette, 1939.

05542. Emard, Paul and Fournier, Suzanne. Les années criminelles
        de Mme de Montespan. Paris: Dencel, 1939.

05543. Mongredien, Georges. Madame de Montespan et l'affaire
        des poisons. Geneva: Edito-service, 1973.

05544. Praviel, Armand. Madame de Montespan empoisonneuse.
        Paris: Alcan, 1934.

05545. Rat, Maurice. La royale Montespan. Paris: Librairie
        Plon, 1959.

05546. Richardson, Joanna. "Madame de Montespan and the Affair
        of the Poisons." History Today 23 (August 1973): 588-592.

05547. Truc, Gonzague. Madame de Montespan. Paris: A. Colin, 1936.

05548. Williams, H. Noel. Madame de Montespan. New York: Charles
        Scribner's Sons, 1903.

        (m) Anne Marie Louise d'Orléans, duchess de Montpensier

05549. Buchanan, Meriel. The great mademoiselle. London:
        Hutchinson, 1938.

05550. Ducasse, André. La grande Mademoiselle la plus riche
        héritière d'Europe 1627-1693. Paris: Hachette, 1938.

05551. La Force, August de Caumont, de duc de. La Grande Mademoi-
        selle. Paris: Flammarion, 1952.

05552. Sackville-West, Victoria Mary. Daughter of France, the
        Life of Anne Marie Louis d'Orléans, duchesse de Montpensier,
        1627-1693. New York: Doubleday and Co., 1959.

05553. Steegmuller, Francis. The Grand Mademoiselle. New York:
        Farrar, 1955.

05554. Vincens, Cecile. La Grande Mademoiselle, 1627-1652.
        New York: G.P. Putnam's Sons, 1902.

05555. _____. La jeunesse de la Grande Mademoiselle
        (1627-1652). Paris: Librairie Hachette et c^{ie}, 1906.

05556. _____. Louis XIV and la Grande Mademoiselle,
        1652-1693. New York: G.P. Putnam's Sons, 1905.

(n)   Elizabeth Charlotte, duchess d'Orléans

05557. Barine, Arvede. <u>Madame, Mother of the Regent, 1652–1722.</u> Translated by Jeanne Mairet. New York: G.P. Putnam's Sons, 1909.

05558. Fuchs, Peter. "Elisabeth Charlotte (Lieselotte), Herzogin von Orleans." <u>Neue deutsche Biographie</u> 4 (1959): 448–451.

05559. Funck-Brentano, F. <u>Liselotte, duchesse d'Orleans, mere du regent.</u> Paris: Nouvelle Revue francaise, 1936.

05560. Henderson, Ernest Flagg. <u>A Lady of the Old Regime.</u> London: Bell and Sons, 1909.

05561. Knoop, Matilde. <u>Madame: Liselotte von der Pfalz: ein Lebensbild.</u> Stuttgart: K.F. Koehler, 1956.

05562. Peterson, Nis A. "'Madame': Elizabeth Charlotte of Orleans." <u>History Today</u> 27 (February 1977): 101–107.

05563. Strich, Michael. <u>Liselotte von Kurpfalz.</u> Berlin: Allstein, 1925.

05564. Vincens, Cecile. <u>Madame, Mother of the regent.</u> New York: G.P. Putnam's Sons, 1909.

Also refer to #4120.

3. ECONOMIC

"If the matter had fallen into your hands earlier, my business would have been much better conducted, because there is nothing like a woman for taking good care of matters like that." Suzanne de la Porte

05565. Franklin, Alfred Louis Auguste. <u>La vie de Paris sous Louis XIV; tenue de maison et domesticité.</u> Paris: E. Plon, Nourrit et Cie, 1898.

05566. Haussonville, Gabriel Paul Othenin de Cleron, comte d'. <u>L'Emigration des femmes aux colonies.</u> Paris: A. Colin et c^{ie}, 1897.

4. RELIGION

"Because the troubles of the wars had been so great and
had caused such disorders in the province that many
people succumbed to witchcraft." Father Symard, 1657

a) Generic

05567. Gueudre, M.C. "La Femme et la vie spirituelle." XVIIe
        siècle 62-63 (1964): 47-77.

05568. Norberg, Kathryn. "Women, the Family, and the Counter-
        Reformation: Women's Confraternities in the Seventeenth
        Century." Proceedings of the Western Society for
        French History 6 (1979): 55-63.

05569. Tavenaux, René. La vie quotidienne des Jansenistes aux
        XVIIe et XVIIIe siècles. Paris: Hachette, 1973.

b) Saints/Religious Women

(1) Women

05570. Augereau, J. Jeanne Absolu: Une mystique du grande siècle.
        Paris: Les Editions du Cerf, 1960.

05571. Cognet, Louis. "La spiritualite de Madame Guyon."
        XVIIe siècle 12-14 (1951-1952): 269-275.

05572. Devos, Roger. Vie religieuse, féminine et société. L'origine
        sociale des Visitandines d'Annecy aux XVIIe -XVIIIe siècles.
        Annecy: Academie salesienne, 1973.

05573. Febvre, Lucien. "Aspects meconnus d'une renouveau religieux
        in France entre 1590 et 1620." Annales: économies, sociétés,
        civilisations 13 (October-December 1958): 639-650.

05574. Gueudre, G. Au coeur des spiritualités: Catherine Ranquet,
        mystique et educatrice (1602-1651). Paris: B. Grasset, 1952.

05575. Himmelfarb, Hélène. "Féminité, fortune terrienne et Contre-
        Reforme: Marie-Félice de Budos." XVIIe siècle 114-115
        (April-June 1977): 99-105.

05576. Hoffman, Paul. "Le Féminisme spirituel de Gabrielle Suchon."
        XVIIe siecle 121 (October-December 1978): 269-276.

05577. Lecouturier, Ernestine. Françoise-Madeleine de Chaugy et la
        tradition salesienne au 17e siecle. Paris: Bloud et Gay,
        1933.

05578. Leflaive, A. Sainte Jeanne de Chantal. Paris: Editions
        France-Empire, 1962.

05579. Lovat, Alice. Life of Mere Marie Eugenie Milleret de
        Brou, Foundress of the Assumption Nuns. London:
        Sands and Co., 1925.

05580. Muller, A. Une mystique dominicaine du XVIIe siecle. La
        Venerable Mere Agnes de Langeac. Langeac: Monastere de
        Sainte-Catherine, 1963.

05581. Plongeron, Bernard. "Concerning Mother Agnes of Jesus:
        Theme and Variations in Hagiography (1665-1963)."
        Concilium 129 (1979): 25-35.

05582. Ribadeau-Dumas, F. Fenelon et les saintes folies de
        Madame Guyon. Geneva: Editions du Mont-Blanc, 1968.

05583. Roux, Janine. "Une page de l'histoire religieuse du
        [XVIIe] siecle: Mademoiselle d'Epernon et Bordeaux."
        XVIIe siecle 78 (1968): 41-47.

                    (2)   Port Royal

05584. Cognet, Louis. "Le mépris du monde a Port-Royal et
        dans le jansenisme." Revue d'ascetique et de
        mystique 41 (1965): 387-402.

05585. _____. La mère Angelique et saint François de
        Sales 1618-1626. Paris: Editions Sullvier, 1951.

05586. _____. La mère Angelique et son temps. Paris:
        Sulliver, 1950.

05587. _____. La reforme de Port-Royal, 1591-1618.
        Paris: Sulliver, 1951.

05588. Gazier, Cecile. Les belles amies de Port-Royal. Paris:
        Perrin, 1930.

05589. Woodgate, Mildred Violet. Pascal and his sister
        Jacqueline. St. Louis: B. Herder Book Co., 1945.

        Also refer to #5569.

(3) Louise de Marillac

05590. Broglie, Emmanuel, prince de. The life of Blessed
Louise de Marillac, co-foundress of the Sisters of
Charity of Saint Vincent de Paul. Translated by
Rev. Joseph Leonard. London: Burns, Oates, & Wash-
bourne, Ltd., 1933.

05591. Dirvin, Joseph I. Louise de Marillac of the Ladies and
Daughters of Charity. New York: Farrar, Straus, and
Giroux, 1970.

05592. Lovat, Alice. Life of the Venerable Louise de Marillac
(Mademoiselle Le Gras), foundress of the company of
Sisters of Charity of St. Vincent de Paul. London:
Simpkin, Marshall, Hamilton, Kent and Co., Ltd., 1916.

05593. Woodgate, Mildred Violet. St. Louis de Marillac,
foundress of the Sisters of Charity. London: B. Herder
Book Co., 1942.

c) Religious Orders

05594. Lamotte, F. "Les femmes du XVIIe siècle et la tentative
monastique. De la difficulté d'être fondatrice dans la
Manche." Annales de la Normandie 28 (December 1978):
351-352.

05595. Rat Maurice. "L'Abesse de Fontevrault." La Revue des deux
mondes (15 August 1966): 564-574.

05596. Weaver, F. Ellen. "Cloister and Salon in the 17th Century
Paris." In Beyond Androcentrism New Essays on Women
and Religion, edited by Rita M. Gross, PP. 159-180.
Missoula, Mt.: American Academy of Religion and Scholars'
Press, 1977. Also in Ohio Journal of Religious Studies
4 (March 1976): 44-57.

d) Mariology

05597. Hoffer, Paul. La dévotion à Marie au déclin du XVIIe
siecle. Paris: n.p., 1938.

e) Witchcraft

05598.   Chaunu, Pierre. "Sur la fin des sorciers au XVIIe siècle."
         Annales: économies, sociétés, civilisations 24 (1969):
         895-911.

05599.   Delcambre, E. and Hermitte, J. L. Un cas énigmatique de
         possession diabolique en Lorraine au XVIIe siècle:
         Elisabeth de Ranfaing, l'énergumene de Nancy, fondatrice
         de l'ordre du refuge. Etude historique et psychologique.
         Nancy: Société d'archéologie Lorraine, 1956.

05600.   Henningsen, G. "The Greatest Witch Trial of All: Navarre,
         1609-1614." History Today 30 (November 1980): 36-39.

05601.   Mandrou, Robert. Magistrats et sorciers en France au
         XVIIe siecle : Une analyse de psychologie historique.
         Paris: Librairie Plon, 1968.

05602.   Mongredien, Georges. Leonora Galigai. Un procès de
         sorcellerie sous Louis XIII. Paris: Hachette, 1968.

05603.   Parker, G. "European Witchcraft Revisited." History Today
         30 (November 1980): 23-24.

05604.   Renard-Gottraux, Danièle. "Les procès des sorciers et
         des sorcières de la Montagne des Diesse au XVIIe
         siècle." Actes de la société jurassiene d'émulation
         78 (1975): 235-329.

Also refer to #2728, 4271, 4590, 4591, 4597.

5. SOCIAL

"It is all very well to say daughters should be
married . . . the merchandise is beautiful and
good but one needs money in order to dispose of
it."   bourgeois' wife concerning a dowry

a) Generic

(1) Non-specific

05605. Babeau, Albert. La Vie rurale dans l'ancienne France.
        2nd ed. Paris: Didier, 1885.

05606. Becker, Georges. "La bienséance au Grand Siècle:
        naissance, education, amours, mariage," Aesculape
        54.2 (1971), 2-61; 54.3 (1971), 1-62; 54.4 (1971),
        41-59; 54.5 (1971), 2-57.

05607. Benichou, Paul. Morales du Grand Siecle. Paris:
        Gallimard, 1948.

05608. Biraben, Jean Noel. "A Southern French Village: The
        Inhabitants of Montplaisant in 1644." In Household
        and Family in Past Time, edited by Peter Laslett and
        Richard Wall, pp. 237-254. Cambridge: University Press,
        1972.

05609. Bussy, Roger de Rabutin. Histoires amoureuse des Gaules.
        Edited by G. Mongrédien. Paris: Athens, 1949.

05610. Crane, Thomas Frederick, ed. La Société française au
        dix-septième siècle. New York: G. P. Putnam, 1889.

05611. Dulong, Claude. L'amour au XVIIe siècle. Paris:
        Hachette, 1969.

05612. Fagniez, G. "L'Assistance publique et la charité féminine
        dans la première moitié du XVIIe siècle." Revue des
        questions historiques 3rd ser. 5 (July 1924): 7-38.

05613. Hildesheimer, Francoise, "Nice au XVIIe siècle (économie,
        famille, société)." Recherches régionales 14 (1974):
        23-30.

05614. Magendie, Maurice. La politesse mondaine et les théories de
        l'honnêteté en France au XVIIe siècle, de 1600 à 1660.
        Paris: F. Alcan, 1925.

05615. Magne, Emile. La Vie quotidienne au temps de Louis
        XIII. Paris: Hachette, 1942.
        [See especially ch. 7, "La vie mondaine--les salons,"
        pp. 206-248.]

05616. Mongrédien, Georges. La vie quotidienne des comediens au
        temps de Molière. Paris: Hachette, 1966.

05617. Mongrédien, Georges. La Vie quotidienne sous Louis XIV.
        Paris: Hachette, 1948.

05618. Richard, Jules Marie, La vie privée dans une province
        de l'Quest: Laval aux XVIIe et XVIIIe siècles. Paris:
        E. Champion, 1922.

05619. Wismes, Armel de. La Vie quotidienne dans les ports
        bretons aux XVIIe et XVIIIe siecles (Nantes, Brest,
        Saint-Malo, Lorient). Paris: Hachette, 1973.

                        (2) Women

05620. Babou, H. "De la vertu des femmes au XVIIe siècle."
        Revue nouvelle 9 (1846): 53-90, 279-293.

05621. Belcher, Margaret. "The Compleat Woman: a Seventeenth
        Century View of Women." Atlantis 2 (Spring 1977): 16-32.

05622. Circourt, A. de "La société française et les femmes illustres
        au XVIIe siècle." Bibliothèque universelle 7 (1860): 5-40;
        8 (1860): 34-71.

05623. Du Boscq, Monsieur, The Compleat Woman. 1639. Reprint.
        New York: Da Capo Press, 1968.

05624. Fosseyeux, Marcel. "La Vie au XVIIe siècle: Julie
        d'Angennes en ménage." Mercure de France 85 (1910):
        636-649.

05625. Gahier, Joseph. La journée d'une dame de qualite au
        XVIIe siècle. Nantes: Impr. de L. Mellinet, 1894.

05626. Ronzeaud, Pierre. "La femme au pouvoir ou le monde a
        l'envers," XVIIe siècle 108 (1975): 9-33.

                    b) Demography

05627. Arbellot, G. Cinq paroisses du Vallage aux XVIIe et
        XVIIIe siècles. Paris: Micro-editions Hachette, 1973.

05628. Baulant, Micheline. "The Scattered Family: Another Aspect
        of 17th Century Demography." In Family and Society,
        edited by Robert Forster and Orest Ranum, pp. 104-116.
        Baltimore: Johns Hopkins University Press, 1976. Also
        in Annales: économies, sociétés, civilisations 27 (July-
        September 1972): 959-968.

05629. Bideau, Alain. "A Demographic and Social Analysis of
        Widowhood and Remarriage: The Example of the Castellany
        of Thoissey-in-Dombes, 1670-1840." Journal of Family
        History 5 (1980): 28-43.

05630. Bongaarts, J., "Intermediate Fertility Variables and Mari-
        tal Fertility Rates." Population Studies 30 (1976):
        227-242.

05631. Bourdin, Pierre-Marie. "La plaine d'Alençon et ses bor-
        dures forestières:essai d'histoire démographique et
        médicale (XVIIe-XVIIIe siècles)." Cahier des annales
        de Normandie 6 (1968): 205-520.

05632. Bouvet, Michel. "Thoarn: Etude de démographie historique
        (XVIIe-XVIIIe siecles)." Cahier des annales de Norman-
        die 6 (1968): 17-202.

05633. Chamoux, Antoinette. "La reconstitution des familles:
        espoirs et réalités." Annales: économies sociétés,
        civilisations 27 (1972) 1083-1090.

05634. Charbonneau, Hubert. Tourouvre-au-Perche aux XVIIe et
        XVIIIe siècles: Etude de démographie historique.
        Paris: Presses universitaires de France, 1970.

05635. Chaunu, Pierre. "Les elements de longue durée dans la
        société et la civilisation du XVIIe siècle: la
        démographie." XVIIe siecle 106-107 (1975): 3-22.

05636. Courtès, Georges. "Un village du Condomois aux XVIIe et
        XVIIIe siècles: Gazaupouy. Étude démographique et
        sociale," Bulletin de la société archéologique,
        historique, littéraire et scientifique du Gers 67 (1966):
        7-55.

05637. Dupaquier, Jacques. "Réflexion sur la mortalité de passé:
        mésure de la mortalité des adultes d'après les fiches
        de famille." Annales de démographie historique 1978:
        31-48.

05638. _____. "Sur la population française au
        XVIIe et au XVIIIe siècle." Revue historique 239
        (1968): 43-79.

05639. _____. Statisques démographiques du Bassin
        parisien 1636-1720. Paris: Gauthier-Villars, 1977.

05640. Goubert, Pierre. Beauvais et le Beauvaisis de 1600 à
        1730. Paris: S.E.V.P.E.N., 1960.

05641. _____. "En Beauvaisis: problemes démographiques
        du XVIIe siècle," Annales: économies, sociétés, civilisa-
        tions 7 (1952): 453-468.

05642. Gouesse, Jean-Marie. "Migrations féminines et mariages. Quelques examples basnormands (XVIIe-XVIIIe siecles)." Annales de démographie historique(1976): 319-339.

05643. Huet, Alain. "Annebault et Bourgeauville aux XVIIe et XVIIIe siècles: contribution à l'étude démographique du pays d'Auge." Annales de Normandie 22 (1972): 277-300.

05644. Kordi, Mohamed El. Bayeux aux XVIIe et XVIIIe siècles. Paris: Mouton, 1970.

05645. LeBrun, François. "Les crises démographiques en France aux XVIIe et XVIIIe siècles." Annales: économies, sociétés, civilisations 35 (March 1980): 205-234.

05646. Lepetit, B. "Démographie d'une ville en gestation: Versailles sous Louis XIV." Annales de demographie historique(1977): 49-83.

05647. Sudré, M., "Aspects démographiques de la paroisse Saint-Miches de Bordeaux (1660-1680)." Annales de démographie historique (1974): 231-248.

Also refer to #4604, 4608.

c) Family

(1) Non-specific

05648. Ainson, Vera, "Enquête sur la société et la famille vers 1640 d'après les testaments." Recherches régionales, Centre de documentation des Alpes-Maritimes 3 (1963): 1-9.

05649. Duchêne, Roger, "La famille au XVIIe siècle: à propos de quelques mots d'enfants." Information historique 37 (1975): 211-216.

05650. Goubert, Pierre, "Family and Province: A Contribution to the Knowledge of Family Structure in Early Modern France." Journal of Family History 2 (Fall 1977): 179-197.

05651. Gouesse, Jean-Marie. "Parenté, famille et mariage en Normandie aux XVIIe et XVIIIe siècles. Présentation d'une source et d'une enquête." Annales: économies, sociétés, civilisations 27 (July-September 1972): 1139-1154.

05652. Grenouiller, J.F., "Communautés et familles en Bas-
        Dauphine: les cotes d'Arey et sa region (XVIIe siècle-
        1815)." Bulletin du centre d'histoire économique et
        sociale de la région lyonnaise 2 (1972): 62-68.

05653. Hildesheimer, Françoise, "L'organisation familiale à Nice
        au XVIIe siècle." Revue historique de droit français et
        étranger 4th ser. 54 (1976): 177-202.

05654. Mousnier, Roland. "Les survivances médiévales dans las
        France du XVIIe siècle." XVIIe siècle 106-107 (1975):
        59-79.

05655. Orcibal, Jean. "Mademoiselle de Mouléon (Catherine Gary)
        et la famille de Bosseut." Revue d'histoire littéraire
        de la France 56 (July-September 1956): 321-341.

05656. Richard, Paul. "Les avantages réserves aux familles
        nombreuses de 1667 à 1720." Echo de Saint-Pierre
        d'Auxerre 25 (1960): 14-18.

05657. Wheaton, Robert. "Affinity and Descent in Seventeenth-
        Century Bordeaux." In Family and Sexuality in French
        History, edited by Robert Wheaton and Tamara K. Hareven,
        pp. 111-134. Philadelphia: University of Pennsylvania
        Press, 1980.

        Also refer to #4603, 4609, 4611, 5628, 5632.

(2) Childhood

05658. Berthieu, René. "Les nourrissons à Cormeilles-en-Paris
        (1640-1789)." Annales de démographie historique(1975):
        259-289.

05659. Bourdelais, Patrice and Roulot, Jean-Yves. "La reprise de
        fécondité après décès: indicateur des conditons
        d'accouchement?" Annales de démographie historique
        (1977): 207-213.

05660. Caspard, Pierre. "Conceptions prénuptiales et développement
        du capitalisme dans la Principauté de Neuchâtel (1678-
        1820)." Annales: economies, sociétés, civilisations 29
        (July-August 1974): 989-1008.

05661. Grimmer, Claude, "Les bâtards de la noblesse auvergnate
        au XVIIe siècle." XVIIe siècle 117 (1977): 35-48.

05662. Hunt, David. Parents and Children in History, the Psy-
        chology of Family Life in Early Modern France. New
        York: Basic Books, 1970.

05663.   Marvick, Elizabeth Wirth. "Nature versus Nurture: Patterns
         and Trends in Seventeenth-Century French Child-Rearing."
         In The History of Childhood, edited by Lloyd deMause,
         pp. 259-302. New York: Harper Torchbooks, Harper &
         Row, 1975.

05664.   Molinier, Alain. "Enfants trouvés, enfants abandonnes et
         enfants illégitimes en Languedoc aux XVIIe au XVIIIe
         siècles." In Sur la population francaise au XVIIIe et au
         XIXe siècles, pp. 445-473. Paris: Société de démographie
         historique, 1973.

                          d) Marriage

05665.   Bertin, Ernest. Les Mariages dans l'ancienne société
         française. 1879. Reprint. Geneva: Slatkine, 1975.

05666.   Gaudemet, Jean. "Legislation canonique et attitudes sécu-
         lières à l'égard du lien matrimonial au XVII siècle."
         XVIIe siècle 102-03 (1974):15-30.

05667.   Gouesse, Jean-Marie. "La formation du couple en Basse-
         Normandie." XVIIe siècle 102-103 (1974):45-58.

05668.   Hilaire, Jean. "L'évolution des regimes matrimoniaux
         dans la region de Montpellier aux XVIIe et XVIIIe
         siècles." Le droit des gens mariés 27 (1966): 133-194.

05669.   Káczmarek, Léon, and Savelon, Guy. Problemes matri-
         moniaux dans le ressort de l'officialité de Cambrai:
         1670-1762. Paris: Hachette, 1973.

05670.   Lévy, Claude, "Nuptialité, natalité, limitation des
         naissances à la cour de Versailles (1650-1800)."
         Concours medical 83 (1961): 5755-5763.

05671.   Lottin, Alain. La Désunion du couple sous l'ancien
         régime: L'Exemple du nord. Université de Lille III.
         Paris: Editions universitaires, 1975.

05672.   _____. "Vie et mort du couple; difficultés conjugales
         et divorces dans le nord de la France aux XVIIe et
         XVIIIe siècles." XVIIe siècle 102-103 (1974): 59-78.

05673.   Vivier, Em. "Les pactions de mariage des paysannes de
         l'Avranchin aux XVIIe et XVIIIe siècles." Annales de
         Normandie 3 (1953): 149-161.

         Also refer to #4615, 4616, 4626, 5432, 5641, 5651.

e) Sex Life and Morals

05674. Lacroix, Paul. Mémoires curieux sur l'histoire des moeurs
         et de la prostitution en France aux dix-septième et dix-
         huitième siècles. Brussels:Imp. C. de C. Vanderauwera,
         1855-1861.

05675. Solé, Jacques. "Passion charnelle et société urbaine
         d'Ancien Régime. Amour vénal, amour libre et amour fou
         à Grenoble au milieu du règne de Louis XIV." In Villes
         de l'Europe méditerranée et de l'Europe occidentale du
         moyen âge au XIXe siècle, edited by M. Bordes and J.
         Gautier-Dulche, pp. 211-232. Annales de la faculté des
         lettres et sciences humaines de Nice, nos. 9-10. Nice:
         University of Nice, 1969.

f) Health/Medical

(1) Birth Control

05676. Gouesse, Jean-Marie. "En Basse-Normandie aux XVIIe et
         XVIIIe siècles: Le refus de l'enfant au tribunal de la
         penitence." Annales de demographie historique(1973):
         231-261.

(2) Women in Medicine

05677. Gelis, Jacques. "La formation des accoucheurs et des sages-
         femmes au XVIIe et XVIIIe siècles: Evolution d'un material
         et d'une pédagogie." Annales de démographie historique
         (1977): 153-180.

05678. _____. "Sages-femmes et accoucheurs:
         l'obstétrique populaire aux XVIIe et XVIIIe siècles."
         Annales: économies, sociétés, civilisations 32
         (September-October 1977): 927-957.

(3) Women and Health

05679. Laget, Mireille. "La naissance aux siècles classiques. Pratique des accouchement et attitudes collectives en France au XVIIe et XVIIIe siècles." Annales: économies, sociétés, civilisations 32 (September-October 1977): 958-992.

g) *Fashion/Manners*

05680. Carr, John Laurence. "The Bourgeois Way of Life." and "The Bourgeois at Table." In Life in France under Louis XIV, pp. 58-67. New York: Capricorn Books, 1970.

6. CULTURAL

"Superstition is undoubtedly to be feared for woman, but nothing uproots it or prevents it more effectually than good instruction."   Fenelon

a) *Education*

(1) Non-specific

05681. Brown, Irene Q. "Phillipe Ariès on Education and Society in Seventeenth and Eighteenth Century France." History of Education Quarterly 7 (1967): 357-368.

05682. Snyders, Georges. La Pédagogie en France au XVIIe et XVIIIe siecles. Paris: Presses universitaires de France, 1965.

(2) Women

05683. Aubry, Marie-Elisabeth. "La congregation de Notre Dame à Nancy et l'éducation des filles aux XVIIe et XVIIIe siècles." Annales: économies, sociétés, civilisations 26 (1974): 75-96.

05684. Deltour, F. "De l'éducation littéraire des femmes aux XVIIe siècle." Revue des cours littéraires 2 (1864-1865): 249-261.

05685.   Dubois, Elfrieda T.   "The Education of Women in Seventeenth-
         Century France."   French Studies 32 (January 1978): 1-19.

05686.   Georges-Renard, L.   "La femme et l'éducation sous la
         minorité de Louis XIV."   Revue internationale de
         l'enseignement 49 (1905): 206-220.

05687.   Greard, O.   L'education des femmes par les femmes.
         Etudes et portraits.   Paris: Hachette, 1886.

05688.   Lewis, W. H.   "Female Education."   In The Spendid Century,
         Life in France of Louis XIV, pp. 214-262.   New York:
         William Morrow and Co., 1953.

05689.   Strassburger, Ferdinand.   Die Mädchenerziehung in der
         Geschichte der Padagogik des 17. und 18. Jahrunderts
         in Frankreich und Deutschland.   Strasbourg: J. Singer,
         1911.

                         (3) Fénelon

05690.   Barbard, H. C.   Fénélon on Education.   New York: Cambridge
         University Press, 1966.

05691.   Compayre, G.   Fénélon et l'éducation attrayante.   Paris:
         Delaplane, 1911.

05692.   Danielou, Madeleine (Clamorgan).   "Fenelon educateur."   XVIIe
         siècle 12-14 (1951-1952): 181-189.

05693.   Fénélon, Francois de Salignac de la Mothe.   The Education
         of Girls.   Translated by Kate Lupton.   Boston: Ginn
         and Company, 1891.

05694.   Lougee, Carolyn.   "Noblesse: domesticity and agrarian
         reform: the education of girls by Fenelon and Saint
         Cyr."   History of Education Quarterly 14 (1974): 87-113.

05695.   Sallwurk, E. de   Fenelon und die Literatur der weiblichen
         Bildung in Frankreich, Von Cl. Fleury bis Fr. Necker
         de Saussure.   Langensalza: Beyer, 1886.

                   (4)   Poulain de la Barre

05696.   Grappin, Henri.   "A propos du féministe Poulain de la Barre."
         Revue d'histoire littéraire de la France 21 (1914): 387-389.

05697.   _____.   "Notes sur un féministe oublié: le carte-
         sien Poulain de la Barre."   Revue d'histoire littéraire
         de la France 20 (1913): 852-867.

05698.   Hine, Ellen McNiven.   "The Woman Quesion in Early
         Eighteenth-Century French Literature: The Influence of
         François Poulain de La Barre."   Studies on Voltaire
         and the Eighteenth Century 116 (1973): 65-79.

05699.   Lefevre, G.   "Poulain de la Barre et le féminisme au
         XVIIe siècle."   Revue pédagogique n.s. 64
         (1914): 101-113.

05700.   Seidel, Michael A.   "Poulain de la Barre's The Woman as
         Good as the Man."   Journal of the History of Ideas 35
         (July-September 1974): 499-508.

         Also refer to #5176, 6631.

                         (5)   Saint-Cyr

05701.   Barnard, H.C.   Madame de Maintenon and Saint-Cyr.
         London: Black, 1934.

05702.   Daniélou, Madeleine (Clamorgan).   Madame de Maintenon
         éducatrice.   Paris: Bloud & Gay, 1946.

05703.   Lavallée, Théophile.   Histoire de la maison royale de
         Saint-Cyr (1686-1795).   Paris: Furne, 1856.

05704.   Noailles, Paul, Duc de.   Saint-Cyr.   Histoire de la
         Maison royale de Saint-Louis établie à Saint-Cyr
         pour l'éducation des demoiselles nobles du royaume.
         Paris: n.p., 1843.

05705.   Sée, Camille.   L'Université et Mme de Maintenon.   Paris:
         L.Cerf, 1894.

05706.   Vindry, Fleury.   Les Demoiselles de Saint-Cyr (1686-
         1793).   Paris: H. Champion, 1908.

         Also refer to #6620.

b) Literature

(1) Non-specific

05707. Ehrmann, Jacques. Un paradis désespéré: l'amour et
l'illusion dans l'Astrée. New Haven: Yale University
Press, 1963.

05708. Hobert, Erhard. Die französische Frauensatire 1600–1800
unter Berücksichtigung der antiken Tradition. Marburg:
Kleinoffsetdruck Görich & Weiershauser, 1967.

05709. Maclean, Ian. Woman Triumphant: Feminism in French
literature, 1610–1652. Oxford: Clarendon Press, 1977.

05710. Storer, Mary Elizabeth. "Madame Deshoulières jugée par
ses contemporains." Romanic Review 25 (October–December
1934): 367–374.

05711. Toinet, R. "Les écrivains moralistes au XVIIe siècle: essai
d'une table alphabétique des ouvrages publiés pendant le
siècle de Louis XIV (1638–1715), qui traitent de la
morale." Revue d'histoire littéraire de la France 23
(1916): 570–610; 24 (1917): 296–306, 656–675; 25 (1918):
310–320, 655–671; 33 (1926): 395–407.

05712. Treloar, Bronnie. "Some Feminist Views on France in the
Seventeenth Century." Australasian Universities Modern
Language Association Journal 10 (May 1959): 152–159.

Also refer to #4372.

(2) Drama

(a) Women

05713. Fournier, Edouard, ed. Les Caquets de l'accouchée.
Paris: P. Jannet, 1855.

05714.   Harvey, Lawrence E.   "The denouement of Melite and the
          role of the nourrice." Modern Language Notes 71
          (March 1956): 200–203.

05715.   Nadal, O. Le sentiment de l'amour dans l'oeuvre de Pierre
          Corneille. Paris: Gallimard, 1948.

                         (b) Molière

05716.   Chill, Emanuel S.   "Tartuffe, Religion and Courtly
          Culture." French Historical Studies 3 (1963–1964):
          151–183.

05717.   Gilder, Rosamond.   "Madeleine and Armande Bejart
          Moliere's Mistress and His Wife." In Enter the
          Actress The First Women in the Theatre, pp. 100–131.
          Boston: Houghton Mifflin Company, 1931.

05718.   Lacour, Leopold.   Les maîtresses de Molière.   Paris:
          Malfere, 1932.

05719.   Lanson, G.   "Les stances du mariage dans l'Ecole des
          femmes." Revue politique et littéraire 4th ser. 12
          (1899): 718–720.

05720.   McBride, R.   "The skeptical view of marriage and the
          comic visions in Molière." Modern Language Forum 5
          (1969): 26–47.

                         (3) Prose

                      (a) Non-specific

05721.   Flutre, L. F.   "Du rôle des femmes dans l'elaboration des
          Remarques de Vaugelas." Neop hilologus 38 (October 1954):
          241–248.

05722.   Hoffman, P.   "Préciosité et féminisme dans le roman de
          Michel de Pure." Travaux et linguistique et de littérature
          5 (1967): 25–34.

05723.   La Bruyère, Jean de. The Characters of Jean de La Bruyère.
          Translated by Henri van Laun. London: G. Routledge and
          Sons, 1929.
               [See especially "Of Women," pp. 58–85.]

(b) Women

05724. Calame, Alexandre. Anne de La Roche-Guilhen, romancière huguenote, 1644-1707. Geneva: Droz, 1972.

05725. Palmer, Melvin D. "Madame d'Aulnoy in England." Comparative Literature 27 (1975): 237-253.

(c) Individuals

[1] MADAME DE LAFAYETTE

05726. Allentuch, Harriet Ray. "Pauline and the Princesse de Cleves." Modern Language Quarterly 30 (1969):171-182.

05727. Brody, Jules. "La Princesse de Cleves and the Myth of Courtly Love." University of Toronto Quarterly 38 (1969): 105-135.

05728. Dédéyan, Charles. Madame de La Fayette. Paris: Societe d'édition d'enseignement superieur, 1965.

05729. Fabre-Luce, Alfred and Dulong, Claude. Un amour dechiffre: La Rochefoucauld et Madame de La Fayette. Paris: Grasset, 1951.

05730. Lanfredini, Dina. "Madame de La Fayette e Henriette d'Angleterre: l'histoire de madame, con documenti inediti trattati dall' Archivio di Stato di Firenze." Archivio storico italiano 116 (1958): 178-206;511-543.

05731. Pingaud, Bernard. Madame de La Fayette. Paris: Ed. du Seuil, 1978.

05732. Raitt, Janet. Madame de Lafayette and 'la Princesse de Cleves'. London: Harrap, 1971.

05733. Scott, J. W. "The 'Digressions' of the Princesse de Cleves." French Studies 11 (1957): 315-322.

05734. _____. Madame de Lafayette: a selective critical bibliography. Research Bibliographies and Checklists, vol. 7. London: Grant and Cutler, 1974.

05735. Weightman, John. "Madame de la Fayette." Listener 75 (1966): 305-307.

[2]   MADELEINE DE SCUDERY

05736.   Cousin, Victor.   <u>La société française du</u> XVIIe <u>siècle</u>
d'après <u>Le grand Cyprus de</u> Mlle <u>de Scudéry</u>.   Oxford:
Clarendon Press, 1909.

05737.   McDougall, Dorothy.   <u>Madame de Scudéry</u>.   London:
Methuen, 1938.

05738.   Mongredien, Georges.   <u>Madeleine de Scudéry et son salon</u>.
Paris: Tallendier, 1946.

05739.   Niderst, Alain.   <u>Madeleine de Scudéry, Paul Pellison et
leur monde</u>.   Paris: Presses Universitaires de France,
1976.

Also refer to #5712.

[3]   MADAME DE VILLEDIEU

05740.   Aldbaïs, Michelle.   "La Paternité du <u>Journal Amoreaux
d'Espagne</u>." XVIIe <u>siècle</u> 84-85 (1969): 79-96.

05741.   Cuénin, Micheline.   "A propos de Madame de Villedieu et
du <u>Journal Amoreaux d'Espagne</u>." XVIIe <u>siècle</u> 88 (1970):
79-87.

05742.   Hipp, Marie-Thérèse.   "Fiction et realité dans les Mémoires
de Henriette-Sylvie de Molière et Madame de Villedieu."
XVIIe siecle 94-95 (1971): 93-117.

05743.   Magne, Emile.   <u>Mme de Villedieu</u>.   Paris: Mercure de
France, 1907.

05744.   Morrissette, Bruce Archer.   <u>The Life and Works of
Marie-Catherine Desjardins (Mme de Villedieu): 1632-
1683</u>.   St. Louis: Washington University, 1947.

c)   Literary Salons

(1)   Non-specific

05745.   Aragonnes, Claude.   "Chez Madame Cornuel: un salon bourgeois
au XVIIe siecle." <u>Revue de Paris</u> 6 (1931):   578-597.

)5746   Batiffol, Louis et. al. <u>The</u> <u>Great</u> <u>Literary</u> <u>Salons</u> <u>of</u> <u>the</u>
         <u>XVII</u> <u>and</u> <u>XVIII</u> <u>Centuries</u>. Translated by Mabel Robinson.
         London: Thornton Butterworth, 1930.

05747.   Lougee, Carolyn. <u>Le</u> <u>Paradis</u> <u>des</u> <u>Femmes</u>: <u>Women,</u> <u>Salons,</u>
         <u>and</u> <u>Social</u> <u>Stratification</u> <u>in</u> <u>Seventeenth-Century</u> <u>France</u>.
         Princeton, N.J.: Princeton University Press, 1976.

05748.   Picard, Roger. <u>Les</u> <u>Salons</u> <u>littéraires</u> <u>et</u> <u>la</u> <u>société</u>
         <u>francais</u> <u>(1610-1789)</u>. New York: Brentano, 1943.

05749.   Robinson, Mabel. <u>The</u> <u>Great</u> <u>Literary</u> <u>Salons</u> <u>of</u> <u>the</u>
         <u>XVII</u> <u>and</u> <u>XVIII</u> <u>Centuries</u>. London: Thornton Butter-
         worth, 1930.

         Also refer to #5596, 5737-5739, 5746, 5748, 5749.

(2)   Madeleine de Sablé

05750.   Cousin, Victor. <u>Madame</u> <u>de</u> <u>Sablé</u>. Paris: Didier et c^{ie},
         1882.

05751.   Eliot, George. "'Women in France, Madame de Sablé', West-
         minster Review, LXII (October 1854)." In <u>Essays</u> <u>of</u> <u>George</u>
         <u>Eliot</u>, edited by Thomas Pinney, pp. 52-81. New York:
         Columbia University Press, 1963.

05752.   Ivanoff, Nicola. <u>La</u> <u>Marquise</u> <u>de</u> <u>Sablé</u> <u>et</u> <u>son</u> <u>salon</u>. Paris:
         Les Presses Modernes, 1927.

d)   Intellectuals

(1)   Les prétieuses

05753.   Adam, Antoine, "Baroque et préciosité." <u>Revue</u> <u>des</u> <u>sciences</u>
         <u>humaines</u> n.s. 55-56 (July-Dececember 1949):208-224.

05754.   Avigdor, Eva. "La vraie préciosité d'une véritable pre-
         cieuse." <u>XVII</u>^{e} <u>siècle</u>. 108 (1975): 59-74.

05755.   Backer, Dorothy Anne Liot. <u>Precious</u> <u>women</u>: <u>a</u> <u>feminist</u>
         <u>phenomenon</u> <u>in</u> <u>the</u> <u>age</u> <u>of</u> <u>Louis</u> <u>XIV</u>. New York: Basic
         Books, 1974.

05756.   Bray, René. <u>La</u> <u>préciosité</u> <u>et</u> <u>les</u> <u>précieux</u>. Paris: A.
         Michel, 1948.

05757.   Conrart, Valentin. La Journée des madrigaux, suivé de
          la gazette de tendre et du carnaval des prétieuses.
          Paris: A. Aubry, 1856.

05758.   Debu-Bridel, Jacques. "La Préciosité: conception heroique
          de la vie." Revue de France 5 (1938): 195-216.

05759.   Fidao-Justiniani, J. E. L'esprit classique et la
          préciosité au XVIIe siècle. Paris: n.p., 1914.

05760.   Lathuillère, Roger. La Préciosité étude historique et
          linguistique. Geneva: Droz, 1966.
              [See especially 1, ch. 5, pp. 652-675.]

05761.   Livet, Charles Louis. Precieux et les precieuses. Paris:
          Didier, 1859.

05762.   Mongrédien, Georges. Les précieux et les précieuses.
          Paris: Mercure de France, 1939.

05763.   Pintard, Rene. "Préciosité et classicisme." XVIIe siècle
          50-51 (1961): 8-20.

05764.   Pure, Michel de. La prétieuse;ou le mystère des ruelles.
          Paris: E. Droz, 1938.

05765.   Schwarz, Fritz. Somaize und seine Précieuses Ridicules.
          Koenigsberg: n.p., 1903.

05766.   Somaize, Antoine Baudeau de. Le Dictionnaires des
          prétieuses. Paris: P. Jannet, 1856.

05767.   Thérive, André. "Les Précieuses non ridicules." Revue
          des deux mondes 24 (1959): 641-648.

          Also refer to #5441, 5712, 5722.

                    (2) Madame Dacier

05768.   Farnham, Fern. Madame Dacier: Scholar and Humanist.
          Monterey, Calif: Angel Press, 1976.

05769.   Mazon, P. Madame Dacier et les traductions d'Homère
          en France. Oxford: Clarendon Press, 1936.

                    (3) Madame de Sévigné

05770.   Allentuch, Harriet Ray. Madame de Sévigné: A Portrait
          in Letters. Baltimore: Johns Hopkins Press, 1963.

05771. Avigdor, Eva. Madame de Sévigné: un portrait intellectual et moral. Paris: A. G. Nizet, 1974.

05772. Bailly, Auguste. Madame de Sévigné. Paris: A. Fayard, 1955.

05773. Baldensperger, Fernand. "L'Heureaux Paradoxe de Madame de Sévigné: Sa continuite de culture." Romanic Review 32 (February 1942): 32-40.

05774. Duchêne, Roger. "Affaires d'argent et affaires de famille au XVIIe siècle: Madame de Sévigné et Guillaume D'Harays." XVIIe siècle 53 (1961): 3-20.

05775. _____. "Du destinaire au public, ou les metamorphoses d'une correspondance privée." Revue d'histoire litteraire de la France 76 (January-February 1976): 29-46.

05776. _____. "Une reconnaissance excessive?" Madame de Sevigne et son Bien Bon." XVIIe siècle 74 (1967): 27-53.

05777. Gérard-Gailly, Guillaume. Madame de Sévigné. Paris: Hachette, 1971.

05778. _____. Les sept couches de Mme. de Grignan. Abbeville: n.p., 1926.

05779. Gorman, M. Adele, O.S.E. "Madame de Sévigné: Woman of Many Talents." Cithara 4 (1965): 43-59.

05780. Hérard, Madeleine. Madame de Sévigné, demoiselle de Bourgogne. Dijon: n.p., 1959.

05781. Herz, Michelline. "Madame de Sévigné telle qu'elle fut." Modern Language Notes 74 (November 1959): 621-629.

05782. Marcu, Eva. "Madame de Sévigné and Her Daughters." Romanic Review 51 (1960): 182-191.

05783. Mayer, Denise. "Le Portrait de Madame de Sévigné par Madame de la Fayette." XVIIe siècle 101 (1973): 69-87.

05784. Nicolich, Robert N. "Life as theater in the Letters of Madame de Sévigné." Romance Notes 16 (Winter 1975): 376-382.

05785. Noyes, Alfred. "The enigma of Madame de Sévigné." Contemporary Review 189 (March 1956): 149-153.

05786. Pradel, Genes. Madame de Sévigné en Provence. Paris: Figuiere, 1936.

05787. Ritchie, Anne Isabella (Thackeray) Lady. <u>Madame de
        Sévigné</u>. Edinburgh: W. Alackerwood, 1898.

05788. Tilley, Arthur. <u>Madame de Sévigné: some aspects of her
        mind and character</u>. New York: Macmillan, 1937.

e) Art

(1) Women Artists

05789. Chasles, Ph. "Les Femmes chansonnières sous Louis XIV."
        <u>Revue de Paris</u> 8 (1824): 191-202, 325-41.

05790. Gibson, W. "Women and the Notion of Propriety in the
        French theatre (1628-1643)." <u>Forum for Modern Language
        Studies</u> 11 (1975): 1-14.

05791. Wilhelm, Jacques. "Louise Maillon." <u>L'Oeil</u> 21 (Sept.
        1956): 6-13.

Also refer to #4666, 5717.

D. THE GERMANIES

1. POLITICAL

"Govern you then, Madame."
The Great Elector to his wife

a) Legal

05792. Berkner, Lutz K. "Inheritance, Land Tenure and Peasant
        Family Structure: A German Regional Comparison." In
        <u>Family and Inheritance: Rural Society in Western Europe,
        1200-1800</u>, edited by Jack Goody, Joan Thirsk and E. P.
        Thompson, pp. 71-95. Cambridge: University Press, 1976.

05793. Roth, Franz Otto. "Anna Catharine von Graltenau, geb.
        (Freiin) von Putterer—ein steirisches Witwenschicksal,
        1682-1692: Zur Auswertung von Verlassenschaftsinventaren
        und Akten." Zeitschrift des historischen Vereins Steier-
        mark 68 (1977): 81-104.

b) Criminal

05794. Hampe, Theodore. "Crimes and Punishment of Barbara
        Schlumpfen." In Crime and Punishment in Germany,
        pp. 159-165. New York: E.P. Dutton and co., 1929.

c) Political Roles

(1) Women

05795. Adalberto de Baviera, Príncipe. "Mariana de Neoburgo y la
        pretensiones bávaras a la sucesión española." Boletin de
        la Real Academia de la Historia Madrid 80 (January 1922):
        22-40; (February 1922): 107-122; (March 1922): 219-246;
        (April 1922): 328-340; and (May 1922): 497-514.

05796. Bedford, Jessie. A Sister of Prince Rupert: Elizabeth
        princess palatine and abbess of Herford. New York:
        J. Lane, 1909.

05797. Blaze de Bury, Marie Pauline Rose, baroness. Memoirs of the
        Princess Palatine. London: Richard Bentley, 1853.

05798. Bunnett, F. Louise Juliane, Electress Palatine. London:
        J. Nisbet and Co., 1862.

05799. Crevelier, Jacques. La vie romanesque d'Aurore de
        Königsmarck. Paris: n.p., 1929.

05800. Dammert, Rudolf. Aurora von Königsmarck; ein
        Frauenschicksal um August den Starken. Hamburg:
        Hoffmann und Campe, 1936.

05801. Haake, Paul. Christiane Eberhardine und August der Starke.
        Eine Ehetragödie. Dresden: C. Heinrich, 1930.

05802. Heck, Robert. Die Regentschaft der Gräfin Sophie Hedwig.
        Diez: n.p., 1923.

05803.   Horric de Beaucaire, Charles Proper Maurice, comte. A
          mésalliance in the House of Brunswick. London: Reming-
          ton and Co., 1866.

05804.   Justi, Carl Wilhelm. Amalie Elisabeth, Landgräfin von Hessen.
          Giessen: n.p., 1812.

05805.   Marelle, Luise. Eleonore d'Olbreuse, Herzogin von Braun-
          schweig-Lüneburg-Celle, die Grossmutter Europas.
          Hamburg: Hoffman and Campe, 1936.

05806.   Neigenbaur, Johan Ferdinand. Eleanor d'Olbreuse die Stammut-
          ter der Könighauser von England, Hannover und Preussen.
          Braunschweig: E. Leibrock, 1859.

05807.   Renner, Anna Marie. Sibylla Augusta, Markgräfin von Baden.
          Die Geschichte eines denkwürdigen Lebens. Stuttgart:
          Strecker and Schroder, 1938.

05808.   Saring, Toni. Luise-Henriette, Kurfürstin von Brandenburg,
          1627-1667. Die Gemahlin des Grossen Kurfürsten. Göttingen:
          Deuerlichsche Verlag, 1939.

05809.   _____. "Kurfürstin Anna (von Preussen)." Forschungen
          zur brandenburgischen und preussischen Geschichte 53 (1941):
          248-295.

05810.   Seraphim, August. Ein Schwester der Grossen Kurfürsten,
          Luise Charlotte, Margräfin von Brandenburg, Herzogin von
          Kurland (1617-1676). Berlin: 1901.

05811.   Smidt-d'Orrenberg, Irmgard. Margarita Maria Infantin
          von Spanien, romisch-deutsche Kaiserin. Vienna:
          Bergland Verlag, 1966.

05812.   Sommerfeldt, Gustav. "Der Frau Elisabeth von Borck
          Beteiligung an der Landesfension in Preussen 1602.
          Archiv für Kulturgeschichte 4 (1906): 303-309.

05813.   Taylor, Gladys. The Little Infanta. London: Phoenix
          House, 1960.

05814.   Ward, Adolphus William. Elizabeth, Princess Palatine.
          London: n. p., 1901.

05815.   Wegführer, Johann. Leben der Kurfürstin Luise. Leipzig:
          E. P. Melzer, 1838.

          Also refer to #5456.

(2) Individuals

(a) Elizabeth of Bohemia, the Winter Queen

05816. Benger, E. Memoirs of Elizabeth Stuart, Queen of Bohemia.
London: Longman, Hurst, Rees, Orme, Brown and Green,
1825.

05817. Buchan, Alice. A Stuart Portrait, being a brief study of
a Stuart princess, Elizabeth, daughter of James I and
queen of Bohemia. London: Davies, 1934.

05818. Everett Green, Mary Anne. Elizabeth, Electress Palatine and
Queen of Bohemia. London: Methuen & Co., 1909.

05819. Gorst-William, J. Elizabeth the Winter Queen. London:
Abelard-Schumann, 1977.

05820. Hauck, Karl. Elisabeth, Königin von Böhmen. Heidelburg:
C. Winter, 1905.

05821. Oman, Carola. Elizabeth of Bohemia. London: Hodder and
Stoughton, 1964.

05822. Opel, Julius Otto. Elisabeth Stuart. Munich: n.p., 1870.

(b) Sophie of Hanover

05823. Baily, F. E. Sophia of Hanover and her times. London:
Hutchinson, 1936.

05824. Fester, Richard. Kurfürstin Sophie von Hannover. Hamburg:
Verlagsanstalt und Druckerei, 1893.

05825. Knoop, Mathilde. Die Kurfürstin Sophie von Hannover.
Hildesheim: A. Lax, 1964.

05826. Kroll, Maria. Sophie, Electress of Hanover: A Personal
Portrait. London: Gollancz, 1973.

05827. Schaumann, Adolph Friedrich Heinrich. Sophie Dorothea
Prinzessin von Ahlden und Kurfürstin Sophie von
Hannover. Hanover: Klindworth, 1879.

05828. Ward, Adolphus William. The Electress Sophia and the
Hanoverian Succession. New York: Longmans, Green and
Co., 1909.

Also refer to #4120.

(c)   Sophie Charlotte

05829.   Brentano, Bernard. Sophie Charlotte und Danckelmann:
eine preussische Historie. Wiesbaden: Limes, 1949.

05830.   Erman, Jean Pierre. Memoires pour servir à l'histoire
de Sophie Charlotte. Berlin: G. F. Starcke, 1801.

05831.   Koser, Reinhold. "Sophie Charlotte, die erste
preussische Königin." Deutsche Rundschau 52 (1887):
353-369.

05832.   Krauske, Otto. "Konigin Sophie Charlotte." Hohenzollern
Jahrbuch 4 (1900): 110-126.

05833.   Varnhagen von Ense, Karl August Ludwig Philipp. Leben
der Königin Sophie Charlotte von Preussen. Berlin:
Dunker und Humblot, 1837.

2. RELIGION

"However much the princes burn, they can never burn
out the evil."

Spee

a)   Saints/Religious Women

05834.   Irwin, Joyce. "Anna Maria van Schurman: From Feminism
to Pietism." Church History 46 (1977): 48-62.

Also refer to #5260-5266.

b)   Witchcraft

05835.   Brück, Anton Ph. "Hexenprozesse in Aschaffenburg und Damm
in den Jahren 1603/4 and 1628/9." Aschaffenburger
Jahrbuch 6 (1979): 241-270.

05836.   Crecelius, W. "Frau Holde und der Venusberg (aus
hessischen Hexenprozessen)." Zeitschrift für deutsche
Mythologie und Sittenkunde 1 (1853): 272-277.

05837. Grebner, Christian. "Hexenprozesse im Freigericht Alzenau (1601-1605)." Aschaffenburger Jahrbuch 6 (1979): 137-240.

05838. Ladame, P. ed. Procès criminel de la dernière sorcière brûlée à Genève le 6 avril 1652. Paris: Delehaye, 1888.

05839. Otto, Eduard. "Ein Protest gegen Hexenverbrennung aus der Zeit des Dreissigjahrigen Krieges." Archiv für Kulturgeschichte 6 (1908): 83-89.

3. SOCIAL

My mother "cared more for her dogs and pet monkeys than for her children."   Sophie of Hanover

a) Generic

05840. Kuczynski, Jürgen. Geschichte des Alltags des deutschen Volkes. Vol. I. Cologne: Pahl-Rugenstein Verlag, 1980.

b) Demography

05841. Berkner, Lutz K. "Peasant Household Organization and Demographic Change in Lower Saxony, 1689-1766." In Population Patterns in the Past, edited by Ronald Demos Lee, pp. 53-69. New York: Academic Press, 1977.

05842. Goertz, Adalbert. "The Marriage Records of Montau in Prussia for 1661-1704." Mennonite Quarterly Review 50 (July 1976): 240-250.

c) Family

05843. Lehners, Jean-Paul, "Haus und Familie im Markt Stockerau am Ende des 17. Jahrhunderts," Unsere Heimat: Zeitschrift des Vereins für Landeskunde von Neiderosterreich und Wien 45 (1974): 222-235.

Also refer to #5792.

d) Marriage

05844.   Staufenegger, R.   "Le mariage à Genève vers 1600."
Mémoires de la société pour l'histoire du droit et des
institutions des ancien pays bourguignons 27 (1966):
319-329.

Also refer to #5842.

e) Fashion/Manners

05845.   Haug, Fl. H.   "Der Schmuck einer fränkischen Gräfin um
1611." Archiv für Kulturgeschichte 12 (1916): 97-103.

4. CULTURAL

"This Princess has the genius of a great and the
knowledge of a learned man."
Frederick II said of Sophie Charlotte

a) Education

05846.   Fertig, Ludwig. Die Hofmeister. Stuttgart: Verlag J.B.
Metzler, 1979.

b) Literature

05847.   Stern, Gerhard Wilhelm. Die Liebe im deutschen Roman des 17.
Jahrhunderts. 1932. Reprint. Nendeln/Leichtenstein:
Kraus, 1967.

05848.   Uhde-Bernays, H.   Catharina Regina von Greiffenberg (1633–
          1694). Berlin: Fontane, 1903.

05849.   Petit, Léon. Descartes et la princesse Elisabeth. Paris:
          A. G. Nizet, 1969.

E. IBERIA

1. POLITICAL

"The Court has provided his Catholic Majesty [Carlos II]
a third wife, the Emperor's daughter, being about fifteen
years old. Poor lady! If it be her fortune, I most
heartily pity her."

                                        Stanhope

a) Political Roles

(1) Women

05850.   Guazza, R.   Margherita di Savoia duchessa di Mantova e vice-
          regina di Portogallo. Turin: Paravia, 1930.

05851.   Llano y Torriglia, Felix de.   "Notica de hallazgo de los
          restos de Isabel Clara Eugenia." Boletin de la Real
          Academia de la Historia Madrid 120 (January–March 1947):
          126–130.

(2) Marie Louise of Orléans

05852.   Aubarede, Gabriel d'. La prisonnière de Madrid. Marie-
          Louise d'Orléans, reine d'Espagne. Paris: Editions
          nationales, 1936.

05853.   Izquierdo Hernández, Manuel.   "El régimen alimentario de una
          Reine de España, en 1696." Boletin de la Academia de la
          Historia Madrid 122 (January–March 1948): 351–359.

05854.   Maura y Gamazo, Grabriel Duque de. Maria Luisa de Orleans,
          Reina de España. Madrid: Editions Calleja, 1943.

2. RELIGION

"The great lords and most illustrious people cannot marry
off more than one of their four or five daughters because
of the excessive dowries demanded. There is no other
course but to send the younger sisters to convents."
                              Fray Hernando del Castillo

a) Saints/Religious Women

05855. Bordeaux, Henry. Marianna, la religieuse portugaise.
        Paris: Michel, 1934.

05856. D'Auvergne, Edmund B. "The Nun Ensign (Catalina de Erauso)."
        In Adventuresses and Adventurous Ladies, pp. 15-44. New
        York: J. H. Sears and Company, Inc., 1927.

b) Witchcraft

05857. Caro Baroja, Julio. "Las Brujas de Fuenterrabia (1611)."
        Revista de dialectologia y tradiciones populares 3 (1947):
        189-204.

3. SOCIAL

"She has these positions
First she keep a tavern
A perfume and soap shop,
She is a procuress of fornications. . ."
                    Verse from 17th century Seville concerning
                    a street hawker

a) Generic

05858. Deleito y Piñuela, José. La Mujer, la Casa y la moda (en la
        España del Rey Poeta). 2nd ed. Madrid: Espasa-Calpe, 1954.

Also refer to #4844.

b) Demography

05859. Martínez Perona, José Vincente. "Demografía y alimentación
en la baronia de Pedralba y Bugarra (1610-1720)." Estudios
6 (1977): 27-69.

4. CULTURAL

"Let us praise their pretty turn of phrase and their
learning and give them a place in the library, but
not in our hearts."

Quevedo

a) Literature

(1) Non-specific

05860. DeArmas, Frederick A. The Invisible Mistress: Aspects
of Feminism and Fantasy in the Golden Age. Charlottes-
ville, Va.: Bibliotheca Siglo de Oro, 1976.

05861. Mas, Amédée. La caricature de la femme, du mariage et de
l'amour dans l'oeuvre du Quevedo. Paris: Ediciones
Hispano-Americanas, 1957.

(2) Drama

05862. Bravo Villasante, Carmen. La mujer vestida de hombre
en el teatro español. Madrid: Revista de Occidente,
1955.

05863. McKendrick, Melveena. "The Bandolero of golden-age drama:
a symbol of feminist revolt." Bulletin of Hispanic
Studies 46 (1969): 1-20.

05864. _____. "The 'mujer esquiva' - A Measure of
the Feminist Sympathies of Seventeenth Century Spanish
Dramatists." Hispanic Review 40 (1972): 162-197.

05865.   Matulka, B.   "The Feminist theme in the Drama of the Siglo
          del Oro."   Romanic Review 26 (1935): 191-231.

05866.   Podol, Peter.   "Non-conventional Treatment of the Honor theme
          in the theatre of the Golden Age."   Revista de estudios
          hispanicos 7 (October 1973): 449-463.

                          (3) Prose

05867.   Lasperas, Jean-Michel.   "Personnages et récit dans les
          'novelas amorosas y ejemplares' de Maria de Zayas y
          Sotomajor."   Melanges de la Casa de Valsquez 15
          (1979): 365-384.

05868.   Griswold, Susan C.   "Topoi and Rhetorical Distance: The
          'Feminism' of Maria de Zayas."   Revista de estudios his-
          panicos 14 (May 1980): 97-116.

05869.   Lara, M. V., ed.   "De escritores españoles--II: Maria de
          Zayas y Sotomayor."   Bulletin of Spanish Studies 9
          (January 1932): 31-37.

05870.   Serrano Poncela, Segundo.   "Casamientos enganosos Doña Maria
          de Zayas, Scarron y proceso creacion literarra."   Bulletin
          hispanique 64 (July-December 1962): 248-259.

05871.   Sylvania, Lena E. V.   "Doña Maria de Zayas y Sotomayor A
          Contribution to the Study of her Works."   Romanic Review
          13 (April-June 1922): 197-213; 14 (April-September 1923):
          199-232.

05872.   Vasileski, Irma.   Maria de Zayas y Sotomayor: Su Epocha
          y su Obra.   Madrid: Playor, 1974.

                      F. ITALY

                      1. POLITICAL

          "The highest ornament of woman is silence. They are
          made only to stay at home, not to go abroad."
                              Elena Lucrezia Cornaro

a) Political Roles

05873.   Bayer, Ferdinand. "L'infanzia di Maria Felice Orsini
         a Firenzi e il suo matrimonio con Enrico II di
         Montmorency (1599-1613)." Archivio Storico Italiano 121
         (1963): 237-254

05874.   Fusai, Giuseppe. "Trattative di matrimonio tra Casa
         Savoia e Casa Medici." Archivio storico italiano
         76 (1918): 178-190.

05875.   Spanò, Serena. "Per uno Studio su Caterina da
         Bologna." Studi Medievali 3rd ser. 12 (1971):
         713-759.

2. RELIGION

"Obedience shall be her enclosure, the fear of God her
grate, and modesty her veil."
                              St. Vincent de Paul
                              speaking of the Sisters
                              of Charity

05876.   Ciammitti, Luisa. "Una santa di meno. Storia di
         Angela Mellini, cucitrice bolognese (1667-17..)."
         Quaderni Storici 41 (March-August 1979): 603-639.

05877.   Petrucci, Armando. "Nota sulla scrittuta di Angela
         Mellini." Quaderni Storici 41 (March-August 1979):
         640-643.

Also refer to #4593.

3. SOCIAL

"The Spaniards with their artificial 'code of honor'
introduced the formal duel and the custom of wife
murder for real or imagined infidelity [into Italy]."
                              Jameson

a) Family

05878. Corsini, Carlo. "Materiali per lo studio della famiglia en
        Toscana nei secolo XVII-XIX: gli esposti." Quaderni
        storici 33 (September-December 1976): 998-1052.

b) Sex Life and Morals

05879. Accati, Luisa. "Lo spirito della fornicazione: virtu
        dell' anema e virtu del corpo." Quaderni storici 41
        (March-August 1979): 644-672.

05880. Cavallo, Sandra and Cerutti, Simona. "Onore femminile
        e controlla sociale della riproduzione in Piemonti tra
        sei Settocento." Quaderni storici 44 (August 1980):
        346-383.

4. CULTURAL

        "It is a miracle if a woman in wishing to overcome her
        sex and in giving herself to learning and then lan-
        guages, does not stain her soul with vice and filthy
        abominations."   17th century doctor

05881. Fusco, Nicola. Elena Lucrezia Cornaro Piscopia 1646-
        1684. Pittsburgh: United States Committee for Elena
        Lucrezia Coronaro Piscopia terentary, 1975.

05882. Labalme, Patricia H. "Women's Roles in Early Modern
        Venice: An Exceptional Case." In Beyond their Sex,
        Learned Women of the European Past, edited by Patricia
        Labalme, pp. 129-152. New York: New York University
        Press, 1980.

05883. Maschietto, Francesco Ludovico. Elena Lucrezia Cornaro
        Piscopia 1646-1684. Padua: Antenore, 1978.

05884. Santi, Angelo de. "Elena Lucrezia Cornaro Piscopia (1646-
        1684): Nuove Ricerche." Civiltà cattolica 17th ser.
        4 (1898): 172-186, 421-440, 678-689; 5 (1899): 176-193,
        433-447.

G. LOW COUNTRIES

1. POLITICAL

The party at court feared no one except Amalie of
Solms "and that was not without reason."
                          French ambassador at the Hague

05885. Geyl, Pieter. "The Princess Dowager, 1661-1668." In
        Orange and Stuart 1641-1672, pp. 163-300. 1939.
        Reprint. London: Weidenfeld and Nicholson, 1969.

05886. _____. "The Princess Royal, 1650-1661." In
        Orange and Stuart 1641-1672, pp. 72-162. 1939.
        Reprint. London: Weidenfeld and Nicholson, 1969.

05887. Klingenstein, L. The Great Infanta Isabel Sovereign of
        the Netherlands. New York: G. P. Putnam's Sons, 1910.

2. SOCIAL

"Their [Dutch] women live with general good fame; a certain
sort of chastity being hereditary and habitual among them,
as probity among men."
                          Sir William Temple
                          British ambassador to Holland
                          17th century

a) Generic

05888. Zumthor, Paul. Daily Life in Rembrandt's Holland. New
        York: The Macmillan Company, 1963.

b) Demography

05889. Slicher van Bath, B. H. "Contrasting Demographic Development in Some Parts of the Netherlands during the depres-
sion period of the 17th and 18th Centuries." In
Population Growth and the Brain Drain, Edinburgh Con-
ference on Demography, 1967. Edited by F. Bechhofer,
pp. 209-219. Edinburgh: University Press, 1969.

05889. Van der Woude, A. M. "Variations in the size and
structure of the household in the United Provinces
of the Netherlands in the seventeenth and eighteenth
centuries." In Household and Family in Past Time,
edited by Peter Laslett and Richard Wall, pp. 299-
318, Cambridge: The University Press, 1972.

c) Family

05891. Mook, Barbara. The Dutch Family in the Seventeenth and
Eighteenth Centuries: An Explorative and Descriptive
Study. Ottawa: University of Ottawa Press, 1978.

3. CULTURAL

". . . the education of their children as well daughters
as sons . . . they [the Dutch] take care to bring up to
write perfect good hands . . . have full knowledge and
use of Arithmetic . . ."
Sir Josiah Child, A New Disclosure
of Trade, 1668

05892. Belche, Jean-Pierre. "Anne-Marie de Mansfelt: Pionierin
weiblicher Schulbildung in Luxemburg (ca. 1585-1657)."
Hemecht 29 (1977): 349-381.

VI. EIGHTEENTH CENTURY

A. GENERAL

1. SURVEYS

"More civilized than we are in externals, they [women]
have remained true savages inside, all of them
Machiavellians more or less."   Diderot

05893. Fritz, Paul, and Morton, Richard, eds. Woman in the
        Eighteenth Century and Other Essays. Toronto: Samuel
        Stevens Hakkert and Co., 1976.

05894. Goncourt, Edmond, and Goncourt, Jules. The Woman of the
        Eighteenth Century: Her Life, from Birth to Death, Her
        Love and Her Philosophy in the Worlds of Salon, Shop
        and Street. 1862. Reprint. Translated by Le Clercq and
        Roeder. Freeport, N.Y.: Books for Libraries Press, 1972.

05895. Trowbridge, William Rutherford Hayes. Daughters of Eve.
        New York: Brentano's, 1912.

05896. _____ . Seven Splendid Sinners.
        London: T. F. Unwin, 1908.

2. POLITICAL

"[Married women] with all their movable goods . . . are
wholly in potestate viri."
                    Magnae Britanniae Notitia, 1729 edition.

05897.   Clements, Frances M.   "The Rights of Women in the
         Eighteenth-Century Novel."   Enlightenment Essays 4
         (Fall-Winter 1973): 63-70.

05898.   Humphreys, A. R.   "The 'rights of woman' in the Age of
         Reason."   Modern Language Review 41 (1946): 256-269.

05899.   Schapire-Neurath, Anna.   Die Geschichte der Frauenbewegung
         im Abriss. I. Die Vorgeschichte der modernene Frauen-
         bewegung im 18. Jahrhundert. Kultur und Fortschritt,
         nos. 254-256. Grautzsch bei Leipzig: Felix Dietrich,
         1909.

3. ECONOMIC

". . . that these poor [women] will hardly earn as much
as the value of the day bread they have already eaten
during the previous idle days."
                    Klima, "Role of Domestic Industry."

05900.   Tilly, Louise A., Scott, Joan W. and Cohen, Miriam.
         "Woman's Work and European Fertility Patterns."   Journal
         of Interdisciplinary History 6 (Winter 1976): 447-476.

4. SOCIAL

"If we take a survey of ages and of countries, we will
find the women almost without exception-at all times
and in all places, adored and oppressed."
                    Antoine-Leonard Thomas, 1772.

a) Generic

05901. Gillis, John R. Youth and History: Tradition and Change in
        European Age Relations 1770-Present. New York: Academic
        Press, 1974.

05902. Shorter, Edward. "Female Emancipation, Birth Control, and
        Fertility in European History." American Historical
        Review 78 (June 1973): 605-640.

05903. _____. "Illegitimacy, Sexual Revolution and
        Social Change in Europe, 1750-1900." Journal of Inter-
        disciplinary History 2 (Autumn 1971): 237-72. Also in
        The Family in History, edited by T. K. Rabb and R. I.
        Rotberg, pp. 48-84. New York: Harper and Row, 1971.

        Also refer to #5168, 5169.

b) Demography

05904. Andorka, R. "Peasant Family Structure in the Eighteenth
        and Nineteenth Centuries." Ethnographica 86 (1975):
        341-365.

05905. Berkner, Lutz K. and Mendels, Franklin. "Inheritance
        Systems, Family Structure and Demographic Patterns in
        Western Europe (1700-1900)." In Historical Studies of
        Changing Fertility, edited by Charles Tilly, pp. 200-224.
        Princeton, N.J.: Princeton University Press, 1978.

05906. Habakkuk, H. J. "Population Problems and European Economic
        Development in the Late Eighteenth and Nineteenth Cen-
        turies." American Economic Review 53 (1963): 607-618.

05907. Langer, William L. "Checks on Population Growth, 1750-
        1850." Scientific American 226 (February 1972): 92-99.

05908. McKeown, Thomas; R. G. Brown; and Record, R. G. "An Inter-
        pretation of the Modern Rise of Population in Europe."
        Population Studies 27 (November 1972): 345-383.

c) Family

05909.   Donzelot, Jacques. The Policing of Families. New York:
           Pantheon, 1979.

05910.   Lorence, Bogna W. "Parents and Children in Eighteenth Century
           Europe." History of Childhood Quarterly 2 (Summer 1974):
           1-30.

           Also refer to #5904, 5905.

d) Sex Life and Morals

05911.   Nutzbares, Galantes und Curioses Frauenzimmer-Lexicon.
           Frankfurt a.M.: J.F. Gleditschens Sohn, 1739.

e) Fashion/Manners

05912.   Boehn, Max von. Die Mode Menschen und Moden im 18.
           Jahrhundert. Munich: F. Bruckmann, A.G., 1923.

           Also refer to #5167.

5. CULTURAL

           "The second caution to be given her and which is absolutely
           necessary is to conceal whatever learning she attains with
           as much solicitude as she would hide crookedness or
           lameness."
                                                  Mary Montague

a) Education

05913.   Salmon, David, and Hindshaw, Winifred. Infant Schools: Their
           History and Theory. New York: Longmans, Green, 1904.
           Also refer to #5174, 5175.

b) Literature

05914. Brissenden, R.F. "La Philosophie dans le boudoir; or, A
        Young Lady's Entrance into the World." Studies in
        Eighteenth-Century Culture 2 (1972): 113-141.

05915. Fauchery, Pierre. La destinée féminine dans le roman
        européen du dix-huitième siècle, 1713-1807, Essai de
        gynécomythie romanesque. Paris: A. Colin, 1972.

05916. Stewart, Philip. Le Masque et la parole: Le Langage de
        l'amour au XVIIIe siècle. Paris: Corti, 1973.

        Also refer to #5897, 5898.

c) Art and Artifacts

05917. Borgiotti, Mario. La donna e i bimbi nell-arte del nostro
        Ottocento pittorico . . . Milan: A. Martello, 1969.

B. ENGLAND

1. BIBLIOGRAPHIES

[The truly wise woman] "conceals the superiority she has
with as much care as others take to display the superiority they have not. . ."
                              Gentleman's Magazine, 1737

05918. Schnorrenberg, Barbara Brandon. "Toward a Bibliography of
        Eighteenth-Century Englishwomen." Eighteenth-Century
        Life 1 (March 1975): 50-52.

05919. _____ and Hunter, Jean E. "The
        Eighteenth-Century Englishwoman." In The Women of
        England from Anglo-Saxon Times to the Present, edited by
        Barbara Kanner, pp. 183-228. Hamden, Conn.: Archon
        Books, 1979.

05920.   Steinen, Karl von den. "The Discovery of Women in Eight-
         eenth-Century English Political Life." In The Women of
         England from Anglo-Saxon Times to the Present, edited
         by Barbara Kanner, pp. 229-258. Hamden, Conn.: Archon
         Books, 1979.

2. SURVEYS

         "Shake off this vile obedience they exact and claim an
         equal Empire o'er the World."
                                            Gentlemen's Magazine

05921.   Burton, Elizabeth. The Pageant of Georgian England. New
         York: Scribner, 1968.

05922.   Fyvie, John. Noble Dames and Notable Men of the Georgian
         Era. London: Constable, 1910.

05923.   Hamilton, Catherine J. Notable Irishwomen. Dublin:
         Sealy, Bryers, and Walker, 1904.

05924.   Stebbins, Lucy (Poate). London Ladies: True Tales of the
         Eighteenth Century. 1952. Reprint. New York: AMS Press,
         1966.

05925.   Urdang, Laurence, Associates, compilers. Lives of the
         Georgian Age. New York: Barnes Noble, 1977.

05926.   Vaughan, Herbert M. From Anne to Victoria: fourteen
         biographical studies between 1702 and 1901. London:
         Methuen, 1931.

05927.   Wark, Robert R. Meet the Ladies: Personalities in Hunt-
         ington Portraits. San Marino, Calif.: Huntington
         Library, 1972.

         Also refer to #5178, 5181.

3. POLITICAL

         "Nature has given women so much power that the law has
         wisely given them little."
                                            Samuel Johnson

a) Legal

05928. Greenberg, Janelle. "The Legal Status of the English Woman
in Early Eighteenth-Century Common Law and Equity."
<u>Studies in Eighteenth-Century Culture</u> 4 (1975): 171-182.

b) Criminal

05929. Auvergne, Edmund B. d'. "The Countess-Duchess (Elizabeth
Chudleigh)." In <u>Adventuresses</u> and <u>Adventurous Ladies</u>,
pp. 64-90. New York: J. H. Sears and Company, Inc.,
1927.

05930. Beattie, J. M. "The Criminality of Women in Eighteenth-
Century England." <u>Journal of Social History</u> 8 (Summer
1975): 80-116.

05931. MacKinnon, Sir Frank Douglas. <u>Grand larceny</u>. London:
Oxford University Press, 1937.

05932. Sill, Geoffrey M. "Rogues, Strumpets, and Vagabonds: Defoe
on Crime in the City." <u>Eighteenth-Century Life</u> 2 (June
1976): 74-78.

c) Feminism

(1) Non-specific

05933. Plaisant, Michèle. "Féminisme et poésie en Angleterre à
l'Aube du XVIIIe siècle." In <u>Aspects du féminisme en
Angleterre au 18e siècle</u>, pp. 11-49. Paris: Editions
universitaires, 1972.

05934. _____, Denizot, Paul and Moreaux, Françoise.
<u>Aspects du féminisme en Angleterre au 18e siècle</u>. Paris:
Editions universitaires, 1972.

(2) Individuals

(a) William Godwin

05935. Brailsford, H. N. <u>Shelley, Godwin, and their Circle</u>.
Hamden, Conn.: Archon Books, 1969.

05936. Brown, Ford K. The Life of William Godwin. London: J.M. Dent & Sons, 1926.

05937. Detre, Jean. A Most Extraordinary Pair: Mary Wollstone-craft and William Godwin. New York: Doubleday, 1975.

05938. Fleisher, David. William Godwin: A Study in Liberalism. London: George Allen & Unwin, 1951.

05939. Grylls, Rosalie Glynn. William Godwin and his World. London: Odhams Press, 1953.

05940. Paul, C. Kegan. William Godwin: His Friends and Contemporaries. London: Henry S. King, 1876.

05941. Pollin, Burton R. Education and Enlightenment in the Works of William Godwin. New York: Las Americas Publishing Company, 1962.

05942. Robinson, Victor. William Godwin and Mary Wollstonecraft. New York: The Altrurians, 1907.

05943. Roussin, Henri. William Godwin (1756-1836). Paris: Librairie Plon, Plon-Nourrit et c^{ie}, 1913.

05944. Simon, Helene. William Godwin und Mary Wollstonecraft. Eine biographisch-soziologische Studie. Munich: O. Beck, 1909.

05945. Smith, Elton Edward and Smith, Esther Greenwell. William Godwin. New York: Twayne Publishers, Inc., 1965.

(b) Mary Wollstonecraft

[1] BIBLIOGRAPHIES

05946. Todd, Janet M. "The biographies of Mary Wollstonecraft." Signs 1 (Spring 1976): 721-734.

05947. _____. "Mary Wollstonecraft: a review of research and comment." British Studies Monitor 7 (Fall 1977): 3-23.

05948. _____. Mary Wollstonecraft: An Annotated Bibliography. New York: Garland Publishing Co., 1976.

05949. Tyson, G. P. "A Found Woman: Some Recent Biographies of Mary Wollstonecraft." Eighteenth Century Studies 9 (Winter 1975-1976): 263-269.

[2] CONTEMPORARY

05950.   Godwin, William. Memoirs of Mary Wollstonecraft. New
         York: R. R. Smith, Inc., 1930.

05951.   Wollstonecraft, Mary. The Female Reader. Delmar, N.Y.:
         Scholars' Facsimiles and Reprints, 1980.

05952.   _____. An Historical and Moral View of the
         Origin and Progress of the French Revolution and the
         Effect It Has Produced in Europe. Introduced by Janet M.
         Todd. Delmar, N.Y.: Scholars' Facsimile and Reprints,
         1975.

05953.   _____. Maria or the Wrongs of Women.
         Introduced by Moira Ferguson. New York: Norton, 1975.

05954.   _____. Posthumous Works. 4 vols. Edited
         by William Godwin. (The Feminist Controversy in England
         1788–1810 Series.) New York: Garland Publishing, Inc.,
         1974.

05955.   _____. Thoughts on the Education of
         Daughters: With Reflections on Female Conduct, in the
         More Important Duties of Life. 1787. Reprint. New York:
         Garland Publishing Co., 1974.

05956.   _____. A Vindication of the Rights of Men,
         in a letter to the Right Honourable Edmund Burke. 1790.
         Reprint. Delmar, N.Y.: Scholars' Facsimiles and Reprints,
         1960.

05957.   _____. A Vindication of the Rights of
         Women. Baltimore: Penguin Books, 1975.

05958.   _____. A Wollstonecraft Anthology, edited
         by Janet M. Todd. Bloomington, In.: Indiana University
         Press, 1977.

[3] SECONDARY

05959.   Bouten, J. Mary Wollstonecraft and the Beginning of
         Female Emancipation in France and England. 1922.
         Reprint. Philadelphia: Porcupine Press, 1975.

05960.   Flexner, Eleanor. Mary Wollstonecraft, a Biography. New
         York: Coward, McCann and Geoghegan, 1972.

05961. George, Margaret. One Woman's "Situation": a Study of
       Mary Wollstonecraft. Chicago: University of Illinois
       Press, 1970.

05962. Guralnick, Elissa S. "Radical politics in Mary Wollstone-
       craft's A Vindication of the Rights of Women." Studies
       in Burke and His Time 18 (August 1977): 155-166.

05963. Hughes, Patricia. "Mary Wollstonecraft: Stoic Liberal-
       Democrat." Canadian Journal of Political and Social
       Theory 1 (Spring-Summer 1977): 59-74.

05964. Janes, R. M. "On the Reception of Mary Wollstonecraft's
       A Vindication of the Rights of Woman." Journal of the
       History of Ideas 39 (April-June 1978): 293-302.

05965. Korsmeyer, Carolyn W. "Reason and Morals in the Early
       Feminist Movement: Mary Wollstonecraft." In Women
       and Philosophy: Toward a Theory of Liberation, edited
       by Carol C. Gould and Marx W. Wartofsky, pp. 97-111.
       New York: Putnam's, 1976. Also in Philosophical Forum 5
       (Fall-Winter 1973-1974): 97-111.

05966. Nicholes, Eleanor L. "Mary Wollstonecraft." In Romantic
       Rebels, Essays on Shelley and His Circle, edited by
       Kenneth Neill Cameron, pp. 34-58. Cambridge, Mass.:
       Harvard University Pres, 1973.

05967. Nixon, Edna. Mary Wollstonecraft: her life and times.
       London: Dent, 1971.

05968. Preedy, George. This Shining Woman: Mary Wollstonecraft
       Godwin, 1759-1797. London: Collins, 1937.

05969. Storr, Marthe (Miguel) Seven. Mary Wollstonecraft et le
       mouvement féministe dans la littérature anglaise. Paris:
       Les Presses universitaires de France, 1932.

05970. Sunstein, Emily W. A Different Face: The Life of Mary
       Wollstonecraft. New York: Harper & Row, 1975.

05971. Tims, Margaret. Mary Wollstonecraft, A Social Pioneer.
       London: Millington Books, 1976.

05972. Tomalin, Claire. The life and death of Mary Wollstone-
       craft. New York: Harcourt, Brace, Jovanovich, 1974.

05973. Wardle, Ralph M. Mary Wollstonecraft: A Critical Bio-
       graphy. New York: Coward, McCann and Geoghegan, 1972.

       Also refer to #5405, 5935-5945.

d) Political Roles

(1) Women

05974. Beck, Clark L., Jr. "Romance, Politics or Madness: John Paul Jones and the Countess of Selkirk." Journal of the Rutgers University Library 27 (June 1973): 51-56.

05975. Benjamin, Lewis S. Lady Suffolk and Her Circle. New York: Houghton Mifflin Co., 1924.

05976. _____. Maids of Honor. New York: George H. Dorna Co., 1927.

05977. Biddulph, Violet. Kitty, Duchess of Queensberry. London: Nicholson and Watson, 1935.

05978. _____. The Three Ladies Waldegrave (and their Mother). London: Peter Davies, 1938.

05979. Bleackley, Horace. The Beautiful Duchess, Being an Account of the Life and Time of Elizabeth Gunning, duchess of Hamilton and Argyl. London: John Lane, 1907.

05980. Bretherton, Francis Fletcher. The Countess of Huntington. London: Epworth Press, 1940.

05981. Burnet, Regula., ed. Ann Cook and Friend. New York: Oxford University Press, 1936.

05982. Calder-Marshall, Arthur. The Two Duchesses. New York: Harper and Row Publishers, Inc., 1978.

05983. Curtis, Edith Roelker. Lady Sarah Lennox, an irrepressible Stuart, 1745-1826. New York: Putnam, 1946.

05984. Dobree, Bonamy, ed. From Anne to Victoria. New York: Scribner's, 1937.

05985. Doran, John. Lives of the Queens of England of the House of Hanover. 1875. 4th ed. Reprint. New Haven, Conn.: Research Publications, Inc., 1977.

05986. FitzGerald, Brian. Emily, Duchess of Leinster, 1731-1814. London: Staples Press, 1949.

05987. _____. Lady Louisa Conolly, 1743-1821: an Anglo-Irish biography. New York: Staples Press, 1950.

05988. Greenwood, Alice Drayton. Lives of the Hanoverian Queens of England. London: G. Bell and Sons, 1909-1911.

05989. Halsband, Robert. "The Noble Lady and the Player." History Today 18 (July 1968): 468-472.

05990. Haslip, Joan. Lady Hester Stanhope. New York: Stokes, 1936.

05991. Hill, Patricia Kneas. The Oglethorpe Ladies and the Jacobite Conspiracies. Atlanta: Cherokee Publishing Company, 1977.

05992. Hopkinson, M. R. Married to Mercury. A Sketch of Lord Bolingbroke and his wives. London: Constable, 1936.

05993. Iremonger, Lucille. Love and the Princess. London: Faber, 1958.

05994. Keppel, Sonia. The Sovereign Lady: A Life of Elizabeth Vassall, Third Lady Holland, with her family. London: Hamilton, 1974.

05995. Leslie, Shane. Mrs. Fitzherbert; A life chiefly from unpublished sources. London: Burns Oates, 1939.

05996. Lindsey, John. The lovely Quaker. London: Rich and Cowan, 1939.

05997. Lynch, Kathleen M. "Henrietta, Duchess of Marlborough." Publications of the Modern Language Association of America 52 (1937): 1072-1093.

05998. Marples, Morris. Six Royal Sisters. London: Michael Joseph, 1969.

05999. Mayne, Ethel Colburn. A Regency chapter; Lady Bessborough and her friendships. London: Macmillan, 1939.

06000. Mitchiner, Margaret. No Crown for the Queen. Louise de Stolberg, Countess of Albany and Wife of the Young Pretender. London: Cape, 1937.

06001. Napier, Lady Sarah (Lennox) Bunbury. The Life and Letters of Lady Sarah Lennox, 1745-1826. New York: Scribner, 1902.

06002. Palmer, Iris Irma (Leveson-Gower). The Face Without a Frown: Georgiana, Duchess of Devonshire. London: F. Muller Ltd., 1947.

06003. Phillipson, Wulfston. "Homage to Mrs. Fitzherbert." Downside Review 58 (1940): 17-28.

06004. Richardson, Joanna. "The Princess Charlotte." History
        Today 22 (February 1972): 87-93.

06005. Stuart, Dorothy Margaret. The Daughters of George III.
        London: Macmillan, 1939.

06006. _____. Dearest Bess: The Life and Times
        of Lady Elizabeth Foster, afterwards Duchess of Devon-
        shire, from her Unpublished Journals and Correspondence.
        London: Methuen, 1955.

06007. _____. Molly Lepell, Lady Hervey.
        London: Harrap, 1936.

06008. Tayler, Henrietta. Lady Nithsdale and her family. London:
        Lindsay Drummond, 1939.

06009. Vining, Elizabeth Gray. Flora; A Biography. Philadelphia:
        Lippincott, 1966.

06010. Wilkins, W. H. A Queen of Tears: Caroline Matilda, Queen
        of Denmark and Norway, and Princess of Great Britain and
        Ireland. New York: Longmans, Green and Co., 1904.

06011. Wilson, J. Harold. "Rochester's marriage." Review of
        English Studies 19 (1943): 399-403.

                        (2) Individuals

                        (a) Anne

06012. Bevan, Bryan. "Queen Anne 1665-1714." Contemporary
        Review 205 (1964): 432-435.

06013. Brown, Beatrice Curtis. Alas, Queen Anne, a Reading of
        her Life. Indianapolis: Bobbs-Merrill, 1929.

06014. Connell, Neville. Anne: the last Stuart monarch. London:
        Thornton Butterworth, 1937.

06015. Curtis, Gila. The Life and Times of Queen Anne. London:
        Weidenfeld and Nicolson, 1973.

06016. Gearey, Caroline. Royal Friendships, The Story of two
        Royal Friendships. London: Digby, Long and Co., 1898.

06017. Green, David. Queen Anne. London: Collins, 1970.

06018. Gregg, Edward. Queen Anne. Boston: Routledge and Kegan
        Paul, 1980.

06019.   Gregg, Edward. "Was Queen Anne a Jacobite?" History 57
         (October 1972): 358-375.

06020.   Hodges, Margaret. Lady Queen Anne. New York: Farrar
         Straus and Giroux, 1969.

06021.   Hopkinson, Marie Ruan. Anne of England. New York: Mac-
         millan, 1935.

06022.   Paul, Herbert. Queen Anne. London: Hodder and
         Stoughton, 1912.

06023.   Snyder, Henry L. "The Last Days of Queen Anne; The Account
         of Sir John Evelyn Examined." Huntington Library Quarterly
         34 (May 1971): 261-276.

06024.   Toynbee, Margaret. "Princess (Afterwards Queen) Anne as
         Patroness of Painters." Burlington Magazine 112 (March
         1970): 149-153.

(b)   Caroline of Ansbach

06025.   Arkell, Ruby L. Caroline of Ansbach. George the Second's
         queen. London: Oxford University Press, 1939.

06026.   _____. "Des Hauses Oesterreich Werben um Caroline
         von Ansbach, spatere Gemahlin George II." Niedersach-
         sisches Jahrbuch fur Landesgeschichte 15 (1938): 114-141.

06027.   Colton, Judith. "Merlin's Cave and Queen Caroline: Garden
         Art as Political Propaganda." Eighteenth-Century Studies
         10 (1976): 1-20.

06028.   Quennell, Peter. Caroline of England. New York: Viking,
         1940.

06029.   Wilkins, W. H. Caroline the Illustrious, queen consort of
         George II. London: Longmans, 1904.

(c)   Caroline of Brunswick

06030.   Bowman, William Dodgson. The Divorce case of Queen
         Caroline. London: Routledge, 1930.

06031.   Holme, Thea. A Biography of Caroline of Brunswick. New
         York: Atheneum, 1980.

06032.   Imann, Georges. Caroline de Brunswick, reine d'Angleterre
         (1768-1821). Paris: Calmann-Levy, 1939.

06033. Imann, Georges. "Caroline de Brunswick, reine d'Angleterre
        (1768-1821)." Revue de Paris 45 (1938): 301-333, 584-611,
        873-911.

06034. Parry, Sir Edward Abbott. Queen Caroline. New York:
        Scribner's, 1930.

06035. Richardson, Joanna. The Disastrous Marriage: A Study of
        George IV and Caroline of Brunswick. London: Cape, 1960.

06036. Tisdale, E.E.P. The Wanton Queen. The story of Britain's
        strangest queen. London: Stanley Paul, 1939.

                    (d) Charlotte

06037. Blakeney, T.S. "Queen Charlotte: Fanny Burney's Employer."
        New Rambler 4, ser. c (January 1968): 24-36.

06038. Hedley, Olwen. Queen Charlotte. London: John Murray, 1975.

            (e) Sarah Churchill, duchess of Marlborough

06039. Butler, Iris. The Great Duchess: The Life of Sarah
        Churchill. New York: Funk and Wagnalls, 1968.

06040. _____. Rule of Three: Sarah, Duchess of Marlborough
        and Her Companions in Power. London: Hodder and Stough-
        ton, 1967.

06041. Campbell, Kathleen. Sarah, Duchess of Marlborough. New
        York: Little Brown, 1932.

06042. Carter, Winifred. Sarah. London: Selwyn and Blount, 1943.

06043. Chancellor, Frank. Sarah Churchill. Glasgow: University
        Press, 1932.

06044. Green, David. "The Duchess (of Marlborough) and the
        Doctors." History Today 19 (May 1969): 332-337.

06045. _____. Sarah, Duchess of Marlborough. London:
        Collins, 1967.

06046. Kronenberger, Louis. Marlborough's Duchess: A Study in
        Worldliness. New York: Knopf, 1958.

06047. Molloy, Joseph Fitzgerald. The Queen's Comrade, The Life
        and Times of Sarah, duchess of Marlborough. London:
        Hutchinson and Co., 1901.

06048. Reid, Stuart J. John and Sarah, duke and duchess of
        Marlborough, 1660-1744. London: John Murray, 1915.

06049. Rowse, A. L. "Sarah Churchill in Old Age." In The
        English Spirit: Essays in History and Literature, pp.
        193-201. London: Macmillan, 1944.

                        e) Military

06050. Athill, Lawrence. "Eccentric Englishwomen: v. Hannah
        Snell." Spectator (14 May 1937): 899-900.

4. ECONOMIC

        "A farmer often estimates his riches by his number of
        sons."
                                        Townsend

06051. Collier, Francis. The Family Economy of the Working Class
        in the Cotton Industry 1784-1833. 1921. Reprint. Man-
        chester: Manchester University Press, 1964.

06052. Hecht, J. Jean The Domestic Servant Class in Eighteenth
        Century England. 1956. Reprint. Boston: Routledge and
        Kegan Paul, 1980.

06053. Loschky, David J. and Krier, Donald F. "Income and Family
        Size in Three Eighteenth-Century Lancashire Parishes:
        A Reconstitution Study." Journal of Economic History
        29 (September 1969): 429-448.

06054. McKendrick, Neil. "Home Demand and Economic Growth: A
        New View of the Role of Women and Children in the
        Industrial Revolution." In Historical Perspectives:
        Studies in English Thought and Society, pp. 152-210.
        London: Europa, 1974.

06055. Marshall, D. "The domestic Servants of the Eighteenth
        Century." Economica 25 (April 1929): 15-40.

06056. Pinchbeck, Ivy. Women Workers and the Industrial Revolu-
        tion, 1750-1850. 1930. Reprint. London: Cass, 1969.

        Also refer to #5254.

5. RELIGION

"Sir, a women's preaching is like a dog walking on his
hind legs. It is not done well, but you are surprised
to find it done at all."

Samuel Johnson

a) Saints/Religious Women

06057. Balleine, George Reginald. <u>Past Finding Out: The Tragic
Story of Joanna Southcott and her Successors.</u> New York:
Macmillan, 1956.

06058. Booth, Christopher C. "Ann Fothergill: The Mistress of
Harpur Street." <u>Proceedings of the American Philosophical Society</u> 122 (1978): 340-354.

06059. Braund, Elizabeth. "Mrs. Hutchinson and Her Teaching."
<u>Evangelical Quarterly</u> 31 (1959): 72-81.

06060. Forster, E. M. "Eccentric Englishwomen: vii. Luckie
Buchan." <u>Spectator</u> (28 May 1937): 986-987.

06061. Hamblin, F. J. "A Minister's Wife of the Eighteenth
Century." <u>Transactions of the Unitarian Historical
Society</u> 10 (1954): 185-192.

06062. Stein, Stephen J. "A Note on Anne Dutton, Eighteenth-
Century Evangelical." <u>Church History</u> 44 (December
1975): 485-491.

06063. Thomson, Ronald W. "Anne Steele, 1716-1778." <u>Baptist
Quarterly</u> 21 (1966): 368-371.

b) Methodists

06064. Brailsford, Mabel P. <u>Susanna Wesley, the mother of
Methodism.</u> London: Epworth Press, 1938.

06065. Harmon, Rebecca L. <u>Susanna: Mother of the Wesleys (1669-
1742).</u> London: Hodder and Stoughton, 1968.

06066. Morrow, Thomas W. <u>Early Methodist Women.</u> London: Epworth
Press, 1967.

06067.   Rogal, Samuel. "John Wesley's Women." Eighteenth Century
          Life 1 (September 1974): 7-10.

06068.   Swift, W.F. "The Women Itinerant Preachers of early
          Methodism." Wesley Historical Society Proceedings 28
          (1952): 89-94 and 29 (1953): 76-83.

06069.   Wearmouth, Robert Featherstone. Methodism and the Common
          People of the 18th Century. London: Epworth Press, 1947.

                        c) Witchcraft

06070.   Carnochan, W. B. "Witch-hunting and Belief in 1751: the
          Case of Thomas Colley and Ruth Osborne." Journal of
          Social History 4 (Summer 1971): 389-403.

                        6. SOCIAL

          "The very nature of the marriage contract was . . .
          nothing but giving up liberty, estate, authority and
          everything to the man, and the woman was indeed a mere
          woman ever after-that is to say, a slave."
                                            Defoe, Roxana

                        a) Generic

                      (1) Non-specific

06071.   Anderson, Michael, "Household Structure and the Industrial
          Revolution: Preston in Comparative Perspective." In House-
          hold and Family in Past Time, edited by Peter Laslett and
          Richard Wall, pp. 215-235. Cambridge: University Press,
          1972.

06072.   Ashton, John. Social Life in the Reign of Queen Anne.
          2 vols. London: Chatto, and Windus, Piccadilly, 1882.

06073.   Bayne-Powell, Rosamund. Eighteenth-Century London Life.
          New York: E. P. Dutton Co, Inc., 1938.

06074.   _____. English Country Life in the
          Eighteenth Century. London: J. Murray, 1935.

06075. Bayne-Powell, Rosamund. Housekeeping in the Eighteenth
        Century. London: Murray, 1956.

06076. Bovill, Edward Wm. English Country Life 1780-1830. New
        York: Oxford University Press, 1962.

06077. Burton, Elizabeth. The Georgians at Home: 1714-1830.
        London: Longmans, 1967.

06078. Fussell, George Edwin. Village Life in the Eighteenth
        Century. Worcester: Littlebury, 1947.

06079. George, Mary Dorothy (Gordon). London Life in the Eighteenth
        Century. New York: Capricorn Books, 1965.

06080. Lochhead, Marion Cleland. The Scots Household in the
        Eighteenth Century: A Century of Scottish Domestic and
        Social Life. Edinburgh: Moray Press, 1948.

06081. Lockitt, Charles Henry. The Relations of French and English
        Society (1763-1793). New York: Longmans, Green and Co.,
        1920.

06082. Marshall, Dorothy. The English Poor in the Eighteenth
        Century: A Study in Social and Administrative History.
        London: Routledge and Kegan Paul Ltd., 1969.

06083. Mingay, G. E. English Landed Society in the Eighteenth
        Century. London: Routledge and Paul, 1963.

06084. Parreaux, Andre. Daily Life in England in the Reign of
        George III. Translated by Carola Congreve. London:
        G. Allen and Unwin, 1969.

06085. Plant, Marjorie. The Domestic Life of Scotland in the
        18th Century. Chicago: Aldine, 1952.

06086. Taylor, G. Rattray. The Angel Makers; a Study in the
        Psychological Origins of Historical Change. New York:
        Dutton, 1974.

06087. Thompson, E. P. "The Moral Economy of the English Crowd
        in the 18th Century." Past and Present 50 (February
        1971): 76-136.

06088. Turberville, A. S. English Men and Manners in the
        Eighteenth Century. New York: Oxford University Press,
        1957.

        Also refer to #5287, 5290, 5291, 5293, 5295, 5296.

(2) Women

(a) Contemporary

06089. Bennett, John. Letters to a Young Lady. 10th ed. Philadel-
        phia: Lippincott, 1856.

06090. Dickson, Lane E. Introduction to Treatise of Feme Covert:
        Or the Lady's Law. 1732. Reprint. Littleton, Col.: Fred
        B. Rothman and Company, 1974.

06091. Gregory, John. A Father's Legacy to His Daughters.
        1774. Reprint. New York: Garland Press, 1974.

06092. [Haywood, Eliza (Fowler)]. Epistles for Ladies. 1765.
        Reprint. New Haven, Conn.: Research Publications, Inc.,
        1975.

06093. [Kendrick, William.] The Whole Duty of Woman. Georgetown,
        D.C.: S. S. Rind, 1831.

(b) Secondary

06094. Bass, Robert D. The Green Dragoon: The Lives of Banastre
        Tarleton and Mary Robinson. New York: Holt and Company,
        1957.

06095. Benkovitz, Miriam J. "Some Observations on Woman's Con-
        cept of Self in the Eighteenth Century." In Woman in the
        18th Century and Other Essays, edited by Paul Fritz and
        Richard Morton, pp. 37-54. Toronto: A. M. Hakkert Ltd.,
        1976.

06096. Boyce, Benjamin, ed. The adventures of Lindamira, a
        lady of quality. Minneapolis: University of Minnesota
        Press, 1949.

06097. Burnett, Frances. A Lady of Quality: Being the Most
        Curious, Hitherto Unknown History As Related by Mr.
        Isaac Bickerstaff. 4th ed. London: Warne, 1913.

06098. Calder-Marshall, Arthur. The Grand Century of the Lady.
        London: Gordon and Cremonesi, Ltd., 1976.

06099. Landa, M. J. "Kitty Villareal, the DaCostas and Samson
        Gideon." Transactions of the Jewish Historical Society of
        England 13 (1932-1935): 271-291.

06100.   Legates, Marlene. "The Cult of Womanhood in Eighteenth-
         Century Thought." Eighteenth-Century Studies 10 (Fall
         1976): 21-39.

06101.   Maror, Elizabeth. The Virgin Mistress, A Study in Survi-
         val. New York: Doubleday and Co., 1964.

06102.   Murray, K. L. Beloved Marian. The social history of Mr.
         and Mrs. Warring Hastings. London: Jarrolds, 1938.

06103.   Sherson, Errol Henry Stuart. The Lively Lady Townshend and
         her Friends, An Effort to Set forth the Doings and
         Surroundeings of a Typical Lady of Quality of the
         Eighteenth Century. London: W. Heinemann Ltd., 1926.

                         b) Demography

06104.   Buer, Mabel Craven. Health, Wealth, and Population in the
         Early Days of the Industrial Revolution. London: G.
         Routledge and Sons, 1926.

06105.   Connell, Kenneth Hugh. "Land and Population in Ireland,
         1750-1845." Economic History Review 2nd ser. 2 (1949-
         1950): 278-289.

06106.   _____. "The Population of Ireland in the
         Eighteenth Century." Economic History Review 16 (1946):
         111-124.

06107.   _____. The Population of Ireland 1750-
         1845. Oxford: Clarendon Press, 1950.

06108.   _____. "Some Unsettled Problems in
         English and Irish Population History, 1750-1845."
         Irish Historical Studies 7 (1951): 225-234.

06109.   Crafts, N.F.R. and Ireland, N.J. "A Simulation of the
         Impact of Changes in Age at Marriage before and during
         the Advent of Industrialism in England." Population
         Studies 30 (1976): 495-511.

06110.   Drake, Michael. "Marriage and Population Growth in Ire-
         land, 1750-1845." Economic History Review 2nd ser. 16
         (1963-1964): 301-313.

06111.   Flinn, Michael Walter, British Population Growth 1700-
         1850. London: Macmillan, 1970.

06112.   Glass, David Victor.   The Population Controversy; a collec-
          tive reprint of material concerning the 18th century
          controversy on the trend of population in England and
          Wales.   Farnborough: Gregg, 1973.

06113.   Habakkuk, H. J.   "English Population in the Eighteenth
          Century."   Economic History Review   2nd ser. 6 (1953-
          1954): 117-133.

06114.   Kermack, W. R.   "Did the Marriage Age of Scottish Brides
          Decrease in the Eighteenth Century?"   Scottish Genealo-
          gist 18 (1971): 21-22.

06115.   Krause, J. T.   "Some aspects of Population Change, 1690-
          1790."   In Land, Labour and Population in the Industrial
          Revolution, edited by Eric L. Jones and G. E. Mingay,
          pp. 187-205.   London: Edward Arnold, 1967.

06116.   McKeown, Thomas and Brown, R. G.   "Medical Evidence Related
          to English Population Changes in the Eighteenth Century."
          Population Studies 9 (1955-1956): 119-141.   Also in
          Population in Industrialization, edited by Michael Drake,
          pp. 40-72.   London: Methuen and Co., 1969.

06117.   O'Grada, Cormac.   "The population of Ireland: 1700-1900:
          a survey."   Annales de demographie historique (1979):
          281-299.

06118.   Outhwaite, R. B.   "Age at Marriage in England from the Late
          Seventeenth Century to the Nineteenth Century."   Trans-
          actions of the Royal Historical Society 5th ser. 23 (1973):
          55-70.

06119.   Razzell, P. E.   "Population Change in Eighteenth-Century
          England. A Reinterpretation."   Economic History Review
          2nd ser.   18 (1965): 312-332.

06120.   Sogner, Solvi.   "Aspects of the Demographic Situation in
          Seventeen Parishes in Shropshire 1711-1760."   Population
          Studies 17 (1963-1964): 126-146.

06121.   Ticker, G. S. L.   "English Pre-Industrial Population Trends."
          Economic History Review 2nd ser. 16 (December 1963):
          205-218.

06122.   Wrigley, E. Anthony.   "A Note on the Life-Time Mobility
          of Married Women in a Parish Population in the Later
          Eighteenth Century."   Local Population Studies 18
          (1977): 22-29.

          Also refer to #4314, 6053.

c) Family

(1) Non-specific

06123. Everitt, Alan. "Kentish Family Portrait: An Aspect of the
        Rise of the Pseudogentry." In Rural Change and Urban
        Growth 1500-1800, edited by C.W. Chalklin and M.A. Havinden,
        pp. 169-199. New York: Longmans, 1974.

06124. Hughes, Helen Sard. The gentle Hertford: her life and
        letters. New York: Macmillan, 1940.

06125. Inglis-Jones, E. "A Pembrokeshire Country Family in the
        Eighteenth Century." Journal of the National Library
        of Wales 17 (1971): 136-160, 217-237, 321-342.

06126. Johnston, J. A. "The Family and Kin of the Lincolnshire
        Labourer in the Eighteenth Century." Lincolnshire His-
        tory and Archaeology 14 (1979): 47-52.

06127. Lesourd, J. A. "Situation particulière des familles catho-
        liques en Angleterre XVIIIe siècle-XIXe siècle: lois
        d'exception et isolement." Recherches anglaises et
        américaines 8 (1975): 85-108.

06128. Schücking, Levin Ludwig. "Die Familie als Geschmacks-
        trager in England im 18. Jahrhundert." Deutsche
        Vierteljahresschrift für Literaturwissenschaft und
        Geistesgeschichte 4 (1926): 439-458.

06129. Smelser, Neil J. "The Industrial Revolution and the
        British Working Class Family." Journal of Social
        History 1 (1967): 17-35.

06130. Trumbach, Randolph. The Rise of the Egalitarian Family,
        Aristocratic Kinship and Domestic Relations in
        Eighteenth-Century England. New York: Academic Press,
        1978.

06131. Watt, Ian. "The New Woman: Samuel Richardson's Pamela."
        In The Family: Its Structure and Functions, edited by
        Rose Laub Coser, pp. 267-289. New York: St. Martin's
        Press, 1964.

        Also refer to #5322, 5323, 6275, 6283.

(2) Childhood

06132. Bayne-Powell, Rosamund. The English Child in the
        Eighteenth Century. New York: E. P. Dutton and Co.
        Inc., 1939.

06133. McClure, Ruth K. Coram's Children: London Foundling Hos-
        pital in the Eighteenth Century. New Haven, Conn.: Yale
        University Press, 1981.

06134. Malcolmson, R.W. "Infanticide in the Eighteenth Century."
        In Crime in England 1550-1800, edited by J.S. Cockburn,
        pp. 187-209. Princeton, N.J.: Princeton University Press,
        1977.

06135. Plumb, J. H., "The New World of Children in Eighteenth-
        Century England." Past and Present 67 (1975): 64-95.

06136. Rendle-Short, John. "Infant Management in the 18th Cen-
        tury with a Special Reference to the Work of William
        Cadogan." Bulletin of the History of Medicine 34 (March-
        April 1960): 97-122.

06137. Roe, Frederic Gordon. The Georgian Child. London:
        Phoenix House, 1961.

        Also refer to #6145, 6274, 6276.

d) Marriage

06138. Beckett, J. V. "The Lowthers at Holker: Marriage, Inheri-
        tance and Debt in the Fortunes of an Eighteenth-Century
        Landowning Family." Transactions of the Historical
        Societies of Lancashire and Cheshire 127 (1977): 47-64.

06139. Chandos, John. "Marriage (and One or Two Other Social
        Institutions) Georgian Style." Horizon 16 (Autumn 1974):
        96-101.

06140. Habakkuk, H. J. "Marriage Settlements in the Eighteenth
        Century." Transactions of the Royal Historical Society
        4th ser. 32 (1950): 15-30.

06141. Halimi, S. "Le mariage en Angleterre au XVIIIe siècle."
        Recherches anglaises et americaines 8 (1975): 72-84.

06142. Hayley, William. A Philosophical, Historical and Moral
        Essay on Old Maids. 1785. Reprint. New Haven, Conn.:
        Research Publications, Inc., 1975.

06143. Hopkins, Robert H. "Matrimony in 'The Vicar of Wakefield'
        and the Marriage Act of 1753." Studies in Philology
        44 (July 1977):322-339.

06144. Martin, J. M. "Marriage and Economic Stress in the Felden
        of Warwickshire during the Eighteenth Century." Popu-
        lation Studies 31 (1977): 519-535.

06145. Meteyard, Belinda. "Illegitimacy and Marriage in Eighteenth-
        Century England." Journal of Interdisciplinary History 10
        (Winter 1980): 479-490.

06146. Robinson, Peter. "The Third Earl of Shaftesbury and
        Lady Anne Carberry in 1708." Notes and Queries 221
        (November 1976): 484-486.

06147. Thomas, David. "The Social Origins of Marriage Patterns
        of the British Peerage in the Eighteenth and Nineteenth
        Centuries." Population Studies 26 (March 1972): 99-111.

        Also refer to #5332, 5343, 6109, 6110, 6114, 6122, 6333.

e) Sex Life and Morals

(1) Non-specific

06148. Smith, Norah. "Sexual Mores in the Eighteenth Century:
        Robert Wallace's 'Of Venery'." Journal of the History
        of Ideas 39 (July-September 1978): 419-433.

06149. Thomas, Keith. "The Double Standard." Journal of the
        History of Ideas 20 (1959): 195-216.

        Also refer to #6163.

(2) Prostitutes

06150. Bleackley, Horace. Ladies Fair and Frail: Sketches of
        the Demimonde During the Eighteenth Century. New
        York: John Lane, 1909.

06151. Hamilton, Adrian, ed. The Infamous Essay on Woman: Dr.
        John Wilkes Seated between Vice and Virtue. London:
        Deutsch, 1972.

06152. Radner, John B. "The Youthful Harlot's Curse: The Prostitute
        as Symbol of the City in Eighteenth-Century English Litera-
        ture." Eighteenth-Century Life 2 (March 1976): 59-64.

06153. Rogal, Samuel J. "The Selling of Sex: Mandeville's Modest
        Defence of Publick Stews." Studies in 18th Century Cul-
        ture 5 (1976): 141-150.

f) Fashion/Manners

06154. Brooke, Iris. "Dress" In Life under the Stuarts, edited by
        J. E. Morpugo, pp. 170-178. London: Falcon Educational
        Books, 1950.

06155. Buck, Anne. Dress in Eighteenth Century England. New
        York: Holmes and Meier, 1979.

06156. Cunnington, Cecil Willett. Handbook of English Costume
        in the Eighteenth Century. Boston: Play, 1972.

06157. Laver, James. English costume of the Eighteenth Century.
        London: A. and C. Black, Ltd., 1931.

06158. Quinlan, Maurice. Victorian Prelude: a history of
        English manners 1700-1830. Columbia University Studies in
        English and Comparative Literature, no. 155. New York:
        Columbia University Press, 1941.

        Also refer to #5352.

g) Philanthropy

06159. Cormack, Alexander A. Susan Carnegie, 1744-1821, Her Life
        of Service. Denside: Aberdeenshire, 1966.

h) Health/Medical

06160. Forbes, Thomas Rogers. "The Regulation of English Midwives
        in the Eighteenth and Nineteenth Centuries." Medical
        History 15 (October 1971): 352-362.

06161. Seligman, S. A. "Mary Toft--The Rabbit Breeder." Medical
        History 5 (1961): 349-360.

06162. Viseltear, Arthur J.   "Joanna Stephens and the Eighteenth
        Century Lithontriptics: A Misplaced Chapter in the
        History of Therapeutics." Bulletin of the History of
        Medicine 42 (May-June 1968):199-220.

06163. Waugh, M. A.   "Attitudes of Hospitals in London to Venereal
        Disease in the 18th Centuries." British Journal of
        Venereal Disease 47 (April 1971):146-150.

7. CULTURAL

"I cannot forbear wishing that several writers of that sex
had chosen to apply themselves rather to Tapestry than
                                              Rhime."
                    Spectator

a) Education

(1) Contemporary

06164. Essex, John.   The Young Ladies Conduct; or, Rules for
        Education, under Several Heads. 1722. Reprint. New
        Haven, Conn.: Research Publications Inc., 1975.

06165. Fordyce, James.   Sermons to Young Women. 1766. Reprint.
        New Haven, Conn.: Research Publications Inc., 1975.

06166. Moir, John.   Female Tuition; or An Address to Mothers on
        the Education of Daughters. 1800. Reprint. New Haven,
        Conn.: Research Publications Inc., 1975.

06167. More, Hannah.   Strictures on the Modern System of Female
        Education. 2 vols. 1799. Reprint. New York: Garland, 1974.

        Also refer to #5362.

(2) Secondary

06168. Davis, Mollie C.   "The Countess of Huntington and
        Whitefield's Bethesda." Georgia Historical Quarterly
        56 (Spring 1972): 72-82.

06169. Hans, Nicholas A.   New Trends in the Eighteenth Century.
        London: Routledge and Kegan Paul, Ltd., 1966.
            [See especially ch. 10.]

06170. Lerenbaum, Miriam. "Mistresses of Orthodoxy: Education in
        the Lives and Writings of Late Eighteenth-Century English
        Women Writers." Proceedings of the American Philoso-
        phical Society 121 (1977): 281-282.

06171. Miller, Peter John. "Women's Education, 'Self-Improvement' and
        Social Mobility--A Late Eighteenth Century Debate." British
        Journal of Educational Studies 20 (October 1972): 302-314.

06172. Schnorrenberg, Barbara Brandon. "Education for Women in
        Eighteenth Century England: An Annotated Bibliography."
        Women and Literature 4 (Spring 1976): 49-55.

                        b) Literature

                        (1) Non-specific

06173. Elwood, Anne Katherine. Memoirs of the Literary Ladies of
        England, from the Commencement of the Last Century.
        Philadelphia: G.B. Zieber and Co., 1845.

06174. Fyvie, John. Some Famous Women of Wit and Beauty: A Georgian
        Galaxy. 1905. Reprint. Norwood, Pa.: Norwood Editions,
        1973.

06175. Halsband, Robert. "'The Female Pen.' Women and Literature
        in Eighteenth-Century England." History Today 24 (Oct.
        1974): 702-709.

06176. _____. "Women and Literature in 18th Century
        England." In Women in the 18th Century and Other
        Essays, pp. 55-71. Toronto: A. M. Hakkert, 1976.

06177. Hinkley, Laura. Ladies of Literature. New York: Hastings
        House, 1946.

06178. Hufstader, Alice A. Sisters of the Quill. New York:
        Dodd, Mead and Company, Inc., 1978.

06179. Mayer, Gertrude Townshend. Women of Letters. 2 vols.
        London: R. Bentley & Sons, 1894.

06180. Rogers, Katharine M., ed. Before Their Time Six Women
        Writers of the Eighteenth Century. New York: Frederick
        Ungar Publishing Co., 1979.

06181. Spacks, Patricia Meyer. "The Dangerous Age." Eighteenth-
        Century Studies 11 (Summer 1978): 417-439.

06182. Spacks, Patricia Meyer. "Ev'ry woman is at heart a rake."
Eighteenth-Century Studies 8 (Fall 1974): 27-46.

06183. _____. "Reflecting Women." Yale
Review 63 (1973): 26-42.

06184. Wienbeck, Dorothea. Die Stellung der Frau der oberen und
mittleren Gesellschaftsklassen Englands in der ersten
Halfte des 18. Jahrhunderts; unter Ausschluss der Vers-
und Prosadichtung nach zeitgenössischen Zeugnissen
dargestellt. Halle: E. Klinz, 1931.

Also refer to #5366, 6095, 6100.

(2) Drama

(a) Women

06185. Burgess, C.F. "John Gay and Polly and a Letter to the
King." Philological Quarterly 47 (1968): 596-598.

06186. Conolly, L. W. "Anna Margaretta Larpent, The Duchess of
Queensberry and Gay's Polly in 1777." Philological Quarterly 51 (1972): 955-957.

06187. Hershey, Jane. "Female Playwrights of the Eighteenth
Century: Shaping the Marketplace of Love." American
Journal of Psychoanalysis 35 (1975): 69-74.

06188. Lock, F. P. "Astraea's 'Vacant Throne'. The Successors
of Aphra Behn." In Woman in the Eighteenth Century and
Other Essays, edited by Paul Fritz and Richards Morton,
pp. 25-36. Toronto: A. M. Hakkert Ltd., 1976.

06189. Pearce, Charles E. "Polly Peachum," Being the Story of
Lavinia Fenton (Duchess of Bolton) and "The Beggars
Opera", New York: Brentano's, 1913.

06190. Rhodes, R. Crompton. "The Belle's Strategem." Review of
English Studies 5 (April 1929): 129-142.

Also refer to #5376, 5377.

(b) Susan Centlivre

06191. Anderson, Paul Bunyan. "Innocence and artifice: or, Mrs.
Centlivre and The Female Tatler." Philological Quarterly 16 (1937): 358-375.

06192. Boyer, John Wilson. The celebrated Mrs. Centlivre.
        Durham, N.C.: Duke University Press, 1952.

06193. Mackenzie, John H. "Susan Centlivre." Notes and queries
        198 (1953): 386-390.

06194. Sutherland, James R. "The progress of error: Mrs. Cent-
        livre and the biographers." Review of English Studies
        18 (1942): 167-182.

                          (3) Poetry

06195. Ashmun, Margaret Eliza. The Singing Swan: An Account of
        Anna Seward and her Acquaintance with Dr. Johnson, Boswell,
        and Others of their Time. 1931. Reprint. Westport,
        Conn.: Greenwood, 1969.

06196. Doughty, Oswald. "A Bath Poetess of the Eighteenth
        Century." Review of English Studies 1 (1925): 404-420.

06197. Fullard, Joyce and Schueller, Rhoda Walgren. "Eighteenth
        Century Poets: A Bibliography of Women not Listed in
        CBEL." Mary Wollstonecraft Journal 2 (May 1974): 40-46.

06198. Hughes, Helen Sard. "Elizabeth Rowe and the Countess of
        Hertford." Publications of the Modern Language Associa-
        tion of America 59 (September 1944): 726-746.

06199. Kaplan, Cora. ed. Salt and Bitter and Good: Three
        Centuries of English and American Women Poets. New
        York: Paddington Press Ltd., Two Continents Publishing
        Group, 1975.

06200. Myers, Robert Manson. Anna Seward: an eighteenth-century
        Handelian. Williamsburg, Va.: Manson Park Press, 1947.

06201. Nussbaum, Felicity A. "Pope's 'To a Lady' and the 18th
        century women." Philological Quarterly 54 (Spring 1975):
        444-456.

06202. Wright, H. Bunker. "Matthew Prior and Elizabeth Singer."
        Philological Quarterly 24 (1945): 71-82.

                          (4) Satire

06203. Gubar, Susan. "The Female Monster in Augustan Satire."
        Signs 3 (Winter 1977): 380-394.

(5) Prose

(a) Women in Novels

06204. Donovan, Robert A. "The Problem of Pamela, or Virtue unrewar-

06205. Kaufman, Anthony. "A 'Libertine Woman of Condition's Congreve's Dorothy'." Yearbook of English Studies 3 (1973): 120-123.

06206. Kennedy, Hugh L. "Love and Famine, Family and Country in Trollope's Castle Richmond." Eire-Ireland 7 (1972): 48-66.

06207. Krieger, Murray. "'Eliosa to Abelard': The Escape from Body or the Embrace of Body." Eighteenth Century Studies 3 (Fall 1969): 28-47.

06208. Marshall, Madeleine Forell. "Millwood and Marwood: Fallen Women and the Moral Interest of Sentimental Tragedy." Mary Wollstonecraft Journal 2 (May 1974): 2-12.

06209. Moynihan, Robert D. "Clarissa and Enlightened Woman as Literary Heroine." Journal of the History of Ideas 36 (1975): 159-166.

06210. Rogers, Katharine M. "Sensitive Feminism vs. Conventional Sympathy: Richardson and Fielding on Women." Novel 9 (1976): 256-270.

06211. Schucking, Levin Ludwig. "Die Grundlagen des Richardson'schen Romans." Germanisch-Romanische Monatsschrift 12 (1924): 21-42 and 88-110.

06212. Sejourne, Philippe. Aspects generaux du roman feminin en Angleterre de 1740 a 1800. Gap: Editions Ophrys, 1966.

06213. Shinagel, Michael. "Memoirs of a Woman of Pleasure: Pornography and the Mid-Eighteenth-Century English Novel." In Studies in Change and Revolution, edited by Paul J. Korshin, pp. 211-236. Menston, Yorkshire: Scholar Press, 1972.

06214. Simon, Irene. "Le roman feminin en Angleterre au XVIIIe siecle." Etudes anglaises 27 (April-June 1974): 205-213.

06215. Staves, Susan. "British Seduced Maidens." Eighteenth-Century Studies 14 (Winter 1980/1981): 109-134.

06216. Towers, Augustus R. "Amelia and the State of Matrimony." Review of English Studies n.s. 5 (April 1954): 144-157.

06217. Williams, Murial Brittain. Marriage: Fielding's Mirror of Reality. University, Ala.: Alabama Press, 1973.

(b) Novelists

[1] INDIVIDUALS

[a] Fanny Burney

06218. Adelstein, Michael E. Fanny Burney. New York: Twayne, 1968.

06219. Coolidge, Theresa. "Family concerns of Fanny Burney."
More books 21 (1946): 83–86.

06220. Copeland, Edward W. "Money in the novels of Fanny Burney."
Studies in the Novel 8 (Spring 1976): 24–37.

06221. Delachaux, E. "Fanny Burney, intermédiaire manquée entre
l'Angleterre et la France." Revue de littérature com-
parée 15 (1935): 381–386.

06222. Gérin, Winifred. The young Fanny Burney: A Biography.
New York: T. Nelson, 1971.

06223. Hahn, Emily. A Degree of Prudery, a biography of Fanny
Burney. New York: Doubleday, 1950.

06224. Hemlow, Joyce. "Fanny Burney and the Courtesy Books."
Publications of the Modern Language Association 65
(September 1950): 732–761.

06225. _____. "Fanny Burney: playwright." University of
Toronto Quarterly 19 (1950): 170–189.

06226. _____. The History of Fanny Burney (1752–1840).
New York: Oxford University Press, 1958.

06227. Lloyd, Christopher. Fanny Burney. London: Longmans, 1936.

06228. Macaulay, Thomas Babington. "Diary and Leters of Madame
D'Arblay." In Critical and Historical Essays 3: 331–
395. Boston: Houghton Mifflin Co., 1900.

06229. Masefield, Muriel Agnes (Bussell). The Story of Fanny Burney:
an introduction to the diary and letters of Madame d'Arbley.
Cambridge: University Press, 1927.

06230. Newton, Judith. "Evelina, or, the history of a young
lady's entrance into the marriage market." Modern Language Studies 6 (Spring 1976): 48–56.

06231. Staves, Susan. "Evelina or Female Difficulties." Modern
Philology 73 (May 1976): 368–381.

06232. Tinker, Chauncey Brewster. <u>Dr. Johnson</u> and <u>Fanny Burney</u>. New
        York: Moffet, Yard, & Co., <u>1911</u>.

[b] Elizabeth Inchbald

06233. Littlewood, S. R. <u>Elizabeth Inchbald</u> and <u>Her Circle:</u>
        <u>The Life of A Charming Woman</u> (<u>1753-1821</u>). London:
        Daniel O'Connor, 1921.

06234. McKee, William. <u>Elizabeth Inchbald, novelist</u>. Washing-
        ton, D.C.: Catholic University of America, 1935.

06235. Moreaux, Françoise. <u>Elizabeth Inchbald et la revendication</u>
        <u>féminine au dix-huitième siècle</u>. Lille: Université de
        Lille, Editions universitaires, 1973.

06236. _____. "Elizabeth Inchbald et le courant
        'humanitaire' au XVIIIe siècle." In <u>Aspects du</u>
        <u>féminisme en Angleterre au 18e Siècle</u>, pp. 69-85.
        Paris: Editions universitaires, 1972.

06237. Rogers, Katharine M. "Inhibitions on Eighteenth-Century
        Women Novelists: Elizabeth Inchbald and Charlotte Smith."
        <u>Eighteenth-Century</u> Studies 11 (Fall 1977): 63-78.

06238. Tobler, Clara. <u>Mrs. Elizabeth Inchbald, eine vergessene</u>
        <u>englische Buhnendichterin</u> und <u>romanschriftstellerin</u>
        <u>des 18. Jahrhunderts</u>. Berlin: Mayer und Muller, 1910.

[c] Ann Radcliffe

06239. Arnaud, Pierre. <u>Ann Radcliffe et le fantastique essai de</u>
        <u>psychobiographie</u>. Paris: Aubier Montaigne, 1976.

06240. Grant, Aline. <u>Ann Radcliff</u>. Denver: Alan Swallow, 1961.

06241. McIntyre, Clara Frances. <u>Ann Radcliff in Relation to her</u>
        <u>Time</u>. 1920. Reprint. New York: Archon Books, 1970.

[2] OTHERS

06242. Baker, Van R. "Whatever Happened to Lydia Stern."
        <u>Eighteenth-Century Life</u> 2 (September 1975): 6-11.

06243. Black, Frank Gees. "A lady novelist of Colchester."
        <u>Essex review</u> 44 (1935): 180-185.

06244. Crittenden, Walter Marion. The life and writings of
        Mrs. Sarah Scott, novelist (1723-1795). Philadelphia:
        University of Pennsylvania Press, 1932.

06245. McBurney, William H. "Edmund Curll, Mrs. Jane Barker,
        and the English Novel." Philological Quarterly 37
        (1958): 385-399.

06246. _____. "Mrs. Mary Davys: Forerunner of
        Fielding." Publications of the Modern Language Asso-
        ciation of America 74 (1959): 348-355.

06247. _____. "Mrs. Penelope Aubin and the Early
        Eighteenth-Century English Novel." Huntington Library
        Quarterly 20 (1957): 245-267.

06248. MacCarthy, B. G. The Later Women Novelists 1744-1818.
        Cork: Cork University Press, 1947.

06249. Masefield, Muriel Agnes (Bussell). Women Novelists from
        Fanny Burney to George Eliot. London: I. Nicholson
        and Watson, Ltd., 1934.

06250. Norton, J. E. "Some Uncollected Authors. XXII: Eliza-
        beth Griffith, 1727-1793." Book Collector 8 (1959):
        418-424.

06251. Richetti, John J. "Mrs. Elizabeth Rowe: The Novel as
        Polemic." Publications of the Modern Language Associa-
        tion of America 82 (1967): 522-529.

        Also refer to #5408-5409.

(c) Periodicals

[1] *THE FEMALE SPECTATOR*

06252. Haywood, Eliza (Fowler). The Female Spectator, being
        selections chosen and edited by Mary Priestly. London:
        John Lane, 1929.

06253. Hodges, James. "The Female Spectator, a courtesy Periodi-
        cal." In Studies in Early English Periodical, edited by
        Richmond Pugh Bond, pp. 151-182. Chapel Hill, N.C.:
        University of North Carolina Press, 1957.

06254. Koon, Helene. "Eliza Haywood and the Female Spectator."
        Huntington Library Quarterly 42 (Winter 1978): 43-55.

06255. Whicher, George Frisbie. The Life and Romances of Mrs.
        Eliza Haywood. New York: Columbia University Press,
        1915.

[2] *THE FEMALE TATLER*

06256.   Anderson, Paul Bunyan. "Mistress Delarivière Manley's
         Biography." Modern Philology 33 (1935-1936): 261-278.

06257.   _____. "Splendour out of Scandal: the
         Lucinda-Artesia Papers in The Female Tatler." Philo-
         locical Quarterly 15 (1938): 286-300.

06258.   Graham, Walter. "Thomas Baker, Mrs. Manley, and the
         Female Tatler." Modern Philology 34 (1937): 267-272.

06259.   Kline, Richard B. "Anne Oldfield and Mary de la Riviere
         Manley: The Unnoticed Reconciliation." Restoration and
         18th Century Theatre Research 14 (November 1975): 53-58.

06260.   Milford, R. T. "The Female Tatler." Modern Philology 29
         (1932): 350-351.

06261.   Needham, Gwendolyn B. "Mary de la Rivière Manley, Tory
         Defender." Huntington Library Quarterly 12 (1948-1949):
         253-288.

06262.   _____. "Mrs. Manley: an eighteenth-century
         wife of Bath." Huntington Library Quarterly 14 (1951):
         259-284.

06263.   Snyder, Henry L. "New Light on Mrs. Manley." Philolog-
         ical Quarterly 52 (1973): 767-770.

[3] OTHERS

06264.   Hunter, Jean E. "The 18th Century Englishwoman: According
         to the Gentleman's Magazine." In Woman in the Eighteenth
         Century and Other Essays, edited by Paul Fritz and
         Richard Morton, pp. 73-88. Toronto: A. M. Hakkert, 1976.

06265.   _____. "'The Ladies Magazine' and the History of
         the Eighteenth-Century Englishwoman." In Newsletters to
         Newspapers: Eighteenth-Century Journalism, edited by
         Donovan H. Bond and W. Reynolds McLeod, pp. 103-117,
         Morgantown, W. Va.: School of Journalism, West Virginia
         University, 1977.

06266.   Miller, Peter John. "Eighteenth-Century Periodicals for
         Women." History of Education Quarterly 11 (Fall 1971):
         279-286.

06267.   Stearns, Bertha Monica. "Early English Periodicals for
          Ladies (1700-1760)." Publications of the Modern
          Language Association of America 48 (1933): 38-60.

06268.   Watson, Melvin R. "Mrs. Grey's Family." Periodical post
          boy 14 (November 1953): 2-5.

                    c) Literary Salons

06269.   Hannay, Prudence. "The Redoubtable Lady Holland."
          History Today 23 (February 1973): 94-104.

06270.   Hesselgrave, Ruth A. Lady Miller and the Batheaston
          literary circle. New Haven: Yale University Press,
          1927.

06271.   Tinker, Chauncey Brewster. The Salon and English Letters;
          Chapters on the Interrelations of Literature and Society
          in the Age of Johnson. New York: The Macmillan Co.,
          1915.

                    d) Intellectuals

                    (1) Individuals

                    (a) Daniel Defoe

06272.   Backscheider, Paula. "Defoe's Women; Snares and Prey."
          Studies in Eighteenth-Century Culture 5 (1976):103-120.

06273.   Defoe, Daniel. Conjugal Lewdness; or, Matrimonial
          Whoredom. A Treatise concerning the use and Abuse of
          the Marriage Bed. 1727. Reprint. Introduced by
          Maximillan E. Novak. Gainesville, Fla.: Scholars'
          Facsimile & Reprints, 1967.

06274.   _____. The Family Instructor. 1734. Reprint.
          New Haven, Conn.: Research Publications, Inc., 1975.

06275.   _____. Religious Courtship. 1857. Reprint.
          New Haven, Conn.: Research Publications, Inc., 1975.

06276.   Erickson, R. A. "Mother Midnight and Moll Flanders."
          Studies in Philology 76 (January 1979): 75-100.

06277. Mason, Shirlene. *Daniel Defoe and the Status of Women.*
        St. Alban's, Vt.: Eden Press, 1978.

06278. Mundy, P. D. "The Wife of Daniel Defoe." *Notes and*
        Queries 203 (1958): 296-298.

06279. Rogers, Katherine M. "The Feminism of Daniel Defoe." In
        Woman in the 18th Century and Other Essays, edited by
        Paul Fritz and Richards Morton, pp. 3-24. Toronto:
        A. M. Hakkert, Ltd., 1976.

(b) Samuel Johnson

06280. Craig, William Henry. *Doctor Johnson and the Fair Sex:*
        A Study of Contrasts. London: S. Low, Marston and Co.,
        Ltd., 1895.

06281. Isles, Duncan. "Johnson and Charlotte Lennox." *New*
        Rambler ser. C 3 (June 1967): 34-48.

06282. McAdam, E. L. "Dr. Johnson and Saunders Welch's Pro-
        posals." *Review of English Studies,* n.s. 4 (October
        1953): 337-345.

06283. Molin, Sven Eric. "Dr. Johnson on Marriage, Chastity,
        and Fidelity." *Eighteenth-Century Life* 1 (September 1974):
        15-18.

06284. Rowell, Phyllis. "The Women in Johnson's Life." *New*
        Rambler ser. B 14 (January 1964): 22-28.

06285. Ruhe, Edward. "Birch, Johnson, and Elizabeth Carter: An
        Episode of 1738-39." *Publications of the Modern*
        Language Association of America 73 (1958): 491-500.

(c) Catherine Macaulay

06286. Ditchfield, G. M. "Some Literary and Political Views of
        Catherine Macaulay." *American Notes and Queries* 12
        (January 1974): 70-75.

06287. Donnelly, Lucy Martin. "The Celebrated Mrs. Macaulay."
        William and Mary Quarterly 3rd ser. 6 (1949): 173-207.

06288. Fox, Claire Gilbride. "Catharine Macaulay, an Eighteenth
        Century Clio." *Winterthur Portfolio* 4 (1968): 129-142.

06289. Hill, Bridget and Hill, Christopher. "Catharine Macaulay and
        the Seventeenth Century." *Welsh History Review* 3 (1967):
        381-402.

06290.   Schnorrenberg, Barbara Brandon. "The Brood Hen of Faction:
          Mrs. Macaulay and Radical Politics, 1765-1775." Albion
          11 (1979): 33-45.

06291.   Withey, Lynne. "Catherine Macaulay and the Uses of
          History: Ancient Rights, Perfectionism, Propaganda."
          Journal of British Studies 16 (Fall 1976): 59-83.

                    (d) Elizabeth Montagu

06292.   Blunt, Reginald. Mrs. Montagu "Queen of the Blues," Her
          Letters and Friendships from 1762 to 1800. London:
          Constable and Co., Ltd., 1923.

06293.   Boulton, James T. "Mrs. Elizabeth Montagu (1720-1800)."
          Burke Newsletter 3 (1961-1962): 96-98.

06294.   Climenson, Emily. Elizabeth Montagu, Queen of the Blues.
          London: Constable, 1923.

06295.   Doran, John. A Lady of the Last Century. Boston:
          Nicolls, 1873.

06296.   Hornbreak, Katherine Gee. "New Light on Mrs. Montagu ."
          In The Age of Johnson, edited by F.W. Hilles, pp. 349-
          361. New Haven, Conn.: Yale University Press, 1949.

06297.   Huchon, Rene Louis. Mrs. Montagu and her Friends. London:
          J. Murray, 1906.

06298.   Jones, W. Powell. "The Romantic Bluestocking: Elizabeth
          Montagu." Huntington Library Quarterly 12 (1948-1949):
          85-98.

06299.   Ross, Ian. "A Bluestocking over the Border: Mrs.
          Elizabeth Montagu's Aesthetic Adventures in Scotland,
          1766." Huntington Library Quarterly 28 (May 1965):
          213-233.

                    (e) Lady Mary Wortley Montagu

06300.   Barry, Iris. Portrait of Lady Mary Wortley Montagu.
          Indianapolis: Bobbs-Merrill Co., 1928.

06301.   Gibbs, Lewis. The Admirable Lady Mary: The Life and Times
          of Lady Mary Wortley Montagu (1689-1762). New York:
          William Morrow and Co., 1949.

06302.   Halsband, Robert. "Lady Mary Wortley Montagu and
          Eighteenth-Century Fiction." Philological Quarterly
          45 (1966): 145-156.

06303. Halsband, Robert. "Lady Mary Wortley Montagu as a Friend
        of Continental Writers." Bulletin of the John Rylands
        Library 39 (1956): 57-74.

06304. _____. "Lady Mary Wortley Montagu as Letter-
        Writer." In The Familiar Letter in the Eighteenth
        Century, edited by Howard Anderson, Philip B. Daghlian
        and Irvin Ehrenpreis, pp. 49-70. Lawrence, Ks.: University
        of Kansas Press, 1966.

06305. _____. "Lady Mary Wortley Montagu: Her Place
        in the Eighteenth Century." History Today 16 (1966): 94-102.

06306. _____. The Life of Lady Mary Wortley Montagu.
        Oxford: Claredon Press, 1956.

06307. _____. "New Light on Lady Mary Wortley
        Montagu's Contribution to Inoculation." Journal of the
        history of medicine and allied sciences 7 (1953):
        390-405.

06308. Melville, Lewis. Lady Mary Wortley Montagu: her life and
        letters. Boston: Houghton Mifflin, 1925.

06309. Parreaux, Andre. "L'Angleterre de Lady Montagu." Etudes
        Anglaises 22 (1967): 24-28.

06310. Paston, George. Lady Mary Wortley Montagu and Her Times.
        New York: G. P. Putnam's Sons, 1907.

06311. Pilon, Edmond. "Lady Mary Wortley Montagu ." Revue bleue
        76 (1938): 256-258.

06312. Strohl, E. Lee. "The Fascinating Lady Mary Wortley
        Montagu, 1689-1762." Archives of Surgery 89 (September
        1964): 554-558.

06313. Tillotson, Geoffrey. "Lady Mary Wortley Montagu and
        Pope's Elegy to the Memory of an Unfortunate Lady."
        Review of English studies 12 (1936): 401-412.

                    (f) Hannah More

06314. Aikin-Sneath, Betsy. "Hannah More." London Mercury 28
        (1933): 528-535.

06315. Aldridge, Alfred Owen. "Madame de Stael and Hannah More on
        Society." Romanic Review 38 (December 1947): 330-339.

06316. Child, Philip. "Portrait of a Woman of Affairs--old
        style." University of Toronto quarterly 3 (1933):
        87-102.

06317.   Courtney, Luther Weeks. Hannah More's Interest in Educa-
          tion and Government. Waco, Tx.: Baylor University, 1929.

06318.   Hopkins, Mary Alden. Hannah More and her Circle. New
          York: Longmans, Green, 1946.

06319.   Jones, Mary G. Hannah More. 1952. Reprint. New York:
          Greenwood Press, 1968.

06320.   Meakin, Annette M. Hannah More: A Biographical Study.
          London: Murray, 1919.

06321.   Snodgrass, A. E. "Dr. Johnson's petted Lady." Cornhill
          74 (1933): 336-342.

06322.   Yonge, Charlotte. Hannah More. London: W. H. Allen and
          Co., 1888.

(g) Richard Steele

06323.   Blanchard, Rae. "Richard Steele and the Status of Women."
          Studies in Philology 26 (July 1929): 325-355.

06324.   Heinrich, Joachim. Die Frauenfrage bei Steele und Addison.
          Eine Untersuchung zur englischen Literatur und Kul-
          turgeschichte im 17/18 Jahrhundert. Leipzig: Mayer and
          Müller, 1930.

06325.   Hoagland, Florence. The Women of Steele and Addison: a
          literary and critical interpretation of their status in
          the early eighteenth century. Ithaca: n.p., 1933.

(h) Jonathan Swift

06326.   Davis, Herbert. Stella: a gentlewoman of the eighteenth
          century. New York: Macmillan Co., 1942.

06327.   Deford, Miriam Allen. "Swift and Stella: An Unsolved
          Mystery Story." Modern Age 11 (1967): 400-406.

06328.   Gibbs, Lewis. Vanessa and the Dean. New York: Funk
          and Wagnalls, 1939.

06329.   Gold, Maxwell B. Swift's Marriage to Stella. Cambridge,
          Mass.: Harvard University Press, 1937.

06330.   Heinemann, M. "Swift's 'Corinna' Again." Notes and
          Queries 217 (1972): 218-221.

06331.   Petitjean, A. M. "Swift et Stella." Cahiers du Sud 24
          (1937): 720-733.

06332.   Rogers, Katherine M.   "'My Female Friends':   The Mysogyny
          of Jonathan Swift."   Texas Studies in Literature and
          Language 1 (1959): 366-379.

06333.   Swift, Jonathan.   "A Letter to a Very Young Lady on her
          Marriage."   In Prose Works, edited by Herbert Davis,
          9:84-94.   Oxford: Basil Blackwell, 1948.

                    (i)   Hester Lynch Piozzi Thrale

06334.   Bloom, Edward A.; Bloom, Lillian D.; and Klingel, Joan E.
          "Portrait of a Georgian Lady: The Letters of Hester
          Lynch (Thrale) Piozzi, 1784-1821."   Bulletin of the
          John Rylands University Library 60 (Spring 1978): 303-338.

06335.   Clifford, James L.   Hester Lynch Piozzi (Mrs. Thrale).
          Oxford: Claredon Press, 1941.

06336.   Hyde, Mary.   The Impossible Friendship: Boswell and Mrs.
          Thrale.   Cambridge, Mass.: Harvard University Press, 1972.

06337.   _____.   "The Impossible Friendship (Boswell and Mrs.
          Thrale).   I: Rivalry (1763-1775).   II: Restraint (1776-
          1781).   III: Estrangement (1782-1786).   IV: Enmity
          (1787-1791).   Harvard Library Bulletin 20 (January,
          April, July, and October, 1972) 5-37; 188-221; 270-317;
          372-429.

06338.   _____.   The Thrales of Streatham Park: Journal of an
          Eighteenth-Century Family.   Cambridge, Mass.:   Harvard
          University Press, 1977.

06339.   _____.   "The Thrales of Streatham Park I."   Harvard
          Library Bulletin 24 (April 1976): 125-179.

06340.   _____.   "The Thrales of Streatham Park.   II.   The
          Family Book, (iii) 1775-1776; (iv) 1777-1778."   Harvard
          Library Bulletin 24 (October 1976): 414-474; 25 (January
          1977):   63-100.

06341.   _____.   "The Thrales of Streatham Park.   III.   The
          Death of Thrale and Remarriage of His Widow."   Harvard
          Library Bulletin 25 (April 1977): 193-241.

06342.   Riely, J. C.   "Lady Knight's Role in the Boswell-Piozzi
          Rivalry."   Philological Quarterly 51 (October 1972): 961-
          965.

06343.   _____, and Ribeiro, Alvaro.   "'Mrs. Thrale' in the
          Tour: A Boswellian Puzzle."   Papers of the Bibliographi-
          cal Society of America 69 (1975): 151-163.

06344.   Spacks, Patricia Meyer. "Scrapbook of a Self: Mrs. Piozzi's
          Late Journals." Harvard Library Bulletin 18 (July 1970):
          221-247.

06345.   Vulliamy, C. E. Mrs. Thrale of Streatham. London:
          Jonathan Cape, 1936.

                          (2) Others

06346.   Alspach, Russell K. "Charlotte Brooke: a forerunner of
          the Celtic Renaissance." University of Pennsylvania
          General Magazine and historical chronicle 40 (1938):
          178-183.

06347.   Ashdown, Margaret. "Elizabeth Elstob, the learned
          Saxonist." Modern Language Review 20 (1925): 125-146.

06348.   B., J. "The First Home Student." Oxford Magazine 57
          (1938): 212-223.

06349.   Gaussen, Alice C. A Woman of Wit and Wisdom A Memoir of
          Elizabeth Carter, One of the 'Bas Bleu' Society (1717-
          1806). London: Smith, Elder and Co., 1906.

06350.   Hume, David. Essays, Moral, Political and Literary, edited
          by T. H. Green and T. H. Gross. London: Longmans,
          Green and Co., 1889.
            [See especially "Of Love and Marriage" 2: 383-388.
            "Of Polygamy and Divorce" 1: 231-239.]

06351.   MacGregor, Margaret Eliot. Amelia Anderson Opie: Worlding
          and Friend. Northampton, Mass.: Smith College Studies,
          1932-1933.

06352.   Menzies-Wilson, Jacobine, and Lloyd, Helen. Amelia: the
          tale of a Plain Friend. London: Oxford University
          Press, 1937.

06353.   Parker, W. M. "Lady Davy in Her Letters." Quarterly
          Review 300 (1962): 79-89.

06354.   Ponsonby, Lord. "Letitia Pilkington (1712-50) — a
          curiosity of literature." English 1 (1937): 297-306.

06355.   Shepperson, Archibald Bolling. John Paradise and Lucy
          Ludwell of London and Williamsburg. Richmond,
          Va.: Dietz Press, 1942.

06356.   Small, Miriam Rossiter. Charlotte Ramsay Lennox, an
          Eighteenth Century Lady of Letters. New Haven, Conn.:
          Yale University Press, 1935.

06357.   Stuart, Marie W. "Countess Charming." Cornhill Magazine
         156 (1937): 64-73.

06358.   Vulliamy, C. E. Aspasia: The Life and Letters of Mary
         Granville, Mrs. Delaney (1700-1788). London: Geoffrey
         Bles, 1935.

         Also refer to #5414.

(3)   Bluestockings

06359.   Bodek, Evelyn Gordon. "Salonières and Bluestockings:
         Educated Obsolescence and Germinating Feminism."
         Feminist Studies 3 (Spring-Summer 1976): 185-199.

06360.   Scott, Walter S. The Bluestocking Ladies. London: John
         Green & Co., 1947.

06361.   Wheeler, Ethel Rolt. Famous Bluestockings. London:
         Methuen and Co., 1910.

e)   Art

(1)   Women in Art

06362.   Penny, N. B. "English Church Monuments to Women Who
         Died in Childbed between 1780 and 1835." Journal of
         the Warburg Courtauld Institute 38 (1975): 314-332.

06363.   Schlüter, Henning. Ladies, Lords und Liederjane.
         Berlin: Propylaen, 1966.

(2)   Women Artists

(a)   Actresses

[1]   CHARLOTTE CHARKE

06364.   Peavy, Charles D. "The Chimerical Career of Charlotte
         Charke." Restoration and Eighteenth Century Theatre
         Research 8 (1969): 1-12.

06365.   Strange, Sallie Minter. "Charlotte Charke: Transvestite
         or Conjuror?" Restoration and Eighteenth Century Theatre
         Research 15 (November 1976): 54-59.

06366. Waddell, Helen. "Eccentric Englishwomen: VIII. Mrs.
        Charke." Spectator (4 June 1937): 1047-1048.

                        [2] PEG WOFFINGTON

06367. Dunbar, Janet. Peg Woffington and Her World. London:
        Heinemann, 1968.

06368. Lucey, Janet Camden. Lovely Peggy: the life and times
        of Margaret Woffington. London: Hurst and Blackett, 1951.

06369. Scott, Walter S. "Peg Woffington and Her Circle." New
        Rambler ser. C 2 (January 1967): 14-23.

                            [3] OTHERS

06370. De la Torre, Lillian. The Actress, being the story of
        Sarah Siddons, showing how she began as a strolling
        player . . . . New York: T. Wilson, 1957.

06371. Fothergill, Brian. Mrs. Jordan: Portrait of an Actress.
        London: Faber and Faber, 1965.

06372. Gore-Brown, Robert. Gay was the Pit; The Life and Times of
        Anne Oldfield, Actress (1683-1730). London: Max Reinhardt,
        1957.

06373. Greene, Godfrey. "Mrs. Sarah Gardner: a further note."
        Theatre notebook 8 (1953): 6-10.

06374. Grice, F., and Clarke, A. "Mrs. Sarah Gardner." Theatre
        notebook 7 (1953): 76-81.

06375. Hodgson, Norma. "Sarah Baker (1736/7-1816): 'Governess-
        General of the Kentish Drama.'" In Studies in English
        Theatre History in Memory of Gabrielle Enthoven, pp. 65-83.
        London: Society for Theatrical Research, 1952.

06376. Manvell, Roger. Sarah Siddons: Portrait of an Actress.
        New York: Putnam, 1971.

06377. Nash, Mary. The Provoked Wife: The Life and Times of
        Susannah Cibber. London: Hutchinson, 1977.

06378. Sands, Mollie. "Mrs. Toft, 1685?-1756." Theatre Notebook
        20 (Spring 1966): 100-113.

06379. Steedman, W. "The Early Years of Mrs. Garrick." Theatre
        Research International 4 (February 1979): 94-102.

        Also refer to #5419.

(b) Musicians/Singers

06380. Allchin, A. M. "Ann Griffiths: An Approach to Her Life
        and Work." Transactions of the Cymmrodorion Society
        (1972-1973): 170-184.

06381. Bor, Margot, and Clelland, Lamond. Still the Lark: A
        Biography of Elizabeth Linley. London: Merlin Press,
        1962.

06382. Halsband, Robert. "Virtue in Danger: The Case of Griselda
        Murray." History Today 17 (1967): 693-700.

06383. Matthews, Betty. "The Davies Sisters, J. C. Bach and the
        Glass Harmonica." Music and Letters 56 (April 1975):
        150-169.

06384. Myers, Robert Manson. "Mrs. Delany: An Eighteenth Century
        Handelian." Musical Quarterly 32 (January 1946): 12-36.
        Also refer to #6358.

        Also refer to #5420.

(c) Painters/Sculptors

06385. Evans, Margaret Carey. "Mrs. Sarah Baxter, nee Buck
        (1770-?): Norfolk Portrait-Painter and Miniaturist."
        Norfolk Archaeology 35 (1972): 400-409.

06386. Sydie, Rosalind. "Woman Painters in Britain: 1768-1848."
        Atlantis 5 (Spring 1980): 144-175.

06387. Walsh, Elizabeth. "Mrs. Mary Beale, Paintress." Connoisseur
        131 (April 1953): 2-8.

f) Science

06388. Ogilvie, Marilyn Bailey. "Caroline Herschel's Contribution
        to Astronomy." Annals of Science 32 (March 1975): 149-
        161.

C. FRANCE

1. SURVEYS

"O Women, you are very extraordinary children."
                                         Diderot

a) Non-specific

06389. Garden, Maurice. Lyon et les lyonnais au XVIIIème siècle.
        Paris: Les Belles lettres, 1970.

06390. Goncourt, Edmond and Gancourt, Jules de. Portraits intimes
        du XVIIIe siècle. Paris: E. Fasquelles, 1878.

06391. Hufton, Olwen H. Bayeux in the Late Eighteenth Century:
        A Social Study. New York: Oxford University Press, 1967.

06392. _____. The Poor of Eighteenth Century France,
        1750-1789. New York: Oxford University Press, 1974.

06393. _____. "Towards an Understanding of the Poor of
        Eighteenth-Century France." In French Government and
        Society 1500-1850: Essays in Memory of Alfred Cobban,
        edited by J. F. Bosher, pp. 145-65. London: Athlone
        Press, 1973.

06394. Kaplow, Jeffrey. The Names of Kings: The Parisian
        Laboring Poor in the Eighteenth Century. New York:
        Basic Books, Inc., 1972.

06395. Saint-Beuve, Charles Austin. Portraits of the Eighteenth
        Century, Historic and Literary. Translated by Katharine P.
        Wormeley. 2 vols. New York: G. P. Putnam's Sons, 1905.

b) Women

06396. Dodson, Austin. Four Frenchwomen. 1893. Reprint. New
        York: Arno Press, 1972.

06397. Imbert de Saint-Armand, Arthur Leon. Portraits de femmes
        françaises du XVIIIe et du XIXe siècles. Paris:
        n. p., 1869.

06398. Jacobs, Eva, et. al., eds. Woman and Society in Eighteenth-
        Century France. London: Athlone Press, 1979.

06399. Kavanaugh, Julia. Woman in France during the Eighteenth
        Century. New York: J. P. Putnam's Sons, 1893.

06400. Latour, Therese Louise. Princesses, Ladies and Salonnieres
        of the reign of Louis XV. London: K. Paul, Trench, Trubner
        and Co., Ltd., 1927.

06401. Lee, Vera. The Reign of Women in Eighteenth-Century France.
        Cambridge, Mass.: Schenkman Publishing Co., 1975.

06402. Luppe, Albert Marie Pierre, comte de. Les Jeunes Filles dans
        l'aristocratie et dans la bourgeoisie à la fin du XVII^{ieme}
        siecle. Paris: Ed. Champion, 1925.

2. POLITICAL

"In almost all countries, the cruelty of the civil law
has combined with the cruelty of nature, against women.
They have been treated like imbecile children."
                                        Diderot

a) Legal

06403. Traer, James F. Marriage and the Family in Eighteenth
        Century France. Ithaca, N.Y.: Cornell University Press,
        1980.

        Also refer to #5432, 6495, 6585, 6588, 6590, 6592, 6593,
        6594.

b) Criminal

06404. Cummings, Mark. "Elopement, Family and the Courts: The
Crime of 'Rapt' in Early Modern France." Proceedings of
the Western Society for French History 4 (1976): 118-125.

Also refer to #5435, 5436.

c) Feminism

06405. Abensour, Léon. La femme et le féminisme avant la
Révolution. 1923. Reprint. Geneva: Megariotis, 1977.

06406. Williams, David. "The Politics of Feminism in the French
Enlightenment." In The Varied Pattern: Studies in the
18th Century, edited by Peter Hughes and David Williams,
pp. 333-351. Toronto: Hakkert, 1971.

d) Political Roles

(1) Women

06407. Argenson, Marquis d'. Madame de Montmorency-Laval (sa
famille et ses amis 1767-1791). Paris: Messein, 1931.

06408. Armaillé, Marie Celestine Amelie de Ségur, comtesse d'.
La comtesse d'Egmont, fille de Maréchal de Richelieu.
Paris: Perrin, 1880.

06409. Barthélemy, Edouard Marie. Les filles du Régent. Paris:
Librairie Firmin-Didot frères, 1874.

06410. _____. Mesdames de France, filles de
Louis XV. Paris: Didier, 1870.

06411. Carré, Henri. Madamoiselle, fille du régent, duchesse
de Berry (1695-1719). Paris: Hachette, 1936.

06412. Datta de Albertis, G. La principessa di Lamballe (1749-
1792). Milan: Corticelli, 1935.

06413. Fleischmann, Hector. Madame de Polignac et la cour galante de Marie-Antoinette. Paris: Bibliotheque des curieux, 1910.

06414. Fleury, Maurice, comte de. Louis XV intime et les petites maitresses. Paris: Plon, 1933.

06415. Goncourt, Edmond and Goncourt, Jules de. La duchesse de Châteauroux et ses soeurs. Paris: N. Charpentier, 1879.

06416. _____. Les maitresses de Louix XV. Paris: Firmin Didot frères, fils et c^{ie}, 1860.

06417. Gottschalk, Louis. Lady-in-Waiting: The Romance of Lafayette and Aglae de Hunolstein. Baltimore: Johns Hopkins University Press, 1939.

06418. Imbert de Saint-Armand, Arthur Leon. Women of Versailles: The Court of Louis XV. New York: C. Scribner's Sons, 1893.

06419. _____. Women of Versailles: Last Years of Louis XV. Translated by Elizabeth Gilbert Martin. New York: C. Scribner's Sons, 1893.

06420. Lescure, Mathurin François Adolphe de. La princesse de Lamballe; Marie-Thérèse-Louise de Savoie-Carignan. Paris: H. Plon, 1864.

06421. McCabe, Lida Rose. Ardent Adrienne. New York: Appleton, 1930.

06422. Marquiset, Alfred. La Duchesse de Fallary, 1697-1782. Paris: H. Champion, 1907.

06423. Poignant, S. Les Filles de Louis XV: L'Aile des Princes. Paris: Arthaud, 1975.

06424. Pollitzer, Marcel. La Marquise de Boufflers: La Dame de volupté. Paris: Vernier, 1970.

06425. Raynal, Paul de. Le mariage d'un roi, 1721-1725. Paris: C. Lévy, 1887.

06426. Sabatier, Pierre. "Une instigatrice du mariage de Louis XV: la marquise de Prie." Nouvelle revue deux mondes 10 (October 1974): 94-107.

06427. Saintville, Georges. La confidante de Madame de Pompadour, Madame Haussay des Demaines. Paris: Ancienne librairie Furne, Boivin et c^{ie}, 1937..

06428. Sicard, Roch Ambroise Cucurron. Vie de Madame la Dauphine, mère de S.M. Louis XVIII. Paris: Audot, 1817.

06429. Wright, Constance. Madame de Lafayette. New York: Henry Holt and Company, 1959.

(2)   Individuals

(a)   Louise, duchess de Choiseul

06430.   Maugras, Gaston.   La disgrace du duc et de la duchesse de
    Choiseul.   Paris: Plon-Nourrit et c^{ie}, 1903.

06431.   Orliac, Jehanne d'.   La duchesse de Choiseul.   Tours:
    Arrault, 1947.

06432.   Trouncer, Margaret.   A duchess of Versailles; the love
    story of Louise, duchesse de Choiseul.   London: Hutchin-
    son, 1961.

(b)   Madame du Barry

06433.   Aulneau, J.   La comtesse du Barry et la fin de l'ancien
    régime.   Paris: Denoel, 1937.

06434.   Breitner, Erhard.   Madame du Barry.   Translated by Lord
    Sudley.   London: Cobden-Sanderson, 1939.

06435.   Castries, Rene de la Croix, duc de.   Madame du Barry.
    Paris: Hachette, 1967.

06436.   Douglas, Robert Bruce.   The Life and Times of Madame du
    Barry.   London: L. Smithers, 1896.

06437.   Fromageot, Paul.   Madame Du Barry de 1791-1793.
    Versailles: L. Bernard, 1909.

06438.   Goncourt, Edmond and Goncourt, Jules de.   La Du Barry.   Paris:
    G. Charpentier, 1889.

06439.   Laski, Philip.   The Trial and Execution of Madame du
    Barry.   London: Constable, 1969.

06440.   Leroy, Alfred.   Madame du Barry et son temps.   Paris:
    A. Michel, 1941.

06441.   Levron, Jacques.   Madame Du Barry ou la fin d'une courti-
    sane.   Paris: Perrin, 1973.

06442.   Loomis, Stanley.   Du Barry: A Biography.   Philadelphia:
    J. B. Lippincott Company, 1959.

06443.   Mairobet, Pidansat de.   Memoirs of Madame du Barry.
    London: The Folio Society, 1956.

06444.   Saint-André, Claude. Madame du Barry d'après les docu-
          ments authentiques. Paris: Librairie Plon, 1933.

06445.   Schumacher, Karl von. The Du Barry. London: Harrap, 1932.

06446.   Vatel, Charles. Histoire du Madame du Barry. Versailles:
          L. Bernard, 1883.

06447.   Williams, Hugh Noel. Madame du Barry. New York:
          Scribner's Sons, 1909.

(c) Madame Elizabeth

06448.   [Alleman, Jeanne]. Madame Elizabeth. Paris: Spes, 1935.

06449.   Fuye, Maurice de la and Babeau, Emile-Albert. Madame
          Elizabeth, 1764-1794. Paris: Lethielleux, 1957.

06450.   Vendôme, Henriette. Madame Elisabeth de France. Paris:
          E. Flammarion, 1942.

06451.   Vergne, Yvonne de la. Madame Elisabeth of France. St.
          Louis: B. Herder Book Co., 1947.

06452.   Woodgate, Mildred Violet. Madame Elizabeth of France.
          London: Brown and Nolan, 1943.

(d) Marie Leczinska

06453.   Des Reaulx, (de Saint Ouen). Le roi Stanislas et Maria
          Leczinska. Paris: E. Plon, Nourit et c^{ie}, 1895.

06454.   Jallut, Marguerite. "Marie Leczinska et la peinture."
          Gazette des Beaux Arts 111 (May-June 1969): 305-322.

06455.   Leroy, Alfred. Marie Leczinska et ses filles. Paris:
          A. Michel, 1940.

06456.   Nolhac, Pierre de. Louix XV et Marie Lexzinska. Paris:
          Calmann-Levy, 1930.

(e) Marie Antoinette

06457.   Arnauld-Bouteloup, Jeanne. Le Rôle politique de
          Marie-Antoinette. Paris: Edouard Champion, 1924.

06458.   Belloc, Hilaire. Marie Antoinette. London: Methuen and
         Co., 1951.

06459.   Castelot, André. Marie-Antoinette. Paris: Rombaldi, 1973.

06460.   Funck-Brentano, F. Les derniers jours de Marie-Antoinette.
         Paris: Flammarion, 1933.

06461.   Goncourt, Edmond and Goncourt, Jules de. Histoire de Marie
         Antoinette. Paris: E. Flammarion, 1929.

06462.   Gooch, George Peabody. "Maria Therese and Marie Antoinette."
         Contemporary Review 174 (October 1948): 216-225; (November
         1948): 288-295; (December 1948): 348-356; 175 (January
         1949): 22-29; (February 1949): 91-96; (March 1949): 153-159;
         (April 1949): 214-220; (May 1949): 277-283; and (June 1949):
         342-348.

06463.   Haggard, Andrew C. P. Louis XV and Marie Antoinette.
         2 vols. New York: Appleton, 1909.

06464.   Hearsey, John. Marie Antoinette. New York: E. P. Dutton
         and Company, 1973.

06465.   Huisman, Philippe, and Jallut, Marguerite. Marie Antoi-
         nette. New York: Viking Press, 1971.

06466.   Hupin, Gerard. Une Grande reine, Marie-Antoinette.
         Paris: Nouvelle Editions latines, 1972.

06467.   Kunstler, Charles. La Vie privée de Marie-Antoinette.
         Paris: Hachette, 1938.

06468.   Lafue, Pierre. La Tragedie de Marie-Antoinette. Evreux:
         Le Cercle du bibliophile, 1972.

06469.   Leroy, Alfred. Marie Antoinette. Paris: Societe d'
         éditions françaises et internationales, 1946.

06470.   Loomis, Stanley. The fatal friendship: Marie Antoinette,
         Count Fersen and the flight to Varennes. New York:
         Doubleday, 1972.

06471.   Pilkington, Ian David Bruce. Queen of the Trianon; the
         Story of Marie Antoinette. London: Jarrolds, 1955.

06472.   Vallotton, Henry. Marie Antoinette et Fersen. Paris:
         La Palatine, 1952.

06473.   Webster, Nesta. Louis XVI and Marie Antoinette before the
         Revolution. New York: G. P. Putnam's Sons, 1937.

06474.   _____. Louis XVI and Marie Antoinette During the
         Revolution. New York: Gordax Press, 1976.

06475.   Zweig, Stefan. Marie Antoinette. Budapest: Pantheon,
         1947.

                    (f) Madame de Pompadour

06476.   Aretz, Gertrude. Die Marquise von Pompadour, ein Lebens-
         bild aus dem Rokoko. Dresden: P. Aretz, 1924.

06477.   Bonhomme, Honoré. Madame de Pompadour, général d'armée.
         Paris: Charavay frs., 1880.

06478.   Carré, Henri. La marquise de Pompadour. Paris: Hachette,
         1937.

06479.   Castelot, André. "La Pompadour mieux que reine. Le roi
         etait son amant." Historia 329 (April 1974): 46-55.

06480.   Goncourt, Edmond and Goncourt, Jules de. Mme. de Pompadour.
         Paris: G. Charpentier, 1889.

06481.   Laulan, Robert. "La Foundation de l'ecole Militaire et
         Madame de Pompadour." Revue d'histoire moderne 21
         (April-June 1974): 284-299.

06482.   Leroy, Alfred. Madame de Pompadour et son temps. Paris:
         A. Michel, 1946.

06483.   Levron, Jacques. Pompadour. Translated by Claire Eliane
         Engel. New York: St. Martin's Press, 1963.

06484.   Mitford, Nancy. Mme. de Pompadour. London: Sphere, 1976.

06485.   Nolhac, Pierre de. Louis XV et Madame de Pompadour.
         Paris: L. Conrad, 1928.

06486.   _____. Madame de Pompadour et la politique.
         Paris: Calmann-Levy, 1928.

06487.   Smythe, David Mynders. Madame de Pompadour, mistress of
         France. New York: Wilfred Funk, 1953.

06488.   Soulavie, Jean Louis Girard. Madame de Pompadour.
         Translated by E. Jules Meras. New York: Sturgis and
         Walton, 1910.

06489.   Tinayre, Marcelle. Madame de Pompadour. Paris:
         Flammarion, 1938.

06490.   Trouncer, Margaret. The Pompadour. London: Hutchinson,
         1956.

06491.   Williams, Hugh Noel. Madame de Pompadour. New York:
         Charles Scribner's Sons, 1902.

3. ECONOMIC

"All household chores are left to the women. They milk
the cows, make butter and cheese, go to bed later than
the men, and rise before them."
                    Le Grand Aussy, Voyage d'Auvergne.

06492. Depauw, Jacques. "Immigration féminine, professions fémi-
        nines et structures urbaines à Nantes au XVIIIe siècle."
        Université de Nantes Centre de recherches sur l'histoire
        de la France Atlantique. Enquêtes et documents 1972:
        37-60.

06493. Dubois-Butard, Louis. Les Femmes dans la maîtrise
        d'Amiens au XVIIIième siècle. Amiens: Archives departe-
        mentales de la Somme, 1975.

06494. Gayot, Gerard. "A propos de structures sociales ardennaises
        aux XVIIIe et XIXe siècles, fiscalité et relations
        familiales." Etudes ardennaises 53-54 (1968): 7-28.

06495. Hufton, Olwen. "Begging, Vagrancy, Vagabondage and the
        Law: An Aspect of the Problem of Poverty in Eighteenth-
        Century France." European Studies Review 2 (1972):
        97-123.

06496. _____. "Women and the Family Economy in Eighteenth-
        Century France." French Historical Studies 9 (1975):
        1-22.

06497. See, Henri. La France économique et sociale au XVIIIe
        siecle. 3rd ed. Paris: A. Colin, 1946.

06498. Sussman, George D. "The Wet-Nursing Business in Paris,
        1769-1876." Proceedings of Western Society French
        History 1 (March 1974): 179-194.

4. RELIGION

"Crowds of people . . . began to be seized by similar
frenzied paroxysms. Men, women and children took part
in the proceedings . . . filling the cemetery with
'tears, groans, and frightful screams.'"
                    Kreiser on 18th Century convulsionaries

a) Religious Orders

06499.   Boussoulade, J.   "Soeurs de charité et comités de bienfai-
         sance des faubourgs Saint-Marcel et Saint-Antoine."
         Annales historique de la Revolution française 42 (April-
         June 1970): 350-374.

06500.   Richomme, Agnès.   L'appel de la route: Julie Billiart,
         fondatrice des soeurs de Notre-Dame de Namur.   Paris:
         Editions "Marie-Mediatrice."   1968.

06501.   _____.   Marie Louise Trichet 1684-1759, fonda-
         trice des Filles de la Sagesse, avec Sainte Louise-Marie
         de Montfort.   Lyon: Impr. M. Lescuyer et fils, 1971.

         Also refer to #6717, 6723.

b) Witchcraft

06502.   Garret, Clarke W.   "Witches and Cunning Folk in the Old
         Regime."   In The Wolf and the Lamb Popular Culture
         in France from the Old Regime to the 20th Century,
         edited by Jacques Beauwy, Marc Bertrand and Edward T.
         Gargan, pp. 53-64.   Stanford French and Italian Studies,
         No. 3.   Saratoga, Calif.:   Anma Libri and Co., 1976.

06503.   Mandrou, Robert.   Magistrats et sourciers en France au
         XVIIIe siècle.   Paris: Plon, 1968.

06504.   Wilkins, Kay.   "Attitudes to Witchcraft and Demonic
         Possession in France during the Eighteenth Century."
         Journal of European Studies 3 (December 1974): 348-362.

5. SOCIAL

"There is no kind of vexation which in civilized nations
a husband may not exercise against his wife."
                                        Diderot

(1) Non-specific

06505. Arrighi, Paul. La vie quotidienne en Corse au XVIIIe
        siecle. Paris: Hachette, 1970.

06506. Barber, Elinor. The Bourgeoisie in Eighteenth-Century
        France. Princeton, N.J.: Princeton University Press,
        1955.

06507. Bluche, François. La Vie quotidienne de la noblesse
        française au XVIIIe siecle. Paris: Hachette, 1973.

06508. Castan, Yves. Honnêteté et relations sociales en
        Languedoc, 1715-1780. (Civilisations et mentalites.)
        Paris: Plon, 1974.
            [See especially ch. 3 & 4 on the Family.]

06509. Ducros, Louis. La société française au XVIIIe siecle
        d'après les memoires et la correspondance du temps.
        Paris: H. Hatier, 1922.

06510. Forster, Robert. The House of Saulx-Tavanes: Versailles
        and Burgundy, 1700-1830. Baltimore: Johns Hopkins
        Press, 1971.

06511. _____. The Nobility of Toulouse in the
        Eighteenth Century: A Social and Economic Study.
        Baltimore: Johns Hopkins, 1960.

06512. Franklin, Alfred Louis Auguste. La vie de Paris sous
        Louis XV. Devant les tribunaux. Paris: E. Plon,
        Nourrit et Cie, 1898.

06513. Goncourt, Edmond. L'amour au dix-huitième siecle. Paris:
        G. Charpentier et E. Fasquelle, 1893.

06514. Kunstler, Charles. La Vie quotidienne en France sous la
        Regence. Paris: Hachette, 1960.

06515. _____. La vie quotidienne sous Louis XV.
        Paris: Hachette, 1953.

06516. _____. La vie quotidienne sous Louis XVI.
        Paris: Hachette, 1950.

06517. Lacroix, Paul. France in the Eighteenth Century: its
        institutions, customs and costumes. 1876. Reprint.
        New York: Frederick Unger Publishing Co., 1963.

06518. Meyer, J. La vie quotidienne en France au tempes de Régence.
        Paris: Hachette, 1978.

06519. Sheppard, Thomas F. Loumarin in the Eighteenth Century:
        A Study of a French Village. Baltimore: Johns Hopkins
        University Press, 1971.

(2) Women

06520. Darrow, Margaret H. "French Noblewomen and the New Domes-
        ticity, 1750-1850." Feminist Studies 5 (Spring 1979):
        41-65.

06521. Exposition, Sens. La Condition féminine dans le monde
        rural aux XVIII et XIX siècles: Hôtel de ville de
        Sens, juillet-septembre 1975. Auxerre: Impr. Tridon-
        Gallot, 1975.

06522. Goncourt, Edmund and Goncourt, Jules. "La mujer francesca
        en el siglo XVIII." España moderna 10 (July 1898): 130-157.

06523. Toth, Karl. Woman & Rococo in France, Seen Through the
        Life and Works of a Contemporary, Charles-Pinot Duclos.
        Translated by Roger Abingdon. London: G. G. Harrap, 1931.

        Also refer to #5569, 5619.

b) Demography

06524. Ackerman, Evelyn Bernette. "The Commune of Bonnieres-
        sur-Seine in the eighteenth and nineteenth centuries."
        Annales de démographie historique (1977): 85-100.

06525. Bideau, Alain, "La population de Thoissey aux XVIIIe
        et XIXe siècles." Bulletin du Centre d'histoire
        economique et sociale de la région lyonnaise 2
        (1972): 23-42.

06526. Biraben, Jean-Noël. "Certain demographic characteristics
        of the plague epidemic in France, 1720-1722." In
        Population and Social Change, edited by D. V. Glass and
        Roger Reville, pp. 233-241. New York: Crane, Russak,
        1972. Also in Daedalus 97 (Spring 1968): 536-545.

06527. _____. "Travaux et recherches sur la
        demographie de la France au XVIIIe siècle." Union
        internationale pour l'etude de la population: conference
        internationale de New York en 1961 1 (1963): 556-564.

06528.   Blayo, Yves. "Trois paroisses d'Ille-et-Vilaine."
          Annales de démographie historique (1969): 191-213.

06529.   _____, and Henry, Louis. "Données démographiques
          sur la Bretagne et l'Anjou de 1740 a 1829." Annales
          de démographie historique (1967): 91-171.

06530.   Cahen, L. "La Population parisienne au milieu du XVIIIe
          siècle." Revue de Paris 26 (15 September 1919): 146-170.

06531.   Chaunu, Pierre. "Reflexions sur la démographie normande."
          In Sur la population francaise au XVIIIe et au XIXe
          siècles, pp. 97-117. Paris: Société de démographie
          historique, 1973.

06532.   Daubeze, Yvette and Perrot, Jean-Claude. "Un programme
          d'étude démographique sur ordinateur." Annales: écono-
          mies, sociétés, civilisations 27 (1972): 1047-1070.

06533.   Dupâquier, Jacques. "Les caractères originaux de l'his-
          toire démographique française au XVIIIe siècle." Revue
          d'histoire moderne et contemporaine 23 (1976): 182-202.

06534.   Gabet, Camille, "Etude démographique dans une paroisse
          rurale au XVIIIe siècle: les mariages à Thaire d'Aunis."
          Actes du 90e Congres de la Société des savantes, Nice,
          1965 1 (1966): 151-157.

06535.   Galliano, Paul. "La mortalité infantile (indigènes et
          nourrissons) dans la banlieue Sud de Paris à la fin du
          XVIIIe siècle (1774-1794)." Annales de demographie
          historique (1966): 139-177.

06536.   Ganiage, Jean. Trois villages d'Ile-de-France au XVIIIe
          siècle: Etude demographique. Paris: Presses universi-
          taires de France, 1963.

06537.   Gautier, Etienne and Henry, Louis. "The Population of
          Crulai, a Norman Parish." In Popular Attitudes toward
          Birth Control in Pre-Industrial France and England,
          edited by Orest and Patricia Ranum, pp. 45-52. New
          York: Harper and Row, 1972.

06538.   Girard, Pierre. "Aperçus de la demographie de Sotteville-
          les-Rouen vers la fin du XVIIIe siecle." Population 14
          (1959): 485-508.

06539.   Gouberg, Pierre. "Legitimate fertility and infant mortality
          in France during the eighteenth century: a comparison."
          In Population and Social Change, edited by D. V. Glass and
          Roger Reville, pp. 321-330. New York: Russak, 1972.
          Also in Daedalus 97 (Spring 1968): 593-603.

06540.   Goy, Gérard. "Esquisse de l'évolution démographique de la
         Brede et des ses environs dans la deuxième moitié du
         XVIIIe siècle." Revue historique de Bordeaux et du
         departement de la Gironde 21 (1972): 71-77.

06541.   Henry, Louis. "Monographie paroissiale sur la population
         francaise au XVIIIe siècle. Un faubourg du Havre:
         Ingouville." Population 16 (1961): 285-300.

06542.   _____. "The Population of France in the Eighteenth
         Century." In Population in History, edited by David V.
         Glass and D. E. C. Eversley, pp. 434-456. Chicago: Aldine
         Pub. Co., 1965.

06543.   Houdaville, Jacques. "Trois paroisses de Saint Domingue
         au XVIIIe siècle: étude démographique." Population 18
         (1963): 93-110.

06544.   Jouan, Marie-Helene, "Les originalités démographiques
         d'un bourg artisanal normand au XVIIIe siècle:
         Villedieu-les-Poeles (1711-1790)." Annales de
         démographie historique (1969): 87-124.

06545.   Lachiver, Marcel. "Fecondité légitime et contraception
         dans la region parisienne." In Sur la population fran-
         çaise au XVIIe et au XIX siècles, pp. 382-402. Paris:
         Société de démographie historique, 1973.

06546.   Lefebvre-Teillard, Anne. La population de Dôle au
         XVIIIe siècle. Paris: Presses universitaires de
         France, 1969.

06547.   Livi-Bacci, Massimo. "Les répercussions d'une crise de
         mortalité sur la fecondité: une verificaiton empirique."
         Annales de démographie historique (1978): 197-207.

06548.   Malgorn, Bernadette, "La population d'Ouessant au
         XVIIIe siècle: étude démographique." Annales de
         Bretagne 80 (1973): 289-315.

06549.   Maye, Jean-Martin. "Du soin extreme qu'on doit avoir
         du baptisme des enfants, dans le cas d'une fausse
         couche ou de la mort d'une femme enciente (1764)."
         Annales de démographie historique (1973): 389-391.

06550.   Sur la population française au XVIIIe et au XIXe
         siècles: hommage à Marcel Reinnhard. Paris: Société
         de démographie historique, 1973.

06551.   Szajkowski, Zosa. "Note on the Demography of Sephardism
         in France, 1737-1787." Hebrew Union College Annual 30
         (1959): 217-232.

         Also refer to #5627, 5629, 5631-5634, 5636-5640, 5641-5644,
         5645, 6589.

c) *Family*

(1) Non-specific

06552. Bezard, Yvonne. Une famille bourguignonne au 18e siècle.
        Paris: Michel, 1930.

06553. Blacker, C. P., "Social Ambitions of the Bourgeoisie in
        the 18th Century France, and Their Relation to
        Family Limitation." Population Studies 2 (July 1957):
        46-63.

06554. Collomp, Alain. "Famille nucleaire et famille elargie
        en Haute Provence au XVIIIe siècle, (1703-1734)."
        Annales: économies, sociétés, civilizations 27 (July-
        September 1972): 969-975.

06555. Daumard, Adeline, and Furet, François. Structures et rela-
        tions sociales à Paris au milieu du XVIIIe siècle. Paris:
        Librairie Armand Colin, 1961.
            [See especially ch. 3, "Origines familiales et
            contacts sociaux," pp. 57-90.]

06556. Dupâquier, Jacques and Jadin, Louis. "Structure of house-
        hold and family in Corsica, 1769-1771." In Household
        and family in Past Time, edited by Peter Laslett and
        Richard Wall, pp. 283-297. Cambridge: The University
        Press, 1972.

06557. Forster, Robert. Merchants, Landlords, Magistrates, The
        Dupont Family in Eighteenth-Century France. Baltimore:
        Johns Hopkins University Press, 1981.

06558. Goubert, Pierre. "La famille française au XVIIIe siècle."
        Saggi di demografia storica, serie Ricerche empiriche 2
        (1969): 35-50.

06559. Lannes, Xavier. "Le XVIIIe siècle: l'évolution des
        idees." In Renouveau des idées sur la famille, edited
        by Robert Prigent, pp. 34-49. Paris: Presses univer-
        sitaires de France, 1954.

06560. Philipps, Roderick. "Women and Family Breakdown in
        Eighteenth-Century France: Rouen 1780-1800." Social
        History 2 (May 1976): 197-218.

06561. Pilon, Edmond. La vie de famille aux dix-huitième siècle.
        Paris: A. Michel, 1941.

06562.   Ribbe, Charles de. Les familles et la société en France
          avant la Révolution, la vie domestique ses modèles et
          ses regles. Tours: A. Mame et fils, 1879.

06563.   Sicard, Germain. "Notes sur la famille en Gascogne
          toulousaine à la fin du XVIIIe siècle." In Mélanges
          Roger Aubenas; Recueil de mémoires et travaux publie
          par la société d'histoire du droit et des institutions
          des anciens pays de droit écrit, pp. 683-696. Mont-
          pellier: Faculté de droit et des sciences économiques
          de Montepellier, 1974.

06564.   Valmary, Pierre. Familles paysannes au XVIIIe siècle en
          Bas-Quercy. Etude démographique. Paris: Presses
          Universitaires de France, 1965.

          Also refer to #5436, 5628, 5632, 6403, 6404, 6494, 6496,
          6724.

(2)   Childhood

06565.   Aleil, Pierre-François, "Enfants illégitimes et enfants
          abandonnés à Clermont dans la seconde moitié du XVIIIe
          siècle." Cahiers d'histoire 21 (1976): 307-333.

06566.   Bideau, Alain. "Envoi des jeunes enfants en nourrice.
          L'exemple d'une petite ville: Thoissey-en Dombes.
          (1740-1840)." In Sur la population française au XVIIIe
          et XIXe siecles, pp. 49-58. Paris: Societe de demo-
          graphie historique, 1973.

06567.   _____; Brunet, Guy; and Debos, Roger. "Variations
          locales de la mortalité des enfants: l'example de la
          Chatellenie de Saint-Trivier-en-Dombes (1730-1869)."
          Annales de démographie historique (1978): 7-29.

06568.   Chamoux, Antoinette. "L'enfance abandonnée à Reims à la
          fin du XVIIIe siecle." Annales de démographie histo-
          rique (1973): 263-285.

06569.   Delasselle, Claude. "Abandoned Children in Eighteenth-
          Century Paris." In Deviants and the Abandoned in French
          Society, edited by Robert Forster and Orest Ranum, pp.
          47-82. Baltimore: Johns Hopkins Press, 1978. Also in
          Annales: économies, sociétés , civilisations 30 (January-
          -February 1975): 187-218.

06570.   Drake, T. G. H. "Infant Welfare Laws in France in the
          18th Century." Annals of Medical History n.s. 7
          (January 1935): 49-61.

06571. Drake, T. G. H. "The Wet Nurse in France in the 18th
        Century." Bulletin of the History of Medicine 8
        (July 1940): 934-948.

06572. Lebrun, Francois. "Naissance illégitime et infanticide en
        Anjou au XVIIIe siècle." Annales de Bretagne 87 (1980):
        143-146.

06573. _____. "Naissances illégitimes et abandons
        d'enfants en Anjou au XVIIIe siècle." Annales: écono-
        mies, sociétés, civilisations 27 (1972): 1183-1189.

06574. Lottin, Alain. "Naissances illégitimes et filles-meres
        a Lille au XVIIIe siècle." Revue d'histoire modern et
        contemporaine 17 (April-June 1970): 278-322.

06575. Mercier, Roger. L'enfant dans la société du XVIIIe siècle
        (avant "l'Emile"). Paris: n.p., 1961.

06576. Morel, M. F. "Théories et pratiques de l'allaitement en
        France au XVIIIe siècle." Annales de démographie
        historique (1976): 393-427.

06577. Peyronnet, Jean-Claude. "Les enfants abandonnés et leurs
        nourrices à Limoges au XVIIIe siècle." Revue d'histoire
        moderne et contemporaine 23 (1976): 418-441.

        Also refer to #5660, 6535, 6539.

                        d) Marriage

06578. Burguière, André. "Endogamia e comunita contadine. Sulla
        practica matrimoniale a Romainville nel XVIIIe secole."
        Quaderni storici 33 (September-December 1976): 1073-1094.
        Also in Annales de démographie historique (1979): 313-336.

06579. Cros, Claude. "Les mouvements saisonniers des conceptions
        et des mariages, paroisse de Saint-Priest-le-Betoux
        (1700-1820) en Lemosin (Haute-Vienne)." Etudes
        limousines 60-61 (1976): 37-42.

06580. Dravasa, Etienne. "Les classes sociales au XVIIIe siècle
        à Bordeaux d'après les contrats de mariage." Revue
        juridique et économique du Sud-Ouest, serie économique
        12 (1963): 961-1012.
        Also refer to #6594.

06581. Henry, Louis. "La fécondité des mariages dans le quart
        sud-ouest de la France de 1720 à 1829 (suite)." Annales:
        économies, sociétés, civilisations 27 (1972): 612-640,
        977-1023.

06582. Henry, Louis and Houdaille, Jacques. "Célébat et âge au
        mariage aux XVIIIe et XIXe siècles en France. Pt. I.
        Celebat definitif." Population 33 (January 1978): 43-84;
        "Pt. II. Age au premier mariage." Population 34 (March
        1979): 403-442.

06583. Houdaille, Jacques. "Un indicateur de pratique reli-
        gieuse: la célébration saisonniere des mariages avant,
        pendant, et après la Révolution française (1740-1829)."
        Population 33 (March 1978): 367-380.

06584. _____. "Les signatures au mariage de
        1740 à 1829." Population 32 (January-February 1977): 65-90.

06585. Lelièvre, Jacques. La pratique des contrats de mariage
        chez les notaires au Châtelet de Paris de 1769 à 1804.
        Paris: Editions Cujas, 1959.

06586. Mémin, Marcel. "Conventions de mariage dans la région
        mancelle en 1780." Revue historique de droit francais
        et étranger 4th ser. 43 (1965): 247-271.

06587. Petit, A. M., "Mariages et contrats de mariage à Agen en
        1785 et 1786." Annales du Midi 72 (1960): 215-229.

06588. Poussou, Jean-Pierre. "Experience aquitaine et méthodo-
        logie des contrats de mariage au XVIIIe siècle."
        Annales du Midi 76 (1964): 61-76.

06589. Segalen, Martine. Nuptialité et alliance; le choix du
        conjoint dans une commune de l'Eure. Paris: G.-P.
        Maisonneuve et Larose, 1972.

06590. Sicard, Germain and Sicard, Mireille. "Les contrats de
        mariage de la noblesse toulousaine en 1786." In Droit
        privé et institutions régionales, pp. 623-653. Paris:
        Presses universitaires de France, 1976.

06591. Terrisse, Michel. "Le rattrapage de nuptialité d'après
        peste à Marseille (1720-1721)." In Sur la population
        francaise au XVIIIe et au XIXe siècles, pp. 565-580.
        Paris: Société de démographie historique, 1973.

06592. Van Hille, W., "Contrats de mariage à Dunkerque (1706-
        1790)." Vlaamse Stam 2 (1966): 229-238.

06593. Vincent, Jacqueline. "Richesses et lacunes des actes
        notariés pour la connaissance des anciennes structures
        sociales: les contrats de mariage à Cannes de 1785-
        1818." Revue historique 508 (October-December 1973):
        363-402.

06594.   Wheaton, Robert. "Notes critiques sur les classes sociale
         au XVIIIe siècle à Bordeaux d'après les contrats de
         mariage." Revue historique 241 (1969): 99-114.

         Also refer to #5432, 5641, 5665, 5668-5673, 6403.

                      e)   Sex Life and Morals

                      (1)   Non-specific

06595.   Fairchilds, Cissie. "Female Sexual Attitudes and the Rise
         of Illegitimacy: A Case Study." Journal of Interdiscipli-
         nary History 8 (Spring 1978): 627-667.

06596.   Josephs, Herbert. "Sade and Woman: Exorcising the Awe of
         the Sacred." Studies in Burke and his Time 18 (Spring
         1977): 99-113.

06597.   McLaren, Angus. "Some Secular Attitudes Toward Sexual
         Behavior in France: 1760-1860." French Historical
         Studies 8 (Fall 1974): 604-625.

                      (2)   Prostitutes

06598.   Bloch, Iwan. 120 Days of Sodom and the Sex Life of the
         French Age of Debauchery. Translated and edited by
         Raymond Sabatier. New York: Falstaff Press, 1934.

06599.   Bretonne, Nicholas Edme, Restif de la. Le Pornographe;
         ou, Idées d'un honnête-homme sur un projet de relégment
         pour les prostituées propre à prévenir les malheurs qu
         occasionne le publicisme des femmes. Brussels: Gay and
         Douce, 1879.

06600.   Capon, Gaston. Les maisons closes au XVIIIe siècle:
         Academies de filles et courtières d'amours, maisons
         clandestines, matrones, mères-abbesses, appareilleuses
         et proxénètes. Rapports de police, documents, secrets,
         notes personneles des tenancières. Paris: H. Daragon,
         1903.

06601.   _____. Les petites maisons galantes de Paris au
         XVIIIe siecle; folies maisons de plaisance et vide-
         bouteilles d'après des documents inédits et des rapports
         de police. Preface by R. Yve-Plesis. Paris: H. Daragon,
         1902.

06602. Depauw, Jacques. Amour illégitime et société à Nantes
        au 18e siecle. Paris: Hachette, 1973.

06603. Depauw, Jacques. "Illicit sexual activity and society in
        18th century Nantes." In Family and Society, edited by
        Robert Forster and Orest Ranum, pp. 145-191. Baltimore:
        Johns Hopkins, 1967. Also in Annales: économies, sociétés,
        civilisations 27 (July-September 1972): 1155-1182.

06604. Fleischmann, Hector. Le dix-huitième siècle galant et
        libertin. Recueil de documents curieux et rares sur
        l'amour et les femmes galantes au XVIIIe siècle.
        Paris: A. Michel, 1913?

06605. Herold, J. C. Love in Five Temperaments. New York:
        Atheneum, 1961.

06606. Hervez, Jean. La galanterie parisienne sous Louis
        Louis XV et Louis XVI. Vol 3 Les chroniques du
        XVIIIe siècle. Paris: Bibliothèque des curieux,
        1910.

06607. _____. Maisons d'amour et filles de joie. Vol. 6.
        Les chroniques du XVIIIe siècle. Paris: Bibliothèque
        des Curieux, 1911.

06608. _____. La Régence galante. Vol. 4. Les Chroniques
        du XVIIIe siècle. Paris: Bibliothèque des Curieux, 1909.

06609. Jones, Colin. "Prostitution and the Ruling Class in 18th-
        Century Montpellier." History Workshop 6 (Autumn 1978):
        7-28.

06610. Sade, Marquis de. "La Philosophie dans le boudoir." In
        The Marquis de Sade: An Essay by Simone de Beauvoir,
        edited by Paul Dinnage, pp. 122-167. New York: Grove
        Press, 1953.

        Also refer to #5674.

f) Health/Medical

06611. Chamoux, Antoinette and Dauphin, Cécile. "La contraception
        avant la Révolution française: l'exemple de Chatillon-
        sur-Seine." Annales: économies, sociétés, civilisations
        24 (May-June 1969): 662-684.

06612. Gelis, Jacques. "L'accouchement au XVIIIe siècle: Pratiques
        traditionnelles et contrôle médical." Ethnologie Fran-
        caise 6 (1976): 325-340.

06613. Greenbaum, Louis S. "Nurses and Doctors in Conflict: Piety and Medicine in the Paris Hôtel-Dieu on the Eve of the French Revolution." Clio Medica 13 (1977): 247-267.

06614. Pirami, Edmea. "An 18th Century Woman Physician." World Medical Journal 12 (1965): 154-155.

Also refer to #5676-5679.

6. CULTURAL

"A Woman of wit is the scourge of her husband, her children, her friends, her servants, of everybody."
                                                    Rousseau

a) Education

(1) Non-specific

06615. Bloch, Jean H. "Women and the Reform of the Nation." In Woman and Society in Eighteenth-Century France, edited by Eva Jacobs, et. al., pp. 3-18. London: Athlone Press, 1979.

06616. Laclos, Pierre Ambroise François Cholderlos de. De l'éducation des femmes. Paris: A. Messein, 1903.

06617. Mali, Millicent S. Madame Campan: Educator of Women, Confidante of Queens. Washington, D.C.: University Press of America, 1978.

06618. Mylne, Vivienne. "The Bibliothèque universelle des dames (1785-1797)." In Woman and Society in Eighteenth-Century France, edited by Eva Jacobs, et. al., pp. 123-136. London: Athlone Press, 1979.

06619. Perrel, Jean. "Les écoles de filles dans la France d'Ancien Regime." In The Making of Frenchmen: Current Directions in the History of Education in France, edited by Donald N. Baker and Patrick J. Harrigan, pp. 75-83. Waterloo, Ontario, Canada: Historical Reflections Press, 1980.

06620. Roche, Daniel. "Education et société dans la France du XVIII siècle: l'exemple de la maison royale de Saint-Cyr." Cahiers d'histoire 23 (1978): 3-24.

06621.   Stock, Phyllis H. "The Theory and Practice of Women's
         Education in Eighteenth Century France." Eighteenth-
         Century Life 2 (June 1976): 79-82.

06622.   Versini, L. Laclos et la tradition, essai sur les sources
         et la technique des Liaisons Dangereuses. Paris:
         Klincksieck, 1968.
              [See especially ch. 3, pp. 521-529.]

         Also refer to #5681-5683, 5689, 6684, 6695, 6709, 6724.

                     (2) Madame de Genlis

06623.   Bonhomme, Honoré. Madame la comtesse de Genlis, sa vie,
         son oeuvre, sa mort. Paris: Librairie des biblio-
         philes, 1885.

06624.   Genlis, Stephanie Félicité Ducrest de Saint Aubin,
         comtesse de, afterwards marquise de Sullery. Adelaide
         and Theodora, or Letters on Education. 3rd ed. 1788.
         Reprint. New Haven, Conn.: Research Publications, 1975.

06625.   _____ . De l'influence des femmes dur la littéra-
         ture française comme protectrices des lettres et comme
         auteurs. Paris: Maradan, 1811.

06626.   _____ . Le mari corrupteux suivi de la femme phi-
         losophe, nouvelles. Paris: Maradan, 1803.

06627.   Harmand, Jean. Madame de Genlis. Paris: Perrin et c^{ie},
         1912.

06628.   Raaphorst, Madeleine Rousseau. "Adèle versus Sophie: The
         Well-Educated Woman of Mme. de Genlis." Rice University
         Studies 64 (Winter 1978): 41-50.

06629.   Walker, T. C. "Madame de Genlis and Rousseau." Romanic
         Review 43 (April 1952): 95-108.

                     b) Literature

                     (1) Non-specific

06630.   Bailet, Dietlinde Sigrid. "Séduite ou Séductrice. Image
         litteraire de la femme au xviii siècle." Atlantis 4
         (Spring 1979): 78-90.

06631.   Berkowe, Christiane. "Louis-Sébastien Mercier et les
          femmes." Romanic Review 55 (February 1964): 16-29.

06632.   Lough, John. "Women in Mercier's Tableau de Paris." In
          Woman and Society in Eighteenth-Century France, edited by
          Eva Jacobs, et. al., pp. 110-122. London: Athlone Press,
          1979.

06633.   Zylawy, Roman. "Prévost, Woman and the Ethic of Sensualism."
          Selecta 1 (1980): 37-41.

                         (2)   Drama

06634.   Brady, Valentini Papadopoulou. Love in the Theatre of
          Marivaux. Geneva: Droz, 1970.

06635.   Mason, H. T. "Women in Marivaux: Journalist to Dramatist."
          In Woman and Society in Eighteenth Century France, edited
          by Eva Jacobs, et. al., pp. 42-54. London: Athlone
          Press, 1979.

06636.   Olah, Lillian. Une grande dame auteur dramatique et
          poete au XVIIIe siècle, Madame de Montesson. Paris:
          Champion, 1928.

                         (3)   Prose

                    (a)   Women in Novels

06637.   Duckworth, Colin. "D'Antraigues's Feminism: Where Fact and
          Fantasy Meet." In Woman and Society in Eighteenth-Century
          France, edited by Eva Jacobs, et. al., pp. 166-182. London:
          Athlone Press, 1979.

06638.   Hall, P. M. "Duclos's Histoire de Madame de Luz: Woman and
          History." In Woman and Society in Eighteenth-Century
          France, edited by Eva Jacobs, et. al., pp. 139-151. London:
          Athlone Press, 1979.

06639.   Swiderski, Marie Laure. "La condition de la femme
          française au XVIIIe siècle d'après les romans." In
          Woman in the 18th Century and Other Essays, edited by
          Paul Fritz and Richard Morton, pp. 105-125. Toronto:
          A.M. Hakkert, Ltd., 1976.

(b) Novelists

06640. Bishop, Morris. "The Liberation of Mme. de Tencin."
        Horizon 13 (Summer 1971): 54-56.

06641. Crosby, Emily. Une Romancière oubliée: Madame Riccobini,
        sa vie, ses oeuvres, sa place dans la littérature
        anglaise et francaise du XVIIIe siècle. 1924. Reprint.
        Geneva: Slatkine Reprints, 1970.

06642. Godet, Philippe Ernest. Madame de Charrière et ses amis,
        1740-1805. Lausanne: Editions Spes, 1927.

06643. Jones, Shirley. "Madame de Tencin: an Eighteenth Century
        Woman Novelist." In Woman and Society in Eighteenth-
        Century France, edited by Eva Jacobs, et. al., pp. 207-
        217, London: Athlone Press, 1979.

06644. Rosbottom, Ronald. "Parody and truth in Mme. Riccoboni's
        Continuation of La Vie de Marianne." Studies in Voltaire
        and the Eighteenth Century 81 (1971): 163-175.

06645. Scott, Geoffrey. The Portrait of Zélide. New York: Scrib-
        ner's, 1959.

c) Literary Salons

(1) Non-specific

06646. Aldis, Janet. Madame Geoffrin, Her Salon and Her Times.
        New York: G. P. Putnam Sons, 1905.

06647. Du Sault, Jean. "La comtesse d'Angiviller." La nouvelle
        revue des deux mondes (November 1976): 381-390.

06648. Fischer, Carlos. Les salons. 2 vols. Paris: Seheur, 1929.

06649. Gay, Sophia. "El Salon de la Senorita Contat." España
        moderna 5 (March 1893): 123-148.

06650. Glotz, Margeurite and Madeleine, Marie. Salons du 18e
        siècle. Paris: Nouvelles Editions Latines, 1949.

06651. Gooch, G. P. "Four French Salons: I. Mme. Geoffrin."
        Contemporary Review 180 (June 1951): 345-353.

06652.   Gooch, G. P.   "Four French Salons: V. Mme. Necker."
Contemporary Review 180 (October 1951): 223-233.

06653   Hall, Evelyn Beatrice. The Women of the Salons. 1926.
Reprint. Freeport, N.Y.: Books for Libraries Press, 1979.

06654.   Hamel, Frank. Famous French Salons. New York: Brentano's,
1909.

06655.   Mason, Amelia Gere. The Women of the French Salons. New
York: Century Co., 1891.

06656.   Tallenture, S. G. The Women of the Salons. New York:
G. P. Putnam's Sons, 1926.

Also refer to #6271, 6359.

(2) Individuals

(a) Marie Anne Deffand

06657.   Gooch, G. P. "Four French Salons: II. Mme. Du Deffand."
Contemporary Review 180 (July 1951): 26-33.

06658.   _____. "Four French Salons: IV. Mme. du Deffand and
Horace Walpole." Contemporary Review 180 (September 1951):
148-157.

06659.   Seznec, Jean. "Madame du Deffand Loves Horace Walpole."
Listener 82 (1969): 825-826.

(b) Julie de Lespinasse

06660.   Bouissounouse, Janine. Julie, the life of Madamoiselle
de Lespinasse: her salon, her Friends, her loves.
Translated by Pierre de Fontnourelle. New York:
Appleton Century Crofts, 1962.

06661.   Gooch, G. P. "Four French Salons: III. Julie de Lespinasse." Contemporary Review 180 (August 1951): 93-100.

06662.   Mitchiner, Margaret. A Muse in Love. Julie de Lespinasse. London: Bodley Head, 1962.

06663.   Royde-Smith, Naomi. The Double Heart. A Study of Julie
de Lespinasse. London: Hamish Hamilton, 1931.

06664. Segur, Pierre. _Julie de Lespinasse_. London: Chatto &
        Windus, 1907.

d) Intellectuals/Philosophers

(1) Enlightenment Thought

06665. Brumfitt, J. H. "Cleopatra's Nose and Enlightenment
        Historiography." In _Woman and Society in Eighteenth-
        Century France_, edited by Eva Jacobs, et. al., pp.
        183-194. London: Athlone Press, 1979.

06666. Charbonnel, P. "Repères pour une étude du statut de la
        femme dans quelque écrits théoriques des 'philosophes.'"
        Etudes sur le XVIIIe siècle 3 (1976): 93-110.

06667. Clinton, Katherine B. "Femme et philosophe: Enlightenment
        Origins of Feminism." _Eighteenth Century Studies_ 8 (Spring
        1975): 283-299.

06668. Dupont-Chatelain, Marguerite. _Les Encyclopedistes et les
        femmes_. Geneva: Slatkine, 1970.

06669. Gardner, Elizabeth J. "The _Philosophes_ and Women:
        Sensationalism and Sentiment." In _Woman and Society in
        Eighteenth Century France_, pp. 19-27. London: Athlone
        Press, 1979.

06670. Hoffman, Paul. _La Femme dans la pensée des lumières_.
        Paris: Editions Ophrys, 1977.

(2) Individuals

(a) The Marquise du Chatelet

06671. Barber, W. H. "Mme. du Châtelet and Leibnizianism: The
        Genesis of the _Institutions de Physique_." In _The Age of
        Enlightenment: Studies Presented to Theodore Besterman_,
        pp. 200-222. London: Oliver and Boyd, 1967.

06672. Bertaut, Jules. "La grossesse de Mme du Châtelet."
        Historia 381 (August 1978): 94-101.

06673. Capefigue, Jean Baptiste Honoré Raymond. <u>La marquise Du</u>
        <u>Châtelet</u> <u>et les amies des philosophes du XVIII siecle</u>.
        Geneva: Slatkine Reprints, 1970.

06674. Edwards, Samuel. <u>The Divine Mistress</u>. London: Cassell,
        1971.

06675. Gerson, Noel Bertram. <u>The Divine Mistress</u>. New York:
        D. McKay, 1970.

06676. Hamel, Frank. <u>An Eighteenth Century Marquise; a Study</u>
        <u>of Emilie du Châtelet and her Times</u>. New York: J. Pott
        and Co., 1911.

06677. Iltis, Carolyn Merchant. "Madame du Châtelet's Metaphysics
        and Mechanics." <u>Studies in History and Philosophy of</u>
        <u>Science</u> 8 (1977): 29-48.

06678. Maurel, André. <u>The Romance of Madame du Châtelet and</u>
        <u>Voltaire</u>. London: Hutchinson, 1930.

06679. Philips, Edith. "Madame du Châtelet, Voltaire and Plato."
        <u>Romanic Review</u> 33 (October 1942): 250-263.

06680. Taton, René. "Madame du Châtelet, tradutrice de Newton."
        <u>Archives internationales d'histoire des sciences</u> 22
        (July-December 1969): 185-210.

06681. Wade, Ira. "Madame du Chatelet and Voltaire." In <u>The</u>
        <u>Intellectual Development of Voltaire</u>, pp. 265-291.
        Princeton, N.J.: Princeton University Press, 1969.

06682. _____. <u>Voltaire and Madame du Chatelet</u>. Princeton,
        N.J.: Princeton University Press, 1941.

                        (b) Diderot

06683. Bongie, Laurence L. <u>Diderot's femme savante</u>. Studies on
        Voltaire and the Eighteenth Century, vol. 166. Oxford:
        The Voltaire Foundation, 1977.

06684. Jacobs, Eva. "Diderot and the Education of Girls." In
        <u>Woman and Society in Eighteenth-Century France</u>, edited
        by Eva Jacobs, et. al., pp. 83-95. London: Athlone
        Press, 1979.

06685. May, Georges. "Une certaine Madame Madin." In <u>Literature</u>
        <u>and History in the Age of Ideas: Essays on the French</u>
        <u>Enlightenment Presented to George Remington Havens</u>,
        edited by Charles Garfield Singer Williams, pp. 255-271.
        Columbus, Ohio: Ohio State University Press, 1975.

06686.   Niklaus, Robert. "Diderot and Women." In Woman and
         Society in Eighteenth-Century France, edited by Eva
         Jacobs, et. al., pp. 69-82. London: Athlone Press,
         1979.

06687.   Wilson, Arthur M. "'Treated like Imbecile Children'
         (Diderot): The Enlightenment and the Status of Women."
         In Woman in the Eighteenth Century and Other Essays,
         edited by Paul Fritz and Richard Morton, pp. 89-104.
         Toronto: A. M. Hakkert, 1976.

(c) Montesquieu

06688.   Geffriaud Rosso, Jeannette. Montesquieu et la feminite.
         Paris: Nizet, 1977.

06689.   Magné, B. "Une Source de la Lettre persane xxxviii?"
         Revue d'histoire littéraire de la France 68 (1968): 407-414.

06690.   Mason, Sheila. "The Riddle of Roxane." In Woman and
         Society in Eighteenth Century France, edited by Eva
         Jacobs, et. al., pp. 28-41. London: Athlone Press,
         1979.

06691.   Oake, Roger B. "Polygamy and the Lettres persanes."
         Romanic Review 32 (February 1941): 56-62.

06692.   O'Reilly, Robert F. "Montesquieu: Anti-Feminist." Studies
         on Voltaire and the Eighteenth Century 102 (1973):
         143-156.

06693.   Rosso, Jeannette Geffriaud. Montesquieu et la feminité.
         Pisa: Liberia Goliardica Editrice, 1977.

06694.   Shackleton, Robert. "Madame de Montesquieu, with some
         Considerations on Thérèse de Secondat." In Woman and
         Society in Eighteenth-Century France, edited by Eva
         Jacobs, et. al., pp. 229-242. London: Athlone Press,
         1979.

(d) Rousseau

06695.   Bloch, Jean H. "Rosseau's reputation as an authority on
         child care and physical education in France before the
         Revolution." Paedagogica Historica 14 (1974): 5-33.

06696. Brooks, Richard A. "Rosseau's Antifeminism in the Lettre
        a d'Alembert and Emile." In Literature and History in
        the Age of Ideas: Essays on the French Enlightenment
        Presented to George R[emington] Havens, edited by Charles
        G[arfield] S[inger] Williams, pp. 209-227. Columbus:
        Ohio State University Press, 1975.

06697. Fontenay, Elisabeth de. "Pour Emile et par Emile, Sophie
        ou l'invention du Ménage." Temps Modernes 358 (May
        1976): 1774-1795.

06698. Graham, Ruth. "Rosseau's Sexism Revolutionized." In
        Woman in the 18th Century and Other Essays, edited by
        Paul Fritz and Richard Morton, pp. 127-139. Toronto:
        A.M. Hakkert, Ltd., 1976.

06699. Gribble, Francis Henry. Rosseau and the Women he
        Loved. New York: Scribner's Sons, 1908.

06700. Gutwirth, Madelyn. "Mme de Staël, Rosseau and the Woman
        Question." Proceedings of the Modern Language Associa-
        tion 86 (January 1971): 100-109.

06701. Jimack, P. D. "The Paradox of Sophie and Julie: Contempo-
        rary Response to Rousseau's Ideal Wife and Ideal Mother."
        In Woman and Society in Eighteenth-Century France,
        edited by Eva Jacobs, et. al., pp. 152-165. London:
        Athlone Press, 1979.

06702. Miller, Nancy I. "Female Sexuality and Narrative Structure
        in La Nouvelle Héloïse and Les Liasons dangereuses."
        Signs 1 (Spring 1967): 609-638.

06703. Okin, Susan Moller. "Rousseau's Natural Woman." Journal
        of Politics 41 (May 1979): 393-416.

06704. Rapaport, Elizabeth. "On the Future of Love: Rousseau
        and the Radical Feminists." In Woman and Philosophy:
        Toward a Theory of Liberation, edited by Carol Gould and
        Marx Wartofsky, pp. 185-205. New York: Putnam's, 1976.

06705. Tanner, Tony. "Julie and 'La Maison Paternelle': another
        look at Rousseau's La nouvelle Heloise." Daedalus
        (Winter 1976): 23-46.

06706. Wexler, Victor G. "Made for Man's Delight: Rousseau as
        an Antifeminist." American Historical Review 82 (April
        1976): 266-291.

        Also refer to #6627, 6628.

(e) Voltaire

[1] CONTEMPORARY

06707. Voltaire, François Marie Arouet de. "Les anciens et les
modernes ou la toilette de Madame de Pompadour."
In Dialogues et anecdotes philosophiques, edited by
Raymond Naves, pp. 152-160. Paris: Editions Garnier
Frères, 1955.

06708. _____. "Dialogue entre Mme de Maintenon et Mlle de
Lenclos." In Dialogues et anecdotes philosophiques,
edited by Raymond Naves, pp. 13-17. Paris: Editions
Garnier Frères, 1955.

06709. _____. "L'éducation des filles." In Dialogues et
anecdotes philosophiques, edited by Raymond Naves,
pp. 109-111. Paris: Editions Garnier Freres, 1955.

06710. _____. "Femmes, soyez soumises à vos maris." In
Dialogues et anecdotes philosophiques, edited by Raymond
Naves, pp. 213-216. Paris: Editions Garnier Frères,
1955.

06711. _____. "Maladie, Médecine (La princesse et le médecin)."
In Dialogues et anecdotes philosophiques, edited by
Raymond Naves, pp. 365-368. Paris: Editions Garnier
Freres, 1955.

[2] SECONDARY

06712. Duisit, Lionel. "Madame du Deffand et Voltaire: Le Mythe
du progrès et la décadence du goût." French Review
36 (1963): 284-292.

06713. Raaphorst, Madeleine Rousseau. "Voltaire et féminisme.
un examen du théâtre et des contes." Studies on Voltaire
and the Eighteenth Century 89 (1972): 1325-1335.

06714. Stern, Jean. Voltaire et sa nièce, Madame Denis. Paris:
Palatine, 1957.

06715. Waddicor, Mark. "Voltaire and Ninon de Lenclos." In
Woman and Society in Eighteenth-Century France, edited
by Eva Jacobs, et. al., pp. 197-206. London: Athlone
Press, 1979.

(3)   Others

06716.   Brahimi, D.   "Restif Feminist?"   Etudes sur le XVIIIe
         siècle 3 (1976):   77-91.

06717.   Briggs, E. R.   "Marie Huber and the Campaign against
         Eternal Hell Torment."   In Woman and Society in
         Eighteenth-Century France, edited by Eva Jacobs, et.
         al.,   pp. 218-228.   London: Athlone Press, 1979.

06718.   Falvey, John.   "Women and Sexuality in the Thought of La
         Mettrie."   In Woman and Society in Eighteenth-Century
         France, edited by Eva Jacobs, et. al., pp. 55-68.
         London: Athlone Press, 1979.

06719.   Fletcher, Dennis.   "Restif de la Bretonne and Woman's
         Estate."   In Woman and Society in Eighteenth-Century
         France, edited by Eva Jacobs, et. al., pp. 96-109.
         London: Athlone Press, 1979.

06720.   Hartman, Lydia Claude.   "Esquisse d'un portrait de Sophie
         Volland.   Quelques note sur la vie privée, les amitiés
         du philosophes. Diderot Studies 16 (1973):   69-89.

06721.   Hine, Ellen McNiven.   "Madame de Lambert, Her Sources and
         Her Circle: On the Threshold of a New Age." Studies in
         Voltaire and the Eighteenth Century 102 (1973): 173-190.

06722.   Lescure, Mathurin Francois Adolphe de.   Les Femmes
         philosophes au dix-huitième siècle.   Paris: Dentu, 1881.

06723.   Metzger, Gustave A.   Marie Huber, (1695-1753), Sa vie,
         ses oeuvres, sa théologie.   Geneva: n.p., 1887.

06724.   Pellerin, Lyonel M.   Famille et education dans l'oeuvre
         utopique de Restif de la Bretonne, 1775-1782.   Nantes:
         Faculté de droit et des sciences politiques, 1975.

06725.   Schazmann, P. E.   La comtesse de Boufflers.   Paris: Roches,
         1933.

06726.   Schurmans, H.   "Dom Deschamps et la communaute des femmes."
         Etudes sur le XVIIIe siècle 3 (1976): 111-118.

e) Art

(1) Women in Art

06727. Duncan, Carol. "Happy Mothers and Other New Ideas in
French Art." The Art Bulletin 55 (December 1973):
570–583.

06728. Roberts, Warren E. Morality and Social Class in Eighteenth
Century French Literature and Painting. Buffalo: University of Toronto Press, 1974.

(2) Women Artists

(a) Actresses/Dancers

06729. Capon, Gaston and Yves-Plessis, Robert. Paris galant au
dix-huitième siècle; fille d'opera, vendeuse d'amour,
histoire de Mlle Deschamps. Paris: Plessis, 1906.

06730. Corsi, Mario. Adriana le Couvreur; una vita d'arte e di
passione. Milan: Ceschina, 1935.

06731. Dacier, Emile. Mlle. Sallé: Une Danseuse de l'Opera sous
Louis XV. Geneva: Minkoff, 1972.

06732. Deville, Alberic. Arnoldiana, ou Sophie Arnould et ses
contemporains, par l'auteur de Bievraine. Paris: Gerard,
1913.

06733. Goncourt, Edmond de. La Guimard. Paris: Flammarion, 1929.

06734. Goncourt, Edmond de. Mademoiselle Clarion. 1927. Reprint.
New York: Somerset Publications, 1972.

06735. _____ and Goncourt, Jules de. Madame Saint-
Huberty. 1900. Reprint. New York: Greenwood Press, 1969.

06736. _____. Sophie Arnould.
1857. Reprint. Geneva: Minkoff Reprints, 1973.

06737. Spink, J. S. "Mademoiselle Clarion à Ferney." Bulletin
des historiens du théâtre 3 (July–August 1935): 65–74.

06738. Vince, Stanley W. E. "Marie Salle, 1707–1756." Theatre
Notebook 12 (1957): 7–14.

Also refer to #6649.

(b)   Painters

06739.   Ananoff, Alexandre.   "Propos sur les peintures de Mar-
          guerite Girard." Gazette des Beaux Arts 121 (December
          1979):   211-218.

06740.   Nolhac, Pierre de.   Madame Vigée Le Brun, peintre de la
          reine Marie-Antoinette, 1755-1842.   Paris: Joyant, 1908.

06741.   Portalis, Baron Roger.   "Adelaide Labille-Guiard." Gazette
          de Beaux Arts 43 (1901): 353-367 and 477-494; 44 (1902):
          100-118 and 325-347.

D. THE GERMANIES

1. SURVEYS

"Women have a strong inborn feeling for all that is
beautiful, elegant, and decorated. Even in childhood
they like to be dressed up, and take pleasure when they
are adorned." Immanuel Kant, Observations on the
Feeling of the Beautiful and Sublime

06742.   Biedermann, Karl.   Deutschland im 18. Jahrhundert.
          Deutschlands politische, materielle und soziale Zustande
          im 18. Jahrhundert. vol. 1. Leipzig: Weber, 1854.

06743.   _____. Deutschland im 18. Jahrhundert.
          Deutschlands sittliche und gesellige Zustande im 18.
          Jahrhundert. Vol. 2. Leipzig: Weber, 1858.

06744.   Mollat, G. Von Goethes Mutter zu Cosima Wagner 200
          Jahre deutsches Frauenleben. Stuttgart: Frommann,
          1936-1938.

06745.   Schreiber, S. Etta.   The German Woman in the Age of
          Enlightenment. New York: King's Crown Press, 1948.

2. POLITICAL

I was "without money, without credit, without an army,
without any experience or knowledge of my own and finally
without any kind of advice."   Maria Theresa

a) Legal

06746. Conrad, Hermann. "Die Rechtsstellung der Ehefrau in der
        Privatrechtsgesetzgebung der Aufklarungszeit." In Aus
        Mittelalter und Neuzeit: Gerhard Kallen zum 70. Geburt-
        stag, edited by Joseph Engel and Hans Martin Klinkenberg,
        pp. 253-270. Bonn: P. Hanstein, 1957.

06747. Petschauer, Peter. "Tradition and Enlightenment; Women's
        Legal Position in Southwest Germany." Enlightenment
        Essays 3 (Fall/Winter 1972): 160-168.

06748. Die vorzüglichen Rechte der deutschen Weibsbilder, als
        jungfern Braute, eheweiber, schwanger und gebahrend
        betrachtet. 1791. Reprint. Frankfurt a. M.: Metzner,
        1966.

        Also refer to #6828.

b) Feminism

06749. Hippel, Theodor Gottlieb von. On Improving the Status of
        Women. 1790. Translated by Timothy F. Sellner.
        Detroit: Wayne State University Press, 1979.

06750. Secci, Lia. "I trattati di Theodor Gottleib von Hippel
        sull emancipazione femminile." Nuova DWF (Donna, Woman,
        Femme) 1 (October-December 1976): 127-140.

c)　Political Roles

(1)　Women

06751.　Altenburg, Otto. Elisabeth Prinzessin von Braunschweig.
Eine ungekrönte preussische Konigin. Stettin: Sauniter,
1924.

06752.　Gerard, Frances. A Grand Duchess: The Life of Anna Amalia,
Duchess of Saxe-Weimar-Eisenach and the Classical Circle
of Weimar. New York: E. P. Dutton, 1902.

06753.　Hay, Marie. A German Pompadour; being the extraordinary
history of Wilhelmine von Gräve-Wirtemberg. New York:
C. Scribner's Sons, 1909.

06754.　Pauls, Eilhard Erich. Das Ende der galanten Zeit Gräfin Voss
am preussischen Hofe. Lübeck: Quitzow, 1924.

06755.　Poseck, Ernst. Die Kronprinzessin. Elisabeth Christine,
Gemahlin Friedrichs der Grosse, geb. Prinzessin von
Braunschweig-Bevern. Berlin: Steuben-Verlag, 1940.

06756.　Reck-Malleczewen, Fritz Percy. Sophie Dorothee, Mutter
Friedrichs des Grossen. Leipzig: Kaiser Verlag, 1941.

06757.　Wolf, Adam. Marie Christine, Erzherzogin von Österreich.
Vienna: G. Gerhold's sohn, 1863.

(2)　Individuals

(a)　Queen Louise

06758.　Aretz, Gertrude. Queen Louise of Prussia, 1776-1810.
Translated by Ruth Putnam. New York: Putnam, 1929.

06759.　Arnim, Hans von. Königin Luise. Berlin: Haude und
Spenersche Verlagsbuchhandlung, 1969.

06760.　Bailleu, Paul. Königin Luise. Berlin: Hafen Verlag, 1923.

06761.　Jagow, Kurt. Konigin Luise. Ein Lebensbild. Leipzig:
Verlag Phil. Reclam, 1934.

06762.　Moffat, Mary Maxwell. Queen Louisa of Prussia. New York:
E. P. Dutton and Co., 1907.

06763. Mundt, Klara Muller. _Louisa of Prussia and Her Times_.
        New York: McClure, 1868.

06764. Petersdorff, Herman von. _Königin Luise_. Bielefeld:
        Velhagen und Klasing, 1926.

06765. Rogge, D. Berhard. _Königin Luise._ Liegnitz: Verlag
        von Karl Seyfarth, 1910.

06766. Wright, Constance. _Beautiful Enemy: A Biography of Queen
        Louise of Prussia._ New York: Dodd, Mead and Co., 1969.

                    (b) Maria Theresa

06767. Arneth, Alfred von. _Geschichte Maria Theresias._ 10 vols.
        Vienna: Braumuller, 1863-1879.

06768. Corti, Egon Cesar, ed. _Maria Theresia. Ein Lebensbild in
        Anekdoten._ Berlin: Haude und Spener, 1969.

06769. Crankshaw, Edward. _Maria Theresa._ New York: Viking Press,
        1969.

06780. Franchi, Anna. _Maria Teresa d'Austria._ Milan: Ceschina,
        1934.

06781. Glatzer, J. _Die grossen Herrscherinnen-Maria Theresia._
        Quellenhefte zum Frauenleben in der Geschichte, edited
        by Emmy Beckman and Irma Stoss, vol. 2. Berlin: F. A.
        Herbig, 1927-1933.

06782. Gooch, G. P. _Maria Theresa and Other Studies._ New York:
        Longmans, Green and Company, 1951.

06783. Guglia, Eugen. _Maria Theresia._ Munich: R. Oldenbourg,
        1917.

06784. Holzmair, Eduard. "Maria Theresia als Tragerin 'mann-
        licher' Titel." _Mitteilungen des Instituts für öster-
        reichische Geschichtsforschung_ 72 (1964): 122-134.

06785. Krück von Poturzyn, Maria Josepha. _Maria Theresia, Frau
        und Königin._ Hamburg: Hoffman and Campe, 1936.

06786. Lafue, Pierre. _Marie-Thérèse, impératrice et reine,
        1717-1780._ Paris: Flammarion, 1956.

06787. Macartney, Carlile Aylmer. _Maria Theresa and the House
        of Austria._ London: English University Press, 1970.

06788. McGill, William J., Jr. _Maria Theresa._ New York:
        Twayne, 1972.

06789.   Pick, Robert.   Empress Maria Theresa: The Earlier Years
          1717-1757.   New York: Harper and Row, 1966.

06790.   Reinhold, Peter.   Maria Theresa.   Wiesbaden: Insel-Verlag,
          1957.

06791.   Roider, Karl A., Jr.   Maria Theresa.   Englewood, N.J.:
          Prentice-Hall, 1973.

06792.   Tapié, Victor L.   "Le Legs de Marie-Theresa."   Revue
          d'histoire diplomatique 88 (January-June 1974): 5-20.

06793.   Tschuppik, Karl.   Maria Theresia.   Amsterdam: DeLange, 1935.

          Also refer to #6461.

(c) Sophie Dorothea

06794.   Jordan, Ruth.   Sophie Dorothea.   New York: Braziller, 1972.

06795.   Morand, Paul.   The Captive Princess. Sophia Dorothea of
          Celle.   Translated by Anne-Marie Geoghegan.   New York:
          American Heritage Press, 1972.

06796.   Wilkins, W. H.   The Love of an Uncrowned Queen, Sophia
          Dorothea, Consort of George I.   2 vols.   Chicago:
          S. Stone and Co., 1900.

(d) Wilhelmina of Bayreuth

06797.   Gervais, Otto.   Frauen um Friedrich den Grossen.   Versuch
          einer Deutung des Liebeslebens Friedrichs II.   Graz:
          Deutsche Vereins-Druckerei, 1933.

06798.   Thiel, Heinrich.   Wilhelmine von Bayreuth.   Die Lieblings-
          schwester Friedrichs des Grossen.   Munich: Suddeutscher
          Verlag, 1967.

06799.   Volz, Gustav Berthold.   "Die Markräfin Wilhelmine von
          Bayreuth und ihre Denkwürdigkeiten."   Forschungen zur
          brandenburgischen und preussischen Geschichte 36
          (1924): 164-175.

06800.   Wright, Constance.   A Royal Affinity: The Lives of
          Frederick the Great and Wilhelmina of Bayreuth.
          London: Frederick Muller Ltd., 1967.

3. ECONOMIC

"The vast majority of the proletariat who worked with
machines were women and children."   Kuczynski

06801. Frühsorge, Gotthardt. "Die Einheit aller Geschafte
Tradition und Veranderung des 'Hausmutter'-Bildes in der
deutschen Ökonomieliteratur des 18. Jahrhunderts."
Wolfenbütteler Studien zur Aufklarung 3 (1976): 137-157.

06802. Kuczynski, Jurgen. The Rise of the Working Class. Translated by C.T.A. Ray. London: Weidenfeld and Nicolson,
1967.

4. RELIGION

"The number of ecclesiastical establishments has risen to
an extravagant height. [These people] are the most
dangerous and useless subjects in every state."
Joseph II

06803. Domarus, Max Äbtissin Eva Theresia von Schönborn und das
Adelige Damenstift zur Heiligen Anna in Würzburg.
Würzburg: Kommissionsverlag Ferdinand Schöningh, 1964.

06804. Novak, Norbert. "Die Wahl der Äbtissin Maria Antonia von
Platz im Jahre 1711 in St. Georgen am Langsee. Juris-
diktions- und Präzendenzschwierigkeiten zwischen Staat
und Kirche." Carinthia I, 162 (1972): 375-396.

5. SOCIAL

"I have lost everything. The wife I worshipped, the
object of all my love, is no more."   Joseph II

a) Generic

06805. Engelsing, Rolf. "Dienstbotenlektüre im 18. und 19.
Jahrhundert in Deutschland." International Review of
Social History 13 (1968): 384-429.

06806. Kuczynski, Jürgen. Geschichte des Alltags des deutschen
Volkes. Vol. 2. Cologne: Pahl Rugenstein Verlag, 1980.

06807. Nikisch, Reinhard M. G. "Die Frau als Briefschreiberin im
Zeitalter der deutschen Aufklarung." Wolfenbütteler
Studien zur Aufklarung 3 (1976): 29-65.

06808. Phayer, Fintan Michael. Religion und das Gewöhnliche Volk
in Bayern in der Zeit von 1750-1850. Miscellanea Bavarica
Monacensia, no. 21. Munich: Stadtarchiv München, 1970.

06809. Schultz, Alwin. Das Alltagsleben einer deutschen Frau zu
Anfang des achtzehnten Jahrhunderts . Leipzig: S.
Hirzel, 1890.

06810. Seeger, Lothar Georg. The "Unwed Mother" as a Symbol of
Social Consciousness in the Writings of J. G. Schlosser,
Justus Moser and J. H. Pestalozzi. Berne: Herbert Land
and Company, Ltd., 1970.

b) Demography

06811. François, Etienne. "La mortalité urbaine en Allemagne à
XVIIIe siècle." Annales de démographie historique
(1978): 135-165.

06812. _____. "La population de Coblence au XVIIIe
siècle: déficit démographique et immigration dans une
ville de résidence." Annales de démographie historique
(1975): 291-341.

06813. Gebauer, Curt. "Quellenstudien zur Geschichte der
bürgerlichen Reform der Gesellschaft in Deutschland während
des 18. Jahrhunderts." Archiv für Kulturgeschichte 25
(1935): 61-86.

06814. Knodel, John. "Natural Fertility in Pre-Industrial
Germany." Population Studies 32 (November 1978): 481-510.

06815.   Knodel, John and DeVos, Susan. "Preferences for the sex of
         Offspring and Demographic Behavior in Eighteenth and
         Nineteenth-Century Germany: An Examination of Evidence
         from Village Genealogies." Journal of Family History 5
         (Summer 1980): 145-166.

06816.   _____ and Wilson, C. "The Secular Increase of
         Fecundity in German village Populations: An analysis of
         Reproductive Histories of Couples married 1750-1889."
         Population Studies 35 (March 1981): 53-84.

06817.   Lee, W. R. "Bastardy and the Socioeconomic Structure of
         South Germany." Journal of Interdisciplinary History 7
         (Winter 1977): 403-425; 8 (Winter 1978): 471-476. Also
         in Marriage and Fertility, edited by Robert I. Rotberg
         and Theodore K. Rabb, pp. 121-143, 157-162. Princeton,
         N.J.: Princeton University Press, 1980.

06818.   _____. Population Growth, Economic Development, and
         Social Change in Bavaria 1750-1850. New York: Arno
         Press, 1977.

06819.   Shorter, Edward. "Bastardy in South Germany: A Comment."
         Journal of Interdisciplinary History 8 (Winter 1978):
         459-469. Also in Marriage and Fertility, edited by
         Robert I. Rotberg and Theodore K. Rabb, pp. 145-155.
         Princeton, N.J.: Princeton University Press, 1980.

         Also refer to #5841.

                      c) Family

                  (1) Non-specific

06820.   Berkner, Lutz K. "The Stem Family and the Developmental
         Cycle of a Peasant Household: An Eighteenth-Century
         Austrian Example." American Historical Review 77
         (April 1972): 398-418.

06821.   Moller, Helmut. Die kleinbürgerliche Familie im 18.
         Jahrhundert. Berlin: de Gruyter, 1969.

06822.   Schaub, Walter. "Städtische Familienformen in sozial-
         genealogischer Sicht (Oldenburg 1743/1870)." In
         Sozialgeschichte der Familie in der Neuzeit Europas,
         edited by Werner Conze, pp. 292-345. Stuttgart: Ernst
         Klett Verlag, 1976.

(2)   Childhood

06823.   Peller, Sigismund. "Zur Kenntnis der städtischen Mortalität
         im 18. Jahrhundert mit besonderer Berücksichtigung der
         Sauglings- und Tuberkulösesterbichkeit (Wien zur Zeit
         der ersten Volkszahlung)." Zeitschrift für Hygiene und
         Infectionskrankheiten 90 (1920): 227-262.

         Also refer to #6817, 6819.

d) Marriage

06824.   Dufour, Alfred. Le mariage dans l'école allemande du
         droit naturel moderne au XVIIIe siècle. Paris:
         Librairie générale de droit et de jurisprudence, 1972.

06825.   Herzer, Franz Xavier. Nachricht von Stiftungen zur Aus-
         sterung gut gesitterer und arbeitsamer Mädchen und
         wahrhafte Begebenheiten gut oder ubel gerathener Ehen
         zur Uberlegung für ganz reife Mädchen. 1792. Reprint.
         New Haven: Research Publications, Inc., 1975.

         Also refer to #6746, 6748.

e) Health/Medical

06826.   Becker, W. "Die erste Ärztin in Mitteldeutschland." Die
         Medizinische Welt 9 (4 March 1939): 307-308.

06827.   Runge, Hans. "Contemporary Reports on Germany's First
         Woman Physician, Dorothea Christ." Leporin von Qued-
         linburg." Münchener Medizinische Wochenschrift 87:51
         (20 December 1940): 1435.

06828.   Schubart-Fikentscher, Gertrud. Die Unehelischen-Frage
         in der Frühzeit der Aufklarung. Berlin: Akademie-Verlag,
         1967.

6. CULTURAL

". . . their young daughters . . . did not fail in their
few idle hours to strum old fashioned arias and sonatas
on a tuneless clavichord."
                    Eichendorff, on rural patrician society

a) *Education*

06829. Brandes, E. Betrachtungen über das weibliche Geschlecht
          und dessen Ausbildung in dem geselligen Leben. Hanover:
          Buchhandlung Gebrüder Hahn, 1802.

06830. Gebauer, Curt. "Studien zur Geschichte der bürgerlichen
          Sittenreform des 18. Jahrhunderts, Die Reform der
          häuslichen Erziehung." Archiv für Kulturgeschichte 20
          (1930): 36-51.

06831. Hermann, Ulrich. "Erziehung und Schulunterricht für
          Madchen im 18. Jahrhundert." Wolfenbütteler Studien
          zur Aufklärung 3 (1976): 101-135.

06832. Lurz, Georg. "Die bayerische Mittelschule seit der
          Übernahme durch die Klöster bis zur Sakularisation."
          Beiträge zur Geschichte der Erziehung und Unterrichts
          in Bayern. Mitteilungen der Gesellschaft für deutsche
          Erziehungs-und Schulgeschichte, Beiheft 6, 1905.

06833. Petschauer, Peter. "Improving Educational Opportunities
          for Girls in Eighteenth Century Germany." Eighteenth
          Century Life 3 (December 1976): 36-62.

06834. Raumer, Karl von. Geschichte der Pädagogik vom Wieder-
          aufblühen klassischer Studien bis auf unserer Zeit.
          Stuttgart: Verlag von Samuel Gottlieb Liesching, 1852.

06835. Rudolphie, Caroline. Gemälde weiblicher Erziehung. 2 vols.
          Heidelberg: Mohr und Zimmer, 1807.

06836. Schulz, Gunther. "Elise von der Recke, die Freundin
          Friedrich Nicolais." Wolfenbütteler Studien zur
          Aufklärung 3 (1976): 159-173.

06837. Steinhausen, Georg. "Das gelehrte Frauenzimmer. Ein
          Essai über das Frauenstudium in Deutschland zur Rococo
          und Zopfzeit." Nord und Süd 75 (1895): 46-55.

06838.   Stephan, G. Die häusliche Erziehung in Deutschland während
          des achtzehnten Jahrhunderts. Weisbaden: J.F. Bergmann,
          1891.

06839.   Winkler, Maria Theodolinde. Schulgeschichte von Altötting
          Festschrift zur Feier des zweihundertjährigen Jubiläums
          der Grundung des Englischen Instituts Atlötting 3. Mai
          1921. Fürstenfeldbruck: Buchdruckerei Albert Sighard,
          1921.

          Also refer to #5689, 6749.

b) Literature

(1) Non-specific

06840.   Bach, M. G. Wieland's Attitude toward women and her
          cultural and social relations. Columbia University
          Germanic Studies, vol. 5. New York: Columbia Univer-
          sity Press, 1922.

06841.   Bianquis, G. Love in Germany. New York: Humanities Press,
          1964.

06842.   Gleichen-Russwurm, Alexander von. Vom Zopf zur Romantik
          Beitrag zum Werdigang der modernen Frau. Bucherei der
          deutschen Frau, vol. 3. Berlin: Deutsche Frauen
          Verlag, 1916.

06843.   Haberland, Helga, ed., Frauen der Goethezeit in Briefen,
          Dokumenten und Bildern, von der Gottschedin bis zu
          Bettina von Arnim. Stuttgart: Reclam, 1960.

06844.   Hanstein, Adalbert von. Die Frauen in der Geschichte des
          deutschen Geisteslebens des 18. und 19. Jahrhunderts.
          Leipzig: Freund and Wittig, 1908.

06845.   Kluckhohn, Paul. Die Auffassung der Liebe in der Literatur
          des 18. Jahrhunderts und in der deutschen Romantik.
          3rd ed. Tübingen: Niemeyer, 1966.

06846.   Werner, Oscar Helmuth. The Unmarried Mother in German
          Literature. 1917. Reprint. New York: AMS Press, 1966.

          Also refer to #6629.

(2) Prose

06847. Beaujean, Marion. "Das Bild des Frauenzimmers im Roman des
        18. Jahrhunderts." Wolfenbütteler Studien zur Aufklarung
        3 (1976): 9-28.

06848. Waldeck, Marie-Luise. "The Princess in Torquato Tasso:
        Further Reflections on an Enigma." Oxford German
        Studies 5 (1970): 14-27.

c) Literary Salons

06849. Blaze de Bury, Ange Henri baron. Les salons de Vienne et
        de Berlin. Paris: Michel-Levy freres, 1861.

06850. Hargrave, Mary. Some German Women and Their Salons.
        London: T. W. Laurie, 1912.

06851. Hertz, Deborah. "Salonières and Literary Women in Late
        Eighteenth Century Berlin." New Germanic Critique 14
        (Spring 1978): 97-108; 139-141.

06852. Heuschele, Otto. Herzogin Anna Amalia Die Begrunderin des
        weimarischen Musenhofes. Munich: Munchener Verlag, 1947.

06853. Horvath, Eva. "Die Frau im gesellschaftlichen Leben
        Hamburgs: Meta Klopstock, Eva König, Elise Reimarus."
        Wolfenbütteler Studien zur Aufklärung 3 (1976): 175-194.

06854. Toelpe, Elisabeth. Die Frauen von Weimar. Quellenhefte
        zum Frauenleben in der Geschichte, edited by Emmy Beckmann
        and Irma Stoss, vol. 3. Berlin: F. A. Herbig, 1927.

d) Intellectuals

06855. Assing, Ludmilla. Sophie von La Roche, die Freundin
        Wieland's. Berlin: O. Janke, 1859.

06856. Bäumer, Gertrud. Frau Rath Goethe; die Mutter der Weis-
        heit. Tübingen: Rainer Wunderlich Verlag, 1949.

06857. Bodemann, Eduard. _Julie von Bondeli und ihr Freundeskreis._
        Hannover: Hahn, 1874.

06858. Lürssen, Johanna. _Die Frauen der Romantik._ Quellenhefte
        zum Frauenleben in der Geschichte, edited by Emmy Beck-
        mann and Irma Stoss, vol. 3. Berlin: F. A. Herbig, 1932.

06859. Olfers, Margarete von. _Elisabeth von Staegemann Lebens-_
        bild einer deutschen Frau 1761-1835. Leipzig: von Hase
        and Koehler Verlag, 1937.

06860. Olivier, J. J. and Norbert W. _Barbarina Campanini, eine_
        Geliebte Friedrichs des Grossen. Berlin: Marquart and
        Co., 1909.

e) Art

(1) Artists

(a) Actresses

06861. Gilder, Rosamond. "Carolina Neuber. Germany's Pioneer
        Actress-Manager." In _Enter the Actress The First_
        Women in the Theatre, pp. 202-226. Boston: Houghton
        Mifflin Company, 1931.

(b) Musicians

06862. Ullrich, Hermann, "Maria Theresia Paradis in London."
        Music and Letters 43 (1962): 16-24.

E. IBERIA

1. POLITICAL

"They do not like it here when women occupy themselves
with [political] affairs."
                    Madame de Maintenon about Princess Ursins

06863.   Armstrong, Edward. Elisabeth Farnese. London: Longmans,
          Green and Co., 1892.

06864.   Cermakian, Marianne. La princesse des Ursins; sa vie et
          ses lettres. Paris: Didier, 1969.

06865.   Cheke, Marcus. Carlota Joaquina, Queen of Portugal.
          Reprint. 1947. New York: Arno Press, 1969.

06866.   Combes, Francois. La princesse des Ursins. Paris: Didier
          et c^ie, 1858.

06867.   Danvila y Burguero, Alfonso. Fernando VI y Doña Barbara de
          Braganza. Madrid: J. Ratés Martín, 1905.

06868.   _____. Luisa Isabel de Orleans y Luis
          I. F. Fe, 1902.

06869.   Javierre Mur, Aurea. "Boda de la Infanta Maria Antonia
          de Borbon con Victor Amadeo, Duque de Saboya." Boletin
          de la Real Academia de la Historia Madrid 131 (July-
          September 1952): 181-245.

06870.   Oliveros de Castro, M.T. Maria Amalia de Sajonia,
          esposa de Carlos III. Madrid: Consejo superior de
          Investigacaiones cientificas, 1953.

06871   Pimodan, Claude Emmanuel Henri Marie. Louise-Elisabeth
          d'Orléans, reine d'Espagne (1709-1742). Paris:
          Libraire plon, 1923.

06872.   Taxonera, Luciano de. Isabela de Farnesio. Barcelona:
          Editorial Juventud, 1943.

2. SOCIAL

> "A Law of 1766 ordered that the prior consent of parents
> should be obtained before children could marry."
>   Altamira y Crevea

a) Demography

06873.   Bustelo García del Real, F. "Algunas reflexiones sobre la
          poblacion española de principios del siglo XVIII."
          Annales de Economia 15 (1972): 89-106.

06874.   Bustelo Garcia del Real, F. "La populacion española en la
         segunda mitad del siglo XVIII." Moneda y Credito 123
         (1972): 53-104.

06875.   _____. "El vecindario general de
         Espana de 1712-1717 ol censo de Campoflorido." Revista
         Internacional de Sociologia 7-8 (1973): 83-103.

06876.   Livi-Bacci, Massimo. "Fertility and Population Growth in
         Spain in the eighteenth and nineteenth centuries." In
         Population and Social Change, edited by D.V. Glass and
         Roger Reville, pp. 173-184. New York: Crane, Russak,
         1972. Also in Daedalus 97 (1968): 523-535.

06877.   Nadal, Jordi and Saez, Armand. "La fécondité à Saint Joan
         de Palamós (Catalogne) 1700 à 1859." Annales de démo-
         graphie historique (1972): 105-113.

                          b) Family

06878.   Sanz Samplayo, J.F. "Nuevas Aportaciones al Estudio de la
         Mortalidad Infantil a Fines des Antiguo Regimen: El
         Caso de Granada en el Seglo XVIII." In Actas del I
         Congresso de Historia de Andalucia, Andalucia moderna
         (sieglo XVIII), pp. 265-274. Cordoba: Caja de Ahorros y
         Monte de Piedad de Cordoba, II, 1978.

3. CULTURAL

         "In everything here there is somewhat of barbarism . . .
         One does not know what to talk about with the women,
         their Ignorance is incredible."
                                              Queen Amalie

06879.   Diaz de Escovar, Narciso. "Comediantes de otros siglos:
         María Antonia Fernández 'La Caramba.'" Boletin de la
         Real Academia de la Historia Madrid 96 (April-June
         1930): 774-784.

06880.   March, José Ma. "Los Duques de Alba, Marqueses de
         Villafranco, don José Alvarez de Toledo y doña Maria
         Teresa Cayetana, Señores del Palau." Boletin de la Real
         Academia de la Historia Madrid 149 (October-December 1961):
         153-243.

F. ITALY

1. POLITICAL

"On . . . rare occasions, when the Dogaressa was also
crowned, a second baretta was provided, but after . . .
1700 there was a twofold provision that the consort was
not again to receive this honor."
                            W. Carew Hazlett, The Venetian
                            Republic, 421-1797

a) Feminism

06881. Correnti, Santi. "Femminismo e antifeminismo nella Sicilia
        del Settecento." Nuovi quaderni del meridione 16 (April-
        June 1978): 171-214.

b) Political Roles

06882. Amadei, Amalia Borduia. Maria Carolina d'Austria e il
        Regno delle Due Sicilie. Naples: Cooperativa editrice,
        1934.

2. SOCIAL

"The cicisbo, or married lady's cavalier seemed to dominate
social life. He was her constant companion."
                            Jameson

a) Generic

06883. Andrieux, Maurice. Daily Life in Papal Rome in the
        Eighteenth Century. Translated by Mary Fitton.
        New York: Macmillan, 1969.

06884. Andrieux, Maurice. <u>Daily</u> <u>Life</u> <u>in</u> <u>Venice</u> <u>in</u> <u>the</u> <u>Time</u> <u>of</u>
        <u>Casanova</u>. Translated by Mary Fitton. New York: Praeger,
        1972.

        Also refer to #6505.

b) Demography

06885. Rousseau, Raymond. <u>La</u> <u>population</u> <u>de</u> <u>la</u> <u>Savoie</u> <u>jusqu'en</u>
        <u>1861</u>. <u>Nombre</u> d'habitants <u>pour</u> <u>chaque</u> <u>commune</u> <u>des</u> <u>deux</u>
        <u>actuels</u> <u>departements</u> <u>savoyards</u>, <u>du</u> <u>milieu</u> <u>du</u> <u>XVIII</u>e <u>au</u>
        <u>milieu</u> <u>du</u> <u>XIX</u>e <u>siecle</u>. Paris: S.E.V.P.E.N., 1960.

c) Family

06886. Borelli, Giorgio. "Nozze e doti i una famiglia nobiliare
        durante la prima metà del XVIII secolo." <u>Economia</u> <u>e</u>
        <u>Storia</u> 18 (1971): 321-342.

06887. Levi, Giovanni. "Terra e strutture familiari in una
        communita piedmontese del '700." <u>Quaderni</u> <u>storici</u> 33
        (September-December 1976): 1095-1121.

3. CULTURAL

        "<u>La</u> <u>Trona</u> (Caterina Giacobba Dolfin-Trono) was in her time
        the central figure of the . . . most brilliant society
        in Venice . . . and according to the descriptions of
        her . . . she must have been a highly fascinating woman."
                        W. Carew Hazlett, <u>The</u> <u>Venetian</u>
                        <u>Republic,</u> <u>421-1797</u>

a) Art

06888. Damerini, Gino. <u>La</u> <u>vita</u> <u>avventurosa</u> <u>di</u> <u>Caterina</u> <u>Dolfin</u>
        <u>Tron</u>. Milan: Mondadori, 1939.

06889. Hartcup, Adeline. Angelica: The Portrait of an Eighteenth-
        Century Artist. London: Heinemann, 1954.

06890. Manners, Victoria and Williamson, G. C. Angelica Kauffmann
        R.A.; Her Life and Her Works. 1924. Reprint. New
        York: Hacker, 1976.

G. THE LOW COUNTRIES

1. POLITICAL

Maria Theresa's "firm moderation, adherence to principles
of justice, and avoidance of affronts to Belgian prejudices
had permitted her to make some headway toward a centralized
monarchy."

Walter W. Davis

06891. Nabonne, Bernard. La reine Hortense. Paris: Bonne, 1951.

2. SOCIAL

"...in Holland the wives are so well versed in bar-
gaining, cyphering, and writing . . . they beat the
trade at home, and their words will pass in equal
credit [as their husbands'] . . ." James Howell
Epistolae Ho-Elianae, 1754

06892. Deprez, P., "The Demographic Development of Flanders in
        the Eighteenth Century." In Population in History, edited
        by David V. Glass and D.E.C. Eversley, pp. 608-630.
        Chicago: Aldine Pub. Co., 1965.

06893. Hasquin, Hervé. "La population de l'agglomération bruxel-
        laise au XVIIIe siècle." Etudes sur le XVIIIe siècle 4
        (1977): 13-26.

Also refer to #5889, 5890.

3.   CULTURAL

"Hannetaire's daughters not only attracted adoring crowds
to the theatre but incurred for their salon the jealousy
of other hostesses."

                                        Walter W. Davis

06894.   Shetter, Willaim Z.   "Noontime: Sara Burgerhart." In
         The Pillars of Society Six Centuries of Civilization in
         the Netherlands, pp. 129-138. The Hague: Martinus Nij-
         hoff, 1971.

Also refer to #6642, 6645.

SUBJECT INDEX

Abbesses, 1273, 6803-6804 (Also see Religious Orders).

Abduction, 3005.

Abigails, 1148.

Abortion, 364, 513, 1620-1623, 2697, 3209.

Actresses, 984, 1635, 2504, 4381, 4666, 5117-5118, 5379, 5416-5423, 5717, 5790, 6364, 6379, 6649, 6729-6738, 6861.

Adoption, 3548.

Adultery, 2040, 2426, 2557, 2746, 3373, 4028, 4254, 4764, 5794.

Albigensian (see Catharism).

Amazons, 1688-1698, 1822, 1977, 4380.

Amenorrhoea, 916.

Anapaptism, 4729.

Annulment (Also see Divorce), 2562.

Art-Women in (Also see Mariology), 970-983, 1213, 1357, 1360, 1465, 1489-1490, 1632-1634, 1977-1989, 2276, 2495-2503, 2965-2972, 3365-3366, 4065, 4770, 5111-5116, 5791, 5917, 6362-6363, 6727-6728.

Assumption, Order of the, 5579.

Authors (Also see Intellectuals), 5724-5725, 6173-6184, 6893.

Bas Bleu Society, 6349.

Bastardy (See Illegitimacy).

Begging, 6495.

Beghards/Beguines, 2717-2719, 2721, 3518, 3779-3781.

Bible, Women in, 384-431.

Bibliothèque Universelle des Dames, 6618.

Birth Control (Contraception), 364, 443-444, 447, 510, 512, 846-852, 1122, 1185-1186, 1341-1342, 1346, 2463, 2861, 3208, 3523, 3540, 3996, 4360, 5676, 5902, 6611.

Bluestockings, 6359-6361.

Book Collectors, 4639.

Booksellers, 924.

Breast Feeding, 5312, 5318.

Brideprice, 718.

Education, 932-941, 1129, 1193-1198,
  1349-1351, 1430-1437, 1491, 1626-
  1628, 1872-1873, 2871-2881, 3211-
  3212, 3601-3604, 4060-4063, 4361-
  4370, 4765, 4853-4858, 5061-5062,
  5160, 5163, 5174-5175, 5361-5363,
  5681-5706, 5846, 5892, 5913, 6164-
  6172, 6615-6628, 6684, 6695, 6709,
  6724, 6749, 6829-6839.

Eleusis, 1757, 1766, 1768.

Elopement, 6404.

Enlightenment, 6406, 6665-6726.

Exposure of children (See Infanticide).

Family, 323, 329-330, 380, 415-416,
  450, 591, 598, 614-709, 1076,
  1125-1148, 1240, 1241, 1243, 1300-
  1319, 1408-1416, 1458-1459, 1485-
  1488, 1595-1603, 1713, 1722, 1724,
  1805-1820, 2262, 2265, 2407-2421,
  2493, 2547, 2568, 2581, 2772,
  2793-2808, 2831, 2995, 3002, 3132,
  3170-3181, 3199, 3372, 3374,
  3548-3569, 3693, 3694, 3793-3796,
  3844, 3849, 3886-3891, 3908, 3911,
  3951, 3952-3961, 4317-4334, 4603,
  4609, 4613-4626, 4712, 4758-4760,
  5017, 5027-5047, 5170-5171, 5300,
  5314-5329, 5628, 5632, 5648-5664,
  5792, 5843, 5878, 5891, 5904-
  5905, 5909-5910, 6053, 6123-6137,
  6274, 6403-6404, 6494, 6496,
  6552-6577, 6724, 6820-6823, 6886-
  6887.

Fashion, 268, 816-845, 1164-1184,
  1614-1615, 1854-1856, 2333, 2337-
  2338, 2457-2461, 2856-2857, 3203-
  3205, 3597, 3599, 3806-3807, 4053-
  4054, 4353-4356, 4633, 5059-5060,
  5172-5173, 5352-5356, 5845, 5912,
  6154-6158.

Female Spectator, 6252-6255.

Female Tatler, 6256-6263.

Folklore, 1763.

Folk songs, 1358-1359.

Franciscans, 3922.

Free Spirit, Heresy of, 2716.

Fronde, Women in, 5443, 5457,
  5460-5462, 5479-5481, 5497-
  5500.

Gentleman's Magazine, 6264.

Gilbertine Order, 3107-3108.

Goddesses, 378, 1575-1584, 1770-
  1783, 3085-3087, 3470-3471,
  3723.

Guglielmites, 3941.

Guilds, Women in, 3722, 4961.

Gynaecology, 914, 1859, 3600,
  4359.

Gyneocratic Controversy, 4221-
  4230.

Hairstyles (See also Fashion),
  1174, 2459, 2461.

Heresy, 2710, 2715-2726, 3123,
  3518-3522, 3778-3781, 3940-
  3941.

Hermaphrodite, 1755.

Hetaera (See Prostitute).

Historians, 966.

Homicide (See Crimes).

Hysteria, 917.

Illegitimacy, 508, 702-703, 772,
  1142-1146, 1233, 1315, 1319,
  1415, 1417, 2990, 2993, 4330-
  4331, 5325, 5328, 5660-5661,
  5664, 5903, 6145, 6565, 6572-
  6574, 6595, 6817, 6819, 6828.

Industrialization, 642, 653.

Industry, Women in, 1265, 6054,
  6056.

NAME INDEX

Abelard, Peter, 2662, 3497-3514.

Acarie, Barbe, mystic, 4581, 4583.

Addison, Joseph, 6325

Adelaide of Savoy, duchess of Burgundy, 5470-5472.

Adelheid, 3711-3715.

Adorno, Caterina Fieschi, saint,
4971.

Aelfgifu, 3048.

Aelian, 1848.

Aeschines, 1717.

Aeschylus, 1914-1919.

Aethelflaed, 3045.

Agnes, saint, 2341-2342.

Agnes of Jesus, mother, 5581.

Agrippa von Nettescheim, Henry
Cornelius, 4750, 4755.

Agrippina, 2153-2162.

Alberti, Leon Battista, 5027, 5046.

Albret, Jeanne d', 4468-4476.

Alciphron, 1848.

Alcoforado, Marianna, 5855.

Alexander of Hales, 2861.

Alexis, Guillaume, 4303.

Amalia Elizabeth, countess of
Hessen, 5804.

Amalia of Solmes, wife of
Frederick Henry of Holland,
5885.

Amboise, Renée de Bussy d',
princess of Cambrai, 4446.

Ambrose, saint, 2316-2317.

Ames, Richard, 5401.

Amicitia, 2151.

Anaxagoras, 1909.

Andoins, Corisande d', countess
of Guiche, 4466.

Andreas Capellanus, 3674-3681

Andreini, Isabella, 5118.

Angelina de Grecia, 3868

AUTHOR INDEX

Abarbanel, Albert, 745.

Abbiateci, André, 5435.

Abbot, Willis J., 209.

Abbott, Frank F., 1992, 2035.

Abbott, Jacob, 3021.

Abel, Johann Joseph, 30.

Abel-Smith, B., 1187.

Abels, Richard, 3520.

Abensour, Léon, 299, 300, 6405.

Abrahams, Israel, 2752.

Abrams, Annie, 3076, 3129-3130.

Accati, Luisa, 5879.

Acheson, Arthur, 4392.

Ackerman, Emma M., 853.

Ackerman, Evelyn Bernette, 6524.

Acremont, Henri d', 5479.

Acworth, Evelyn, 31.

Adalberto de Baviera, Principe, 5795.

Adam, Antoine, 5753.

Adam, Paul, 4758.

Adams, Elsie, 32.

Adams, Henry, 1569, 2620

Adams, John B., 1133, 2414, 2415, 3175-3176.

Adburgham, Alison, 5410.

Adcock, F.E., 2466.

Adelman, Joseph, 210.

Adelstein, Michael E., 6218.

Adlard, George, 4094.

Adler, Rachel, 2027.

Aeschines, 1717.

Agapito y Revilla, Juan, 3857.

Agonito, Rosemary, 33.

Agresti, Guglielmo di, 4964.

Agrippa von Nettesheim, Henricus Cornelius, 4750

Ahrem, Maximilian, 1632.

Ananoff, Alexandre, 6739.

Ancelet-Hustache, Jeanne, 3724–3725.

Ancilli, Ermanno, 4965.

Andersen, Jorgen, 3365.

Anderson, Alan, 1078, 4258.

Anderson, Florence Mary, 1688.

Anderson, James, 4004, 5182–5183.

Anderson, Margaret, 945.

Anderson, Marjorie, 3022.

Anderson, Michael, 6071.

Anderson, Paul Bunyan, 6191, 6256–6257.

Anderson, Robert T., 624.

Andorka, R., 5904.

Andreas Capellanus, 3675.

Andrews, Allen, 5249.

Andrews, Marian, 4867–4868, 4934, 5135.

Andrieux, Maurice, 6883–6884.

Angel, J. Lawrence, 1589.

Anglo, Sydney, 516, 4031.

Angoulême, Marguerite d', 4516.

Angwin, Maria L., 855.

Ankarloo, Bengt, 318.

Annas, Julia, 1888.

Anson, John, 2653.

Anthony, Evelyn, 4144.

Antiphon, 1725.

Antoine, Thomas, 39.

Appleton, C., 2003.

Aquinas, Thomas, 2711.

Aragonnès, Claude, 5501, 5745.

Aranguren, Jose Luis L., 736.

Arbellot, G., 5627.

Archambault, Paul, 3497.

Arciniegas, German, 5112.

Arco, Ricardo del, 4863.

Ardiner, Shirley, 40.

Aretino, Pietro, 5073.

Aretz, Gertrude, 816, 1386, 6476, 6758.

Argenson, Marquis d', 6407.

Arici, Zelmira, 4550.

Aries, Philippe, 625–626, 691, 1281, 1341, 3208, 3540.

Aristotle, 1878–1879.

Arkell, Ruby L., 6025–6026.

Arkem, Hans, 3995.

Armaillé, Marie Célestine Amelie de Ségur, 4440.

Armengaud, Andre, 4603, 5444, 6408.

Armistead, M.G., 3858.

Armogathe, Daniel, 1245–1246.

Armour, Richard, 211.

Armstrong, C.A.J., 4614.

Armstrong, Edward, 6863.

Arnaud, Pierre, 6239.

Arnauld-Bouteloup, Jeanne, 6457.

Babcock, Charles L., 2082.

Babeau, Albert, 5174, 5605.

Babeau, Emile-Albert, 6449.

Babelon, J., 2083.

Babelon, Jean, 4561.

Babou, H., 5620.

Bach, M.G., 6840.

Bachi, Roberto, 1480.

Bachmann, Donna G., 990.

Bachofen, Johann Jacob, 1529, 2029.

Backer, Dorothy Anne, 5755.

Backscheider, Paula R., 3, 6272.

Bacon, Helen H., 1926.

Bacon, Janet, 1667.

Bacon, L.D., 456.

Bacquet, P., 4317.

Bader, Clarisse, 1661, 2004.

Bader, Guido, 4731.

Baecker, Louis de, 1570.

Bäumer, Gertrud, 212-213, 1361, 1373, 3711-3712, 3726, 6856.

Bäuml, Franz H., 3826.

Bagg, Robert, 1953.

Bagnani, G., 2065.

Bague, Enric, 3859.

Bahlmann, Dudley, 5288.

Bailet, Dietlinde Sigrid, 6630.

Bailey, Cyril, 2233.

Bailey, Derrick Sherwin, 433-435.

Bailey, F.E., 5823.

Bailey, S.J., 3023.

Bailleu, Paul, 6760.

Bailly, Auguste, 2177, 4477. 5502, 5772.

Baines, Barbara J., 5196.

Bainton, Roland H., 436, 4018, 4060, 4073-4074, 4667, 4745, 4575, 4705, 4727, 4992.

Baird, Joseph L., 3682.

Bakan, David, 41.

Baker, Derek, 2529, 3060.

Baker, Elizabeth C., 999.

Baker, Herschel, 5381.

Baker, M.J., 4652.

Baker, Van R., 6242.

Balde, Jean, 4584.

Baldensperger, Fernand, 5245, 5773.

Balsdon, John Percy Vyvian Dacre, 2005-2006, 2036, 2369.

Baldwin, Barry, 1508.

Baldwin, F.E., 1165.

Ballard, George, 1199.

Balleine, George Reginald, 6057.

Ballesteros-Beretta, Antonia, 3860. 3860.

Ballou, Patricia K., 4.

Baltensweiler, H., 2301.

Baltzer, Rebecca A., 3688.

Bambeck, Manfred, 4519.

Bandel, Betty, 3159.

Bangerter, Otto, 2654.

Banner, Lois W., 100, 568.

Bansley, Charles, 4304.

Baratier, Edouard, 3541.

Barbard, H.C., 5690.

Barber, Elinor, 6506.

Barber, Malcolm C., 3521.

Barber, Richard, 2926.

Barber, W.H., 6671.

Barbey d'Aurevilly, Jules Amedee, 42.

Barchewitz, Jutta, 3719.

Bardèche, Maurice, 43.

Bardet, Jean-Pierre, 586.

Bardis, Panos D., 616, 2265.

Bardon, Françoise, 4542, 5463.

Barine, Arvede, 5557.

Baring-Gould, Sabine,, 490-491.

Barini, C., 2457.

Barker, Albert W., 1854.

Barker, Diana Leonard, 319.

Barker (Bercher), William, 4071.

Barley, M.W., 1093.

Barlow, Frank. 3046.

Barnard, Howard Clive, 1193, 1349, 5701.

Barnard, Sylvia, 1943.

Barnett, Bernard, 517.

Barnett, F.J., 3872.

Barnett, Thomas Ratcliffe, 3061.

Barnstone, Aliki and Barnstone, Willis, 962.

Barranger, Milly S., 5364.

Barrau, Caroline de, 932.

Barry, Iris, 6300.

Bart, Jean, 3982.

Bartels, H., 2084.

Bartels, Max, 149.

Bartels, Paul, 149.

Barthélemy, Edouard Marie, comte de, 5521, 6409-6410.

Bartoli, Marie-Claude, 3925.

Barton, Felix, 1031.

Barton, J.L., 2990.

Baschwitz, Kurt, 518.

Bascou-Vance, P., 4437.

Bascoul, J.M.F., 1954-1955.

Basilius, saint, the great, archbishop of Caesarea, 2322-2323.

Bass, Robert D., 6094.

Bassani, F., 2452.

Bassermann, Lujo, 782.

Bataillon, Marcel, 4864.

Bateson, Mary, 2655.

Batiffol, Louis, 5473, 5531-5532, 5746.

Battandier, Albert, 3753.

Batten, J., 386.

Crankshaw, Edward, 6769.

Cranmer, Thomas, 4235.

Crawford, J.P. Wickersham, 3894.

Crawford, Jane, 3124, 3658.

Crawley, Ernest, 1533.

Crecelius, W., 5836.

Crepaz, Adele, 687.

Cressy, David, 1195.

Crevelier, Jacques, 5799.

Crittenden, Walter Marion, 6244.

Crivelli, Domenico, 4939.

Crofts, Maud Isabel, 1045.

Croix, Alain, 4605-4606.

Crook, J.A., 2045, 2068, 2163.

Crook, Margaret Brackenbury, 339.

Cros, Claude, 6579.

Crosby, Alfred W., 4057.

Crosby, Emily, 6641.

Crosfield, Helen G., 5270.

Crosland, J., 3668.

Cross, Claire, 3123.

Crouzel, Henri, 2268, 2314, 2812.

Crow, Joan, 3607.

Crozet, Rene, 3597.

Crump, C.G., 2519.

Cruttwell, Maude, 5509.

Cuénin, Micheline, 5741.

Cuisenier, Jean, 633.

Culver, Elsie Thomas, 340.

Cumming, Alan, 1877.

Cummings, Mark, 6404.

Cunningham, Peter, 5222.

Cunnington, Cecil Willett, 823, 827, 1171-1172, 3203, 4353, 5354, 6156.

Cunnington, Phillis, 824-827, 1173, 5354.

Cupaiuolo, Nice, 1948.

Cuq, Edouard, 2046.

Curran, Leo C., 2448.

Currie, E.P., 4033.

Curry, Herbert, 1039.

Curtayne, Alice, 4976.

Curtis, Edith Roelker, 5983.

Curtis, Gila, 6015.

Curtius, Ernst Robert, 2929.

Cusack, Pearse Ardan, 3930.

Cuthbert, M., 867.

Cuthbert, R.P., 3936.

Cutler, Kenneth E., 3028.

Cutter, Irving S., 868.

Cuvillier, Jean-Pierre, 3888.

Cyprianus, Saint, bishop of Carthage, 2326.

Dacier, Emile, 6731.

Dacier, Henriette, 2324.

Dahl, Nancy, 614, 621.

Dahlberg, Charles, 3683.

Dahmus, Joseph, 2573.

Dain, A., 4665.

Dalby, Andrew, 2395.

Dale, Amy Marjorie, 1921.

Dale, M., 2011.

Dale, Marian K., 4231.

Dalla Costa, Mariarosa, 1477.

Dal Pino, A.M., 2624.

Daltrop, Georg, 2095.

Dalven, Rae, 2096.

Daly, Mary, 460-462.

Damerini, Gino, 6888.

Dammert, Rudolf, 5800.

Damour, Felix, 4633.

Danielou, Jean, 2593.

Daniélou, Madeleine (Clamorgan),
   5692, 5702.

Dantas, Júlio, 2333.

Dantier, Alfonse, 463.

Danvila y Burguero, Alfonso, 6867-
   6868.

D'Arcy, M.C., 744.

Dargaud, J.M., 4170.

Dark, Sydney, 234, 308.

Darricau, Raymond, 5465.

Darrow, Margaret H., 6520.

Darton, J.M., 1036.

Dasent, Arthur Irwin, 5223.

Datta de Albertis, G., 6412.

Daube, David, 1566, 1572, 2047,
   2425.

Daubèze, Yvette, 6532.

Daudet, Pierre, 3515-3516.

Daugherty, Margaret, 1922.

Daughters of St. Paul, 464.

Daumard, Adeline, 6555.

Dauphin, Cecile, 6611.

Dauvergne, Edmund B., 235, 5191,
   5929.

Dauvillier, Jean, 2303, 2673-
   2674.

Davari, Stefano, 4893.

Davenport, Millia, 828.

Davenson, Henri, 2907.

Davey, Richard Patrick Boyle,
   4171.

Davidson, Clifford, 3367.

Davidson, H.R. Ellis, 3723.

Davidson, Lillias Campbell,
   5215.

Davidson, Terry, 713.

Davies, J.K., 1814.

Davies, John Langdon, 70.

Davies, R. Trevor, 1081.

Davies, Steven L., 2269.

D'Avino, Michele, 2012.

Davis, Audrey B., 5.

Davis, Elizabeth Gould, 71.

Erasmus, Desiderius, 5159-5161.

Ercole, Francesco, 3965.

Erdmann, W., 1823-1824.

Erickson, Carolly, 2514, 2769, 4180.

Erickson, R.A., 6276.

Erikson, Erik, 634, 696-697.

Erlanger, Philippe, 3029, 4490,
    4497, 4544-4545, 4599, 5500.

Erlanger, Rachel, 4907.

Erman, Jean Pierre, 5830.

Ermisch, Hubert, 4675.

Ernemont, Madeleine, 5449.

Errazuriz, Helena, 3883.

Escott, Thomas Hay Sweet, 1095.

Esdaile, K.A., 2209.

Eshleman, Michael K., 4058.

Esmein, Adhemar, 507, 2678.

Espinas, Georges, 3701.

Espinosa, Juan de, 4846.

Esposito, M., 3090.

Essex, John, 6164.

Essig, Olga, 1388.

Estienne, Nicole, 4620.

Estienne, Pierre, 1288.

Etienne, Robert, 1602, 2375, 02805.

Euing, Ludwig, 2242.

Evans, Hilary, 791.

Evans Joan, 3368, 3598.

Evans, Margaret Carey, 6385.

Evans, Mary, 829.

Evans, Michael, 2965.

Evans, W.O., 3363.

Evans-Pritchard, Edward, 1512.

Evelyn, John, 5200.

Everett-Green, Mary Anne, 1060,
    5818.

Everitt, Alan, 6123.

Eversley, D.E.C., 594, 1110.

Evoy, John J., 466.

Ewart, Andrew, 244.

Ewen, Cecil Henry L'Estrange,
    1082-1083.

Exposition, Sens., 6521.

Eyb, Albrecht von, 4050.

Eyben, Emiel, 1603.

Fabre, Lucien, 3431.

Fabre-Luce, Alfred, 5729.

Fábrega Grau, Ángel, 3873.

Facinger, Marion F., 3384.

Fagniez, Gustave, 3461, 5429,
    5612.

Faguet, E., 1248.

Fahrner, Ignatz, 2679.

Fahy, Conor, 3030, 4002.

Fairchilds, Cissie, 6595.

Fairholt, Frederick William,
    1175.

Faith, Rosamund J., 3171.

Griffiths, Ralph A., 3019, 3388.

Grignaschi, M., 3967.

Grillot de Givry, Emil, 531.

Grimal, Pierre, 93, 1515, 2015, 2449.

Grimaldi, Natale, 3915.

Grimmer, Claude, 5661.

Grion, P. Alvaro, 4983.

Gripkey, Mary Vincentine, 2631-2633.

Grisar, Joseph, 5263.

Grisay, Auguste, 3608.

Griswold, Susan C., 5868.

Gross, Rita M., 342-343.

Gross, Walter Hatto, 2198

Grosse, Ernst, 643.

Groult, Benoîte, 94.

Grundmann, Herbert, 2874, 2890, 3778.

Grylls, Rosalie Glynn, 5939.

Gryson, R., 2600-2601.

Guadier, M., 2875.

Guazza, R., 5850.

Gubar, Susan, 4397, 6203.

Guerdan, René, 1336, 4752.

Guerra, F., 4351.

Gueudre, G., 5574.

Gueudre, M.-C., 5567.

Guglia, Eugen, 6783.

Guicciardini, Francesco, 5031.

Guichard, Pierre, 3879.

Guilbert, Madeleine, 1268.

Guilhiermoz, Paul, 3381.

Guillaume, Pierre, 1290.

Guillet-Rydell, Mireille, 2818.

Guillon, Pierre, 1949.

Guilloreau, Dom Léon, 1273.

Guillou, Andre, 3968.

Guitton, Georges, 5511.

Guitton, Jean, 3436.

Gundermann, Iselin, 4689.

Gundersheimer, Werner L., 4887, 4896.

Guralnick, Elissa S., 5962.

Guthrie, Charles John, 1152.

Guthrie, W., 1758.

Gutierez Lasanta, Francisco, 4779.

Guttenberg, Erich, Freiherrn von, 4753.

Gutwirth, Madelyn, 6700.

Guyon, C.M., 1691.

Guyot, Yves, 795.

Guzman, Perez de, 1464.

Gy, Pierre-Marie, 2683.

Haake, Paul, 5801.

Haan, Jean, 2730.

Habakkuk, H.J., 596, 5906, 6113, 6140.

Hanawalt, Barbara A., 2536, 3016–3018, 3020, 3179.

Hand, Geoffrey, 3004.

Handover, P.M., 4217.

Hands, L., 369.

Hanlon, Sister Joseph Damien, 4250.

Hannay, Prudence, 6269.

Hanning, Robert W., 3341.

Hans, Nicholas A., 6169.

Hansbrough, Henry Clay, 314.

Hansen, Elaine Tuttle, 3217.

Hansen, Joseph, 2731–2732.

Hanson, Ann Ellis, 1862.

Hanstein, Adalbert von, 6844.

Haraszti-Takács, Marianne, 5122.

Harding, Davis P., 4340.

Harding, Mary Esther, 97.

Hardman, Sister Anne, 5258.

Hardy, Blanche Christabel, 3032, 4218.

Hardy, E., 4287.

Hardy, E.R., 1585.

Hareven, Tamara K., 645–646, 1314, 2796.

Hargrave, Mary, 6850.

Hargreaves, Reginald, 315.

Harkness, Georgia Elma, 344, 576.

Harksen, Sibylle, 2537.

Harless, Johann Christian Friedrich, 1010.

Harley, T.R., 2388.

Harmand, Jean, 6627.

Harmon, Rebecca L., 6065.

Harrier, Richard C., 4150.

Harriet, W., 796.

Harris, Adelaide E., 3218.

Harris, Ann Sutherland, 998.

Harris, Anthony J., 5280.

Harris, Barbara J., 618.

Harris, Frank, 4399.

Harris, G., 797.

Harris, Joseph, 2900.

Harris, Marvin, 533, 1540.

Harris, William Vernon, 1998.

Harrison, Alick R.W., 1722.

Harrison, Austin, 98.

Harrison, Evelyn B., 1980.

Harrison, G.B., 5281.

Harrison, Jane, 1760.

Harrison, K.P., 4136.

Hartcup, Adeline, 6889.

Hartemann, Jean, 3437.

Hartland, Edwin Sidney, 647, 1598.

Hartley, C.G., 99.

Hartman, Lydia Claude, 6720.

Hartman, Mary S., 100.

Hartmann, Cyril Hughes, 5205, 5485–5486, 5523.

Harvey, David, 1728.

Heinsius, Maria, 4670, 4690.

Heintze, Helga von, 1961.

Heisch, Allison, 4155.

Heise, Ursula, 3833.

Heisner, Beverly, 5534.

Heiss, Gernot, 5154-5155.

Helbig, Althea K., 3086.

Heller, Henry, 4528.

Hellstedt, 877.

Helm, K., 2362.

Helmholz, Richard H., 2993-2994, 3180.

Hemlow, Joyce, 6224-6226.

Henderson, Daniel, 4181.

Henderson, Ernest Flagg, 5560.

Henderson, Helen W., 4547.

Henderson-Howat, A.M.D., 3062.

Hengel, Martin, 2351.

Henne am Rhyn, Otto, 925.

Hennessy, W.M., 3087.

Henningsen, G., 5600.

Henrard, P., 4451.

Henriot, Emile, 252-253.

Henriques, Fernando, 752, 800-801.

Henry, Louis, 1291-1293, 1402, 6529, 6537, 6541-6542, 6581-6582.

Henry-Bordeaux, Paule, 4554.

Hentsch, Alice A., 2877.

Hérard, Madeleine, 5780.

Herbenová, Olga, 833.

Herculano de Carvalho e Arauja, Alexandre, 3896.

Herford, Charles H., 4401.

Herfst, P., 1746.

Herington, C.J., 1761.

Héritier, Jean, 4202, 4499.

Herkommer, Agnes, 5264.

Herlihy, David, 2772-2773, 2785-2786, 2820, 3943-3944, 3947-3949, 3954, 5024-5026, 5032-5034, 5053.

Herm, Gerhard, 2982.

Hermann, Claudine, 2071.

Hermann, Ulrich, 6831.

Hermansen, G., 3049.

Hermitte, J.L., 5599.

Hernández-Léon de Sanchez, Francisca, 3863.

Herold, J.C., 6605.

Herpin, Clara Adele, 5524.

Herr, Ethel, 401.

Herre, Paul, 4679.

Herrmann, Paul, 2363.

Hershey, Jane, 6187.

Herter, H., 1612.

Hertz, Deborah, 6851.

Hervas, Ramon, 802.

Hervez, Jean, 6606-6608.

Herz, Michelline, 5781.

Houston, Mary Gelway, 3204.

Howard, Albert Andrew, 2253.

Howard, George, 4172.

Howard, George Elliott, 1155.

Howarth, W.D., 2558.

Howell, Cicely, 1047.

Hozeski, Bruce W., 3817.

Huarte y Echenique, Amalio, 3864.

Huby, M., 2945.

Huchon, René Louis, 6297.

Hudson, Hoyt H., 4419.

Hudson, William Henry, 3818.

Huebner, Rudolf, 1378.

Hueffer, Oliver Madox, 536.

Huet, Alain, 5643.

Hufstader, Alice A., 6178.

Hufton, Olwen H., 6391-6393, 6495-6496.

Hugel, Friedrich freiherr von, 4967.

Hughes, Diane Owen, 718, 2797-2798, 3955-3956.

Hughes, Helen Sard, 5412, 6124, 6198.

Hughes, Muriel J., 2866.

Hughes, Patricia, 5963.

Hughes, Pennethorne, 537.

Hughes, Richard E., 4417.

Hugo, Thomas, 3112.

Huisman, Philippe, 6465.

Huizinga, J., 2525.

Humbert, Michel, 2432.

Hume, A.S. Martin, 4106, 4182, 4780.

Hume, David, 6350.

Humiliata, Sister Mary, 5362.

Humphreys, A.R., 5898.

Humphreys, S.C., 1815.

Hunt, David, 5662.

Hunt, Morton M., 753.

Hunt, Percival, 2986.

Hunter, J., 3054.

Hunter, Jean E., 6264-6265.

Hupin, Gerard, 6466.

Huppert, M.P., 2866.

Hurd-Mead, Kate Campbell, 878-882, 2868.

Hurstfield, Joel, 4342-4343.

Hutcheson, W.J. Fraser, 4403.

Hutchinson, R.W., 1700.

Hutton, J. Bernard, 310.

Huizing, Peter, 509.

Humy, Fernand Emile de, 255.

Hunt, E.D., 2353.

Huyghebaert, Nicola, 3468, 3994.

Hybels, Judith, 326.

Hyde, Mary, 6336-6341.

Hyman, Paula, 370.

McDonnell, Ernest W., 2717.

McDougall, Dorothy, 5737.

McEvilley, Thomas, 1963-1965.

McFarland, Joan, 328.

Macfarlane, Alan, 4260-4261, 4331, 5316.

McGill, William J., Jr., 6788.

McGrath, Sister Albert Magnus O.P., 472.

MacGregor, Magaret Eliot, 6351.

McGregor, O.R., 1127.

MacGuigan, Maryellen, 1892.

Machiavelli, Niccolo, 5087-5088.

MacIlquham, Harriet, 4755.

McInnes, Ian, 4114.

McIntyre, Clara Frances, 6241.

MacKay, Janet, 5216, 5230.

McKee, William, 6234.

McKendrick, Melveena, 4848, 5863, 5864.

McKendrick, Neil, 6054.

McKenna, Sister Mary Lawrence, 473.

McKenzie, A. Dean, 2643.

Mackenzie, Agnes Mure, 4406.

Mackenzie, John H., 6193.

Mackenzie, Muir, 889.

McKeowan, Thomas, 5908, 6116.

Mackerness, E.D., 4092.

MacKinnon, Sir Frank Douglas, 5931.

Macksey, Joan, 24.

Macksey, Kenneth, 24.

McLachlan, Hugh V., 1090.

McLane, Paul E., 4422-4423.

McLaren, Angus, 6597.

McLaren, Dorothy, 5188, 5312.

McLaughlin, Eleanor Commo, 351, 2603, 2725.

McLaughlin, Mary Martin, 2808.

McLaughlin, T.P., 2662, 2690, 2823.

Maclean, Ian, 4066, 5709.

Maclennan, Hector, 4359.

MacLennan, John Ferguson, 1549, 1606-1607.

McLeod, Enid, 3504, 3631.

McLintock, D.R., 3838.

McLoughlin, Eleanor L., 2285.

McNally, Sheila, 1984.

MacNalty, Arthur Salisbury Sir, 4203.

McNamara, Jo Ann, 2286, 2577, 2604, 2777, 2799, 3799.

McRobbie, Kenneth, 2951.

Macurdy, Grace Harriet, 1739-1742, 2016, 2114, 2165.

Madariaga, Salvador de, 1446.

Madinier, Renée, 1261-1262.

Maertens, Thierry, 411.

Magendie, Maurice, 5614.

Magli, Ida, 1550.

Magné, B., 6689.

Mason, Otis T., 1520.

Mason, Sheila, 6690.

Mason, Shirlene, 6277.

Mason-Hohl, Elizabeth, 3975.

Mastellone, Salvo, 5537.

Masters, R.E.L., 120.

Mate, Mavis, 3077.

Mathew, David, 4174.

Mathew, Gervase, 3188.

Mathewson, Jeanne T., 3347.

Matossian, Mary Kilbourne, 346.

Matter, Joseph Allen, 5194.

Mattessich, Paul W., 705.

Matthew, Donald, 2526.

Matthew, Sir Tobie, 5259.

Matthews, Betty, 6383.

Matthews, William, 3348.

Mattingly, Garrett, 4139.

Mattingly, Harold, 2117.

Matulka, Barbara, 4772, 5865.

Mau, August, 2386.

Maugras, Gaston, 6430.

Maulde la Clavière, R. de, 3392,
    4009, 4557.

Mauny, Michel de, 4485.

Maur Cocheril, P., 3875.

Maura y Gamazo, Grabriel, duque de,
    5854.

Maurel, Andre, 6678.

Mauriac, Francois, 3937.

Maus, Anna, 1432.

Maus, K.E., 5379.

May, B., 939.

May, Georges, 6685.

Maye, Jean-Martin, 6549.

Mayer, Anton, 2738.

Mayer, Denise, 5783.

Mayer, Dorothy Moulton (Piper),
    4558.

Mayer, Gertrude Townshend,
    6179.

Maynard, Theodore, 4186.

Mayne, Ethel Colburn, 263,
    5999.

Mayr, M., 4766.

Mazon, P., 5768.

Mazzarino, Santo, 2118.

Mazzeo, Joseph Anthony, 1883.

Mead, Margaret, 134.

Meade, Marion, 3414.

Meadows, Denis, 4088.

Meakin, Annette M., 6320.

Medick, Hans, 329.

Medicus, Dieter, 2056.

Medin, A., 5096.

Meeker, Arthur, 2255.

Meeks, Wayne, 2287.

Parducci, A., 4955.

Paribeni, Roberto, 2413.

Paris, Pierre, 2124.

Park, Roberta J., 5175.

Parke, H.W., 1788.

Parker, G., 5603.

Parker, W.M., 6353.

Parmisano, Fabian, 2827.

Parreaux, André, 6084, 6309.

Parrinder, Geoffrey, 550-551.

Parry, Sir Edward Abbott, 6034.

Parsons, Elsie Clews, 765, 1130.

Parsons, Frank Alvah, 5172.

Parsons, John Carmi, 3040.

Parton, James, 264.

Parturier, E., 4535.

Parturier, Louis, 1279.

Parvey, Constance, 2292.

Pascal, Carlo, 2779.

Pasolini dall 'Onda, Pietro De-
    siderio, conte, 4952.

Pasquier, Etienne, 2057.

Paston, George, 6310.

Pastorino, A., 2125.

Pastoureau, Michel, 3146.

Patai, Daphne, 958.

Patai, Raphael, 378, 415-416.

Patault, A.M., 3535.

Paul, C. Kegan, 5940.

Paul, Herbert, 6022.

Paul, John E., 4141.

Paulhart, Herbert, 3713-3714.

Paulin, V., 1269.

Pauls, Eilhard Erich, 6754.

Paulsen, Friedrich, 1381.

Paulus, Nikolaus, 2828, 4038.

Pavan, Elisabeth, 3972.

Payen, Jean-Charles, 3585,
    3686.

Payer, Alice de, 5443.

Payer, Pierre, 2605.

Payne, Blanche, 5173.

Payne, George Henry, 706.

Peacock, N., 1493.

Pearce, Charles E., 6189.

Pearce, T.E.V., 2436.

Pearse, Nancy Cotton, 5387.

Pearson, Lu Emily, 4292, 4374.

Peavy, Charles D., 6364.

Pecchiai, Pio, 4879.

Pechmann, M. Gonzaga Fr. von,
    1394.

Peers, E. Allison, 4831.

Pelegrin, Benito, 3902.

Pelicier, Paul, 4463.

Pellegrini, Giovan Battista,
    2829.

Ring, Richard R., 3951.

Ringland, John, 1191.

Riquet, Michel, 347, 447, 2789.

Rist, J.M., 2510.

Ritchie, Anne Isabella (Thackeray)
Lady, 5787.

Ritter, Hans-Werner, 2201.

Ritter, Raymond, 4466, 4492, 4538.

Ritzer, Korbinian, 2565, 2702.

Rival, Paul, 4122, 4539, 5527.

Rivers, Theodore John, 3012, 3702.

Rivers, W.H.R., 580.

Robathan, Dorothy, 5109.

Robbins, Russell Hope, 552.

Robert, Louis, 1779.

Robert, U., 3594.

Roberts, Phyllis B., 2347.

Roberts, Warren E., 6728.

Robertson, Clyde, 266.

Robertson, D.W., 2959, 3511.

Robertson, Jean, 4420.

Robida, A., 840.

Robine, M., 1329.

Robinson, C.E., 1650.

Robinson, David M., 1967.

Robinson, Mabel, 5749.

Robinson, Peter, 6146.

Robinson, Victor, 767, 895, 5942.

Robiquet, Paul, 5469.

Robleda, Olís, 2438.

Roby, Henry J., 2059.

Rocamora, María Luisa, 26.

Roche, Daniel, 6620.

Roche, Paul, 1968.

Roche, T.W.E., 5488.

Rochon, André, 4880.

Roderick, A.J., 3193.

Rodocanachi, E. Pierre, 1491,
4881, 4945.

Rodriguez-Solis, E., 4852.

Rodriguez Valencia, Vincente,
4804.

Roe, Frederic Gordon, 979,
6137.

Roebuck, Peter, 5301.

Roeder, Ralph, 4505.

Roehrich, Timotheus Wilhelm,
4706.

Roelker, Nancy Lyman, 4473,
4579, 4588.

Rörig, Fritz, 2764.

Rösler, E. Robert, 4818.

Rössler, Oskar, 3066.

Rogal, Samuel J., 6067, 6153.

Rogers, Cameron, 267.

Rogers, H.L., 2388.

Rogers, Katherine M., 959,
6180, 6210, 6237, 6279, 6332.

Rogers, Robert Samuel, 2130-
2131, 2160, 2202.

Rogge, D. Bernhard, 6765.

Steinbach, Hartmut, 3455.

Steinberg, Leo, 5115.

Steinberger, S., 903.

Steinen, Karl von den, 5920.

Steinhausen, George, 6837.

Steinmetz, David C., 4023.

Stendahl, Krister, 426.

Stengel, Paul, 1790.

Stenhouse, Evangeline E., 904.

Stenton, Doris May, 1030, 3153.

Stenton, Frank M., 3165.

Stephan, G., 6838.

Stephens, George R., 3044, 3094.

Stern, Bernhard J., 678.

Stern, Gerhard Wilhelm, 5847.

Stern, Jean, 6714.

Steudel, Johannes, 905.

Stevens, John, 3654.

Stevenson, Robert Louis, 4256.

Stewart, Isabel Maitland, 869.

Stewart, Philip, 5916.

Stewart, Susan, 1145.

Sticca, Sandro, 3823.

Stiller, Nikki, 3227.

Stock, Phyllis H., 940, 6621.

Stockmeier, P., 2709.

Stocker, Lydia, 2294.

Stoll, E.E., 4410.

Stone, J.M., 4191.

Stone, Lawrence, 1135-1136, 4325, 4347.

Stone, Merlin, 1581-1582.

Stone, Robert K., 3103.

Stopes, Charlotte (Carmichael), 1051.

Storer, Mary Elizabeth, 5710.

Storr, Marthe (Miguel) Seven, 5969.

Stoss, Irma, 49.

Stouff, Louis, 5132.

Strachey, Rachel Conn (Costelloe), 1052.

Strage, Mark, 4510.

Strange, Sallie Minter, 6365.

Strano, Titina, 4932.

Strassburger, Ferdinand, 5689.

Strassmann, P., 4635.

Straub, A., 3752.

Strauss und Torney, Lulu von, 3790.

Strecker, Gabriele, 1427.

Strich, Michael, 5563.

Stricker, Kathe, 1434, 4692.

Strickland, Agnes, 1063-1065, 4127-4128.

Strohl, E. Lee, 6312.

Strong, Joanna, 275.

Strong, Roy, 4166.

Strübing, E., 3771.

Tavenaux, René, 5569.

Tavernier, Félix, 1280.

Taviani, Huguette, 2710.

Taxonera, Luciano de, 6872.

Tayler, Henrietta, 6008.

Taylor, A.E., 1885.

Taylor, G.S., 2857.

Taylor, Gladys, 5813.

Taylor, Gordon Rattray, 776, 6086.

Taylor, H.O., 2618.

Taylor, K.W., 608.

Taylor, Kathryn, 276.

Taylor, M.A., 4130.

Taylor, William Cooke, 4571.

Teall, John L., 4266.

Telle, Emile Villemeur, 4541, 5162.

Temporini, Hildegard, 2145.

Tenenti, Alberto, 4602.

Terrien, Samuel, 428, 1781.

Terrisse, Michel, 6591.

Terroine, Anne, 3596.

Tertullianus, Quintus Septimium Florens, 2334-2340.

Tervarent, Guy de, 2355.

Teufer, Johannes, 2080.

Thabaut, Jules, 1243.

Thelliez, C., 5133.

Theobald, Robert, 187.

Theopold, Wilhelm, 708.

Therault, Suzanne, 5001.

Therel, M.L., 3483.

Thérive, André, 5767.

Thevenin, André, 3807.

Thibaut, Francisque, 5147.

Thiel, Heinrich, 6798.

Thiel, J.H., 1708.

Thiel, Josef Franz, 732.

Thième, Hans, 1384.

Thième, Hugo Paul, 188.

Thiroux d' Arconville, Marie Geneviève Charlotte, 5545.

Thiselton-Dyer, Thomas F., 961.

Thoma, Albrecht, 4726.

Thomas of Celano, 3935.

Thomas, Antoine Leonard, 189.

Thomas, C.G., 1709.

Thomas, David, 6147.

Thomas, Edith, 190, 3456.

Thomas, Gertrude Z., 5341.

Thomas, Keith, 1091-1092, 3083, 4267-4269, 5276, 5285, 6149.

Thomas, W. Derek, 2295.

Thomas, William, 777.

Thompson, C.J.S., 5342.

Thompson, Claude A., 5343.

Thompson, Dorothy Lampen, 335.

Van Lennep, William, 5225.

Van Leuven, Jon C., 1783.

Vann, Richard T., 612, 1137, 5274.

Van Vuuren, Nancy, 353.

Varnhagen, Hermann, 2349.

Varnhagen von Ense, Karl, 5833.

Varty, Kenneth, 3628, 4649.

Vasari, Georgio, 5130.

Vasileski, Irma, 5872.

Vatel, Charles, 6446.

Vatin, Claude, 1832.

Vauchez, André, 3744.

Vaughan, Agnes Carr, 2230.

Vaughan, Herbert M., 5926.

Veblen, Thorstein, 842.

Vecellio, Cesare, 4054.

Vegas, Liana Castelfranchi, 3484.

Veith, D., 1435.

Veith, Ilza, 917.

Vendôme, Henriette, 6450.

Venturi, 5008.

Vercauteren, F., 3989.

Verdier, Philippe, 2897.

Verdon, Jean, 2515, 3494-3496, 3538-3539.

Verdon, Michael, 681.

Vergne, Yvonne de la, 6451.

Verlinden, Charles, 2838.

Vermeule, C.C., 1903.

Vernant, Jean-Pierre, 1767, 1833.

Vernon, Virginia (Fox-Brooks), 5440.

Versini, L., 6622.

Veverka, Georgina, 4746.

Veyne, Paul, 2419.

Veze, Raoul (Jean Hervez), 2855.

Vierling, Josef Fridolin, 4707.

Vigman, Fred K., 195.

Vigne, Rene Rousalt de la, 1264.

Villa Pastur, Jesus, 1465.

Villefosse, Rene Heronde, 1340.

Villermont, Comtesse Marie de, 843.

Villers, Robert, 1332, 2077.

Villette, Abbé Pierre, 4597.

Villiers, Elizabeth, 1071.

Vinatier, Jean, 486.

Vince, Stanley W.E., 6738.

Vincens, Cecile, 277, 5164, 5554-5556, 5564.

Vincent, Arthur, 278.

Vincent, Jacqueline, 6593.

Vindry, Fleury, 5706.

Vine, Phyllis, 679.

Vining, Elizabeth Gray, 6009.

Vinogradov, P.G., 3157.

Violante, Cinzio, 2839.

Vioux, Marcelle, 5492.

Virolleaud, Charles, 1583.

Viseltear, Arthur J., 6162.

Visky, Karoly, 2442.

Vismara, Guilio, 2840, 3959.

Vitti, Earl D., 3673.

Vives, Juan Luis, 4854-4857.

Vives, Vicens J., 1453.

Vivier, Em., 5673.

Voeltzel, R., 515.

Vogel, Cyrille, 2712, 2841.

Vogel, Johannes, 1440.

Vogelsang, Thilo, 2576.

Vogt, Heinrich, 2062.

Vogt, Joseph, 1734.

Volkmann, Hans, 2186.

Volpe, G., 3940.

Voltaire, 6707-6711.

Volterra, Edoardo, 2063-2064, 2420.

Volz, Carl A., 450.

Volz, Gustav Berthold, 6799.

Von Arx, Walter, 487.

Von Bothmer, Dietrich, 1697.

Voorhies, Barbara, 133.

Vorländer, Dorothea, 5106.

Vos, Clarence J., 430.

Vosburg, Nancy, 3375.

Vries, Jan de, 2366.

Vulliamy, C.E., 6345, 6358.

Wachsmuth, Wilhelm, 585.

Waddell, Helen, 3513, 6366.

Waddicor, Mark, 6715.

Wade, Ira Owen, 6681-6682.

Wadsworth, James, 3593.

Wagner, Anni, 982.

Wainwright, F.T., 3045.

Wakeford, Geoffrey, 1072.

Walcot, Peter, 1658, 1972.

Waldeck, Marie-Luise, 6848.

Waldegg, Richard, 815.

Waldhauer, Oscar, 2503.

Waldman, Milton, 3458, 4167, 4192, 4514.

Walker, Curtis H., 3420-3421.

Walker, D.P., 4271.

Walker, George, 1181.

Walker, Jane, 906.

Walker, Sue Sheridan, 3014, 3200.

Walker, T.C., 6629.

Wall, Richard, 1121.

Wallas, Ada, 5415.

Walser, Hermann, 5107.

About the Compilers and Editors

Linda Frey is an Associate Professor of History at the University of Montana. Marsha Frey, an Associate Professor of History at Kansas State University, has coauthored several books and articles on Western European History with her twin sister, Linda Frey. Joanne Schneider is a Teaching Associate at Brown University and is currently a visiting Assistant Professor of History at Wheaton College.